Our
Sacred
Honor

Prelude to Glory

VOLUME 1

Our Sacred Honor

A NOVEL BY

RON CARTER

BOOKCRAFT

SALT LAKE CITY, UTAH

Library of Congress Catalog Card Number: 98-70388

ISBN: 1-57008-431-9

Printed in the United States of America   18961-4950

10   9   8   7   6   5   4   3

This series is dedicated to the common people
of long ago who paid the price.

★ ★ ★

America was discovered, colonized, and made into a great nation so that the Lord would have a proper place both to restore the gospel and from which to send it forth to all other nations. As a prelude to his coming, and so the promised work of restoration would roll forward, the foundations of the American nation were laid.

—BRUCE R. MCCONKIE

This volume is dedicated to my wife, LaRae.

Our Sacred Honor

We, therefore, the Representatives of the united
States of America, in General Congress, Assembled,
appealing to the Supreme Judge of the world for the
rectitude of our intentions, do, in the Name, and by
Authority of the good People of these Colonies,
solemnly publish and declare, That these United
Colonies are, and of Right ought to be Free and
Independent States. . . . And for the support of this
Declaration, with a firm reliance on the protection of
divine Providence, we mutually pledge to each other
our Lives, our Fortunes and our sacred Honor.

—DECLARATION OF INDEPENDENCE,
JULY 4, 1776

CHRONOLOGY OF IMPORTANT EVENTS RELATED TO THIS VOLUME

1765

Parliament in Britain passes the Stamp Act, which requires payment of a tax on many goods used by the people of the thirteen British colonies in America. The colonies have no representation in the British Parliament.

1766

Because of hot colonial opposition, the Stamp Act is repealed.

Parliament then passes the Declaratory Act, which declares Parliament's right to enact laws for the thirteen colonies.

1767

Parliament passes the Townsend Acts, which require the colonists to pay taxes on such products as glass, paint, and tea.

The colonists protest that the right to tax them without representation is the power to destroy them, and they retaliate with a boycott of British goods.

1768

England sends soldiers to maintain the peace in the face of rising colonial opposition to Parliament's actions.

1770

March 5. In Boston, colonials harass British soldiers and throw snowballs. A fray ensues in which the British shoot and kill five colonials. It will be dubbed the Boston Massacre.

1773

December 16. In protest against the Tea Act, colonials disguised as Indians board British merchant ships and throw 342 chests of tea into Boston Harbor. The event will be known to history as the Boston Tea Party.

1774

Parliament enacts what the colonists will term the "Intolerable Acts."

September. The First Continental Congress convenes in Philadelphia.

1775

April 18. Paul Revere and William Dawes make their midnight rides to rouse the colonial militia and minutemen to arms against the British, marching that night to Concord, Massachusetts.

April 19. The first shot is fired at Lexington, Massachusetts, and the Revolutionary War begins.

June 15. The Continental Congress appoints George Washington of Virginia to be commander in chief of the Continental army.

June 17. The battle of Bunker Hill and Breed's Hill is fought, which the British win at great cost, suffering numerous casualties before the colonial forces abandon the hills due to lack of ammunition.

1776

February-March. Commodore Esek Hopkins leads eight small colonial ships to the Bahamas to obtain munitions from two British forts, Nassau and Montague.

March 17. General William Howe evacuates his British command from Boston and moves to New York to engage and destroy George Washington's army.

July 4. The Continental Congress adopts the Declaration of Independence, and it is delivered to the public.

October 11. General Benedict Arnold leads a tiny fleet of fifteen hastily constructed ships to stall the British fleet of twenty-five ships on Lake Champlain. The hope is that Arnold's forces can at least delay the movement of thirteen thousand British troops south until the spring of 1777 and thus save George Washington's Continental army.

1779

September 23. Commodore John Paul Jones, aboard the *Bonhomme Richard,* engages the larger British man-of-war *Serapis* off the east coast of England in the much-celebrated night battle in which Jones utters the now famous cry, "I have not yet begun to fight!"

Part One

★ ★ ★

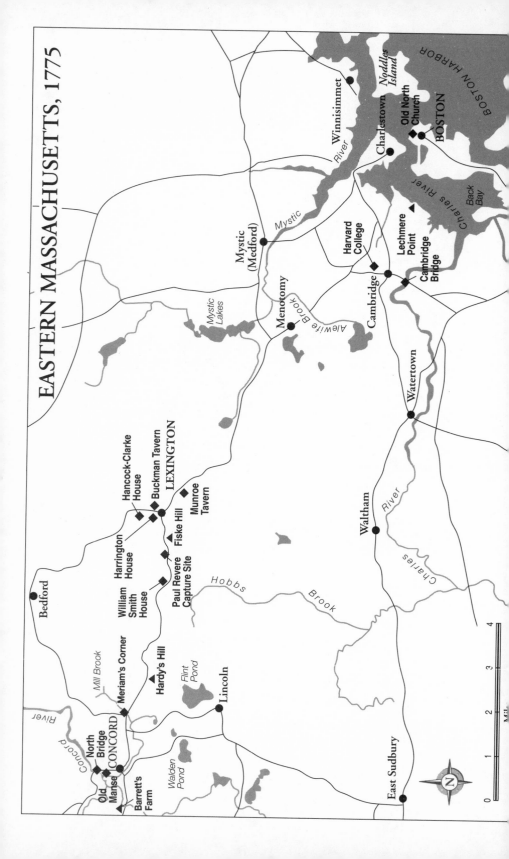

EASTERN MASSACHUSETTS, 1775

BOSTON HARBOR

BOSTON

Noddle's Island

Charlestown

Old North Church

Winnisimmet

Mystic River

Charles River

Back Bay

Mystic (Medford)

Mystic

Medford

Harvard College

Lechmere Point

Cambridge Bridge

Menotomy

Cambridge

Alewife Brook

Mystic Lakes

Watertown

Buckman Tavern

LEXINGTON

Hancock-Clarke House

Fiske Hill

Munroe Tavern

Harrington House

Paul Revere Capture Site

Waltham

William Smith House

Charles River

Bedford

Hobbs Brook

Meriam's Corner

Mill Brook

Hardy's Hill

Flint Pond

Lincoln

North Bridge

CONCORD

Concord River

Old Manse

Barrett's Farm

Walden Pond

East Sudbury

N

0   1   2   3   4
Mile

Saturday, April 15, 1775

CHAPTER I

★ ★ ★

*T*he sharp, urgent rap came unexpected at the front door. With the small brass shovel still in her hand, Margaret Pulsipher Dunson straightened, stared at the huge hand-carved clock in the center of the heavy fireplace mantel and then at the calendar beside it, and brought her racing thoughts under control.

Nine forty-five P.M. Saturday, April 15, 1775.

Late . . . no one but the British comes this late in Boston . . . which one of us are they after?

She had been banking coals in the great fireplace to save for the Sabbath morning fire, and now she hung the small brass shovel back on its peg and turned to peer at her husband, seated on his work stool in one corner of the big room behind the oak dinner table.

John Phelps Dunson raised a warning hand to stop all sound, all movement in the room, and the others waited in silence. His eyes narrowed and his breathing slowed as they sat in the yellow lamplight, the tension rising while John lowered his face to concentrate.

Margaret glanced at the door, then back at John as she worked with her thoughts and fears.

Do they want John? . . . what about Warren and Thorpe and the others on the committee? . . . have they already got Adams and Hancock?

Seconds passed while Margaret waited and watched her husband sitting motionless on his work stool where he had labored to become a master clockmaker and gunsmith. Steady, deliberate, strong, six feet in height, large nose, cleft chin, dark eyed, dark brown hair pulled back and tied behind his head with a leather thong. Elected to the Massachusetts Provincial Congress and placed on the single most critical committee in the entire colony—the Committee of Safety—which was assigned to provide for the safety of the colonial citizens against British oppression. The British had openly vowed to arrest everyone on the committee and hang them all for treason. Only fear of reprisals had prevented it, for at that moment the tenuous, trembling peace was as an open powder keg, waiting for the spark that would explode into an all-out war in the streets and on the farms.

Her breathing slowed as she studied him, and the familiar stir rose in her heart as it always did when he was near.

She pursed her mouth, and for a moment her eyes narrowed to fine points of light.

If they want John, there will be trouble.

She brought her fears under control, and her thoughts continued, shifted.

Or have they come for Matthew?

She glanced at her tall son, sitting at the dining table with a large Mercator sea chart spread before him, just coming into his full man's frame at twenty-one, with his serious, dark eyes and strong, regular features. Home five weeks from Cambridge, he had graduated from Harvard, where he studied naval navigation and international commerce and the sea and stood third in his class. He had spent two summers working on frigates for Franklin Shipping, Ltd., learning the complex currents and winds of the Atlantic coast from Greenland to the West Indies.

She knew the British had need for good navigators, and fear surged as her mind raced.

Have they come to take Matthew? . . . like young Phillip Alsop fourteen months ago . . . just four blocks away? . . . they needed a ship's carpenter . . . took him at bayonet point . . . no one has heard from him since.

Or do they want Brigitte?

She glanced at her daughter, turned eighteen two months ago. Heart-shaped face, blue eyes, light brown hair which she wore long and pulled back by a ribbon, the best student in school. It was she who had secretly drafted a request, which some of the girls in school signed, and presented it to the schoolmaster, Horace Stallings.

Horace had pursed his lipless mouth, tipped his head back to peer through the bifocals perched on the end of his nose, and read it. Horrified, he convened a special public meeting of the school board and the Boston Ecumenical Society and read it aloud in the square, austere assembly hall. The nine men on the board had recoiled, white faced. Young women suggesting they abandon their God-ordained place as wives and mothers to enter colleges? What next? the right to public office and the vote? They blustered, red faced, but in the end they condescended to dismiss the entire confrontation, attributing it all to the misguided energies of children not yet matured, and the matter faded and died in the face of intransigent Boston puritanism.

Or do they want Caleb, or Adam and Priscilla, asleep in their beds?

She slowed her racing thoughts and turned her eyes back to John and waited for him to take charge. Always, always, since the day they married, he had been there to stand between trouble and her nest.

John raised his face to her and silently asked her the question.

She gave her head a nearly imperceptible shake. *No. I do not know who is knocking or why. But if the British have come to take you or Matthew, there will be trouble.*

John shifted his eyes to Matthew with the same silent question.

Matthew shifted his eyes from the door to John and shook his head slowly, mouth a straight line, dark eyes hot. *I don't know who it is, but if it's the British here for you or me, there will be a problem.*

Brigitte sat facing the fireplace in the carved oak upholstered rocking chair. She lowered the embroidery hoops that held the red rose design and waited for her father to turn his inquiring eyes to her.

She shook her head. *I don't know who it is. If it's the British, I have a few things to say.*

"Margaret, are the other children in bed?" John asked in a hushed tone.

"Yes. Asleep."

Quickly he slipped the musket trigger assembly he had been working on into the large drawer in his workbench, along with the tiny gunsmith's file and the strip of emery cloth. In one movement he closed the drawer and slid the inner workings of a clock onto the work space before him, along with the delicate tools of a master clockmaker.

He drew a breath. "Act normal and go on with what you were doing," he said with forced calm. "If it's the British, I'll talk. If they've come to arrest me, do nothing. I'll go with them."

Margaret gasped and clapped her hand over her mouth. "You will *not* go with them," she hissed. "They mean to be rid of you— you and the others." Her voice rose. "If you go with them in the cover of night, we'll never see you again!"

John rose to his full height and glanced about the large, austere, well-ordered parlor, searching for anything that would hint of the seven muskets he had crafted and hidden beneath the floorboards of the pantry, wrapped in oilcloth and tarp against the dampness of a Boston winter and spring. Hidden muskets intended to arm the rebellious militia would be enough evidence for them to throw him into the deepest cell in the hold of the next ship sailing for England, where he would die in an English dungeon. Satisfied there was nothing visible to hint of the hidden muskets, he walked across the bare, stone-sanded, polished hardwood floor, heels clicking in the silence.

"Calm yourself," he said quietly to Margaret. "Gage wouldn't dare imprison us. He might arrest us to show power and then release us, but not prison, nor England." He studied her for a moment while he waited for her to settle. Blue eyed, deep blonde hair, high cheekbones, nose straight and slightly turned up, full mouth, average height. Twenty-three years of marriage and six children—including the one they lost—had taken their toll, but John always saw her as she looked the day in June twenty-three years ago when he peered across Boston Common and she was there, in the full bloom of her eighteenth year. His eyes softened as they always did when he looked at her.

He spoke to Matthew as he reached the door. "If I have to go with them, wait a few minutes and then go find Tom Sievers and have him tell Warren what happened. Understand?"

"I understand, but it's wrong." Matthew half rose from his chair. "Resist them!"

Brigitte suddenly leaned forward, knuckles white as she grasped the embroidery hoops. "What right do they have to pound on our door at this hour?"

John raised a hand in caution. "Settle down. We'll resist, but we'll pick the time and place, and it won't be here and now. If they've come to arrest me, they've brought enough men to do it."

"You're going to let them take you?"

"We'll see." John waited until Matthew settled back onto his chair, rigid, ready.

John raised a finger to his lips, drew a heavy breath, and opened the door several inches. The chill of the night air washed over him with the familiar brine smell of the salt sea of Boston Harbor. A thin wet fog was rising from the ocean and beginning to swirl. The light from the room behind caught his hair and haloed his head.

"Who's there?" he called, squinting into the night. Behind him, no one moved nor breathed as they waited.

"It's me, Tom Sievers," came the low, rough voice from the gloom.

John exhaled loudly and his shoulders sagged as he swung the door wide and stepped to one side. Behind him, Margaret grasped the fireplace mantel to steady herself as she released her held breath, and Matthew leaned back in his chair and tipped his face toward the ceiling with his eyes closed. Brigitte relaxed her death grip on the embroidery needles and rounded her cheeks to blow air. Margaret strode to John's side to peer out past his shoulder.

"Tom!" John exclaimed. "Come in. Hurry!"

Tom appeared as a shadow from the fog and stood outside the threshold with hands clenched at his sides. Damp, matted hair hung loose past his shoulders. His frayed woolen coat and cotton shirt showed stains and dirt, and an eight-day gray beard stubble moved as he spoke. The handle of a knife and the iron head of a tomahawk bulged the coat at his waist. His eyes glowed from beneath shaggy brows like embers in his thin, hawk-nosed, narrow face, with an upper lip that was too long. A slanting scar forced a small gather at one corner of his mouth. Smells of rum and sweat and unbathed body reached John as Tom spoke.

"It would not be seemly for me to come in, the way I am." He raised his deep-set eyes, and his seamed, craggy face glowed earnestly in the shaft of light gleaming from the open door and making a small rainbow in the fog. "Come out. We got to talk. There's movement on the Back Bay."

John tensed.

The Back Bay! The body of water the British had to cross to get from the Boston Peninsula to the mainland. If they intended to move a force onto the mainland, they had to either cross the waters of the Back Bay or march their troops south over the Neck, the narrow strip of land that connected Boston to the continent. Movement on the Back Bay by the British could be the beginning of war.

John turned to Margaret. "I'll be outside for a while with Tom."

"Put on your coat," she said sternly. "It's cold and foggy. And stay in the yard. The British have eyes everywhere in the night." She lifted his coat from the carved and polished coat tree next to the door and handed it to him, and he slipped it on as he stepped out into the wet chill.

He led Tom from the door to the white gate in the front-yard picket fence, near the oak post with the large sign, on which was carved "John Phelps Dunson, Master Clockmaker and Gunsmith" and beneath that the likeness of a mantel clock and a musket. They stood motionless and listened intently to the sounds of the night to be certain they were alone.

The sound of distant bells came clanging as British warships moved cautiously through the fog-shrouded Boston Harbor. To the north, the streetlamps of downtown Boston and the wharves and docks of the Back Bay glowed dull gray in the swirling mist. From somewhere far away came the rhythmic cadence of marching men. Someone bawled indiscernible orders and the marching stopped, then continued. Faint, fragmented sounds of human voices drifted from the town, sometimes muffled, sometimes strangely clear and loud as the drifting, swirling fog worked its magic. Raucous laughter came queerly, and elsewhere someone cursed. Closer, a dog barked; there was a grunt and a sound, and the dog yelped in pain and the sound stopped. Across the narrow dirt street, something small scurried in the veiled darkness and was gone.

"What's moving on the Back Bay?" John asked softly.

"Six British officers finished supper at the Crow's Nest about eight o'clock but didn't go back to their barracks. They went on down towards the old commissary on the Back Bay shore, near the Common."

John nodded and Tom continued.

"You remember the longboats they beached and repaired two weeks ago?"

"Yes."

"That's where they are. Question is, why did they go to those boats tonight?"

"Anybody else there?"

"Maybe sixty, seventy regulars. Came sneaking in the dark."

"Who else knows?"

"Dawes. Revere. Maybe Warren." Tom stopped to wipe at his nose with his sleeve. "But that's not all. Earlier Gage ordered the marines and light infantry off regular duties until Gage says different."

"How do you know?"

"I saw a copy of his orders."

"How?"

"We got friends close to Gage."

John's eyes narrowed. "They're standing down? Why?"

"Not standing down. Doing something hidden. Don't know what it is. And one thing more." Tom's eyes became intense. "A citizen sneaked down to the officers when they was working on them boats and delivered something small, from his coat pocket."

"A message?"

"That's how I'm thinkin'."

"Any idea who it was?"

Tom shook his head. "I was south and he came and went from the north. I couldn't get around the soldiers in time to catch him in the fog."

"Are the streets still crowded?"

"Hah!" Tom grunted. "You know how it is. That Port Act the British laid on us has half the men in town out of work, and they're still in the streets, surly and looking for trouble. If they don't open the harbor soon, there'll be blood spilt on the cobblestones."

John let his eyes drop for a moment. "How many boats?"

"Over twenty."

John made calculations. "Enough for maybe five hundred men and their arms?"

"That's how I see it."

John pursed his mouth as he pondered. "Are they sending a major force inland? We better take a look." He paused to glance at Tom. "Are you hungry? When did you eat last?"

Tom shook his head impatiently. "Don't matter. We need to be about our business."

John strode back into the house. "I'll be gone for a while," he said to Margaret. "Lock the doors and turn out the lights and go to bed as soon as I leave, except for Matthew. I'll tap on the window when I get back."

Matthew asked, "Am I going?"

"Not this time. You sit in the dark and listen. Once an hour walk outside and take a look. Don't go to bed until after two."

Margaret marched across the room to confront him. "Off at night like a common spy, with a hundred soldiers hoping for a reason to take you. Aren't the Provincial Congress and that accursed Safety Committee enough for you?"

"There's no danger. I'll be back before morning."

"You are not taking your musket!" It was an order, not a question.

"No."

"Does Tom have his?"

"No. Get Brigitte and go to bed." He picked his hat from its peg on the rack by the door, paused to look back at Margaret, then was through the door and gone. Behind him, she stood framed in the light with her arms folded across her midsection until she could no longer see him, and then she closed the door.

He raised his coat collar against the damp chill as he and Tom closed the gate and turned south. They walked silently, quickly through the night, watching, listening, pausing at the intersections of the crooked, narrow cobblestone streets to peer ahead. Twice they crouched behind hedges while men walked past, and then they hurried on, working steadily south and west towards the Commons and the waterfront on the Back Bay.

"Feel it?" Tom whispered.

"Feel what?"

"The wind's rising. It'll move the fog out."

Through the mist they heard the lapping of the rising tide against the pilings of the wharves and rocks before they saw the choppy black waters of the Back Bay. Tom stopped suddenly and pointed upward. The moon was a disc behind the wind-driven fog streaming past its white face.

Tom pointed with his chin. "Revere's over at the foot of Beacon Street. The boats are between Beacon and Hollis, at about Fox Hill. We go up Pleasant to the shore and work north to Fox Hill."

John nodded and they crouched low and moved slowly up Pleasant Street. The dark buildings became increasingly shabby, then turned to abandoned derelicts.

Tom stopped twenty feet short of the rocks that lined the

shore and raised his arm to point north. "Up there. Hear?"

The muffled sounds of restrained cursing and grunting reached them. Ahead, something hard struck the hollow hull of a longboat and the sound echoed, unreal in the fog.

"They're doing something with the boats," Tom whispered. "Shall we go closer?"

"Where're the sentries? Did you locate the sentries earlier?"

"No."

"We don't move until we know where they are."

With the wind rising, they settled down to wait. The moon became less obscure, then cleared and shined. The fog thinned in the wind and then it was gone, and the great panorama of the Boston Back Bay lay before them bathed in the brilliant silver light of a full moon that cast a sparkling white bridge across the wind-driven, choppy waters and silhouetted the ships.

To the north, the lights of Boston gleamed. To the northwest, the muted night lanterns of half a dozen anchored British transport ships that had carried British troops from England showed dull, moving rhythmically with the rolling of the rising tide. Farther north the high lanterns of the British man-of-war *Somerset* undulated slightly as the great ship rode the incoming swells. The *Preston* and the *Boyne* flanked the *Somerset* in squadron formation to seal up the single narrow passage that gave deep-water ships access from the Atlantic to the Back Bay, the soft, vulnerable backside of the Boston Peninsula. Loaded for war, they rode deep in the water. Beyond the warships, farther to the north, the lights of Charlestown twinkled on the mainland.

Tom led John north, creeping among the rocks while the lapping high tide covered any sound as they crouched behind a smooth, massive boulder. Tom crept to the edge and slowly looked beyond. For several seconds he studied and counted, then drew back to allow John to look.

Twenty yards to the north, along the shore, John counted eighteen longboats already launched, held by uniformed soldiers standing to their knees in the backwater. Farther on a dozen soldiers grasped either side of the remaining four boats and on signal marched them into the water, then turned and splashed ashore. The broad white bands that crossed on their chests showed dull against the red coats, black in the moonlight, and their tall, pointed hats lent an unreal cast to their heads.

The officers in charge gave signals and the regulars slung their muskets, then clambered into their assigned boats, four men to the boat, including officers. The fifth man remained in the water, braced against the boat to launch it on command. Inside the boats, men set the oarlocks, then raised the huge oars, wrapped in sailcloth to silence them, and dropped them chunking into the locks. The men in the water bowed their backs and heaved, and slowly the beached boats inched forward as the mud released them, and then they were all free and floating while the men scrambled dripping from the water to take their places.

Tom watched intently as they maneuvered into formation. "North! They're strung out headed north!"

The boats hit a rhythm and moved steadily towards the black shapes of the men-of-war. Hushed calls were exchanged and lanterns appeared on the high-riding decks, and hawsers dropped over the railings and uncoiled in the night. Half an hour later all twenty-two boats were secured under the sterns of the ships, and the officers and troops had disappeared into the holds.

A minute later John whispered, "Did you hear any sentries leave?"

Tom shook his head. "Too much wind. I think they all got into the boats." He wiped his dirty sleeve across his mouth. "One way to find out."

He stood upright and strode boldly thirty yards up the shore, visible for two hundred yards in the bright moonlight. "Anybody there?" he called. It echoed slightly and died, and there was no sound above the wind and the driven water. No one challenged. No musket cracked. John trotted after Tom as three figures rose from the rocks near Fox Hill and came running.

"Who's with you, Tom?" came a tense voice.

"Revere, is that you?"

"Yes."

"I got John Dunson." They waited for Paul Revere, who stopped before them, breathing hard. He was flanked by two men.

"How many boats did you count?" Revere asked.

Tom recognized William Dawes, but studied the third man. "Who's this?"

Revere glanced back. "Peter Sheffield. Messenger from Menotomy."

"Been with you all night?"

"Yes. Why?"

"Someone delivered something to the British officers a while ago. Maybe an informer."

"We saw him come and go," Revere said, "but we couldn't follow him because of the sentries. It wasn't Sheffield."

Tom nodded. "Beggin' your pardon, Sheffield. No offense intended."

"None taken."

Paul Revere looked at John. "How many did you count?"

"Twenty-two."

"How many men?"

"Four or five per boat. Maybe a hundred in all."

"I calculated a hundred and ten. Any idea what they're up to?"

"Getting ready to move troops across the Back Bay. Probably Lexington."

Revere nodded emphatically. "I agree. We better get the committee. You get Thorpe and meet us at Warren's house in one hour. I'll get Palmer and Watson."

John nodded and drew his watch from his vest and turned it to the moonlight. "It's about twelve-fifteen. Warren's house in one hour. Be careful."

Ten seconds later the shoreline was vacant and silent as Revere moved east and Tom led John back south to Hollis, then east towards the Common. They crossed Clough Street, and Tom quickened his pace beneath the great boughs of lined oak trees that blotted out the sky. Suddenly he stopped and crouched, and his right hand slipped beneath his coat and drew his knife from his weapons belt. Two steps behind, John stopped, searching, probing. Ten seconds passed, and then John heard it. The whisper of someone moving through high grass. Tom tensed and pointed, and John peered into the deep shadows. There was a faint flicker of movement, and then it was gone and silence closed in.

"What was it?" John whispered.

"Someone watching us."

"British?"

"Not in uniform. Maybe the same man who brought the message to the officers. Want me to try for him?"

John considered for a moment. "Can't. We've got to get to Warren's."

Without a word Tom slipped his knife back into its worn leather sheath with the Huron quill and beadwork, and moved on eastward, then angled south. Fifteen minutes later he stopped at the door of Doctor Henry Thorpe, John beside him. There were no lights within. John rapped lightly at the door, waited twenty seconds, then rapped again. Tom faded back into the shadows and disappeared. The window beside the door suddenly glowed dimly and a strained voice came from within. "Who's there?"

"John Dunson and Tom Sievers."

Instantly the door opened and Thorpe—wrapped in a night robe, slender, barefooted, hair askew—faced John. Thorpe held a lamp shoulder high and peered at John wide-eyed. "John! What's wrong?" he inquired.

"The British are moving at the Back Bay."

Tom appeared behind him from nowhere and John turned.

"No one out there," Tom said. "We're all right."

John turned back to Thorpe and in terse sentences explained what they had seen on the Back Bay.

Thorpe asked, "What do you propose we do?"

"The committee—those we can get—is meeting at Warren's home at one-fifteen. Can you come?"

Thorpe glanced back into the darkness of the room behind him. "Do you want to go ahead or wait?"

"We'll wait out here."

Five minutes later Thorpe walked out, and Tom led them rapidly through the dark streets until they stood at the back door of a darkened home. Three minutes later they were seated at the large table in the study of Doctor Joseph Warren, where a single lamp cast dim light and long shadows on the wall. The windows were covered with thick black drapes.

The name of Joseph Warren was third on the British list of men to be instantly seized and thrown into prison should war break out. Only two were considered greater threats: Samuel Adams and John Hancock.

Thoughtful, educated, charismatic, respected, wise beyond his years, Warren openly strode the streets of Boston, hot and loud in his passion to throw the galling yoke of British tyranny from his beloved Massachusetts. He had publicly thrown down the gauntlet to General Gage himself. "Arrest me if you dare, but count well the price before you do, for the day I am in British irons is the day ten thousand of my countrymen rise and drive you into the sea."

Warren studied the strained faces of the eight men around his table, glowing yellow in the lamplight. "Revere says they took twenty-two longboats out to the men-of-war," he began, "and we don't know why. So let's back up a little. Gage got fresh troops from England ten days ago, grenadiers and marines—the best the British have. Now he's suspended them from all regular duties and got longboats into position. What does that tell us?"

"They're going after Adams and Hancock," Thorpe exclaimed.

"Or the cannon and munitions at Concord, or both," Watson said.

"He knows the arms are at Concord," Warren answered, "but he doesn't know *where* at Concord. I doubt he'd go after them, because he'd have to tear down the entire town to find them and dig up half the county for the ones that are buried." He paused. "Would he do it?" He studied his hands for a moment. "Maybe. I doubt it, but maybe. If he's decided to move, it's more likely he's after Adams and Hancock."

Tom's eyes moved from one man to the next, studying, while Warren continued.

"If that's his game, and he's decided on boats, they won't go south across the Neck to Roxbury, they'll move across the Back Bay, but then which direction? West through the farms and back-roads past Cambridge, or north on the main road past Charles-town, on to Mystic and Menotomy?"

For a moment no one spoke.

Tom broke the silence. "Across the Back Bay to Lechmere Point, then up the backroads past Harvard College and Cambridge and on north. He won't move troops on main roads where everybody'll see. He's scared of the militia and the minute companies."

Warren shook his head. "People at the college and Cambridge will see."

"Not if he moves silent, at night, on secret orders."

For a time no one spoke while they pondered whether Tom had guessed Gage's plan. Their thoughts leaped ahead, and suddenly each tensed as their minds reached the single question that had become a great, dark cloud hovering over the colonies.

Warren cleared his throat and put it to words. "Is this the act that triggers war?"

There it was! After five years of hot, face-to-face confrontation between the colonies and the British, the question lay naked on the table before them like a thing long awaited but too quickly arrived. They recoiled, recovered, then tentatively, hesitantly approached it.

Thorpe spoke, alarmed. "It's too soon. We're not ready. The militia isn't trained, or organized, nor armed well enough. We are not yet ready to take on the strength of the British army. Not yet."

All eyes turned to him and he continued.

"We *must have time!*" His balled fist thumped the table. "Gage intends forcing it now, on his terms. Take Adams and Hancock, and get our cannon and munitions at Concord if he can, and he has us. We won't have leadership or weapons." He stopped to shake his head. "It will be months before we can even *hope* to stand up to the cannon and muskets of the British regulars."

"What are you proposing?" Palmer asked in the silence that followed. "Let him take Adams and Hancock, and our stores?"

"No! Deal with him. Go to him and offer to give up some cannon and gunpowder, but not all."

John's mouth became a straight line, and Warren leaned forward on his elbows. "And what about Adams and Hancock?" Warren asked.

Thorpe shrugged. "Tell him we don't know where they are."

Warren shook his head. "He knows we do."

"Keep moving them. Tell Gage we can't control them."

"Gage won't ask where they are. He'll demand we produce them."

"Tell him we can't."

"He knows better."

Thorpe dropped his eyes and fell silent.

Palmer looked at Revere. "You've been carrying messages, you and Dawes. You know the temper out in the countryside. What do you say?"

Paul Revere looked at William Dawes for a moment before he answered. "If the British go after Adams or Hancock, or the munitions, our people in the country will fight whether they're ready or not."

"What if we gave part of the cannon and powder to Gage to save Adams and Hancock, without a fight?"

Revere's forehead wrinkled in thought, and the silence held until Tom interrupted.

"I'll tell you. Our militia would have the bunch of you in irons as traitors by nightfall, and go looking for Gage. The war would start right here in the streets of Boston, whether or not our people are well enough trained and armed. They'd storm the men-of-war in the harbor and burn 'em. Blood would flow like water."

He paused in silence so thick it was nearly palpable, then spoke again. "You haven't talked about the worst problem you got."

Warren's voice croaked as he spoke. "Which is what?"

"The temper of our own troops. Not Gage's. Ours."

"Meaning what?"

"They're past waiting. They're looking for an excuse. I think Gage just gave it to them. They won't tolerate a deal with Gage. So you've got a choice. Either you lead them into this, no matter how badly trained or badly armed they are, or they do it without you. That's the only decision you got to make."

In shocked silence the eight men stared at Tom. No one moved for a full half minute.

"It's true," John said quietly. "This committee is sworn to provide safety for our towns. We must slow this thing down for a time if we can, until we're better prepared, or we must lead our people into it if we can't; but whichever it is, we do it now or we step down."

Warren leaned forward on his forearms and all eyes fixed on him. He spoke firmly, decisively. "The time has come. Gentlemen, may God bless us in the plans we must now make. Revere, you have a hard ride ahead of you tomorrow. Adams and Hancock are at the home of the Reverend Jonas Clarke in Lexington. Do you know the place?"

"I do, but it's the Sabbath."

"God and Jonas Clarke will both understand. Adams and Hancock must know everything and you're the one to go tell them. Now, let's get on with a plan."

The moon had set before Warren doused the lamp and opened the back door of his home, and the eight men quickly disappeared in separate directions into the sleeping town of Boston. Tom led John back through the darkened, quiet streets, crouching but once, knife in hand, at a movement in the shadows.

The black sky had become deep purple in the east when Margaret heard the soft rap on the bedroom window, and she felt the tension drain as she realized John was home. She silently passed through the kitchen to the back door and swung it open. John entered and quickly closed it, and put out the lamp.

"Did anyone come while I was gone?"

"No."

"Did Matthew see anyone outside watching the house?"

"He thought he did once. Nothing came of it."

John walked silently through the dark room, and moments later sat on the bed working with his shoelaces, Margaret seated beside him.

"What happened?" she asked pensively, clutching her robe closed at her throat in the dim light.

For five minutes John spoke in low tones. When he finished, Margaret sat with downcast eyes, staring unseeing in the darkness.

Finally she spoke. "Why do you have to do these things?" she asked. Her tone was not accusing. It was filled with a sense of baffled wonder, and behind it lay her worst fear—that one day he would not be there.

John hesitated, then chose his words carefully. "I believe that, somehow, all this is happening for a reason. Sometimes I think I see part of the reason, but not all. What little I do understand reaches something inside of me that I cannot deny."

Margaret slowly shook her head. "It's happening because the British want to keep the colonies."

"I think that's part of the plan."

"Yes. Their plan."

"No. Not theirs, and not ours. A higher plan."

Slowly Margaret raised her eyes to his. In them she saw an earnestness she had never seen before and a depth of conviction that chilled her. She knew that the foundations of John's life were his family—her and the children. All he thought, all he did, was for them. If that was true, then why was he risking it all in this impossible business of provoking the British? Thirteen fledgling, untested, disorganized colonies, defying the power of the greatest nation and strongest military force on the face of the earth! Ridiculous! And why? They had every good thing life offered.

Why put it all at risk? Why? Confused in her heart, she said nothing as she hung her robe over the chair beside the bed and slipped beneath the thick goose-down comforter.

John turned out the lamp and stretched out beside her. He drew the comforter up and let out all his breath. He did not look at her, but he knew she would be staring at him in the darkness, unable to control the panic that had risen in her heart while he was out in the fog, moving among the British, then meeting in secret to help form a plan to push the British into the sea. He did not know how to talk to her about it, so he lay on his back in silence, waiting.

A time passed, and he felt the tension drain and his muscles began to relax before Margaret's voice came whispering in the dark. "Is the committee expecting war? Did they make a plan for war?"

John searched for a gentle way to say it, and could fine none. "We made a plan to defend our citizens. It's possible that could lead to war." He finished and lay waiting for her response.

A long time passed while he listened in the black silence to her measured breathing, and then her voice came low and subdued. "John, I'm frightened. Hold me."

Notes

The John Phelps Dunson family is essentially fictitious, although loosely based on one or more families living at the times depicted. Tom Sievers is also fictional, although his life is based on that of a real person.

Among the most reliable and respected historical accounts of the affairs portrayed in Part I are those of the renowned historian Allen French in his two works *General Gage's Informers* and *The Day of Concord and Lexington* (see the bibliography).

The critically important "Committee of Safety" was created by act of the Massachusetts Provincial Congress in October 1774, and was charged with the responsibility of acquiring arms and ammunition to be used on a

moment's notice to resist British aggressions and of providing safety for all citizens. From this beginning, the term *minutemen* evolved, being first used on
November 24, 1774, in the "Journals of the Congress." (See French, *The Day
of Concord and Lexington*, p. 21.)

The chronology and substance of the events described between the
evening of Saturday, April 15, 1775, when Bostonians noticed British regulars
working their way to the Back Bay and launching the longboats, and the night
of April 19, 1775, when the battles of Concord and Lexington concluded, are
historically accurate (see French, *The Day of Concord and Lexington* and *General
Gage's Informers*).

The names of those on the Committee of Safety as given in the novel are
accurate (see Birnbaum, *Red Dawn at Lexington*, p. 82).

Among the British men-of-war stationed at Boston were the *Somerset*, the
Boyne, and the *Preston* (see French, *The Day of Concord and Lexington*, p. 80; Miller,
Sea of Glory, p. 25).

CHAPTER II

★ ★ ★

*T*he wind died in the gray of dawn, and the Back Bay calmed. For a few moments the sun's first rays set high clouds afire. Jays and robins scolded from trees. A dog barked. A rooster cocked its head and saluted the morning, and hens came clucking, button eyes searching for grain in a chicken yard. A Jersey cow with one crooked horn stood by a milking shed, patiently waiting for relief for her dripping udder, while her calf bawled its displeasure at being held in another pen to be weaned. Bells clanged on ships in the harbor, changing the watch.

The snows and winds of the Atlantic winter were past for another season, and green things were awakening from their sleep. The first plowing and planting had been done in the countryside, bringing the scent of fresh-turned earth that mingled with the salt smell of the ocean, each with its promise of bounty for those willing to labor. People swept life's troubles into a guarded corner of their minds, to wait until their souls had tasted the renewal of life sufficient to once again pick up their load and trudge on.

Margaret padded silently through the kitchen in her heavy felt slippers and house robe, and quietly opened the back door. For a moment she stood in the door frame and gloried in the beauty of the fresh, clean, pristine morning, dew sparkling in the sun's first light. She stepped onto the brick pathway and glanced at the cherry and apple trees that bordered the white picket fence to her left. The buds were bursting their hulls, and the green leaves and white blossoms were peeking out, stretching, impatient to get on with their wondrous transition to full, rich fruit. In the flower beds beneath, the tulip bulbs so carefully planted by Brigitte in unconventional patterns and color schemes had pushed upwards to the warmth of the spring sun, and the green pods were splitting to reveal full blossoms in a breathtaking mosaic of red and yellow.

Margaret looked at the great oak tree at the rear of the spacious yard, a full sixty feet from base to top. The tree had grown with the family, and it seemed to her that the great, spreading arms now embraced the entire yard with a sense of comfort and security. Thirteen years ago, John and Matthew had built a circular bench around the massive trunk, and it soon became the special place for the entire family. The bench that girdled the old tree had witnessed the hushed whispering of secrets, the remorse of confessions, the mending of hurts, the laughter of excited children at play, the silent, somber reflections of troubled minds, and the first kiss of true love four years ago, when Matthew had secretly led Kathleen from a family supper to the bench and awkwardly kissed her, a quick, wide-eyed peck—the first for both of them. Neither of them could look at the other for the next two days at school without diverting their eyes while they blushed, and neither of them could sleep for two nights, remembering the sweet, stunning shock of it.

Margaret smiled with the remembrance of John and Matthew working with the saw and hammer and measuring tape to build the bench. At age eight, Matthew was so excited with self-importance at doing a man's work that he was everywhere, into everything, wide-eyed, peering constantly into his father's face, seeking any hint, any sign of approval. John grinned ruefully the second day as they put away the tools and came to the kitchen for supper. "Much more help from Matthew and that bench will take all year," he muttered. "You think you're building a bench?" Margaret retorted. "You're building a man." John smiled and never again spoke of the nuisance of working with the children.

She glanced at the greening shrubs along the fence to the right and at the thick grass in the yard with its first showing of yellow dandelions. Even the sunken root cellar six feet from the back door, with its pitched roof, was grass covered. The shingle-roofed well, with its circle wall and oak windlass, stood in the near right corner of the backyard; in the far right corner stood the outhouse, with the brick path leading to its door. The house and the well and the outhouse, all brick, were whitewashed every second year by John and the boys.

For a moment her eyes took in the wood yard, as John called it, to the right of the door. One cord of soft yellow pine and one cord of cured maple were cut to kindling size and stacked against the rear wall of the house. Pine burned quick and hot, maple slow, and each served a purpose in the chores of the day. The scarred, battered chopping block stood close by, and the single-bitted axe, handle shiny from use, and the one-man crosscut saw with the turnbuckle to adjust blade tension hung from their pegs on the wall. A household of seven required an unending supply of firewood; John had cut it all until Matthew was of age, and Matthew cut it until last year when Caleb had come strong enough to set cured logs on the sawhorses and cut them into eighteen-inch rungs with the saw, and then swing the axe with enough authority to split the rungs into kindling. The chips were raked and gathered into a pan and carried with the clean white kindling sticks to the wood box by the gaping entrance into the great fireplace. At day's end Margaret banked the live coals to hold their heat in order to start the cooking fires the next morning, and so the fires never died, and the wood box had to be refilled each evening. Brigitte was assigned to sweep the daily ashes into a brass bucket to be dumped into a large box outside, where they were picked up monthly by the ash man in his large, horse-drawn, two-wheeled cart. He delivered them to the smelly soap factory near the east docks, where they were leached and cured, mixed with lye and tallow, and fashioned into large yellow-brown bars of strong laundry soap.

Margaret drew deeply at the sweet air and casually, thoughtfully, walked the brick path to sit on the bench beneath the oak.

How she treasured the quiet solitude of earliest morning, before any of the children were awake, when she could let her mind run free and unfettered to sort out and make sense of the troubles and problems that had piled up during the daily rush. Occasionally, in good weather, she would simply sit motionless on the bench and reflect in the peace and quiet while gray and red squirrels chattered and scurried; other times she chose to sit in her own clean, familiar, orderly kitchen—her kingdom, her dominion—where she knew the deep joy of preparing the food that fed the bodies of her family, a task she performed with the love that fed their souls. In those private moments the night faded in the light of a new day, and reality drove away the demons, and problems dwindled, and life become manageable once again.

A somberness crept over her now as the remembrances of the night came flooding. John and Tom gone—the British on the Back Bay—a midnight meeting with Warren and the Committee of Safety—plans—muskets under the pantry floor—all of it shaping into a head-on, armed confrontation—war. John among the leaders—Matthew at risk. War, war, war—it echoed relentlessly in her brain.

And there was absolutely nothing she could do to stop it, change it, protect her own. Always, always, she had found a way to stand between her nest and trouble. But now, facing the most unthinkable threat of all—the possibility of losing John or Matthew—she was utterly helpless. There was no remedy for the dark foreboding that had wakened her an hour ago, trembling and sweating from dreams of them dead on some distant battlefield.

She sat for a time, searching for an answer that would not come. Then she squared her shoulders and released a great breath and stood and drew her robe tighter and looked towards the house with firm, practical New England resolution.

There's nothing I can do about it, and breakfast will not prepare itself and beds will not make themselves and children won't be ready for church by themselves. She pursed her mouth. *There's no rest for the wicked, and the righteous don't need it. I wonder which I am.*

As she retraced her steps towards the kitchen door, an unexpected thought suddenly emerged and a wry smile flashed. *I wonder if Homer Ellers will be at church this morning, after Brigitte wounded him last Sunday.*

Small, dour, supremely confident in his pseudo-intellectualism, Homer had made the mistake of challenging a casual remark made by Brigitte about geography and politics. "The Azores are too far from American shores to be of significance to the colonies," she had said.

"Not so," Homer had chortled. "Their strategic location is important to all Atlantic navigation."

Brigitte rounded her eyes in humble surprise and retorted, "Oh, I forgot! They certainly are important to navigating Cape Horn."

Homer glowed. He had corrected Brigitte Dunson, brightest of the bright. "Precisely what I had in mind," he said grandly, his chest expanded and his nose too high.

"Of course," Brigitte continued, loudly enough for anyone within thirty feet to hear, "it would be helpful if someone would move the Azores from the North Atlantic to the tip of South America, where Cape Horn is located, don't you think, Homer?"

Giggles tittered as Homer reddened and his face fell.

What's to be done with that girl? She's affronted half the respectable boys in Boston with her brain and sharp tongue. She'll be a spinster if she doesn't stop humiliating them. And this business of girls wanting to go into nursing and accounting and all—what's this new generation coming to?

She remembered well the hours she and John had spent, talking far into the night in their efforts to dissuade Brigitte from plunging into nursing before she even understood what life was about. They had finally struck a compromise. She would remain at home for one year to help Margaret. If she still felt compelled to go into a profession, they would discuss it again.

Margaret entered through the back door into the parlor and plucked the leather bellows from its peg on the wall near the fireplace. Patiently she worked the oak handles to pump air against the banked coals, gently at first, then stronger as sparks flew and flames licked. She placed shavings, then larger pieces of split, dried pine, then maple, then the big rungs on each of the four fires in the great opening. She hung three fire-blackened kettles on the arms, dipped water from a bucket into two of them, and set the lids.

She carried a broad, shallow copper pan out the back kitchen door and lifted the heavy door to the root cellar, descended the five steps, and selected a cabbage, carrots, and turnips. Climbing the steps back to the light and sounds of the beautiful morning, she found a smile tugging despite the dark shadows that had ridden heavy. She set the vegetable pan on the worktable and returned to the root cellar for the gallon jar of cool milk to be poured into the one empty kettle to scald. With the Thorpes coming for dinner, there would be a clamor for her famous custard.

She chuckled and shook her head at the remembrance of how the invitation had been extended to the Thorpes for today's dinner.

It had happened the previous Sunday. The Reverend Silas Olmsted—aging, slight, round-shouldered—had droned through his colorless sermon, and services had ended. The austere, high-ceilinged South Church chapel was buzzing with the usual exchange of greetings and news and gossip while the congregation patiently filed out the high double doors into the churchyard. Matthew and Kathleen were lost in each other as they worked their way towards an oak tree near the corner of the churchyard. Henry Thorpe's eyes narrowed in satisfaction as he watched them go, and his wife Phoebe smiled modestly. The four younger Thorpe children were chattering as they tugged and romped with Adam and Priscilla and Caleb. Henry and Phoebe were chatting with John and Margaret while they waited until Matthew and Kathleen returned, and the families started on their way home, the Thorpes leading the way, since they lived two blocks past the Dunson home. Before they had cleared the churchyard, Matthew suddenly trotted ahead and called to Henry Thorpe, who stopped and turned, puzzled.

"Sir," Matthew exclaimed, "it would be most appreciated if you and your family would share dinner with our family next Sunday afternoon."

Phoebe stared wide-eyed at Margaret while John stared at Matthew. Henry's eyebrows arched in utter surprise, and for a moment his mouth dropped open. He snapped it closed and looked at John inquiringly.

Matthew did not flinch. He looked steadily into Henry's eyes and concluded, "Would that be agreeable, sir?"

Henry glanced at Kathleen for an explanation, but she stared at the ground and refused to raise her head. He turned to Phoebe, who signalled she was as stunned as he. Invitations by one family to another to share a Sunday dinner never came from other than the head of the house, or at least the wife. What ailed Matthew?

"Why, uh, of course," Henry blurted. "That would be nice." He recovered some presence of mind and battled a smile as he spoke to John, just approaching with the family. "I presume Matthew speaks for the master of the house?"

John was caught flat-footed. He choked down a smile and answered, "I presume he does."

Henry threw back his head and laughed, and a moment later John joined him. Margaret and Phoebe clapped their hands over their mouths in their struggle to avoid loud laughter on the Sabbath, and the Reverend Silas Olmsted appeared to quietly remind the two men that it was unseemly for two of the pillars of the church and community to engage in such an uproar on the Lord's Sabbath.

Both men sobered and apologized, and then battled to contain another outburst while they gathered their families for the walk home.

Kathleen Thorpe was the eldest of the Thorpe children. Dark eyed and dark haired, approaching her twenty-first birthday, she was tall, striking, spirited, capable, a born mother. In her third year at school she somehow knew in her child's heart that she would one day marry Matthew, despite the fact she was then a confirmed tomboy, to the unending consternation of her modest, quiet, reserved mother. In her fourth year, with two front teeth so large they seemed to fill her entire smile, she beat Alvin Wasselman at hoops, then hoisted her skirt to her knees and wrestled him to the ground when he accused her of cheating. In her sixth year she changed; no longer the tomboy. In her eighth year she knew the pain of ultimate tragedy when Matthew told her he would be going to sea the next summer. She knew in her heart that he would be shipwrecked on a desert island, where he would languish without food or water and die, never knowing the breadth and depth of her love. And she would never love another; rather, she would waste away until she was old and gray, a martyr to her all-consuming love. When he didn't go to sea, she pouted for a week, angry at him for cheating her of her one shining opportunity for martyrdom.

In their ninth year Matthew had used his father's clockmaker's tools to carve a small, beautiful snow owl for her birthday gift, with painted eyes and the feathers veined and delicate and snow-white. It instantly became her treasure of treasures. She kept it locked in her cedar chest, to be taken out and held tenderly while she gently stroked it and pressed it to her heart when she knew she was alone. In the tenth grade she had spent two months patiently creating for Matthew a watch fob of royal blue silk with his initials beautifully cast in red letters edged in white. His eyes shined when he saw it, and he put it away in his drawer, to be used only when he got his first gold-plated watch.

When he left for college she told him she would be waiting when he returned. He wrote faithfully, and she tied his letters and put them with the owl; and she wrote him every week, and waited for his visits. Four times his first year he walked from Cambridge to Boston, just to see her. The two summers he later spent on the sea mastering maritime navigation were endless, and she waited at the window for the postman to bring news of what exotic port he had last visited.

Margaret smiled at the warm memories, and her thoughts

settled on the dinner she was preparing. Matthew's spontaneous invitation to the Thorpe family had caught everyone by surprise, including Kathleen. *Is he planning to make the big announcement? No, not yet. That will come after he's been approved to graduate in September, and discussed it with John and me. He wouldn't just suddenly jump into it without talking to us. Would he?* Her forehead wrinkled in frustration. *Would he?*

In the week since the startling invitation, she had noticed him glancing restlessly at the calendar, then the clock, and she knew the thought that was running through his mind like a chant, like an impatient drumbeat: Kathleen's coming . . . Kathleen's coming . . . Kathleen's coming. She softened as she remembered the sweetness of it twenty-three years ago when it pulsed in her blood—John's coming . . . John's coming . . . John's coming.

She heard the soft padding of feet behind and turned. "What brings you into the kitchen so early?" she asked.

Matthew, fully dressed, settled onto a chair by the big table. "Couldn't sleep. You're up early."

"A lot to do. Can't stop thinking about Kathleen, can you?"

Matthew ducked his head for a moment and reddened. "Making custard?"

"No," Margaret said, "I thought I'd serve ashes and seashells."

Matthew snorted.

Margaret glanced at the clock on the massive oak mantel above the fireplace. About seven forty-five, Sunday morning, April 16. John had made all the clocks in the house, and they were among the most accurate in the colonies. They were Dunson clocks, sought after over the entire Chesapeake Bay and in shipping ports as far north as Portland, Maine.

She remembered the day she saw John across the Boston green—June, over twenty-three years ago. He was standing alone, dressed in moccasins and buckskin breeches and a homemade woolen shirt, one arm cocked over the muzzle of his musket, long hair pulled back by a buckskin string, staring at her. Though she had pondered it many times, she could never decide what had stopped her, made her return his frank gaze. His features were regular, firm, strong set to his shoulders, and his feet were planted like tree stumps. Was it the total honesty she felt from him? Or was it the solid feeling that he knew what he wanted, and that whatever it was he would get it? He had learned to read and write and cipher in the tiny log school of the hamlet of Marsden, forty miles north, where he was orphaned by Indians. He was a crack woodsman, and could drive nails at fifty feet with a ball from his musket. He had come to Boston to learn a trade, and within days was an apprentice clockmaker and gunsmith. They had married at the end of one year, and steadily, relentlessly he pursued his chosen trade until Dunson clocks and muskets were renowned throughout the colony. He chafed at the oppression of the British and spoke out. His common-sense steadiness and resolve were soon recognized—the Provincial Congress, the Committee of Safety—and inevitably, one day at a time, he was emerging as a natural-born leader, prominent and popular in town meetings.

Margaret spoke to Matthew without turning. "Go tell Brigitte to come. I need her help and she needs to learn."

Matthew stood. "When did Father return?"

For a moment Margaret's face clouded. "Nearly four o'clock."

Matthew blew air softly through rounded lips. "Trouble?"

"He'll tell you, but don't wake him. He needs sleep."

Matthew quietly wakened Brigitte, then returned to the kitchen and sat down and asked again, "Was there trouble? Last night, I mean."

"Not the kind you mean."

"Then what kind?"

"The British may be planning a troop movement."

Matthew leaned forward, voice suddenly tense. "Where? When?"

Margaret shook her head. "Wait till your father is awake."

Brigitte walked into the kitchen wearing her robe, her long blonde hair tied back with a bit of ribbon. Her heavy woolen slippers were silent on the polished floor.

"Good morning, sunshine," Margaret said cheerfully. "Put on

your apron. We've work to do if we're feeding half of Boston this afternoon."

"Oh, Mother, it's just the Thorpes," Brigitte groaned. "Feed them hominy grits and well water."

Margaret shook with a silent laugh. "That's an improvement on the ashes and seashells I'd planned. Get the leg of lamb from the root cellar."

Brigitte reached for the large, shallow copper pan and walked out.

Margaret opened the door to the firebox beneath the oven, built into the front of the fireplace, beside the great opening. She scooped burning coals in a copper shovel and dumped them onto the floor of the firebox, then stuffed in shavings, then larger sticks, and watched until they caught. She closed the door and set the draft openings on the front.

Brigitte walked back in with the pan. Her eyes glowed, and she was smiling. "Beautiful out there."

"The Lord's own Sabbath," Margaret said. "Now, wash the meat and get busy with the basil leaves and thyme." She turned to Matthew. "Busy hands are happy hands. Go fetch a pan of potatoes and knock the sprouts off."

"My hands are happy the way they are."

"Then they'll be overjoyed when you fetch the potatoes. Move." Her eyes snapped. Matthew picked up the copper pan and walked out.

Margaret turned back to Brigitte and watched with approval as her daughter worked the spices into the leg of lamb. Matthew walked in the back door with the potatoes.

"Now scrub the potatoes," she said to Brigitte, "and then get started on the griddle cakes. I'll wake the children."

She stopped to lift the lid on the milk kettle to be certain it was not boiling, then started for the archway to the bedroom wing as John entered.

"You can sleep for twenty more minutes before breakfast," Margaret said.

"I'm fine."

She continued through the archway and then down the hall to awaken Caleb, growing daily at age fourteen, and the seven-year-old twins, Adam and Priscilla.

Matthew faced John. "What happened last night?"

John glanced at Brigitte and gave Matthew a head signal. "Let's take a walk."

Brigitte straightened and stopped working with the potatoes. "Something I can't hear?"

"No, something others can't hear." John led Matthew out the back door, past the root cellar, to the rear fence, while Brigitte stood for a moment at the back door with her hands on her hips and called, "What do you think I'd do? Shout it from the pulpit at church? Humph! Men!" She finished with the potatoes and went to the pantry for flour, sugar, and salt.

Outside, the two men settled onto the bench that circled the oak.

"What happened last night?" Matthew asked.

For five minutes John spoke while Matthew listened intently, and he sat silent for a few moments while the facts settled in. "Revere's gone?" Matthew asked.

"Left before daylight."

"Tom Sievers?"

"Trying to find out who's spying for Gage."

"Tell me about Tom. Why is he the way he is? What is there between you and him? Why do you feed him and let him sleep here when he needs it?"

John leaned forward, elbows on knees, and for a moment slowly rubbed his palms together in deep thought.

"Maybe you're old enough." Again he paused. "Have you ever heard of the snowshoe men?"

"A little."

"I was seventeen, and Tom was twenty-one. He was married and had a son a year old. We lived north of here in a little village named Marsden. It's gone now. The Indians raided those small towns to get rid of us. We had to fight them. We found out they didn't like to fight in the winter because we could track them in the snow. So we made snowshoes and organized patrols. We carried the fight to them and drove them farther north. We became known as the snowshoe men."

John paused.

Matthew stared. "You never talked about this before."

"There was no reason to."

"Look at Tom now! A filthy drunkard that talks to himself and wears a knife and tomahawk all the time. What happened?"

"Tom and I were assigned together. He was one of the finest woodsmen I ever knew. He was a dead shot at one hundred yards. I never saw anyone handle a knife or tomahawk the way he could. He was without fear. He loved his wife and his son with all his heart. Her name was Elizabeth, the boy was Jacob."

Matthew stared in disbelief.

"The Indians hit our town in February, and several of us followed them. We caught them—Huron—about fourteen miles north of town and there was a fight. We killed over half of them before the others ran. We thought we had seen the last of them until we returned to Marsden, or what was left of it."

Matthew licked dry lips.

"The party we followed had been a decoy. About a hundred others had waited until we were gone before they moved on Marsden. No one was left alive in town. My family was all killed. So was Tom's."

"I knew about Grandmother and Grandfather, but no one ever said how it happened nor that Tom lost his family too. You didn't become a drunkard. What happened to Tom?"

Moments passed before John answered. "We found his wife in the yard and his son by the milking shed. Everything had been burned to the ground and the livestock slaughtered."

"But why has he become—"

John cut him off. "Let me finish. I said we found his wife and son dead. The truth is, we found part of them. It took us over an hour. There were parts of them we never did find."

Matthew choked.

John stared hard at his hands. "We buried what we had, and two days later Tom disappeared. A year later we heard there was a wild man up north, killing every Huron he could find. I guessed who it was. The following summer I spent two months tracking him. I think he was insane when I found him, and I understood why because I saw what they did to his wife and son. No one ever knew how many Huron he killed. He had eaten part of some of them."

Matthew did not move.

"He said he wasn't coming back until he found Elizabeth and Jacob. What he meant was, he wanted to find what had been missing."

Matthew closed his eyes and his head rolled back.

John continued. "It took me another month to get him to come back. He never stopped mumbling about Elizabeth. Sometimes he'd disappear all day in the woods, looking for her."

John drew a deep breath and released it. "I came to Boston, and Tom came with me because he had no other place to go and no one else who understood. In time, he changed enough to be in town. He still mumbles to Elizabeth once in a while, but he doesn't realize it. He drinks to forget."

"I didn't know," Matthew whispered.

"Your mother knows most of it, so she feeds him and lets him sleep here once in a while. Despite what he is, Tom's still one of the best fighting men I know." John stopped and for a time stared unseeing at his hands. "Keep this to yourself. Not many in town know about it, and they don't need to."

They sat quietly in the warmth of the morning sun for a time while Matthew struggled. He raised his head and looked at his brick home, square and solid and whitewashed, and at the tulip and hyacinth beds along the white fence, and the giant oak spreading above his head, and the pruned cherry and apple trees just bursting into blossom. He looked, and he thought, and said nothing.

He turned back to John. "I didn't know you had fought the Indians—that you were a fighting man."

"There was no reason to tell you until now. It's far behind me."

"You carried a musket? a knife and tomahawk? You killed?"

"Yes."

"Is that how you became a dead shot?"

"Yes. Tom taught me most of it."

Matthew stood for a moment and walked away. He gathered his thoughts and returned. "I never knew that."

"It happened. It was necessary." He reflected for a moment. "Or at least we thought it was."

Matthew slowly sat down beside his father and studied the ground for a time. He raised his head and spoke firmly. "You said Revere was riding to tell Adams and Hancock what's happening."

John realized Matthew was changing the direction of their thoughts. The talk of Tom Sievers and of the events from long ago was closed, and Matthew had accepted it.

"Yes. He is."

"Is this the beginning of the war?" Matthew asked.

"No one wants it, but it could happen. We're not ready for it. But if they go after Adams and Hancock, or our arms, it will probably end in a fight, and if it's bad enough it could bring on war."

"When will we know?"

"No way to tell. We stall and prepare. But one thing we all agreed on last night. They have to provoke it. They have to fire on us first."

"Why?"

John studied the deep-set eyes. "Principle. We must have the advantage of being the victims."

"They've already done that at the massacre on King Street."

"Too long ago."

"What's happening today?"

"Wait for their next move, and for Revere."

The back door swung open and both men turned. Margaret walked out and called, "Come get ready for breakfast, and bring four eggs."

The men looked at each other, and both recognized that in their time together beneath the oak something new, something binding had occurred between them. They started back to the house together.

"What about you and Kathleen?" John asked.

"I intend to marry her this spring."

"Good. Have you told your mother?"

"No. I was going to wait until later this week."

"They're coming for dinner today." John grinned at the remembrance of the unplanned invitation. "Didn't you get all this backwards? The talk first, the announcement dinner after?"

Matthew shrugged through an embarrassed grin. "Well, you know, I didn't mean to. It just came out that way."

"I thought so." John chuckled softly, then sobered and spoke again. "Your mother said someone might have been prowling last night."

"About two o'clock I thought I heard something, but I don't know. Nothing happened."

John stopped at the root cellar for the eggs before walking into the kitchen. He set them on the worktable as Margaret opened the oven door and carefully slid the meat pan inside. She latched the door, adjusted the draft in the firebox, and turned back to the worktable. Expertly she cracked the four eggs into the griddle-cake batter, and then she stirred with her large wooden spoon and raised it above the bowl to let the thick batter drip back while she watched to see if it was lumpy enough. It was.

She quickly settled the four-legged griddle over the fourth fire, dropped a spoonful of lard onto it, and watched it melt and spread. She tucked the batter bowl under one arm, leaned forward, and rapidly scooped six large, round portions of the batter onto the griddle and watched to see how rapidly the bubbles formed on top and burst. Satisfied the griddle was not too hot, she called, "Matthew, get the children to the table."

Five minutes later they all bowed their heads and John clasped his hands before his face and offered grace. The first twelve cakes were buttered, drenched in sweet New England maple syrup, and half-eaten when Margaret brought the next twelve. She helped the twins butter theirs, poured the syrup, and began cutting the steaming cakes for them.

"Let them do it, Mother," Brigitte interrupted. "They're old enough."

"I'll help," she answered defensively, knowing it was no justification, but afraid to speak of why she hovered over her two youngest, doing too much for them, refusing to let them grow up. Ever present in her mother's heart was the ache left behind when Sarah, three years younger than Caleb, had come home from school in January four years ago, fevered and coughing. Nine days later she died of pneumonia. Months passed before Margaret smiled, and it was a year before she quit changing the sheets on Sarah's bed along with the other beds in the house. From the day of the funeral, Margaret hovered over the twins. She knew she was wrong, that she had to let them grow up, but promised herself daily that there was time and that her need to protect them would lessen. But it had not.

"Clear the table while I start the dough for muffins," she said to Brigitte.

Brigitte turned to Adam and Priscilla. "You two help, and be careful with the dishes."

"Caleb, fetch a dozen eggs in that bowl," Margaret directed, "and be careful. Drop them and we won't have custard."

Caleb laid down his fork and rose. At fourteen he was suffering the torments of a body that was out of control and a mind that did not know from one minute to the next who or what he was. His knuckles, knees, and elbows seemed nearly deformed in their rush to full manhood, and coordinated movement from any of them was a thing he could only vaguely remember. Life had become a nightmare of clumsiness. None of his clothes fit his frame, nor could Margaret alter them rapidly enough to catch up. He never knew from hour to hour whether he would be brave or burst into tears over nothing. He had stopped singing in school or church after his voice cracked for the third time and wandered off into sounds he had never heard before. He would be as tall as John and Matthew, but his facial features favored the fine, high cheekbones and aquiline nose and generous mouth of Margaret.

"Yes'um," he said quietly, and reached for the bowl. Margaret stopped to watch him carry it out the back door, then released held breath and shook her head with sympathetic understanding.

The dough had risen before the clanging of the church bell, five blocks to the north, brought Margaret up short as she laid out her church clothes in her bedroom. "Where has the morning gone?" she exclaimed. "Brigitte, come here. Adam, Priscilla, church in fifteen minutes. Finish dressing." She handed a brush to Brigitte and reached for a comb. "You do Priscilla, I'll do Adam."

Ten minutes later she ran a critical eye over Priscilla and said, "Now, go stand in the parlor and don't muss yourself." Then she walked quickly to the kitchen, punched the dough, watched it collapse, and covered it again with heavy cheesecloth. She added eight average sticks of kindling to the oven firebox and twisted the drafts in the front door two-thirds closed. It took years to learn an oven.

She called to Brigitte as she strode back to her bedroom, "Watch the twins while I do my hair."

John waited at the front door until they were all assembled, then gave them the usual inspection and stern reminder, "Mind your manners and restrain yourselves. This is the Sabbath."

Brigitte's impish grin flashed. "Like you and Henry Thorpe last Sunday?" she chortled.

John fixed her with a stern stare. "That's enough, young lady."

"Oh! Sorry, Father," she said demurely. Looking demure usually bridged any rifts.

John turned on his heel to hide a smile, and marched out the front door, Margaret on his arm, the children following in the standard, accepted Boston formation. Past the front gate, John turned north into the processional of other proper families, dressed in their Sunday best, women in their Sunday bonnets, walking through the narrow cobblestone streets to Old South

Church. Matthew called and waved to his lifelong closest friend, Billy Weems, who shouted from half a block and waved back and came running. From earliest recollection, Matthew and Billy had been inseparable. Billy, shorter, husky, freckled, sandy haired, was impetuous, impulsive, and when he grinned, irresistible. Somehow the boys had sensed that Billy's open, cheerful view of life was the perfect counterbalance for Matthew's serious side, and at twenty-one, they had no secrets from each other.

"Good morning to you all," Billy grinned to the family, and fell in beside Matthew.

"Good morning, Billy," Margaret said. "Looking well."

"Thank you, Mrs. Dunson," Billy replied, "and you're lovely as always." He grinned until his eyes closed, and Margaret blushed and ducked her head and Brigitte groaned and John smiled.

"Matthew, how are you?" He whacked Matthew between the shoulder blades.

Matthew winced. "I have a broken back, thank you."

"Well," Billy said, studying Matthew's back, "a hunch back there will add something to your natural good looks."

Families called greetings, hats were tipped, gossip exchanged, and children scolded, as the magic of a beautiful Sabbath spring morning spread through Boston.

They were two blocks from the church when Matthew touched John's shoulder from behind and his quiet words gripped the entire family. "We're being followed."

John turned. Half a block behind, four British grenadiers with their muskets slung, bayonets mounted and pointing upward, were keeping pace with the family. Their red coats and the white crossed bands gleamed in the bright sun. John turned back and his eyes swept the street ahead. Two British officers stood on the next corner watching the family approach. The epaulets of a captain gleamed on the shoulders of one, and those of a lieutenant on the other.

Margaret clutched at John's arm, panic and fear in her eyes. *They know about last night—they're after John.*

"Keep walking," John said evenly, "as though nothing were happening."

Notes

The general description of the great fireplace in the Dunson home (such fireplaces being the area where, in colonial times, nearly all cooking was done in pots and pans hung on heavy, swinging arms) and of the root cellar (where milk and other perishables were kept cool) was gathered from several sources, chief among them Ulrich, *Good Wives* and *A Midwife's Tale;* Furnas, *The Americans;* and Colbert, ed., *Eyewitness to America.*

The reference to the snowshoe men and their resistance to the Huron Indians is historically accurate.

The sending of Paul Revere on Sunday, April 16, 1775, to warn Samuel Adams and John Hancock of the launching of the British longboats the night before is historically correct. Sam Adams and John Hancock were hiding at the residence of the Reverend Jonas Clarke in Lexington (see French, *The Day of Concord and Lexington,* p. 66).

Sunday, April 16, 1775

CHAPTER III

★ ★ ★

*T*hey held their steady pace, eyes locked onto the two officers ahead, Margaret clinging to John's arm. She gasped when the
officers stepped into the cobblestone street and two regulars
appeared from the corner to follow the officers, in military step,
muskets slung on their backs. Margaret's eyes widened when the
officers turned directly towards them, their shiny black boots
clumping a steady cadence on the brick sidewalk. Margaret craned
her neck to look behind where the four grenadiers marched thirty
feet in back of them. Half a dozen families on both sides of the
street slowed and conversations became hushed while fingers
pointed as the soldiers closed on the family, front and back.

The officers stopped when they were ten feet from John and
blocked the sidewalk, side by side. John slowed and stopped, with
Margaret white-faced, clutching his arm. They waited.

The captain studied John dispassionately, without a word. For
long moments the buzzing of bees and the quarrelling of jays
seemed too loud in the silence. Behind Margaret, Brigitte's mouth
was clenched shut and her eyes were points of light as she tenu-
ously held control of her temper, and then she could take no
more. She strode forward in her white high-waisted Sunday dress
and white bonnet, and opened her mouth to hotly confront the
two officers and demand an explanation for being stopped in the
streets of Boston. And then she slowed, and her face thrust forward slightly as her eyes grew large, and she stopped in her tracks.

She was facing the young lieutenant, less than six feet away, who stood at attention in his red tunic with the white belts crossed over his chest, wearing the tall hat of an officer in the Royal Marines. He was taller than average, built well, and moved with a natural grace. His young face was not handsome, but it was regular, and strong, and striking. A noticeable scar showed in his right eyebrow, which was dark, as was his hair. It was his eyes that stopped her, froze her. They were hazel, and in them she saw gentleness and humility, and frankness and innocence, and a firmness, and she saw nothing of the condescending superiority that now glowed in the face of his captain next to him. Her eyes locked with his for a brief moment, and his nod of acknowledgment of her was nearly imperceptible. Then he shifted his gaze back to John, and for the first time in her life Brigitte felt her arms prickle, and she was unable to form words. She stood rooted beside her mother, mesmerized.

Margaret had missed nothing of the silent exchange between the two.

The captain's eyes went over John, head to toe, and an ugly smile flitted for a moment, and then, without having spoken a word, he turned on his heel and began marching towards the church, the lieutenant beside him, with the two armed regulars in front of him. John waited for a moment, then moved forward, following, with the remaining four grenadiers marching thirty feet behind.

The strange processional marched past white fences fronting square brick houses, one with a great maple in the yard, whose branches arched over the sidewalk and cast a filigree of sunlight on them as they passed. Margaret held her white-knuckled grip on John's arm, scarcely breathing while John kept his face a smiling mask, watching ahead. They approached the first corner, crossed the cobblestones, and started the long journey of the last block to the church.

Margaret turned her white face upwards towards John's. "Why are they doing this?" she whispered.

"To frighten us and show everyone else what happens when you oppose them."

"They're succeeding," Margaret muttered. She counted the unending paces for the last block, and suddenly they were at the corner and the tall, square, white frame church was across the cobblestone street. The high stained-glass windows glowed in the sunlight, and the big brass bell in the pointed steeple gleamed. Twenty families made their way on the walks and across the half acre of grass that surrounded the church towards the big open double doors. "Sanctuary," Margaret breathed.

John's eyes were narrowed, scanning the entire churchyard. "Maybe, maybe not. Something's wrong." And in the instant of speaking he saw. Spaced throughout the incoming congregation were the tall hats and red coats and white crossed belts of British grenadiers with their muskets slung on their backs and bayonets mounted. The usual social buzzing and called greetings were missing while the congregation gathered in strained silence. John's head turned while he looked for Warren and Thorpe and Palmer and Watson, but there was only Warren, walking with measured step towards the gaping church doors with his family, face a study of alert control. The captain and lieutenant leading John gave hand commands, and the soldiers that had boxed in the family for the last two blocks marched to their positions in the churchyard, while the two officers walked towards a sergeant near the street.

"Keep walking," John commanded his family, and they moved up the worn brick path through the open doors and down the narrow center aisle, following the family ahead of them. John slowed while his eyes adjusted to the light inside, waited until those ahead took their places, then continued towards the pew on the right side, fourth from the front, where the family usually sat. His eyes flicked over those already seated. Relief flooded as he picked out Thorpe and Palmer and Watson, each in his place, wives and children with them.

The family settled into their seats, John on the aisle, Margaret next, Brigitte, the three children, and Billy beside Matthew. John waited for a moment, then turned to look. Spring sunlight flooded through the east bank of high stained-glass windows and cast a kaleidoscope of color on the congregation. The people sat wide-eyed, bewildered, whispering. The last person arrived and closed the main doors and took his place.

Margaret closed her eyes, concentrating on the sounds outside in the churchyard. She heard faint, muffled commands of a British officer, then the sound of boots on the brick walkway, and then a muffled voice.

"They're not leaving," she whispered to John.

He pursed his mouth and nodded once and said nothing.

"Would they dare come in here during church services with muskets and bayonets?" she breathed.

"I don't know. They're here for a reason but I don't know what."

"To arrest the committee?"

At that moment the large clock on the wall behind the raised pulpit read ten A.M., and the small door beneath it rattled and the Reverend Silas Olmsted entered, cradling a large Bible in his right arm. His shock of white hair shined against his black robe, and he grasped the railing with his left hand as he climbed the two steps into the pulpit. He set the Bible down with a thump, and for a moment he struggled to set his wire-framed spectacles squarely on his nose before he tilted his head backwards to stare through them at his congregation. He laid his handwritten notes on the pulpit and raised his head to speak, when the rear doors burst open. Every person in the building jumped, their heads pivoted about, and they all gasped at once. Olmsted's eyebrows arched in stunned surprise.

The captain and the young lieutenant strode into the chapel, turned, and gave hand commands to the waiting regulars. The soldiers marched in, their boots clicking on the hardwood floor, and moved quickly, efficiently, down both outside aisles along the walls, groups of them dropping off at intervals. One marched past Olmsted to stand beside the exit door behind the pulpit. Another stopped squarely in front of the east exit door and stood at attention. The two officers remained at the head of the aisle by the big doors, facing Olmsted.

Twenty men in the congregation came to their feet as one. Instantly Olmsted raised both hands and signaled them to sit down. Then he faced the captain at the far end of the center aisle. "Sir, this is a house of worship. What is the meaning of this?"

"I have my orders," the captain replied, and waved a folded document. "Control your congregation and the matter will be finished quickly with no one harmed." His face once again showed the insolence that comes with authority and the force of arms. With the lieutenant beside him, he marched down the center aisle, stopped directly before the pulpit without looking at Olmsted, and pivoted on his heel. Then the two officers started back up the aisle side by side, the captain peering into the face of every person seated on his right, the lieutenant the left.

"What are you doing?" Olmsted demanded. "Who are you looking for?"

"Traitors!" the captain exclaimed, and his voice rang off the hard walls as he continued slowly up the aisle without looking back at Olmsted.

The young lieutenant moved back up the aisle slowly, steadily, looking into every face. His eyes were noncommittal, probing, missing nothing. Margaret's grasp on John's arm became a death grip as he came to their pew. Brigitte felt her breath coming short, and suddenly her thoughts became confused and she felt the color rising in her face, and she did not know why. She could not focus her bewildered thoughts, and she stared straight ahead, feeling the outer fringes of fear for the first time in her life. John breathed shallow as the lieutenant stared into his face, and then the young, serious eyes moved on to Margaret, and then to Brigitte. The lieutenant paused in the instant of recognition, and suddenly Brigitte turned her face to his and she knew her face was flushed and that her eyes screamed her confusion and fear. She jerked her face forward and stared directly ahead while the lieutenant scanned the others and moved on. John drew a long, silent breath, waited five seconds, then turned to look at Warren, to his left, five rows back, on the far side of the aisle. Warren sat tall and rigid, staring defiantly at the captain moving towards him. The officer paused, nodded slightly to Warren, then passed on.

"Adams and Hancock," John whispered to Margaret. "That's who they're after. They know about the meeting last night and they think Adams and Hancock might be in town."

Margaret exhaled and loosened her grip and went limp.

The officers reached the rear doors, turned once again to face Olmsted, and again gave hand signals to the regulars. The captain pushed the main doors open, and sunlight cast a bright rectangle into the chapel while the regulars marched clumping to the rear of the building and passed through the doors two by two, stooping to clear their bayonets through the door frame. The doors closed, and pandemonium exploded.

Dawes leaped to his feet hot, fist jammed into the air. "*Outrage!*" he bellowed, and fifty loud voices echoed it. His wife reached to grasp his coat sleeve and tried to pull him back into his seat and he shrugged it off, face crimson, neck veins bulging. "Weapons of war in a house of God! Frightening our women and children! How much more? How much longer?"

A chorus of voices swelled and rang off the hard, bare walls.

Warren stood and raised his hands and shouted, "Order!" then stood on his bench and shouted again. Olmsted seized the pulpit bell and shook it high, clanging. Slowly the outcry subsided.

"William Dawes is right," Warren exclaimed. "A deliberate act of desecration and insult to provoke us. But do we rise to their bait and deliver control of this affair to them?"

All talk ceased.

Warren continued. "I think not. Fight we will, but restraint is our assurance of winning. Wait until we are ready! Keep your passion for freedom alive, but restrain it until our time has come!"

The congregation sobered. Dawes settled back into his seat.

The Reverend Mr. Olmsted seized the moment. He shook the

pulpit bell again and waited until everyone was facing the pulpit and all talk ceased before he clacked it back onto its shelf. His high nasal voice came piercing. "We shall begin services this morning by singing."

John looked back at Warren, who rounded his lips and blew air as they felt the congregation settle and the mood change, and they knew the flash point had passed.

Instantly Olmsted launched into "A Mighty Fortress Is Our God," his thin voice quavering. Hesitantly at first, then in strength, the congregation picked it up. The sound reached outside where the British soldiers paused and exchanged questioning glances and shook their heads as they fell into ranks and waited further orders from the officers.

The song finished, Olmsted gave no space for interruption. "Let us pray," he said instantly, and bowed his head. "O God, who dwells in the heavens," he began, and for a full minute invoked the spirit of the Almighty to fill the chapel. With his lusty "Amen" still in the air, he opened the Bible.

"I have prepared this morning's sermon from the second letter written by the Apostle Paul to the Corinthians, chapter three, verse seventeen." He stared down his nose through his spectacles while his finger tracked down the column on the Bible page and stopped. Carefully he read, " 'Now the Lord is that Spirit: and where the Spirit of the Lord is, there is liberty.' " He raised his head, mouth a straight line, and waited.

Liberty! The word reached into every heart with its magic! A resounding "Amen" filled the chapel, and Olmsted continued.

"The Lord God is spirit, without form or substance, large enough to fill the immensities of eternity, small enough to dwell in your heart, and it is his spirit that has moved upon this land and inspired an unquenchable thirst for liberty!"

Caught up in the sudden, unexpected thrust of Olmsted's sermon, John leaned forward, eyes narrowed as he listened intently.

"The earth is his footstool, the heavens his throne. Oh, the marvels of God, the unknowable secrets of his power!"

John did not move in his fierce concentration.

"If you would throw off the yoke of oppression and have the liberty your souls thirst for, then draw close to God. He is spirit, and you will know him only through spirit, which knowledge awaits all who come to him through obedience to his divine will and word. You can bring him here to dwell in your hearts, in this chapel, in this fair land, through obedience, and where he is, there also is liberty." His finger thumped the Bible. "God has declared it. If we will humble ourselves to his will and word, God has promised us liberty in this life, and the unknowable blessing of dwelling in his presence in the eternities, singing endless songs of praise to his holy name with throngs of angels."

Olmsted continued while John slowly eased back in his pew. His eyes dropped as startling new thoughts settled into the depths of his soul, and he pondered. Margaret turned to study his face, and he was unaware of her frank stare.

At five minutes past eleven Olmsted closed the book and concluded. "God has inspired our passion for freedom. We must continue our struggle, peacefully if possible, by whatever means necessary if not." He paused and pursed his mouth for a moment. "Let us pray."

The congregation added their "Amen" to Olmsted's, and then they rose from the pews, one and two at a time, tentative, not knowing what waited outside. Someone opened the rear doors and squinted into the bright sunlight, then led out, and the chapel began to empty. Still lost in his thoughts, John was unaware when those in front of him stopped, and Margaret tugged his arm to avoid a collision. John blinked back to reality and looked about, startled, and only then did he see that the people were standing in the churchyard in silence.

British soldiers stood in the streets, in pairs, at intervals. The congregation milled about, uncertain of the meaning, hesitant of what to do.

John turned to Margaret. "Stay here with the children until I'm back," he said, and then he trotted to Warren. "Any idea what this is about?"

Thorpe arrived, eyes darting to watch the soldiers.

"No," Warren answered. His eyes were slits, his face growing red.

Dawes arrived running. His eyes flashed and his voice was too loud. "What do they think they're doing?" He jammed an accusing finger towards the officers.

Palmer and Watson stopped behind Thorpe. Eyes in the crowd turned to the men, asking for direction.

"We've got to get these people to go home," John exclaimed. "If they become a mob we could be in trouble."

"Agreed," Warren said.

Quickly the six men spread through the crowd. "Go home in groups. Act normal. Start nothing. Come back and go into the church if they interfere. Go. Now."

Olmsted appeared in the chapel door, Bible under one arm. Thorpe was nearest him and called, "Help get this crowd moving before something happens." Olmsted's head thrust forward for a moment in surprise before he raised his voice and moved among the people. Families grouped together and moved out, past the soldiers, not looking back. The crowd thinned and was suddenly gone, leaving John and the other five alone in the churchyard with their families.

John said, "Dawes, come with me. You others pair up and let's go."

Wives on their arms, they started their separate directions, John leading his family, with Dawes and his wife, Sarah, following behind. Sarah, whose beauty was legend in Boston, and William had privately borne their deep personal sorrow of being unable to have children, and seeing her broken heart, William had become ever more protective.

John held a steady pace until the British officers and four regulars marched directly in his path, stopped, faced him, and waited beneath a great maple gleaming in the sun. John slowed and stopped and waited as the British officer spoke. "Up a bit late last evening, wouldn't you say?"

John remained silent.

"A shame that Revere couldn't be here today," the officer continued, a condescending smile tugging at the corners of his mouth. "And the other member of your committee—lost his bloody name—oh yes, Sievers. Now, where would Sievers be? Drunk in what pub?"

Behind Dawes, unseen, a sergeant of the regulars quietly swung his musket from his shoulder and lowered the bayonet. He carefully slipped the point beneath the hem of Sarah's ankle-length dress and began to lift it. He had it halfway to her knee before she felt the tugging and turned. She gasped and slapped at her skirt and jerked away.

Dawes spun to see the cause. He stared uncomprehending at his wife, then at the soldiers, and then saw the unslung musket. "What happened?" he demanded of Sarah.

"Nothing. It was nothing."

"You're frightened half to death! Did he touch you?"

Sarah shook her head, hand at her throat, eyes downcast.

The sergeant grinned. "No need to embarrass your lady," he drawled. "She ain't goin' to say. 'Twas nothin', really. All that happened was I used me old Brown Bess to take a peek at the ankle of this fair lass." He thrust the rifle down and forward. "Like this, y'see, g'vnor?"

The tip of the bayonet touched the hem on Sarah's skirt, and Dawes's movement was a blur. His foot came down with all his weight on the gun muzzle, driving it downward, and the bayonet point hit the cobblestones. The blade bowed, snapped in two, and spun clanging into the street. Sarah screamed and clapped her hands over her mouth. Margaret gasped, and Brigitte shouted, "Stop it!" John and Matthew grabbed the women and pulled them clear of the action and held them crying as the sergeant lost his hold on his musket and it went clattering at his feet. Dawes swept it up and in one fluid movement swung it over his head with all his strength. It caught the sergeant on the downstroke, just above his ear, and ripped it half off his head before it struck his shoulder at the base of his neck. The sergeant went down backwards with a groan.

"Shoot him!" bellowed the captain, and the soldier nearest the sergeant grabbed for the strap to bring his musket around. Dawes slammed the brass-plated butt of the ten-pound musket into the soldier's face and he went down in a heap, blood spurting as Dawes took a stride to the maple tree and swung the musket with all his strength. The first blow smashed the hammer and the powder pan completely off the weapon, and the second blow bent the barrel six inches out of line.

He threw the ruined weapon bouncing into the cobblestone street and spun back to leap for the last two armed British regulars, who were desperately fumbling to bring their muskets to bear. They threw up their hands, stumbled backwards, lost their footing, and went down sprawling. Dawes turned and lunged towards the British officers.

John caught him from behind around the middle with both arms, lifted him off his feet, and held him struggling. "Dawes, Dawes, get control," he shouted. Dawes wrenched against John's hold and battled, and then he slowed and stopped. He exhaled, and it was as though all the wind went out of him.

"I'm all right now, John."

John set him down and watched for a moment, and Dawes took one pace and thrust his face nearly into that of the captain. "Tell Gage the next British soldier who touches my wife is dead," he said evenly. "I'm William Dawes. Tell him."

The captain blinked as though coming from some far place in his mind. "You'll be under arrest before nightfall," he blustered, "for assaulting a soldier of the Crown." The young lieutenant moved to one side and spread his feet, balanced, ready.

Warren and Thorpe both arrived, breathless from their run across the church lawn, wide-eyed, pensive, waiting for an explanation.

John pushed Dawes aside and fronted the officer and spoke, his voice thick with rage. "Your soldier used a bayonet to force an indecency upon a gentlewoman in public. Count yourself lucky he's still alive. If you charge Dawes with anything, I'll charge the soldier with assault with a deadly weapon upon a defenseless woman in a public street on a Sabbath morning. He will be tried in a Massachusetts court despite Gage's order to the contrary, and as God is my witness, *I will see him hang!*" John did not realize his clenched fist was raised into the face of the officer.

John stopped and the captain looked into his eyes and recoiled. He licked suddenly dry lips and involuntarily took half a step back. The young lieutenant glanced at his captain and held his ground. John lowered his fist, and his next words were quiet but struck deep. "I suggest, sir, you gather up your wreckage and move on."

The captain puffed himself up and his eyes were wild and his face flushed red, but he said nothing. Then he turned and barked orders. The young lieutenant hauled the sergeant to his feet while the other soldiers picked up the other battered man and the useless musket, and they followed him as they marched down the narrow street without looking back, and disappeared.

John watched for a moment, then exhaled and battled to regain a sense of calm. He turned to Sarah. "Are you all right?"

"Yes. He did no harm." She was still trembling, clinging to William.

"What happened?" Warren demanded.

"The sergeant made a mistake," John answered. "Dawes corrected it. That's all." An unexpected smile flashed. "I doubt he'll do it again." He sobered again. "William, you'll have to learn to govern that temper. I think that sergeant knew about the cannon."

For a moment Dawes puzzled at the statement before the remembrance came back to him. It was he who had flared hot when the British seized all the colonial cannon on the Boston Back Bay to prevent their use against British ships if war broke out. That night Dawes led seven men in from the Back Bay, where they silently scaled a twenty-foot stone wall, lifted a two-ton cannon from its mounts, lowered it into their waiting boats, and disappeared, all with a British sentry less than forty feet away. In the heavy lift, Dawes had driven a cuff button into his wrist, and went to Warren, the physician, for treatment, refusing to tell Warren how it happened. The sheer bravado of the unbelievable, daring feat made a laughingstock of the British in every newspaper in the thirteen colonies, and every pub, every inn, and half the church meetings rocked with laughter at the telling and retelling. The truth of who led the audacious raid was finally known, and overnight Dawes became a folk hero.

Dawes looked John in the eyes. "I didn't intend to harm that man," he said, "but when he went after Sarah . . ." His voice trailed off.

"No one faults you," John said. "It's over and best forgotten." He glanced at his own Margaret and the thought came, *If it had been Margaret, what?* John shuddered and pushed it away.

"John, I would have killed him if you hadn't stopped it," said Dawes. "Thank you."

John nodded his head once. "We'll walk with you to your home."

"It's out of your way," Dawes protested. "You've done enough. We'll be all right."

"I'm sure you will, but we'll walk you home anyway."

Warren said, "If this is under control, I better get back to my family."

"Wait," John said.

Warren and Thorpe stopped and all eyes were on John.

"That captain knew about the meeting last night. He knows that Revere and Sievers are gone." He paused and watched the concern grow in Warren and Thorpe. "How did he know?" He paused again before he continued. "Has Gage done anything about it? Does he have Revere and Sievers now?"

They stood for several moments in the beauty of the spring morning, the silence broken only by the songs of the jays and robins in the sunlight and the trees.

Warren shook his head. "I don't know how Gage found out about the meeting last night. I doubt Gage has Revere or Sievers.

If he did, we'd know about it by now, one way or another. There's nothing to do but trust and go about our business."

"You're right."

Warren and Thorpe hurried back across the church lawn.

John turned to Margaret. "Are you all right?"

She saw the concern in his face. "Yes, but don't ever do that again."

"Do what?"

"Stand in the streets of Boston and threaten a British officer with your fist in his face."

John's eyebrows rose. "Did I do that?"

Brigitte spoke, her voice strained, too high. "You certainly did! 'Gather up your wreckage and move on'—that's exactly what you told him, and he didn't say a word! He just did it!" Rarely had Brigitte ever shown unabashed admiration to anyone, but now her face shone with pride.

John turned to her. "How about you? All right?"

"Fine." She tugged at her bonnet. "I thought the war had started!"

John straightened his vest and turned once again into the winding street. Ten minutes later the Dunsons left William and Sarah standing in their doorway waving while they continued down the walk through the twisting streets towards their own home. With the explosive moments behind them, the children began to cautiously shape and form the stories they would tell for years to come.

"Did you see it?" Caleb croaked hoarsely to Adam. "Dawes stamped that musket to pieces and knocked those two soldiers kicking—*bam, bam*—just like that, and the women were yelling, and Father and Matthew jerked them out, and then Father put that British officer in his place for fair! Did you see it? Did you?"

Eyes huge and earnest, Adam exclaimed, "And did you see when he picked William up like he was nothing—picked him up and made him be good!" He stared at John's straight back as though he were seeing his father for the first time.

Margaret turned her face towards John's. "Why did this all have to happen on such a beautiful spring morning with the Thorpes coming for dinner?"

Lost in the startling, deadly events of the day, the thought came rolling forward, crowding past the tension and fears. *The Thorpes are coming!* Steaming leg of lamb! Custard! Talk and games and running in the yard. Matthew's eyes sparkled. *Kathleen is coming. Kathleen is coming.* At that moment, no thought in the world other than this one would have pulled his mind from the explosive minutes that had just passed.

John opened the front door, and Margaret said, "Change," and everyone went to their bedrooms.

While John loosened the buckles and ties on his square-toed shoes, Margaret worked the buttons on her shoes.

"I hope to never again pass through such a strange Sabbath," she said.

"Strange?"

"Soldiers marching us to church, soldiers inside the church, soldiers on the way home, disagreement with Olmsted's sermon, you and William in a street battle, and now we have to put all that behind us and get ready for dinner guests! Strange."

A wry smile crossed John's face. "A little different."

She stopped for a moment. "Different, you say? Much more different and I would have died of fright!" She hung her bonnet in the closet and turned back to him. "Did you see Brigitte and that young soldier? the one in the street, and then in the church?"

John's hands stopped. "What soldier?"

"The young one that marched us to church, the officer."

"The lieutenant?"

"Yes, if that's what he was."

"No. What happened?"

"The way she looked at him, and he looked at her. She's taken by him."

"You sure? I didn't see it."

"I did. In her entire life, have you ever seen Brigitte with nothing to say?"

John smiled. "No."

"Well, she was dumbstruck today. Twice."

John put his shoes in the closet and turned back thoughtfully. "I don't see any problem coming from it. She'll likely never see him again."

Margaret shook her head. "Something tells me she will."

John shook his head. "I doubt it." He worked with the buttons on his vest. "What did you mean, disagreement with Olmsted's sermon? Who disagreed?"

"You did."

John's eyebrows arched and he stopped and turned to her. "I did? I haven't said a word."

"It was all over your face. What was it you disagreed with?"

John blew air and shook his head, baffled. He stopped for a moment and carefully avoided answering the question. "Describe God," he said to her. "What does he look like?"

"Is that what you disagreed with?" Margaret retorted. "His description of God?"

"Just answer the question."

Margaret's eyes widened. "I don't recall ever seeing him!"

"It's important."

Margaret sobered. "I can only say what the church says. He is everywhere and nowhere. Three yet one, somehow. Indescribable. Unknowable." She shrugged. "Is that what possessed you, when everything else was going on with those soldiers?"

John stared unseeing at the floor. "Describe heaven. If we go there, what do we do?"

Margaret's forehead wrinkled. "Are you all right?"

"What do we do?" he repeated.

"We are blessed to sing the praises of God with angels."

"What else?"

Margaret pondered. "I don't know. I've never heard of anything else. I never thought about it."

"How long do we sing songs?"

"Eternity."

"What of wives and children? Will we know them?"

"No one ever said."

"Will we have them?"

Margaret shrugged. "Families? I suppose we're all God's family there." She stopped working with the buttons on her dress. "Where are these strange questions coming from?"

John grunted and hung his coat and vest in the closet, and tugged at the large knot in the tie about his neck.

"All right," Margaret said, "if you won't answer that, then you describe God."

"I can do no better than you," he replied softly. "I know the teachings."

Margaret suddenly stopped. "Then describe heaven." There was creeping concern in her voice.

He did not look at her as he folded the tie and laid it on the bed. "The teaching is as you said."

"Are you having thoughts other than the teachings?" she asked. Seconds passed while her concerns grew.

"No."

She stared at him for a moment. "There is something you're not telling me."

He turned to her. "No. The Bible is true."

She studied his face, his eyes. He broke off, and she knew the moment was gone and that it would be useless to press him further. She resumed working with the dress buttons. "Good. They put heretics in the stocks down on the Common, you know, and I would not come to visit you." She watched him from the corner of her eye. A smile flickered across his face and was gone.

The discussion was closed for now, and Margaret put it away in her mind to be recalled again.

Brigitte was waiting in the kitchen when Margaret strode in and took command. Aprons reaching nearly to their ankles, they plunged into the work.

"Matthew, two more leaves in the table. Adam and Prissy, start polishing the silver, and don't miss places. Brigitte, get out the great tablecloth."

For more than eighteen months, Margaret and Brigitte had worked to crochet a tablecloth large enough to cover their dinner table, with all the leaves, fourteen feet long, six feet wide. They lost track of the needle strokes when the count passed 120,000. They hung it on the wall for a week after they finished, and tenderly touched it each day, and from that time they called it simply the great tablecloth. It came from its special drawer only on special occasions.

"Matthew, be careful and fetch the milk from the fireplace and pour it here. Brigitte, punch the dough and set it by the stove to rise again. John, lift the plates and goblets from the cupboard—the crystal ones."

The work hit a rhythm and chatter arose, and Margaret hummed a line from a church hymn. Brigitte joined in, and they smiled as they finished together. The rich, pungent smells of roast lamb and custard and steaming vegetables filled the room. Twice Matthew stole away to peer out the front window up the street.

"Matthew, they'll be here when they get here, and Kathleen will be just as beautiful then as she is now. Get out the linen napkins and fold them. And set the chairs at the table. Thirteen of them, patriarchs at both ends. Caleb, keep your finger out of the custard!"

"Mama," Adam whined, "I can't get these spots off the knives."

"Caleb, help Adam. Brigitte, you come here and watch. Add vanilla when the milk thickens—you know how. John, add two sticks to the oven firebox. Brigitte, the dough is high enough. Get out the muffin molds."

Margaret opened the oven and partially pulled out the pan with the leg of lamb, punched it with a fork, sniffed at it, then drew it out, balanced on thick hot pads in either hand. She set it inside the fireplace, near one of the fires, settled the lid onto it, and closed the oven door.

"Brigitte, when the muffins have risen, put them in the oven and watch—golden, not brown."

Brigitte's nose wrinkled. "I know, Mama. I know." She shaped the dough into the depressions in the muffin tins.

"Go change while they're rising," Margaret said, and Brigitte walked briskly to her bedroom.

The custard went into the root cellar to cool and set. The muffins were coming to a golden finish in the oven. The meat had simmered, and the drippings blended into thick brown gravy. The vegetables were tender but not soft. Margaret paused for a moment to smile inwardly and indulge herself in a feeling of pride in the mark of a master chef. Everything she had prepared was reaching perfection at the same time.

"They're coming," Caleb exclaimed, and Margaret muttered, "Oh, mercy, I still have my apron on," and scurried to change.

There was a rap at the door and John opened it. "Henry, please come in. What a pleasure to have you!"

As tall as John, fine boned, handsome, enigmatic, politically popular, educated in London by the best medical doctors, Doctor Henry Thorpe had used his gift of wit and humor in writings to chide the British and support the citizens in their slow and painful rise against the iron grip of King George. Readily elected to the Massachusetts legislature (later the Provincial Congress), and eventually placed on the crucial Committee of Safety, Thorpe had risen to prominence in Boston, and his leadership was being noticed in neighboring colonies. His aristocratic wife, Phoebe, had born him five children, the third of which had been stillborn. The four remaining were well favored, talented. The oldest, Barton, was married and living in New York. Kathleen had a younger brother, Charles, age thirteen, and Faith was the youngest at age eight. Henry Thorpe's medical practice flourished.

He removed his hat and shook John's hand warmly. "The pleasure is ours," he said.

Matthew saw only Kathleen, who entered last. Her long dark hair was beautifully braided into a coil at the back of her head, and a few stray wisps curled against her forehead. She closed the door and turned to Matthew. At the moment their eyes met,

Matthew felt his breath come short and knew he had reddened and he did not care. Kathleen's eyes shined as she smiled, and for a moment she stood transfixed, lost in the sight of him, aware of nothing more than that the next few hours would be spent with him. They stood thus, sharing the rare sweetness of the moment, while the others moved into the room.

Then Matthew quietly said, "Hello," and Kathleen curtsied slightly and said, "Hello."

Margaret strode through the archway, still tucking wisps of hair, and hurried directly to Phoebe. "Oh, how good to have you come!" she said, and hugged her. "Let me take your wraps."

They all shrugged from their spring coats, and Margaret carried them into a bedroom and returned. "Please do sit down," she said, and gestured to the sofa and upholstered chairs. "Dinner will be served shortly."

Phoebe followed her into the kitchen. "Henry told me about the confrontation between the British and William Dawes, and about John stopping it. You must have been frightened."

Margaret filled bowls with steaming food. "Terrified! It all happened so fast!"

"And those soldiers in the church. Did you ever think they would be so bold?"

"Never. What's this all coming to?" Margaret picked up a bowl of vegetables, and Phoebe and Brigitte picked up others. They walked to set them on the dinner table, and Phoebe paused to examine the great cloth. Plump, round faced, pleasant, tending to be fragile and naive, Phoebe was accepted everywhere simply because she was always pleasant, even when circumstances demanded otherwise. "I see you finished it. It is absolute perfection."

Margaret blushed. "It turned out well."

Phoebe leaned forward to examine the small, precise stitching. "Such needlework! It's marvelous."

John and Henry, lost in a deep discussion of the events of the morning, were oblivious to the women. Caleb had gathered the

children into his room, where he and Adam were giving demon-
strations of how Dawes and John had whipped the British and
sent them marching back to their compound, while the Thorpe
children stood wide-eyed, mouths gaping open.

Matthew quietly opened the front door and reached for Kathleen's hand, and she reached to him and they revelled in the touching as he led her outside. For a moment they stood shoulder to
shoulder in the quiet warmth of late afternoon of the sweet New
England spring day, and looked and did not speak. Nothing
stirred. Sunlight caught the new leaves in the oaks and maples and
cast lacy shadows. The tulip beds were green and yellow and red.
They stood for a time, lost in the touch of their hands and the
awareness of each other, and basked in the profound beauty of the
day.

Matthew led her to the front gate and they stopped. "I'm glad
you could come."

Her dark eyes shined as she smiled. "It was nice to be asked."

The words meant nothing; the sound of their voices, everything.

For a moment Matthew fumbled. "Church this morning was
. . . different."

"It was frightful."

"Did you hear about William Dawes?"

"Father told us. And about your father and the British captain."

"That was a bit tense. For a moment I thought we were going
to war right there in the streets."

"Father says it's coming soon enough."

They both started as the front door of the house opened and
Margaret called, "Dinner. Come get ready."

Everyone gathered at the table and stood behind the chairs
until each was ready. John knelt beside his, and all the others went
to their knees.

"Almighty God . . ." The prayer was sincere and not long.

John rose and took his seat at one end of the table, Henry

took his at the other, their wives took theirs to the right of their husbands, and on John's nod the children sat down, Matthew next to Kathleen.

John sliced the leg of lamb while steaming bowls of potatoes and vegetables were passed. Woven baskets lined with white linen and filled with golden muffins emptied and Brigitte refilled them. Silver bowls of applesauce and crushed, sweetened cranberries were handed about, emptied, and refilled. Rich gravy was spread dripping over potatoes, and talk flowed, and a warm glow filled the room.

Adam looked at Margaret with pleading eyes. "Is it time for the custard?"

Matthew brought the large, square silver pan from the root cellar, and bowls appeared on the table. Margaret cut and scooped large squares of the quivering custard into the bowls while Brigitte dipped hot maple syrup. Talk dwindled while they spooned small portions and closed their eyes to savor it. Margaret watched, smiling, deep joy shining in her eyes.

All too soon it was over. Talk continued while the women tied aprons and cleared the table, saved the remains, and dropped the dirty dishes into a large pan of steaming water. The children darted into the backyard to perfect their enactment of the battle in the streets, while John and Henry settled into large overstuffed chairs to talk. Matthew watched Kathleen working with the women, then caught her by the hand and gestured towards the front door.

"I have to help," she said, tugging back.

"They can do it," Matthew replied.

Margaret raised her head. "We're nearly done. You two go on."

Kathleen pulled her apron over her head, tucked at her hair, and reached for Matthew's outstretched hand. They closed the door behind them and in the early dusk walked through the gate and turned. They walked slowly, stride for stride, to the corner and crossed the cobblestones. Windows lighted and glowed in the lengthening shadows, and in the distance a dog barked.

Nighthawks overhead began their nightly ballet on whispering silken wings, while ships rumbled to each other on the Back Bay.

"It's hard to think of war," Kathleen said quietly.

"Out here like this, it is," Matthew answered.

"What will happen to Boston if fighting comes?"

Matthew exhaled a great breath. "No one knows. I hope nothing."

"If it comes, will you join in?"

Matthew studied the ground for a moment. "Probably."

"In the shooting?"

"It could happen. I haven't thought that far."

They walked on slowly for a time. "I can hardly stand the thought," Kathleen said. "I don't know what I would do if . . ."

He looked down at her and she turned her face upwards to his, and he saw the fear in her wide dark eyes and the slight tremble in her chin.

He had not planned to have it happen this way. It was supposed to happen at home, in the backyard, her seated on the bench beneath the great oak, him before her with his heart on his sleeve and a ring in his hand. But it did not happen that way.

He stopped and turned to her and the words rolled out. "Kathleen, I love you with all my heart. Will you marry me?"

Kathleen blinked in total surprise. For years they had known this moment was coming, but Kathleen had always envisioned it with her dressed in a beautiful, flowing gown, beneath a sheltering tree, with Matthew on one knee before her, a beautiful ring in a small, exquisitely designed box, delivering a flawlessly prepared speech while she waited for the right moment when she would blush, nod, and say, "Yes. I will marry you."

She gasped and struggled with the realization that it was happening here and now, with no ring, no prepared speech, her with the aroma of the kitchen still lingering. She suddenly understood that her visions had been the dreams of a child and that this moment, as with most of life's great events, had occurred on its own schedule. She swallowed and gasped, and her breathing came short for a moment while her heart and mind caught up with the realities of the moment. "Yes. Yes. Oh, Matthew, of course."

He held her and her arms circled his neck and he kissed her, and she kissed him, and the feelings burned into their memories forever.

"Soon?" he asked. "Before there's a chance for the war?"

"Yes."

They stood in the deep shadows of the unlighted street, alone, clinging to each other, sharing their moment. Time was lost as they drew strength from the touch and the smell and the closeness. "Thank you," Matthew breathed. "Thank you." They walked back to the front gate, caught up in the strange, wonderful feelings that had been born with their commitment, talking quietly in their new world.

"When shall I talk with your parents?" Matthew asked.

Kathleen paused. "Have you talked to your own?"

"Father. Not Mother. Father consented."

"We can't marry without her blessing."

"She'll consent. I could talk with your parents before you leave tonight."

"Oh, Matthew!" She caught her breath. "So fast! I can't catch up."

"Tonight?"

She squared her shoulders. "Yes. If Margaret will give her blessing, talk with my father and mother tonight."

"Do you want to talk with them first?"

She thought for a moment. "No. Better it comes from you."

He took her hand and led her into the house.

Margaret glanced at them, then stopped to look. Phoebe looked at Kathleen, and her eyes dropped and she turned away for a moment. When she turned back, her eyes were too bright.

"Matthew," Margaret said, "I need some help for a moment in the root cellar."

Matthew followed her out, and she stopped in the shadows by the back door. "When is it to be?"

"When is what to be?"

"The wedding. It was written all over you two when you walked in the front door."

Matthew's mouth dropped open for an instant. "Do we have your blessing?"

"Of course."

Matthew folded his mother inside his arms and held her close, his cheek on hers. "Mother, I love you so much. Thank you for everything. Thank you."

She held her eldest for a long moment, and he felt her shake with a mother's sob, and then she drew back.

"She's a fine girl. She will do you honor. Love her always."

"I plan to talk with her parents tonight."

Margaret reflected and then chuckled. "It will certainly catch Henry and Phoebe by surprise, but it seems a good time. It's the Sabbath. We have just had a special day with her family."

They walked back into the house, and Matthew said firmly, "Father, could I see you a moment?"

John's eyes narrowed as he followed Matthew into the kitchen.

"Father, I have asked Kathleen to marry me, and Mother has consented. This morning you approved. Do we have your blessing?"

John reflected for a moment. "Isn't this a little abrupt? You have my blessing, of course, but what about Henry and Phoebe?"

"I plan to ask them tonight, before they leave."

Concern showed in John's face. "Shouldn't the Thorpes be given a little time to get used to the idea?"

"Kathleen says it's all right."

John let his eyes drop to the floor for a moment. "Talk with Henry."

Matthew brought his eyes to his father's, and in them he saw the memories that rose in John of a dark-haired little boy at his knee, and then a child, and then a young man who left for college, and returned grown, steady and strong. Matthew thrust his hand forward and John ignored it; he embraced his son, and for a moment they stood in the kitchen, knowing they were closing a precious chapter in life and opening a new one.

John followed Matthew back into the great room, where Matthew faced Henry Thorpe. "Mr. Thorpe, could I see you and your wife for a moment in the kitchen?"

Henry glanced at John, and Phoebe walked to her husband and waited, and they followed Matthew into the kitchen.

"I wish to ask you for the hand of your daughter in marriage."

Phoebe's eyes dropped. Henry stiffened.

"I have asked Kathleen and she agreed. I have talked with my parents and they have given us their blessing. I know this is usually done at the home of the bride, but I did not want to wait." He stopped, and for a moment the room was silent.

Henry cleared his throat and glanced at Phoebe. "This catches us a little unprepared."

"I know it does, sir. It caught me unprepared."

Henry stared at the floor for a moment. "Yes, I give permission." He reached with his hand and Matthew shook it warmly, then turned to Phoebe.

"May we have your blessing too, Mrs. Thorpe?"

Phoebe's chin trembled as she nodded. "Yes. Gladly." She put her hand over her mouth and a sob caught in her throat.

Instantly Kathleen burst through the doorway, where she had been waiting breathlessly. She threw her arms about her mother, and Phoebe clutched her close and burst into tears. Margaret followed and in a moment joined the other two women, and the three of them stood embracing and dabbing at their eyes with handkerchiefs.

Henry cleared his throat. "These things never do work without ten minutes of weeping women." He glanced at Matthew. "That's because they're so happy, you understand."

Matthew laughed nervously, and John walked in and shook Henry's hand. The children clambered into the room and stood aside, eyes wide in wonder at why the women were weeping while they smiled and the men were standing tolerantly, talking among themselves.

Brigitte herded the children back into the parlor explaining, "They're weeping because they're happy."

"About what?" Caleb asked.

"Kathleen and Matthew are getting married."

Caleb's nose wrinkled. "*That's* why they're crying?"

"Someday you'll understand," Brigitte said. "Right now, you stay here and help with these children."

Talk went on for fifteen minutes while the two families let the idea grow and take shape and root.

Henry turned to Margaret. "It's getting late. We should be going."

Margaret brought the coats, and the Thorpes slipped them on, and both families walked outside into the still, cool spring evening, cast in the silver glow of a full moon.

"Sir, may I walk Kathleen home, alone?"

"Of course."

They opened the front gate, and the Dunson family stood silhouetted in the yellow shaft of light coming from their open door as they waved to the Thorpes until they were out of sight. John watched Matthew and Kathleen disappear into the shadows and turned back. He dropped his arm around Margaret's shoulders and drew her to him as they walked together towards the open door.

"It's been a long day," he said wistfully.

"I don't remember one like—"

A hiss came sharp from the shadows and they jerked to a stop. Margaret gasped and John peered into the silvery darkness.

"John. It's me."

John's eyes narrowed in puzzled surprise. "Tom?"

"Don't talk and don't look. Walk normal on into the house and put out the lights in the kitchen and meet me at the back door."

John continued with measured step, Margaret still held to his side, through the open door. The instant it closed he gave hand signals to Margaret to gather the children, trotted into the kitchen and put out all the lamps, and silently opened the back door. It took a moment for his eyes to adjust, and he stepped into the yard and closed the door.

Thirty seconds passed, with only the whisper of nighthawks above and the ships in the Back Bay, before Tom rose from beside the root cellar. "Come with me," he whispered.

"Wait," John answered, and disappeared silently back inside the house to where Margaret was waiting with the children. "I'll be gone for a while. Put the children to bed." He turned on his heel and once again disappeared out the back door. He followed Tom over the back fence, through the neighbor's yard, then south, towards the Neck, to where open fields and woods began.

Tom stopped at the tumbled-down remains of an old tavern, burned and abandoned years ago. He held his finger to his lips, listened for a moment, and then, satisfied they were alone, faced John. "Sorry for the fright," he said quietly. "I been followed half the day. Things are happening."

He paused, and John peered about for movement in the shadows. There was none.

"I been watching Gage since before sunup. A civilian went to his living quarters early, and left, and twenty minutes later Gage went to his office at headquarters in a hurry and then on to talk to a major and a captain. Fifteen minutes later the major left with four mounted soldiers headed north at a gallop. The captain went to the barracks and mustered a twenty-man company, armed, ready to fight. They left marching. Then, about noon the same civilian came back to Gage's office. I don't know who he was."

Tom paused to wipe his sleeve across his mouth. "He left after about ten minutes, and a few minutes later Gage went back to his living quarters. I figured two trips by the same civilian meant he was carrying information."

John interrupted. "This morning a British captain and twenty regulars harassed us at church, and he knew about the meeting last night and that Revere's gone. He knew you were there."

Tom's mouth clamped tight for a moment. "It figures. After the civilian left I waited to see who would come back, but no one did, so I got Abe Cullens. He's the old cripple that keeps Gage's headquarters clean. He's sworn allegiance to the Crown and Gage thinks he's harmless, so he pretty much comes and goes when he wants and nobody minds, and they don't know yet he's with us. Abe rummaged through Gage's office and found a paper in an envelope in a drawer. The paper wasn't there yesterday. He snuck it out to me. It's in French. I took it to Jacque and he translated it."

Again he paused, and John didn't move.

"Jacque said it was written by an Englishman who knows French but not enough to write it good. He gave me the translation. Here it is." Tom hunkered down. "Now, get down here and I'm going to strike a light and you're going to read it."

John dropped to his haunches, and Tom struck flint to steel and nursed the spark to life in the tinderbox. John turned the paper to the light, and while Tom watched in all directions, John silently read.

Four Brass Cannon and two Mortars or Cohorns with a Number of small arms in the Cellar or out Houses of Mr. Barrett a little on the other side the Bridge where is also lodged a Quantity of Powder & Lead.

Ten Iron Cannon before the Town-House and two within it which Town-House is in the Center of the Town. The ammunition for said Guns within the House.

Three Guns 24 Pounders, lodged in the Prison yard with a Quantity of Cartridges and Provision.

A Quantity of Provision and Ammunition in other Places, the Principal Deposits are the Houses of Messrs. Hubbard, near the Meeting, Butler, Jones the Tailors, near Hubbards, two men of the name of Bond, and particularly at Mr. Whitneys who lives on the Right Hand near the Entrance of the Town, at a House plaistered white a small yard in Front and a railed Fence a large Quantity of Powder and Ball is reported to be deposited in his store adjoining the House.

Cannon hid in a wood a mile & half from the Center of the

Village between the River and Malden Pond. The wood thick a good deal of underwood. The Ground no little wet, but not a Marsh. Three Guns still mounted, the rest dismounted and carefully hid and even buried. In the same place some Boxes of Arms hid like the Cannon.

The Medicine Chests & Powder Barrells, Tents, etc, distributed in the chief Houses, particularly Mr. Barretts, Capt. Wheelers, Mr. Hubbards Stores and the two Bonds.

The three Guns in the Prison Court remain there besides many different Articles.

John's mind numbed and he lowered the paper, and Tom snapped the lid shut on the tinderbox. They stood and stared at each other in the moonlight while John licked dry lips, his mind reeling.

"Concord!" he whispered. "This tells where we hid everything at Concord! All of it, in detail! Only the committee knows all this, and we didn't learn some of it until Friday!"

He stopped and forced his thoughts into a semblance of order. His mind leaped and he suddenly thrust the paper forward. "Where's the original of this—the one in French?"

"Cullens put it back. Gage can't know we saw it."

John exhaled held breath and continued. "One of us at that meeting last night told the civilian you saw and he took it to Gage. It wasn't you or me. That leaves Revere, Warren, Thorpe, Palmer, Watson, Dawes, and Sheffield. Which one?"

"I don't know much about Palmer or Watson," Tom answered. "And Sheffield isn't on the committee."

"Adams and Hancock vouched for Palmer and Watson before we put them on the committee."

"Maybe it's not one of the committee. Maybe it's one of their wives or kids who can't control their tongue, or who is in with the British."

"Either way, it comes from the committee."

"I don't know how they're doing it."

John heaved a defeated sigh. "Did Revere get out of town? Did you see him go?"

"I watched him leave in his boat. He had a horse waiting on the other side."

"Any British follow?"

"Not that I saw."

"Have you seen him return?"

"No."

John stared north towards the lights of Boston. "Does Gage know where to find Adams and Hancock at Lexington?"

Tom saw the thoughts forming in John's eyes, and John spoke. "If Gage takes Adams and Hancock, and our arms and supplies, we're beaten before we start."

Tom shifted his feet. "That's why I came to find you tonight."

Silence held for several seconds before John held up the paper. "This gives him what he needed. He has enough now to undo us."

Tom asked, "What of those muskets under your pantry? You better get them out now, because it will be trouble after this all starts."

John nodded. He folded the paper, opened the buttons on the front of his shirt and slipped it inside, and asked the final question. "Did that mounted patrol catch Revere? Does Gage have Revere?"

Tom shook his head. "I don't know."

In the moonlight Tom saw the faraway look and the heavy questions come into John's eyes. *Who is Gage's informer, and when will Gage move?*

Tom interrupted his thoughts. "I'll go wait for Revere. We've got to know if he made it, and what Adams and Hancock said."

John nodded. "I'll go tell Warren what we know."

Both men melted into the darkness. Twenty minutes later John rapped on Warren's door, and a light moved inside and the door opened. Thirty minutes passed before the light went out and John slipped back into the night and made his way through the street sounds back to his own home. Lights glowed inside and John slowed, puzzled that lamps would still be burning at this late hour.

He paused at the door and heard the voices of Brigitte and Margaret, and he rapped and the door opened and he entered. Brigitte, sitting at the dinner table, leaned forward on her elbows. Margaret closed the door behind John without a word and walked back to the table.

John glanced at both of them. "Trouble?"

Margaret shook her head. "No. Just talking. What did Tom want?"

John shook his head. "It's moving too fast. Gage knows too much. We've got to find a way to slow it down, take control." He hung his coat on the coatrack. "What are you doing still up, Brigitte?"

Margaret stood silently waiting, and John looked at her, then back at Brigitte.

Brigitte finally shrugged. "Just talking."

"At midnight? About what?"

Again Margaret waited, giving Brigitte her chance.

Brigitte took a heavy breath. "Nothing. I better go to bed." She stood and started towards the archway to the bedroom wing, and John looked at Margaret, silently inquiring. Margaret shook her head, and John said nothing and waited until he heard the bedroom door quietly close.

"What's wrong?" he asked Margaret.

Margaret pursed her mouth for a moment while she picked her words. "Remember that young lieutenant this morning? the one in the street, and then at the church? the one I mentioned?"

John's eyes narrowed as he searched his memory. "Yes. What about him?"

"Brigitte can't get him out of her mind."

"She told you that?"

"Yes. She couldn't sleep. We've talked over an hour."

John's eyebrows rose. "Nothing can come of it. Doesn't she understand that?"

Margaret shook her head. "What she understands means nothing! For the first time in her life, she is deeply taken by a man. She's frightened, and she's ecstatic, and the last thing she wants to think about is, does she understand nothing can come of it? I told you earlier, she will see him again, and I'm telling you the same thing now. She will see him again. Somehow it's going to happen."

John frowned. "She's young. It'll pass."

"Don't be mistaken. She's eighteen, and she's beyond her years. She has the heart of a grown woman. We better take this seriously, because she certainly is."

John's smile disappeared. "That bad?"

"Yes, that bad."

"She's only seen him twice. She's never spoken to him—doesn't even know his name."

"John, sometimes that's enough."

John let out all his breath, and his shoulders slumped from weariness. "We'll talk more about it. Right now we better get to bed. If this thing with the British goes wrong, we'll need all the rest we can get."

Notes

The incident wherein William Dawes thrashes a British soldier for insulting his wife is based on a real event (see French, *The Day of Concord and Lexington,* p. 77).

The incident described wherein William Dawes led a group of colonials to steal a cannon from under the noses of British guards—in the process driving a cuff button into his wrist and later needing medical attention from Doctor Joseph Warren, whom he refused to tell how he sustained the wound—is historically accurate (see French, *The Day of Concord and Lexington,* p. 78).

The name of the colonial spy who succeeded in penetrating the office of General Thomas Gage to obtain his secrets and messages could not be found; thus the name Abe Cullens is used in this volume. It is not the true name.

Background concerning the information and documents with which General Gage's informers were supplying him at this time can be found in French, *General Gage's Informers.* One of those providing Gage with intelligence concerning the colonial weapons stores did write his communications in the French language. (See *General Gage's Informers,* pp. 10–14, 28–30.)

Sunday, April 16, 1775

CHAPTER IV

★ ★ ★

*T*he rapid, insistent rapping came again. Margaret Kemble Gage opened her eyes and for a moment stared into the gray blackness of her second-floor bedroom, caught in the twilight world between deep, dreamless sleep and an awareness that someone was at the downstairs door. She listened and it came again, and she reached to grasp the shoulder of her husband. "Someone's knocking."

His eyes flickered and opened, and for a moment he stared at her while his brain registered her touch and her words. "Who?"

"I don't know. I just heard it."

He waited and it came again. He glanced at the clock—five-fifteen A.M., Sunday, April 16, 1775—and he threw back the thick comforter and swung his feet onto the round, hand-braided rug. His slippers made a slapping sound as he walked down the hardwood stairs to the back door. He was tying his robe belt when he tugged the window blind to one side and peered out. Instantly he drew the dead bolt, turned the brass key, and opened the door.

"Come in," he said with sharp urgency and paused long enough to look beyond the man who entered. Nothing moved in the silent yard. "Sit." He pointed to the kitchen table, and the small man pulled a chair and dropped onto it, tense, nervous, eyes constantly moving.

"You know you were never to come here." Gage was still standing, frowning in hot disgust. The man sat silent while Gage drew out his own chair and settled onto it. "What was so important?"

"Someone saw the longboats go out to the men-of-war. Within half an hour nine colonials met at Warren's home."

"You saw them?"

"I saw them."

"Who?"

"Warren, Thorpe, Dunson, Palmer, and Watson, all from the committee, and Revere, Dawes, Sievers, and one other man I didn't know."

"For how long?"

"Until nearly four—more than three hours."

"What happened after they left?"

"They scattered and I think they all went home but Revere. He crossed the river in his boat."

Gage eased back in his chair and ran his hand through his unkempt hair. "North?"

"North."

His head settled forward and his jowls rested on his chest as he stared at his clasped hands before him on the table and worked with his thoughts in the silence of the austere, orderly New England kitchen.

General Thomas Gage, personally selected by King George to be governor of the rebellious colony of Massachusetts, had arrived under direct orders of Lord Dartmouth, secretary of state for the American colonies, in May 1774, with four regiments of British regulars. He audaciously declared to King George in writing that "if we will but assert ourselves firmly, the Americans will submit meekly."

His declaration was a spectacular catastrophe.

In the years before Gage's arrival, the British Parliament had passed various measures to collect taxes from the colonies. In 1765 came the Stamp Act, which required the colonists to pay a tax on most paper goods, from newspapers down to the cards used by the sailors to play whist. When the colonials ripped up the tax stamps and hung tax collectors in effigy, the Stamp Act was repealed. In hot retaliation, Parliament passed the Declaratory Act in 1766, declaring the right of Parliament to enact laws for the colonies "in all cases whatsoever." This was followed in 1767 by the Townsend Acts, requiring colonists to pay taxes on a host of goods, including paper, glass, paint, and tea. "Tyranny!" screamed the colonies, and the British eventually repealed the Townsend Acts—with the exception of the tariff on tea. Then in 1773, when Parliament gave to the East India Company a tea-trade monopoly in the colonies, incensed Bostonians disguised as Indians raided three British ships and dumped over three hundred boxes of the company's tea into Boston Harbor. With tensions building, the British struck back with the Intolerable Acts, asserting their power to close Boston Harbor with a Port Act, quarter British troops in colonial homes, appoint members of the Massachusetts legislature, appoint judges, and stop all town meetings.

A firm disciple of following the letter of the law, Gage enforced the Port Act, essentially shutting down Boston Harbor. Shipping stopped, and with it commerce, and Boston City ground to a halt. Gage was startled when the colonials refused his beneficent offer to reopen trade if they would swear allegiance to the Crown and submit to his rule, and he was shocked when the stores of gunpower in Boston began to disappear into the countryside to be used against the British if war came.

Gage seized the Boston powder magazine northwest of town, midway between Mystic and Cambridge. Within twenty-four hours, three thousand men flooded from the countryside into Boston in raucous, angry protest. Instantly Gage wrote a shaky letter to General Haldimand of New York. "Bring all your gunpowder and troops to Boston at once."

None came. Haldimand desperately needed all he could get to hold off a threatened rebellion in New York.

Gage, detesting the thought of war, sought counsel from Brigadier General Percy and from a trusted officer, Major John Pitcairn, then sent a special, urgent message to Lord Dartmouth in London. "If I am to execute my orders to contain and control the citizenry in the colony of Massachusetts, I must have an additional twenty thousand troops, armed and battle ready, instanter."

Troops arrived five months later on April 3, 1775. Eleven regiments of light infantry and five hundred marines, with little artillery. The addition brought Gage's total army to just under four thousand soldiers under arms. Parliament could not believe that his request for twenty thousand men was justified.

His own men began calling him "Old Woman" and "Tommy." He felt a growing apprehension that he had already proven himself a failure as a politician, and that he was about to prove himself incapable as a military commander. He cast about for something that would save his wounded career. It came to him in the early hours of April 14, after he had paced the floor through the night.

Take their munitions at Concord, and the rebellion would be over, and if Adams and Hancock were at Lexington, might as well pick them up too. Samuel Adams! He had been offered the governorship of the colonies for life, and a fortune in gold if he would but denounce the colonials and swear his allegiance to the Crown. He had shouted his refusal and defiance in every newspaper. He could not be bought. Hancock was another matter. He well understood the wealth and power game, but in the end, he too defied the king.

Gage speculated. *Now they'll learn of their own folly! Their ragtag colonial militia might show token resistance, but let's see what they do with an advance regiment of marines followed by half a dozen regiments of grenadiers. The whole affair should be over in one day, and Boston and the entire colony of Massachusetts will be on their knees. Then let's hear what Sam Adams and John Hancock have to say.*

With growing confidence in his plan, Gage worked tirelessly on the details until midafternoon; then he called in only the officers who had need to know.

Saturday, April 15, you will select thirty trusted men for a sensitive maneuver. Secrecy is critical. Do not tell any of them until six o'clock P.M. They are to be on the Back Bay south of Cambridge Street at ten o'clock P.M. Have them leave in small groups so they will pass unnoticed. A messenger will deliver written orders to you at ten o'clock. You will memorize the orders and then destroy the paper. That is all.

Then he called in his messenger to deliver the ten o'clock P.M. message, and it was delivered at precisely ten o'clock. Now, at five-fifteen A.M. on Sunday morning, a scant seven hours and fifteen minutes after his officers and troops put the boats in the water, his secret messenger was sitting across the kitchen table telling him not only that the moving of the longboats out to the men-of-war in preparation for the daring raid on Concord and Lexington was seen by the colonials, but that their leaders had already met for three hours after watching the entire process. Worse, Revere was headed north, which could only mean one thing. Adams and Hancock would know by breakfast, and the militia at Concord before noon.

Gage scowled and cursed and his fist pounded the table. He rose and paced, then returned and dropped heavily onto his chair and brought his eyes to those of his messenger. His words were angry in the dead silence. "Did you get the list of details about Concord from the informer?"

Angry or not, as a matter of meticulous discipline, Gage never spoke the name of his paid informer on the Committee of Safety, nor the name of his messenger. Those names uttered by accident in the wrong place could cut off a pipeline to information without which his entire governorship would collapse. At all cost, he had to protect his sources. He had never mentioned those names to a single member of his staff, or even to his wife. Despite the fact she was American born, he trusted her implicitly, but knew that without those names, she could not reveal them in an idle moment of forgetfulness as she chatted with the wives of other officers, or even with her American friends.

The messenger's eyes brightened and a tight smile spread. He drew an envelope from his inside coat pocket and handed it to Gage, who slipped out the paper and flattened it on the table.

It was written in French. For more than a minute he studied the stiff, unnatural pen strokes, the only sounds the rhythmic ticking of the clock and their breathing. He knew enough rudimentary French to make out the general text.

"When did you get this?"

"Forty minutes ago. I took three detours coming here to be certain I was not followed."

A smile spread and he leaned back in his chair. "All right. I can translate most of this, but I want it exact. Take it to the translator and bring it back as soon as possible."

The messenger left, and fifteen minutes later Gage, in full uniform, strode rapidly up the brick walkway to the officer's quarters and entered. Three minutes later he faced two officers behind closed doors.

"Major Strumman, you are to find Paul Revere and arrest him. Select four of your best horsemen immediately and move north to Lexington, then on to Concord if necessary. Revere will be riding his gray mount. Don't spare your horses. I want that man back here before noon. Arrest him on sight. Here is my arrest warrant, charging him with acts of treason against the Crown. Leave immediately."

"Captain Cutler, pick one lieutenant and twenty armed and uniformed regulars and march to the South Church where citizens Warren and Thorpe and Dunson regularly attend services. When you get there, this is what you will do."

For three minutes he methodically repeated his orders, then handed the captain a letter with the same orders in writing.

"Do you understand?"

"Yes, sir."

"Very well. Proceed at once."

Gage stood at the front door of his headquarters when the major led his four horsemen north across the compound at a gallop, saluting smartly as they swept past the general. Twenty minutes later he watched the captain muster his troops into a double column and march them south out of the compound, and they disappeared into the streets.

He took his breakfast at his quarters with his wife, and returned to his office to wait while she attended church services at the chapel on the compound. At noon his orderly answered the rap at his headquarters, accepted the sealed envelope, and delivered it to Gage. By twelve-fifteen P.M. Gage was elated, nearly gleeful.

He allowed himself a moment of pure exultation as he strode about his large, square, sparsely furnished office waving the translated document in the air.

It's all here—cannon, powder, shot—all of it. I can pull their fangs! Without their munitions they can bark but they cannot bite! I have them, and it can be done in one day just as I planned it! A small force—six, eight hundred crack troops—a lightning march in the night—total surprise—they'll wake up in Concord to the sound of musket butts on their doors, and we'll have their stores by noon and be back by nightfall!

He drew a great breath and exhaled sharply.

We can also pick up Adams and Hancock, but that is now of little consequence. Without munitions, they're hamstrung! Oh, the buzzing we will hear then from these hot-blooded little bees who have lost their stingers!

And the king! Ah, the letter to the king! "Your Royal Majesty King George. It is my great honor to inform His Royal Majesty of the events of the day. This date the Royal Marines and light infantry have seized the entire supply of munitions, medicines, supplies, and food upon which the citizenry of the city of Boston and the surrounding countryside have wholly depended to begin and maintain hostilities. Consistent with the advice of Lord Dartmouth, secretary of state for the American colonies, this extremely successful military maneuver was conducted in one day with a minimum of casualties on both sides. Further details will follow timely. Your obdt. svnt. General Thomas Gage."

Perhaps it should be longer. No, humility is the key. Short and humble.

He looked at the paper clutched in his hand and sobered. He folded the original document in French back in the envelope and placed it in the right drawer of his massive, polished oak desk, closed it, locked it, and hung the desk key back on its peg on the underside of the desk, next to the position his right knee assumed when he was sitting at the desk. The second document, the translation, he folded and placed in the inside pocket of his officer's coat, over his breast.

He settled into his large, carved, leather-covered chair and for many minutes sat with his hands clasped across his paunch while he worked with his thoughts. He scratched notes with a quill, crossed some of them out, added others, and continued refining his plan. Finished, he folded the written notes and put them in his inside coat pocket.

He rose and called his orderly. "I will be taking my midday meal at my quarters. Remain here. Allow no one in except those authorized. I will return later. If anyone needs me, come inform me immediately."

He walked towards his quarters in bright, warm sunlight, lost in his thoughts. He was thirty yards from his front door when the sound of marching men turned him about and he stared south-, ward, across the compound. The captain was returning with his twenty-man detail from the assignment at the South Church, and even at seventy yards Gage could see that two of the regulars were bloodied and one was being carried by the others. Gage crossed the compound at a trot, and the captain barked orders that stopped his column at Gage's approach. The captain snapped to attention, boot heels clicking, toes spread, chest out, shoulders back, his chin jammed down tight. His arm whipped up in a salute as Gage slowed.

"Report!" Gage demanded.

"Sir, we executed our orders. A colonial attacked two of the soldiers with a musket. As ordered, we refused to be drawn into an open conflict. We repulsed the attack and left the scene with our wounded. There were no shots fired. The soldiers sustained wounds, one serious. That is all. Sir."

"What wounds?"

"Sergeant Cope is believed to have a broken collarbone, and something's wrong with his neck, and his right ear is badly torn. Corporal Betters has four teeth missing, four more smashed, and needs stitching about his mouth."

"Whose musket? Colonials don't carry muskets to church."

The captain licked dry lips and hesitated. "Sergeant Cope's musket."

"To be sure! Who was this colonial and how did he get Cope's musket?"

"William Dawes, sir, and he took it away from Cope."

"For what reason?"

The captain exhaled and his shoulders sagged. "Sir, Sergeant Cope made a . . . questionable maneuver with his bayonet and Dawes took exception."

"What maneuver?"

"I'd rather not say, sir."

"You will tell me now, or later before a board of inquiry."

"He attempted to lift the skirt of Mrs. Dawes."

Gage's head jerked forward. "He *what?*"

"I would rather not repeat it, sir."

"Do I understand that one of our regulars attempted to lift the skirts of a colonial gentlewoman in the streets with a bayonet, and her husband took the musket from him and disabled two of our troops?"

"That's not all, sir."

"Go on."

"Dawes broke the bayonet, smashed the musket, and bent the barrel."

Gage's mouth sagged open for a moment before he clamped it shut.

"And there's more, sir."

"What more could there be?"

"Mr. Dawes advised me to tell the general that the next time one of our soldiers so much as looks at his wife, that man is dead."

"He threatened us?"

"Yes, sir, he did, and I think he meant it."

"Be assured he did!"

"And one thing more. Citizen John Dunson swore on his oath that if any charges are brought against William Dawes, Mr. Dunson will see Sergeant Cope tried in a Massachusetts court and hanged for his armed assault on a gentlewoman."

Gage shook his head in stark disbelief. "This little adventure will cost Sergeant Cope the price of a new musket and bayonet, Boston prices, and a reprimand in his record. Perhaps his sergeant's chevrons. Take your wounded to the infirmary. Carry on."

Gage watched the rigid red backs of the soldiers as they marched on towards the infirmary, then trudged back to his living quarters, shaking his head in disgust at the wild story. He paused at his front door and for a moment pondered. *Has the patrol caught Revere? Did Revere get to Adams and Hancock first? What about Concord?* For a moment his eyes involuntarily darted north, and then he reached for the doorknob.

Eleven miles northwest, Revere jumped his mare splashing through green cattails and reeds growing in a low marsh and spurred her up a gentle rise into a cluster of oak saplings and pulled her to a stop. She threw her head and munched at the bit, mud-splattered, wanting to run. Straight ahead four hundred yards, across the Bedford Road, stood the two-storied white frame house of the Reverend Jonas Clarke. To the left six hundred yards was the junction of the Bedford Road and the Concord Road.

Revere dismounted and spoke low to his mare, "Good girl, good girl," while he stood stock-still and studied every thing, every movement in the village from the cover of the sprouting oaks. Nothing red was moving. There were no soldiers.

Eight times since daybreak he had ridden away from the road onto hills and taken cover behind stone fences or trees or hedgerows to wait and watch his back trail. Twice he had seen mounted British patrols ahead, before they saw him, and had hidden—once in a corncrib, with his hand clamped over the mare's nose to prevent a whicker, and once in a tributary to the Mystic River, he and the horse both belly deep in water, shielded by willows, while the patrol rode past twenty yards away.

The mare blew and tossed her head, fighting the tight reins. "Huuu," Revere crooned to settle the mare, and reached for the onside stirrup. Mounted, he let her run on the gentle decline to Bedford Road, across it, and into the yard of Jonas Clarke.

"Hello the house!" he called, and trotted the mare to the rear, where the barn and horse stalls stood square with the house and the road. He led her into the barn and closed the door, then threw the stirrup over the saddle seat while he loosened the girth and jerked the saddle and blanket off and racked them.

He turned and stopped when the barn door opened and Jonas Clarke entered.

"Paul Revere! Have you come with news?"

"Yes. Have British soldiers been here today?"

"No."

"Let me tend the horse and we'll go in."

He rubbed her down with a burlap bean sack, then brushed her damp hide and led her to a stall where he unbuckled the bridle and hung a nose bag with cracked corn and oats. Three minutes later he walked shoulder to shoulder with Clarke back into the house.

Adams and Hancock met them at the door.

"Is it good or bad news?" Adams asked without greeting.

"You judge." They sat down at the kitchen table, and for fifteen minutes Revere spoke. They were interrupted by an elderly woman and a younger woman, who suddenly appeared in the kitchen archway.

Revere stopped and turned to Adams for an explanation.

"This is Mrs. Thomas Hancock, John's aunt, and Dorothy Quincy, his fiancée."

Revere rose and bowed. "It is my pleasure." He resumed his seat and turned to Hancock. The ladies walked back to the reception room. "Warren sent me so you could prepare for whatever's going to happen."

"Is Gage after us, or the munitions at Concord?"

"We don't know."

Hancock raised one eyebrow. "We'll assume he's after both."

"Does anyone know when he's coming?" Adams asked.

"No."

"The question is, do we stay or do we leave?" Adams responded.

Hancock bristled. "I'm staying. I'll carry a musket against them."

Adams shook his head. "You're needed elsewhere."

Revere interrupted. "Anything you want me to carry back? any message?"

Adams stood. "Keep us informed."

Revere nodded and reached to shake the hands of both men and of Jonas Clarke. Revere had his hand on the doorknob when the sound of a running horse brought him up short and he turned, trying to see through the next room out the front window. The horse slid to a stop and the rider hit the ground running, banging on the front door.

"It's Ira Halsted," Clarke exclaimed and strode quickly and threw the front door open.

"There's a British captain and four regulars down at the tavern asking about a man riding a gray horse. Is Revere here?"

"Yes."

"They're armed. I don't know what they want."

"Are they coming here?"

"They're asking where this place is. No one's told them yet."

Clarke turned to Revere. "Go a quarter mile east of where you came in. There's a rise there, and you'll be hidden behind it for the first half mile. Go now."

Revere darted out the back door and sprinted for the barn. Two minutes later the barn doors burst open and he swung onto the back of the mare and kicked her into a run, across the road, angling left, cresting the rise with the horse stretching at every stride, and then he was out of sight.

He held the mare to a stampede gait for a mile, feeling the smooth reach and pull of her driving haunches, then took the slack out of the reins and slowly worked her back, talking to her, and then he pulled her to a stop. She stood spraddle legged, blowing, battling for wind, sweat running, nose dripping. He dismounted and walked her for several minutes while her breathing slowed, and she stopped and shook herself hard and the saddle rattled and popped. He led her to a small stream and let her drink for a moment, then pulled her head up, waited, and let her take more.

He remounted and turned her southeast, angling back for the

road to Menotomy at a walk. Then he raised her to a trot for a time, then a walk. He glanced up at the sun and gauged the time to be a little after one o'clock. He looked about at the gentle roll of the greening hills and the spring flowers opening their blues and reds and yellows, and he could not remember a more beautiful spring day. He rode on in the sunshine.

The buzzing whirr of the ball and the pop of the musket six hundred yards distant came nearly as one and froze Revere for a split second. The mare jumped, frightened, and Revere socked his blunted spurs into her flanks and lay low on her neck as she leaped to a full-out gallop. He looked back over his right shoulder and saw the white smoke from the road and the red coats of the twelve mounted soldiers. Two more clouds of white smoke appeared and two more balls sang and missed, and then he heard the thump of the distant muskets.

Patrol! I chanced into a patrol! Why are they shooting? Do they know? It doesn't matter. They'll never catch me. I'll be at the Mystic in five minutes, and once I hit the river they'll never find me. Come on, catch me if you can!

He slowed the mare to a hard lope until he sighted the pond north of the Menotomy Road, then angled south, skirting the lake, to the upper waters of the Mystic River. He followed the river down past Cooper's Tavern, then northwest to Mystic, across the Medford Road. He angled south, following the river until he came to the place it opened wide and shallow, and he jumped the mare in and plowed through to the east side of the river. He stopped in a huge, dense growth of oaks and waited, the only sounds the lapping of the river and the squeak of the saddle as the mare caught her wind.

He patted the sweated neck and murmured, "We wait here until the roads are clear."

The sun had set and long shadows were creeping when he tightened the saddle girth and remounted the tired horse. He walked her south along the river to the second fording place, waded back across where the Meford Road passed Winter Hill, and again dismounted to listen and watch.

In full darkness he remounted and turned southwest on the Medford Road, a weary man riding a weary horse in the darkness. The full moon was rising when he reached Charlestown. He worked his way through the narrow streets and stopped near the outskirts, with the smell of Boston Harbor and the Charles River strong. He dismounted stiff before a small white house and cautiously rapped on the door.

"Who's there?"

"Revere. Open up, Conant."

The door opened and a man slipped out and closed it quickly, and the two stood facing each other in the moonlight.

"What brings you here?"

"Things are happening. We think Gage is sending troops to take our munitions, and maybe Adams and Hancock."

"When?"

"No one knows."

"How? March troops down through Roxbury and then up through Cambridge?"

"We don't know. We think maybe by longboat, across the Back Bay to Lechmere and then across open farmlands, at night, so no one sees. When they do it, they might barricade the Neck and seal up the harbor so no one can leave Boston to tell about it."

Revere paused. "When they move, we've got to spread the alarm out to our people in the country. I'll try to get through myself to warn people, but we need something in addition to that. I've got a plan. I'll see to it that lanterns are hung in the North Church steeple on the Boston side of the Back Bay. If they move by land, one lantern will be hung. If they move across the Back Bay, two lanterns. You watch at night. When you read the lanterns, spread the word to get the militia and the minutemen up for action. Do you understand?"

"Yes."

"One more thing. If the British troops move, I'm going to get across the river in my boat in the dark and hope they don't see.

Meet me down at Putnam's pier on your side and have a horse ready. I'll ride to Concord to help spread the alarm."

"I understand." Colonel William Conant looked closely at Revere in the moonlight. "Where have you been? You're a mess and you look exhausted."

"To Lexington, and dodging British patrols all the way back. They're shooting. Be careful. Take care of yourself, Conant. And watch for the lanterns."

"Done."

Revere remounted and picked his way to the Charlestown ferry and watched to be certain there were no British troops patrolling or guarding before he boarded in the dark. The moonlight turned the bay to countless jewels, and Revere breathed deep in the clean sea air. The ferry jammed into the dock on the Boston side and the ramp dropped, and Revere led the mare down to the dock with her hooves stamping hollow on the heavy planking, and he remounted. He tapped lightly with his spurs and the mare moved east and south through the outskirts of town, and then he angled back west to his home. He led her quickly into the small barn, stripped the saddle and blanket, and was unbuckling the bridle when he sensed sound behind. He spun and faced the black silhouette of a man in the doorway, the silver moonlight behind, and he crouched, ready.

"It's me, Sievers. Warren sent me to find you. We were worried maybe the British took you."

"They tried."

"Warren said to tell you. The British got the list of everything buried or hidden at Concord. They know about the cannon and powder and supplies. All of it. The committee's making a plan to move it all before the British can take it. He wants you to be ready to ride as a messenger on a minute's notice. You and Dawes."

Notes

It was suspected that General Thomas Gage was dominated by his handsome American wife, Margaret Kemble Gage (see French, *The Day of Concord and Lexington*, p. 61).

The attitude of General Gage that asserting his power firmly would cause the Americans to submit meekly and the reaction of his own troops to his lack of firmness and decision by calling him "Tommy" and "Old Woman" when not in his presence are established in French, *The Day of Concord and Lexington*, pp. 11–16.

The incident depicted in this chapter in which the British shoot at Paul Revere on the night of April 16, 1775, is fictional.

As shown in the novel, Revere did make arrangements to alert those across the river from Boston regarding British troop movements. The plan involved showing lanterns in the Boston North Church steeple if the British moved their forces at night: one lantern if they marched their troops south over the Neck, then northwest to Concord; two lanterns if they moved the troops across the Back Bay by boat to Lechmere Point. (See French, *The Day of Concord and Lexington*, pp. 66–67.)

CHAPTER V

★ ★ ★

*M*atthew." John's whisper came sharp in the dark, and Matthew stirred in his bed, then settled.

"Matthew, wake up." John gently shook his shoulder.

Matthew's eyes opened, and for a moment he stared unseeing in the blackness before his brain identified the voice and the faint, square, gray shape of his open bedroom door.

He looked up at John, crouched over his bed, still holding his shoulder. "What's wrong?" he said, and swallowed dry.

"I need your help. Get dressed. Be quiet."

Three minutes later Matthew walked fully dressed, carrying his shoes, into the shadows of the parlor, where John sat at his workbench with one lamp glowing. John was hunched forward, working the metal of the trigger assembly of the seventh, and last, musket. The trigger pull was too stiff; the sear had to have a whisper of metal removed and smoothed. It would take fifteen more minutes of delicate work.

John spoke without looking up. "Get the unfinished musket from the pantry."

Matthew set his shoes on his work stool next to John's and walked to the pantry. He rolled the long, oval-braided rug to one side, raised the trapdoor with the recessed brass ring, and lifted the top musket, wrapped in oil cloth and tarp, from beneath the floorboards. John untied it on his workbench while Matthew glanced at the clock. Nearly five o'clock, Monday morning.

"What's happened?" Matthew asked. "What time did you get home?"

"After midnight."

"Did they get Revere?"

"No, but they tried. A patrol shot at him out west of Menotomy."

"How did you find out?"

"Tom was here twenty minutes ago."

Matthew stiffened and his eyes widened. "Has the shooting started?"

"Probably not. The soldiers were nearly half a mile away, probably shooting just to shoot. A patrol was in Lexington looking for him." John paused for a moment. "It's too close. We need time but we can't slow it. It's happening on its own terms."

"Did he get to Adams and Hancock?"

"Yes."

Matthew took a moment to order and weigh his thoughts.

Frustration was in John's voice. "We could be at war any time—today, tomorrow." He pointed at the musket. "Once it starts, we'll be too late with the muskets in the pantry. Too many British patrols in the streets. We've got to get these to the church today so Silas can get them to the militia. We may be too late now."

Matthew's face clouded. "Five blocks? You're worried about five blocks?"

John nodded, eyes narrowed. "There were four British patrols in the streets when I came home, and they were stopping everyone, checking everything. That's what I need you for. Walk from here to the church right now and count the patrols. I have to know."

Matthew glanced at the musket while he worked with his shoes.

For fifteen months John had worked quietly at his workbench in the night by candlelight, setting up the vises to lock the long barrels in place, then twisting the drill bits by hand to bore them out. With the precision of a master clockmaker, he fit the smoothbore barrels exactly to the .60-caliber balls they would fire. Such precision was necessary in order to prevent gas leakage around the ball and to increase speed, range, and accuracy. At seven pounds, the Dunson muskets were three pounds lighter than the cumbersome Brown Bess issued to British regulars, and at distances above eighty yards, more than twice as accurate. The bore in the Brown Bess was bigger than the .75-caliber balls, and allowed gas leakage as the ball rattled up the barrel, bouncing slightly from side to side. At fifty yards the Brown Bess ball began to drift; at eighty yards it was out of control; at one hundred yards, marksmen agreed that what you aimed at usually had little to do with what you hit. The single virtue of the Brown Bess was that the huge .75-caliber ball struck like the kick of a mule. The .60-caliber Dunson musket ball was big enough; the Brown Bess ball was excessive.

Matthew quickly brushed and tied back his shoulder-length hair with a leather thong, shrugged into his coat, and disappeared out the front door.

At five-twenty John slipped the finished trigger assembly into its port in the smooth, oiled oak stock, settled the musket barrel into place, and tightened the setscrews. By five-thirty the hammer, powder pan, pan cover, and frizzen were in place, with the V-shaped spring locked beneath to operate the pan cover. John forced a tiny steel pin through the touchhole to be certain the passage was clear from the pan to the firing chamber, then sorted through half a dozen flints to select one. He loosened the thumbscrew on the hammer, set the flint, and twisted the setscrew tight, solid.

He started at the sound of padded feet entering from the bedroom wing and turned to face Margaret, wrapped in her robe, standing in the archway in her thick felt slippers. He glanced at the clock.

"Where's Matthew?" she asked, and yawned.

"Outside."

Her eyes widened. "Doing what?"

"Looking for British patrols. We've got to get these muskets to the church."

She strode to his side, eyes suddenly alert, serious. "Has something happened? Did they get Revere?"

"No, but they shot at him. We're out of time."

For long moments their eyes locked as the impact settled into Margaret. Her eyes dropped for a moment, then shifted to the musket, and her thoughts went to Matthew, and then to John, and she spoke quietly. "John, I'm terrified. What would I do if . . ." Her voice trailed off, and she stood next to him in the lamp glow, vulnerable, defenseless, sick in her soul with the growing realization of what was coming.

He had no reply. He sat quietly, wishing he knew what to say, wanting to reach out, but he had no words, no assurances, no comfort.

She swallowed and turned in the silence and walked to the fireplace. She worked with the leather bellows until the banked coals glowed and caught, and she fed shavings, then sticks, until flames licked. She stared into the bright, dancing flames for long moments in silence, unmoving, needing to cry out, to have someone pluck the dark foreboding from her heart, knowing it could not be. She sighed, then padded silently back to the bedroom to get dressed.

John stared into the dark archway after her passing, wrenched, torn, because he could not stand between her and her fears as he always had. This time, forces beyond control were only moments away from a cataclysmic collision that would send their world reeling and would leave their life, their family, their home, their country changed forever. There was no comfort in the truth. He could only push the blackness from his mind and try to endure the grab in his heart while he continued work on the musket.

He cocked the hammer, slowly squeezed the trigger, felt with approval the smooth working of metal on metal in the action, and watched the hammer fall. The flint struck the steel frizzen and drove it upwards while it knocked sparks into the exposed pan.

John set the finished musket on his workbench and sat in the lamplight for a moment, shoulders slumped, staring at the musket in deep thought. Within days the weapon would be used to kill. No matter whom it killed, no matter the cause, he felt the tightening in the pit of his stomach with the knowledge that he had created it. He jumped and sucked air at the sound of the door opening.

Matthew stepped into the room, eyes wide in the early-morning light. "Four patrols between here and the church, one right at the churchyard. We're not going to get the muskets down there today."

John jerked from his work stool and paced. "We have to."

"How?"

John ran his hand over his hair, anxious, frustrated. "I don't know yet."

Margaret walked through the archway and looked at Matthew. "Help with the kettles and get the water."

While John rewrapped the finished musket and hid it beneath the pantry floor, Matthew and Margaret hung two huge, fire-blackened kettles on the heavy swivel arms in the fireplace, anchored in the stone and cement wall by two iron bolts, each arm being eighteen inches long and one inch in diameter. Matthew picked two water buckets from beside the kitchen door and walked out into the hush of early morning. He returned in minutes with both of them full, dripping, set them down on the braided rug at the back door to let the drip absorb for a moment before he walked to the fireplace, poured the water into the kettles, and then turned to go back out.

Margaret dipped water into a pan and set it on the stove, then transferred burning sticks from the fireplace to the stove firebox, followed by kindling, and closed the firebox door clanging and set the draft. She worked in silence, preoccupied, apprehensive.

John studied her and remained silent, comprehending vaguely the awful compulsion rising in her mother's heart to protect her own, her nest. She saw meaning in the chaos of the Boston streets only as it affected her offspring, her husband, her home. And should war come, it would be she who would have to accept and hide the soul-destroying fear while she kept her offspring fed and clothed; and it would be she who wore a brave face and said brave words to shield them from the demons that rode heavy in the daylight and waked them crying in the night.

Margaret tapped the stove top gingerly with her fingertips to test how it was warming, and three minutes later scooped rolled oats into the simmering pan of water, replaced the lid, waited for a minute, then moved the pan off the heat to steep. She fed more wood to the fires beneath the water kettles, then went to the root cellar for a jar of milk, a block of her own homemade cheese, leftovers from the leg of lamb, and three apples.

She stopped for a moment at the kitchen door to look at the heavens and feel the air. It would be a sunny day, good for drying clothes. Fifteen minutes later she placed wrapped leg-of-lamb sandwiches in three woven-reed lunch baskets, with a small chunk of wrapped cheese and an apple, and put all three baskets on the big dining table. She checked the oatmeal, added a pinch of salt and stirred, then replaced the lid.

Three minutes later she finished stripping the sheets and pillowcases from her bed, gathered the soiled clothing from the previous week into a large woven basket, and set it down by the back door. She set bowls and spoons and glasses on the table, then walked briskly down the hall and rapped on Brigitte's door.

By rigid Boston custom, Monday was wash day. "Goodwives" were measured by their observance of such sacred customs, and on fair-weather Mondays, vacant clotheslines brought wagging tongues and pointing fingers. For the hard, exhausting work of scrubbing and hanging the weekly wet wash for a family of seven, Margaret wore a thick apron, a broad blue bandana to hold her hair back, and high buttoned leather shoes.

"Brigitte, get your wash load and come along." She waited until Brigitte's bare feet were on the oval rug before she went back to the kitchen.

"John, you and Matthew set up the tubs." War or no war, clothing had to be washed, dried, ironed; children had to be fed— the business of life ground on, giving no quarter to fears, no time to brood. When weather permitted, doing the wash in the backyard saved the work of mopping the kitchen floor afterwards.

John and Matthew walked out the back door. Margaret set honey, brown maple sugar, and the bread-cutting board on the table, then walked back into the bedroom wing and tapped on Caleb's bedroom door, then Priscilla's. "Time for school. Breakfast in fifteen minutes."

She returned to the kitchen, where wisps of steam rose from the big water kettles, and she felt the moist heat begin to fill the room, and the inside of the windows began to fog. She opened the back door and spoke to John and Matthew. "Leave it open . . . let some steam out."

Brigitte brought her basket of bedding and soiled clothing and added it to Margaret's, and went back to strip the children's beds and gather their soiled clothing. John and Matthew entered with buckets in their hands and began carrying the steaming water out to the two washtubs, one for scrubbing, one for rinse. They filled the tubs, then drew more water from the well and refilled the kettles.

Margaret took the first basket of bedding and soiled linens out, dumped it into one tub, shaved slices of brown bar soap into it, poked the sheets down with a water-bleached oak stick, and stirred until the soap dissolved and froth appeared. She stirred until the steam stopped, then reached for the corrugated scrub board and thrust it into the tub, upright against the near edge, then walked back inside.

"Places at the table," she called.

Three minutes later they all knelt beside their chairs and John nodded to Matthew, who offered their morning prayer and said grace.

It was a school day, a work day, and everyone knew what was expected. In efficient silence they passed the porridge and brown sugar, poured the milk, cut thick slices of bread and spread butter and honey, ate, and drank. With John's permission the children went to their rooms, with Brigitte and Margaret following to put finishing touches on their hair. Then all reappeared in the parlor for Margaret's inspection before they left for school.

"Mama, are the soldiers going to steal us?"

Margaret saw the fear in Adam's wide, frightened eyes as she reached for the two small lunch baskets on the kitchen table.

"Of course not," she said firmly. "Don't you worry about the soldiers. Caleb will be with you." She handed one lunch basket to each of the twins, then the third, larger one to Caleb. "Now, out the door, you three. On to school and come straight home." She marched them out the front door, to the front gate, and watched them start south towards the small, square frame school building. "Caleb," she called, "you watch them." They reached the first corner before the school bell clanged the five-minute warning, and the children broke into a trot for the last two blocks. Margaret looked up and down the streets for flashes of red coats in the bright sunlight, but there were none.

She walked back into the house and closed the front door, and the hot, humid air washed over her. She glanced at the two large black kettles with water boiling and drew and released a great breath and braced herself.

While Brigitte did the dishes, Margaret walked on out the back door and jabbed the stick into the soaked sheets, lifted one on the oak stick, and felt it. "Soaked enough," she murmured, and dropped it sloshing back into the tub. She laid the stick on the washstand, grasped the dripping sheet with both hands, and began grinding it up and down on the scrub board, shifting it steadily as she did, until it was finished. She wrung it, then dumped it splashing into the rinse tub and started on the next sheet. Brigitte walked out with the clothespins.

The two of them hit a rhythm, and the clothes began to fill the lines strung beside the west fence of the yard, while John and Matthew carried more water from the well to refill the big kettles in the fireplace.

With the kettles full and wood on the fires, John went back to his workbench and motioned to Matthew and spoke quietly. "I'm going down to see Silas. Maybe he knows a way to get the muskets to the church. You stay here. If Tom or any of the others come, hold them here. I'll be back soon."

Matthew nodded, and John picked his hat from its peg on the engraved hat rack by the door, and walked out into a world of budding trees and greening grass and bursting flower beds washed with the bright sunlight of a new spring morning. He felt a rise as he drew the clean ocean air into his lungs. He walked out the gate and turned right, towards the church, watching ahead for anything that moved.

At the corner he nodded a greeting and paused to let Amos Poulter, pushing three large covered milk cans in his creaking two-wheeled milk cart, pass on to his next customer. Halfway down the block he watched Enid Ferguson walk out the front door of her bakery with a dozen hot fresh loaves of bread covered in a woven basket and turn towards him, hurrying to deliver them before they cooled. A patrol of four British regulars followed her out the gate and spoke to her. She stopped and turned. They lifted the basket cover, looked and counted, and turned back while she hurried on. John spoke and lifted his hat to her, and she nodded her "Good morning, Mr. Dunson" to him as they passed. The four soldiers watched and waited at the bakery door for John's approach.

"'E's one of 'em what did it."

John heard the guarded accusation and saw the pointed finger, and studied the four soldiers as he walked, searching his mind for an explanation. There was none.

"'Im and Dawes, it was. Like to 'ave took poor Cope's ear off and broke his neck, they did."

In John's mind came the image of Dawes's foot driving the musket muzzle down, the bayonet snapping, Dawes swinging, the musket ripping the ear, the solid hit, the groan, the sergeant sagging to the ground.

John recognized neither man and kept walking. He was three steps past them when he heard the challenge.

"'Ow about it, g'vnor? Want to take my musket and bash me like you done Cope? C'mon, give it a try."

John ignored the challenge and walked on and heard the slur, "Bloody cowards, the lot of 'em," and he did not look back.

He passed the open door of Purdom's sausage and cheese store with the sharp smell of spiced meats and continued across the street, moving steadily to the church. The clack of iron horseshoes on the cobblestones came from behind, and he turned to see two mounted British officers riding the big-boned bay horses preferred by English light grenadiers, uniforms bright in the sun, their golden shoulder epaulets sparkling. One was a slightly built captain, the other a young lieutenant, taller than average, solidly built, regular features, with a scar in his right eyebrow. They studied John as they rode past, and recognition flashed in the eyes of the captain.

John slowed at the corner and felt the rise of tension in his chest. The two officers had tied their horses to the iron rings set in the stone shafts beneath the great oaks and maples lining the street in front of the church. The captain said something to the lieutenant, who nodded, and they studied John as he walked towards the two regulars who guarded the big double doors with slung muskets. John glanced at the officers and then faced the regular with the two chevrons on his sleeve, and waited.

"State yer name and business."

"Citizen John Dunson to see the reverend."

"About wot?"

"Church matters of confidence."

"I got me orders to search everyone goin' in and comin' out. Stand 'ere." He pointed, and John stood still and turned his pockets out on demand. The solider had him remove his coat so they could search it, and then tossed it back to him.

"Ten minutes, g'vnor, then we come in 'n get you," the corporal said, and stepped aside.

John walked into the silent chapel, and the sound of the doors closing behind him echoed. Bright sunlight on the high stained-glass windows cast color on the empty pews as he walked down the aisle, past the pulpit, through the small door behind, and down a narrow passage to the living quarters of the reverend. He rapped on the door.

"Who's there?" came the thin, high voice.

"John Dunson."

The door rattled and opened, and the reverend drew John in quickly.

"They've been out there since morning, and two at the back door. We're prisoners." He gestured to his wife, Mattie, small, wiry, who raised faded eyes to smile tiredly at John. She sat round-shouldered on a straight-backed chair rapidly working a needle up and down through a needlepoint mat.

"Is anyone listening?" John asked.

"We're alone."

John paced in the small room, agitated, nervous. "Silas, I've got seven muskets finished, but I don't know how to move them from my house to here." He stopped and stared at Silas intently. "Any ideas?"

"When?"

"Today."

The reverend's eyes grew large, and he took half a step back. "Has shooting started?"

"They shot at Revere last night. It's coming too quick. We've got to get the muskets out to the militia."

Silas's hand covered his mouth, and then it dropped and he shrugged. "I don't know how. There's British all around."

"How did others do it?"

"Brought them after midnight, but that's when the British weren't everywhere."

John shook his head. "It can't wait." He paused. "Where do you hide them?"

"In the well, in oilskin, on a rope. Militiamen pull them out just before dawn."

John licked dry lips. "If we did get them here, could you get them to the militia?"

The reverend hunched his shoulders. "Risky. They had soldiers around here all night."

John shook his head. "It has to be done. I don't know how we're going to do it, but we'll get them here. Get ready to hide them and tell the militia to come get them."

Two minutes later John strode up the aisle through the silent, vacant chapel and out the main doors.

"'Old 'er right there," the corporal growled. The search took two minutes, and John continued out past the officers and down the cobblestone street, stopping for no one in his hurry.

Matthew met him at the door. "Any hope?"

John strode to his workbench, then back to the center of the room, where he stood on one foot, then the other. "Not much. Four patrols, one at the church. I was searched going in and coming out. If we did get them inside the church, I don't know how Silas could get them out to the militia."

The back door swung open and the two men turned as Brigitte walked in with her woven laundry basket on her hip, wisps of hair showing from beneath the white bandana tied about her head. She saw John's face and slowed, staring. "Something's wrong."

John said nothing as Margaret walked in behind Brigitte, her empty basket on her hip. She stopped. "Why is everyone standing around? What's happened?" Her eyes were wide, puzzled.

"I can't find a way to get the muskets to the church," John said, "and the militia has got to have them."

"Why?" Margaret asked. "Has someone started shooting?" She set her basket on the large table.

"They shot at Revere last night, boats on the Back Bay, the streets filled with British patrols, four of them between here and the church, one of them stationed at the church doors." He ran a nervous hand over his hair. "Yes, they're starting something."

Brigitte set her basket inside Margaret's on the table and studied John's face and movements. "The muskets you made? under the pantry?"

"Yes."

Brigitte stood with her hand on her laundry basket for a moment, then walked back into the kitchen to drink from the dipper.

John turned to Matthew. "Could we get Karl Heilman to hide them in a load of firewood? He delivers to the church."

Matthew shook his head. "If they inspected the load they'd hang Karl."

Brigitte walked back in from the kitchen, dipper still in her hand, forehead creased in thought. "How long are those muskets?"

"Why?" John stopped pacing to look at her.

"How long?"

"Fifty-eight inches."

She raised the dipper and sipped, then lowered it. "Four feet and ten inches," she said to herself.

"Yes. Why did you ask?"

She placed one hand on her hip, cocked her head slightly, eyes snapping, and spoke bluntly. "You men will never get those muskets into the church, but women could."

John shook his head and turned away from her with a wave of his hand.

"Well," she said defiantly, "we could!"

John turned back. "We're not going to put women at risk over those muskets."

"What risk? The British are going to make the same mistake you're making right now." She raised both hands in mock horror and plunged on. "What? Women? Never! Why, women are for washing and ironing and meals and having babies! Women lack the intelligence to think. Smuggling muskets? Ridiculous! Never." She paused to let her theatrics settle in before she jabbed an accusing finger at her father. "They'll never suspect women. We could march down the streets with a musket in each hand and they'd never—"

Margaret cut her off, her voice ringing. "Stop it, Brigitte! You're not going to get involved in this."

"Nonsense," Brigitte spouted, and plowed on. "This family is already involved. If they found those muskets in this house, how many of us would they have in jail?"

"That's enough! This is for your father and the militia to do."

Unable to stop herself, Brigitte barged ahead. "They've already admitted they can't do it," she insisted, her voice too loud. "Women could."

"No," John said with finality, "we aren't going to—"

"Wait a minute," Matthew said. "Give her a chance." He turned to Brigitte. "How would you do it?"

Brigitte blinked, caught with only a hazy, undefined idea for a plan. Always—always—she had depended on her nimble wit and quick brain to rescue her from her own impertinent mouth, and once again she reached inside herself. "Wrap them in something! Quilts. Blankets. Anything. They'd never suspect."

"Muskets in quilts, into the church?" Matthew exhaled and rolled his head back. "Forget that."

In the two seconds Matthew had given her, her thoughts leaped. She thrust a pointed finger into the air. "No, it would work," she exclaimed. "Listen to me. Put them with quilting frames and wrap them all together inside an unfinished quilt! We roll quilting frames inside unfinished quilts all the time to carry them around, and they're longer than the muskets, so only the quilting frames would show at the ends. And we carry them down to the church for quilting bees half a dozen times a year. The British have seen us do it forever, and their women do it themselves, and they'd never suspect there's a musket inside with the frames."

She stopped triumphantly, and her eyes swept from Matthew to Margaret, and then settled on John while she waited in the stunned silence.

"It might work," Matthew exclaimed.

John's eyebrows arched in utter surprise.

"That's enough nonsense," Margaret asserted, eyes boring into Brigitte. "You are *not* taking muskets to the church, and that's the end of it."

Brigitte spun towards Margaret. "But Mother," she pleaded, "Father says those muskets are important, and the idea will work!"

John raised a hand and the others fell into silence. "Does anyone have a better idea?"

Margaret gasped and looked at him, pleading in her eyes. "John, you aren't going to get the children involved in this, are you?"

He studied her for a moment. "I don't like it any better than you, but I can't think of a better plan. Those muskets have to go."

Brigitte's eyes were wide, alive, dancing, and she continued on, encouraged by John. "It wouldn't just be us. By afternoon we could get Kathleen, and Dorothy Weems and Trudy and Anna— they all have quilting frames—make one trip to the church together. Go there now and tell Silas we're going to have a quilting bee at the church sometime next week, and tell the British patrol we'll be coming in with the frames this afternoon so they won't be surprised. It will work! I know it will!"

Margaret blustered. "You're going to expose half the congregation in this smuggling scheme? You've lost your mind!"

Brigitte rushed to Margaret and seized her arm. "Mother, it will work! You *know* it will." Her face was pleading, begging. "If Silas tells that British patrol the women are holding a quilting social next week, and they're coming with the quilting frames this afternoon, and then a dozen of us come with those frames wrapped in quilts like always, there's no possible way it can fail. They'll let us in. I know it!"

Margaret opened her mouth to speak, then closed it, and Brigitte exclaimed, "Mother, you'll have to help. We can't do this without you. Think of it! Right under their noses! Even telling them before we come!" Brigitte was exultant with the thought, eyes wide, shining. "The men can't do it, but we can!"

Margaret huffed, "That's what you're after! Shaming the men! A great adventure just to prove you can do it while they can't."

"*No*," Brigitte exclaimed. "A chance to do something to help the colonies! To fight tyranny."

John fought a smile at the high rhetoric. He looked at Matthew. "What do you think?"

Matthew shook his head. "Brilliant and scary. Only Brigitte could dream it up. But it might work. Probably would."

Brigitte beamed!

John spoke quietly to Margaret. "It will never work without you leading."

Margaret's jaw dropped for a split second. "You want *me* to lead this insanity?"

John said nothing as all three of them stared at Margaret.

She turned her eyes, staring back at each of them individually, her eyes growing wide. "No. Absolutely not." She set her chin stubbornly and again surveyed the three of them. They neither moved nor spoke.

She swallowed and took half a step backwards. "Absolutely not. Why, there's no chance, no faint possibility we could get this all organized today, and if we did try, someone would say something and the British would know all about it before we ever got the muskets wrapped in the quilting frames."

Brigitte threw her arms wildly about Margaret. "Then you agree? You'll help?"

"Not without answers to a lot of questions," Margaret said defensively.

"What questions?" Brigitte exclaimed.

"The children. They'll be coming home from school by the time all this business with quilts and muskets is ready. What do we do about them?"

"Take them with us!" Brigitte answered. "No British patrol would stop six or eight women with quilting frames and a dozen children along."

John interrupted. "It will work."

Margaret drew and released a determined breath. "How do we know a musket won't make the bundle too big?"

"Let's try it," Brigitte said, and ran into the bedroom for the set of quilting frames while John cleared back the chairs from the table. They spread a quilt on the table and stacked the four long oak frames with the bolts, nuts, and washers, and laid a musket with them, and John and Matthew carefully folded one edge of the quilt over the pile and rolled it over and over inside the quilt.

"Here," Margaret said, and handed them four lengths of heavy hemp cord. They tied each end, and twice between, and stepped back to peer at it. The long oaken frames protruded from both ends; the musket did not show, and John picked it up gingerly.

"Look too big?" he asked tentatively.

"No," Brigitte exclaimed. "You'd never know."

"I wouldn't know the difference," Matthew added.

Margaret took it from John and held it. "It's heavier, but no one would know." She laid it thumping on the table. "Matthew, you better go see Dorothy Weems and then down to Phoebe while Brigitte and I finish the wash. Tell them to be here with their frames and their children after school's out. John, go tell Silas and be sure he tells the British patrol we're coming for a quilting bee."

Brigitte was beside herself! Danger! Adventure! Smuggling! Contraband! Women doing what men couldn't! Soldiers! She beamed, clapped her hands, hugged Margaret, and turned to Matthew. "Hurry! And don't tell another soul." She spun towards John. "Tell Silas we'll be there around four o'clock, and he's not to breathe a word to another living person." Her eyes were alive, her face flushed, and she could not stand still.

Margaret shook her head. "Come on, Brigitte. We've got wash to finish, and we better get at it before you explode."

For forty minutes Margaret scrubbed clothes while Brigitte chattered and went through the motions of rinsing, and they hung the last of the wash.

"Let's change," Margaret said as she walked to the kitchen door. "We have to go find out if Sarah Willums and Mercy Hobson want to get hung for smuggling."

Brigitte giggled and Margaret looked at her and chuckled.

At five minutes past two Margaret and Brigitte walked in from the bright afternoon sunshine, and Matthew and John rose from the table, waiting.

Margaret untied her bonnet and dropped it on the table. "Sarah and Mercy will be coming after school. What did Dorothy and Phoebe say?"

"They'll be here," Matthew said. "Kathleen's coming to help."

Margaret nodded. "We have a problem. We have five sets of quilting frames and seven muskets. We've got to find out if two muskets will make the bundle too big."

Ten minutes later they stared at their own quilting frame bundle and John shook his head. "That looks pretty bulky."

"Would a British soldier know that?" Margaret asked.

"I doubt it," Matthew answered.

"Of course not," Brigitte scoffed. "You could wrap a horse inside there and a soldier wouldn't know it."

Margaret pursed her mouth for a moment. "There're a few more things. It seems to me there's a chance they might open one of these bundles to look. If they do, I expect it will be the first one. So we'll not put a musket in the first one, then put two muskets in the next three bundles, and one musket in the last one."

"Of course!" Brigitte exclaimed. "That's exactly how we'll do it."

"What else?" John inquired.

"Before we leave, Matthew goes up and finds a place across the street from the church where he can watch us. If they do find the muskets and arrest us, he raises the alarm."

Matthew nodded and Margaret spoke again. "We're not going to tell the children a word about muskets. As far as they know, we're taking our quilting frames for a quilting bee. We're going to let them carry the small bags with the needles and thread and thimbles. That ought to persuade the soldiers the whole thing is just what it appears."

"That's good sense," John said, and Margaret gave him a look that said, *Of course it is! What did you expect?* She looked at each of them, waiting for any response, and there was none.

At three-twenty P.M. a rap came at the door and Phoebe

entered with Kathleen and nine-year-old Faith, the last to arrive. John took their quilting frames, and three minutes later laid the wrapped bundle on the table with the others. He glanced at the faces of the five mothers, and in their eyes he saw the fear of the terrible risk they were taking, knowing that one wrong word, one wrong move, would tear them from their families and land them in a British jail. But deeper than that, he saw the resolve and the determination and the willingness to risk it all if it would help lift the galling yoke of British tyranny. He cast his eyes at the floor and struggled with the lump in his throat.

Margaret stepped forward and smiled and casually dropped her arm about Priscilla's shoulder. "My, my, with all your children we look like an army!" She laughed, and the women laughed, and the children laughed because their mothers had.

Margaret spoke to the children. "We're going to have a quilting bee Thursday night at the church and maybe a potluck supper. So we're going to take the quilting frames down this afternoon, and we need you to help carry the sewing bags. There are soldiers, so we thought we'd go together so they won't bother us. Can you do that?"

The children stared at each other for a moment, then burst into excited chatter. "Yes. Oh yes."

The women handed small carrying bags to each child. "Now, carry them carefully."

Margaret straightened and smiled. "And if it's all right with everyone here, I think it would be nice if we would all bow our heads for a moment in silent prayer."

The room fell silent as all heads bowed for a time, and then Margaret raised hers and said, "Thank you. Now, Brigitte, you and I will take our frame first, and—"

"Wait," Kathleen interrupted. "Brigitte and I agreed we would take the first one. Please. You and Mother can take the second one."

"What on earth for, child?"

"We just want to carry the first one."

Margaret glanced at Phoebe, who nodded, and Margaret saw the bright look of defiance in Kathleen's eyes and the open rebellion in Brigitte, and caught a glimmer of the need in the two girls to be first in the daring plan to smuggle muskets into the church in broad daylight, under the noses of the British army.

Margaret took a deep breath. "All right. Let's get started."

Brigitte released held breath and her eyes danced as she looked at Kathleen.

Talking casually for the sake of the children, each pair accepted the seven-foot bundles from John and Matthew and walked out the front door, the youngsters beside them, wide-eyed, skipping, chattering with delight at their unexpected departure from chores and studies.

John followed them to the gate and scarcely breathed as they reached the corner where a four-man British patrol stood watching the afternoon foot traffic. The women gossiped and laughed and gestured as they walked, crossed the cobblestone street, and paraded past the soldiers, each in turn nodding her respects as the regulars studied them in puzzled surprise.

John returned to the house and stood by the front window, watching the street for long moments. Bobby Thorpe trotted past, heading towards the church. John ran a nervous hand over his hair and began to pace. He stopped, took hold of himself, and walked to his workbench. He reached for a work tray at the back of the bench, with a mantel clock in it and his work card clipped to it. "Quincy," it read. "Losing time. Due April 25."

He used a small, fine-tipped screwdriver to loosen the back plate, then removed the face and the hands and carefully slid the clockworks out into his hand. He paused and glanced at his clock above his workbench. Twelve minutes past four o'clock. *They should be back by five o'clock. They can walk five blocks and return in forty minutes, can't they? Five o'clock.*

He clamped the wire frame over his head, swung the clockmaker's lens down before his eye, and studied the delicate gears of the broken clockworks that meshed with the spindle to turn it.

There. The balance gear. Two teeth missing. Two out of ten. Twenty percent. It's losing twelve minutes each hour. I can replace it in two hours.

At four-thirty he laid down the screwdriver, walked to the window, and peered towards the church, while Enid Ferguson hurried the other direction, across the street, her basket again filled with fresh hot bread. Her head was down, preoccupied as she walked on. John grasped the door handle to open and call to her to ask if she had seen the women and children, and he stopped before he opened the door, and returned to stare out the window.

Five blocks north, Brigitte slowed as she came into view of the church. The late-afternoon sun caught the white steeple, and the big brass bell shined. The green grass was a checkerboard as the budding trees filtered sunlight and shadow.

Hope leaped in her heart. There were no soldiers! The churchyard was vacant, silent. She nearly trotted across the street, while the other women quickened their pace to follow. She reached the first great oak in the churchyard before the crimson-red coats rounded the corner of the building and the soldiers slowed to study the column of approaching women and children, suspicion and surprise in their faces.

In the next few minutes the women were going to pass through the crucible, and each of them knew it.

Brigitte resumed a normal pace, turned her head, and said, "There they are," and laughed, and Kathleen laughed and said, "I see them," and turned her head to call back over her shoulder, "Be careful," and laughed again. The warning was passed to the end of the line with light banter and laughter. Brigitte walked briskly across the lawn, onto the path to the main door, and did not stop until she was facing the soldiers. The women were in a line on the path behind her, the children standing near their mothers, awed by the sight of the red coats and the tall pointed hats and muskets.

"Good afternoon," Brigitte said boldly. "We've come with our quilting frames for the quilting bee. I do hope the reverend told you to expect us."

"So 'e did, m'um, so 'e did." The corporal leaned on his

musket. "And wot 'ave we got in those bundles, m'um?" He was condescending, domineering, a small man with a big musket and authority to tease and toy as he wished.

"Quilting frames. See?" Brigitte held up her end of the bundle, from which protruded more than a foot of the wooden frames, with grooves and bolts connecting them.

"And what else, m'um? A cannon?" The soldier threw back his head and roared at his humor, and Brigitte laughed with him. Kathleen smiled, and Margaret ducked her head to hide her disgust.

"Yes, Captain," Brigitte exclaimed. "A cannon on wheels and a horse to pull it."

The corporal doubled over in laughter, and the private next to him reached to steady his musket.

"Well, m'um, we'll just 'ave to take a look at yer cannon and horse."

"Very well, Captain," Brigitte said, and set her end of the bundle on the ground and signalled to Kathleen. They quickly untied the cords and unrolled the quilt and extra batting.

"Is it all right, Captain?" she asked, eyebrows raised fetchingly in question. "May we take them on in?" She and Kathleen hastily rewrapped and tied the quilt.

"These other bundles, m'um," the corporal said, not ready to relinquish his rare chance to exercise authority over someone else, "wot's in them, if yuh don't mind?"

Brigitte shrugged. "Just more cannon and horses."

The corporal chuckled, and Brigitte laughed and opened both doors into the church. "May we go in now? These are getting rather heavy, Captain."

"Corporal, m'um. Not captain. And I'd appreciate it mightily if you wouldn't confuse me with a bloody officer. Go on in."

Holding her breath, Brigitte walked from the bright sun into the dim coolness, praying in her heart the other women would crowd in behind her. If the corporal demanded to open any of the other bundles . . . Brigitte looked wildly at the pews and chairs in the chapel for something—anything—to distract them if it happened.

The corporal's voice froze her in her tracks. "'Old it there, m'um."

Brigitte glanced over her shoulder. His back was turned and he was speaking to Margaret. "I said the first one could go in. Got to 'ave a look at yer bundle before you go in."

For a split second Brigitte's mind froze in stark terror, and then she looked at the row of hard straight-backed chairs three feet ahead of her that were lined up behind the back pew in the chapel and instantly raised her foot and kicked with all her strength. The chair smashed into the pew ahead of it, and Brigitte screamed and fell heavily against the next chair. It knocked the next two clattering, and she threw her end of the bundle slamming into the next chair and screamed once more in mortal pain. She and the chairs and her end of the bundle ended in a scramble on the hardwood floor, Brigitte clutching her leg, writhing, moaning, eyes clenched shut.

Then, with all her strength, she shrieked, "*Mother!*"

Without hesitating, Kathleen threw her weight against her end of the quilting frame and rammed it forward through the door onto the jumbled chairs, then stepped to one side to clear the doorway. The other women shoved the soldiers aside and jammed their way into the chapel, casting their frames into the aisle and gathering around Brigitte, who was curled in a ball on the floor, knees drawn up, arms thrown about her right shin and foot.

"Brigitte!" shrieked Margaret. "Is it broken? Did you break it?" She turned to Phoebe. "Fetch Doctor Soderquist." Phoebe spun on her heel and lunged out the door.

The children drew back, white-faced, and Priscilla began to whimper.

Mercy Hobson stood bolt upright and fixed the corporal with lightning in her eyes. "The very idea! You've crippled this child! I'll see you in irons, sir! In irons!"

The stunned corporal staggered backwards a full step. "Me, m'um? I didn't touch her, m'um. I—"

Mercy shook her fist in his face. "Are you shameless? In irons, sir."

The corporal licked his lips and tried to speak but no sound would come.

Kathleen gave quick, silent hand signals, and while gentle hands worked with Brigitte, other hands, unnoticed, moved the bundled frames down the main aisle in the church and laid them on benches, out of sight.

The door behind the pulpit rattled open and Silas Olmsted bolted out into the chapel and stopped dead still. "In the name of heaven, what was that crash and scream?"

"It was him," exclaimed Mercy and thrust an accusing finger at the bewildered corporal. "He assaulted poor Brigitte and crippled her! Phoebe's gone for the doctor. Someone ought to get the sheriff."

Kathleen dashed down the aisle to the reverend and grasped his arm to lead him back to the group around Brigitte. She spoke to him quietly as she turned. "The frames are on the benches. Look on the benches." She walked him hastily back to the gathering, and as he passed the benches he counted the bundles without turning his head. He nodded faintly and Kathleen relaxed.

"Let me help you, child," the reverend said to Brigitte, and stooped to reach for her. Capable hands lifted her to her feet, and she stood for a moment, right foot off the ground.

"Can you put your foot down?" the reverend asked.

Brigitte carefully lowered it and uttered a small cry as it touched the hardwood floor. "It hurts so!" she said.

"Bring her back to my quarters," the reverend said. "We have hot water and salts that will help."

Margaret and Mercy looped Brigitte's arms over their shoulders and carried her, while Trudy Willums herded the children behind them, down the aisle, through the small door and narrow passageway into the reverend's quarters. Mercy took the children on out the back door, onto the back lawn of the church, and sat them down and calmed them.

Kathleen remained behind and faced the corporal, her eyes flat, face without emotion. "I suggest, Corporal," she said evenly, "that you take up your post at the front doors until the doctor comes. It will go much better for you if you are found at your assigned post rather than inside this church with your musket and an injured girl."

The soldier swallowed hard, gave the private a hand signal, and backed out the doors and closed them. Kathleen spun on her heel and raced down the aisle and through the passageway to the reverend's chamber, where Brigitte was seated in Mattie's rocking chair, surrounded by the women, who stood silent, white-faced, shaking.

She grasped Brigitte's shoulders. "Are you hurt?" she demanded.

"No, but we can't let anyone know it."

Kathleen's eyes rolled back into her head and her shoulders sagged as she exhaled all her breath. "I saw the kick, but I thought you broke both legs the way you went down."

Brigitte leaned forward, eyes flashing, intense with the thrill of risk and mortal danger, now passed. "Was it good?"

Sarah Willums finally found her voice. "Don't ever do that again! You took ten years off my life!"

Brigitte looked up at her. "I had to do *something!* He was going to open all the bundles. We'd have all been in jail."

Kathleen shook her head. "You were magnificent. Flawless! You convinced me, and I saw the whole thing!"

The others had recovered from the near mortal fright and the shock, and the murmuring began, and then the words came tumbling in nervous streams.

"It terrified me," Margaret said. "When that soldier stopped me I thought we were all going to prison forever."

A heavy knock came at the door and instantly the room fell silent while the reverend called, "Who is it?"

"Walt Soderquist. Is someone hurt in there?"

Mattie opened the door, and Doctor Soderquist, plump and balding and sweating from his hurry, bustled in and looked at Brigitte, Phoebe right behind.

"Are you the one that's hurt?"

Brigitte looked at Margaret, and Margaret spoke. "We can tell Walter." She turned to him. "She's not hurt. She faked an injury to save us all when we smuggled muskets into the chapel."

Doctor Soderquist stopped dead still and studied Margaret for several seconds. "Someone better tell me what's going on here."

Five minutes later Walter Soderquist started to chuckle, and then he laughed until he wheezed and tears ran. "You mean you women brought seven muskets right past two British soldiers, faked this injury, and browbeat that corporal out front?"

Phoebe's eyebrows rose. "It appears we did, though I don't yet understand how. And never, never will any of us ever try something like this again!"

Doctor Soderquist set his black bag by Brigitte's foot and knelt down. "I better wrap that good so it'll look right. And I'll send you a bill." He laughed as he unbuttoned her shoe. "No, on second thought, I won't send a bill." He began wrapping a massive bandage. "This one's free. Hearing that wild story was worth it." He shook his head. "Nobody's going to believe it."

The doctor finished and examined his work. "Take that off whenever you want. It's only there to help your story." He closed and picked up his black bag, then looked around at the faces of the women and shook his head. "Right under their noses," he said to himself, and walked out the door.

Margaret looked at the others. "The longer we stay here, the more risk. We better see if we can back out past those soldiers." She raised a warning finger and the room fell silent. "Nobody breathe a word of what happened here. It could be our undoing!"

Every face sobered and they all silently nodded.

They gathered the children, and the moment they started back through the chapel Kathleen and Margaret took Brigitte's arms around their shoulders and walked her, with her bandaged foot raised. They reached the large front doors, and Kathleen turned the knob and swung open the doors. The sunlight flooded in and they stopped in their tracks.

A British captain and a young lieutenant filled the door frame. The lieutenant, taller than average, had blue eyes and dark hair, and a scar in his right eyebrow. He was not handsome, but striking. Brigitte stared into his face and recognition struck. She gasped and stiffened, and Kathleen's head swivelled to look at her. The lieutenant's eyes narrowed for a moment, searching his memory, and then he remembered. Kathleen saw it in his eyes, and he shifted his gaze to the women behind.

"What's the meaning of this?" the captain demanded.

Kathleen faced him cooly. "There was an accident. Doctor Soderquist treated this young lady's injured foot and said we must take her home and get her into bed. We're taking her home."

Behind them, Silas Olmsted silently walked up the aisle and stood listening.

"I can see that. What did you bring into the church? The corporal said you brought something in."

Kathleen's eyebrows arched in surprise. "Ask him! He was told hours ago we were bringing quilting frames for a quilting bee. He didn't believe us, so he opened a bundle to look. Ask him!"

Behind, Sarah grasped Faith and Priscilla by the hands and watched and listened and waited.

The captain's forehead creased in question. "Did he inspect all the quilting frames?"

Kathleen opened her mouth to answer when Sarah barged forward with the two children and exclaimed belligerently, "We have children here who are hungry. We have husbands coming home and supper to prepare and wash to take from the lines. Isn't it enough that you've injured this girl?"

Dorothy pushed forward, clutching the hands of Adam and Trudy. "What's the reason for keeping these children from their homes and suppers?"

The captain shifted his weight and licked his lips. "We have our orders. We must—"

Dorothy cut him off, her voice loud, hot. "Did they include injuring young women and keeping children from their homes, sir?"

"Ma'am, we are *not*—"

Dorothy gave him no quarter. "You most certainly *are!* What is your name, sir? I'm taking your name to the Committee of Safety!"

"Ma'am, I am only obeying—"

Again Dorothy chopped in. "And we are only taking our children and this injured girl home, sir, and we're leaving now." Dorothy pushed past Kathleen and Margaret and Brigitte, and the captain and lieutenant stepped aside. Sarah followed, and Mercy Hobson came behind, herding the children. As Mercy passed the officers she tipped her nose into the air and grunted a resounding "Humph."

Kathleen and Margaret, with Brigitte between them, followed the others out onto the brick walkway when the young lieutenant's voice stopped them. "One moment." He turned to the captain. "Sir, if our troops caused this, would it be in order to have one of our physicians examine the damage?"

Behind them, Silas Olmsted quietly closed the big doors and set the great oak bar into its brackets. He ran to the nearest bundle of quilting frames, frantically threw it over his thin, wiry shoulder, trotted down past the pulpit, jammed the bundle beneath the sacrament table, then returned for the second bundle.

Brigitte blurted, "No! Doctor Soderquist took care of it. I just need to go home."

The lieutenant brought his eyes to hers, and they were penetrating, incisive. She felt he was looking into the very depths of her soul, that there was nothing, no secret he did not comprehend, and in that brief instant she saw the slightest hint of a smile, and a look of understanding crept to linger for the briefest moment.

He knows! He knows! Brigitte felt the blood drain from her face, and she battled to maintain a noncommittal mask.

He dropped his eyes for a moment, then turned back to the captain. "Perhaps not."

Kathleen seized the moment. With Brigitte's arm still over her shoulder, she started up the pathway. "Come on. We've got to catch up with the others."

They had gone five paces when the lieutenant called after them, "May we call for a carriage to take her home? One can be here from the base in five minutes."

"We'll manage," Kathleen answered, without looking back. They marched to the corner with shoulders squared, heads high. Margaret turned to search across the street to the north, and Matthew appeared for a brief moment beside a great oak, then disappeared.

The five blocks from the church to the Dunson home had never seemed so brutally long. They passed one British patrol that stopped and eyed them suspiciously, then another. Brigitte counted every step, every brick, every breath, expecting the voice of the captain or the lieutenant every instant, commanding them to stop, arresting them. She was certain they had gone into the church, unwrapped the quilting frames, discovered the muskets, and gathered soldiers to arrest them. She was petrified at the thought of looking back, and she listened to every sound from behind, waiting for the pounding of countless heavy black boots as the soldiers came running.

But there were no boots, no voices, no running soldiers, no arrest.

Dorothy and Sarah herded the children through the front gate, up the sunken brick walkway. John threw open the door and they plunged inside, Kathleen and Margaret last with Brigitte supported between them. The women collapsed on the sofa and chairs, silent, shoulders slumped, unable to believe they had delivered the muskets and escaped arrest and capture. The children stood silent, knowing something frightening had happened but not aware what it was.

Matthew grasped Kathleen by the shoulders, and she sagged against him for support. Caleb backed into a corner, totally confused. John lifted Brigitte into his arms, white-faced. "You're hurt!"

"No. I'm fine."

He stood rooted to the spot, Brigitte still in his arms, and faced Margaret. "What happened?" He held his breath, waiting.

Margaret rounded her lips and blew air. "Caleb, take the children into the backyard. Give them each a gingersnap. Take the jar."

She waited until the door closed behind Caleb, then turned to John. "Brigitte's not hurt. The muskets are there. I don't know if they've figured it out yet."

John closed his eyes, and all the air drained from him as he lowered Brigitte to her feet. "Tell me."

Margaret started, and Brigitte broke in, and Dorothy interrupted, and it was as though the dam had burst. Sarah chuckled, and then Phoebe laughed, and then they were all laughing, nervously at first, then uproariously. For ten minutes John listened intently as the details came spewing.

The telling played itself out, and as the voices subsided and talking settled, John sobered. "If they found the muskets, they'd be here by now. So far so good." He looked at each of the women for a moment. "You've done a remarkable thing. Don't breathe a word of this until the time is right. You'll know when. I don't know how to thank you."

The women glanced at each other. They needed no thanks. They all knew they had something, a bond, that they would share forever, because they had volunteered for something deadly and dangerous, and for the right reasons, and they had succeeded. As long as memories endured, they would have this one thing, this one bright deed, quietly shining in their hearts. It was enough.

Dorothy stood and squared her shoulders. "I've got clothes on the line and supper to prepare. I must be on my way."

Margaret held up a hand for silence. "Not a word to anyone."

They all nodded. Five minutes later John and his family stood in the front yard and watched the women lead their children through the gate, and waved to them until they were all out of sight. Matthew walked to the middle of the cobblestone street and stood looking both directions while John led the others back inside.

Matthew followed them in. "There are no British in sight."

Margaret served supper late, in the lengthening shadows of sunset, amid unending chatter from the children. Caleb sat bewildered, groping to understand, and Margaret and John cleared the dishes while Brigitte sat at the table with the children with a book. They knelt together for evening prayers, and Margaret tucked the children into bed.

At ten o'clock John blew out the lamp in their bedroom and slipped beneath the thick comforter, and reached to stroke Margaret's hair in the dark. "You did a remarkable thing this afternoon."

"A foolish thing, you mean." She paused for a moment and then shuddered. "Never again. It was too close."

He touched her cheek. "Thank you. For everything."

The sharp rap at the window sounded loud in the darkness, and Margaret gasped as John rolled from the bed and reached the window in one fluid movement, where he crouched on one knee. He moved the edge of the curtain enough to see out into the silver light of a full moon, and his eyes widened for a moment.

He was looking into the shadowy face of Tom Sievers. Tom raised a hand to point towards the kitchen door and John stood.

"It's Tom," he said, and trotted barefoot in his nightshirt down the hall, through the kitchen, and to the back door, which he threw open.

Tom's voice came low, urgent. "There's trouble. The British have Silas shackled and are wrecking the church searching. Warren's headed there now."

"Wait." John spun and ran silently back to his bedroom and began changing back into his street clothes.

Margaret sat bolt upright in bed, comforter drawn to her chin, her voice strained, too high. "What's wrong?"

"The British are at the church searching. I've got to go."

Brigitte thrust her head inside the door. "Something's wrong. What's wrong?"

"Nothing," exclaimed Margaret. "What are you doing up?"

"Couldn't sleep. Someone's here. What's wrong?"

"The British are at the church," John said.

Brigitte gasped and clapped both hands over her mouth, then spun and ran back into her bedroom and locked the door.

Notes

The details about the British military musket called the Brown Bess are correct (see French, *The Day of Concord and Lexington*, pp. 27–30).

There were many colonial women who were patriots, often spying and carrying secret, important messages and performing other acts for their country. Thus, while the smuggling of the Dunson muskets into the church as described in this chapter is fictional, it is nonetheless well within reality to believe that women would volunteer, and succeed, in such an act.

Monday, April 17, 1775

CHAPTER VI

★ ★ ★

*J*ohn turned the corner, pushed through the gathering, shouting, ugly crowd, and stopped dead in his tracks, stunned, unbelieving, chest heaving from his run. Tom stopped beside him, eyes glittering, mouth an ugly slit as he battled for breath. For long moments they stood without moving, without speaking, trying desperately to make sense of the citizens gathered across the street from the chapel, shouting, waving fists and axe handles and pitchforks.

Fifty large torches on six-foot standards were jammed into the grass at intervals around the churchyard, and the flames cast long, dancing shadows. More than one hundred British regulars ringed the church, their red coats and white belts bright in the firelight. They faced outward, muskets in their hands, bayonets lowered and ready, shining yellow in the fire's glow. Ten officers paced inside the ring of soldiers, sabers drawn and flashing, shouting the repeated order, "Fire if they step into the street!"

The big double doors into the church stood open like a yawning entrance into a cavern. Lanterns inside the chapel lighted the high stained-glass windows and cast colored lights into the surrounding trees, while sounds of booted feet, hollow on the hardwood floors inside, echoed out into the night.

Someone jostled through the crowd to John's side, and he looked. It was Warren, breathless, sweating, angry. "What are they doing?" he shouted above the din.

"I don't know. I just got here."

Warren sucked air, set his jaw, and shoved his way into the street. John was at his side, Tom one step behind, his hand beneath his coat clutching the head of his tomahawk.

A British officer pivoted, set his feet, pointed his saber at the three men, and shouted, "Halt or we fire!"

Warren stopped in the street, turned and raised both hands to the surging crowd, and waited for them to quiet.

"Hold your peace until I find out the meaning of this," he called, and slowly they settled. Warren turned back to the British officer, John paced straight towards the bayonets, and Warren caught up with him and Tom.

"Prepare to fire," shouted the officer, and the musket muzzles levelled.

"Sir," Warren shouted, "I am Joseph Warren and this is John Dunson, both of us members of the Committee of Safety of the Massachusetts Provincial Congress. We come in peace to determine the reason for this outrage against our house of worship. Shoot if you dare!" None of the three men slowed.

"Cock your pieces," the officer commanded, and the double clicks of the heavy musket hammers being drawn came loud and sharp.

"Murder us in this street and the consequences of the blood-bath will be on your heads. If you believe your soldiers can reload in time to stop those behind us, then fire and be done with it."

They continued their steady pace towards the bayonets and musket muzzles of the regulars between them and the officer. The muzzles wavered.

"Do we shoot 'em, sir?" one regular croaked, voice cracking.

Dead silence settled in the unbearable tension. The only sound was the measured stride of the three men on the cobblestones and the hollow thump of boots drifting from inside the church. The officer's chin trembled for a moment, but he did not speak. The three men reached the bayonet of the soldier who had spoken, and John pushed it aside. The man did not resist, and they walked past him towards the officer. They reached him and he lowered his sword and they stopped.

"Where is the Reverend Mr. Olmsted?" Warren demanded, his voice ringing.

"Inside," answered the scowling officer. "He is being questioned."

"On what authority?"

The officer thrust out his chin belligerently. "A warrant of the Crown."

"A warrant to do what?"

"Search this church for contraband arms."

"I will see that warrant, sir!" Warren thrust out his hand and stood still, staring at the officer, waiting.

"The colonel has the warrant."

"Then I will see the colonel."

Thorpe strode up behind them and they turned for a moment, and Thorpe barked, "What is the meaning of this travesty?" His jowls shook with anger.

The officer bit down on his anger, turned on his polished boot heel, and with the four men following, marched through the soldiers, to the open doors, and into the church. When they cleared the doors and their eyes adjusted to the dancing firelight, the four colonials instantly slowed in disbelief.

Twenty soldiers armed with muskets and bayonets held burning torches at intervals down both walls, with dirty, oily smoke rising to collect against the ceiling. In the dancing yellow firelight, thirty more armed soldiers were systematically moving through the chapel, one row of pews at a time, leaving nothing untouched in their search for the muskets. Two soldiers had lifted the pulpit from its foundation, searching. Silas Olmsted stood defiantly behind the pulpit, beside the door to his quarters, mouth clamped shut, chin high, eyes staring straight ahead, while Mattie clung to him, silent tears running. A soldier stood beside them, musket and bayonet at the ready.

To the left of Silas, in the choir cove, the five sets of quilting frames were leaned unbolted against the wall, the quilts torn. From overhead, in the bell steeple, came sounds of guttural cursings and boots on the stairs and things behind moved. Near the center of the chapel stood an officer, hands on hips, face a study in dispassionate efficiency as he watched and directed the regulars. The four men strode down the center aisle, pushing soldiers aside as they confronted him.

"I am Joseph Warren of—"

The officer cut him off. "I know who you men are." His eyes were flat and cold, his face disciplined, controlled, disinterested.

"By what authority are you—"

Again he cut Warren off by thrusting a folded sheet of paper forward, and Warren took it and unfolded it. The single word "WARRANT" was printed at the top in large, bold letters.

To: Colonel Arnold Norse,
42nd Regiment,
His Majesty's Royal Marines

This date you will instantly select a detail of men sufficient in number and arms to search the South Church in the City of Boston for contraband arms, specifically, seven muskets, which are reliably reported to be stored or hidden within said church or on the grounds thereof. You are authorized to take whatever reasonable actions are necessary to enforce this warrant, including the use of firearms or other weapons as seems appropriate, avoiding if possible, of course, the harming or destruction of private property or the shedding of blood.

Dated Monday, April 17, 1775, 8:20 p.m.
Signed, General Thomas Gage.

Warren handed the document to John and paused a moment while John quickly read it and handed it on to Thorpe. Warren turned hot eyes back to the colonel. "I presume you are prepared to pay for the damage to the quilts and frames."

A smile flickered for a moment. "Petition the king for damages."

Warren pointed. "Why is our minister detained by an armed soldier?"

"Resisting the warrant."

"You know he's harmless. Release him."

"If we find those muskets he will be arrested and tried for treason."

"You've desecrated this church enough! Yesterday morning, and now again tonight. There is nothing here for you to find. I demand you stop this blasphemy and leave now."

A broad, condescending smile spread as the officer spoke. "Only General Gage can stop us before our search is finished, unless you choose to lead that rabble in the streets to try."

"What do you plan to do? occupy our church permanently?"

"Until the search is completed."

"I demand to talk with our minister."

"You have one minute, and I will be present." Colonel Norse turned and led them down the aisle to Silas.

"Are you all right?" John asked, pain in his eyes.

Olmsted smiled. "Fine. Mattie's just frightened."

"Did they harm you?"

"No harm."

"Did you resist the warrant?" Warren asked.

Silas paused to pick his words and glanced at John for a split second before he spoke. "I told this officer there were no muskets in the church. He put me under this armed guard and brought in all these men, and you see what they're doing." He gestured to them as they continued their systematic search.

Warren turned squarely to the colonel. "How did he resist your warrant?"

One corner of the colonel's mouth curled for a moment. "General Gage will get my full report. If you have a protest, file it with the general."

"Release this man now."

"Your minute is up. Leave now or you will all be detained under armed guard with your minister." He reached to pluck the warrant from Thorpe's hand and pointed towards the big chapel doors. "You have one half minute to be off the church grounds."

Warren spoke to Silas. "We'll be back."

He turned on his heel, and they picked their way back through the bustle of soldiers and out the front doors, when John reached to slow Warren, and spoke with quiet intensity as they walked. "That officer means to provoke us into a confrontation. He all but invited us to lead the people outside into a fight that will result in shooting. That's what this is all about. He wants us to start it."

Warren turned narrowed eyes towards John as he considered. "You're right. We've got to clear the streets before that happens."

He strode boldly into the street and raised his arms to the milling, sullen crowd and waited for silence.

"Our minister has not been harmed. They are searching the church under a regular warrant. We will petition the king for redress of the wrongs they have done, but for now, go back to your homes. Leave now. Abide the law. Go back to your homes."

John and Tom walked to his left side, Thorpe to his right, and they raised their hands with Warren.

"Let it be on their shoulders to breach the peace, not ours," John called. "They are here under a warrant. Let them finish their business. We will have our day later."

Revere and Dawes stepped from the crowd and turned and began calling, "Go home. We're finished here for tonight. Go back to your homes."

For twenty tenuous, explosive seconds the six men in the street stood their ground, fearing that the detaining of their minister under force of arms and the occupation and search of their church were too much, that this time the British had pushed too hard, gone too far. The grumbling crowd milled, and then, first one at a time, then in small groups, they began to break away and disappear into the dark streets. John felt the muscles between his shoulder blades begin to relax, and then he quietly exhaled his held breath, while Dawes and Revere worked with the dwindling crowd until they faded away from the torches and were gone. Unnoticed, one figure remained hidden in the shadows of the trees, a shawl drawn about her head, watching, waiting.

The six men stood on the cobblestones and waited until the street was vacant and silent. Then John said quietly, "We need to talk."

"My home," Warren said.

Ten minutes later they were seated around his dining table with one lamp burning.

At the church, the lone figure huddled in the shadows across the street from the churchyard quickly darted forward and crouched behind a great oak while she carefully studied the officers inside the ring of regulars. She moved back into the shadows and dodged to the corner, then down the side street, and again hid behind a tree while she went over every detail of each officer. Suddenly she froze and waited until a young lieutenant turned his face in her direction in the yellow torchlight and she saw the deep-set eyes and the scar in the eyebrow. He was working his way down towards the well at the rear of the yard, talking with the regulars as he moved. She moved silently as a shadow opposite him, waiting.

At Warren's home, John leaned forward on his forearms on the table while the others faced him, waiting, watching intently while he spoke. "This afternoon my wife and some women took seven muskets to the church for Silas to deliver to the militia. That was between four and five o'clock."

Tom started and Warren reared back in his chair and Thorpe opened his mouth to speak, but John held out a hand to keep them silent while he continued. "The women succeeded. They got the muskets in without the British knowing."

Thorpe exclaimed, "I heard about it later, and I think it should have been discussed before those women and children were used that way."

Warren was incredulous. "You had women smuggle seven muskets into the church in broad daylight?"

"Yes. The militia has to have them. It was the only way any of us could think of."

Warren stared at the tabletop while he worked with his racing thoughts. "The risk! Did you think of the risk?"

"I did. The plan was theirs, not mine, but I was responsible. I let them do it."

Warren shook his head. "Brilliant, but fearful. It was a lot to ask of women."

John continued, face drawn, eyes flat. "That warrant was signed by Gage at eight-twenty P.M. It says 'seven muskets.' He knew the number, and he knew the description, all within three hours."

Warren sobered. "If the women got them past the soldiers, how did he know?"

The question stopped all sound, all movement for several moments.

Tom grasped John's arm. "Besides Margaret, who else?"

The ticking of the clock could be heard as John collected his thoughts. "Phoebe and Kathleen. Willums. Hobson. Weems. Some of the children."

"Which children?"

"Priscilla. Mercy. Trudy. Faith. Adam. I think that was all."

"Did their men know?"

Thorpe interrupted. "I didn't know until Phoebe and Kathleen got back with a wild story. I took strong offense I was not told, John." For a moment Thorpe's face darkened. "There was risk. I should have been told."

John's eyes dropped for a moment. "I decided the fewer who knew, the better. I left it to the women to tell their husbands, and to decide. If that was wrong, I'm sorry."

Thorpe settled back in his chair.

John spoke. "The children were never told what was going on. That leaves the women. Which of them could have leaked it?"

Thorpe jerked forward. "I can vouch for Phoebe and Kathleen. They weren't out of my sight from the time they got home until I left to come here."

Tom cleared his throat and all eyes turned to him. "If one of them leaked it by accident, it might have reached Gage by morning, but not within two hours. He signed the warrant at eight-twenty, and that means Gage found out about it earlier, maybe an hour." Tom paused, and his eyes swept the faces of the others before he set it squarely in front of them. "That wasn't an accident."

A prickly sensation moved up their spines to set them tingling with the sick realization. If Tom was right, there was a traitor among those who knew about the muskets, someone close enough to General Gage to get secrets to him on an hourly basis, perhaps a minute-by-minute basis. They glanced quickly at each other in the dim lantern light and felt the hair on their necks rise, and for a moment they looked away, or at the tabletop, unprepared for what eyes might reveal, and then they looked at Tom.

"Who, Tom?"

Tom shook his head in frustration. "I don't know. But one thing I don't understand. If whoever told Gage knew the exact number of muskets, then that person also had to know who took them in and how. If that's true, then why didn't Gage arrest the women?"

Silence hung thick.

Warren cleared his throat. "Maybe he feared public reaction, or he's waiting for morning, or he wants to arrest their husbands too. We don't know that, and we don't know how he learned about the muskets. It could have been accidental, but I don't think so. No matter how it happened, we can't wait. We have things that must be handled now. What do we do about the church? about Silas?"

At the churchyard, in the dancing torchlight, the lone figure watched as Lieutenant Buchanan made his way to the last regular, glanced at the well, and then started to return towards the front of the building. She stood and strode rapidly into the street, and the nearest regulars levelled their muskets and ordered, "Stop or we shoot."

She did not stop.

The lieutenant turned, eyes narrowed as he watched her approach. He glanced up and down the street, then walked directly towards her.

"As you were," he said quietly to the regulars. "Go on back to your posts. I'll take care of this." The regulars brought their muskets back to order arms, and moved back to their stations, to stare back with suspicion at a young British lieutenant meeting a colonial girl in the night.

The lieutenant stopped on the sidewalk, and Brigitte stopped in the cobblestone street, six feet from him. She did not hesitate. "You told them, didn't you?"

"Beg your pardon, ma'am. Told who what?"

"About the muskets. You knew."

The lieutenant thrust his head forward, studying Brigitte's face in the shadow of the shawl, and suddenly his eyes widened. "You're the young lady who was here this afternoon and—"

He remembers! He remembers me! Brigitte cut him off. "Yes, I am. You knew and you told them, and they've seized our church." Her eyes were hot, indignant.

The lieutenant glanced downward towards her feet, and a faint smile flickered. "Quick recovery. Your foot, I mean."

Brigitte tossed her head, and her mouth became a straight line. "You knew I wasn't hurt and you knew about the muskets. You informed, and you came to help violate the church."

The lieutenant's face sobered, and his eyes narrowed, and he spoke with quiet intensity. "I suspected your foot wasn't hurt, but I told no one, because suspicions prove nothing. And I knew nothing to tell about the muskets. That came from someone else, not me."

Brigitte's heart leaped. *He did not betray!* She cast her eyes downward for a moment. "Then, sir, I apologize. I thought—"

"Your name, ma'am."

Her breath caught in her throat. "Is that important?"

"It is. I have to detain you to be questioned by Colonel Norse."

She recoiled. "What?"

"You said too much. You seem to know about the muskets. The colonel will want to find out where they are now."

Brigitte blanched and shrank back a step, and realized for the first time that she had been so intensely caught up in her need to know if the lieutenant had reported her that she failed to see the obvious. She stopped and squared her shoulders. "I am Brigitte Dunson, daughter of John Dunson of the Committee of Safety. I was the one who brought the muskets. I'm responsible."

"We know you brought them in those quilting frames. What we don't know is who has them now. I'll have to take you to—"

Again she cut him off. "What is *your* name, sir?"

"My name?"

"It will be important to our militia, and they'll certainly hear it."

He shrugged. "Lieutenant Richard Arlen Buchanan, Forty-second Regiment, Royal Marines. Will you please come with me?"

"I will not. You can arrest me and take me by force, but I will not come." She stood erect, feet planted apart, head high, eyes blazing defiance.

He paused for a time, pondering the delicate question of whether he was going to drag a colonial girl kicking and screaming in the night to Colonel Norse.

In frustration he said, "Do you know where the muskets are now?"

"I do not. I believe the militia has them."

He glanced at the regulars, then at the other officers for a long moment, then turned to Brigitte. "Miss Dunson, go home. Just turn around and get home as fast as you can."

"You're not going to arrest me?"

"What's the point? We know how the muskets got here and that you and half a dozen women and children did it, and we know who they are. What we're after now is the men who got them. If you don't know that, what's the point in arresting you?"

"You're not taking me to colonel whoever-you-said?"

"No. You said you don't know who has the muskets now. I believe you."

"Just like that? You believe me? Why?"

In the long pause, Brigitte stared into his eyes deeper than she had ever stared at anyone, and in them she saw compassion and honesty, and she thought she saw need, and her heart leaped.

The brisk, piercing voice startled both of them. "Lieutenant Buchanan! Is something wrong?" Their heads turned to see Colonel Norse walking towards them.

"No, sir. The young lady was looking for her family. She's just leaving."

He turned back to her and saluted and growled, "Move. Now."

She backed into the street, spun, and was gone.

Ten minutes later she silently entered her room through the window she had left open, changed into her nightclothes, and slipped between the freshly laundered sheets. She lay on her back for a long time, staring at the ceiling, remembering. Lieutenant Richard Arlen Buchanan.

Halfway across town, at the home of Joseph Warren, the men who had gathered around the table in the candlelight silently struggled with Tom's question. If Gage knew who the women were who had smuggled the muskets into the church, why were they not arrested?

There was no time to ponder. Their church had been desecrated and their minister held under armed guard like a criminal, and what they intended doing about it had to be decided and accomplished by dawn. The talk began slowly, then gained momentum as they argued and debated and hammered out a plan for redress. It was after one o'clock, with dark questions still nagging, when Warren blew out the lamp and they walked back into the street and turned north, towards the church.

The hated sound of commands and marching boots reached them as they turned the corner, and they slowed. In the dancing light of torches carried high above the soldiers' heads, Colonel

Norse marched the last squad of twenty men in double file away from the churchyard towards the British military base. The colonials stopped squarely in his path and he halted his column.

"Where's the minister?" Warren demanded.

"In his quarters."

"You found no muskets, of course."

"Correct." Norse was smiling.

"We intend speaking with the minister."

"As you wish. We left no guards at the church."

"You're afraid of reprisals."

Norse sneered. "Step aside. I have troops to move." He barked orders over his shoulder and the column marched forward, and the four men let them pass. They trotted up the path, through the large front doors, and down the aisle towards the rear door to the living quarters of Silas Olmsted and Mattie. John knocked.

"Who is it?"

"Warren."

Silas opened the door a crack, then threw it wide and the men entered.

Mattie was seated in the corner, white, shaking, still in shock. Warren placed his hand on her shoulder and looked into her frightened eyes. "Are you all right?" he demanded, controlling his anger.

"Yes."

Warren turned to Silas. "Are we alone? Can we talk?"

"Only Mattie and I are here."

John interrupted, urgency in his voice. "The muskets?"

"Gone. The militia got them five minutes before the soldiers forced their way through the front doors."

"How did you get word to the militia?"

"Molly Telford. Her husband's in the militia. She sends Amy every afternoon with fresh milk. I send notes back hidden on Amy. She's seven years old."

"Did you hide the muskets in the well?"

"Yes."

"I thought the militia didn't come to the well until after midnight."

"They usually don't. This time I said come as soon as it was dark."

"Why?"

"Fear. The British are learning of such things too quickly."

"How did you get the muskets past the guards, out to the well?"

"They let us go to the well and the outhouse when we want. We waited until dark. Mattie and I went together and they didn't pay any attention."

John paused and asked, "Who besides the Telfords did you tell?"

"No one. Why?"

John considered his words before he answered. "Someone got word to Gage within two hours of when you got the muskets."

Silas glanced at Mattie and then back at John, and said, "I don't believe it was Ben Telford. I've known Ben since he was born. He's a captain in the militia."

John exhaled a weary sigh, and his eyes ran over the sparse furnishings in the small, humble quarters. "Silas, I'm responsible for them coming here today and putting you under armed guard and frightening Mattie. I don't know how to say how sorry I am to have brought this down on you."

Mattie took Silas's hand, and Silas squared his thin, pinched shoulders. His gray eyes came alive. Imperceptibly at first, then growing, a feeling crept into the room. No one spoke as they felt it settle into them.

"No need," Silas said. "The church wasn't harmed. Mattie and I will be all right. But I fear the cost we will pay—all of us—when we finally rise against them in the streets and in the fields. I see blood and tears in this land, and great sorrow lying like a dark cloud, and then a new land being born."

It was as though his unexpected words struck into the very core of each of them. The strange, new spirit settled into the tiny, austere room, and it overwhelmed them, subdued them. For long seconds they shrank from the bright and awful truth that burned into their beings with a sureness never before known by any of them. None could withstand it, nor did they try; it cut them low, humbled them, awed them.

It was coming, imminent, at the very door. There would be war. Blood would flow. Many would die. Their fair land would suffer much destruction. From the blood and pain and devastation would rise a new, shining land to take its place as a guiding star for the weary people of a tired and battered world. They knew it more clearly than any other truth in their lives, from some unknown source they dared not challenge, nor could they explain.

They could become part of the struggle and the pain and the sorrow and of the birth of the brave new land, or they could withdraw to safety and let others bear the terrible burden and gain the incomparable victory. The choice was theirs. More than that they did not know, could not see, but it was enough.

Seconds passed while the spirit slowly withdrew, and they did not look at each other or speak or move. It was as if they had no will, no thought of their own—only an impression so powerful that it robbed them of being conscious of any other thing. So powerful was the impression that they dared not speak of it.

Finally John swallowed and spoke. "Will you be all right, Silas?"

Silas nodded.

"Then we have work to do. People will be here tomorrow to straighten up whatever they disturbed in the chapel, and to take your statements. We have a petition to prepare, and much that we must find out and do. Are we all agreed?"

All of them sensed in their hearts that in this austere, humble place, John had placed the choice squarely, inescapably before them. Their decision would somehow turn the history of the colonies irrevocably. They could force the battle, or they could seek safety, and once they decided, there would be no turning back. For long moments the air was charged in the thick silence.

Tom faced John. "Let's be about it."

Silently, as one, the men walked out of the small quarters, through the dark chapel, and into the stillness of the warm Boston night, and for a moment they paused in the bright moonlight. They looked about and up at the endless stars in the heavens, and oddly, knowing in their souls the holocaust that was coming, they felt a sense of peace. They separated, Tom walking with John and Thorpe the five blocks to John's home, each man working silently with his own thoughts. They stopped at the front gate and said their good-byes, and Thorpe continued on towards his home.

John asked Tom, "Do you want to come in? You can stay here tonight."

"No, but I need to tell you some things. I followed that citizen that comes and goes from Gage's quarters. He has a room at Sailor's Cove Inn. Calls himself Amos Ingersol. Stops at Hubbard's ale house, over at Enid's bakery for bread, buys tobacco at Hilda's, cheese and sausage at Reichman's, but never comes close to anyone that would know things that are getting to Gage. Maybe I'm wrong about him."

"Does anybody else come and go at Gage's quarters? maybe a scrubbing maid?"

"No. Soldiers do the cleaning."

"Did that man come tonight?"

"If he did, it was after dark and I missed him."

"Keep looking. We've got to find out."

Tom nodded and faded into the shadows and was gone. John pushed through the gate and rapped gently on the front door. Matthew opened it, with Margaret behind, and she stepped forward and threw her arms about him and buried her face in his chest. For a moment he held her.

"What's happened?" he asked. "Are you all right?"

She stepped back. "We're all right. What happened at the church? We heard the soldiers were there with bayonets and they had Silas under armed guard, and then you didn't come home."

John sat them down at the table, and for several minutes

Margaret and Matthew did not move as he talked. He did not speak of the powerful, strange experience they had shared in Silas's small living quarters, because he did not yet understand it, nor could he put it into words.

When he finished, Margaret's shoulders slumped. "It's coming. The shooting is coming."

John knew no words to help, and he covered her hand with his. They remained silent for a moment, and John said, "There's nothing more we can do tonight. We need to go to bed." He stood and helped Margaret to her feet and started for the bedroom, when Matthew stood.

"Father, could we talk a minute?"

Margaret nodded consent, and continued through the archway to the bedroom, and John walked back to the table and sat across from Matthew and waited.

"Today Mother and Kathleen could have gone to prison."

John nodded.

"What would we have done if they had?"

"Try to get them out. The muskets had to go to the church. The women made their own choice. Why do you ask?"

Matthew stared at his hands. "So far this thing with England has been mostly talk, but today it could have become more than that, and I realized something." He raised his eyes to John's. "Some of us could be killed."

John held a steady gaze but said nothing.

"Is it worth that?" Matthew settled back into his chair and waited.

John leaned forward, forearms on the table, fingers laced. "What do you think this thing with the British is all about?"

Matthew shrugged. "Tyranny. Freedom."

"Anything else?"

"No. Not that I know about."

"Get the Bible."

Matthew blinked, startled. "What does that have to do with this?"

"Get it."

Matthew picked the heavy family Bible from the fireplace mantel and set it before John and waited, eyes narrowed, questioning, while John turned pages and then pushed the Bible to Matthew.

"The Apostle Paul's letter to the Hebrews. Read it. Start here at chapter nine, verse seventeen." He pointed.

Matthew turned the Bible around and studied the words for a moment, then began to read deliberately. " 'For a testament is of force after men are dead: otherwise it is of no strength at all while the testator liveth. Whereupon neither the first testament was dedicated without blood. For when Moses had spoken every precept to all the people according to the law, he took the blood of calves and of goats, with water, and scarlet wool, and hyssop, and sprinkled both the book, and all the people, saying, This is the blood of the testament which God hath enjoined unto you. Moreover he sprinkled with blood both the tabernacle, and all the vessels of the ministry. And almost all things are by the law purged with blood; and without shedding of blood is no remission. It was therefore necessary that the patterns of things in the heavens should be purified with these; but the heavenly things themselves with better sacrifices than these.' "

"Stop," John said, and Matthew looked up, startled. "What was the first testament?"

"The law of Moses."

"What was the new testament?"

"The law of Christ."

"Neither came without the shedding of blood."

Matthew nodded. "What does that have to do with the British?"

"The two events in history on which all mankind will be judged are connected with the shedding of blood. Do you know how Christ's Apostles died?"

Matthew reflected. "Most of them were killed."

"Eleven out of twelve. We don't know what happened to John

the Beloved. They couldn't deny what they knew, and it cost them pain and sorrow that tested their souls and finally took their lives. The price for what they knew was their lives, and they paid it."

Matthew slowly settled back in his chair, eyes wide in the yellow glow of the lamp, mind racing. "What are you saying?"

John's voice was quiet, but there was an intensity as never before. "There is more to this than throwing off tyranny. There is more than freedom. I don't know all of it, only part, but what I do know is that somehow what we do now, in the next days and weeks, is part of a plan made by the Almighty, and that plan is beyond anything any of us can dream. Somehow this struggle is going to affect the history of this world forever. I don't know how, only that it will." John paused, eyes like lightning, face bright in the lamplight. "And I know in my soul it will not happen without the shedding of blood."

Matthew released held breath, stunned by the conviction he felt coming from his father, like nothing he had ever felt before. He spoke quietly. "Has something happened?"

Instantly John answered. "Yes. Tonight. In Silas's parlor. Standing in the chapel, we all felt it. We all knew."

Matthew swallowed. "Knew what?"

"That the need to be free of the British is of God! Something is supposed to happen soon, and it can't happen until we're free of them. I don't know what it is, only that it is coming."

The spirit that had pervaded Silas's humble quarters slowly settled over Matthew and John, and Matthew dared not move or speak as it grew. It held them for a time and then slowly withdrew.

Matthew remained silent for a time, then finally spoke. "You intend carrying a musket when the war begins?"

"If needed, yes, I do." John's eyes were steady.

"You'd risk being killed—leaving Mother and the family without you?"

John did not hesitate. "Yes, if I have to."

"Is that part of God's plan?"

"I don't know. What I do know is, what is now before us has to be, and because I know it I cannot refuse to be part of it. If it costs me my life, I will have to go. I would never be a whole man again, for your mother or for anyone, if I don't do this thing."

Matthew's eyes fell for a long time. "I don't know if I can go to battle, and leave Kathleen. I can't think of leaving her."

"I understand. You're young. The sweet years of life are ahead for you two. You will have to look inside yourself for your own answer. I can only decide for myself."

Again Matthew's eyes dropped while he considered. Then he raised them and said, "You taught us not to shed blood. How do I justify it now?"

"I taught you what God said to Moses on Sinai and what Jesus said in the Beatitudes. Killing men is wrong. The teaching is right, but it is not the whole teaching. The whole teaching is, there is a time for all things. There is a time to rise up and do what is necessary to bring God's plan to pass, and sometimes that may require standing up against tyranny and putting our lives on the line. I believe we are facing such a time now."

"What happened at Silas's place?"

John stared at his hands for long seconds. "I don't know. Standing there in his parlor I told Silas I was sorry for bringing it all down on him, and he said it was all right. No one had been hurt."

He raised his eyes to Matthew and continued, his voice low, his words paced, thoughtful. "Then he said he saw great sorrow and pain coming, to lie on this land like a dark vapor. And something happened. I don't know what it was, but all of us at that moment saw and felt what he saw and felt, and we all knew, and we didn't move or speak for a time because it was too powerful. I know he was right. It is coming, and it is of God. I felt the same spirit, not as strong, here with you."

Neither man knew how long they sat, unaware of time or surroundings. Finally John drew a deep breath and let it out. "Was there anything else you wanted to talk about?"

Matthew shook his head and rose and walked silently to his room.

Notes

The events that take place at the Old South Church are fictional, as is the character Richard Arlen Buchanan.

CHAPTER VII

★ ★ ★

A chill east wind arose from the Atlantic in the gray before sunrise, and swells rolled into the harbor and Back Bay to set every vessel rocking. Seagulls quarrelled over things the tides had abandoned on the beaches and shoreline in the night, while the four o'clock watch on ships changed to the cadence of the clean sound of brass bells. High clouds in the east quadrant of the sky thickened and settled and came scudding on the raw wind to hide the rising sun, and the new day was born chill and gray.

Shoulders hunched against the bite of the wind, Tom Sievers stood beneath the greening branches of a large maple tree across the street from the huge British military compound. Inside the stone wall, barracks formed the north and south boundaries, with infirmary, mess halls, stockade, and stables on the east, and officers' quarters on the west. The square created by the buildings was centered by a flagpole, with drill and parade grounds on all sides. Sleepy-eyed sentries stood at the wrought-iron gates into the streets, occasionally shaking their legs against the stiffness and cramps of four hours of guard duty.

At five-thirty A.M. a bugler with his tunic half-buttoned and hair awry blasted the morning wakeup call, and lights began showing through shaded barracks windows. At six-fifteen the soldiers emptied from the barracks in full uniform, red coats and white belts crossed bright on their chests, and the tall, pointed hats of the light grenadiers square on their heads. They fell into ranks on four sides of the flagpole while two drummers sounded the assembly drumroll. On command every arm was raised in salute while the drums crescendoed and two soldiers raised the Union Jack proud in the cold wind. Officers barked more orders, and the hands snapped down from the salute. Lieutenants shouted to their companies, and the ranks and files marched smartly in order to the mess halls.

Boston City stirred and stretched, and life began to trickle into the streets. A large dog harnessed to a two-wheeled milk cart leaned into the leathers and scratched the cobblestones, stopping from time to time on voice command while his master dipped fresh milk into pails on doorsteps. A man in heavy rubber farm boots trudged towards Gerhard's cheese house with two forty-pound rounds of cheddar cheese sealed in half an inch of wax and wrapped in linen in his backpack. Women with hand-knitted shawls wrapped about their shoulders hurried from bakeries with baskets of smoking bread loaves to be delivered to the inns and boardinghouses in time for breakfast.

Tuesday was ironing day for all goodwives. Inside homes, women dipped hands into open pans of cold water and sprinkled yesterday's wash stacked high on dining tables. Then they rolled it tightly and packed it in woven baskets to mellow while they built fires in their stoves and set four flatirons on top to be rotated when the ironing began. Smoke from chimneys all over Boston rose to be caught away by the wind. A thin mist of rain settled in to turn faces clammy and make the cobblestones slick.

No one paid much attention to Tom Sievers. Not crazy Tom, who smelled foul in his ragged clothes, and carried an ancient knife and tomahawk beneath his threadbare coat, and mumbled through an eight-day beard stubble to a figment named Elizabeth. He was a curiosity that wandered the streets of Boston, to be ignored when possible, greeted when necessary, and allowed to go and come as he would. To see him standing hunch-shouldered across the street from the British military compound in the early hours of a Tuesday morning brought little more than a glance and a head shake from Bostonians and British soldiers alike.

An hour later, no one noticed or cared when he stopped moving and his head jerked forward slightly as his eyes tracked a rather small man dressed in civilian clothes. The man crossed the street half a block away and walked quickly to a sentry post, past the sentries, who did not challenge him, through the gate, and into the compound. He worked his way through the press of soldiers going to or coming from their duty, turned on the brick path to the command building, spoke to the guards at the big shiny doors with the black-lettered sign above, "COMMAND HEAD-QUARTERS. GEN. THOS. GAGE. MASSACHUSETTS PROVINCIAL GOVERNOR," and they let him pass unrestricted.

Tom wiped his sleeve across his mouth and ambled across the street, slowing to let a mounted rider leading a sorrel mare pass on his way to the farrier. On the British side of the street, he walked towards the sentries at the nearest gate, and they watched his approach with expressions that were a mix of tolerance and disgust. He stopped at the gate, peering inside at the big double doors of Gage's headquarters building.

One of the sentries looked at him. "'Ere, you can't stand there gawkin' through the gate like 'at. Keep movin' on up the street, g'vnor."

Tom said nothing and did not move.

"Move along, I say," the sentry repeated, his voice stiffening. "Move or I'll have to stick you with this 'ere bayonet!" He shook his musket.

Tom's hand slipped under his coat.

The sentry grinned and spoke to his companion at the other side of the gate. "D'you see? I believe the old coot would make a fight of it, I do. 'E's reachin' fer that knife, or maybe the tomahawk 'e carries under that bloody coat."

His companion remained at attention, rifle slung. "Don't be provokin' trouble without reason. We got enough as it is. 'E's harmless. Leave 'im be."

Still grinning, the sentry swung his rifle strap back over his shoulder and resumed his disciplined stance at attention. "Just 'avin' a bit o' fun to break the blinkin' boredom."

Tom's arm dropped from inside his coat and he remained as he was, on the sidewalk, watching the doors into Gage's building.

Inside, General Gage sat at his desk in his high-ceilinged office, hunched forward on his forearms, intense in his third reading of the five-page report of Colonel Norse. He started at the unexpected knock on his door, raised his head and sighed, and called, "Enter."

His orderly stood at rigid attention. "Sir. You 'ave a visitor."

Gage's eyebrows arched, and he slowly straightened in his great leather-covered chair. There was but one man allowed to see General Gage at any time without giving his name. "Show him in."

"Yes, suh!" The orderly did an about-face with heels clicking and said, "You may see the general!"

Amos Ingersol quickly entered the door and walked to the chair facing Gage's desk. The tap of his heels on the hard floor echoed slightly in the cavernous room while the door closed behind him. Small, hawk-faced, with beady, nervous eyes and nervous movements, Ingersol removed his hat and stopped opposite Gage.

"Be seated," Gage said. "Were you followed?"

"I think not. I took detours."

"What brings you here?" Gage's face was clouded.

"Information about the affair at the South Church last night."

"Yes. I have the report. Is there something else?"

"Yes." The man leaned forward, eyes bright with the glow of self-importance. "The seven muskets were there, all made by John Dunson of the Committee of Safety."

Gage pursed his mouth. "I know who John Dunson is. Why didn't Colonel Norse find them?"

"They were hidden." The man waited, savoring his power to force the general, governor of the colony of Massachusetts, to take the inferior position of asking questions.

Gage controlled his resentment. "Where?"

"In the well."

"Sunk?"

"Not sunk."

"Then how?"

"Wrapped in oilskins and lowered on a rope."

Gage leaned slightly forward. "Colonel Norse reports his soldiers looked in the well."

"They were gone before your soldiers arrived."

"How did they know we were coming?"

"They didn't. The reverend was fearful because of other searches. He got them out as soon it was dark enough."

"To whom?"

"Benjamin Telford."

"Isn't he a captain in the provincial militia?"

"That he is."

Gage waited, but could not control his impatience. "Go on, go on."

"The colonials are planning to petition for redress for the search of the church, and if their terms are not met, they plan to stop payment of all taxes until they've held out enough to meet their demands. And they're going to require punishment for the soldiers who put Mr. Olmsted under armed guard while he was questioned."

Gage snorted and slammed his clenched fist banging on the desktop. "Stop paying taxes, will they! That will last until we seize their businesses and livestock to pay them! And as for Olmsted, he refused to answer questions, and brought it on himself. The colonel was absolutely justified in everything he did."

"They've started on their petition. The full Committee of Safety, including Adams and Hancock, will sign it and deliver it here this week. They plan to bring some of the militia with them."

Gage recoiled. "Armed militia coming here?"

"I don't know if they'll be armed."

Gage rose to his feet, paced to the rear bank of windows to

stare out at the stone wall for a moment, then came back to his desk and remained standing. "If Adams and Hancock sign it, will they also come to deliver it?"

"They didn't say."

"Was there anything else of importance?"

"Yes!" Ingersol leaned forward, buoyant with the knowledge that his next revelation to Gage would shake him. "They know you have been informed about their arms and supplies stored at Concord."

Stunned, Gage spun, then settled into his chair. "How do they know?"

"I presume an informer."

For long moments Gage searched his memory for any conversation, any person with access to his office that could have given the information to the colonials. There was no one. "It did not come from this office," he said emphatically. "Did anyone learn it from you?"

"Absolutely not."

Gage pondered for a moment, then suddenly stood and leaned forward, palms flat on his desktop. "Do they plan to move the cannon and munitions away from Concord?"

Ingersol shook his head. "I was not told."

Gage's voice rang. "It is absolutely critical that I know. The entire campaign depends on those stores being at Concord!" He sat back down and quickly scrawled the critical questions on an unsigned paper, and thrust it towards Ingersol. "Deliver that at once and return with the answer in writing as soon as you can. Bring that back with you."

Ingersol stood, surprised. Rarely did Gage trust him with messages in his own handwriting. He folded the paper, inserted it inside the sweatband of his hat, and quickly walked out the door, while Gage slumped back into his chair and for long moments studied the closed door, unseeing. Then he grasped his quill, dipped it in ink, and wrote rapidly for several seconds before he called, "Orderly."

The door opened instantly. "Yes, suh!"

"Have these officers report here in an hour."

"Yes, suh!"

Outside, Ingersol trotted through the nearest gate into the street, slowed to a rapid walk, and continued west, working his way through the morning buggy and foot traffic. He did not notice the thin, shabby man at the next sentry gate turn to watch him go, and then fall in behind, moving unnoticed, turning the same corners, fading into the crowd, always behind him dogging his trail. Ingersol stepped into Welty's tavern, and emerged five minutes later to stand beside the door while he studied the faces and the movement of the crowd, then crossed the street and hurried west two blocks, then back north. He disappeared into Reichmann's sausage shop, then reappeared back into the sunshine with a small wrapped package in his hand, and again stood near the door while he turned his head slowly, missing nothing before he resumed his rapid pace.

Ten minutes later he passed the South Church, continued down two blocks, and walked through the open doorway into Ferguson's bakery. Tom stopped and leaned casually against an oak tree, nearly hidden while he watched and waited.

Three minutes later Enid Ferguson walked into the street, turned, and hurried south with half a dozen loaves of hot bread covered in her basket. Ingersol was not to be seen. Tom studied Enid as she hurried south, face downcast, working her way through the street traffic. Suddenly he straightened and his eyes narrowed and his mouth pursed. He looked back at the bakery and waited to see if Ingersol would reappear, and when he did not, Tom turned on his heel and started after Enid at a trot. He saw her pass the Dunson home, watching the sidewalk as she hurried, and he held his distance while she continued.

To the northeast, at the British military compound, Gage flinched at the sudden rap at his door, settled, and called, "Enter."

"Suh! The officers have arrived as requested."

Gage took a deep breath and released it. "Show them in." He

stood as they filed in, splendid in their red tunics and crossed white belts and white trousers, hats clamped under left arms, gold epaulets of rank glistening on their shoulders. Lieutenant Colonel Francis Smith. Major John Pitcairn. Brigadier Hugh Percy. Lieutenant Frederick Mackenzie.

They saluted, Gage returned the salute, and they stood at rigid attention, staring past him at the back wall.

"Be seated, gentlemen." He pursed his mouth for a moment while they drew up chairs and sat, spines rigid, shoulders square. He stared into their eyes for a moment before he spoke.

"You're aware of the preparations made the night of April fifteenth for a sudden movement of our troops to accomplish an undisclosed mission. It appears it may be imminent, and you will be involved."

He paused, and in the hush each officer shifted on his chair, startled by the abrupt announcement and the sobering realization they would be among the officers charged with command. They instantly recovered their composure and remained silent, waiting.

"I would appreciate your frank response to two vital questions." Again they shifted and waited, wide-eyed and silent.

"How many of their militia and minutemen do you expect they could muster on, say, twelve hours' notice?"

Smith glanced at Pitcairn as they both made instant speculations on the reason for the question.

"Where? between here and Concord?" Smith asked, probing. "Yes."

Smith's breath came short. *Concord! He's finally going after their arms, and maybe Adams and Hancock too! Finally!* He took a deep breath and continued. "Armed militia?"

"Yes."

"Perhaps four or five thousand."

Pitcairn pursed his mouth for a moment and nodded concurrence.

Mackenzie shook his head. "Closer to eight thousand. Maybe ten."

"So many?" Gage asked, eyebrows raised in surprise.

"Yes. In the streets right now are minutemen from Mystic, Cambridge, Menotomy, Charlestown, Lexington, Meriam's Corner, Concord, waiting for word our troops are marching. They can gather close to ten thousand armed militia within hours of the time our troop formations leave the compound."

"Only if they know about it," Gage interjected and raised a pointed finger, "and that is the key. They *must not know.*" He paused, and his eyes swept those of the officers, driving the message home. Then he continued. "The second question. Should shooting start, what quality of fighting force do you expect from the colonials?"

Smith shrugged. "Moderate, maybe even weak. Their leaders have fought Indians but never a disciplined army. Most of the militiamen have never been in battle, and they have seldom trained or drilled. I expect them to be a ragged lot that will present little trouble to a trained army."

Percy leaned slightly forward. "Begging the colonel's pardon, I disagree. True, their leaders have little experience and the men have never faced an army in battle, but they are a sly bunch, and mean. They'll fight us like they fought Indians—from hiding. And do not underestimate them. I have personally observed squirrels decapitated at seventy yards, and a running deer dropped at two hundred by a colonial musket."

Gage stared hard at his hands, fingers interlaced on his desktop for a moment. "Major Pitcairn? Do you have an opinion?"

Pitcairn shrugged his shoulders. "Perhaps six thousand militiamen. If we move quickly and with authority, we will be in and out before they can mount any meaningful resistance."

"Very good, gentlemen. This conference is to be kept in absolute confidence. Do not leave your quarters until you hear further from me. You are dismissed."

Passing through the outer door into the light of a sun breaking through thinning clouds, Smith walked shoulder to shoulder with Pitcairn. "If Concord is involved, something's happened."

Pitcairn nodded his head. "Maybe Norse was too harsh at the church."

"Whatever it was has started things moving, fast."

They walked on to the officers' quarters in silence, laboring with the quiet, overpowering conviction that all the prologue and politics were past. They were hurtling towards a shooting war with an enemy, the strength and number of which they could only guess.

At that moment, halfway across the bustling city of Boston, Tom Sievers's eyes narrowed in puzzlement as he watched Enid Ferguson, half a block ahead and on the far side of the street, waiting on the doorstep of the home of Doctor Henry Thorpe. Five minutes earlier she had walked through the gate and up to the front door of the large, two-storied, whitewashed brick home, and her knock had been greeted by one of the children, who turned back into the house. Ten seconds later Henry Thorpe had appeared in the doorway, accepted her bread, and turned back into the house, leaving the door open while Enid waited. For five full minutes she stood on the doorstep, silent and nervous, before Henry Thorpe again appeared in the doorway and handed her what appeared to be money. She counted it, tucked it into the purse in the bread basket, curtsied slightly and thanked him, and walked hurriedly back out the gate and turned north, back towards the bakery, her ankle-length skirt moving with her long stride. The rain stopped and the clouds broke and disappeared, and the warm sun raised wisps of steam in the streets.

From across the street Tom followed her, hanging back, watching intently. She looked neither right nor left until she reached the bakery door, where she stopped and turned, and for long moments her eyes darted up and down the street before she disappeared through the door frame.

Across the street, Tom leaned aimlessly against a tree and mumbled to the passersby, who eyed him as they walked on without comment. The sun settled towards the line where earth meets sky west of the city, and still Tom waited, watching everyone who entered the bakery and came out. Ingersol did not appear. Lamps began to glow behind shaded windows, and then the last of the customers left the bakery and Enid Ferguson closed and locked the door and turned the sign.

For a time Tom stared unseeing at the cobblestone street in the lengthening evening shadows, face clouded while he struggled for a conclusion that would not come. Then he shook his head and started north and east at a trot, towards the high-walled military compound. Dusk had settled before he crossed the street and stopped, peering through the black iron bars of the great gate while two sentries studied him.

"Crazy Tom," one said. "'E's 'armless." They ignored him.

Purple shadows of night crept and shaded windows in the officers' quarters began to glow as lamps were lighted inside. Street traffic thinned.

A barked command from Tom's right brought his head around, eyes squinting to see in the darkness.

"'Alt and identify yerself!"

Forty yards farther down the high, thick wall, at the next gate, Tom made out the forms of two sentries facing a small man who was not in uniform. Tom jerked erect and he caught his breath. *I got ahead of him! I didn't wait long enough at the bakery, and I got ahead of him!*

Tom watched as the small man showed something to the sentries and they turned the large brass key in the lock and gave him entrance. Ten seconds later, through the gate bars, Tom picked up the small form trotting across the compound and watched as he stopped at the door to the headquarters building and banged with his clenched fist. The door opened and the irregular rectangle of yellow lamplight flooded outward, and Tom saw the face clearly as the small man darted inside.

Tom settled to wait.

Inside, the orderly held the door open and Gage stood at his desk to motion Ingersol inside. Ingersol threw the paper on Gage's desk and stood breathing heavily while Gage seized it with trembling fingers and opened it. He read the brief scrawled message twice, then sagged back into his chair, wild-eyed, while he felt his thoughts disintegrate and fleeting panic seize him for a moment. He took a deep breath and by force of will took charge of himself.

"Orderly!" he barked, and Ingersol recoiled.

The big door burst open and Gage stood. "Get the four officers who previously assembled here today and have them here in five minutes."

"Yes, suh!" The orderly spun and sprinted.

Gage turned to Ingersol. "You should not be here when they arrive. Use the rear entrance to leave this building, and use the small north gate to leave the compound."

Ingersol pivoted on his heel and disappeared through the door, and Gage listened for the quiet closing of the rear door.

Five minutes later the officers were seated opposite Gage, backs ramrod straight as they stared, waiting.

Gage's strained voice sounded too loud in the dead silence. "Gentlemen, you know about the colonial arms cached at Concord. I am informed they are aware of the plan to seize those supplies and are moving them to other locations. So we move now, tonight."

A forced night march! For a moment none of the officers breathed.

Gage shifted his eyes to Smith's and continued. "Colonel Smith, you will take command of the operation." He paused while the men shifted, then settled. "Immediately when we finish here, send out half a dozen mounted patrols with orders to clear the roads between here and Lexington of any colonials. They must not see troops marching at night."

Smith nodded once, in deep concentration.

"The troops will assemble on the Back Bay at precisely ten P.M. and be towed across in boats. They will land at Lechmere Point and march cross-country, avoiding villages and any place they can be detected. They will take the Lexington Road at Menotomy and move on to Concord, where they will confiscate the munitions."

"Sir—," Smith began and Gage cut him off.
"Here are your written orders. Read them aloud."
Smith broke the seal and unfolded the document.

Boston, April 18, 1775.
Lieut. Coll. Smith, 10th Regiment foot,

Sir
Having received Intelligence, that a Quantity of Ammunition, Provision, Artillery, Tents and small Arms, have been collected at Concord, for the Avowed Purpose of raising and supporting a Rebellion against His Majesty, you will March with the Corps of Grenadiers and light Infantry, put under your Command, with the utmost expedition and Secrecy to Concord, where you will seize and destroy all the Artillery, Ammunition, Provisions, Tents, Small Arms, and all Military Stores whatever. But you will take care that the Soldiers do not plunder the Inhabitants, or hurt private property.

You have a Draught of Concord, on which is marked, the Houses, Barns, &c., which contain the above Military Stores. You will order a Trunion to be knocked off each Gun, but if its found impracticable on any, they must be spiked, and the Carriages distroyed. The Powder and flower, must be shook out of the Barrells into the River, the Tents burnt, Pork or Beef destroyed in the best way you can devise, And the Men may put Balls or lead in their pockets, throwing them by degrees into Ponds, Ditches &c., but no Quantity together, so that they may be recovered afterwards.

If you meet with any Brass Artillery, you will order their Muzzles to be beat in so as to render them useless.

You will observe by the Draught that it will be necessary to secure the two Bridges as soon as possible, you will therefore Order a party of the best Marchers, to go on with expedition for that purpose.

A small party on Horseback is ordered out to stop all advice of your March getting to Concord before you, and a small number of Artillery go out in Chaises to wait for you on the Road, with Sledge Hammers, Spikes &c.

You will open your business, and return with the Troops, as soon as possible, which I must leave to your own Judgment and Discretion. I am,

Sir,

Your most obedient
humble Servant
Thos. Gage.

Smith drew a heavy breath and slowly released it.

"Questions?" Gage asked.

Smith raised his eyes. "Where's the draught?"

"Here." Gage spread the map on his desk before them, and instantly all four men hunched over it, silently studying every detail.

Smith asked, "Do we take cannon?"

"No."

"How many rounds per man?"

"Thirty-six."

"What other provisions?"

"Haversacks only, with rations for one day."

Mackenzie straightened. "Am I reading this right? We are taking light grenadiers and marines from eleven different battalions?"

"Yes."

"Under officers they have never seen before? There will be confusion."

"I do not think so. The plan is simple. The entire column should be back in their barracks twenty hours after they leave. I see little room for problems of command."

Mackenzie's eyes narrowed. "What are our orders regarding engaging the colonials?"

"Avoid confrontation if possible. Do not fire on them unless fired upon. I repeat, fire on them only if you are fired upon. I cannot stress that too much. They must fire the first shot."

Smith raised his eyes from the map. "Only eight hundred men?"

"Yes."

"Earlier today the lowest estimate we made of the men they could muster was four thousand; the high estimate was ten."

"That is correct."

"That would be five to one at best, twelve to one at worst, and our men would have just thirty-six rounds each and no cannon. There is a possible disaster in those numbers." Doubt showed in his eyes and his voice, and the other three officers raised their eyes, waiting for the reply.

Gage shook his head confidently. "Speed and surprise are our greatest weapons, gentlemen," he exclaimed, his voice ringing. He leaned over the map and began thumping his plump index finger repeatedly on the Concord crossroad. "Moving more troops from Boston to Concord will take too much time and rouse the countryside. A small, fast-moving, elite strike force of grenadiers and marines can be at Concord by sunrise, execute the orders, and be back here by sunset tomorrow. It will be over before the colonials can raise any appreciable force. That is the plan."

He paused for a moment, then continued. "Obviously, secrecy and stealth are the key to success. You must not notify the troops until five minutes before time to march. Have them leave the barracks without lighting any lamps, and waken none of the other troops. They are to move through Boston to the boats on the Back Bay in small groups of three or four, and if they are challenged they are to answer that they are simply a night patrol. Do you understand?"

The officers nodded.

Smith spoke. "I find nothing here about Adams or Hancock. Do we arrest them?"

"Only if you can do so without a major engagement, and I leave that to your discretion. This mission is intended to remove their ability to wage war. Adams and Hancock will come later, once they realize they have an army without arms."

Tense, focused talk continued for twenty minutes before Smith folded his orders and the map, slipped them inside his coat, and faced Gage. "If there is nothing else, sir, we have much to do."

"There is nothing else. Have those mounted patrols out clearing the roads between here and Concord in twenty minutes. I will be here or in my quarters until you return."

The click of boot heels on hardwood floors sounded loud in the silence as the four officers filed out of Gage's office and through the foyer, then opened the door into the blackness of a night in which the moon had not yet risen. In the seconds they were framed in the yellow light from the foyer, Tom strained to count them, counted again, and realized the little civilian was not among them. He watched as they closed the door, and he closed his eyes for a second to adjust to the darkness, then opened them again and saw the black shapes moving rapidly in separate directions.

I missed Ingersol! Either he's still inside or he got out some other way.

He dropped his head forward to stare at the ground in the darkness, his thoughts racing. *What were those four officers doing in there so long? Is this the night they go to Concord?*

For long seconds he agonized.

I wait. I stay here and wait.

Five minutes later lanterns flickered on in the stables. Ten minutes later light grenadiers in full battle uniform and arms trotted from the barracks and mounted the nervous horses. Tom watched as officers barked orders, and counted as the mounted soldiers divided into squads.

Six squads! Mounted, armed! Why? Where to?

Tom stood stock-still as they separated, half approaching the west gate, half the north. Officers called to sentries, the gates swung open, and the mounted squads raised their horses to the canter, their iron shoes clattering on the cobblestone streets. Tom trotted to the corner to see their direction, but they had disappeared, and once again darkness and silence shrouded the streets and the compound. Tom stopped and by strength of will slowed his thoughts and forced them into some semblance of reason.

Start at the beginning—Ingersol—took something in to Gage—Gage sent him back to get something more—the sausage shop—tavern—bakery—never came out of the bakery—I followed Enid—to Thorpe's—missed Ingersol—got back to the compound before him—he brought something back to Gage—officers went in—one hour—came out—six mounted, armed squads—what did Ingersol get? from whom? sausage house, tavern, bakery?

Tom took a deep breath and concentrated. *Where's the package Ingersol got at the sausage shop? Who got it? Where did they take it? Did Enid carry something to Thorpe in the bread? Is Thorpe the traitor? Thorpe on the Committee of Safety, is he the one?*

Deep in his consciousness a tiny buzz began, and Tom pushed his thoughts aside and gave way to it. It gained and Tom began to work with it, and slowly it took shape and form until suddenly it was there, fully formed, and Tom's head jerked up and he caught his breath and exclaimed, "It's Thorpe!"

Movement inside the compound caught Tom's eye, and once again he squinted into the blackness to make out shapes moving from the officers' quarters to the dark barracks. He settled, concentrating.

Inside the barracks, officers moved silently down the rows of bunks, pausing to shake the shoulders of sleeping soldiers, then clamp their hands over their mouths while they whispered blunt, abbreviated orders. Startled troops soundlessly dressed in full battle gear and carried their boots out of the barracks to pull them on outside. Officers huddled with them in companies and gave quiet orders, and the companies fragmented into small groups and moved in different directions, towards the gates in all four walls.

Tom breathed light as he counted the shapes he could see. In ten minutes, more than four hundred battle-ready light grenadiers and some marines silently left the compound.

Tom turned on his heel and started for the Back Bay at a trot.

At ten minutes past nine o'clock, a dog growled at half a dozen marines walking soundlessly across the Common, then bristled and broke into barking. The nearest marine unslung his

musket and faced the dog and made one swift stroke with his bayonet. There was a loud, startled yelp of pain and whimpering and
then silence as the marines moved on.

At twenty minutes past nine o'clock, grenadier Harvey Gibson
and four others from his battalion marched past the open door of
the Oaks tavern. Inside, lamps glowed yellow, and raucous laughter
spilled out into the night. Gibson wiped his sleeve across his
mouth and slowed. "Keep movin', lads. I'll catch up in a minute."

"You better stay with us," Corporal Lee growled. "There's
only trouble in the taverns for us this night."

Gibson grinned at him rakishly. "Won't be but a second." He
trotted into the tavern. The pint of dark bitter went down easy,
and Gibson slapped his money on the bar, wiped his sleeve across
his mouth, and was gone, running to catch up.

"See? Like I told ye, lads, only a minute."

Lee looked back at the dark shape standing in the doorway,
hands on hips, watching the soldiers disappear in the dark. Then
the shape disappeared at a run, east and south.

Ten minutes later the man pounded on the door of Dr. Joseph
Warren and waited.

Warren threw the door open. "Who's there?"

"Barkley Walsh. British troops are moving in the streets,
towards the Back Bay. Muskets and haversacks."

Without a second's hesitation Warren exclaimed, "Get Revere
and Dawes here as fast as you can."

Walsh turned on his heel and was gone.

At nine forty-five P.M. a nearly full moon rose in a clear, black-
velvet sky and bathed the Back Bay in silvery shadows. A cool
wind rose, blowing in from the ocean to riffle the water. Tom came
onto the shore south of Fox Hill, well below the beached boats.
On the Back Bay waters he counted the waiting boats offshore
where sailors sat huddled with oars shipped, straining to see the
troops assembling on the shore twenty yards away, anxious for
orders to loop hawser lines over the bow hooks of the boats on
the beach and tow them across the Back Bay.

There was no mistaking the tall hats of the light grenadiers as they assembled in the darkness. Tom heard the hushed cursing as the troops sought their own companies in the confused muddle. Lieutenant Frederick Mackenzie of the Twenty-third Battalion counted the boats and shook his head in disgust. Half enough boats. No organization as to where each unit was to assemble. No officers yet arrived to take command. Troops growing rebellious in the disorganized confusion.

Tom silently backed away and ran south along the shoreline, then east.

Far to the east, Walsh banged on the door of Paul Revere.

"British troops are moving across the Back Bay," he blurted, gasping for breath. "Warren says come." He turned and sprinted.

Fifteen minutes later William Dawes answered the pounding on his door.

"British troops—moving on the Back Bay. Warren says come."

Five minutes later Tom slammed through John Dunson's front gate and pounded on the front door.

Notes

The customs of washing on Monday and ironing on Tuesday with flatirons warmed on stoves, as well as other staid Boston habits, are described in Ulrich, *Good Wives.*

Lieutenant Colonel Francis Smith was the officer in command of the British forces who marched on Lexington and Concord. The officers under his command included Major John Pitcairn and Lieutenant Frederick Mackenzie. Brigadier Hugh Percy was part of the force but was held in reserve in the event of an emergency. Further, the opinions held by these various officers of the capabilities of the colonials is accurately represented in the novel, with Major John Pitcairn showing the highest regard for colonial marksmanship and fighting ability. (See French, *The Day of Concord and Lexington,* beginning with chapter 9.)

The written orders from General Thomas Gage to Lieutenant Colonel Francis Smith as given in the novel are an accurate and verbatim copy (see

French, *General Gage's Informers,* pp. 31–32). The written orders refer to a "Draught of Concord," meaning a draft, or map, of Concord as it appeared on April 19, 1775. A photocopy of the "draught," or map, or one comparable to it, appears between pages 78 and 79 of *General Gage's Informers.*

General Gage was emphatic that the British column was not to fire until fired upon. They were not to fire the first shot. Similarly, the colonial force was under orders not to fire until fired upon. (See French, *The Day of Concord and Lexington,* pp. 105, 109.)

The true name of the traitor who was on the Committee of Safety was not Henry Thorpe but Doctor Benjamin Church. The specific circumstances surrounding Church's discovery as a traitor and the events that followed are different from those surrounding the fictional Thorpe. A copy of a document written by Church in his own hand and which establishes his guilt as a traitor appears in French, *General Gage's Informers,* between pages 156 and 157.

The incident wherein a dog detects the British forces gathering at the Back Bay for transportation across to the mainland—which dog barks and is killed by a bayonet—and the incident in which a British soldier named Gibson, in full battle gear, stops at the Oaks tavern for a pint of bitters are accurate (see French, *The Day of Concord and Lexington,* pp. 75–76).

CHAPTER VIII

★ ★ ★

*J*ohn threw open the door and Tom stood framed in the light, sweating, hair tangled and windblown, chest heaving as he fought for breath. "Five hundred grenadiers and marines moving across the Back Bay," he blurted before John could speak. "More coming."

For an instant John stood transfixed as his thoughts ran wild. Behind him Margaret gasped and Matthew raced to his side to stare at Tom.

John's voice came too high, strained. "Who told you?"

"I was there. I counted."

"Are they armed?"

"Full battle gear. Haversacks."

"Have any gone yet?"

"First gathering has gone. Second gathering was getting ready when I left fifteen minutes ago."

"Gone where?"

"Across towards Lechmere Point. I figure they're headed towards Concord. They sent out patrols earlier, and I figure they were going to clear the backroads."

"Who else knows?"

"Anybody who seen them, I guess."

"Does Warren know?"

Tom shrugged. "I didn't stop to tell him."

"We better get over there."

"Let's go."

John spun on his heel to Margaret. "You heard. I'll be back as soon as I can."

He jerked his coat from the coat tree and Margaret grasped his arm. "Don't go out in the streets. If they're marching tonight, there will be trouble."

"We'll take backstreets," he answered and seized his hat from its peg. "It's come too fast. The committee has got to get control."

"John," she pleaded, her grasp like a vise, "don't leave. Don't go."

He stopped and faced her, pain in his eyes, and he spoke gently. "I have to. I'd stay if I could." He turned to Matthew. "You're in charge here until I get back. Whatever happens, you and your mother will have to use your own best judgment."

Matthew nodded as John turned and strode out into the silvery gray of the nearly full moon, and the door closed. He followed Tom trotting to the front gate. Tom stopped, and John saw the turmoil in his large, troubled eyes.

"There's more," Tom said, and his face dropped as he stared at the ground. "I didn't want to say with Margaret and Matthew right there."

John's face clouded. "What's wrong, Tom? Something's wrong."

Tom brought his tortured eyes back to John's. "It's Thorpe. He's the informer. He's the one been telling Gage."

John gasped at the searing stab of pain, and long seconds passed before he moved or spoke. "No, not Thorpe," he said, his voice thick with disbelief. He shook his head. "It can't be Henry."

Tom stared at him steadily in silence.

John lowered his eyes. "How do you know?"

"I followed the go-between all day. They use Enid Ferguson to get messages in and out when she delivers bread to Thorpe's house."

"Enid Ferguson! At the bakery? You saw it? You're sure?"

"Certain. I saw it but I didn't believe it until I stopped to figure."

"Figure what?"

"Sunday morning the British knew the committee met Saturday night. Half the committee knew about the meeting, and any of them could have told the British. But only you and Thorpe knew the women took the muskets to the church yesterday. It had to be Thorpe told Gage. That's why they never arrested the women. He wouldn't let them arrest his wife and daughter."

John's breath came short as the truth of it settled over his soul like a great, evil, stifling shroud. For long moments he stood staring at Tom as his mind raced unchecked. *Matthew—Kathleen— Phoebe—the children, those poor children—what will our people do? hang him? no time, no time—the British are marching—no time.*

By sheer force of will John brought his stampeding thoughts under control and forced his brain into some sense of order. He squared his shoulders and spoke decisively. "Warren has to know."

Tom shoved the gate open and started for the corner, John following at a trot. Three times they dodged behind hedges and into side streets to let small groups of grenadiers move past quietly towards the Back Bay. Thirty yards from Warren's home Tom suddenly stopped and grasped John's arm, and they watched two shadowy figures open Warren's front gate and rap twice on his front door. Lights flickered on behind drawn curtains and the door opened, and in the brief moments before the two figures strode through the door, recognition flashed.

"Revere and Walsh!" Tom exclaimed.

Seconds later John rapped on the front door, and in a moment he and Tom were inside the room, eyes squinted against the sudden light while they identified the silent, intense faces staring back at them: Warren, Revere, and Walsh.

Warren sat them at his table, and his words were terse, tense. "The British are moving tonight for Concord and we've got to warn our people, so listen well. We have no time to say it twice."

He paused in the silence. "Dawes left ten minutes ago to ride south down through the guard lines, across the Neck if the British haven't already closed it, to Lexington to tell Adams and Hancock and Parker—Parker's in charge of the militia there. Then on to Concord to tell James Barrett and John Buttrick. He'll stop at every farmhouse along the way to tell them what's happening, and to get ready."

He raised his eyes to Revere. "We can't leave this to chance, so I'm asking you to do the same thing, only you go north, across the water to Charlestown, then on to Lexington and Concord with the same message. Do you understand?"

"Yes."

"At each village, each farm close to the roads, pause long enough to raise someone in charge of the militia if you can, and call the news to them and tell them to spread it, but don't stop. Keep moving. I've already sent the message out to the farther towns—Winchester, Woburn, Tewksbury, and down south to Watertown, Newton, Framingham."

He paused until the room became silent. "And whatever you do, be certain Parker and Barrett and Buttrick understand clearly, we are not to fire unless the British do. They must fire first. Is that clear? They must fire first."

Revere nodded. "I understand."

Tom interrupted. "The British sent out six mounted patrols a couple of hours ago. I figure they went to clear the backroads. You're bound to run into one of them."

Warren pursed his mouth and paused for a moment, then shrugged. "Watch for those patrols, and if you run into one, you'll just have to handle it. Don't spare your horse. You can get a fresh mount at most any of the farms if you have to."

Warren paused to look briefly into the eyes of Paul Revere. In them he saw the fire and the will and the commitment, and he felt his soul open to embrace him, to fear for him. "God bless you. Only he knows what waits for all of us out there, but as he is my witness, we are doing his work this night."

For a moment the small group sat in the stillness, awed by the sudden feeling that seized them, melded them into a oneness.

Then Revere stood. "If I'm to get ahead of the British army, I'll have to go. I've alerted Newman and Pulling and Thomas Bernard about the signal from the church. They'll be waiting."

Robert Newman was sexton, and John Pulling vestryman, for the Old North Church, directly across the street from Robert Newman's home. The Anglican rector had lately been forced out of the church because of his vehement loyalty to the Crown, and the old building, the tallest in Boston City and easily visible from the Charlestown side of the Charles River, was closed and locked. Both Newman and Pulling had keys.

Without another word he strode to the door, threw it open, and silently disappeared into the night. Warren closed the door and turned to glance at the great clock on his mantel. It was approaching ten P.M., April 18, 1775. He turned to Walsh. "You've done your work. Who's the captain of your militia?"

"Samuel Smith."

"The one who's chairman of the Tea Committee? In charge of powder and ball?"

"Yes. Sam's ready."

"I know he is. Go report to him for duty. You'll be in good hands. God bless you."

Walsh nodded and walked out into the bright wash of moonlight.

To the north, Revere worked his way through the crooked streets to the home of Robert Newman at the corner of Salem and Sheafe Streets, directly across the street from the Old North Church. Revere slowed and stopped, listening, watching for movement, and there was nothing. He silently walked past the front windows of the brick home and peered inside, and his breath came short. British soldiers sat at a table with Mrs. Newman, playing cards, boisterous, laughing. Robert Newman was not to be seen.

Revere felt a split second of panic as he continued down the street and pushed through a heavy iron gate into the darkness of the garden at the rear of the home, mind groping.

Where's Robert? Have they taken him? Do they know the plan?

He sensed more than heard a sound and then a movement in the deep shadows, and instantly he was balanced, braced, ready for the hunched figure that suddenly appeared in the dim moonlight, and then recognition flashed.

"Robert!" he exclaimed in a hoarse whisper.

"Didn't mean to frighten you." Robert turned and signalled and two more men appeared at his side. "I've got Pulling and Bernard. What do you want us to do?"

Revere exhaled air and his shoulders slumped in relief. "I thought the British had taken you."

Newman shook his head. "When they came I told them I was going upstairs to bed early. I dropped out my window and waited for these two."

"Dropped from the second floor? Are you hurt?"

Newman shook his head.

"Good. Did you get the lanterns?"

"Yes. Hidden in a church closet."

"Go to the steeple and show two lights on the Charlestown side."

"The British are crossing the Back Bay?"

"Yes. Two lights. They're waiting on the Charlestown side."

The three men nodded silent understanding, and Revere continued. "I'm going home to change clothes and then across to Charlestown."

"How will you cross the water?"

"Joshua Bentley and Tom Richardson are waiting at my boat. It's hidden under a wharf at the north end. You take care of the signal. I'll do the rest."

"Done."

Quickly, silently, the four men pushed through the iron gate and moved into the street, and Revere disappeared while the other three darted across to the shadows of the Old North Church.

Newman whispered to Bernard. "You stand guard. Pulling and I will go to the tower."

Newman drew the great brass sexton's key from his pocket and silently twisted it in the massive lock and the door swung open. Pulling followed him in, and Bernard drew the heavy door closed and faded into the shadows to watch and listen.

Inside, Newman felt his way to the closet where he had hidden two square metal lanterns with clear glass lenses, so small they barely had place for the stumps of two candles he had set inside. He handed one lantern to Pulling, and they hung them around their necks by the leather loops Newman had tied. Each stuffed flint and steel and tinderboxes into their pockets before Newman turned and worked his way to the stairs leading upwards, Pulling close behind.

They set their feet silently as they climbed the 154 stairs, and the only sound was the creaking of the old staircase as it complained of the unexpected nocturnal intrusion. At the top of the stairs both men crouched, opened their tinderboxes, and with deft, practiced strokes, struck sparks into the tinder with flint and steel and gently blew on them until small curls of flame glowed. They passed flame from the tinderboxes to the candles and waited for a moment while the flame became strong before they closed the lantern gates.

With their glowing lanterns hung about their necks, resting on their chests, Newman pointed to a narrow ladder that led upwards to the top of the bell tower. Rung upon rung, the men carefully climbed to the topmost windows in the steeple, while the tiny glow from the lanterns made giant, grotesque shadows from the huge oaken beams and the great, silent brass bells.

They stopped at the top landing, pulled the leather loops over their heads, and held the lanterns in their hands. Newman nodded to Pulling, and then threw open the sash, opening the northwest window on the Charlestown side of the steeple. Each man thrust his lantern out the window and held it, swinging slightly, for only a few seconds, fearful that British eyes in the streets below might see. Then they quickly pulled them back inside, closed the window sash, blew out the candlewicks, looped the lanterns back around their necks, and clambered back down the ladder, then the stairs. They jammed the lanterns back into the closet and ran to the great door, just as Bernard came barging through and closed it behind him, breathing heavily.

"British patrol! Is there another way out of here?"

Newman spun on his heel. "This way!"

He charged back into the dark sanctuary of the church, where he leaped onto a bench near the altar. He twisted the lock on a window and jerked it open and dropped through, Pulling and Bernard right behind.

Newman paused for one second to shake their hands, grinning in the moonlight. "We're finished! Scatter. We can't be caught together."

The sound of feet running in different directions faded, and in a few moments the Old North Church stood silent in the night.

Across the Charles River, colonial eyes had waited in silence, never leaving the black needle-pointed spire of the Old North Church while they strained to see lights—one, or two. At the moment Newman threw open the window sash and the two lights were thrust out, half a dozen patriots caught their breath, eyes narrowed to be certain before they broke and sprinted, each in a separate direction to be ready when Revere's boat touched the Charlestown shore.

South of the church, Revere had changed his clothing to riding boots, spurs, and surtout while Joshua Bentley and Tom Richardson waited, and the three had then quickly, silently worked their way towards the wharf on the north end of the peninsula, beneath which Revere had hidden his boat. While yet thirty yards from the wharf, they stopped, crouched in the dull moonlight, to watch and listen. The only sound or movement was the water, lapping against rocks and wharf pilings.

They wasted no time. In seconds they were beneath the wharf, a man on either side of the boat, one behind, moving it towards the black water. The bow had reached the shoreline when Richardson suddenly stopped and the other two raised their faces in alarm.

"We forgot cloth to muffle the oars in the oarlocks."

"Is it important?" Revere asked, impatient.

"We can't chance it. We're going through the squadron of British gunboats, probably within yards of the *Somerset*."

Richardson pointed back to the street and Bentley followed him, trotting, while Revere waited with the boat. They crossed the cobblestones, and Richardson stopped at a house and tossed pebbles clacking against a second-story window. Seconds later the dark window opened and Richardson hissed, "We need cloth, enough to wrap two oars."

Again there was a pause, then the rustle of cloth on cloth, and through the window came a set of woolen underwear, floating down, still warm from the lady who had been wearing them. Richardson held them up long enough to identify them, while Bentley gaped.

"Thank you," Richardson whispered loudly, and the window closed without a word. Bentley said not a word as the two ran back to the anxious, waiting Revere.

Two minutes later the oars were wrapped and working silently in the oarlocks as Bentley and Richardson stroked strongly, evenly, barely breaking water with their oars to avoid sound, while Revere sat in the stern of the boat, watching the huge men-of-war, listening for the dreaded challenge from one of them. The *Somerset* was dead ahead.

Earlier that evening, according to rules enforced by the British, all ferries, boats, mud-scows, and canoes in town had been tied to the *Somerset*, to stop all craft from crossing the Charles River after nine o'clock P.M. As they rowed they heard the clear clang of the bell on the great warship, strangely clear in the night—twice, a pause, twice, a pause, and then once more. Ten-thirty P.M. Twice they looked over their shoulders, south, and in the moonlight could see the low black shapes of longboats in the distance, silently moving the British troops west in a line across the Back Bay.

The tide was rising, the ships rocking gently in the swells. The nearly full moon had risen, a great ball, but oddly more south than east on that night. Boston Town lay between the low moon and the great warships, and the town cast a long, wide shadow across this part of the river, while at the same time it created a million sparkling diamonds dancing on the waters elsewhere. Revere's boat moved steadily northward, nearly invisible in the unexpected shadow. The *Somerset* grew larger, then towered ahead, and the two men kept their heads down so that no light would reflect off their faces. They scarcely breathed as they angled slightly east, expecting every second to hear the command "Halt! Who goes there?" from the watch on the top deck of the great man-of-war.

Then they were abreast of the monster, with her 520-man crew, and they could see the ugly snouts of her sixty-four cannon black against the moonlight. Then they were past the bow, and then they quietly glided on north, leaving the ship behind. At one hundred yards Bentley glanced at Revere, and Revere looked back at him, and then Richardson, and they all exhaled held breath while the two oarsmen continued the steady dip and pull on their oars.

Far to the south, Dawes jerked the knot tight in the rope that served as a belt around his middle and tugged his shirttail down around his battered brown woolen trousers. He pulled the bill on his worn leather cap low, then reached for the tied, half-filled sack of rolled oats and threw it up behind the seat of his saddle and lashed it tight. Then he stopped to inspect himself. From his old, cracked high-top leather shoes to his leather cap, he looked the part of an illiterate mill hand.

In the lamplight of his barn, he turned to Elizabeth, standing in the yellow light, shawl wrapped tight. Tenderly he drew her to him and held her. For long moments she was rigid, and then she relaxed and her arms slipped around him.

"I'll be back," he said to her quietly.

She started to speak, but then her chin trembled and suddenly she buried her face in his chest and she sobbed. For long moments he held her, and then the trembling and the sobbing slowed, and stopped.

"I'll be back," he repeated. He kissed her and turned, and she stepped back, and he led the dappled gray gelding out into the moonlight. He swung up onto the nervous mount and paused to look back at Elizabeth, silhouetted in the yellow lamp glow, and then he spun the horse and kicked it to a lope, due south, towards the lines at the Neck.

He held the horse at a lope and wondered, *Will they have the barricade up and stop me? Will they recognize me, or will they believe I'm a Mystic miller trying to get home?* He held the steady lope, listening and watching intently for the first sign of a British patrol that would challenge him.

To the north, at his home, Joseph Warren faced John and Tom. "We need to get the committee gathered. We have a lot to do."

John's eyes dropped and he spoke quietly. "There's a matter we have to handle first."

Warren felt the heavy darkness in John and stopped and waited.

"Tom says Henry Thorpe is the one who's been informing Gage."

Warren's mouth dropped open for a moment before he clamped it shut and turned to Tom. "Tell me."

Warren's eyes glowed like fires as Tom spoke, and when he stopped, Warren stood in silence for long moments. Then his eyes closed, and a deep sadness settled into his being. His shoulders sagged and his head dropped forward.

"Henry Thorpe. Why? Why?" He raised tortured eyes to John and shook his head in baffled bewilderment. "Do you know why?"

John shook his head and remained silent.

"Matthew and Kathleen know?"

"Not yet."

"Does Phoebe know?"

"Probably not. She helped take the muskets into the church."

"John, I'm so sorry. So sorry. Your families are close." Warren heaved a sigh and straightened. "We have no choice. We have to do something about it now, tonight." Again he looked at John. "Do you want to stay out of it? want me to handle it?"

"No. You have too much on you as it is. Tom and I can handle it."

"The sheriff?"

"Yes. We'll have to get a Massachusetts warrant for his arrest and let the law handle it. It will be better for him if he's in custody when some of our people find out about it."

"Do you want your name on the papers that are used to arrest him?"

"Better me than someone else."

"Maybe you're right."

"I'll go for the warrant now. Get the rest of the committee together and do what you think best. You have my support, whatever you decide."

"After they arrest him, come back here. The committee will probably be finished and gone, but you'll need to know what went on."

John took a deep breath. "By that time both sides will be committed and moving. There's nothing I could do to help here. I'm going to Concord."

Warren's eyes opened wide in surprise. "To face the British?"

"Yes. There's no way to know what might happen."

"There's risk."

John shrugged. "Tom and I better go see the magistrate and get the warrant."

They worked their way north, past the church, to the small office with the sign "HON. ROBERT MCMANN, MAGISTRATE, SOVEREIGN COLONY OF MASS." above the door. Ten minutes later they sat at a table with a single lamp to their left and McMann digging sleep from his eyes, hair awry, robe wrapped tightly about his corpulent being.

Twenty-five minutes later McMann signed his name with a flourish and raised his eyes to John. "There's the warrant. It's a Massachusetts warrant, and the British can overrule it if they find out." He paused to shake his head. "Henry Thorpe and Enid Ferguson! I can hardly believe it. Before the Almighty, I would never have suspected. I don't know of this third person, this Amos Ingersol." He stood. "I'll tell no one of this, but when word of the arrests gets out it will spread like wildfire. Thorpe and Enid Ferguson may be in danger."

John nodded. "I know. The sheriff will probably have to hide them."

At five minutes past one o'clock A.M. the sheriff opened his front door and held a lamp high. "Who's there?" At one-thirty, fully dressed, he drew a deep breath and faced John and Tom. "I'll get two deputies to make the arrests. You men stay out of it."

John nodded. "Will they be arrested tonight?"

"Within the hour."

"Will they be protected?"

"If there is need."

A hint of wind had arisen, chill and fresh from the Atlantic as they walked back into the night and moved south.

Far to the north, Bentley and Richardson shipped their padded oars, the boat glided into the Charlestown ferry landing, and the bow thumped against the planking. The men sat silent, shoulders hunched, listening, watching, and suddenly there was slight movement and a shape appeared.

"Revere?"

"Conant! You got the signal?"

"Yes. Are they moving across the Back Bay?"

"Eight hundred and more. The horse?"

"In Larkin's barn. Let's go."

Revere turned to Bentley and Richardson and the men shook hands. Revere stepped onto the ferry landing and in a moment disappeared into the shadows with Conant, Richard Devens, and John Larkin.

Joshua Bentley listened for a full minute and heard no challenge, no musket crack, and with Richardson's help he pushed off. They settled onto the wooden seat and dropped both oars into their oarlocks, pulled hard with the right oar until the boat had turned, and then began the steady, even, rhythmic stroking back towards the squadron of British fighting ships.

Back on the Charlestown shore, the four men walked rapidly through the dark streets towards the home of John Larkin, deacon of the Charlestown First Congregational Church, in whose barn they had prepared a strong, big-boned, deep-chested mare named Brown Beauty for the ride Revere was about to make.

"Be careful of British patrols," Devens warned. "I met one earlier this evening—nine officers, well mounted, headed towards Concord. Keep a sharp eye."

Inside the barn Devens tightened the saddle cinch, then untied the reins and handed them to Revere.

"Huuu," Revere crooned to the mare as he accepted the reins and carefully studied her build. She moved her ears uneasily and tossed her head, unsettled at being saddled in the night and approached by strangers. Revere waited until she settled and then spoke to her again while he carefully, slowly reached to touch her jaw, then worked his hand up to her ears, where he scratched for a moment.

He turned admiring eyes to Larkin. "She's a fine mount."

Pride showed in Larkin's eyes. "She can outrun anything the British have in Massachusetts."

Revere turned back to Conant. "I'm on my way. I don't know when I'll be back."

Conant nodded. "We sent riders to the outlying towns when we saw the lanterns in the church tower. Devens is right. Watch for British patrols. Three of them came across late today on the ferry. They're out on the roads somewhere right now."

"I know. William, thank you. Thanks for everything."

Conant shook his head. "It is you we must thank. You're the one that bears the burden tonight. God bless you, Paul."

Revere swung onto the mare and took a good seat and found the stirrups. He reined the horse around and angled just west of due north, avoiding the lights of Charlestown as he headed for the

Medford Road where it nearly touched the Mystic River. He knew every building, every tree, and he watched and listened as he held the mare to a steady lope, feeling the rhythm of her breathing and the steady reach and pull of her stride. He held a firm rein; the nervous mount wanted to stretch her legs and run.

Far to the south, where the Boston Peninsula narrowed to a thin neck, Dawes pulled the gelding to a trot, then a walk, and waited until it had caught its wind. The briny smell of the salt-water beach came strong on the easterly breeze as he continued. He dropped his head forward and rode loose and easy, as one exhausted, nearly asleep, and the gelding plodded on.

Dawes watched the guard, which straddled the road at the narrowest point on the Neck, where the British had movable barricades that they used to block the road when they wanted to stop all ground traffic into and out of Boston. The barricades had been used to isolate Boston from the world after the Boston Tea Party, and again lately when Boston City rebelled against the Port Act, which stopped commerce into and out of Boston cold, dead in its tracks. With the barricades in place, and one hundred soldiers behind them with muskets, this place became a nearly impregnable fortress.

Are the barricades up? If they are, do I pass for a miller or do I get shot for a traitor?

One hundred yards from the lines he raised his head and leaned forward in the saddle, searching, and he saw the faint glow of a lantern and then four figures moving, and then he saw the barricades set across the road. He pulled his horse to a stop, and for long moments he sat looking at the four British guards, weighing his chances in his mind.

He had to go on.

He tapped spur gently to the horse and held it to a plodding walk in the darkness while he sat slumped in the saddle, head lolling forward as though he were nearly asleep.

One hundred yards later the heavy challenge came ringing in the darkness. "Halt and declare yourself."

Dawes jerked erect and hauled the horse to a halt. He stood in the stirrups and leaned forward as though concentrating to see in the darkness. Two of the four British soldiers moved towards him, muskets at the ready, bayonets mounted.

"What?" Dawes blurted. "Who's there?"

"Dismount or be shot."

Dawes's head jerked back and he called, "Don't shoot, I'm getting down." He dismounted awkwardly, as though inept at handling a horse. "Who are you?"

"State your name and reason for being on this road."

"Martin Hoffman. I'm a miller headed for home."

"Advance."

"Are you soldiers?"

"British grenadiers. Advance."

"Oh! Soldiers." He led the horse forward and stopped six feet from the men and thrust his head forward as though studying them. "Did I do something wrong?"

"Where is your home?"

"Mystic. Well, just west of Mystic."

"What's in the sack on your saddle?"

"Oats. I got part of my pay in oats back at the mill."

"What mill?"

"Boston. Hawkens's mill, by the docks."

The soldier looked at the rough-cut shirt and the battered leather cap and the baggy trousers, then walked close to study the horse. "That's no miller's horse. Where did you steal it?"

Dawes straightened. "Sir, I did not steal it. It belongs to Hawkens. I've got to return in two days to finish my job there, and he loaned it to me to ride. Part of our bargain."

The soldier looked at his companion, who shrugged and shook his head.

"Pass," the soldier said, "but don't be caught out again at night. You'll be shot."

"Oh, yes, sir. I'll travel in the daylight from now on. It was my wife I was worried about. She's been alone now for—"

The soldier interrupted. "Just move on."

Dawes scrambled back onto the gelding and gathered up the reins and waited while two soldiers opened the barricade enough for him to pass through. Then he urged the horse to its plodding walk and held it for two hundred yards. He stopped and turned to look, and exhaled through rounded lips, and then raised the horse to a high lope southward towards Roxbury. He reined in at the home of the captain of the minutemen and banged on the door.

"The British are moving north!"

He left the Roxbury minuteman captain scrambling to get dressed and turned northwest at a run to Brookline, where he pounded on the door of the militia leader.

"The British are crossing the Back Bay!"

Twenty minutes later the gelding's hooves rang hollow on the bridge over the Charles River, and Dawes slowed to a walk to let the horse blow and catch its wind before he raised it again to a run, past Harvard College to Cambridge, where he once again sought out the home of the minuteman leader and roused him.

At that moment, on the west side of the Back Bay, at the Lechmere Point landing, Lieutenant Frederick Mackenzie swore bitterly under his breath. His Twenty-third Regiment, for which he was responsible, had arrived ninety minutes earlier with the first group to cross the Back Bay. Under his command, his men had quickly gathered at his orders and were in rank and file, ready, waiting. But they were the only ones. In the darkness four hundred fifty other grenadiers and marines in full battle dress with haversacks on their backs, now under the command of officers they had never seen in daylight nor heard at any time, were a confused, cursing, lost mass of officers bawling orders to regulars who could not hear nor understand, nor could they find any familiar faces in the darkness to gather to.

The boats had gone back for the second group, and had just returned and beached, and just over two hundred more confused, cursing, irate regulars had jumped into the surf and mud to come ashore, piling on top of those already there. Any colonial passing within three-quarters of a mile could hear the angry tumult; any sense of secrecy had long since been lost and forgotten.

Mackenzie, a soldier's soldier, shook his head in angry disgust. "We were supposed to be a column moving west by now. Cambridge by two o'clock. Lexington by daybreak. Concord by nine. This mess won't be a column for two more hours! Where are the officers? Where's Smith?"

Neither Mackenzie nor any British soldier could know that south of them, William Dawes had already crossed the Charles River on his run to Cambridge; he was ahead of them. North of them, Paul Revere was past Charlestown, cautiously approaching the Mystic River where the road forked, north to Mystic or west to Cambridge. He also had passed them in the night. No British patrol had yet sighted either rider as their running horses steadily ate up the dark road.

In Boston City, Tom reached to grasp John's arm at the front gate of the Dunson home. "You're going to Concord?"

John drew a heavy breath. "I think I have to."

Tom reflected for long moments. "You've risked enough. You are one of the only committeemen who been in battle. They'll need you here to share what you know about fighting."

"What I know will save lives out where the shooting is. I have to go."

"I'll come later and find you. There's one thing I have to do first."

"What?"

"Ingersol. He's sly. If he hears about the arrest of Thorpe and Ferguson, he'll run."

"Come in and get a warm meal."

Tom patted his coat pocket. "I got cheese and hardtack." He paused and looked into John's face. "John, you be careful. Promise me."

The frank expression of deep concern startled John, and he looked into the grizzled, lined face of the old Indian fighter and in an instant a hundred scenes flashed through his mind. The snowshoes—Tom pausing countless times to point at marks in the snow, teaching him to track—sitting huddled around small campfires, talking low—learning to read the stars at night—Tom patiently teaching him to lead a moving target with the musket—teaching him the knife, the tomahawk—mending worn moccasins, making new ones—snaring rabbits in the snow to stay alive—hiding in snow holes while thirty Hurons within fifty feet hunted them—the quick, devastating attacks on Huron war parties—the seven times Tom's musket and tomahawk had saved John—the three times John's musket had saved Tom.

John looked into the craggy face and he grasped Tom and pulled him in, and for a moment the two men stood in an embrace they had never before shared.

"I will, Tom. You be careful."

Tom turned and in a moment had disappeared in the shadows, while John once again marvelled at his ability to move silently and disappear as by magic. John rapped on the front door and it opened and Margaret stood in the lamplight. She exhaled held breath and her shoulders dropped as relief flooded.

John hung his hat and coat and walked to the large table. Margaret went to the stove and poured steaming tea and set the cup before him and waited. He worked the hot cup between his palms for a moment while Margaret sat down opposite him and studied his face in the lamplight. She saw the flat look in his eyes and the rigid set of his jaw.

"What's wrong? Is it the British?"

John continued working with the cup for several seconds while he organized his thoughts. Then he set it down and raised his eyes to hers, hating, loathing what he had to tell her. "Not the British," he said quietly. "The man who has been telling Gage our plans is Henry Thorpe."

Margaret recoiled as though struck, and her face was a mask of utter disbelief. "You're wrong!" she exclaimed. "Henry would never do such a thing."

"The sheriff is on the way to his home right now to arrest him on a Massachusetts warrant, along with Enid Ferguson and a man named Ingersol."

"Enid from the bakery? Have you lost your senses?" She stared at John, and his expression did not change. Slowly she comprehended what he had said, and her eyes dropped and she stared unseeing at the tabletop. Then her head jerked up. "What of Kathleen? Phoebe?"

John's shoulders sagged. "I'm sure neither Kathleen nor Phoebe knows." He was suddenly weary, tired, sad in the eyes. "I don't know what to do. I've got to tell Matthew tonight, now."

Margaret felt the unbearable stab of pain it would bring to her firstborn, and for long moments she lost all reason, all control. "You can't tell him! We've got to prepare him first. He'll find out when the time comes."

John saw the wild, unbridled need in her eyes and the abandonment of reason, and for a moment he stared at the teacup. "You know we have to tell him." He raised his eyes again to hers and watched her silently concede what she had known since John told her the truth. She bowed her head, and for several seconds her shoulders shook with quiet sobs.

"There's one more thing," John said, and she heard the urgency in his voice and she wiped her eyes and waited.

"I'm going on to Concord tonight."

Moments passed before she spoke. "Why? You're on the committee."

"They'll need men who have been in battle. They'll lose too many otherwise."

"Battle? You mean twenty-five years ago, when you were with the snowshoe men?"

He nodded in silence.

"That was too long ago. You never fought an army, only Indians. They need you here!"

John shook his head. "I have to go. And Matthew will have to make up his mind whether he's coming or not."

"Matthew? Both of you?" She was incredulous.

"He'll need to make his own choice."

"He's staying here!"

"He has to decide." John rose and started towards the archway into the bedroom wing, and Margaret lunged to her feet and stood in front of him, barring his way.

"You can't take him! If trouble starts here in Boston, I'll need him." Her eyes were wild as she jammed her open hand against John's chest to stop him.

John gently took her hand in his. "He's of age. This decision is too important. We can't rob him."

A door creaked in the dark hallway and Matthew's voice came in the darkness. "What's the matter? What's going on?" He came squinting into the lamplight, barefoot in his nightshirt.

"Sit down," John said, and turned back to the table. Margaret followed and wrapped her robe tightly and sat down, arms folded tightly across her chest. Matthew sat down and John waited until his eyes had adjusted.

"We learned some things tonight that you need to know." He paused to search for words to make it easy, and there were none.

Matthew interrupted. "Something's wrong."

John nodded and raised his eyes to Matthew's. "Yes. We found out who's been giving information to Gage." He paused, hating the words. "It's Henry Thorpe."

Matthew's face went dead. No one moved. The only sound was the quiet ticking of the clock on the heavy oak mantel.

"That's impossible," Matthew said under his breath.

Margaret reached to grasp his arm. "Matthew, it will be all right."

John continued. "The sheriff's on his way now to arrest him on a colonial warrant, along with Enid Ferguson from the bakery."

"Enid?"

"And a man named Ingersol."

John watched the shock in Matthew's eyes turn to pain and suddenly they widened. "Does Kathleen know?"

"I doubt it."

"I've got to go over there! Someone has to be there!" He started to rise.

John grabbed his forearm. "Think through it first."

"What do you mean, think through it?"

"I doubt any of Thorpe's family knows about it. The charge is treason, and there's no worse crime. Will they want anyone there for that?"

Margaret cut in. "Of course Kathleen will."

Matthew continued. "Kathleen will need me."

John cut him off. "You're the last one she'll want to see."

Matthew shook his head and his eyes glowed defiantly. "You're wrong. I've got to go."

"Matthew, *think!* The shame of it will nearly kill both Phoebe and Kathleen. They won't want anyone around while they suffer that humiliation. Think past your own need to what's best for them."

Matthew started back for his bedroom to change clothes and John called, "There's more. The British crossed the Back Bay a while ago with a large force. Revere went north, Dawes went south, to raise the militia. I think this is the beginning of some sort of confrontation with the British. I'm going to Concord."

Matthew stopped short and slowly turned back. "The British? Concord? There could be trouble."

"Yes, there could be. You need to make up your mind about it."

Matthew shook his head. "I only know I've got to see Kathleen." He turned on his heel and disappeared in the dark hallway.

John turned to Margaret and exhaled a weary breath. "Too much too fast. This thing with Henry—none of us were ready." He shook his head. "Matthew will have to do it his own way." He pointed to the pantry. "I'll need a little bread and meat and cheese wrapped in something, and some clean cotton rags. Nothing else. I'll change clothes and get the musket."

In his bedroom John lighted a lamp and knelt beside an old leather trunk in one corner. He loosened the buckles on the broad leather straps and threw them back, lifted the lid and tilted it back against the wall, and raised the lamp to look.

On top were pillowcases and bedsheets, with matching delicate, beautiful needlework, and napkins and tablecloths of fine
linen, with matching hand-sewn designs, for the dowries of
Brigitte and Priscilla. He gently lifted them aside. Beneath were
two packages wrapped in parchment and string. He lifted them
out and laid them on the bed and loosened the strings.

Inside the smaller package were knee-length moccasins, hand-
sewn and double soled from the hide of a bull moose. John lifted
them and touched the bead-and-quill design carefully stitched
with deer sinew before he laid them back on their wrapper. The
larger package held a soft tanned deer-hide hunting shirt with
bead-and-quill work at the cuffs and collar. He carefully refolded
the shirt and tied the package and put it back into the trunk, with
the parchment from the moccasins, and kept the moccasins out.
He replaced the beautiful linens, closed and rebuckled the trunk
lid, then turned to the closet. He picked a loose-fitting deep gray
woolen shirt and dark woolen trousers. He changed into the shirt
and trousers and then into the moccasins, wrapped to his knees,
stiff with age. He pushed his square-toed shoes into the closet and
strode out down the hall to the pantry. Three minutes later he
walked out and laid his musket, leather bullet pouch, and powder
horn on the large table. Matthew was near the front door, shrugging into his coat.

Margaret's eyes were locked onto the musket.

Matthew paused to stare at John's moccasins. "Where did you
get them?"

"Made them."

"When?"

"About twenty-five years ago."

"Snowshoe men?"

"Yes. They're easier for traveling distances."

Matthew buttoned his coat.

"When you've seen Kathleen, what's your plan?"

"It depends on what happens over there."

"Do you plan to come to Concord?"

Matthew shrugged. "If she needs me, no."

"If she doesn't?"

"I don't know."

Margaret turned her face to John and broke in. "He's staying!"

John studied Margaret's face and saw the dead look, the fear, the hopelessness in her blue eyes, and his heart rose in his throat. He swallowed and started to speak, but said nothing. He turned back to Matthew and eyed his white shirt. "If you decide to go, you might want to change to a darker shirt. A white shirt will draw fire in a crowd. The British are fools for having those white belts crossed over their hearts, and gold on their officers' shoulders."

Margaret turned from him and slumped into a chair at the table, and suddenly she leaned forward and put her head on her arms and began to sob. John could stand no more. Gently he knelt beside her chair and pulled her head into his shoulder and wrapped her inside his arms while she wept uncontrollably. He waited until the sobbing stopped and then pulled up a chair and motioned to Matthew, who sat down at the table with them.

"Margaret, please listen to me. I will do all in my power to make you understand. Things are happening that are much more than the colonies breaking from the British. A spirit is moving over this land, a sense that there is a hand guiding us. There is a design, a plan higher than any of us knows."

A strange feeling crept from nowhere.

"In the church yesterday, with Silas and the others, we all felt it. It was a power beyond anything I've ever known. It ran against all good sense, but none of us could deny it. It settled into our hearts and our minds as nothing ever did before, and we knew what we had to do."

He paused. Margaret was staring at him as though she had never seen him before. The spirit that had crept in only moments before had reached inside her.

John continued. "I don't know where it will end, but I don't need to know. It is enough that I know we must do this thing, by treaty if we can, by blood if we cannot. I don't want to die. But if I must, I will, and I know in my soul that if that happens, you will be all right, you and the children. Don't ask me how I know. Only that I do know."

Matthew was hardly breathing. Margaret stared, gripped by a power that reached deep, and she knew John had spoken the truth. He had to go, and she had to let him.

John finished. "I can't add more. I can only pray you will understand."

Margaret stood and threw her arms about him and clutched him to her desperately. Tears came welling down her cheeks, and they clung to each other silently until the tears stopped.

John stepped back and Margaret spoke quietly. "You have to go." With a bursting heart she held him again until the trembling stopped. Then she stepped back and wiped the tears away. "I have the food and bandages ready, there in the pouch." She pointed to a leather bag with a shoulder strap on the table.

Matthew released held breath and stared, astonished at what he had seen and felt, unable to form words, and then he turned and wordlessly opened the door and walked out into the shadows.

John turned to Margaret. "I'll be a minute."

He picked a lamp from the table and started for the archway into the bedroom wing, and Margaret grasped his hand and walked with him. He stopped at the door to Brigitte's bedroom, Margaret took the lamp, and John silently entered. His moccasins made no sound as he walked to Brigitte's bed and knelt. The dim yellow lamplight caught the long lashes, the heart-shaped face, and the few damp curls of hair on her forehead. Memories came flooding. The tiny babe reaching to grasp his finger—her first steps—her first and second lisped words, mama, dada—the impish toddler underfoot—six years old, dropping a bowl of eggs— two missing front teeth—school—the overnight change to a young lady—an emerging beauty—a copy of her mother—the muskets at the church.

Tenderly John leaned to brush his kiss on her forehead and she stirred. He silently walked out and down the hall to Caleb's room to kneel beside the bed.

The peaceful, sleeping face belied the turmoil inside Caleb, caught in the awkward, uncertain stage beyond the child but not yet the man. In the face John saw the man that would be. Strong chin, thoughtful eyes, high cheekbones, prominent nose. He would be a good husband, good father, good leader. John touched the soft cheek and rose and walked to the bedroom where Adam and Prissy slept on opposite sides of the room.

Inside he knelt by Prissy. She stirred and her eyes opened in the soft shadows. "Father? Is that you?"

"It's me. Go back to sleep." He kissed her on the cheek and he felt the soft warmth of her breath. She smiled and pulled her quilt higher, and her large blue eyes closed in the warm, safe security of his presence.

John knelt beside Adam, and in his heart he heard the childish, worshipful exclamation, "And did you see Father? Picked William up like he was nothing! Picked him up and made him be good!" John leaned to kiss the thatch of hair, then rose and walked back into the hall with Margaret. He closed the door, and they strode back into the parlor together.

"If Matthew decides to come, tell him to bring at least sixty musket balls and eighty patches. Be sure his powder horn's full and that he has four extra flints."

He slipped the shoulder straps of his own bullet bag and powder horn over his shoulder and then the small food pouch. He turned to Margaret. "Listen carefully. If Tom comes here, tell him I took the north way, across the Charles, up past Charlestown. At Winter Hill I'll go west, cross-country to Menotomy, and take the main road on to Lexington and then Concord. Can you remember?"

"Yes."

"If Matthew comes, tell him."

"I will. How will you cross the river?"

"Borrow a rowboat. Maybe from John Pulling."

John picked up his musket, and Margaret watched him slip the leather straps of his powder horn and bullet pouch, then the food and bandage bag, over his shoulders. He drew her to him with his free arm and looked into her face for long moments, memorizing, and then he kissed her. "I should be back within one day. God bless you."

He walked out into the light of the nearly full moon, and Margaret stood framed in the door until he was out of sight, working his way north in the narrow cobblestone streets of Boston City.

Notes

The warning to Lexington and Concord that the British were coming the night of April 18, 1775, was delivered by two messengers: William Dawes, Jr., and Paul Revere. Joseph Warren sent Dawes first, to travel south across the Neck and then turn back northwest to Lexington and on to Concord. Minutes later, when Revere arrived at the Warren home, as a matter of being certain the message would get through if either Dawes or Revere was captured, Warren sent Revere north to cross the Charles River in Revere's own boat, then take a horse provided by John Larkin and ride to Lexington and Concord. Warren specifically ordered both men to deliver the message to Sam Adams and John Hancock, at the home of the Reverend Jonas Clarke at Lexington, so they could avoid capture by the British. (See French, *The Day of Concord and Lexington*, beginning with p. 75.)

Revere had previously arranged for three men to help give the prearranged lantern signal from the Old North Church tower, namely, Robert Newman, John Pulling, and Thomas Bernard. They were to meet at the home of Robert Newman, on the corner of Salem and Sheafe Streets, across the street from the church, where Newman was the sexton and Pulling was a vestryman, each of whom had keys into the church. British soldiers who rented rooms from Newman caused a minor problem, which Newman resolved by going to his second-floor room and dropping to the ground, where Pulling and Bernard were waiting and where Revere found them. Acting on Revere's orders, the three of them crossed the street to the church, where Bernard stood watch while Pulling and Newman climbed to the top of the old steeple and gave the signal with two lamps Newman had found and hidden in the church. As they finished their mission and were ready to leave, a British patrol happened by, and the three men escaped through a back window in the church. (See Fischer, *Paul Revere's Ride*, beginning on p. 99.)

The boat used for Revere's ride across the Charles River was his own; however, he had arranged for two friends to help, one a boat maker named Joshua Bentley, the other, Thomas Richardson. The incident in which they obtain the undergarments of an unnamed woman, from the second floor of a home near the wharf where the boat was hidden, is viewed with some suspicion by historians; however, it is part of the Boston folklore surrounding the famous incidents of that night, and therefore included in the novel. It was Bentley and Richardson who rowed the boat, with the oars wrapped in the woman's undergarments to silence them in the oarlocks. The boat docked at the Charlestown ferry wharf, where the men were met by William Conant, who had been watching for the signal from the Old North Church tower and who had arranged for Revere to ride the powerful mare, Brown Beauty, owned by John Larkin, deacon of the Charlestown First Congregational Church. (See Fischer, *Paul Revere's Ride*, beginning on p. 103.)

In the same time frame, William Dawes knew he had to pass through the barricades at the Neck, which were guarded by British sentries. In all probability he masqueraded as a simple miller, which he had done previously with success, with a half sack of oats tied to his saddle, to persuade the British soldiers he was harmless. (See French, *The Day of Concord and Lexington*, p. 78.)

The disorganized confusion of the landing of the British column at Lechmere Point after crossing the Back Bay is chronicled briefly in French, *The Day of Concord and Lexington*, pp. 100–101.

CHAPTER IX

★ ★ ★

*P*hoebe Thorpe rose on one elbow, eyes wide in the dark. Silver moonlight framed the window curtain, and she looked and listened, unsure what had awakened her. The pounding came again at the front door, loud and incessant, and she grasped Henry's shoulder. He rolled in the bed to look at her as his brain registered the sound of the fist on the front door.

"Who's at the door?" he asked.

"I don't know. It woke me."

Quickly Henry slipped into his robe and heavy felt slippers, ran his fingers through his hair, and lighted a lamp. A minute later he walked to the front door, turned the heavy brass key in the lock, and swung it open. He held the lamp high as he peered out, trying to focus. "Who's . . . Sheriff Samuels! What's happened?" The lamplight caught the faces of the two deputies standing behind the sheriff.

"Henry Thorpe, I am required to serve this warrant on you for your arrest."

Thorpe gaped and stood riveted while his mind reeled. "You're *what?*"

"I have a warrant for your arrest. I am required to serve it and take you to jail to be held for arraignment and trial." Samuels stood firm, face expressionless, the folded paper in his hand.

Thorpe stammered, "David, this utter nonsense! You don't

come around at three o'clock in the morning making light of an arrest! Why are you here?"

"Mr. Thorpe, this is a warrant for your arrest. You will come peacefully or we will have to take you by force."

Thorpe's head shifted forward, his eyes incredulous. "You're *serious?*"

"Absolutely."

"Preposterous!" Henry exclaimed. "Is the warrant British or colonial? I demand to see it."

"The colony of Massachusetts." David Samuels handed him the paper, and Thorpe fumbled it open with hands that trembled in outrage.

"*Spying?*" he blurted. "Arrested for *spying?*"

"Yes. Get dressed if you wish. We'll wait."

"Henry, what in the world is all the shouting . . ." Phoebe stopped in her tracks at the sight of Sheriff Samuels. "Sheriff! What's wrong? Is it the British?" She stood with her robe wrapped tightly about her, still wearing her nightcap.

Samuels dropped his eyes and shifted his feet. "No, ma'am. You will need to talk with your husband."

Phoebe's hand shot to her mouth and she hurried to Henry's side. "Henry?"

"Mother, what's the commotion?" Kathleen walked up behind Phoebe barefooted, her robe wrapped tightly, with her long hair braided down her back in a single french braid.

Henry's eyes were on fire as he shoved the warrant within inches of Samuels's face. "Who obtained this warrant?" he thundered.

"Magistrate McMann."

"I can see who signed it! Who swore on their oath to facts that obtained it?"

Phoebe gasped. "Warrant! Warrant for whom? For what?"

Kathleen's voice came too high, too loud. "An arrest warrant?" She pushed her mother aside and fronted Samuels.

"Yes, ma'am."

"For whom?"

"Ask your father."

"Answer my question," Thorpe raged at Samuels. "Who obtained this warrant?"

Samuels raised his eyes to Thorpe's. "I do not issue warrants. I serve them."

"Is that warrant for the arrest of my father?" Kathleen planted her feet and locked Samuels with her glare.

"Ask him."

She grasped Thorpe's arm. "Father?"

Thorpe brushed her aside and shook the warrant in Samuels's face. "I demand to know who obtained this warrant! I'll have them in irons!"

Samuels squared his shoulders and stared Thorpe in the eye. "That warrant was obtained by John Phelps Dunson and Thomas Sievers. It is for your arrest on the charge of spying against the colony of Massachusetts. Now, sir, you will get dressed immediately and come with us or we are prepared to shackle you now and take you by force. The choice is yours. Pronounce yourself."

Kathleen gasped. Phoebe's face blanched white and she sighed and her knees buckled. Kathleen caught her and held her on her feet.

Thorpe's mouth dropped open in utter disbelief, and he lowered his hand with the warrant and stared blindly into the face of David Samuels while his mind numbed. For five seconds he stood unable to move, to speak, his face a blank. "Dunson? Dunson did this?"

"Yes, sir."

"On what proof?"

"I don't know. I do know Enid Ferguson is now in my jail, and she has freely written and signed a full confession against you. It implicates you in giving information directly to General Gage."

Thorpe's head rolled back and his eyes closed and everything inside the man crumbled. He sagged against the door frame, and Samuels reached to hold him erect.

Kathleen laid her mother on the sofa and turned back to her father, shock and utter terror in her eyes. "Is it true? Is John right? Is Enid right?"

Thorpe tried to speak but sound would not come, and he swallowed and tried again. "Of course not, child. A mistake! This is grotesque beyond words!"

She turned to Samuels. "What is he accused of giving to Gage? What information?"

"I don't know, ma'am."

"Of course you do!" Kathleen cried. "If Enid wrote out a confession, you know what she said. Tell me. Now!" Her voice rang and her eyes were points of light.

Samuels's mouth became a straight line for a moment before he spoke. "I do recall mention of the muskets that were taken into the church on Monday."

Kathleen spun to face her father. "Did you do it? You knew! Someone told them and they searched the church. Was it you, Father?" Her eyes bored into his face.

Thorpe could not meet her eyes. He stammered and stopped, then said, "Of course not."

Behind them, the children came padding on bare feet, digging at sleepy eyes. "Mama, what's wrong? Why is everybody shouting?" They walked to Phoebe, slumped on the sofa.

Kathleen backed away from her father, staring at him as though she did not recognize him. "Spying," she hissed. "Spying," she repeated as though the word were a poison, bitter on her tongue. "You've destroyed us! All of us! There will be no place we can go! Like lepers!"

Samuels started at the sound of the sobbing and shoved Thorpe aside and strode to Phoebe. She started to rise, then sank back onto the sofa. She clutched Samuels's arms and her racking sobs filled the room. Her cries were unintelligible as she screamed, and then she turned her face upward and began to call to God to take her and the children from the pain. Samuels seized her shoulders and she slumped. Kathleen ran for water and returned, and Phoebe struck the dipper and it flew clattering against a wall.

"Get Doctor Soderquist," Samuels called to a deputy, and Kathleen stepped in close and wrapped her mother in her arms to stop her. Phoebe stared at Kathleen as though she did not know her, and she suddenly sagged into a huddled lump on the sofa and dissolved into pitiful moans and tears. Kathleen sat down beside her mother and gathered the frightened, crying children under one arm, her mother under the other, and started the instinctive rocking back and forth, talking low.

Samuels turned back to Thorpe, deep anger in his eyes and face. "You, sir, had better get dressed if you intend to. You have three minutes."

Thorpe walked to the bedroom as though in a trance, a deputy beside him, and minutes later emerged, dressed. The deputies clamped the manacles onto his wrists and led him out into the night while Samuels went back to the sofa.

"Kathleen, only God knows how sorry I am. Is there anything I can do?"

She tried to speak and could not. She shook her head.

"Can I send someone? Margaret? Matthew?"

Kathleen turned tortured eyes up to his. "No. No. There's no one you can send."

He placed his large, awkward hand on her shoulder and patted her, then walked from the room and closed the door on the wrenching sounds of Phoebe moaning and the children, huddled against Kathleen, wailing in their anguished fear. He trotted to the carriage waiting in the street, checked to be certain Thorpe was seated beside a deputy, and climbed to the driver's seat. He grasped the reins, clucked to the horse, and the carriage started up the street, its iron-rimmed wheels clattering on the cobblestones. He raised the horse to a steady trot, and from the corner of his eye caught a glimpse of a tall, slender, shadowy figure sprinting towards the Thorpe home. He eased back on the reins, lost the figure in the dark, considered for a moment, and continued on into the night.

Matthew threw open the front gate and hammered on the front door of the Thorpe home. Moments passed in silence and he raised his hand again, when he heard the handle turn and the door opened slightly.

"Who's there?"

"Me, Matthew. Kathleen, in the name of heaven, open the door!"

He heard the breath catch in her throat, and slowly the door opened. Kathleen stood facing him, feet slightly apart, cheeks tear-stained and eyes brimming. Instantly he seized her and pulled her inside his arms and held her, his cheek against her hair, and he felt her stiffen, arms at her sides. Slowly he released her and backed away to look deeply into her face. Behind her, hidden by the door, he heard the sounds of Phoebe moaning and the children sobbing.

"Kathleen, I came as soon . . . what's wrong?"

He watched her chin tremble and knew she could not trust herself to speak, and tears silently ran down her cheeks to make dark spots on her robe.

"Where's your father?"

She choked out two words. "Arrested. Gone."

"Arrested! You can't stay here alone. Come with me. All of you. Come home with me." He reached to push the door open and she caught his arm.

"No. We can't."

Stunned, Matthew stepped back. "What are you talking about? Of course you can. You know how—"

The strangled sound that came from deep in her throat struck Matthew like the thrust of a dagger, and she cried, "Don't you know what's happened? They've taken my father for spying! Spying! We can't come with you or anyone else! Go home. Stay away from us."

Matthew's mouth fell open at the agony in her voice, and he stood rooted for a time before he could form words. "I love you and—"

The pain in her face and her voice was beyond anything

Matthew had ever known. "Don't say it, don't say it!" she moaned. "It's gone. Gone. I can't stand you being here, knowing you will never be mine! It will kill me! If you feel anything for me, go! Leave and don't come back! I couldn't stand the pain again!"

He reached for her, and she pounded clenched fists on his chest and shoved him back roughly and her voice rose. "I'm a leper! Don't you understand? My father is a traitor! We are unclean!"

Overwhelmed, Matthew tried one more time. "I need to be here with you. I can help."

"No, no, no. Go, Matthew. If you feel anything for me, go."

She closed the door and Matthew heard the oak bar drop. He stared at the door, his mind blank, his heart numb. He heard Kathleen's agonized sobbing from within and then her footsteps as she gathered her mother and the children and walked with them into the bedroom wing of the home.

Slowly Matthew backed away from the door, then turned and walked through the front gate and turned north at a regular, firm stride.

North and east, Sheriff David Samuels hauled the carriage to a halt before his office and climbed down. The deputies helped Thorpe to the ground while Samuels unlocked the door and stepped back to let the deputies lead Thorpe inside the bare, austere room. A single lantern glowed, and the deputy turned up the wick.

"Take him on back to the first cell," Samuels ordered, "and then Jonathan, you stay to guard these two while Will and I serve the last warrant."

While the deputies worked with the huge, flat brass keys and the clanging cell door, Samuels walked back outside to look up and down the street. Nothing moved. Satisfied, he walked back inside, closed the door, and dropped the thick oak bar into its brackets.

Across the street, a slight, stooped figure leaped from a dark doorway and sprinted west. Amos Ingersol ran the half mile to his rented room and threw open the door, fighting for breath, sweating, face pasty white. He lighted a single lamp, jerked a woven wicker suitcase from beneath his bed, threw it open, and jammed clothing from his closet and dresser drawers inside. He slammed it closed and buckled the straps, then threw his toiletries into a second small fabric bag. For a moment he surveyed the room to be certain he had not left papers that would incriminate, then turned the lamp wick off and backed out the door into the darkness. He closed the door and turned on his heel to run, and stopped dead in his tracks.

Five feet away, a thin, shadowy figure faced him in the moonlight, eyes glowing like embers. His hair was long and stringy, shoulders pinched, face lined and unshaven, coat worn and tattered. His right hand held a tomahawk loosely at his side.

"Run if you've a mind," the quiet voice declared, and waited. Ingersol did not move nor speak.

"Then get back inside. We'll wait for the sheriff."

Ingersol fumbled the door open and backed into his dark room, eyes never leaving the tomahawk.

A chill breeze moved in from the Atlantic and whispered through the oaks and maples and moved their leaves, which made lacy silver patterns of moonlight on the ground and rooftops. Matthew opened the front gate and rapped on the door. Margaret opened it, and Matthew moved past her without a word and sat down at the table. Margaret followed him and sat down facing him, and waited. They sat in silence for a time before Matthew raised his eyes from the tabletop and looked directly at his mother.

"She sent me away." He could think of nothing else to say.

Margaret's eyes dropped for a moment. "She's been wounded. Give her time."

"She said never come back."

"That wasn't Kathleen. That was pain. Try to understand."

"She said they were lepers. Unclean."

"It will pass."

The muscles on his jaw made little ridges for a moment, and he swallowed against the lump in his throat. He looked into his mother's eyes and she saw the deep fear. "I can't lose her. I can't."

Margaret's chin quivered for a moment, and she impulsively reached to touch his cheek. "You won't lose her. Give her time."

Matthew dropped his head forward to stare unseeing once more at the tabletop, and then he raised his head and drew in a great, ragged breath and released it slowly. He wiped his sleeve across his eyes and stood and ran his hand through his hair, feeling a rise of anger at the black hopelessness. "I don't know what to do," he exclaimed. "I can't go back over there."

"Sit here and we'll talk."

He shook his head and paced to the middle of the room. "She wouldn't even let me past the door. Pushed me out." He turned back to Margaret and she saw the angry points of light in his eyes. "I can't . . ." Suddenly Matthew raised a hand and stopped and turned his head to listen. "Someone's coming."

A soft rap came at the door, and Matthew was there in two strides while Margaret stood.

"Who's there?" he called through the door.

"Tom Sievers."

He threw the door open and Tom stood in the yellow light.

"Has John left yet?"

Margaret spoke as she hurried to the door. "Yes. About half an hour ago."

Matthew paced back to the center of the room, agitated, battling the anger that was building.

Tom nodded to Margaret. "Thank you, ma'am. I stopped to tell him the sheriff arrested Amos Ingersol. He has all three in the jail now." He paused for a moment and glanced at Matthew. "I'll be on my way."

"Wait," Margaret said. "John left a message for you. Come in. Tell us what happened."

Tom backed up half a step. "Ma'am, I oughtn't be inside your house, looking like I am. I can tell you that Ingersol is signing a statement about what he done, like Enid Ferguson. It looks bad for Mr. Thorpe."

At the words "Mr. Thorpe," Matthew stopped dead in his tracks and his head pivoted towards Tom. For a moment their eyes locked, and then Tom looked back at Margaret.

"There's not much more to tell. What message did John leave for me?"

Matthew listened intently.

"He said he's gone to Concord. Across the river, past Charlestown, west at Winter Hill, cross-country to Menotomy, and then onto the main road into Concord."

Tom tracked John's path in his mind as Margaret spoke, and he nodded his head. "Thank you. I'll go find him." He turned to go, then hesitated. "Ma'am, I'm sorry about Henry Thorpe. I know you was close. I hated doing what John and me had to do, but it had to be done."

"It wasn't your fault."

Tom bobbed his head. "I'll be on my way."

"Wait," Matthew commanded. "I'm going with you."

Margaret clutched at his arm. "No, you stay here. This thing with the Thorpes is clouding your thinking. We'll need you."

Matthew shook his head. "No. I can't take it—being here and not being allowed to help her. I'm sick to death of this whole thing. Muskets, the church desecrated, war coming, Father gone, Henry arrested, Kathleen talking crazy. If I stay here I'll do something bad. I'm going." He turned to Tom. "Give me five minutes."

Tom shook his head. "You'll need a clear head if trouble starts at Concord. You oughtn't go if it's just to get away from things here."

Matthew shook his head firmly. "I'm going. With you or alone."

Tom shrugged and stepped inside and remained silent while Matthew trotted back to his bedroom. Five minutes later he returned, dressed in dark woolen pants and shirt, musket in hand. He stopped at the table long enough to slip the straps of his powder horn and bullet pouch over his shoulder.

Margaret walked to him, shoulders slumped, and spoke quietly. "Take sixty balls, eighty patches, four extra flints, and a full powder horn. Father said."

"I have them."

"I'll get some food." She filled a small bag with cheese and dried apples and meat and bread from the pantry, and Matthew tied it to his belt. "Will you need a bottle of water?" she asked.

"No, ma'am." Tom answered. "There's streams."

Matthew slipped the shoulder strap of his musket over his shoulder and faced Tom. "Let's go."

Margaret gently took him by the arm and looked up into his face, her eyes filled with a sadness, and wonder. "It's all come too fast," she said thoughtfully. "Henry arrested, the British, and now both you and John going to war." She shook her head. "I never thought of you and John going to war." She paused, and Matthew saw the flat look in her eyes. "I don't know if I'll ever see either of you alive again."

She did not weep. The feeling in her heart was beyond tears. Without warning, her warm, safe nest, the center of her life, her reason for living, was being wrenched into pieces. Her husband and best friend had gone in the night, carrying a musket to kill other men if he must or be killed. And now her firstborn, her beautiful, tall, obedient firstborn was walking out the door with a musket in his hand to shoot men or be shot. How could such dark and evil things rear their ugly heads so quickly and in a moment steal from her the very foundations of her life? What law of heaven had she offended that brought such soul-destroying punishment down on her head? How had she provoked God that he would allow it to happen?

She slipped her arms about Matthew and for long moments held him close, feeling the warmth and the life and the strength of him, and savoring the smell of him, and remembering countless little things in his life that are precious only to a mother.

She released him and stepped back. "God bless you and bring you home, son."

"I'll be back," he replied, with the blind innocence that hides from all youth any hint of their own mortality.

"Take care of him," she said to Tom.

"I'll try, ma'am. I surely will."

She watched as the two men walked out the door, into the night. She walked out into the chill east breeze and stood in the irregular rectangle of light with her robe wrapped tightly about her and stared after them for long seconds after they disappeared. Then she walked back into the house and closed the door and dropped the heavy oak bar into the brackets, and started at the soft sound of slippers on the hard polished floor from behind. "Brigitte! What are you doing up?"

Brigitte stood at the archway in her nightclothes, arms at her sides, frowning, suspicious. "Couldn't sleep. Where're Father and Matthew?"

Margaret heaved a sigh. "Sit down at the table."

A few moments passed while Brigitte sat rigid at the side of the table, Margaret next to her in John's big chair at the end. Margaret leaned forward on her elbows facing her, arranging her thoughts. "Your father has gone to Concord, and Tom Sievers and Matthew followed."

Brigitte's eyes widened and a shadow passed over her face. "Why?"

"The British have moved hundreds of troops across the Back Bay."

Brigitte gasped. "To do what?"

"No one knows."

"Which troops did the British send? the marines?"

Margaret slowly straightened in her chair, forehead drawn down in puzzlement. "Why do you ask that question?"

There was alarm in Brigitte's voice. "I want to know. Did they?"

"I don't know. I suppose so. But that's not the worst of it."

Brigitte waited.

"They found out that Henry Thorpe is the one who has been informing Gage. He's been arrested. Kathleen closed the door against Mathew."

Brigitte clenched both hands beneath her chin. "Henry

Thorpe!" Seconds passed while she neither moved nor spoke. Then she whispered, "Mother, that can't be true! I don't believe it."

"Enid Ferguson and a man named Ingersol were arrested along with him. They've both signed confessions and they include Henry."

Brigitte melted. Her shoulders slumped and then began to shake as silent tears fell. She raised her head. "Did Kathleen know? or Phoebe?"

"Of course not."

"Will he be hanged?"

Margaret shrugged. "He could be."

Brigitte sagged against the back of her chair. "Kathleen and Phoebe. The poor children! How is Matthew?" She stopped, unable to find words.

"Heartbroken."

"She just turned him away?"

"She's trying to protect him."

"From what?"

"Disgrace."

"Does Matthew care about disgrace?"

"No. But what can he do about it if she does?" Margaret waited a few moments.

"We'll give it a little time, and then we'll go visit." She bowed her head for a moment, sick in her soul with thoughts of the bottomless abyss of black pain into which Kathleen and Phoebe had been plunged without warning.

She raised her head, eyes narrowed, calculating, suspicion growing. "When I told you our men had gone to Concord, you didn't ask about them. You asked about the British marines. Why?"

Brigitte recoiled and fumbled for words. "I was just . . . I . . . I don't know. I just asked."

Slowly Margaret shook her head. "No, not you. What was your reason?"

Brigitte's head slowly nodded forward and she buried her face in her arms on the table. With hot tears flowing, she sobbed, "Mama, I've done a wicked thing. I'm so sorry."

Margaret pursed her mouth and waited.

"I sneaked out of the house Monday night and I went to the church and I found the young lieutenant we saw Monday—the one at the church when we took the muskets. He knew my foot wasn't hurt, and I had to find out if he had told his superior that I had pretended and if that's why they invaded the church. I had to know. I had to!"

"What happened between you two?"

"Nothing. He hadn't reported me. I wasn't responsible for what they did to the church. When the colonel came over, Richard told him I was only looking for my family, and sent me home. Mama, he's honorable. He's fine and honorable!"

"Richard?"

"That's his name. Lieutenant Richard Arlen Buchanan. He's a marine."

"You've seen him twice, and he's fine and honorable?"

"Yes! I *know* it."

Margaret waited and said nothing, and watched the defensive light in Brigitte's eyes fade. Self-doubt crept into Brigitte's steady gaze, and her cheeks flushed as she stared into Margaret's eyes. She leaned forward and seized Margaret's arm. "Mama, what's wrong with me? I went up to the church at night, alone, in the dark, looking for a British soldier I've seen twice. What's happening?"

"Listen to yourself," Margaret said quietly, and waited.

"Listen to *myself*?"

"Yes. Why would a colonial girl go looking in the night for a British soldier she had seen twice?"

Brigitte's fingers bit into Margaret's arm, and she leaned forward and spoke with intensity. "Mama, it doesn't happen that way."

Margaret held her steady gaze, and a hint of a smile formed for a moment, but she said nothing, and waited.

"Well," Brigitte demanded, "isn't it true? It doesn't happen that way."

"Love happens on its own terms, and it can bring trouble."

Brigitte recoiled. The flush left her cheeks and her face turned white. She put both hands over her face and covered a sob. Margaret reached to hold her for a moment. The sobbing quieted, and Brigitte raised frightened eyes to Margaret's. "It's all wrong, Mama."

Margaret nodded. "A colonial girl and a British soldier? Probably. Love doesn't recognize uniform or country, but I doubt it will make any difference anyway."

Brigitte tensed. "Why?"

"I doubt you'll ever see him again."

Brigitte straightened, startled. "You think he'll be killed?"

Margaret held a steady gaze. "I meant that sooner or later he'll go back to England. No matter what happens, he will not be here very long."

Brigitte leaned forward. "You don't know that."

"I do, and so do you." Margaret could not mask the deep fear that was rising inside as she watched and listened to Brigitte. She spoke low, measuring every word. "Child, don't do this to yourself. He's an enemy soldier. You carried muskets to the church to fight him. Let it go. It can only break your heart."

Brigitte stood facing her mother with her feet spread slightly, eyes locked with Margaret's, struggling for control. Never had she disobeyed or been divided from her mother. Suddenly, for the first time in her life her self-confidence wavered and her thoughts fragmented. She groped for words that would not come and then bowed her head, and silent tears rolled down her cheeks.

Margaret felt the pain and gently held Brigitte until the trembling and the sobs and tears quieted. Brigitte pushed back and looked at her, and Margaret handed her a handkerchief. Brigitte wiped her tear-stained face while a sense of calmness settled on her, and she spoke quietly. "What am I going to do?"

Margaret was surprised by her own reply. "Wash your face and go to bed."

Brigitte stopped for a moment. "I mean about Richard."

Margaret let a moment pass in silence. "There's nothing you can do tonight, and tomorrow is a new day and it will look different in daylight. Wash your face and go to bed."

Brigitte shook her head but said nothing. Margaret slipped her arm about her waist and together they walked through the archway, down to Brigitte's bedroom, and Brigitte faced her mother. "And if I don't see it differently?"

Margaret's eyes dropped for a moment. "You will."

To the north, at the British military compound, Lieutenant Richard Arlen Buchanan lay in his bunk in the junior officers' quarters, lost in turmoil, staring vacantly at the ceiling in the darkness. The sounds of sleeping soldiers went unnoticed. The light of a nearly full moon turned the drawn window blinds a dull gray and faintly defined objects in the large, sparse room.

Brigitte Dunson. Brigitte Dunson. The name ran through his brain out of control. Blue eyes. He closed his eyes and her face was there and he studied it. He saw her as he had seen her last, standing in the dark street at the church, proud, defiant, frightened. *She came back because she had to know I had not betrayed her. She had to know.*

He laid his hand across weary, tormented eyes in the darkness, and thoughts and remembrances came reaching from his past. Lichfield, the dirty little coal town in central England—his mother dead on his twelfth birthday—going to the mines with his father at fourteen—his stepmother with the mean eyes and the heavy hickory stick—his father dead the next year of miner's black lung—his stepmother claiming the ancient, crumbling family home—leave, get out—the freezing two-week walk north to Liverpool in January to find work on the shipping docks—no work to be found—starving—then one day the soldiers marching past the docks and in uniforms with muskets—young—following them—the lie about his age—signing the enlistment—a uniform—a bed—warm food every day—pay—not enough but more than he had ever known—and then the drunken private asleep on graveyard guard duty at the ordnance depot—the fire— the explosion that shook the entire garrison and blasted windows out of his barracks—the sprint in his stocking feet and pants to the fire—knocked off his feet by the second blast—into the inferno with ordnance exploding all around—there's one—onto his shoulder and outside to drop the limp body out of harm's way—back into the inferno three more times—three more burned, semi-conscious bodies—the last with the braid of a major on his shoulders—the third blast that levelled the depot—the red-hot metal hitting, burning a dozen places—the cut to the bone above his eye, in his eyebrow—unconscious—waking in the hospital—the colonel beside his bed—the commendation for conspicuous bravery—the order to appear before the brigadier—the rare invitation to enter officers' training—the four years of rising above his beginnings—receiving his officer's commission.

He swung his feet to the hard, cold floor and sat up, hunched forward, hands on his knees, staring at the floor in the murky twilight.

Orders to sail for the colonies—the preparations for war that could be coming—assigned to Percy's cannon—the rising tension with the colonials—Brigitte Dunson and the smuggled muskets—the church desecrated in the search—Brigitte returning to the church at night. And in his mind he saw her again.

Once again the wondrous feeling welled up inside, and then he felt the cold perspiration forming on his forehead as the agony came hot.

A colonial girl—a British officer—it can never be—it can never be. How did it happen? Why did it happen? Why, why? Where's the answer?

He sat thus for a long time, and then he lay back down on his bunk, pulled his blanket up, and lay staring into the dark void until heavy weariness came and his eyes closed to troubled sleep.

CHAPTER X

★ ★ ★

*T*he two mounted men appeared as by magic in the one o'clock A.M. moonlight, and in the instant of seeing them Revere saw the crossed belts on their chests. He hauled back too hard on the reins of his running mare, and she dropped her hindquarters nearly to the dirt of the crooked road and slid to a stiff-legged stop, throwing her head high against the bite of the bit.

"Halt!" came the shouted order from the British officers.

Revere jerked the mare around and jammed both spurs into her flanks and raised her to a stampede gait heading northeast, retreating from Cambridge, back towards the fork in the road near the Mystic River.

The blue-caped British officers slammed their spurred boot heels into their horses' ribs and kicked them to a headlong run in the moonlight, into the dust left hanging in the air by the pounding hooves of Revere's mare. For more than half a mile they held their reckless pace, watching the faint image of horse and rider ahead of them slowly begin to pull away.

Revere looked back over his shoulder, then straightened in his saddle. *Eight hundred more yards,* he thought, *just eight hundred more yards.* He rode easy in the saddle, feeling the power in the thrust of the haunches and the smooth reach and gather of the forelegs of the mare, and he knew they would not catch him.

Four hundred more yards. He stood in the stirrups, searching for the hard turn to the east in the road, followed by a second hard turn back north, around the oozing muck of the natural clay pits. And then it was there. He reined the mare in to make the turn as he swept past the pits and the thick, rank smell. Thirty yards farther he made the second abrupt turn back north, towards the river, and once again he twisted in the saddle to watch. He held his breath as the two officers came hurtling into the east turn.

"Take the shortcut, take the shortcut," he breathed to himself, and set his teeth to watch. The charging officers separated, one leaving the roadbed at the east turn to charge straight north, cutting across what in the moonlight appeared to be smooth, open ground, directly towards Revere. Revere slowed his horse to watch. The officer held his wild pace for thirty feet before his horse plowed into the thick, sticky clay up to its belly. It sucked the horse down, floundering, and the officer pitched headlong over its head into the slime. The terrified horse turned back, buck jumping, churning, reaching for solid footing, and its hooves struck bottom and it dragged itself out, while the officer shouted and cursed, battling to get the ooze out of his eyes. It was up to his shoulders before he spread his arms to keep from sinking, and began working his way back towards his horse, which stood trembling, covered with the sticky muck. The officer on the road reined in his stamping, winded mount for a moment to watch aghast until his slime-covered companion staggered from the clay pit to slump on the ground, finished. Then he spun his horse and once again kicked it to a high run, straining to see Revere ahead.

Revere allowed himself one wry smile at the sight before he turned his horse and raised her to a steady, ground-eating run and watched her distance the pursuing officer. He turned at the fork, and one mile later pulled the mare to a stop and dismounted to watch and listen while she caught her wind. There was no further sign of pursuit. He remounted and passed Prospect Hill to his left, then climbed the gentle incline of Winter Hill and followed the road north towards Mystic, riding easy, listening, watching for anything that moved. He stopped at Maughan's inn on the right side of the road approaching Mystic, and leaned from the saddle to bang on the door.

"The regulars are on the move to Concord!"

Owen Maughan bobbed his head and watched for a moment as Revere spurred the mare to a run on into Mystic. He slammed the door and pivoted and ran to his bedroom for his clothes and his musket.

The hammering of the iron horseshoes on the Mystic cobblestones sounded loud in the darkness as Revere held the mare to a run into town, where he pounded on the door of the captain of the militia.

"The regulars—coming to Concord!"

Lights began to glow behind drawn shades. Second-story windows opened and heads appeared as Revere rode on, clattering on the cobblestones. At the Mystic common he suddenly tensed and leaned forward, peering into the darkness at a mounted rider facing him, and he jammed his spurs home and reined the running mare straight at the rider. If it was a British soldier, he intended running over the top of him.

From forty feet he saw the three-cornered hat and pulled the mare down.

"Who are you and what's your business?" he challenged.

"Martin Herrick. Medical student under Doctor Tufts."

"From where?"

"South Reading."

"Are you loyal to the crown?"

"To the colonies. I heard the regulars are coming."

"Will you a carry the word north?"

"I will."

"They're marching for Lexington and Concord. Rouse the militia."

"I will. I can pass through Stoneham and South Reading."

"Do it. Watch for British patrols. They're out tonight."

"I will. Who are you?"

"Revere. Paul Revere. Boston."

"I'll tell them." Young Herrick spun his horse, and Revere watched and listened as Herrick pounded off into the night before he once again raised his mare to a run, due east, on the road to Menotomy. The nearly full moon was now directly overhead, and the easterly breeze settled and died, and Revere was running free in the moonlight. To his left, in the distance, he could see the thin silver thread that was the Mystic River, and there were no British patrols as he held the mare to her steady run.

He crossed a bridge over a brook leading to the Mystic River and saw the moonlight reflecting off the lakes to his right where the road angled southwest. He slowed as he approached the junction with the Boston Road, and reined the mare into the yard of Cooper's tavern, where he leaned from the saddle to hammer on the front door.

"The regulars are marching for Concord!"

Benjamin Cooper walked outside in his nightshirt to watch Revere gallop on northwest into Menotomy, soon lost in the night. As he galloped through town, he reined in the mare eight times to lean from the saddle and pound on doors. At the far end of town he once more let her out to a lope, holding her in, feeling for the first time a raggedness in her breathing and a slight break in the rhythm of her stride.

The whirr of the ball and the muzzle flash from the trees near the road came in the same instant and then the pop of the musket, and Revere flinched and then leaned low over the neck of the mare and kicked her to a hard gallop. He held the pace for more than half a mile before he reined into a thicket of low oaks seventy yards from the road and waited, listening while the horse battled for breath. Slowly the mare's breathing settled, and there was no sound from behind, no pursuit. He mounted and once again continued west towards Lexington.

Six hundred yards from the place where the Lexington and Bedford Roads joined, forming the junction around which the town of Lexington had grown, Revere pulled the mare to a halt and studied the road ahead and the town.

If they intend stopping the road traffic, they'll do it either here or just this side of Concord. He stared at the ground while he considered. *I have no time to waste finding out which.*

He set the horse at a steady lope, standing tall in the stirrups, watching everything ahead for movement in the shadows, but none came. He reined in at the junction of the Bedford Road and banged on the door of Buckman's tavern. A light flickered on in the first-floor bedroom window, and Ruth Buckman opened it and leaned out, a lantern in her hand, digging sleep from her eyes.

"Who are you?" she called to him.

"Paul Revere. Boston. The regulars are marching to Concord. Tell your husband to spread the word."

The window closed and the lights came on in the tavern as Revere crossed the road to the huge two-and-one-half-story meetinghouse, with the belfry built just to the northwest, its spire pointed into the heavens. He stopped at the home of John Parker, captain of the Lexington militia, near the southwest corner of the town. Big, rawboned, with broad, plain features and a booming voice that rang with authority and command, Parker answered Revere's pounding with a lantern in his hand. His hair was messed and his nightshirt was open at the neck.

"Who's there?"

"Revere. The regulars are on the road, coming here now."

Fair, fearless, tough, Parker bellowed, "You sure?"

"I watched them cross the Back Bay at Boston."

"You seen Warren?"

"He sent me."

"What message?"

"Get ready, but don't start a fight. Protect the town if they start something, but do not provoke them. Under any circumstance, do not fire a shot unless they fire first. Send word on up to Bedford."

"I will. When will the regulars get here?"

"I don't know. Maybe an hour, maybe later in the morning. Depends on what trouble they've had."

"Do you know how they're armed?"

"Grenadiers and marines with muskets. Maybe a few cannon."

"I'll be ready!" Parker exclaimed.

"Are Adams and Hancock still up at Clarke's?"

"Yes."

Revere nodded and turned the weary mare and once more raised her to a lope. He made his way up the Bedford Road, and reined the horse into the yard of the Reverend Jonas Clarke and dismounted. He patted the mare's hot neck. "Good girl," he said to her quietly. He tied her by the front door and banged with his fist. Lights came on inside the house and he waited and knocked again. Cautiously the front door opened and the voice of Sergeant William Munroe spoke through the crack.

"Who's there?"

"Paul Revere."

Munroe threw the door open. "Come on in!"

Revere stared at him. "What are you doing here?" He squinted about the room while his eyes adjusted to the sudden light, and he counted eight more armed men.

"I heard the regulars were moving and we came to guard Adams and Hancock if they intended coming here."

"They're behind me, but they're coming. We've got to get Adams and Hancock out of here."

From the back section of the house came Hancock's booming voice. "Revere, is that you? Come on back here. We're not afraid of *you.*"

Dorothy Quincy, Hancock's fiancée, led Revere back to the kitchen, where Adams and Hancock rose from the table to greet him.

"How far behind?"

"I don't know. More than an hour, at least."

Hancock paced and ran his fingers through his hair. "By the Eternal, I'm going to fight. I'm going with the militia. I'll get my musket."

"No such thing," Adams cut in. "That's exactly what Gage hopes you'll do."

"Forget Gage! Those devils think they're going to come in the night, terrorizing the countryside, taking what they want! No, I'll fight."

Revere interrupted. "Warren wants you and Adams to let the militia do the fighting. Anyone can carry a musket. We have only one John Hancock and one Sam Adams."

Hancock glanced at Revere with hot eyes. "We'll see about that."

Adams suddenly raised his hand to quiet everyone, and in the silence they heard the roll of distant drums. "That's Parker's drummers calling the militia," Adams said.

"I told him on the way here," Revere answered.

Again Adams raised a hand and the sound of a running horse became louder and stopped at the front door, and in an instant came incessant banging.

Munroe quickly opened the door a crack and challenged the intruder. "Dawes!" he exclaimed and opened the door.

Dawes walked in, breathing heavy from his run. He stopped short at the sight of the room filled with men and then he saw Revere. "You made it!"

Revere's shoulders slumped with relief. "I see you did too."

Dawes looked at the armed men. "Who are these men?"

"Militia here to protect Adams and Hancock."

"Good." Dawes looked at Adams. "Are you ready to leave?"

"Yes, but Hancock's being stubborn."

Dawes took a step towards Hancock. "Sir, we need you. You better move on out farther into the country."

"I don't think so." Hancock shook his head and would say no more.

Dawes shrugged and turned back to Revere. "Parker's gathering his militia down on the Green. We better go on down and talk to them."

Revere looked at Adams. "We've got to get on to Concord. Persuade Hancock, and leave before the regulars come."

Remounted in the dooryard, Revere and Dawes stopped for a

moment to look at the gathering that stood in the large, irregular rectangle of light that shined through the door onto the ground. They raised their hands to a salute, and Adams and Hancock, the militiamen, and Dorothy Quincy raised their hands to wave them off. They turned their horses and loped them south back down the Bedford road towards the lights that were shining in Lexington.

On the Green, west of the big meetinghouse, Parker had 130 of his men in rank and file, muskets over their shoulders, waiting, when Revere and Dawes rode up and dismounted.

"We're ready," Parker growled. "Where are the regulars?"

"They'll be here. Maybe late."

Impatient, Parker shook his head. "We can't wait all night."

"We've got to move on to Concord," Revere responded.

"I'm going to send out a patrol and see if they're coming," Parker said.

"Stay alert. Remember Warren's orders. Get word to Bedford."

"It's on the way."

"Good luck."

Revere and Dawes rode back to the road and again turned west, towards Concord.

"Any trouble?" Dawes queried as they rode side by side.

"I left one British officer in the clay pits. Someone shot at me near Mystic."

"Militia or regulars?"

"Don't know. I only saw the gun flash and heard the ball come past. How about you?"

"I was stopped at the barricade. They let me pass."

"A lot of them are out tonight. I expect we'll yet meet some of them."

His words were barely spoken when suddenly Revere reined in his mare and Dawes stopped, eyes darting, searching for what Revere had seen. Revere spun the mare and stood in the stirrups, peering back towards Lexington. Dawes started to speak and Revere stopped him and cocked an ear and concentrated. His arm jerked up and he pointed.

One hundred yards back Dawes saw the dark shape of a rider coming, and then he heard the hoofbeats and Revere pointed to the side of the road and they split, Revere going east, Dawes west, to hide and wait. At twenty yards they saw the three-cornered hat, and Revere spurred the mare back onto the road and the rider pulled his winded horse to a stop.

"Who are you and what's your business?" Revere called.

"Doctor Samuel Prescott. I was in Lexington visiting my fiancée. I'm going home to Concord. Who are you?"

"Paul Revere and William Dawes of Boston. Have you seen any regulars tonight?"

"No, but I saw the militia on the Green in Lexington. A British patrol came through earlier. They're somewhere ahead."

"Are you loyal to the Crown?"

"No. Massachusetts. I'm returning home to get ready for the regulars."

"Do you know the road and the people?"

"Yes. Well."

"We're headed for Concord to give the alarm. Will you ride with us?"

"Yes."

The three of them continued west, and Revere reined off the road to a farmhouse, where he banged on the door and gave the alarm before he returned to the road and caught up with the others.

"Huddleston lives there," Prescott said, pointing, and rode to the house to give the alarm.

They continued west, Prescott pointing out the homes and calling out the names. "Fiske lives there, Whittemore there, Mansfield on up there," he said, pointing to opposite sides of the road. Prescott reined left, Dawes right, to dark homes, and Revere loped on up the road towards the next one.

It happened fast. Revere saw two riders coming straight at him at a full gallop and knew his mare had little left to give. He stood in the stirrups and shouted, "Come on, Lexington men, here are two we can take!" He spurred forward, playing out his bluff, but it was not to be. Within two seconds two more appeared, and then two more, and Revere twisted in his saddle to shout a warning to Dawes and Prescott to escape, but they were coming at a run and in three seconds pulled to a stop in a cloud of dust beside him.

The six British officers surrounded them with cocked pistols. For a moment the three sat working the reins to hold their nervous horses, groping to understand they had been captured.

One officer pointed his pistol to the side of the road. "Get over those bars, out into that field." The top three rails of a split-rail fence had been thrown down, leaving but the lowest one. Two officers led, followed by Prescott, then Dawes, and Revere last, their horses stepping over the low rail and out into the field. The other four soldiers followed, and ten yards into the field they all stopped.

The officer who had given the orders again started to speak. "Who—"

He got no further.

Prescott shouted, "Break for it!" and instantly jerked his horse to the left and drove his spurs home, and the horse leaped to a stampede gait in two jumps. Revere jerked his mare to the right and drove hard for a thicket of trees one hundred yards ahead. Dawes spun his horse completely around and the gelding cleared the low bar at the edge of the field, and Dawes headed back for Lexington at a full-out gallop.

The British soldiers split, two following each man as hard as their horses would run.

Prescott slowed his horse only long enough to drop into a dry creekbed known to him but not the two hot behind him, and angled west up the creekbed for Concord. The two behind him overran the creekbed and had to turn back. They jumped their frightened mounts into it and spurred after Prescott, shouting, "Halt!" Prescott held his horse at a run until he approached a bridge that was high enough to allow a horse beneath it but not a rider, and he slowed, spurred the horse up the bank, around the bridge, and headed on, away from the creekbed, beside a stone fence, and through an orchard, and then hauled the winded horse to a stop. He tied the horse to a tree and ran back ten yards and hunched low to listen.

Behind him the two soldiers had run their horses pell-mell up the creekbed, but not knowing the bridge lay ahead, they had seen it too late in the dark. They jerked back too hard on their reins, and the horses reared and threw both before they stampeded on beneath the bridge, riderless.

There was no pursuit. Prescott remounted and galloped to the door of the orchard owner, Samuel Hartwell, a sergeant in the Lincoln minutemen, under Captain Smith. Hartwell's cousin John lived at the next farm.

"The regulars are on the way. Get word to Lincoln. I'm going on to Concord."

While Prescott rode on to Concord, Hartwell left his barn, mounted on his own sorrel gelding, headed for Lincoln.

Behind Prescott, on the road back to Lexington, Dawes felt his horse begin to labor, and then the rhythm of the driving hooves began to break and Dawes knew he had a horse ready to drop. He twisted to look, and the two soldiers were less than one hundred yards behind, pistols drawn, closing on him rapidly. Fifty yards ahead was the Huddleston home they had aroused but twenty minutes earlier. He spurred his horse forward and at the last instant reined the jaded animal into the yard, with the soldiers less than sixty yards behind.

He hauled back hard and brought the horse to a sliding stop and leaped from the saddle, stumbling, falling, rolling back onto his feet. At the top of his lungs he shouted, "I've got two of them, boys, surround them!"

The house lights were on. There was a light in the barn. The two soldiers took one look, and whatever they thought, whatever they believed, they instantly spun their horses and ripped out of the dooryard back onto the road and headed back towards Concord at a high run, never looking back.

Huddleston opened his front door and looked. He saw a sweating, jaded horse with a man standing beside it. Then the man slowly sat down in the dust of the yard, and Huddleston saw his shoulders start to shake and then he heard the chuckle and then the laugh.

Back to the west, in the field where the three messengers had made their break for freedom, Revere held his horse at a gallop, headed for the black skyline of a gentle rise covered with oak and maple where he intended turning the horse loose and hiding on foot. He had no way of knowing he was running straight for the one place where six more officers lay in ambush. Twenty yards from the woods they charged towards him, and before he could stop or turn they had his bridle reins and two of them had cocked pistols four feet from his head.

"Dismount!" one of them ordered. "We'll teach another rebel a lesson!"

"Traitors!" another exclaimed. "All of them! Let's shoot this bloody traitor here and now and be done with it!"

They dismounted and jerked Revere roughly from his horse.

"What's your name, g'vnor, so we'll get it right on your tombstone."

One grabbed his coat and jerked it open, searching for weapons. "'E's got no pistol."

"Didja see a knife? These bloody colonials are no better than Indians."

Revere remained silent and did not raise a hand in his own defense.

"Easy, gentlemen," another officer interrupted. "We don't yet know why this man was on the road. Perhaps he's harmless." He faced Revere. "We're out here under orders to look for some deserters from the Twenty-third Regiment. We've been surprised at the traffic on this road. What is your name, sir?"

Revere looked at him, and at the others, and made his decision. "Paul Revere."

"I've heard the name. From Boston?"

"Yes, sir."

"You're with the colonials?"

"Yes, sir, I am."

"What's your business on this road at night?"

Revere took a deep breath. "I know full well what you and your soldiers are doing on this road tonight, and it doesn't concern deserters. It concerns Colonel Francis Smith and eight hundred of your grenadiers and marines marching to Concord. You're out here to intercept anyone carrying the news, and that, sir, is what I was doing. I've already put out the word to every town within thirty miles of Lexington."

The officer's mouth dropped open and they all fell into a stunned silence.

Revere waited for a response but they could make none.

"And that isn't all of it, sir," Revere continued, his voice firm. "I have—"

At that moment, to the east, on the Lexington Green, Captain John Parker shook his head in impatient disgust and he bellowed his orders to his militiamen, who had been standing in rank and file with loaded muskets for more than an hour, waiting for the red-coated army which had not appeared.

"The regulars are nowhere near," Parker shouted. "All of you, go on home and wait. I'll sound recall when they get here. Dismissed. Go on home."

"Our muskets are loaded, sir," Sergeant Fowler responded. "Shall we discharge them?" It was close to impossible to dig the ball out of a musket barrel, once it was seated on a patch, and none of the men fancied carrying loaded muskets about on the Green through the night.

"Yes," Parker answered, "fire your muskets into the ground to unload them."

One hundred thirty men pointed their long-barreled muskets into the ground and pulled the triggers, and the muskets blasted like thunder in the night. The sound rolled out from the Green and carried for miles, and it reached the woods where Revere was facing his captors. Every man among them recognized the sound of a musket volley.

Revere continued. "I have five hundred men within two miles of here, riding this way to meet your regulars when they get to Concord. They'll be here within minutes. You have two choices. Run, or be captured."

The officer snapped his gaping mouth shut. "Get Major Mitchell."

A second officer sprinted away, and returned in a moment with Major Edward Mitchell.

"Sir, this man says he has spread the word about Colonel Smith to every militiaman within fifty miles of here. Did you hear the volley just a moment ago?"

"I did."

"He says six or seven hundred of the militia are headed this way at this moment."

"Who is this man?" Mitchell walked to Revere. "What's your name?"

"Paul Revere, of Boston."

"Revere! You caught Revere?" He stared at the captain in the moonlight, then turned back to Revere. "You've been out gathering the militia?"

"I have, sir."

"You say several hundred are headed this way now?"

"They are. I expect that volley we just heard was their first, at a British patrol like yours."

Mitchell's mouth became a straight line as he considered the implications.

"And that's not all, sir," Revere continued. "I should also tell you that twenty-one of your longboats ran aground in the Lechmere marshes before they ever got your grenadiers ashore. I have no knowledge as to how many of your men were lost, or how much of your supplies are at the bottom of the bog right now." He held a stone face, waiting to see if his bluff would work.

Mitchell turned to two lieutenants. "Keep your pistols on this man. If he moves, shoot him." He gathered the other officers around, ten yards away, and they huddled.

"That volley—it couldn't have been our troops," he said quietly. "It was less than two miles from here. It had to be theirs. Maybe he's telling the truth. If he is, we had better not be caught here with Paul Revere as a prisoner."

"Agreed."

Mitchell walked back to Revere and gave orders. "Sergeant, trade horses with this man, and get the other prisoners and cut the saddle girths and bridles and stirrup leathers on all their horses and turn them loose, including Revere. Release all the prisoners and get the patrol mounted. We're leaving."

Four more prisoners were led from the trees, and Revere stared, unaware they had even been there. He recognized only one of them, Solomon Brown, who had been sent earlier by Hancock to scout the road. Revere watched as the sergeant hastily cut the saddle cinch and the stirrup leaders and bridles on the five horses, and then mounted Revere's big bay mare. Three minutes later the hoofbeats of the British patrol faded to the east, and Revere and the four prisoners were left alone in the silence with horses they could not ride.

"Go on to Concord and get with the militia," Revere told the others, while he turned and set off at a trot eastward, back towards Lexington.

The nearly full moon had set and the eastern sky was turning from black to deep purple when Revere again banged on the door of the Reverend Jonas Clarke and waited until the door opened.

"Revere! What happened?"

They all gathered in the parlor while Revere explained. Then Revere turned resolutely to Hancock, who had stormed about the house like a caged lion half the night, and spent an hour cleaning his musket and pistol and packing his bullet pouch and powder horn for the fight.

"The roads are alive with regulars. If they get the munitions at

Concord, and you and Adams besides, we've lost. Go north with Adams, away from here."

Hancock slammed his fist down on the table and lunged to his feet. "I hate it. You're right, but I hate it." By force of will he stopped and gathered himself. "All right, I'll go, but only the Eternal knows how I need to get into this fight."

Notes

While on his famous ride on the night of April 18, 1775, Paul Revere was confronted by two British officers before reaching the town of Mystic. One of the officers did attempt to cut cross-country to intercept Revere, and mired himself and his horse in a clay bog. Revere outran the other officer on the splendid mare loaned to him by John Larkin. (See French, *The Day of Concord and Lexington*, p. 89; Fischer, *Paul Revere's Ride*, pp. 107–8.)

During the ride, Revere did happen onto a young patriot named Martin Herrick and another named Samuel Prescott, both of whom joined Dawes and Revere in spreading the message. Following the visit of Dawes and Revere to the home of the Reverend Jonas Clarke, Revere, Dawes, and Prescott were captured. However, in a daring break for freedom, Dawes and Prescott escaped, while Revere was captured again immediately but released when he bluffed the British officers into believing the militia was on its way and they would be captured. (See French, *The Day of Concord and Lexington*, chapter 10.)

Wednesday, April 19, 1775

CHAPTER XI

★ ★ ★

*J*ohn Dunson silently eased down the overhang of the bank of the Mystic River, west of Menotomy where Alewife Brook joined, and slowly settled into the water to his neck. The rings rippled out into the river current and disappeared. He clamped his teeth at the bite of the cold water and then moved against the grass and willows and cattails on the overhang, making no ripples, no sound, and he stood rigid, holding his musket and powder horn above his head.

The high-pitched voice came from above and behind him, past the overhang. "The bloody colonial was right 'ere, 'e was," called a grenadier. "I seen 'im plain, I did, 'im and his musket, sneakin' in the moonlight!"

"Then find him!" barked an officer.

"Maybe 'e's in the water by now, workin' downstream."

The officer's voice rang. "Deevers, take your squad downstream one hundred yards and wade out. If anything appears, shoot to kill."

John heard the pounding of feet fading as six grenadiers ran north, and then the thrashing continued as twenty-two others tromped the riverbank, ramming their bayonets into the willows and cattails and underbrush thick on the riverbank. He heard the officer dismount and then the unmistakable sound of his sword ripping through the growth as he hacked it down.

John breathed shallow through his open mouth, making no

sound. He kept his head tipped forward to prevent moonlight from reflecting off his face, and he kept his eyes on the water. He saw the moon-cast shadow of a regular on the water directly in front of him and knew the man was standing less than three feet directly above his head. He shifted one foot, getting braced to push off into the current underwater if the man raised the alarm. He heard a bayonet clang on a stone directly above, and then the blade rammed downward four inches from the front brim of his hat. He watched the blade jerk back and he braced for the next thrust. It missed his left shoulder by a foot, and then the grenadier moved on, jabbing the undergrowth, tromping his way north.

The thrashing and cursing continued, and John felt the muscles in his legs and arms begin to stiffen in the cold water and then to cramp, and still he stood motionless.

In his mind he saw Tom Sievers twenty-two years earlier, hiding beneath an overhang in an unnamed river far to the north in a bitter cold January, while eight Huron warriors tried for two hours to flush him. Separated from Tom earlier in the raid, John had circled back and spent half an hour watching before he understood what they were doing. He shot one of them at two hundred yards, and the other seven came jumping, howling after him. He led them away from Tom and lost them when full darkness came on a moonless night. The cramps from the icy water did not leave Tom's legs for two days.

John moved his legs slightly in the water, then his arms, and then remained motionless.

Long moments passed before the officer barked his next order. "We've lost this one. Tompkins, go get Deevers and meet us back at the road. The road's full of them tonight."

John heard the thumping boots and the jangle of Tompkins's canteen and powder horn and bullet pouch as he ran north to get Deevers.

"Sergeant," the officer continued, "reassemble the men immediately and march them back to the road. I'll be waiting there." The sound of the running horse faded as the sergeant bawled his orders. The men fell into rank and file, and he called the cadence as he marched them back to the road to Menotomy.

John waited until the only sound was the quiet murmur of the river before he worked his way upstream twenty feet and up onto the bank. He quickly squeezed the water from his moccasins and picked up his musket and started east, away from the dark line of willows that marked the river. His soaked clothing caught the chill night air, and John shivered as he began the ground-eating trot that Tom had taught him so long ago, with the peculiar slight side-to-side sway familiar to men who have learned to cover long distances.

He slowed atop the gentle groundswell east of town and stopped, counting too many lights, sensing something had happened. He hunched forward and followed a stone fence, bent low, invisible, and came quartering in on the rear of Cooper's tavern, where lights glowed inside behind drawn curtains. He stopped at the front door and listened. There was sound inside but no voices. He rapped quietly.

"Who's there?" It was a woman's voice.

"John Dunson from Boston."

The door opened a crack. "Are you with the militia?"

"I'm joining them in Concord. What's happened here tonight?"

The door opened. "Paul Revere came through and said the regulars are coming. My husband's gone north to spread the warning."

"Have the soldiers been here?"

"Not yet."

"Thank you. I'll move on." The woman followed him out into the night and watched until he was out of sight.

He trotted across the road and on through the town, where lights glowed in every house. Near the church he was challenged by militia before they saw his hat and his musket, and he continued on west. One hundred yards past town he climbed a stone fence and resumed his pace west through open fields, never more than fifty yards from the road. Twice he saw British patrols and dropped to the ground to watch them pass on the road before he continued working his way through the greening fields, head turning constantly to catch any movement in the waning moonlight. His thoughts went back, and he let them run their own direction as he went.

That woman came out to watch me go to war—as she watched her husband—as Margaret watched. Women bear sons and sons leave them to go to war—what causes war? They start in someone's heart—change human hearts—that's the answer. Too hard to change hearts—we push it away—too hard—easier to kill each other than change our hearts—Christ tried to teach us—crucified him—easier to crucify him than change—how many times have we crucified him since? ten thousand? ten million?

The snort and stamp of the horse and the shout from the Lexington Road came in the same instant, and John dropped to the ground like a stone as he heard the voice in the dark.

"There's somethin' movin' out in that field, sir. Looks like a bloody colonial t' me, sneakin' to Lexington."

John sucked air and took off his hat and raised his head far enough to see the patrol on the road, twenty-five yards away. Six mounted men and two officers, all standing stock-still, studying the field where he lay. Desperately he peered into the waning moonlight, looking for a ditch, a rise, trees—anything for cover if he had to run. He held his position and watched, and waited for the officer to give orders.

The officer said, "Move on! I see nothing out there. We've got to get back to warn Colonel Smith."

John's shoulders slumped and he exhaled slowly as he watched them raise their horses to a canter eastward, and he waited until they were gone before he rose.

Fool! Daydreaming with British patrols swarming. I do that again and I'll find out soon enough about changing human hearts. The dead don't have a human heart to change! He shook his head in disgust and once again picked up his pace west.

He crested the rise north of Munroe's tavern and saw the

lights of Lexington. He returned to the road to cross the west bridge and came into town facing the meetinghouse that blocked the view of the big green common. Lights glowed in every house, every building, and militia were in the streets with muskets.

"Where can I find Captain John Parker?"

"Buckman's tavern waiting for the regulars."

The cavernous room in the tavern was crowded with militia, some sleeping on the floor, muskets leaned against the walls. John's eyes adjusted to the light as he made his way to Parker.

"I'm John Dunson from Boston. Has Revere been here?"

"Him and Dawes. They said the soldiers are coming, but we haven't seen a sign of them yet."

"They'll be here."

"We'll be ready."

"Are Adams and Hancock safe?"

"They're up at the Reverend Mr. Clarke's home with nine men on guard."

"Thanks."

"Going up to see them?"

"No, I'm headed for Concord."

In dawn's earliest gray light John made the turn on the groundswell at Meriam's Corner, and he paused in startled disbelief as he stared down at Concord. Every road north, west, and south was jammed with carts and wagons moving away from Concord, loaded with gunpowder, cannonballs, musket shot, muskets, medicines, dried fish, dried beef. Militia and colonials filled the cobblestone streets in Concord Town, carrying munitions and supplies from barns, attics, wells, sheds, stables, the church, and root cellars to more carts and wagons, or placing them on pack saddles strapped to horses and mules.

John trotted the half mile into town and worked his way through the bustling traffic to the first man who carried a musket.

"Where can I find Major Buttrick or Colonel Barrett?"

Lieutenant Frederick Mackenzie, Twenty-third Regiment,

Royal Welch Fusiliers, looked at the eastern skyline, where the beginnings of dawn separated the earth from the sky, and he cursed again under his breath.

His regiment had been in the first longboats to leave Boston and cross the Back Bay, to land at the Lechmere farm staging point and watch the longboats disappear back into the black water to shuttle the second contingent across. The chaos of matching officers with troops they had never seen before was compounded when the longboats returned and dumped another two hundred fifty confused regulars in the dark.

Colonel Francis Smith shouted his orders above the bedlam. "Tenth Regiment of light infantry will lead, with the remaining regiments following in numerical order."

"If that's the marching order 'e wanted, why didn't 'e 'ave us load up that way," came the murmuring from the regulars as they struggled in the dark to find where one regiment ended and the next began.

One hour and forty minutes later Smith rose in the stirrups of his horse at the head of the column, looked about for a moment, and then gave the order.

"Forrrard, march."

Thirty minutes later the entire column was bogged down in the backwater marshes of the Lechmere landing, where low tide had left tide pools and deep mud. For over an hour they carried their ten-pound muskets over their heads while they slogged through water and muck to their hips before they found a solid road and stopped. Covered with marsh mud to their chests, dripping, they once more cursed in the dark as they tried to regroup into the marching order while Mackenzie marveled at the lack of skill he was seeing in the officers. Forty minutes later Colonel Smith once again gave the order and the column moved on past Harvard College towards Cambridge.

It seemed the roads, fields, and woods were filled with either British patrols or colonials, and the column stopped again and again. On the fifth stop for no reason he could see, Mackenzie muttered, "Concord before daylight!" He shook his head. "It's nearly daylight now and we haven't yet made Lexington. Surprise the militia? Most likely they'll have a surprise for us." He shook his head again and marched on.

At the head of the column, Lieutenant Waldron Kelly turned his head to listen, then spoke to Colonel Smith. "There's someone coming at the gallop, sir."

Smith leaned forward in his saddle and peered into the gray darkness. "Challenge him, Lieutenant."

"Halt and identify yourself or be shot," Kelly shouted.

There was no response. Kelly turned to Sergeant Roscoe Wells. "Sergeant, prepare your squad to fire."

Wells and his squad raised their muskets to the ready. The sounds grew louder, and then they could see the shapes of men hunched low over the necks of running horses in the deceptive light. The sergeant and his squad cocked the big hammers on their muskets.

The shout came high above the sound of the pounding hooves, "Major Mitchell coming in," and the men uncocked their muskets and lowered them.

Mitchell's squad pulled their winded mounts to a stop in a cloud of dust, and Mitchell demanded, "Lieutenant, where is Colonel Smith?"

Kelly jerked a thumb over his shoulder. "Right there, sir."

Mitchell straightened in his saddle. "Beg your pardon, sir. I didn't recognize you in this light."

"Report."

"Sir, we've been west past Lexington as ordered. There are . . ." Mitchell hesitated at the sound of more horses nearly upon them at a run, and watched Major Pitcairn pull his mount to a stand-still, with its muzzle a scant four feet from Mitchell's mount, Lieutenant William Sutherland right behind.

"Colonel Smith," Pitcairn exclaimed, "what's wrong? I heard running horses."

"Mitchell was just reporting. Continue, Major."

Mitchell's voice was high, strained. "The whole countryside is aroused between here and Concord. More than five hundred militia have gathered at the Green in Lexington, and more are pouring in. We saw them moving on the ridges. They fired a volley. Sir, it is my estimate that we are facing numbers vastly larger than our column, and they're well armed."

"Are you certain?"

"Yes, sir. I saw them. And the volley they fired was at least two hundred muskets."

"Any casualties?"

"No, sir. It was dark."

Pitcairn twisted in his saddle to look at Sutherland. "Lieutenant, repeat what you told me half an hour ago."

Sutherland reined his horse in closer to Colonel Smith. "Sir, when the column was stopped to send out flankers, I scouted ahead with Lieutenant Adair and we met a colonial driving a load of wood. He said there were a thousand men at Concord ready to defend the town."

"Where is the man now?"

"Gone. But on our return Adair and I saw great numbers of colonials along the ridges and backroads, moving towards Concord."

Smith slumped in his saddle, staring at his hands while he considered. "Gentlemen, it appears we have some things to ponder. Pitcairn, keep the first six companies and flankers out and continue the march."

Pitcairn shouted the orders, and the six lead companies resumed the march. The long column, three abreast, followed the country road while Smith rode thoughtfully, feeling the loneliness of command as he weighed the information given by Mitchell and Sutherland.

He spurred his horse forward, beside Pitcairn. "Stop the column."

While Pitcairn gave the orders, Smith drew pencil and paper from his saddlebag and composed a brief note, sealed it, and once again called to Pitcairn. "I need a messenger."

Thirty seconds later Lieutenant Ambrose of the Twenty-third Royal Welch Fusiliers faced Smith.

"Take this back to General Gage in Boston. Don't spare your horse."

The young lieutenant stuffed the paper inside his red coat, spun his horse, and galloped east in a cloud of dust.

"May I ask, sir," Pitcairn said, "what was the message?"

Smith reflected for a moment. "I told Gage the numbers we're facing and asked him to send reinforcements. Resume the march."

Like a great, flowing river of red coats, the column moved west once more. The clouds on the eastern horizon were shot through with rose and gold by the sun, not yet risen. Smith rode beside the six lead companies, Pitcairn and Sutherland two hundred yards ahead, leading them.

Suddenly Smith straightened in his saddle and studied Sutherland. He had turned his horse back and was coming at a run, while Pitcairn had stopped the first three companies and they were loading their muskets.

Sutherland reined in beside Smith, breathing heavily. "Sir, Major Pitcairn thought you should know. There was a militiaman in the field to the right, up ahead, about fifty yards from the road. We saw him. He aimed his musket at me and pulled the trigger. It misfired, but he intended to shoot me, sir."

Smith reined his horse to a stop and Sutherland stopped beside him.

"Let me be certain of what you're saying," Smith said steadily. "A colonial militiaman aimed his musket at you and attempted to shoot you?"

"That is correct, sir."

"Did Pitcairn give the order to the first three companies to load their muskets?"

"He did, sir. In his opinion the colonials have assaulted his troops."

For a split second Smith considered, then spurred his horse forward at a lope and reined in beside Pitcairn. "Lexington is just ahead. Under any circumstance you are not to fire unless they do. I repeat, do not provoke a fight. If one comes, it must be on their shoulders, not ours."

"Sir, a colonial has already attempted to shoot at us."

"So Sutherland said. Give your troops my orders, just as I gave them to you."

"Yes, sir."

Pitcairn loped his horse to the captains and repeated the orders, which were then given to the regulars, while Smith waited. Pitcairn rode back and reported.

Smith drew and exhaled a tense breath. "Resume the march."

They moved onto the top of the rise in the road, cradled between two low hills, and started the slight descent into the town of Lexington.

The first arc of the sun had just cleared the eastern skyline.

"Down! Get down!"

Tom hissed the words, and Matthew plowed through the willows and cattails and dropped into the sand and stones of the dry streambed beside him and waited, listening. The sound of a running horse came louder from the west, and then a British officer raced past them, hunched low over the horse's neck, cape flying in the moonlight as he galloped east towards Menotomy.

"Messenger," Tom murmured, and stood. He listened a moment, tentative, waiting to see if others were following.

None were.

Tom climbed from the shallow, dry streambed and started east at a trot, Matthew following. They climbed the rock fence at the end of the field, jumped a small seep stream, and continued westward across another field with grain sprouts ten inches up.

"Wonder what the message was," Tom mused.

Matthew remained silent, following Tom blindly, without thought or question, not caring about direction. He saw only Kathleen as he had last seen her, face stained with tears, eyes filled with fear, pain. He heard nothing but her last words that rang in his ears like an unending chant—Go, Matthew, if you feel anything for me, go if you feel anything for me, go—over and over again. He felt the need to fold her inside his arms and hold her until she was all right. He remembered the feel of her arms about him and the smell of her as she clung to him and then looked into his face and said yes, she would marry him, and he ached to have that moment back once more.

But she was in Boston with her life shattered, and he was near Lexington in a spring wheat field in the night, carrying a musket to war, and nothing they had ever known would ever again be as it was. Matthew's brain was blank, unable to leave what had been, to accept what was now. He stumbled on behind Tom like a machine.

Tom stopped and stood upright. "Quiet," he said, and turned his head to catch sound coming on the west wind.

It was there, far in the distance. The unmistakable cadence of drums and the measured tread of hundreds of men marching. Tom glanced over his shoulder eastward, where the black earth met the deep purple of heaven in the first nudgings of dawn.

"They'll be in Lexington by sunup," he said, "and we'll be right behind them." Movement to his right caught his eye and he turned, crouched. On the skyline he saw a dozen men trotting west towards Lexington, and then he saw their three-cornered hats and for a moment a smile flickered.

"Come on," he said, and led on at his peculiar, swaying trot. Matthew followed without a word.

Six hundred yards later Tom angled south and stopped twenty yards short of the winding dirt road for a moment before he once again turned west and continued on towards Lexington. Lights shined in the windows of every farmhouse; people moved in every farmyard. To his left, on the Lexington Road, eight men rode by travelling west, muskets in their hands. Behind him a skiff of clouds caught the first rays of sun and turned the heavens into a great dome of rose and yellows that for a moment bathed the world in indescribable shades. He looked at the farmhouses and the green fields and the stone fences and oaks and maples and the spring flowers, and he slowed to feel the rare beauty and the power of the land seep into his soul.

A mile to his left he watched twenty men trot over the skyline towards Lexington, muskets in hand, and knew there was no longer reason to stay off the road. Four hundred yards farther he rounded a curve and crested a rise, and half a mile ahead they were there. He was looking at the rear echelons of the column of British regulars. Beyond the column lay the small town of Lexington, sparkling like a jewel in the morning sun.

Notes

The bungled crossing of the Back Bay by the British, getting mired in mud up to their chests, and their late start north towards Concord are all chronicled accurately (see French, *The Day of Concord and Lexington*, beginning at p. 100).

Lieutenant Colonel Francis Smith and Major John Pitcairn were both emphatic in their orders to the British troops that they were not to fire unless they were fired upon—in short, they were not to fire the first shot. However, as the British column neared Lexington, Pitcairn believed that a colonial lying in wait by the road had raised his musket and attempted to fire but that the weapon had misfired. Thus Pitcairn believed his command had been assaulted; whereupon he ordered them to prime and load. (See French, *The Day of Concord and Lexington*, pp. 103 and 105.)

Upon approaching Lexington, Lieutenant Colonel Smith was aware that the surrounding countryside was aroused against him, and therefore he selected a messenger, Lieutenant Ambrose of the Twenty-third Welch Fusiliers, to gallop back to Boston, requesting General Thomas Gage to send a support column to assist. This single act of requesting support was all that saved any of his men that day; otherwise not one of them would have returned to Boston that night. (See French, *The Day of Concord and Lexington*, p. 104.)

The names of the officers on both sides and the sequence of events as the day of April 19, 1775, began are accurate (see chapter 12 of French, *The Day of Concord and Lexington*).

Wednesday, April 19, 1775

CHAPTER XII

★ ★ ★

*T*hey're coming, they're coming!"
The distant shout and sound of a horse at stampede gait brought Captain John Parker to a standstill on the Lexington Green. He raised a hand to shade his eyes against the rising sun and squinted to make out the cloud of dust on the road. The dust became a man on a horse, waving his hat, kicking his mount at every stride.

The east road, from Menotomy to Lexington, passed between two low rises before it crossed Vine Brook and came straight on into the town. At town's edge, the road forked. The left fork led to Concord, the right fork to Bedford. In the V formed by the two roads lay the Lexington Green. Those who had seen it declared it to be the most beautiful green in Massachusetts. Deep grass ran for more than one hundred fifty yards. The big meetinghouse was close to where the roads forked, blocking the view of most of the Green from those approaching from Menotomy. Just to the left of the meetinghouse was the white belfry with its spire. Across the Bedford Road, facing the Green, was Buckman's tavern. The homes and farms and businesses that were Lexington surrounded the Green on both forks of the road. On the morning of April 19, 1775, the Green was a dazzling sea of yellow dandelions, sprung to blossom by the warm spring rains.

Captain Parker stood in the dandelions, across the road from Buckman's tavern, and studied the incoming rider intently, and suddenly dropped his hand. "That's Thad Bowman, back from patrol!" Parker broke into a trot towards the place where the road forked, to wait.

Bowman came in whooping, sweating, horse lathered and fighting for wind, and he pulled the horse to a stop and leaped to the ground. "They're coming right now, back at Vine Brook. Maybe fifteen minutes." His eyes were wild, voice high, cracking.

"How many?"

"I don't know. Column must be a half mile long, maybe more."

Parker rounded his mouth and blew air. "Tend that horse and get a musket." He pivoted and ran back up the Bedford Road to Buckman's tavern and burst in where militiamen were dozing after their long vigil in the night.

"Awake and on your feet!" roared Parker. "Drummer, get down to the Green as fast as you can go and sound assembly. The British will be on us in fifteen minutes."

"How many, sir?"

Parker shook his head. "Enough! Hundreds!"

The drummer grabbed his drum and sprinted through the door barefoot and was pounding out assembly while he ran for the Green. Men jerked shoes on and left them untied as they grabbed muskets and lunged out the door into the beautiful spring morning. All over Lexington doors were thrown open and men ran into the streets still buttoning their pants, shrugging into shirts, while they clung to their muskets and ran for the Green. Women and children walked to the roadway to watch.

Parker stood in the center of the Green rubbing his suddenly dry mouth with the back of his hand while he studied the empty road from Menotomy, and then they were there, coming down the rise between the two hills. The small dot of red became the first rank of regulars, and then Parker heard their drummers beating out the cadence, and the first rank was followed by another and another. One hundred yards to the right and left of the column, the flankers moved with the drum cadence, and Parker breathed light when he realized what the formation meant. This column was not moving troops from one place to another. With flankers out, this column was ready to fight. He licked dry lips while the drum cadence continued, and the column became a great, deadly red snake creeping steadily, relentlessly toward Lexington.

Parker stared at the ground for three seconds while his orders from Warren and Sam Adams flashed in his mind. Do not provoke a fight. If they mean only to pass through town, let them. Unless they destroy private property, do nothing. Under any circumstance do not fire unless they do.

I've got to keep them away from the meetinghouse, away from the center of town!

He turned and shouted his next order. "Follow me."

He led his command one hundred yards north of the meetinghouse on the Green near the Bedford Road and waited for them to fall into two ranks, and he quickly counted seventy-six men. He faced them and took a deep breath and spoke. "Our orders are to avoid a fight if we can. Protect the town, but let them pass through if that's all they intend to do. We do not fire unless they do."

He paced for a moment, then continued. "They're headed for Concord, but if we block the road, they'll fight. If we wait here we can defend the town if they attack, but if they only want to pass on to Concord, they can. So I say we wait here."

He waited a moment and then followed the time-honored custom of all colonials. He asked for counsel. "If any of you have a different plan, speak up now."

A murmur rose for a moment, then died.

"Are we agreed?"

"Yes," came the shout.

"Load your muskets," Parker answered.

From behind came a small voice and Parker turned. There stood a man scarcely five feet tall, with a musket taller than he. Parker looked at him quizzically and spoke gruffly. "Who are you?"

"Sylvanus Wood, sir. I want to volunteer."

Despite the crushing responsibility of defending Lexington with seventy-seven men against eight hundred, Parker could not stifle a grin. "Where are you from?"

"Woburn, sir. I got Revere's message last night and came as fast as I could."

Parker shook his head in amazement. He was not sure the man could even shoulder the musket, yet there he stood, eyes big and soulful, wanting only to get into the fight. As he stared at the little man, Parker felt a surge of pride. "Load your musket and fall into that second rank."

"Yes, sir!" Sylvanus Wood was in the second rank in five seconds, at rigid attention, clutching his musket.

East of the Green, across the Bedford Road, half a mile behind Buckman's tavern, Tom Sievers slowed and stopped on the gently sloping hillside, Matthew beside him. For more than a minute Tom studied the British column, locating the officers, identifying the first three companies as marines, realizing that with flankers out they were prepared for battle. Across the road he watched Parker standing firm before his two ranks, and Tom knew.

"The British mean to fight!" he exclaimed. "Parker's got no chance!" He started down the hill at a run, heedless that he and Matthew might be seen by the British column.

On the Green, Parker surveyed his men one more time. "Stand fast until I say," he told them, and turned to study the incoming British, scarcely breathing as he waited to see if they would continue west on the Concord Road or turn onto the Green or into the town for a confrontation.

Steadily they came, red coats shining in the bright sunlight, white belts gleaming over their chests, canteens and powder horns swinging with their stride. Women seized their children and hurried them through open doors that closed instantly, while window curtains were pulled back and small faces appeared.

When they were eighty yards from the fork in the road, Parker realized every soldier in the column was mud stained from the waist down, and he remembered the marshes at the Lechmere landing and a grim smile flashed for a moment. At fifty yards from the fork, the meetinghouse blocked the column leaders from Parker's view, and he waited to see which road they would take, and he heard himself saying, "Concord. Go on to Concord."

It was not to be.

Parker stared in disbelief at what happened next.

The column of regulars, led by three companies of marines, turned right onto the Bedford Road, while Pitcairn and the other officers of the lead companies—Mitchell, Cochrane, Lumm, Sutherland, Adair—loped their horses to the left, taking the Concord Road for twenty yards, then swinging back to their right, around the meetinghouse. They emerged onto the great open space of the Green, resplendent with the carpet of tall dandelions, and the officers hauled their horses to a stop facing Parker and his men one hundred twenty yards ahead.

To the right of the officers, hidden by the meetinghouse and out of sight of the officers, the column marched onto the Green and continued directly towards the waiting militia, but the column was without leadership.

The officers had separated themselves from their command!

As though he finally realized what he had done, Pitcairn set spurs to his horse and galloped towards Parker, shouting, "Disperse your men! Disperse your men!"

At the same time, both he and Mitchell were shouting to their own regulars, "Disarm the militia. Disarm them."

The other officers were hot behind them and joined in the conflicting orders, some shouting to their own soldiers, "Disarm the rebels," while others shouted to Parker, "Disperse your men."

Junior officers and sergeants who had never before been under the command of Pitcairn or the other officers shook their heads in confusion. A grizzled veteran sergeant looked at the lieutenant in charge of his squad. "Now, 'ow do we disarm 'em if they're dispersing?"

The young, smooth-faced lieutenant had no answer.

Far back in the column, Colonel Smith could not believe what he was seeing, and started forward at a gallop. The column of regulars had by that time stopped twenty yards short of the militia, and the first two companies had spread to face them, rank for rank. Parker stood his ground in front of his men while the British assembled in battle formation.

Pitcairn, with the other officers, was approaching at the gallop, still shouting his orders while the regulars brought their muskets to the ready, and suddenly Parker was looking down the barrels of over one hundred muskets.

Avoid a fight. Defend the town if you must, but do not provoke a fight. It ran through his head like the beat of the British drum cadence. To obey that direct order, there was but one command Parker could give his white-faced militiamen, and he gritted his teeth in loathing as he turned to his men and gave it. "Stay in formation and fall back. *Do not fire.*"

The militiamen began backing up without turning, watching every move made by the regulars, waiting for one of them to shoulder a musket and fire.

For both sides, it seemed the very air was charged with an all-consuming tension as the regulars stood in their battle squares, muskets loaded and ready, while the militia backed away, trying to avoid a fight, each side watching like hawks for the other side to make the move that would ignite the powder keg. Not a man among them could know that the history of the world hung in the balance while they stood thus in the yellow dandelions on the Lexington Green that beautiful spring morning. Seconds were an eternity as the militia backed up one step at a time. It seemed a hush seized the Green, and nature held her breath as the gap between the two sides widened.

Then, in the thick tension, from a source no one ever knew, the cracking bang of a single shot rolled out over the Green and echoed off the meetinghouse, and in that moment the world was changed forever.

For an instant that seemed unending both sides stood stone still, unable to comprehend that the inevitable had happened, and then the British regulars leveled their muskets and fired the first devastating volley, and one hundred musket balls ripped into the militiamen. A dozen men in the front rank groaned and went down when the big .75-caliber slugs hit.

The militia still standing returned fire while the second rank of British regulars fired their second volley over the heads of the kneeling first rank, and again militiamen went down.

Tom Sievers was five hundred yards behind Buckman's tavern when the sound of that first shot came rolling across the Bedford Road. He stopped short in his headlong rush and stood still, horrified, unable to do anything other than stand with held breath. He watched as the regulars raised their muskets, and from deep in his throat came the shout "No!" but it was lost in the thunder of the first volley. He watched the front rank of militiamen wither and shrink as the dead and wounded crumpled, and he saw those still able return fire just before the second rank of regulars delivered the second volley. Other militiamen dropped, and those still surviving broke for the trees to the north, save for one lone colonial midway in the file.

Tom watched in disbelief as that one man, who appeared to Tom to be one of the older members of the militia, jerked his hat from his head and threw it on the ground before him and dropped his powder horn and bullet pouch into it. Tom saw him form the words and shout his defiance at the sea of red-coated regulars as they reloaded. *"I will not run!"* He scooped his powder horn from his hat and tapped a load into his musket muzzle and was jamming his ramrod home when the regulars shouted the charge and sprinted forward with their bayonets fixed. The man was seating a ball on the patch when the first regular reached him and rammed his bayonet through the man's right side. The man grasped the British musket and felt his side go numb, and then his vision blurred and he toppled onto his side while the soldier jerked his bayonet out and continued the charge.

Pitcairn and the officers rode storming among their own troops, shouting, "Cease fire," but the order was unheard and

unheeded in the mad bedlam. Colonel Smith came galloping into the battle and instantly shouted to the drummer, "Sound cease fire, sound the cease fire," and the drummer pounded it out.

The militiamen still standing fired their last volley as they ran, and disappeared northward into the trees and fields bordering the Green while the firing from the regulars slowed and stopped. Colonel Smith ordered the soldiers to fall into rank and file, and they began to reassemble from their bayonet charge.

Across Bedford Road, an indiscernible cry of anguish surged from Tom as he lurched forward, down the incline, towards the Green across the road, Matthew following.

On the Green, Smith confronted Pitcairn. "Get the column reassembled and continue on to Concord."

While the regulars were reforming, the townspeople of Lexington threw open their doors and ran towards the cloud of gun smoke that hung white in the still morning air. Women wept and men cursed as they moved among the militia left on the field of battle, seeking those who still lived.

"This one's still alive! Help!" The call came ten times. For the others, there were only the anguished cries of widows and children as they dropped to their knees beside the dead body of a husband or father.

Tom reached the battlefield and worked his way through to the man who alone had stood his ground and now lay on his side, unmoving. A great blot of blood stained the right side of his shirt. Tom knelt and pressed his fingers against the throat, under the slack jaw, then dropped his ear to the chest. There was still warmth, but no heartbeat, no breath. Tom raised his head, frantically looking for Matthew.

Twenty yards behind, Matthew had slowed, then stopped as he came to the first of those who had fallen. He saw the flat, eternal stare in the open eyes of the dead, and their open mouths, and the unnatural lay of their arms and legs in the yellow dandelions and green grass, and he saw the blood from their mortal wounds, and the torn flesh. He heard the moans of the wounded, and saw their movements, and the fear and pleading in their eyes. He saw it and his face paled and he choked at the rise of his gorge.

"Help me!" Tom shouted, and Matthew stared at him for a moment, uncomprehending, before he came running.

A sturdy, round-faced woman dropped to her knees beside Tom, face white, and three teenaged girls stopped behind her, breathing hard, mouths clamped shut at the sight of their father.

"Is he dead?" the woman asked, and Tom heard the deep fear in her voice and saw the pleading in her eyes. He looked down, and in that second the woman knew. Her head rolled back and she bit down to stifle a sob as the searing pain struck. Behind her the girls began to whimper and then sob in the strange, new, grotesque world of dead and wounded, and gun smoke, and groans, and their father at their feet, bloody, not moving.

"I think he's gone," Tom said quietly, and he wanted to reach to touch her, to comfort her, but he could not. Tom and Matthew lifted him between them, and the woman reached to touch the slack face, and she gasped and sobbed. Tom turned at the sound of heavy running feet from behind, and John Parker came to a stop, breathing heavily, eyes wide.

"Is he alive?" Parker boomed.

Tom shook his head.

The massive shoulders dropped and the big, homely face bowed, and Tom saw the single shudder and heard the gasp. When Parker raised his face, his brows were peaked, and his mouth was a straight line as he struggled for control. He gathered the weeping woman into his arms like a child, and held her against his chest, softly repeating over and over, "Lucy, Lucy, Lucy . . ."

He straightened, and by strength of will took possession of himself and turned to Tom. "He's Jonas Parker, my first cousin. Lucy's his wife. Their home is just across Bedford Road."

The three men carried Jonas Parker to his home, with Lucy walking beside, holding the limp hand, and they laid him on his bed. Lucy opened his shirt and Tom watched as she stared at the single purple-rimmed puncture wound in his side.

Tom did not know what to say but knew someone had to explain, and he said simply, "It was a bayonet, not a bullet." It sounded like too little, and awkwardly Tom added, "I don't know how deep," and wished he had not said it.

Lucy slumped onto a chair beside the bed and grasped her husband's square, callused hand in hers. She held it to her face and began to rock back and forth. The three girls stood at the foot of the bed, with sounds of whimpering and choked sobs. Parker stood behind Lucy, silent, giving her time, with a rare tenderness shining from his square, strong face.

He turned to Tom. "Who are you?"

"Tom Sievers, and this is Matthew Dunson. Boston militia."

Suddenly the door flew open and a young man, musket in hand, burst into the room. "Ma? Where's Pa? Someone said he—" He stopped short at the sight of the lifeless figure on the bed. He looked with anguish at Lucy, then at John Parker.

"Jonas," Parker said softly to the young man, "I'm sorry."

With head bowed, twenty-one-year-old Jonas, Jr., walked slowly over to stand beside his mother, laying a hand on her shoulder.

After a moment of painful silence, the three girls began quietly crying once more.

Then John Parker turned again to Tom. A sense of pleading flitted across Parker's face as he spoke. "They shot. There was nothing else I . . . I had to . . ." He did not know how to complete his statement, his defense, his question.

Tom's eyes locked with Parker's. "I seen it all," he said steadily. "You did right. You were seventy men and a few more, and you faced eight hundred, and you ordered your men back to avoid a fight just like you was ordered. You did right. I'll tell them."

Tom caught the brief flash of gratefulness in Parker's eyes before Tom turned to Lucy Parker. "Ma'am, you and your family got to know. When the order was given to fall back, it was your husband who covered the retreat. It was him threw his hat on the ground and said he wouldn't run, and he covered for the militia-men and he took the bayonet charge alone. All alone. Ma'am, I never seen nothing like it, anything so brave. You and your family got to remember that."

Lucy raised startled, searching eyes to Tom. "Jonas did that? My Jonas did that?"

"I seen it, ma'am."

Jonas, Jr., eyes wide, looked first at Tom, then with silent wonder at his father. The three girls stopped their sobbing, and they stared at their father as if they were seeing him for the first time. Jonas, Jr., spoke up. "Ma, I'll go get the rest of the family."

Lucy nodded, and as her son left, she clutched Tom's arm. "Thank you. Thank you."

Tom nodded and turned back to John Parker. "The soldiers was regrouping to move on to Concord."

"I need to get back to my command."

Tom shook his head. "Let the soldiers go. Your command needs time with their dead and wounded, and you need time here."

"I got to send someone to tell them at Concord."

"Me and Matthew are going."

"Tell them the regulars fired while we were trying to fall back to avoid a fight."

"I saw it," Tom answered. "I'll tell them."

"Tell them not to wait. Shoot!" Parker's voice rang with anger.

"I'll tell them. You did right."

Tom and Matthew walked out the door into the bright sunlight, and they looked at the beautiful, flower-covered Green, and the gentle hills to the east, and at the homes and businesses of Lexington. Then Tom once again started west on the Concord Road at his relentless trot, Matthew following.

Ahead one mile, where the road turned as it passed Fiske Hill, Private Samuel Lee, marching in the last company of regulars, mumbled, "It ain't what they said, this soldierin'. Marchin' all night through swamps and bugs. Eatin' hardtack. Shootin' common folk wot ain't doin' nothin'. It ain't wot they said when I joined."

He spoke to the soldier next to him. "Is this here soldierin' to your likin'?"

The man shook his head and said nothing, and they kept step with the drum.

"Ain't wot they promised," Lee continued. "Shootin' folk wot's retreatin'. Ain't wot they promised."

Three minutes later Lee simply slowed. The man next to him turned to look, and Lee shook his head at him, sat down on a rock at the side of the road, and leaned his musket against a tree while the column continued.

"I ain't goin' to shoot at no more people," Lee vowed, "no sir. It ain't wot they promised, and if they lied to me, I ain't doin' nothin' wrong by quittin'." He sat for a while, weighing his argument, testing it to see how it would sound if he were caught and brought to a court-martial. The column continued and disappeared in the distance.

Lee was not prepared for the voice that came from directly behind, and he jumped at the single word.

"Sir."

Lee did not turn. He slowly moved his hands away from his body and said, "I got a rock in my shoe an' I was just gettin' ready to catch up. I ain't no deserter, no sir."

The voice came again. "Sir."

Slowly Lee turned to look. Behind him, Sylvanus Wood stood with feet planted and his musket, held at waist level, pointed where the white belts crossed on Lee's red coat.

Lee's mouth fell open and his eyes popped. He could hardly see Sylvanus for the musket.

"Sir, you're my prisoner."

"I'm your bloody *what?*"

"I'm one of the militia from Lexington. You're my prisoner. I'm taking you back."

Lee threw back his head and roared with laughter. Tears streamed down his cheeks. He brought himself under control and looked at Sylvanus. "So I'm your prisoner."

"Yes, sir. I've got a musket."

"So have I."

"Well," Sylvanus said hesitantly, "don't touch it. I wish you wouldn't touch it."

Lee pondered for a moment. "Wouldn't think of it. Point that thing somewhere else. 'Ere, take mine. I'm your prisoner. Let's get on back to Lexington. I might turn out to be a bloody hero over this, who knows?"

Lee started back towards Lexington with Sylvanus trudging along behind, one musket strap over each shoulder, trying to keep up.

Tom saw them coming and slowed, unable to see Sylvanus until Lee was ten yards away. Lee smiled and waved to Tom. Tom stopped to watch them pass by, and Sylvanus looked proudly up at him.

"He's my prisoner."

Sylvanus Wood had taken the first British captive of the war.

Ten minutes later Tom heard the British drums ahead, and for the first time sporadic shots cracked out far in the distance.

"Militia," he said, "shooting at the column." He turned to Matthew. "We've got to get around them to Concord first."

He left the road and travelled parallel on the north side, slowing occasionally, waiting for Matthew. While still four miles from Concord they saw militia moving through the trees and fields by the score, watching the column, running to get ahead of them. Half an hour later Tom came abreast of the column. Behind him, shots still cracked out from behind trees and rocks.

On the road, Colonel Smith cast worried eyes into the open fields and rolling hills on both sides of the road, watching the militiamen working their way north to Concord. In twos and threes and whole companies they came, watching the column move. Smith had flankers out one hundred yards on both sides, marching through fields, wading streams, climbing rock fences, moving steadily towards Concord, but militia sharpshooters waited for the flankers to pass before they slipped close enough to rest their musket barrels across a rock or tree limb and fire at the passing column.

Smith felt the gathering turmoil in his column, and sensed the reluctance to continue forward to what now appeared to be a head-on, pitched battle with numbers of militia none of the British had ever dreamed possible. How had they gathered such numbers in twelve hours? And worse, what had the point-blank killing at Lexington done to the resolve in the militia? He drew a deep breath and turned at the sound of a horse loping in from behind.

Ensign De Berniere reined in short of Smith. "Sir, some of us are concerned. We underestimated the numbers of militia, and after Lexington, there's going to be fighting at Concord. It may be good judgment to turn back."

Smith's eyes snapped. "I have my orders, and I intend carrying them out. Return to your command."

De Berniere opened his mouth to reply, then clamped it shut and turned back to relay Smith's orders to the regulars.

Smith straightened in his saddle and cantered his horse to the head of the column, then fell back even with the flankers out on his left and right and continued on. The column marched up the east slope of Brooks Hill, and at the crest they looked down the west slope.

There, peaceful in bright sunlight that beautiful spring morning, Concord lay spread before them.

None of them noticed the two militiamen to their right, one wiry, the other tall and slender, trotting down the slope toward the Meriam house at Meriam's Corner, and the town cemetery, and the liberty pole, where the Massachusetts Colony flag shifted in the gentle breeze.

Notes

The description of Lexington Green on the morning of April 19, 1775, including the dandelions, is accurate. The formation of the British troops by Smith and Pitcairn, including the fact that they separated the officers from the regulars when they passed the big meetinghouse at the south end of the Green, with the resulting confusion, is also accurate (see French, *The Day of Concord and Lexington*, p. 108).

Captain John Parker, commander of the minutemen and militia at Lexington, specifically ordered his men not to fire unless the British fired first (see French, *The Day of Concord and Lexington*, pp. 98–99, 109).

Within a few days after the shooting at Lexington, sixty-two colonial witnesses were gathered and their depositions taken. Each declared under oath that it was the British who confronted the minutemen and militia and who fired the first shot. However, British accounts suggest it was a colonial who fired the first shot. No one has ever proved which side was actually responsible, and the subject has been a source of hot debate ever since. (See French, *The Day of Concord and Lexington*, pp. 109–28.)

The incident in which militiaman Jonas Parker, cousin of Captain John Parker, throws down his hat and declares he will not run, while he covers the retreat of the militia, with the resulting fatal bayonet wound in his right side, is accurate (see French, *The Day of Concord and Lexington*, p. 119 n. 3, and p. 143).

The rather comical event involving a colonial Woburn volunteer named Sylvanus Wood, described in this chapter, is also accurate. Wood, just five feet tall, took the first prisoner of war when he happened onto a much larger British grenadier named Samuel Lee, who had simply sat down beside the road to Concord and refused to go further. When Wood, substantially shorter than the two muskets he carried, appeared in Lexington with his captive, the hilarity of the situation did much to raise the spirits of the colonials. (See Galvin, *The Minute Men*, pp. 122–30.)

Wednesday, April 19, 1775

CHAPTER XIII

★ ★ ★

A buzz began in the dark, warm regions of the slumbering brain of Corporal Jeremiah Sotheby, orderly to General Thomas Gage, and it battled its way into his consciousness. He understood someone had taken hold of his shoulder, and he moved in his bunk and murmured his protest. The hand shook his shoulder, and someone spoke sharply. Sotheby rose on one elbow to stare into the face of a young lieutenant, sweating, panting, holding a lantern.

"Get Gage. Now."

Sotheby swallowed at the cotton in his mouth. "What time is it?"

The lieutenant ignored the question. "Get Gage. I'm from Smith's column."

Instantly Sotheby bolted upright and seized his pocket watch from the nightstand and stared until his eyes focused. Ten minutes past five o'clock. "I'm sorry, sir. General Gage was up late. I can't disturb him."

"On your feet," the lieutenant ordered. "You're taking me to him now."

"Who are you, sir?"

"I told you. I'm from Smith's column, headed for Concord. They're in trouble. He sent me back with a message. Get moving."

Sotheby's feet hit the cold, polished floor of his quarters, and five minutes later he jerked the door open and the lieutenant followed him into the gray of early dawn. They trotted to Gage's quarters, and Sotheby paused at the front door to straighten his tunic and his hat before he knocked, then knocked again. A light appeared inside, and Gage opened the door, clad in his royal blue robe with the gold trim. He scowled at the two men.

"Do you know the time? What brings you here?" He glanced past them into the vacant drill and parade ground. Satisfied no one else was there, he waited for Sotheby's answer.

"Sir," Sotheby said, "with due apologies, this officer claims he has a message from Colonel Smith."

For the first time Gage saw the slit eyes and the sweat and the hard set of the lieutenant's face, and he felt the grab in the pit of his stomach. A badly used up messenger from Smith arriving at dawn could mean only one thing.

"Identify yourself."

The man snapped to attention. "Lieutenant Randall Milhouse Ambrose, Twenty-third Welch Fusiliers, sir."

"What's your message?"

"Written, sir." He thrust the paper to Gage.

With quivering fingers Gage unfolded the small paper and read it, then reread it. His mouth compressed, and he stood for a moment in deep thought. "Wait here."

Five minutes later Gage strode from his bedroom, passed them without a word, and walked quickly to his office, the others following.

"Orderly, wait outside. Lieutenant Ambrose, be seated." Gage settled into his great chair, Ambrose opposite him. "Where was the column when you were sent back?"

"About one mile this side of Lexington, sir."

"When did you leave the column?"

"Over an hour ago, sir. I used my horse hard."

"They got to Lexington about four o'clock this morning?"

"Yes, sir."

"They were supposed to be there between one and two o'clock. What happened?"

Ambrose dropped his eyes. "Confusion at loading and un-loading. Bogs at Lechmere."

Gage smacked the flat palm of his hand on the tabletop and cursed, and Ambrose jumped. "What do you mean, confusion at loading and unloading?"

"The troops were not ferried in the marching order. The troops didn't know their officers. No one told them about the Lechmere marshes. We spent an hour in the bog up to our waists."

Gage stood and thumped his desk with his clenched fist. "What do you know personally about the number of militia?"

"We captured a few colonials. They told us the numbers. More than six thousand."

"What's this about a volley being fired in the night?"

"I heard the volley. It had to be over 150 muskets."

"Shooting at what?"

"I don't know, sir. None of us knew."

Gage sagged back in his chair. *Disorganized—late—outnum-bered—this whole campaign in disarray.* "Orderly," he called, and Sotheby was instantly in the room.

"Yes, sir."

"Have Brigadier Percy here within ten minutes."

"Yes, sir." Sotheby ran out the front door, and ten minutes later returned with Percy behind.

"Be seated," Gage invited, and Percy sat down beside Lieu-tenant Ambrose while Sotheby walked out and closed the door.

"This is Lieutenant Ambrose, a messenger from Smith's column," Gage said. "Smith is convinced he's facing vastly superior numbers. He's continuing but asks for reinforcements."

Percy felt his breath come short. *The colonials don't wage war, they wage ambushes. No command, no organization, no training, no discipline—swarm and shoot from hiding.* Percy remained silent, intent, waiting.

"Earlier I ordered your First Brigade on standby alert, in case something like this happened. Did you execute that order?"

"I did, sir."

"Take the First Brigade and proceed to support Smith." Gage

turned to Lieutenant Ambrose. "Can you guide Brigadier Percy back?"

"Yes, sir. I'll need a fresh mount."

"Arrange it. Brigadier Percy, do you have any questions?"

"Yes, sir. Do I pursue Smith until I catch him, or do I set up to cover his return?"

"That will be your decision based on what you observe in the field."

"Yes, sir."

"Anything else?"

"No, sir. Your standby order was clear."

"Move your regiment out at earliest opportunity."

"Yes, sir."

At six o'clock A.M. Percy signed the order for the First Brigade, including the infantry, grenadiers, and marines, to be in marching formation in full battle gear, with cannon on their carriages and teams of horses to pull them by seven-thirty A.M. At seven o'clock Percy was riding his tall, high-blooded sorrel horse before the troops as they assembled. There was not a marine in sight.

Percy reined in his horse before the sergeant major. "Where're the marines?"

"I don't know, sir."

"Find out."

"Yes, sir."

Five minutes later the whiskered sergeant major returned to Percy, shoulders heaving as he fought for breath. "Sir, the marines are under the command of Major Pitcairn, who is already with Smith. The messenger forgot and laid the orders on Pitcairn's desk. They're still there, sir. They were never delivered to his second in command. The marines are still asleep, sir."

Percy cursed and thundered from his saddle, "Tell those marines the whole brigade is assembled and waiting, and they had better be here by the time we march."

"Yes, sir."

The marines trickled in until eight twenty-five A.M., turning grim but silent faces to the shouted wrath of the grenadiers and light infantry, who had been standing for over an hour in full battle gear, waiting.

In full, beautiful morning sunlight, Percy sat his tall gelding and considered. He looked north towards the Charlestown ferry, then south, back towards the guard lines and the Neck, and made his decision. The ferry was too small; it would take four trips to move the brigade across the Back Bay. It would be faster to march them down across the Neck, then back west past Cambridge to Lexington. Farther but faster.

"Regular marching pace," Percy ordered his drummers. "Three miles per hour. We don't want to alarm the countryside, and we have to keep the men fresh enough to fight when we get there. Three miles per hour. Ready! Forrrrard, march."

The drummers hit the cadence and the column moved south, through the barricades, south down across the Neck to Roxbury, then turned hard right, northwest, towards Brookline.

Percy reined in his horse and called for Captain John Montresor, the brigade engineer. "Pick four men and load a pack horse with bridge-repairing equipment and immediately go to the Great Bridge over the Charles River, by Harvard College. See to it the bridge is passable."

"Yes, sir." Half an hour later Montresor pulled his horse to a stop on the south side of the bridge, facing a pile of ripped-up bridge planking. He studied the bridge for a moment, then cursed. "They tore it up! It's impassable."

"But they left the planking on this side," volunteered a lieutenant. "We can nail it back down."

Percy and the incoming column were a scant four hundred yards away when the five men nailed down the last plank, and they mounted their horses to watch the column march onto the bridge, break step, then pick it up again on the north side and march on until the entire column had passed. They worked their way north towards Harvard College, with Percy growing steadily aware that something was wrong. He loped his horse to the front of the column, and as they marched past the buildings and school grounds of Harvard, drums pounding, it struck him.

The college grounds were vacant. Nothing moved. The windows were closed, curtains drawn, the flagpole bare. He glanced at the few scattered homes about the college, and the single movement came from a spotted dog that barked once and slunk away, out of sight.

"We haven't seen one living soul on any of the farms," he exclaimed. "The countryside is deserted!"

They continued in the eerie silence, with a foreboding sense of uneasiness creeping into the column as they passed homes and farms with the windows staring back vacantly and nothing, no one, moving. No sound. No animals. Nothing.

"Keep a sharp watch," Percy ordered. "The colonials won't come out in the open and fight. They shoot from ambush. Watch sharp."

Margaret Dunson waited in Brigitte's bedroom until Brigitte was in her bed and the lamp was out before she closed the door and walked back through the shadows to the parlor. For long moments she stood in the lamplight, staring at the glow of the banked coals in the great fireplace, weary in mind and soul, thoughts in a whirl of confusion, not knowing what she should be thinking or doing. Finally, because she could think of nothing else to do, she walked down the hall in the bedroom wing and quietly entered the room of Caleb, then the twins' room. She knelt beside their beds and gently touched their faces and their hair, and she kissed each of them and felt the warmth of their touch.

Then she rose and went to her own bedroom and sat on the bed in the darkness for a time before she put on her nightgown, braided her hair, and knelt in prayer. Then she got into the bed, refusing to look at the pillow on John's side. For more than an hour she lay without moving, staring upward in the darkness. She could not remember drifting into troubled sleep, only lunging up when the images of Matthew and John dead in the green grass and spring flowers of a battlefield flashed bright in her brain. She sat in the dark for minutes, feeling the clammy sweat on her face and between her shoulder blades and the dampness of her nightgown about her shoulders.

She rose in the dark and washed herself with cool water and put on a fresh, dry nightgown. Then she wrapped a blanket about her shoulders and sat rigid in the rocking chair, slowly rocking back and forth with the drawn curtains a dull gray from the bright light of the nearly full moon. When her eyelids became heavy she walked about the dark room, forcing herself to stay awake, fearful of what her dreams would be. In the deep twilight of the room, sitting in the rocking chair, staring at the gray curtains, thoughts came uninvited, and she let them run because she was exhausted, with no strength nor will left to control or manage them.

Genesis, war—Isaiah, war—war in heaven—Lucifer at war with God—men have sons to go to war—for honor or pride or country—any reason, no reason—always war.

She sighed, and her thoughts continued with a will of their own.

Women know—the message of the womb—nurture your offspring—not war—women know, and they bear the sorrow of the world.

The room was cast in the dusky gray that precedes sunrise when Margaret jerked her head up and her eyes opened wide as she looked about and remembered why she was sitting in the rocking chair. She looked at the mantel clock—six-twenty A.M., Wednesday, April 19, 1775—and she rose quickly as the image of John and Matthew dead in battle once again rose in her mind.

She awakened Brigitte, and they had hot griddle cakes waiting for the children when they were dressed for school. Margaret told them only that John and Matthew were gone for a while on business with the British. She kissed them and locked their lunch baskets under their arms, and followed them to the front gate to watch them until they crossed the first street and were soon lost to view. Brigitte cleared the breakfast table while Margaret set a kettle of water on the stove for the dishes.

Finished, Brigitte settled onto a chair at the table, absentmind-edly working one hand with the other, lost in her own thoughts. Margaret returned the milk pitcher to the cool of the root cellar, and walked back to the kitchen to quietly study Brigitte. Never had she seen her so morose. Always, always, Brigitte had been the one so sure of her own mind. Slowly Margaret walked to the table, her shoes clicking loudly on the hardwood floor in the silence, and sat down in John's large chair. Brigitte continued slowly working her hands on the table without looking.

Margaret opened her mouth to speak, when they heard the first faint rumble of heavy iron-rimmed wheels on cobblestones, and then the rattle of drums and the shrill of fifes, and then the rhythm of marching men.

Brigitte's head jerked towards Margaret. "What is it?" she blurted.

"It sounds like soldiers marching," Margaret murmured.

"I'm going to go see," Brigitte exclaimed.

"See what? that young officer?"

Without a word Brigitte snatched her shawl from the coat tree and threw it around her shoulders as she rushed out the door and blinked in the bright sunlight of a beautiful spring day in Boston City. At the front gate she paused to look up and down the street, and slowed when she realized the street was vacant. Nothing moved beneath the reaching boughs of the oak and maple trees lining the cobblestones. She pulled the shawl tighter and walked rapidly to the corner, then turned east and trotted towards the sounds of an army in motion. She had covered two blocks when a few hesitant citizens ventured from their doors to look eastward, and then she was on the corner and she stopped, facing north.

Other colonials stood near the street, some partially hidden behind trees or fences, mouths set, eyes flat, faces vacant as the British came to the sounds of drum and fife and boots and horses drawing cannon. Then the leaders were there, and she felt the ground tremble as the broad-wheeled gun carriages rumbled towards her. Brigadier Hugh Percy, sitting tall and rigid and oblivious to the colonials in the streets, grand in his spotless crimson coat, led his relief column south on his high-headed sorrel gelding.

She turned to look at the ugly snouts of the first two cannon as they passed and at the strong, iron-bound oak boxes filled with the black twenty-four-pound cannonballs and the black powder that would hurl them at the Massachusetts ragtag militia and minutemen, and she swallowed and turned back to the column following and suddenly her breath stopped and she froze.

Her eyes locked with those of Lieutenant Richard Arlen Buchanan, and her hand darted to cover her mouth. She tried to tear her eyes from his and she could not, nor did his eyes leave hers as he held his horse at a nervous walk, leading the two horses harnessed to the gun carriage of the fourth cannon. In that stunned, unprepared moment the open frankness of their wide eyes held back nothing.

He saw the deep conflict in her soul, and she saw him torn between duty and heart. She sensed his need and she fought the urge to reach out her hand as he rode past her, his stirrup less than five feet from her as he stared down. And then he snapped his head up and forward, and once again he was a British soldier committed only to his duty.

She was oblivious to the next gun carriage as it came rumbling. She saw only his rigid back as he moved on, and she started to call to him but didn't. Then he turned for one moment and once more stared into her eyes. She felt her breath catch, and then he was gone as the grenadiers and marines came marching smartly in their shining uniforms and tall hats, and the drums and fifes and boots drowned all other sound. She stood rooted, unmoving until the last of the column passed and the sounds faded and died, and they were gone. Slowly, doors opened and citizens ventured into the street to peer south, to be certain the British column had passed without stopping.

Brigitte suddenly became aware there were those nearby pointing and staring, and she turned on her heel and walked, slowly, then rapidly, back through the quiet beauty of the morning, through her front gate and into the parlor.

Margaret walked in from the kitchen. "Regulars?"

Brigitte hung her shawl on the coat tree and answered, refusing to look at her mother. "Yes. Cannon and foot soldiers. Going south."

Margaret saw the devastated expression. "What's wrong? Was he among them?"

Brigitte's shoulders slumped and she raised her eyes. "Yes."

"Did he see you?"

"Yes."

"What was said?"

"Nothing. He rode past."

Margaret walked slowly towards her and for long moments searched for words. "What are you going to do?"

Brigitte slumped onto a chair at the table and shook her head and remained silent, staring at her clasped hands.

Margaret sat down next to her. "You know nothing can come of it." The words were quiet, and Brigitte could hear the deep compassion. Seconds passed, and a silent tear crept down Brigitte's face, and Margaret felt the pain. Still Brigitte remained silent because she could find no escape from the torture of where she found herself.

"He's an enemy officer. He's gone to fight the militia—your father and Matthew and Tom."

Brigitte faintly nodded her head.

"Have you thought that maybe he has a wife waiting in England?"

Brigitte shook her head. "He doesn't."

"How do you know?"

Brigitte shrugged. "I know."

"Tell me what you know about him."

"He's honorable."

"You've seen him three times and spoken to him once, and you know?"

"Yes, I know."

"You've listened to your heart, now listen to your head. If he came courting, where would you go? To church with a British officer, or walking on the green? What would he and your father talk about? shooting each other? What would you and he talk about? his view of the war or yours? the oppression his army has put on us, and us trying to drive them back to England? Where would you go to live? him here, or you there?"

Brigitte sat impassively, wiping silent tears, staring at her hands.

"Tell me about his family in England."

Brigitte said nothing and Margaret sat quietly, letting seconds tick into a full minute.

"This has happened all wrong, child. You've never even looked at a boy before, and now something in this young officer has touched you. Most of your life hangs on how you handle it, and no one—not even me—can tell you what to do, because that has to come from you."

Brigitte wiped her eyes. "I don't know what to do."

"Then will you take enough time to find out?"

"How long? How do you know when?"

"You'll know."

Brigitte nodded. "All right. I'll take time."

Margaret released her grip on Brigitte's hand and stood. "There are things I have to do." She turned and walked to her bedroom and dropped onto her bed, sitting with her shoulders slumped, face impassive, staring at the floor. She did not move when she heard the footsteps in the hallway, nor did she look up when Brigitte walked into the room and sat beside her on the bed. Brigitte said nothing, and the two women sat in the rich silence for a time, each lost in her own thoughts and fears.

Margaret stirred. "You need to keep busy. Go to the garden and dig around the tulips. They need it and so do you."

For several moments Brigitte did not move, and then she went to her room and changed clothes, and Margaret listened as she walked through the parlor and the outside door closed.

Margaret did not know how long she sat on her bed. She only knew that a great black cloud was crushing her mind and heart and thoughts. *John gone—Matthew—Tom—shooting—a second British column—Brigitte moving headlong into heartbreak.* Slowly Margaret took control of her swirling thoughts and brought them under control and faced the single question that she had steadfastly avoided.

If John doesn't come back?

She could invent no answer. Her hands began to tremble and she felt beads of perspiration, but she could not force her mind into a world without John. She rose and started for the door, then turned back to the bed and dropped to her knees.

"Dear God . . ." Minutes passed while she pleaded with all her heart, and finally she finished and dropped her face forward onto her clasped hands. Her shoulders trembled with quiet sobbing while she waited for an answer, a feeling, anything, and it would not come. The heavens were sealed against her.

By force of will she stood and wiped her eyes and walked to the kitchen. She finished the breakfast dishes, and made the beds, and started back for the kitchen.

The men will be back for supper. I better start supper. She glanced at the clock. Eleven-fifty A.M., Wednesday, April 19.

Too early. If I fix supper now it will be cold. I'll wait.

She stopped to listen. *Is that the children coming? No, it's only noon. Did Matthew wear his walking shoes?* She hurried down the hall to his bedroom and looked in his closet. *Yes, he did. Good. He'll need them, walking home.*

Suddenly she gasped and stopped. *What's wrong with me? Supper in the morning—the children coming home at noon—Matthew's shoes! If I keep this up I'll lose my mind!*

She walked purposefully to her room and quickly changed clothes, then opened the back door and called to Brigitte, "I'm going to see Phoebe. You wait here for the children. Give them honey and bread and milk, and keep them here. I'll tell them about Father and Matthew."

She tied her bonnet tightly under her chin and picked her shawl from the coat tree as she walked out the door into the beauty of the day. Ten minutes later she opened the gate into the Thorpe yard and walked to the front door and rapped. The door swung open and Kathleen stood in the door frame, face impassive, mouth set. For a moment the women faced each other, and then Kathleen's chin began to tremble and Margaret stepped forward and folded her inside her arms, and Kathleen clung to her and began to sob. A time passed before Kathleen quieted and stepped back, and Margaret followed her inside and closed the door.

"How can I help?" Margaret asked quietly.

Kathleen's eyes didn't leave the floor. "You can't. No one can."

"It can't be that bad," Margaret said, and touched Kathleen's cheek.

"It is. We've had visitors. With threats."

"Who would do such a thing?"

"We didn't recognize them."

"Did they harm any of you?"

"They threatened to burn the house."

"I'll tell the sheriff. Is Phoebe awake?"

"The doctor gave her a powder. She's sleeping. She should be awake soon."

Margaret folded her shawl and hung it over the back of a chair. "Matthew said you sent him away." She looked into Kathleen's eyes, probing.

"I did. For his sake."

"No, not for his sake. Matthew wants you."

"I will never hold him to his promise."

"He doesn't want your release. He needs you."

Kathleen shook her head slowly, and again her eyes fell. Then she raised them to Margaret's. "There is no place my family can go. We have become outcasts among all we love." She battled to hold back the tears.

"That's not true."

"It is true. Father could be hanged. The name Thorpe will be infamous. I would not put that on Matthew."

"Do you love him?"

"More than life."

"Then go west with him. Begin a new life."

"It would follow us."

Margaret drew and exhaled a weary breath. "One week ago our world was good. Now look. Henry gone. John and Matthew off to war. Neither of us knows if we will ever have our men back again."

Kathleen recoiled, and her hand leaped to cover her mouth for a moment. "Matthew has gone to Concord?"

"Yes. John too. They left early this morning."

"With muskets?"

"Yes. To fight, if it starts."

Kathleen could not stifle the moan that rose to choke her, and she buried her face in her hands and her shoulders shook. Margaret remained still and silent, allowing her her moment of grief.

Finally Kathleen wiped her eyes with the heels of her hands and squared her shoulders. "If anything happens to either of them it will be partially the fault of my father."

"Child, don't think like that! John and Matthew made their choice, and they're responsible for what comes of it."

"Kathleen!" Phoebe's voice reached from the master bedroom. "Is someone there?"

Margaret started for the bedroom wing. "I've got to see her," she said, and Kathleen hurried to follow.

The door swung open and Phoebe rose on one elbow. Her eyes were wild, distraught, her face drawn and sallow. She saw Margaret and slumped back onto her pillow and turned away and covered her face as she sobbed. Margaret sat on the side of the bed and tenderly took hold of her shoulder and waited. The racking sobs died, and Margaret spoke. "Can I help? Can I do something? Anything?"

Phoebe twisted and reached to grab Margaret with both arms, and she clung to her as she wept. "Forgive us. Forgive us. Forgive us," she repeated over and over.

Margaret held her close and stroked her hair. "There's nothing to forgive. We all had choices to make. We can't judge what's in the hearts of others, or why they chose as they did. That is for God."

"Margaret, Margaret, what am I going to do? Where will we go? Where can we take the children?"

"For now, nowhere. Stay here."

"We've had threats."

"The sheriff will watch."

"What if they come at night to burn my home?"

"I'll have the sheriff send a deputy to watch at night."

Phoebe settled back onto her pillow and wiped red eyes with a handkerchief.

"Have you sent food to Henry?" Margaret asked.

Phoebe's eyes widened. "I never thought of it."

"I'll send a basket," Margaret said.

"Has John talked about Henry?" Phoebe asked hesitantly.

"John is gone to Concord. Matthew too."

"To fight?"

"If fighting starts, yes."

Phoebe's tortured eyes turned to Margaret's. "Our husbands are enemies. How did it ever happen?"

Margaret shook her head. "They both followed their loyalties. They are not enemies."

The front door rattled and the sound of the children reached the bedroom.

Phoebe sobered. "The children are home from school." Her face went white. "Kathleen, fetch them here, this instant."

Kathleen led them into the room, and they stood facing their mother. They looked at Margaret for a long moment, then back to their mother. They were silent, subdued. Charles's clothing was rumpled.

"What happened to you, Charles?" Phoebe demanded.

"Nothing." Charles's eyes dropped.

"Yes, it did," Faith said. "Jeremy Gould said Father was in jail, and Charles wrestled him."

Phoebe gasped, and Kathleen knelt beside Charles and brushed off his clothing and tucked in his shirttail.

"Mama," Faith said hesitantly, "what is a traitor?"

Phoebe clamped her mouth closed to cut off a cry, and Kathleen faced Faith. "Why do you want to know?"

"Because that's what Jeremy called Papa."

"You two go on out to the kitchen and I'll be out in a minute to get bread and jam. Go on."

Faith hesitated. "Why is Mama in bed? Is she sick?"

"We'll talk about that later," Kathleen said and took them both by the shoulders, turned them around, and gently pushed them towards the door. She waited until their footsteps stopped in the kitchen; then she closed the door and turned to Phoebe. "We have to tell them."

Phoebe's eyes closed and tears flooded. Margaret sat on the bed, leaned over and slipped her arms about her, and held her for a time while the silent tears rolled.

Margaret could find nothing to say. She stood and faced Kathleen. "I should go. You will be in my prayers."

Kathleen nodded and led Margaret out the front door of the house, and Margaret paused and turned and looked deeply into Kathleen's eyes. "I don't know why this all happened—why you have to bear all this on your young shoulders. I don't know. I will take food to your father. Can I bring food to you?"

Kathleen shook her head. "No. I love you, Margaret. For all you have been, and for being here now. But I can't let you be drawn into this."

Margaret reached and touched her cheek, and Kathleen grasped her hand and kissed it and held it, and tears came, and Margaret's heart was bursting. She waited until Kathleen released her hand, and then she turned and walked with firm, measured stride to the front gate and turned up the street towards home.

Notes
___

Brigadier General Hugh Percy was given command of the relief column sent out by General Thomas Gage upon receipt of the message from Lieutenant Colonel Smith, delivered by Lieutenant Ambrose, requesting a support-and-relief column (see French, *The Day of Concord and Lexington*, p. 226).

CHAPTER XIV

★ ★ ★

*W*arm spring rains had greened the wooded hills that cradled Concord valley and drawn the grasses and flowers on the low, rolling meadows and fields of the valley floor into a brilliant mosaic of reds and yellows and blues.

Concord Town had grown near the center of the valley. The cemetery and liberty pole, courthouse, tavern, millpond, and meetinghouse formed the south end of the town, where the road from Lexington entered, curving around the base of the south hill. At the north end of town, the Assabet and Sudbury Rivers joined to form the Concord River, and the North Bridge spanned the Concord to give access from the town into the north end of the valley. Some distance north of the bridge, Punkatasset Hill rose to give a commanding view of the town. Just south of the bridge, the beautiful Emerson mansion stood at the head of the great, open green. The west side of town straddled the Mill Brook that flowed south from the Concord River to power the mill. The east side of town clustered about the road that carried traffic northward from the Lexington Road.

Concord was the county seat of Middlesex County, the center of politics, commerce, government, and colonial society for miles around. For decades it had been the hub to which all Middlesex roads led. Armies had ventured forth from Concord to punish marauding Indians and the French. For a century, news of the profound events that had changed the face of the new and struggling nation had proceeded from Concord. Thus it was that when the Massachusetts colonials stubbornly dug in their heels against the British, no one questioned that the munitions and cannon and supplies to fight would be gathered in Concord, to be hidden in barns and wells and attics, and the cannon buried in furrows plowed in fields. And no one questioned that inevitably, sooner or later, as certain as the tides of the sea or the rising of the sun, the British would come to Concord to get them.

As the British column on the Lexington Road marched steadily towards the south end of town, and the colonial militia and minutemen streamed into Concord from all points of the compass to meet them, a strange, unsettled feeling crept through the valley, as though it were in the very air they breathed. It was to be British regulars against largely untested farmers and craftsmen, with a single question riding heavy on both sides.

If shooting started, would the colonials buckle?

Tom Sievers felt the crackling tension as he led Matthew past the cemetery and millpond and courthouse into the south fringes of town, three-quarters of a mile ahead of the British. He stepped off the road to allow a colonial officer to lead a short column of militia trotting at double time directly towards the incoming British, and then Tom slowed to study the jumbled confusion that was Concord.

People with horse-drawn carts and wagons jammed with hogsheads of dried fish and salt beef, half barrels of gunpowder, kegs of shot, barrels of flour, and crated medical supplies moved away from Concord on every road, while men from outlying villages and towns trotted into Concord, clutching their muskets as they searched for the gathering point for their militia units. Some women and children mixed among them on the Green, and more stood near the homes that fronted on the roads to watch the gathering of the colonial army.

"There," Tom exclaimed, and pointed to a knot of officers near the center of the Green, south of the Emerson mansion. They were shouting orders and giving emphatic hand directions as they struggled to get their confused command organized into rank and file.

"Follow me, and keep a sharp eye for your father." Tom worked his way into the bustling throng. He grasped the arm of a stocky young man as he trotted past and asked, "Where's Barrett, or Buttrick?"

"Right up there giving the orders," he replied, and pointed, and was gone.

From earliest memory, the names of five families had been woven deep into the fabric of the history of Concord. Barrett, Buttrick, Hosmer, Prescott, and Davis. In times of war and peace, of famine and plenty, in politics or church, in joys and sorrows, the men and women of those families had taken their beloved valley on their shoulders and carried it, at any cost. Their dead lay in honored glory in the small cemetery on the hill south of town. And now it was Colonel James Barrett and Major John Buttrick who had been elected to assume command of the untried, unproven militia as they prepared to face the flower of the British army. Joseph Hosmer was appointed adjutant, and Captain Isaac Davis commanded the minuteman company from the tiny village of Acton.

Tom worked his way through the confusion and stopped in a press of milling men who were gathered around Barrett and Buttrick, listening for directions as to where the companies were assembling. Barrett was shouting the names of the towns represented and pointing in various directions, and Tom listened intently. Lincoln, Bedford, Lexington, Carlisle, Westford, Cambridge, Waltham, Menotomy, Mystic, Littleton, Chelmsford, Groton, Stow, and more—the men listened until Barrett called the name of their unit and pointed, then worked their way outward, looking for their officers and familiar faces.

"Boston," Barrett shouted, and pointed toward the mansion of the Reverend William Emerson on the Green close to the North Bridge.

"Come on," Tom said to Matthew, and worked his way out of

the crowd and walked hurriedly toward the mansion, watching for the first familiar face from the Boston militia.

"Matthew!"

The shouted name and the familiar voice stopped Matthew short, and he exclaimed, "Billy! That was Billy Weems!" At that moment he saw the grinning face as Billy shoved his way through the crowd towards them. "Billy!"

Billy Weems threw his free arm about Matthew, and for a moment the two boys stood locked in the embrace of oldest and most beloved friends, and then they stepped apart.

"Billy! You're here?" Matthew was incredulous.

"Wouldn't miss it! I thought you'd be home with Kathleen."

Matthew's eyes dropped. "Things aren't good."

Billy's face clouded. "Your father told me about Henry. I could hardly believe it." He looked at Tom. "How are you, Mr. Sievers?"

"Good. Seen John?"

"Come on," Billy said, and spun on his heel and started north at a trot.

They were there, east of the Emerson mansion—Telford and a host of the Boston militia—and as they approached, John Dunson emerged from their midst and trotted to meet the incoming trio.

He threw his arm about Matthew's shoulder. "You're safe!"

Matthew nodded. "You're all right?"

"Yes." John looked at Tom. "Everything all right at home?"

"They got Ingersol. Margaret is holding up."

"Thank you, Tom."

John turned back to Matthew, studying his face, his eyes, searching for a sign that would tell him if his son was whole and sound, his mind free to work unfettered in the crisis that could come any moment. He saw the flat look in Matthew's eyes, the clenched mouth, the preoccupation, and he felt a rise of concern. He opened his mouth to speak, but was cut off by a shout from a thin man who came running.

"Boston militia!"

All eyes shifted to the thin-faced man. There was no time to talk to Matthew.

"Over here," someone answered.

"Who's in charge?"

"Captain Ben Telford," John answered, and pointed.

The man turned to Telford. "Colonel Barrett wants you right now. And he wants John Dunson from the Committee of Safety, and Tom Sievers."

Telford and John started back towards Barrett, and John turned and motioned to Tom, who fell in beside them as they worked their way to the colonel.

"Why does Barrett want me?" Tom asked, his face drawn in puzzlement.

"Barrett wants me to repeat the orders from the Committee of Safety, and he might ask you to talk to these men about the things we learned to stay alive in battle. Be ready."

"You told him about me? us?"

"You can save lives by telling them."

Tom shrugged.

Colonel Barrett, with Major Buttrick on his right, raised his hands and shouted, "Quiet! We have no time to waste."

Thirty-eight men, the leaders of every unit of militia and minutemen, gathered close around him, brows furrowed, mouths straight lines as they concentrated.

At sixty-four years of age, Colonel Barrett stood just under six feet in height and was sturdy, with regular features and blue eyes that missed nothing. He was a born leader, called by unanimous vote to take command, despite his own protest that his age was against him. He raised his hand to silence the group and spoke. "John Dunson from the Committee of Safety is here. I've asked him to give you our orders." He turned to John.

John drew a heavy breath. "I talked with Sam Adams and John Hancock this morning. Their orders were to defend the stores and the town. Avoid a fight if possible. Do not fire unless they do."

John looked back at Barrett, who again raised his hand to the group. "Now, listen well! The British will be here soon. You've heard our orders, and I intend carrying them out. We've got three hundred tons of food, and cannon and gunpowder and grain hidden all over this valley, and I've got cannon and twenty tons of food hidden at my farm two miles north. They want it, and they won't get it."

He paused, and the men moved, then settled again.

"This is the plan. Let them come into town. Let them look. Let them take whatever they can find, because I do not think they can find much of it. If they start harming our citizens, or burning or destroying private property, we'll stop them, or if they find too much of it we'll stop them, but if they do not, we'll simply stand by and hold our peace."

Again he paused, and there was murmuring.

"Do any of you disagree?"

A powerfully built man near the front exclaimed, "Parker let them into Lexington and they killed some of his men. I say we stop them down at the millpond."

"I understand you," Barrett replied, "but our orders are specific. Protect the munitions and supplies, but do not fight if we can avoid it." He brought his eyes directly to those of the husky man. "Do you agree?"

His eyes dropped. "I agree."

Barrett drew a deep breath. "I'm going to let them into town. We'll surround the town out of musket range but where they can see us. I doubt they'll press too hard if they're surrounded."

He broke off and turned back to John and Tom.

"We've got a seasoned fighting man with us. I've asked him to give us some instruction on some things that will save lives if we have a battle." He turned and nodded to Tom. "Step out here in front, Mr. Sievers."

Tom looked at John before he moved out to the front of the group. The officers huddled close, silent, intense in their concentration.

"I'm sorry how I look," Tom began. "I been travellin' all night. I don't know much about military thinking, but I did learn some things from the French and the Indians." He stared at the ground for a moment, selecting words and thoughts. "If we drive them out of this valley, they'll form a column and march back the way they came, and they'll expect us to follow in a column because that's how they've been taught wars are fought."

Tom paused for a moment. "Keep them off balance. Don't fight them like they been taught. Their companies have been trained to shoot one direction at a time. Get on all sides of the road and shoot from everywhere. Shoot the ones with the gold on their shoulders first. Aim where the white belts cross. Get behind rocks or trees or bushes, or in ditches, or just anywhere you can find cover to shoot. Once you've shot, there's going to be a white cloud of musket smoke hanging out there telling them where you are. So move! Shoot and move! Load while you're running on down to the next cover. Shoot again, and keep moving. They don't have no idea how to fight you if you shoot and move. If they form a box, or a wedge, and charge, just run back until they stop, and get behind something, and shoot again. If they got cannon, make a big circle around and come in behind them. They can't move cannon fast enough to do any good if you circle fast."

Tom paused again. "They got eighteen miles to cover between here and Boston. If they do it peaceful, we let them go. If they shoot, we can punish them every step of the way."

He stopped and turned to John. "I miss anything?"

"Just a couple of things," John answered. "Don't move in big groups. It's easier to hit a big group than a small one. And don't look over the top of a rock or a log. Look around one side or the end, if you can. You're easier to see if your head shows over the top. And darker clothes are harder to see than light ones."

Tom nodded, then turned back to Barrett and waited.

Breathing began again in the group, and Barrett nodded his head. "Thank you." He looked at the group. "When you get back to your companies, repeat what you have been told. Make sure they understand. Now, listen close while I make assignments for your companies."

Methodically, clearly, he called the names of the towns whence the militia and minutemen had come, and pointed to the hills surrounding the valley, except to the north. On each call, the leader nodded his understanding.

"When you're all in position we'll have the valley surrounded except to the north. My Concord companies will take a position just this side of the North Bridge. Does anyone have a question?"

The sound of distant drums brought everything on the Green to an instant standstill, and every eye swung to stare south. The column of colonials that had passed Tom as he came into Concord was now marching back, around the bend by the millpond and the cemetery. Six hundred yards behind them, beating their drums to the identical cadence, the leaders of the British column matched them stride for stride, their red coats and white belts gleaming in the sun.

Barrett shouted to the assembled leaders, "That's Brown leading the British in. Get your commands to your assigned positions. Move!"

The company commanders scattered on the run, John and Tom following Telford back to the Boston company. Telford shouted his orders, the men fell into formation, and he quickly marched them east across the road, scrambling up to the hill to take a position on the ridge, where they turned and stood in plain view of the entire valley.

John turned to Tom. "How's Matthew?"

Tom shook his head slightly. "Too much has come down on him too quick. Thorpe's gone, and Kathleen put him out. We covered eighteen miles last night. He saw the Lexington fight, and we walked right in among the dead and wounded and helped with Parker's cousin Jonas. He took a bayonet charge alone. Brave man. He's dead. Too much too fast for Matthew. He hasn't caught up yet."

"We've got to watch him if shooting starts."

Tom nodded. "Him and Billy. Killing a man is a hard thing. Even if God wants you to do it, it's still hard. We'll have to watch the boys."

John opened the small packet of food and took out cheese and meat, and moved to Matthew's side and glanced at his drawn face. "How is it with Kathleen?"

Matthew shook his head but did not look at John. "She made me leave."

John worked on the food. "You better eat while you can."

Matthew shook his head. "I'm not hungry."

John continued. "You have to understand, her life—her family—has been destroyed. She'll need time."

"I don't think time will matter."

"Be patient. Did you see the Lexington fight?"

"I saw. We went down afterwards, among the dead and wounded."

John dropped his eyes, and he was suddenly back twenty-four years with Tom Sievers, on snowshoes twenty-six miles northeast of Marsden, hidden in the tangled branches of a great windfall maple near a frozen brook. A hill was to their backs, a small, snow-choked valley before them. A force of Indians had hit the Goosequill trading post and left four dead, and Tom and John and five other men found them thirty hours later and laid an ambush. They scarcely breathed as they watched the six Huron warriors trotting on snowshoes beside the brook ice, moving north. They would pass less than fifteen yards from where the men lay, white faced, scared, muskets cocked. The Huron had their fur-lined parkas up, and never stopped turning their heads, looking everywhere, sensing the trap but not expecting it yet. They were directly in front of the great heap of the fallen tree when the first musket cracked, and then the others cracked, all but John's. John felt the sweat freezing on his face as the Huron tumbled, all but one, and the last one swung his ancient French musket to bear at the tree, and Tom screamed, "Fire!" John buried the front sight of his musket in the midsection of the last Huron and pulled the trigger. He took the solid kick and raised his eyes, and he saw the Huron fling his musket to the side and grasp at his chest as he staggered back and tripped over his snowshoes and hit the snow, twisting, moving, trying to rise, and then slumped and moved for a moment and then lay still.

As though in a dream, John rose with the other men to go walk among the enemy dead, and John knew he would never forget the bright, hot, searing burn in his chest as he stared down into the flat, dead eyes of the man he had killed, and in his soul he knew he had committed an act forbidden by God and nature. His eyes blurred as he stared, and he felt the scalding tears freezing on his cheeks and he didn't care. And then he felt Tom's gentle hand on his shoulder, and Tom looked into his eyes and said nothing, and Tom's eyes were too bright and he wiped at them and walked away and left John alone.

John looked at Matthew, and he wished from his soul that he could shield him, take the burden from him and bear it on his own shoulders, but he knew he could not. He could only watch and wait and be there when life forced Matthew to decide for himself if he would commit acts that would test him in the crucible. Tom had called it right. Even if God wants you to kill a man, it's a hard thing. Even if it has to be done to bring about God's work, it's a hard thing.

John said softly, "There's not much that's worse to look at than men killed in battle."

Matthew looked into John's eyes, and John saw the pain and the fear and the doubt and the need for relief.

"I've done it," John continued. "Too many times. Only one thing gets me through it."

Matthew sucked in air and his eyes pleaded with his father.

"I have to know taking their lives was necessary for the right reasons. If I didn't have that, I think I would lose my sanity."

Matthew swallowed hard against the rise in his chest, and he said, "Did those men die for the right reasons at Lexington? Are we here for the right reasons?"

John looked more deeply into his son than ever in his life and spoke with measured words. "Yes. We're where we belong, doing what must be done. This is in the hands of the Almighty."

"The killing—those dead men—are part of God's work?" Matthew's voice was too high, strained. In his mind he was seeing men who had fallen, arms and legs thrown at odd angles, mouths loose and open, eyes wide, flat, dead. Men who had had wives and children, who only moments earlier had been alive, with hopes and dreams, joys and sorrows. He saw no glory, nothing noble. Only broken, bleeding bodies that were dead and would be put in the ground.

"Yes. So was the death of his Son."

Matthew gasped as the thought struck him as never before. From the earliest dawn of his memory he had known of the crucifixion of Jesus, but never, never had it been so real as it was to him at this moment. Jesus had looked like one of those men on the ground on the Lexington Green! Bleeding and grotesque, with unseeing eyes, and dead! Jesus, the Son of God!

He stared at John, and John saw the breaking of new understanding in his son, and he waited and he saw Matthew's mind leaping to accept it. Matthew dropped his eyes and raised his hand to wipe at his mouth, and John remained silent while Matthew's thoughts raced.

Their thoughts were interrupted by the booming voice of Colonel Barrett from down on the Green, and they turned and fell silent as the Boston company listened and watched.

"Captain Fowler," they heard Barrett shouting, "take your company and get these women and children off the Green, to Punkatasset Hill. Go now! The rest of you assemble at the North Bridge in rank and file."

They watched him as he turned to Buttrick. "You come with me to the North Bridge."

Barrett's command started north, and Barrett turned once to watch Brown as he led his incoming command past the cemetery and the millpond and Wright's tavern and headed straight north across the Green towards the North Bridge to assemble with Colonel Barrett's command. Five minutes later the colonial forces had reached their assigned positions, and they all stopped to see what the British would do when they found the town vacated.

They watched as the British column stopped at the cemetery and quickly the flankers seized the liberty pole and cut it down. The colonials held their wrath at the sight of their beloved flag in the dirt, and they continued their stoney silence as they watched the flankers move into town, up the streets, and across the Green, with the column following, drums banging and fifes playing.

They grimly watched as the British column began its systematic movements. Two companies secured the South Bridge to seal up the south end of the valley. Six companies turned east, crossed the road, and started up the hill towards the militia so visible on the ridge. Before the British reached the top, the militia had disappeared, to reappear farther north, again out of musket range.

Six companies moved straight ahead, directly towards Barrett. Barrett turned and spat orders, and his command crossed the North Bridge to take up position four hundred yards out in the valley. While he watched, all six British companies crossed the bridge, then three of them dropped off and quickly took up positions to seal up the bridge, while the remaining three companies angled left.

Suddenly Barrett reared up. "They're headed for my farm!" he cried. "Buttrick, take command. I've got to go warn my people." He spun his horse and rammed his spurs home, and his mare hit racing stride in three jumps. Buttrick fell back another two hundred yards to let the British pass unchallenged, and watched as they continued their two-mile march to Barrett's farm.

In town, the regulars had begun their door-to-door search. They did not find six barrels of gunpowder covered by feathers in an attic, nor twelve barrels of dried fish buried in a compost pile, nor salt beef, medicine chests, harnesses, rifle balls, bayonets, cartridge paper, ropes, salt pork, 318 barrels of flour in fifty barns, 80 barrels of salt in the church cellar, and spades, axes, canteens, and wooden spoons in a hundred pantries and outhouses and stables.

But they did find gun carriages behind the blacksmith shop, and they quickly dragged them to the yard beside the town house and set them on fire, while others continued to bang on doors with their rifle butts. If the door opened they entered to search. If it did not open they smashed it and forced the colonials into a corner at bayonet point and ransacked the place.

On the ridges ringing Concord, the militia remained motionless and silent, but they were beginning to seethe within. Their flag had been stripped and thrown down. They had retreated from the east ridges when the British regulars came up. They had yielded the North Bridge when the six companies made their march to Barrett's farm. And now they were watching their women and children face British bayonets while the systematic search went on in their town. Worse, the town house was jammed full of munitions and supplies. If it caught fire, barrels of gunpowder inside would level half of Concord. They held their breath and watched.

At his farm, Barrett gave orders to his foreman and checked the fields where cannon were buried, the orchard where 206 barrels of wheat and rye were buried, and attics and hay lofts where clothing and gunpowder were hidden. Then he gathered all his people that were nearby.

"They're coming. Stay calm. Do what they say. Do not provoke a fight. I have to go back to Concord. God bless you all."

He again spun his mare and sank spurs into her flanks and headed back to Concord in a cloud of dust on a backroad that would avoid the incoming British column. He pulled his lathered mare to a stop beside Buttrick and leaped down to study the position of the British and of his command. For the half hour he was gone, the two opposing forces had remained each in its place, staring at the other.

In town, the grenadiers had smashed the doors of the town house and entered. Two minutes later they began hauling out barrels of fish and beef and flour, bolts of cloth, wooden spoons, medicine chests, and axes and spades. They stacked them near the burning gun carriages and set them on fire, and the flames leaped and sparks flew into the still-morning sunlight. Within minutes the eaves of the building were smoldering, and then bright flames licked at the roof.

Martha Moulton peered from the window of her home across the street from the town house and clapped her hand over her mouth. "The gunpowder," she exclaimed. She threw her front door open and ran into the street and up to the nearest British officer.

"Sir, there is no need to burn the town house. You can take the supplies, but spare the building."

The officer studied the white-faced, panic-stricken woman, and gave orders to a sergeant. Five minutes later a bucket brigade of British regulars had formed, and the eaves and roof of the town house were soaked. It was saved.

Two blocks away, Reuben Brown refused to open the door to his livery. The regulars smashed it and set it on fire, and Reuben Brown gathered his sobbing wife and terrified children away from the flames to comfort them as they watched their life's work burn and the smoke and sparks rise above the greening, budding trees.

At the North Bridge, Barrett, Buttrick, Davis, and Hosmer stood with gritted teeth, watching the systematic search and the black smoke rising above the trees in the center of town. They could not see what was burning; they only knew buildings were being razed and citizens bullied and supplies destroyed.

Barrett dropped his eyes for a moment. "Do we take the North Bridge?" he asked quietly.

Hosmer turned. "Will you let them burn the town down?"

Barrett looked at his pocket watch—ten thirty-five A.M. on the morning of April 19, 1775—and he gave his orders. "We take the North Bridge. Buttrick, you lead with your command. Go three hundred yards past the bridge and take defensive positions. I'll keep my companies here and wait for the regulars coming back from my farm."

Buttrick turned, and before he could give his orders Captain Isaac Davis quietly said, "My Acton men will lead."

There was no finer, more respected officer than Isaac Davis— quiet, soft-spoken, absolutely dedicated to his men, and fiercely proud of their spirit and determination. There could be no better man and no finer company to lead the fight for the North Bridge.

"Done," Buttrick said.

Five minutes later they were in marching order, and each man remained silent, aware that for the first time militia were taking the fight to British regulars. The question again rose to the top of their thoughts like a bright light. Would the militia buckle under fire from the heavy Brown Bess muskets?

At the bridge, Captain Walter Laurie of the British grenadiers watched as the colonials formed their column and started their march straight at him. He glanced back at the bridge, then once more at the colonials, and gave his orders. "We can defend the bridge better from the other side. Fall out and reassemble on the south side, and assume the street-firing formation and prepare to rotate."

Five minutes later the British regulars had formed on the road leading to the bridge from the south, but they were in a column. Those in the rear could neither see the bridge nor fire on it. Laurie did not realize he had limited the number of muskets his command could bring to bear on the bridge!

A low, swampy bog forced the colonials to march one hundred yards east, then circle back to the bridge, and they approached it from the side, with their column stretched out sixty yards from the bridge entrance, along the bank of the Concord River. Buttrick was in the lead, Davis and Hosmer right beside him, when Buttrick gave his next order. "Halt!"

The British column was on the south end of the bridge, the colonials on the north end, and for seconds that seemed endless they stood thus, less than fifty yards apart, facing each other. On command the regulars began tearing up the bridge planks to stop the colonials from crossing, and Buttrick shouted at them, "Don't tear up the bridge."

Then, without any command given, from nowhere three musket shots cracked out from the British side of the bridge. For one second of shock and disbelief it seemed as if the world were in suspended animation, and then the British fired their first full volley.

Captain Isaac Davis and Private Abner Hosmer went down with four other militiamen, and Buttrick suddenly realized what was happening and screamed his next order. "Fire! In the name of heaven, *fire!*"

The colonials were strung out along the north riverbank, and from their position they could see the entire length of the British column. Their first volley rolled out like thunder and raked the British column from one end to the other. Of the eight British officers facing them, four went down instantly, with more than twenty regulars. Spread as they were, the colonials reloaded faster than the British, and their second volley knocked more than thirty regulars off their feet.

Captain Laurie took one look at his column, one-third of them casualties in the first ninety seconds of the fight, and shouted, "Fall back," but he was too late. The regulars had already broken ranks and were in full retreat, panic-stricken, terrified at the deadly accuracy of the colonial muskets and the fearlessness of the men firing them.

"Follow me," Buttrick shouted, and led his command across the bridge and marched three hundred yards towards the town, where he called a halt and told his men to dig in and wait.

In town, Colonel Francis Smith heard the musket fire to the north and immediately led four companies to secure the North Bridge and stop the firing. As he cleared the edge of town, what he saw across the Green stopped him in his tracks. His regulars were in a full, disorganized, panicked retreat, and he could see red-coated bodies strung out for two hundred yards on his side of the bridge. He hauled his command to a stunned halt and waited for Laurie.

"Report."

The white-faced Laurie stammered, "The North Bridge is lost, sir. The colonials overran our position."

"They *what?*"

"They had superior numbers and better field position, sir."

"Casualties?"

"I don't know, sir. Lieutenants Sutherland, Hull, Kelly, and Gould are back there, sir. And a sergeant—I don't know which one—and a lot of regulars."

Sitting his horse, Colonel Smith battled to keep a cool head. He looked at the surrounding hills with colonials on every ridge, then at the North Bridge where Buttrick was now dug in to hold it, Barrett beyond the bridge, waiting, and at Laurie's command, shattered in less than two minutes. He looked north, past the bridge to where he had sent Parsons and three companies to search the Barrett farm. They were somewhere out there, but in what condition he had no idea. He glanced back at Concord and gave his orders. "Fall back into Concord. We wait for Parsons and his three companies."

His bewildered command turned and marched back to the center of town and stood in confused, white-faced rank and file. Minutes stretched into half an hour, with Smith and his command slowly realizing they were surrounded and pinned down and could not leave until Parsons and his three companies returned from the Barrett farm. He turned to look south towards the millpond and the cemetery.

"Get me a runner," he barked to his adjutant, and a moment later a young lieutenant stood at rigid attention before him.

"Go to the South Bridge. Tell the commander to bring his forces to this place immediately, for reinforcements if the militia attack us."

The young officer vaulted into his saddle, and twenty minutes later the South Bridge command halted beside Smith's troops, and the officer in charge saluted. "We heard shots. What happened?"

"They took the North Bridge."

The officer's mouth dropped open and he clacked it shut, then said, "I don't understand. The colonials took the North Bridge from us?"

"Yes. And inflicted heavy casualties."

The young officer's cheeks ballooned and he exhaled slowly. He said nothing. He turned back to his own command.

Another thirty minutes went by while the British stood in the town center, sweating, white-faced, feeling the rise of tension as all eyes scanned the north hills looking for Parsons's command to return. On every ridge surrounding the town they watched fresh militia arrive from outlying villages to hunker down and stare back at them in ever increasing numbers.

At the North Bridge, a sixteen-year-old boy appeared from nowhere, running across the bridge with a hatchet in his hand, apparently to join Barrett and Buttrick and the colonials. He slowed at the sight of the dead and wounded British regulars, sprawled in their red coats, lifeless and dying, and he blanched and began to tremble. It was not supposed to be like this. It was supposed to be glorious and noble. A British corporal groaned and raised a hand to him for help, and the horror-stricken boy gasped and instinctively swung the hatchet, and the blade struck the mortally wounded soldier at the hairline and peeled back the scalp. Sickened, the boy threw the hatchet down and ran crying back whence he had come.

Colonel Smith's eyes had not left the north reaches of the valley for half an hour while he endured the torments of imagining what would happen when Parsons tried to get past Barrett's force, across the bridge, then past Buttrick's men, dug in and waiting, and in his mind he was seeing Laurie's command, decimated in less than two minutes by this untrained, ragtag gathering of citizens.

He began to pace, then signalled to Pitcairn. "Come with me." Hastily they rode south to the cemetery hill, where their view would be unobstructed, and Smith extended his field glass and locked it onto the road to Barrett's farm. For long minutes he stood still, watching for the first movement on the road, and then it was there.

He lowered the glass and pointed and exclaimed, "There! He's coming! Parsons is coming!"

He raised the glass once more and watched as Parsons saw that the British regulars were no longer at the North Bridge. Parsons came to a full halt when he saw that Barrett's command stood ready and waiting, blocking his approach. Smith watched as Parsons pointed across the bridge at Buttrick's companies, dug in three hundred yards south of the bridge, and he saw Parsons freeze when he caught sight of the red coats littering the road south of the bridge. Parsons stopped his column and for long, agonizing minutes consulted with his officers, and then he gave orders, and Smith watched the column advance at double time towards the bridge.

Smith held his breath as he watched Barrett give orders to his men, and then Smith's eyes widened in utter disbelief. Barrett's militia was moving aside to give Parsons and his three companies free passage across the bridge!

"A trap!" Smith exclaimed in anguish. "They're going to trap Parsons between the two commands!" Pitcairn raised his hand and shook his head, and the two officers watched as Parsons gave orders and raised the pace of his column from double time to a full-out trot. Their boots thumped hollow on the bridge until they cleared the south side, and Parsons paused a moment when he saw the dead corporal at the roadside with his scalp peeled back where the boy's hatchet had struck. Smith watched him drop to one knee, feel the man's throat, then rise to run back to the head of his column, and it continued towards Buttrick's command at a trot.

Smith jerked the glass down, and his head thrust forward at what happened next. Buttrick's men were dividing, falling back two hundred yards on each side of the road. They were giving safe passage to Parsons's outnumbered, tired command, and Parsons did not hesitate. He trotted his men through the divided militia, into town, and did not stop until he reached the safety of Smith's command.

"They had him and they let him go!" Smith exclaimed. "Why?

Why?" Smith and Pitcairn leaped to their saddles and dug in their spurs and held their horses to a gallop from cemetery hill until they were at the town house, where they pulled their blowing mounts to a stiff-legged stop and dismounted.

"Report," he exclaimed to Parsons.

"We searched the Barrett farm. We found trivial amounts of flour and spread it on the ground."

"How much time did you spend?"

"Not long, sir."

"The reason?"

"The hills and ridges were filling with militia. We were outnumbered, sir."

"Do you know why the two militia forces gave you safe passage at the North Bridge just now?"

"No, sir, I do not."

Smith turned to speak to the rest of his officers but Parsons stopped him. "There's something else, sir. There's a dead corporal back at the bridge. They tried to scalp him."

The cluster of gathered officers heard the report, and the word spread throughout the column. The barbarian colonials are scalping! Scalping!

Smith started to speak but stopped at the sound of a horse running from the north end of town. A lieutenant reined in his prancing mount and saluted while he spoke in gasps. "Sir, the two militia forces have joined and the entire force is marching directly towards town. They'll be here in minutes."

Smith instantly barked orders to his officers. "Prepare your commands to march immediately. We have but thirty-six rounds per man, and we absolutely cannot undertake a major engagement with this force of colonials without running out of ammunition. We have about seven hours of daylight left. The reinforcements I sent for are not in sight, and gentlemen, we are leaving here, immediately."

All too gladly the tired, dirty, thirsty, frightened British regulars jumped to the task of putting their forces into marching order, while the officers mounted their horses and supervised.

On the ridges east of town, the Boston command under Telford had watched it all. They had leaped to their feet shouting when the militia returned the British volley at the North Bridge and officers and regulars had dropped all along the column, and they raised their fists in triumph when the British regulars broke under the second devastating militia volley and turned their backs and ran! The single question that had haunted them for two days had been answered. The militia had not buckled under fire; the vaunted British regulars had! A full-out, panic-ridden retreat!

They had settled back into position in studied silence while Barrett and Buttrick gave Parsons's outnumbered men safe passage over the bridge and into town, and they understood.

Barrett's orders still held. Do not fire unless they do.

Now they were watching the entire British force reassemble with their faces south. They were leaving Concord valley, going back through Lexington to Boston.

If they go in peace, let them go. But if they shoot, hit them hard.

Captain Telford remained still and studied the troop movements until he understood that Barrett and Buttrick meant to march straight into the British and force them to make a decision. Stand and fight, or turn around and go back to Boston while they still could. And Barrett intended to hold his fire until the British fired first.

Telford turned to his own Boston command. "There are homes and families on the Lexington Road, and our orders were to protect them and that's what we're going to do. Fall into rank and file. We're going to march!"

In the center of town, Colonel Francis Smith took one last look at Barrett's advancing company and then at the militia jammed on the ridges surrounding Concord, and he waited no longer. "Forwarrrd, *march!*"

Their drummers made no cadence; their fifes were silent. The single sound was of their tramping feet, moving south. Smith ordered out his flankers, and they marched past the millpond and the cemetery and swung nearly due east, with the long, low hill on their left. The flankers moved out one hundred yards on each side of the road and trotted through the yards of the homes as they moved east, watching for the place where the hill dropped off into the open fields that formed Meriam's Corner where the road forked, north to Bedford, east on to Lexington.

On the opposite side of the hill, Telford gave his orders. "We're going to be at Meriam's Corner ahead of them. Stay out of sight on this side of the hill. Let's go."

The Boston company took the lead, running through the tall spring grass, dodging through the scrub oak and maple, leaping small seep streams, watching the ridge to their right for the first sign of redcoats. Bedford and Waltham men came behind, following them, grim faced, watching the skyline, grasping their muskets as they ran. Four hundred yards from the place where the hill sloped off into the meadows of Meriam's Corner, Telford slowed and pointed, and Tom and John, at his side, saw the fresh militia ahead, from Reading and Billerica and Wilmington, formed in the meadows and fields, waiting. Shouts came from behind and they looked back, and parts of the Barrett and Buttrick command were coming hot on their trail to join them.

The British were not yet in sight.

Telford took command. "Spread all along the Lexington Road, three hundred yards back. Do not fire unless fired upon!"

The militia hesitated for a moment, then began taking positions all along the Lexington Road in rank and file. They settled in facing west, watching for the first sign of the redcoats. Flies buzzed and bees came seeking the spring flowers, and still the men stood in silence, waiting for the first glimpse of red on the road, and then it was there.

The flankers came first, one hundred yards from the road, and those on the north side saw the militia and slowed and then angled back towards the road, watching over their shoulders as they approached the single bridge that crossed the stream near the fork in the road, and hurried across in single file. While they crossed the bridge, Telford gave orders and the militia began a slow advance, closing the gap until the flankers reached the main column on the road, and then Telford stopped his company, two hundred yards distant from Smith's command, leading the British column. Smith's command was moving slowly towards Lexington, but every man among them held his musket at the ready, and every eye was watching each move of the colonials with bright memories of seeing Laurie's command reeling, staggering, officers and regulars dropping under the blasting roar of the two volleys at the North Bridge.

Telford remained still, watching intently as the column moved on. The leaders passed the fork in the road and continued on with the column close behind. Telford could see their drawn, tired, frightened faces as they stared at the colonial forces stretched out for a quarter mile facing them.

Telford held his breath. *They might do it. They might pass without firing. They might. I hope they do. I hope they do.*

It came too quick. Suddenly the leading British company pivoted and fired, and the first volley of the heavy .75-caliber balls came whistling at the nearest militia, most of them too high.

For one heartbeat the echo sounded and then the colonials raised their muskets, and Meriam's Corner rang once more with the blasting shots, and the white smoke hung heavy in the warm, still afternoon air. The volley slammed into the section of the column not hidden behind the hill, and British officers and regulars on the near side of the first three companies buckled and staggered and went down on the roadbed. Those behind them shrank away, then turned to retreat but could not because the column behind them was still marching forward. Instantly the officers drew their sabers and spurred their horses into their own men, shouting, "Regroup, regroup and keep marching," and under the threat of the raised sabers the shaken, white-faced troops moved back into formation and slowly resumed their march eastward towards Lexington.

Notes

The description of Concord on the morning of April 19, 1775, is accurate, and the description of the events as they unfolded at the battle of Concord is also accurate. Further, the names of the five families Barrett, Buttrick, Hosmer, Prescott, and Davis—whose people for generations had served their beloved Concord as patriots of the finest order—were prominent in the battle of that day, when the colonials met the British head to head at the North Bridge and turned the battle of Concord into a total rout in which the British retreated in near panic. The words, "Will you let them burn the town down?" uttered by Lieutenant Joseph Hosmer, were the turning point. (See French, *The Day of Concord and Lexington,* chapters 17 through 22, and particularly p. 187.)

The incident wherein the sixteen-year-old boy assaults a wounded British regular with an axe is depicted generally consistent with the account provided by French, *The Day of Concord and Lexington,* pp. 211–12. However, other equally competent sources report the incident not as the act of a startled, distraught boy, but as a deliberate atrocity perpetrated by the militia on the wounded soldier, killing him. The account and the possible reasons for the boy's actions given by French are used as the basis for the novel's account only because they seem to cast the militia in a more humane attitude.

Wednesday, April 19, 1775

CHAPTER XV

★ ★ ★

M̶ove!"

John grasped Matthew's arm and pushed him, then Billy
Weems, and they broke from the ditch where they had crouched,
and John crowded them to a trot ahead of him, with Tom following. The men around them stood still, gaping at the British as
though mesmerized by the realization they were in battle, and
John grabbed the nearest one as he passed him and turned him
east and shoved him roughly.

"*Move!* Load while you run! Head for Hardy's Hill!"

The man shook his head as though coming back from a far
place, then fell in behind John.

"*Move!*" Tom shouted to others they passed. "*Shoot and move!*
Get away from the gun smoke. Load while you move. Find cover
and fire and keep moving."

Slowly the militiamen began to shake off the shock of the first
moments of cracking muskets, and their brains began to function
once more, and those nearest John and Tom began to follow, loading while they ran, looking for a place to stop and fire once more.
It spread outward from the few, and small groups of the colonial
force began to move eastward from Meriam's Corner.

"Small groups," John shouted again. "Gather at Hardy's Hill!"

On the road, the British officers spurred their horses into their
own men, sabers raised high, herding them into a semblance of

order. "Keep marching!" they shouted above the din. "Do not stop—keep marching!"

By threes and fours, the militiamen ran ahead, watching the British as they continued their march, and they saw them raise their muskets once more and fire their second ragged volley. And once again the big lead balls whistled high, over their heads.

Tom slammed his ramrod back into its slot beneath his musket barrel, primed the pan, snapped the cover down, and went to one knee beside an oak. John stopped beside him, and they both levelled their muskets and fired. A British captain flung his sword high and sagged in his saddle and toppled to the ground, and a sergeant carrying the Union Jack grasped his chest and sat down. The proud flag dropped into the dust, and no one noticed or stopped to pick it up.

John took one quick glance at the pans on the muskets of Matthew and Billy. They had not been fired. He glanced at their eyes and saw the boy inside trembling as they faced the white-hot fires, searching to know if they could cross a line drawn in their souls by lifelong teaching and their own conscience against killing a man. The talk by kings and generals of the glories and drama of war was forgotten with lead balls whistling and men dropping. At that moment, the single harsh reality for both boys was the war within themselves. Could they kill? Only they could decide. John saw it and he turned away and said nothing.

With John leading, they dodged from the cover of the oak and continued east at a trot, measuring powder from their powder horns and seating the patch and ball for the next shot as they moved.

Tom paused for one moment to look back. The militia were strung out behind them for half a mile, but they were moving, and they were beginning to develop a rhythm. Take cover, shoot, move, load, take cover, shoot. Tom saw the beginnings of coolheadedness and the first hint of confidence. The British volleys had both been high—the universal sign of panic-stricken, untested troops firing too quickly. The return volleys by the militia had not been high, and the British were leaving dead and wounded at every step. And not one British officer had yet shown the first sign of knowing how to fight a fragmented army that would not stay in one place long enough to become a target and that kept up an unending stream of fire.

"Keep moving!" Tom shouted once more to those behind. "Small groups."

The last company in the British column cleared the low hill at Meriam's Corner and took their first volley. They raised their muskets to return fire, only to see the militiamen streaming east, loading as they ran, moving in small groups, using every rock, tree, ditch, and groundswell for cover to stop and fire again and keep moving.

A grizzled sergeant raised an anguished fist against the colonials and shouted, "Stand and fight, you bloody cowards!" and a moment later a colonial musket ball slammed into his right shoulder and he groaned and spun and crumpled to the ground. The corporal nearest him tried to pick him up and could not, and he laid down his musket and stayed with his fallen sergeant, using his red coat to try to bind the torn, bleeding wound.

At the front of the column, half a mile ahead, the leading company raised frightened eyes to peer eight hundred yards up the road, at Hardy's Hill, where a groundswell rose forty feet on the left side of the road and a heavy stand of oak and maple trees came to road's edge on the right. The regulars glanced at their officers, pleading in their faces, but one thing was clear to Colonel Francis Smith: if he stopped his column, he would be instantly committed to a fight he would lose because his regulars were already beginning to count their ammunition. If he left the roadbed he would be on ground with which he was not familiar, while militiamen knew every tree, every creek, every rock. If he unwittingly marched his men into a bog or a marsh, he could lose every soldier in his command. Boston was yet seventeen miles distant, and the reinforcements he had sent for had not appeared. Smith had no choice. He barked orders. "Stay on the road, and at all costs do not stop!"

The column doggedly continued marching while the incessant firing poured in from their left, from muskets they could not see fired by hidden men who were ever moving in small groups. The British flankers were driven back into the column. The regulars fired when they could see a target, and finally they began firing without one. The taste of acrid gun smoke was thick on their tongues, and rivulets of sweat streaked their faces as they moved on, reloading, searching for a way to stop the nightmare. Thirst began to set in, and they drained their canteens and then licked parched lips while they marched.

Ahead at Hardy's Hill, the minutemen from Sudbury and Framingham hid in the dense maple and oak grove on the south side of the road and studied the incoming column for several minutes. "Scatter and hide," came the command, and one minute later both companies were scattered for one hundred yards, invisible behind trees and rocks and in a small streambed that ran parallel to the road.

On the north side of the road, John and Tom led militia to the lip of the hill, studied the British, now a scant four hundred yards distant, and gave hand signals. Within moments, two hundred militiamen lay in the warm spring grass, just over the crest of the hill, invisible from the road.

The leading British company was nearly past Hardy's Hill before the first musket volley came blasting from the woods, and they turned to look as the balls smashed into them. An instant later, while they were frantically trying to locate targets to return fire, John led the militia ten feet forward to the crest of Hardy's Hill, and two hundred men knelt to steady their muskets and pulled the triggers. Regulars went down all up and down the roadbed, and those left standing surged on, confused at the incoming fire from both sides, unable to decide which direction they should return fire.

"Move!" John shouted, and stood and waved the militia farther on, glancing once at the pans on the muskets of Matthew and Billy. The covers were open. They had fired. He glanced at their faces and read the set of their jaws and the look in their eyes, and he watched as they worked mechanically, reloading while their minds and hearts tentatively accepted the fact they had fired and they waited to see if they could approve the act of killing another man. Once more John signalled and they stopped and took cover and waited, and as the regulars came beneath them, they once again sent a volley ripping into the column leaders.

Regulars all through the first three British companies gasped and sagged and went down, and they turned and tried to run back into the column. The officers in the column drew their pistols and aimed them point-blank at their own troops and shouted, "One more step and we shoot you on the spot!" The regulars stared into the bores of a score of aimed pistols and then into the eyes of their own officers, and turned back and once again started east, while the colonials on both sides fired their second volley. Then the colonials broke cover and moved on east, past Hardy's Hill.

Beyond the hill, the road continued through open meadows and fields, only to pass beneath the crest of another hill on the left where the road made an abrupt left turn around the base of the rise, ran for five hundred yards, then turned sharply once again to continue east. At the turn, the trees on the right side of the road again came to road's edge.

The regulars in the British column looked and dropped tortured eyes for a moment, and groaned.

Ahead of them, at the place where the road made the sharp-angle turn to the left, Major Loammi Baldwin lay behind the decaying remains of a fallen oak. Scattered through the dense growth of trees behind him, his Woburn company lay hidden while they studied the incoming British. Baldwin watched them continue on the road, and he knew they dared not leave it. He gave his orders.

Across the road, the first of the militia arrived and came to the crest of the hill and looked back to watch the British moving steadily towards them. With the unending rattle of musket fire driving them on, it was clear they would not leave the roadbed. A moment later John and Tom arrived, and John gave orders, and although he had no command authority over the militia, not one man, including the officers, failed to instantly obey.

Coming into the abrupt turn, the companies leading the British column, out of formation, struggling with their walking wounded, tried to watch both sides of the road, knowing in their hearts they were about to be caught again in a deadly, point-blank cross fire.

On the crest of the hill, John signalled the militia forward, and in five seconds the ridge was lined with kneeling colonials, and before the British could raise their muskets the first volley plowed into them. Three seconds later Major Baldwin's musket roared on the wooded side of the road, and instantly every man in the Woburn company fired. Once more the first three battered British companies reeled from the barrage of bullets.

Then the colonials were on their feet, moving around the abrupt turn, loading, taking cover, waiting, and two hundred yards past the turn they blasted out their second volley and moved on. One hundred yards past the second sharp turn in the road, the colonials ripped loose with their third volley, and this time men went down the entire length of the British column. The sole remaining captain of the Forty-third Infantry slumped in his saddle and pitched headlong, and the single remaining officer in that company—a young, white-faced lieutenant—assumed command. Of the eight officers assigned to the Forty-third, seven were dead. The British had not yet learned that the gold on the shoulders of their officers drew the heaviest fire.

Nearly three miles ahead, at Lexington, a breathless militiaman pulled his horse from a stampede gait to a sliding halt at the front door of Captain John Parker, leaped to the ground, and pounded on the front door. A moment later Parker threw the door open.

"Sir, we turned 'em around at Concord, and we been chasin' 'em all the way back, and they're comin', sir. They're comin', and we're pourin' the fear into 'em!"

Instantly Parker spun on his heel, and five minutes later he marched onto the Green with his drummer and ordered him to sound assembly. Within ten minutes Parker had the remains of his Lexington command facing him.

"Men, the column of regulars is coming down the road, and by the Almighty, we're going to go meet them and give them what they gave us this morning. Are you with me?"

Their shout became a roar as Parker led them west on the Lexington Road, striding briskly at the front of his command and carrying his musket in his left hand, with his right arm and hand held tightly against his wounded side.

West of Lexington the road crossed Nelson's Bridge, which spanned a small stream, and the approach to the bridge was beneath another hill, over one hundred yards in length, fifty feet above the road. As Parker approached Nelson's Bridge he could hear the distant cracking of musketry, and he stopped for a moment to consider. Past Nelson's Bridge, the land was open and rolling, with stone fences and a great field of boulders on the right, and scattered brush and scrub oak on the left. He hesitated but a moment.

"Up the hill, men. Form a skirmish line on this side, just below the top, and hide. Don't fire until I do."

Minutes later the Lexington men were strung out for the full hundred yards, fifteen feet below the crest of the hill, every man invisible behind a rock or some brush. Parker was in the center of the line, flat on his belly behind a boulder, peering around one side for the first sign of the British. Then they were there, and Parker saw the white musket smoke from the invisible militia on both sides of the road and watched the column take the unending punishment. A look of grim satisfaction crossed his face, and he waited, with the image of Jonas, dead, clear in his mind.

On the roadbed, Colonel Smith turned in the dust and looked at the rear of his column. He saw the orange musket flashes from the militia on the roadsides and the white smoke from their muskets, and he understood but one thing: he had to keep the column moving or the rear companies were going to be annihilated. He watched his men, stumbling, ignoring their wounded, thoughts fragmenting, and he knew that if he did not keep the column moving fast, none of them would see Boston again.

Once more he ordered out his flankers, one hundred yards into the fields and woods at the sides of the road, in the desperate hope they would be able to engage the militia and take some of the pressure off the column. The flankers moved out, but the colonials simply fell back one hundred yards and moved on. When the flankers pursued, other militia moved in where they had been, and there was hardly a break in the firing.

Anxiously Smith peered ahead and his heart sank when he remembered the Nelson Bridge crossing, with its hill on the north side. His only hope was to get past it as fast as he could. He galloped to the head of the column, giving orders to his officers as he passed them. "Move past the bridge as fast as possible!"

Coming to the bridge, the regulars were obsessed with but one thing: if they moved fast enough they might outrun the holocaust. The leading company ran across the bridge, with those behind breaking into a trot, then a run, following, heedless of the hill to their left or the threat it posed.

Parker did not move as he studied the incoming column, picking out the officers, and suddenly his eyes widened. *That's him! He was at the Lexington Green this morning. He commands this column!* He shifted his musket and brought it to bear on Colonel Francis Smith. He waited until Smith was directly below him, less than thirty yards away, and he sighted and pulled the trigger. Instantly every man in Parker's command fired, and Parker moved his head to look beneath the rising cloud of white gun smoke and saw Smith grab his upper thigh and pitch from his horse into the dirt. Behind him a captain grasped his throat and toppled backwards from his horse. Major Pitcairn came forward at a gallop to assume command, while two regulars pulled Colonel Smith to his feet and attempted to put him back on his rearing, prancing horse but could not.

Pitcairn shouted his orders. "Lead companies, charge them!

Up the hill!" He spun his horse and sprinted back four hundred yards and shouted to his marines, "Climb that hill and rout those militiamen!" The marines surged forward from the field and across Nelson's Bridge, and started up the hill.

Parker's men held their ground and maintained their deadly, point-blank fire, and the regulars charging up the hill directly below them sagged. Then the marines came at them from their right, and the militia shifted their fire. The marines began dropping but continued up the hill.

Parker cooly stood and shouted to his Lexington men, "Fall back to the far side of the hill and regroup and wait for them."

The marines watched them disappear over the crest of the hill and followed them, scrambling, and reached the crest and looked down the north slope. They saw no one, and suddenly from behind the trees and rocks another volley came whistling. The marines stopped in their tracks and took cover, and not one of them returned fire.

When Parker's first and second volleys stopped the column at Nelson's Bridge, the rear companies had kept marching and had run into those in front and stopped. The militia, swarming both sides of the road, had now nearly pinned down the six companies at the rear, and Smith understood that if they were pinned, unable to move, it would all be over before sunset. Desperately he shouted to Pitcairn, "Keep them moving!"

Pitcairn nodded his understanding and once more galloped back to the rear of the column, with incoming musket balls whistling on all sides. "Move on to the Bluff. Take the Bluff. Rally on the far side of the Bluff."

Five hundred yards past Nelson's Bridge a single hill known as the Bluff rose beside the road, and it was Pitcairn's desperate hope that if he could take it and make a stand, he could create a little time for his beaten army to breathe and regroup. He charged again from the rear to the front, frantically shouting the same orders, and slowly the column once more began to advance.

The light grenadiers marched up the Bluff, taking heavy fire and casualties, and the colonials fell back and gave the hill to them. Pitcairn held his breath as other companies of his regulars followed to the commanding position of the high ground, and the balance of the column continued until they were under the pro- tection of the muzzles of their own grenadiers and marines at the top of the Bluff. For the first time since they took the heavy volley at Meriam's Corner, they had time to regroup and do what they could for their walking wounded.

What Pitcairn did not recognize was that in buying the time for his own bleeding, decimated army, he had given time to the colonials. Those at the rear of the column now came sprinting past the Bluff, on towards Fiske Hill nearly a mile beyond, and began selecting the rocks and trees and bushes where they would once again be invisible and within fifty yards of the road on both sides.

Twenty minutes later Pitcairn ordered his column back onto their feet and started them east towards Lexington, and before they had moved ten yards another colonial volley raked them from one end to the other. A musket ball cut a channel across the hindquarters of Pitcairn's horse and it screamed and reared, and Pitcairn was thrown rolling into a ditch, while the horse stam- peded away from the road.

From that moment, neither Pitcairn nor Smith was able to again take control of their command. The column started forward with no thought of organization or formation, no thought of who was in command, ignoring the frantic orders of their own officers. They saw Fiske Hill and they marched on, knowing what lay ahead but no longer caring. At that moment none of them could remember a world that was not filled with muskets blasting in their faces and men crumpling to the ground and the groans and cries of the dead and the dying. They moved forward knowing only that they would eventually either be killed or reach Boston, and they did not care which came first.

As they came abreast of Fiske Hill, fresh militia from Cam- bridge and Gardner, under the command of Captain Samuel Thatcher, were waiting. Crouched behind stone fences and rocks and trees on both sides of the road, they waited until the column was squarely in the middle of the trap before they fired.

The regulars in the column broke. They did not raise their muskets as they ran forward, stumbling, ignoring their officers, abandoning their wounded, with but one instinct and that was to find a place where the unending musket blasts and the whine of incoming musket balls would go away.

Two miles east, past Lexington, Brigadier Hugh Percy, travelling west with his relief column, raised his hand and his drummers sounded the halt. One thousand troops from the Fourth Foot, the Forty-seventh Foot, the Twenty-third Royal Welch Fusiliers, and the First Battalion of Royal Marines came to a stop. Sitting his horse, he turned his head to listen, and heard the distant, continuous rattle of muskets. He was half a mile short of reaching Lexington, just approaching the low, gentle hill that commanded the town on the east side. For long minutes he sat listening and pondering how he could best accomplish his mission of rescuing Smith's devastated column. Should he continue on through Lexington and meet the militiamen in open meadows and fields, or set up his cannon and let them come to him? He made his decision and gave his orders.

Twenty minutes later his cannon were aligned on the crest of the hill overlooking Lexington, and his column flanked the cannon on both sides, red coats shining, muskets and bayonets glittering in the late afternoon sunlight. The sounds of the fighting were becoming louder, more distinct, and Percy dismounted and took a position in front of the cannon muzzles. He watched the Lexington Road through his telescope and waited for Smith's battered column to appear.

Moments later he gasped and peered intently through his telescope. "Militia!" he exclaimed. "Where's Smith's command?"

Militia and minutemen from every command were running into the open fields and meadows half a mile past Lexington, where they crouched behind the stone fences and trees, and in ditches and streams, and waited, muskets pointed at the roadway.

And then the first flash of red showed on the roadway, and the red coats of Smith's command came stumbling on with no hint of officers or any semblance of military decorum. They were a disintegrated, beaten army in full running retreat. Regulars broke from the accursed roadway into the meadows and fields on both sides of the road in the desperate hope they could escape the cross fire, and the colonials once again appeared from nowhere and everywhere to fire at point-blank range.

From a ditch where he had crouched to fire, John leaped back into the grassy meadow and ran on towards Lexington, reloading as he moved. He glanced back only long enough to see Tom and Matthew and Billy following, strung out behind him, and beyond them the red-coated regulars scattering into the meadow to escape the cross fire on the road. Reloaded, John stopped to once again take cover behind a low stone fence, and a moment later Tom dropped beside him and then Matthew. John turned to look for Billy, and he was not there.

Billy had been last in line, and none of them had seen him grasp his left side and go down behind them and lie twisting in the grass, trying to rise, nor had they heard his cries for help above the heavy sounds of battle.

"Where's Billy?" John shouted desperately, and Tom and Matthew instantly turned panic-stricken eyes to look. Three retreating red-coated regulars were nearly on top of Billy before they saw him. The leader raised his musket, made one stroke downwards, and drove his bayonet home, then jerked it out for a second stroke.

"*Billy!*" Matthew screamed, and his musket barely touched his shoulder before he fired, and the regular flung his musket high and fell, twisting. The two behind him slowed for a moment, and Tom fired and the second one buckled and went down. John sprinted towards the third, musket held at chest level, and the third redcoat stopped five feet short of Billy and turned, slipping, falling, scrambling back to his feet as he ran blindly back towards the roadbed.

In a moment the three men were crouched around Billy. Tom ripped Billy's shirt open and gritted his teeth at the sight of the blood running from the bullet hole low in his left side, and John winced at the purple-ringed hole in his chest where the bayonet had plunged through. Matthew choked in rage as he looked into the face of his lifelong friend.

Billy opened clenched eyes and recognized Matthew. "He killed me, he killed me, I don't want to die, Matthew, don't let me die," Billy pleaded. His eyes were large, panicked.

John shoved his musket into Matthew's hand and grasped Billy under his arms and stood him on his feet, then draped him over his shoulder.

"Watch my flanks," he shouted to Tom and Matthew, and started across the meadow for Lexington at a run.

On the hilltop at the far side of Lexington, Brigadier Percy studied the battle scene for ten seconds through his telescope, then jerked it from his eye in total, stark disbelief as he struggled to understand what he was seeing.

"They're surrounded, in a full retreat!" he exclaimed. "They're beaten! They'll be annihilated within minutes!"

He spun and shouted orders to his cannoneers. "Load and fire!"

Lieutenant Buchanan, fourth cannon from the north end of the line, barked orders, and his sergeant measured powder into the cannon muzzle, rammed it home, seated the cannonball, and nodded to Buchanan. "Fire," ordered Buchanan, and the corporal smacked the match onto the touchhole, the powder caught, and the heavy gun bucked and roared. The other cannon blasted, and the first fusillade whistled over the Lexington Green and crashed into the trees on the far side.

Instantly every eye on the battlefield turned east to look, and they saw the red-coated fusiliers and marines lining the crest of the hill east of Lexington and the white smoke drifting from the cannon muzzles. A moment later a ragged cheer rolled out from every throat among the regulars down on the roadbed. Never had they seen a more beautiful sight! They moved back to the roadbed and on towards Lexington on feet and legs trembling from exhaustion, counting the moments until they would be under the protection of the cannon and muskets of Percy's relief column.

Tom took one look and fell back, watching as the colonials scattered, uncertain what to do in the face of cannon fire. Tom waved his arms and shouted, "Divide and go around! Divide! Go around! The cannon can't hurt you if you're moving around. Get behind them!"

He waited to watch the militia recover from the sudden shock of cannon, and those in front rallied and began to divide, moving north and south, angling around the hill dominated by Percy's redcoats. The others behind followed as the cannon roared again and the cannonballs ripped harmlessly into the meadow and the woods beyond. Not one militiaman had been injured by the cannon fire.

On the road, one wounded British regular could go no further. He simply sat down, slumped over, unable to rise. Another threw down his musket and collapsed beside him. Within seconds four more had gathered in the group, bloodied, exhausted, tongues swollen from thirst, unable to move further. Colonial hands grasped them, lifted them, carried them as the militiamen continued their relentless pursuit, and they stopped at the first farmhouse and banged on the front door. A terrified woman opened the door, and the militiamen begged entry and laid the wounded British on the floor of her parlor.

"Can you help these men?" they asked. She nodded her head vigorously, and the militiamen were gone as the woman and her children set water to heat and began tearing bedsheets into strips.

Tom turned once more and sprinted to catch up with John and Matthew, and he grasped John's shoulder and pointed. "Take him there! Jonas Parker's house." They crossed Lexington Green amid militia moving north to circle Percy's cannon, then crossed the Bedford Road. Tom hammered on the door of Parker's home. Lucy Parker peeked from behind a window curtain, recognized Tom and Matthew, and threw the door open.

"Ma'am, we got a boy hurt bad, and—"

Tom got no further. Lucy Parker exclaimed, "Bring him here," and led them running to a bedroom. She stepped aside while John gently lowered Billy onto the bed and straightened his feet, Tom and Matthew by his side. Lucy Parker's three teenaged daughters gathered behind them, silent, wide-eyed.

Lucy turned to the oldest of the three daughters. "Prudence, boil water," and to the other two, "Get bedsheets," and the three left at a run.

Tom spoke again. "Ma'am, it was Matthew and me brought your husband home—"

"I know who you are, God bless you! Where is this boy hurt?"

"Here, ma'am." Tom pulled open the shirt, and Lucy looked and closed her eyes and groaned, then asked, "Bullet?"

"One. One bayonet wound. Is there a doctor?"

"There are half a dozen doctors here to help from towns all around. There are bound to be some down at the meetinghouse on the Green or at Buckman's tavern just up the road."

Without a word Matthew darted from the room and left the front door standing open as he sprinted down to Buckman's tavern, one hundred yards south.

The two younger daughters returned with bedsheets, and John rolled the limp, unconscious Billy onto his side while Lucy slipped double layers under him. John settled him back onto the sheets, then worked Billy's shirt off and folded it with the blood inside and laid it beside the bed.

Prudence returned with the first kettle, with steam rising from the spout. Lucy poured half an inch of water into the porcelain bowl on the nightstand, soaked a torn bedsheet and wrung it out smoking, and expertly began washing around the two wounds. She signalled for John to once more roll Billy onto his side while she looked at his back to see if either the bullet or the bayonet had gone through. There was no sign.

"The bullet's still in him," she said and dropped her eyes for a moment.

Tom rolled him once more partially onto his side and gently laid the flat of his fingers against Billy's back and pressed and shifted and pressed again. "I think I can feel the ball, not deep."

Lucy continued to wash the wounds with the steaming water, then left for a moment to return with a bottle of wood alcohol and poured it into the bowl with fresh hot water and continued washing. While she was gone John felt Billy's throat and found the faint, irregular pulse and the beginning of fever.

Five minutes later Matthew was back in the bedroom leading a small, wiry man with a black satchel. He was coatless, his shirt blood spattered, sleeves rolled up, and his hair askew. He had not shaved, and his thin, sweating face showed fatigue and irritation. His spectacles had tiny flecks of blood.

"I'm Doctor Atwood from Woburn. Who's hurt?" he demanded. "There are twenty men on the Green that need help and I need to get back there."

John and Tom moved aside, and he saw Billy.

"Dead?" he asked.

"No," John answered. "Bullet and bayonet wounds."

The little man dropped to one knee beside Billy and felt his pulse, then his throat, and he shook his head but said nothing. He rolled Billy far enough to see that neither the bullet nor the bayonet had gone through. Then he looked at the bullet hole for some indication of angle, and pressed gently on Billy's back, above the belt for several seconds, before his fingers stopped.

"Bullet's right there. We better get it out while he's unconscious."

He rolled Billy onto his stomach, then opened his satchel and drew out a scalpel and a probe. He dropped them into the porcelain basin and poured the last of the steaming water in, then half of the remaining alcohol. He draped torn bedsheets on Billy's back and spoke as he drew the scalpel from the bowl.

"You folks better look away."

None of them turned or moved.

Billy groaned and twitched as the scalpel bit, and the doctor gave John a head sign and John kneeled to hold Billy still as the doctor dropped the scalpel back into the bowl and took out the probe. He slipped the pointed probe into the incision and struck the bullet on the first try. One minute later he had it in the palm of his hand, and the big .75-caliber ball seemed monstrous as he dropped it plunking into the porcelain bowl and once more reached into his satchel. He soaked a needle and gut in the alcohol and water, and eight stitches later washed Billy's side with alcohol.

"That's all I can do for now. Leave him on his stomach for a while. He's going to fever badly. It's up to him now."

Matthew asked, "What are his chances?"

The doctor dropped his head forward to look over the top of his glasses. "I don't know. If he can taste blood when he wakes up, he may have a punctured lung, and if he passes blood in his bowels, that bullet could have destroyed his kidney, and either one of those could be fatal. Or if either one of those wounds hit an intestine, that could be fatal too. But he's young and strong. He has a chance. Keep cold packs on him when he fevers. I'll come back as soon as I can." He started for the door.

Matthew accepted it. "Thanks."

The doctor raised a hand without looking back and was gone.

Outside, on the east hill, Percy's cannon blasted again, and one errant cannonball ripped completely through the meetinghouse on the Green, where the colonials had laid out their dead from the morning's battle. Miraculously the ball struck nothing but the wall going in and the opposite one going out, disturbed nothing inside, and gouged a ten-foot furrow in the dandelions. Not one of Percy's cannonballs had harmed a colonial.

Billy groaned and moved his legs, and Matthew dropped to his knees beside him. "Can you hear me, Billy?"

Billy's eyes fluttered open and he tried to focus. His face was flushed and twisted in pain. "Matthew?"

"Billy, can you understand me?"

"It hurts awful."

"Billy, can you taste blood?"

Billy worked with his tongue and swallowed. "No."

Matthew's head rolled back in relief. "You're in a bed with a good family in Lexington. A doctor got the bullet out."

"My chest burns, and my side."

"You were wounded. Don't talk."

Billy forced his eyes to focus. "Matthew, am I going to die? Tell me true."

Matthew reached to touch the flushed cheek. "The doctor doesn't think so. Now, lie still."

Matthew rose, and Billy tried to raise his head. "Matthew, are you going? Don't leave me here."

John glanced at Tom, then spoke quietly to Matthew. "You've done your share. Stay with Billy. He needs you more than we do. Come home when you can. Here. Take these bandages." He handed Matthew the torn strips of sheeting he had brought from home.

Matthew drew up a chair and settled beside Billy and reached to take hold of his hand. "I'm here, Billy. I'm not leaving."

Billy smiled and his eyes closed, and he tightened his grasp on Matthew's hand.

Tom spoke to Lucy. "Ma'am, could we leave him here?"

"Of course!"

John extended his hand, and Lucy shook it strongly. "Thank you, Mrs. Parker."

"It is us that owes you men," she replied.

John and Tom picked up their muskets and quietly slipped from the bedroom and out the front door. They walked onto Bedford Road and stopped, startled at what they saw.

Lexington was surrounded! On every hill, in every meadow and field, from the Green down past the hill where Percy and his command and the tattered remains of Smith's column had taken their stand, colonials were concealed behind everything that would afford cover, pouring an unending stream of fire into the regulars' positions.

John and Tom trotted north on the Bedford Road, then cut

east when they came to the Reverend Mr. Clarke's home. Twenty minutes later they had circled past Percy's hill and were once again within one hundred yards of the Lexington Road.

Percy stood before his cannon and surveyed the town of Lexington, studied both sides of the road, then turned to his adjutant. "Get Rooke."

"Who, sir?"

"Lieutenant Rooke. Fourth Regiment. General Gage's aide-de-camp."

Five minutes later Lieutenant Rooke stood before him at rigid attention.

"Go back to General Gage with this message. We found Smith and we're returning to Boston and will arrive late this evening, probably heavily engaged. We will probably need further reinforcements. Do you understand?"

"Yes, sir." Rooke saluted and vaulted onto his horse and was gone in a cloud of dust, covering nearly the identical route Revere had covered but fifteen hours earlier, but in the opposite direction.

Then Percy turned to study the Lexington Road he had travelled earlier. Near the road were a dozen large homes and barns, and while he watched, white musket smoke came from the windows and around corners.

He turned to Colonel Maddison. "Take your company and go burn those buildings and knock down those stone fences and walls. Too much cover for sniper fire."

The buildings were deserted when the regulars knocked the front doors down, and for the first time the soldiers disobeyed Smith's standing orders against looting. Before they dropped their torches, the soldiers looted the homes, taking anything of value they wished, and moved on to the next. When they returned to report to Percy they did not mention the looting, only that the buildings were vacant and burning and the stone fences were kicked down. But the regulars all knew. They saw the stolen jewelry and coin, and they held their silence and waited.

At three-thirty P.M. Percy made one last round of his hilltop position, studying the position of the rebels and reflecting on what he knew. He had passed through Menotomy but three hours earlier, and it had been deserted and shuttered. There was no chance the militia could raise enough men at Menotomy in three hours to pose a threat. If he waited longer where he was, the colonials would have time to take positions on both sides of the road back to Boston as they had done with Smith's column as it came from Concord, and if they did so and blocked the road, they could pound his command into the ground as they had done Smith's, perhaps annihilate both.

He made his decision and gave his orders. Freshest troops at the rear of the column, since that was where the fighting was expected to be, and resume the march immediately.

The road from Lexington to Menotomy passed through rolling hills, some of which overlooked the road on the north, with woods on the south side of the road. As Percy's column plodded onward, the firing increased with each mile, and when finally Percy saw Menotomy in the distance he was certain he would be free of the unending musket fire once he was past the small town. He ordered an advance company to move into the empty and shuttered town to be certain it was not filled with colonials waiting in ambush.

The advance company moved into the town and began battering down doors, looting and plundering at will as they had seen done in Lexington. The third door they smashed was the home of Jason Russell, and inside, a dozen militiamen waited. The fight was short-lived and intense, with eleven militia killed or wounded, and twelve British, and as the advance company continued, they were stunned to find militia in nearly every building, hiding in barns and hay lofts and attics, waiting.

Onward Percy marched, past Peirce's Hill and Foot of Rocks, and the weary companies stumbled towards Menotomy, unaware of what lay ahead, taking courage and relief from their belief there would be little resistance.

Behind Percy, two thousand militiamen were decimating his

rear companies. Ahead, men from Framingham, Newton, Beverly, Cambridge, Westford, Watertown, Salem, Danvers, Mystic, Roxbury, Concord, Needham, Lynn, Dedham, and Menotomy were hidden everywhere, dug in, waiting for him to try for Boston.

Percy had his cannon at the head of his column where he could position them instantly to give cover for the column behind if needed. The officers in command were twisting in their saddles, watching the incessant musket fire continue to shred the ranks. Buchanan's face was twisted in torment as red-coated infantrymen staggered and went down, and those who filled in the gaps buckled and fell.

He turned anxious eyes back to Percy, waiting for orders to stop and set the cannon and cover the column until they reached Menotomy, but the order never came.

"Do not stop," Percy shouted. "Keep moving on through the town. It is deserted."

Flanked by open fields on both sides of the road as it approached town, Buchanan spurred his mount to the near horse harnessed to his cannon and grabbed the bit and kicked his horse to a trot, jerking, pulling the harnessed team. The lieutenant in front of him could not control his mount in the wild confusion, and Buchanan came back on his reins and slowed his cannon to avoid running over the one ahead.

"Move," he shouted to the white-faced lieutenant ahead of him.

The young officer jammed his horse into the near horse of the team pulling his cannon and made a wild lunge for the bit, but the horse shied and reared and came down with his right foreleg over the withers of the horse harnessed beside him. They went down in a tangle, and the cannon careened onto one wheel and would not settle.

Buchanan jammed his spurs home, and in four jumps his horse was beside those that were down. He leaped to the ground to grab the bits of the scrambling horses. In thirty seconds he had them separated and standing, and he led them twenty feet off the road and jerked the kingpin from the double tree and released the cannon. Then he slapped the horses on the rump with the reins, and they bolted away into the adjoining field.

Twenty seconds later Buchanan was back at his cannon and had the column moving forward once more, at a trot. They cleared the outskirts of the small town, and then they were at Cooper's tavern, and suddenly, from nowhere, the town was filled with colonials, and the cannoneers and infantry directly behind them were looking into the muzzles of a thousand muskets.

It seemed the world was instantly filled with blasts from every place a man could hide, and once again the British regulars were sent reeling back in a mindless retreat into their own troops following behind. And once again, those behind continued marching to escape the hot fire from the two thousand militia now firing at near point-blank range from behind, and the British column began to collapse onto itself.

At the front, Buchanan saw what was happening. He stood in his stirrups and shouted, "Forward at the trot," and he tried to lead the column through the ambush at a run but it was too late. On the second volley he felt the smashing hit above his left elbow and his arm dropped numb, useless, and he knew it was badly broken. Then his sergeant was beside him, trying to hold him in the saddle, and then the sergeant gasped and clutched his throat and fell backwards. Buchanan half fell, half dismounted to help him, and he saw that he was dead. He somehow remounted with the white-hot wires in his left arm burning, and something slammed into the right side of his head and the world went dark. He felt himself falling, and he reached with his right arm to hold his left tight to his body and tried to kick his feet free of the stirrups to keep from being dragged. Then the sounds and sights of war faded into black silence.

One hundred yards behind, Percy's mouth dropped open in utter terror. He had made the same tragic mistake made by Smith, Pitcairn, and Laurie. None had believed the colonials could gather an army within hours, and to a man, none of them could believe they were now facing over four thousand colonials, each waiting for his chance to fire at the hated redcoats. In Menotomy, the fighting became savage, face to face, hand to hand, and the regulars found themselves swarmed by men who had no fear.

Chief among those was seventy-eight-year-old Sam Whittemore, who heard them coming and quickly cleaned and loaded his two pistols and his musket, and shoved his saber in his belt. When they reached his home he jerked the door open and stepped into the yard facing more than fifty regulars. He fired both pistols simultaneously, and two redcoats dropped. He threw the pistols aside and swept his musket from the doorjamb and fired, and a third regular dropped. He cast the musket aside and jerked his saber out and was advancing to meet them when a Brown Bess musket ball tore into his face, taking flesh and bone from the left side. Sam went down and the regulars ran over him, pausing only to bayonet him thirteen times, then ransack and set fire to his house. Half an hour later Sam regained consciousness, pulled himself into the half of his house that had not burned, cleaned and bound up his own wounds, and reloaded his two pistols and his musket and made ready for the next regulars that ventured into his yard.

In the midst of the heaviest fighting, Joseph Warren of the Committee of Safety and General William Heath, who had come from Boston to join the fight, stood in open sight of the British. Warren shook his fist at them as he shouted his defiance. A British marksman took careful aim and fired, and the big slug knocked the pin loose that was holding Warren's hair. Warren did not miss a step as he continued to parade before them, waving his fist, encouraging the colonials, defying the British.

Colonel Smith called for Percy. "It's happening all over again," he said through the pain of a leg torn by Parker's musket ball. "In the name of heaven, keep the column moving. If we're stopped here, we'll never see another dawn. Take the road to Charlestown and stop there for the night. We'll never make it through Cambridge to the longboats."

Percy gave orders, but few of the regulars heeded or obeyed. The column began to fragment as the lead companies cleared Menotomy. Galloping to the front, Percy wheeled his gelding before the officers in the lead and shouted to them.

"You will regroup your men or stand for a court-martial, and you will take the road to Charlestown, where we will spend the night."

Slowly the column began to regroup into some semblance of organization, and the men plodded on, with the sun reaching for the western rim of the world.

John and Tom worked their way past the place where the road turned south at Mystic and, with the Mystic River at their backs, once again reloaded and waited, with four hundred militiamen clustered about. They fired in the gathering dusk, and the orange flame leaped two feet from the muzzles of their muskets, and they were instantly on their feet moving farther south, reloading. They passed Winter Hill on their right, across the road, and then Prospect Hill, and they saw the orange muzzle blasts and heard the popping of militia muskets from the far side of the road and watched the British column take the volley and shuffle on, demoralized, decimated, beaten.

"They're going into Charlestown," Tom said as they trotted on.

"They'll stay there tonight," John replied. He looked ahead at the lights of Charlestown less than half a mile distant. The roads leading out of town were plugged with outbound citizens who had heard the battle for the last hour and knew the regulars were going to take refuge in town. Reports had trickled into town during the day—the colonials had mauled the regulars with an eighteen-mile ambush; the redcoats had taken the worst beating in North American history. The Charlestown citizenry feared reprisals, and they did not want to be in town when the British arrived. They packed what they could in an hour and were leaving town in droves, by foot, horseback, carriage, wagon, cart.

John slowed. "I think it's finished. They're beaten. We can't see to shoot in this light. Watch for anyone who got separated from their companies, ours and theirs." He wiped his sleeve across his face and glanced at Tom and allowed himself a brief smile. "We made it."

Their faces were both streaked from sweat and dirt and grime and gun smoke. Their clothing was filthy with caked mud from the river and stream crossings and with dirt from crawling on their bellies behind rock fences.

Tom grinned back at him, open and easy. "That was a long day, but—"

He sensed it and a premonition struck terror in his heart, and then he heard the faint click of a musket hammer coming to full cock somewhere behind them, and Tom was turning when John tensed and started around.

The crack of the Brown Bess and the heavy thud of the big ball striking and John's grunt all came on top of each other, and John pitched forward onto his hands and knees as Tom wheeled around and peered into the deep dusk, balanced, ready. He saw the white crossed belts in the gloom and then three regulars running directly at him, and he understood that behind them somewhere was an officer mounted on a horse, and that they had gotten separated from their column in the wild fighting and the fading light, and that he and John had unknowingly walked between them and the road.

Tom saw the orange muzzle flame of a second musket, and the ball tugged at Tom's shirt as the blast rolled past him. Tom fired and the lead regular buckled and went down. Tom threw down his musket and grabbed John's and fired from the hip at the two running men, and the second one went down, finished. The third regular came sprinting to reach Tom with his bayonet before Tom could reload, and Tom measured powder into John's musket barrel, rammed it home with the ramrod, left the ramrod in the barrel, primed the pan, slapped it shut, planted the butt of the gun in the hollow of his hip, levelled it, and cocked and pulled the trigger. The blast twisted Tom back a step and blew the ramrod halfway through the man, who fell at Tom's feet, his eyes wide in surprise as he tried to move and then lay still.

The mounted officer, twenty-five yards behind the regulars, jerked his saber from its scabbard and rammed his spurs home and came thundering, hunched forward over the neck of his horse, saber held at full arm's length, levelled at Tom.

Tom's hand darted beneath his coat and his tomahawk was out. He danced to one side, waiting, gauging distance and speed, and when the officer was forty feet away Tom's arm flashed back and then forward and the tomahawk leaped from his hand. It struck just above the place the belts crossed, and the officer recoiled, his saber fell into the grass, and he pitched headlong from his horse. The horse slowed as the officer hit the ground and rolled, and Tom stepped into its path and raised both hands. It threw back its head and set its front feet and then danced to one side, and Tom lunged and caught the dragging reins and held on while the horse fought, jerking. Tom spoke low to it, "Huuuuu, huuuu," and slowly the horse came to a trembling, nervous stop, eyes wide and white rimmed with fear. Tom spun and led it running back to John, who was still on his hands and knees, head down, gasping, and Tom saw the great gout of blood on John's shirt below his right shoulder blade. Tom fought back the sick panic as he dropped to his knees beside John, still holding the reins with his left hand while he reached under John with his right to support him and exclaimed, "Can you hear me?"

John nodded weakly and said, "Yes," and Tom choked back his rage. "Can you stand up?" John tried to rise and couldn't, and Tom felt a sob surge from his chest and he cried out in anguish, "John, don't you die on me, don't you die!" He quickly thrust his arm through the looped reins and reached to lift John to his feet.

"I'm putting you on a horse," he told John, and John raised his head and Tom lifted him onto the horse behind the saddle, then threw the reins over the horse's head and mounted the saddle seat. He reached behind and found John's hands and brought them around his own midsection and grasped them with his right hand, and with John leaning his weight against his back, Tom turned the horse towards the lights of Charlestown and kicked it to a high gallop.

He held the horse to a gallop up the middle of the street through Charlestown and people gave way, and he did not stop until he reached the docks on the shore of the Charles River. He leaped from the lathered, exhausted animal, caught John over his shoulder, ran to the first rowboat tied to a wharf, and laid John in the bottom. He ignored the British gunboat *Somerset* and the shouts from her crew as he rowed beneath her stern, directly to the north shore of the Boston Peninsula. He caught up the first horse he found and mounted it with John behind and raised the horse to a clattering gallop through the dark cobblestone streets of Boston, ignoring the challenges of British regulars as he stampeded through their patrols, down past the South Church, and hauled the winded horse to a stop at the gate of the Dunson home. He dismounted and lowered John from the horse, then looped John's arm over his shoulders and slid his arm about John's waist and half carried him to the front door and hammered with the flat of his hand.

Notes

The battle that ensued after the colonial minutemen and militia drove the British from Concord has been termed the "longest continuing ambush" in the history of North America. Within one and one-half miles of Concord, colonial forces ambushed the British column at Meriam's Corner, and thereafter at Hardy's Hill, the Bloody Angle, Parker's Revenge, Fiske Hill, Lexington, and Menotomy. The term "Parker's Revenge" came into being after Captain John Parker, informed that the British column was retreating from Concord and was on its way to Lexington, marshalled his command that had met the British on the Lexington Green that same morning, and marched his men more than two miles to where he personally laid an ambush that devastated the British column. By that time the British force was a decimated, reeling army in full, panic-ridden retreat. Brigadier Percy did appear with his cannon and did delay the colonials for a short time, and probably saved the British column from total annihilation. However, the delay caused by the British cannon allowed the colonials to circle the guns and lay further ambushes, as far as Menotomy. The events described in chapter 15 are accurate, save for the activities of the fictional characters John Dunson and his son Matthew and Tom Sievers. (See French, *The Day of Concord and Lexington*, pp. 193–264.)

Wednesday, April 19, 1775

CHAPTER XVI

★ ★ ★

*H*ead bowed in somber and foreboding thoughts, Margaret sat at the dining table staring out the window into the gloom of deep dusk gathering in the street. She had not drawn the shades, nor had she yet lighted the evening lamps. Since morning, when the British column had marched south with the cannon, Margaret had become quiet, then silent, and Brigitte saw the terrible apprehension growing. Half a dozen times in the late afternoon mounted criers had ridden horses through the streets, shouting the latest news of the battle. Lexington—Concord—the British in full retreat—heavy fighting—cannon—they will be back in Boston during the night. And each time Margaret's hands had trembled and she had busied herself with housework to hide her terror from the children. After the supper dishes were finished Brigitte had quietly taken the children to her bedroom to read to them, to give Margaret time to herself.

Margaret slowly worked her hands together, one with the other, struggling to keep control of her fears. *They will come back. God hears the prayers of those who love him, and he answers. He will not let harm come to them. He will not. He will not.*

She raised her eyes to again peer out the front window, and there were more buggies and wagons in the streets than before, working their way south, leaving the city in fear of what was to come.

Suddenly Margaret's hands stopped and she straightened in

her chair, and then she bolted to her feet and her chair skittered backwards, scraping on the hardwood floor. For a fleeting moment she saw it in her mind—John in a field, on his hands and knees, unable to rise—and then it was gone. Her face turned white, and for a time she could not breathe as the image burned into her heart.

He's hurt!

The knowledge was certain.

In the bedroom Brigitte paused in her reading at the sound of the chair skidding.

"Caleb, keep the children here." A moment later she stopped in the archway to the parlor, struck by the image of her mother standing rigid, white-faced, staring out the front window in the twilight of the room.

"Mother?" she said quietly.

Margaret did not turn as she spoke. "He's hurt."

A look of puzzlement crossed Brigitte's face. "Father? How do you know?"

"I saw it."

For a moment Brigitte did not understand, and then realization struck and she stood rooted. For a time it seemed the room was charged, and then Brigitte sat down at the table and Margaret sat down beside her, and neither woman spoke. Finally Brigitte stood and lighted the lamps and drew the shades, and silently walked back to be with the children.

Margaret sat in the silence, face drawn, until she was startled by the sound of footsteps in the hallway and Brigitte appeared with the children.

"Shall I get them ready for prayer and bed?"

Margaret stood and said, "Yes, I'm coming," when the sounds of a running horse came from the street, and then they heard the front gate slam open and a moment later the fearful pounding at the front door. Margaret ran and threw up the latch and jerked the door open, and Tom stood framed in the light holding John on his feet, head slumped forward.

Margaret gasped and stiffened and blurted one word. "Alive?"

"Alive!" Tom exclaimed and did not wait for a reply or permission to enter the home. He walked John past Margaret, into the bedroom wing, and settled him sitting onto his bed, then laid him on his stomach while Margaret straightened his legs and Brigitte removed his moccasins, battered and caked with dried mud. Tom looked at John's back, and Margaret saw the shirt sodden with blood from his shoulder to his belt. She clapped both hands over her mouth to stifle her anguished cry, and Brigitte backed up a step and said nothing. Behind Margaret, Adam and Priscilla began to sob quietly, aware that something tragic had happened but unsure what it was. Caleb swallowed and stood silently behind the children.

Tom turned to Brigitte. "Get the doctor." Brigitte spun on her heel to leave.

"No," Margaret exclaimed. "You shouldn't be in the streets tonight."

Brigitte didn't hesitate. "I'm going," she replied and ran from the room.

Margaret squared her shoulders and reached to touch John's throat and felt the slow, weak pulse. "When did it happen?" she asked Tom.

"About an hour ago."

"I saw it," she said quietly.

Tom gaped, stunned, until he saw her eyes.

She spoke to Caleb. "Put kindling in the firebox and bring the teakettle the minute it steams. Hurry!"

Margaret disappeared for a minute, and returned with her large sewing scissors, a stack of bedsheets, alcohol, and soap. With her jaw set like granite she cut John's clothes from him and rolled them into a ball and dropped the bundle to the floor.

"Help me," she said, and Tom rolled John while Margaret tucked fresh sheets under him. She leaned over and carefully studied the pucker of the purple wound and the black blood that had clotted and the fresh, bright blood that was beginning to show. "Did it go on through?"

R.G. MICHAELS

Tom shook his head and Margaret's shoulders slumped. Caleb ran into the room, and Margaret took the large teakettle and poured steaming water into the china bowl on the nightstand and soaked and wrung out a large washcloth, soaped it, and began to clean away the blood. While she worked, Tom gently touched John's cheek.

"Can you hear me?"

There was no reply and Tom repeated it. "Can you hear me?"

Slowly John's eyes opened, and he tried to focus. He knew it was Tom, and he formed the words, "Where are we?"

"You're home in your bed. Margaret's here."

John turned and tried to look up, and Margaret dropped to her knees beside him and laid her hand on the side of his head. "I'm here."

He worked his tongue and swallowed. "How long have I been here?"

"Ten minutes."

He started to speak again and he coughed and tried once more, and Margaret leaned forward to press her cheek against his. "Don't talk. We have to wash you. Brigitte's gone to get Walter."

John slowly asked, "Tom, did it go on through?"

Tom hesitated. "No."

John closed his eyes, and Margaret fought back tears and rinsed the washcloth and continued washing. Minutes passed while she cleaned his face and hands, then his body. She soaked the washcloth with alcohol and wiped him and folded clean linen and packed the wound and covered him carefully with sheets.

Then she turned to Caleb. "Take the children into the parlor and read to them."

Caleb took the children by the shoulders and herded them from the room, and Adam began to whine as Caleb walked him down the hall.

Margaret suddenly stopped and stared at Tom, panic in her eyes. "Where's Matthew?"

"Lexington. Billy Weems got hurt. Matthew stayed with him."

Margaret pressed her fingers against her mouth for a moment. "Matthew's not hurt?"

"No, ma'am. It was Billy."

She released held breath and her shoulders settled. "Did anyone tell his mother?"

"Not me. I came here."

"Someone has to go tell Dorothy."

"Will you be all right here for a while, ma'am?"

"Hurry," Margaret said, and Tom walked out into the night.

Margaret turned back to John and for a moment stood working her hands together, indecisive, wondering what she should do next, and there was nothing, so she got a comb and carefully combed his hair and tied it back. Then she drew a chair close to the bed and reached to hold his hand, and his fingers tightened on her hand. She watched the slow, rhythmic rise and fall of his breathing. She touched his face and forehead and they were warm.

Fever. Where's Brigitte? Where's Walter? Where's Tom? He's had time to tell Dorothy and be back. Brigitte should have been back ten minutes ago. The British have her. I should never have let her go into the streets tonight. They have her.

Margaret jumped as Caleb's voice called, "Mama, Prissy won't stop crying."

Margaret rose and hurried to the parlor, feet apart, her voice high, firm. "Your father's been hurt. You children get ready for bed this minute, and we'll have prayer and you're to get into bed and stay there."

"Is Papa going to die?" Prissy wailed.

"You are not to worry about that," Margaret exclaimed. "You get ready for bed. I will take care of your father."

Caleb marched the children to their bedrooms, and Margaret returned to John's side and again laid the back of her hand against his face and forehead.

She flinched at the sound of the front door bursting open, and Brigitte came pounding into the bedroom with Doctor Walter Soderquist behind, his black satchel in hand. He was panting, his clothing rumpled, his hair awry, and his shirt showing stains of working with wounded. He came directly to the bedside.

"Move, Margaret," he said, and reached for John's wrist. He closed his eyes for thirty seconds while he counted and felt the strength of the pulse. He drew the sheet down and pulled the packing from the bullet hole, and Margaret saw the muscles in his jaw make small ridges when he looked at the location and size of the bullet hole. He looked carefully at the blood on the packing, and said nothing, and repacked the wound with fresh sheeting. He laid his hand on John's forehead, then the side of his face, then on both sides of the wound.

He looked at Margaret. "Did it go on through?"

She shook her head, and he sucked air and for a moment his eyes closed.

"Has he had anything to eat or drink?"

"Not since he got home."

"When was that?"

"An hour ago. Maybe less."

"How did he get here?"

"Tom Sievers."

The front door rattled, and a moment later Tom strode into the room and stood at the end of the bed, staring at the doctor, waiting.

"When was he hit?" Walter asked him.

"Maybe two hours ago."

"Has he talked since?"

"Yes. He talked after he got here."

Doctor Walter Soderquist settled onto the chair beside the bed and folded his hands in his lap, and slowly his head bowed and he sat for long moments with his eyes closed. Then he raised them to Margaret and Tom, and they saw the sadness and the anger.

"The bullet's punctured his right lung, and it's somewhere in there now. I can probe for it, but I might do more damage than good. I can operate, but I don't know where the bullet is, and if I don't find it quickly, chances are strong he wouldn't survive. I can leave it where it is and hope the damage to the lung isn't so bad he will die, but I fear for the worst. Those are the choices we have. For now I think we better wait and see."

"How bad do you think it is?" Margaret asked firmly.

Walter's eyes would not meet hers for a moment; then he stared at her steadily. "Bad. The blood on the packing I took off was bright red. He's bleeding into that lung now."

Margaret raised her chin. "How much time does he have?"

"No way to tell. I expect he will rally sometime soon, and he'll talk and look like he's going to recover. After that either he'll begin to recover or we'll lose him. No way to tell."

"I'll need time to think about what to do. Can we come get you later?"

"I'll be at home waiting."

"Is there anything we should do now?"

"Try to get him to drink a little water. Keep cold packs on his head and around that wound to fight fever."

"Thank you, Walter. Thank you. We'll come when we've decided."

"Let me know if he rallies," Walter said, then studied John for a long moment, and turned and walked from the room.

Margaret turned to Brigitte. "Get Caleb and the children and bring them here. We'll kneel around the bed for evening prayers. Hurry."

Brigitte started from the room and suddenly turned, eyes frantic. "Matthew! Where's Matthew?"

"At Lexington. Billy was hurt and Matthew stayed with him. He'll be home soon."

Brigitte returned with the children, and they silently knelt around the bed, Adam and Priscilla on either side of Margaret, pressed against her, and Margaret offered the prayer.

"Now, off to bed with you," she said, and the children walked from the room, pausing at the door for a moment to look back before they padded softly up the hall into their bedrooms. Brigitte tucked them in and read them a story, then returned to Margaret to sit quietly in a corner. Margaret sat on the chair next to the bed and touched John's face and forehead again.

"He's hot."

Tom said, "I'll fetch fresh water." He went out the back door to the well, and returned with cold water in a kitchen kettle. Margaret soaked and wrung out a large pack and spread it over John's back, then a smaller one and laid it on the side of his head, while Tom watched. She finished with John and looked at Tom, face streaked with sweat, dirty from gun smoke, clothing a shambles, bloodied from carrying John.

"If you'd like, you can go into the kitchen and wash. Brigitte can bring you some of John's clothes."

"That would be good, ma'am."

Twenty minutes later Tom softly walked back into the bedroom and sat down quietly in the corner, washed, hair combed and tied back, in a clean shirt.

Margaret soaked the packs in cold water and again laid them on John's back and side, and touched his face. His breathing remained slow and shallow. Her chin trembled for a moment, and she cleared her throat and turned to Tom. "Tell me about Billy."

"A musket ball hit him in the side, up by the Lexington Green. A soldier bayonetted him. We carried him to Jonas Parker's home and left him with a doctor and the Parker family."

"Will he die?"

Tom's forehead wrinkled for a moment. "I don't think so. He was awake and talking."

"Is Matthew all right?"

"He wasn't hurt."

"I don't mean shot. I mean is he all right inside?"

Tom's eyes dropped for a moment while he weighed his words. "I think so. Too much of life caught up with him in too little time. But I think he got through it. He had a good look about him when we left him. He's sturdy. A good son."

"Did you see Dorothy Weems?"

"Yes."

"Is she all right?"

"She cried, but then she took hold and she'll be all right."

"Oh!" Margaret exclaimed. "I didn't think! You must be hungry." She turned to Brigitte. "Can you get something for Tom?"

"Ma'am, that's nice, but I couldn't eat. I couldn't."

Brigitte settled back into her chair and folded her arms as women do when they must sit quietly and silently bear grief.

Talk slowly dwindled, and Brigitte nodded off. Tom brought fresh water twice while Margaret sat in the yellow lamplight, face set, drawn, and he changed the cold packs. At twenty minutes past one o'clock A.M. there was a gentle rap at the front door, and Tom rose and answered. A moment later he returned and ushered Joseph Warren into the room.

Warren looked at Margaret, then John, and removed his hat and stood still with it in his hand. "I heard he was hurt. I had to come see. May I look?"

Margaret stood and gave Warren space, and he knelt beside the bed and tenderly felt John's face, and pulled the damp sheets down to look at the cold pack on his back. His chin trembled and he worked his jaw and swallowed and wiped at his eyes, and then rose.

"I shouldn't stay. I had to come. Our Boston militia told me what he and Tom did today. Led us all the way. One of the best men I know." His voice broke, and he waited until he had control. "Margaret, if there's anything I can say or do, promise you'll come to me."

Margaret nodded. "I will."

Warren stood with his hat in his hands for a moment, wanting to say more, knowing he should go, and finally he turned and walked from the room. Tom followed him while Margaret sat back down on the chair beside John. Tom latched the door behind Warren and returned to the bedroom.

At three-thirty Tom brought fresh cold water and Margaret continued changing the cold packs, and they once more settled down to their vigil. At five-fifteen, with the gray of early dawn filtering into the streets, Tom started at the sound of the front door opening, and he strode into the parlor.

"Matthew!"

Matthew stopped in his tracks. "What's wrong? Where's Father?"

Tom faced him. "He's in his bed. He's been shot."

Matthew's eyes closed and his head rolled back for a moment. "Is he alive?" He started for the bedroom, Tom following.

"Yes."

Margaret met him at the door, and she threw her arms about him and clung to him with all her strength. She buried her face in his chest, and he folded her inside his long arms. She shook with sobs for long minutes while Matthew looked past her at his father, lying on his stomach in the light of the two lamps, breathing shallow and rapid. He stroked Margaret's hair and waited until the trembling and the sobbing slowed before he spoke. "Where was he hit?"

"In the lung. Right lung."

"Has Walter been here?"

"Yes."

"Is it bad?"

Margaret looked him in the eyes. "Yes. It is."

Matthew gently pushed past Margaret and dropped to both knees beside the bed, and felt his father's face and forehead. He raised the cold packs, and his face clouded at the sight of the purple hole in his father's back and the fresh froth of blood. He looked at Brigitte and said nothing, and he stood.

"I better bring Walter."

"Not yet. We're supposed to wait for some sign of change."

Matthew shook his head. "I better get him. The change may come too late."

He turned and started for the door, and Tom gently took his arm.

"I'll bring Walter. You stay here."

Tom left the room, and Matthew moved a chair to the bedside and sat down beside Margaret to wait.

At five minutes past six o'clock Tom followed Doctor Soderquist into the bedroom, and Matthew and Margaret moved away from the bed. He sat down on one of the chairs and set his satchel on the floor and grasped John's hand and closed his eyes while he counted thirty slow heartbeats. Then he felt John's face and head, and pulled the wet bedsheet down and lifted the cold pack. He looked at the bright blood and rinsed it and wrung it out and settled it back in place.

He spoke while he looked at John. "I thought he would rally before now, but he didn't." He pursed his lips and hated what he had to say. "It's worse than I thought. An operation would kill him. The bullet has to stay in."

Margaret's voice was steady. "Will he die?"

Walter drew and released a great sigh. "The truth? I think so." Only then did he raise his eyes to Margaret.

She stared back into his eyes for a moment, then looked away. She clamped her mouth closed as she battled tears, then cleared her throat and spoke firmly once again. "Thank you. Someone will come for you when we need you again."

Walter rose and picked up his black bag and started for the door, and his house slippers made slapping noises on the polished hardwood floor. He stopped at the archway and turned back.

"Margaret, I don't know a better man than John. I don't know what to say. I wish I could . . ." His voice trailed off.

"Thank you for coming."

Walter studied his black bag for a moment, then turned and shuffled out into the night, while Matthew and Margaret again sat beside the bed and Tom stood silently in a corner, watching.

The drawn window shades began to lighten, and Brigitte drew them back and sunlight streamed into the room. For a moment they all looked out at the backyard, where the great oak caught the light of the rising sun in its top and the bursting buds and greening leaves were ablaze, and the flood of pink and white blossoms on the cherry and apple and peach trees glowed like gems in the fresh morning. Jays and robins argued, and squirrels chattered. As though caught in a spell, they all stared for a time, awed by a beauty they had not seen before. Then they broke it off and looked at the floor or the bed, but not at each other, and they settled back into their vigil.

Five minutes later Tom thought to turn down the lamps.

At six fifty-five A.M. Margaret spoke to Brigitte. "Would you get something for the children's breakfast? We had porridge yesterday. Maybe griddle cakes?"

Brigitte stood. "Shall I get them ready for school?"

"No. They stay here today."

Brigitte silently walked out into the kitchen.

A knock came at the front door while Caleb was helping Adam cut his griddle cakes. Brigitte wiped her hands on her apron and opened it.

Kathleen stood before her, and Brigitte instantly flew into her arms, and the two girls stood in an embrace for a time while Brigitte sobbed. Then she backed up and wiped her eyes, and Kathleen spoke. "I heard about your father. Has Matthew come home?"

"Yes."

"Could I see him?"

"Oh yes, yes, come in."

"I think it would be best if I talked to him here."

Brigitte turned to run to the bedroom, when Matthew came through the archway and walked steadily to the front door. "I heard your voice. Will you come in?"

"I think not. I had to come find out. How is your father?"

Matthew looked back at the children and motioned to Kathleen, and followed her outside and closed the door. "Bad."

Kathleen recoiled. She could hardly bear what she must ask next. "Will he live?"

Matthew studied her eyes for a long time. "I don't think so."

She gasped and her eyes closed. She swayed on her feet for a moment, and Matthew reached to steady her.

"Will you send one of the children to tell me what happens?"

"Yes."

She fell silent for a moment and raised her eyes to his, and he saw the need in her and knew she would not be able to say what was in her heart. He chose his words carefully. "Is your family all right? your mother?"

"She's asleep. The doctor gave her some powders. She was not in her right mind for a time last night."

"Your father?"

She spoke firmly. "He's in prison. He confessed. He was an informer to General Gage."

Matthew studied Kathleen's face for a moment. In her dark eyes he saw there was nothing left except the instinct to survive. Every other meaningful part of her life had been wrenched from her within the past two days and left her utterly devastated, adrift, reduced to existing in a thick blackness from which she saw no escape, no faint gleam of light or hope. He saw it, and he yearned with all his soul to pull her within his arms and hold her and talk to her gently until she knew it would be all right.

But he could not. He could only frame the single question that would let Kathleen choose the direction their lives would travel—together, or apart. "Could I come visit you later today?"

She looked steadily into his face for a time before she answered, and her voice was firm. "I think that would not be good."

Matthew did not move or respond, and she continued.

"There would always be the question standing between us. Did my father bring about the death of yours?" She paused. "We may never speak of it, but it would always be there. I will not do that to you."

Matthew's eyes dropped for a moment, and he accepted it. "I will always love you."

"I will always love you too, Matthew. More than life itself."

"There's no other way?"

She shook her head. "None. I must go. I would give my life if it would save your father."

"I know you would."

"Tell your mother—"

"Kathleen, is that you?" Margaret's voice came from behind Matthew, and Matthew stepped aside as Margaret approached. She did not stop, but walked directly to Kathleen and embraced her and kissed her on the cheek and held her, and Kathleen clung to her.

"Are you all right, Kathleen? Is Phoebe?"

"Mother's not well. She's under doctor's care. I heard about John. I don't know how to say how sorry I am."

"Don't try, child. I know. Come in."

"I can't. I have to get home to Mother and the children." Kathleen was desperately clinging to self-control, and suddenly she could no longer hang on and she collapsed in Margaret's arms and stood for long minutes, sobbing uncontrollably. Margaret embraced her and stroked her hair and waited. Kathleen leaned back and stared into Margaret's eyes and sobbed, "What's happened to us? What's happened to the world? It's all gone! Gone! Everything we loved, ever dreamed of, ever wanted! How, Margaret? How?"

There was no answer. Margaret could only hold her and wipe her tears.

Kathleen shuddered as she brought herself back under control. "I love you, Margaret. No matter what happens, know that I and my family love you."

"I know, child. And we love you."

Kathleen backed away and wiped her eyes on her sleeve and looked at Matthew, and then she turned and walked to the gate and into the street and did not look back.

"Mother!"

Margaret jerked at Brigitte's frantic cry, and Matthew ran to the bedroom with Margaret following. John was moving, turning onto his side. His eyes were open, trying to focus, and Tom was on his knees beside him, preventing him from rolling onto his back. Margaret knelt beside Tom, and Tom moved so Matthew could take his place.

"Margaret, is that you?"

A sob welled from Margaret's chest and she choked, "I'm here, John. I'm here."

He brightened. "Matthew?"

"He's right here."

John squinted, and slowly his eyes came into focus and he smiled. "You're back. How's Billy?"

"Good. His fever broke in the night. The doctor said he'll be all right. I'll go back for him in a few days."

"Have you told his mother?"

"I stopped there on the way here."

John turned to look at Margaret, then past her at Tom. "Are you all right?"

Tom came to his side. "I'm fine. Don't wear yourself out talking."

"I won't. My back's sore. How bad is it?"

There was the slightest hesitation before Tom said, "You've got a bullet in your lung. Now that you're awake I'll go get Doctor Soderquist."

John caught the hesitation, and realized Tom's words did not answer the question, and in that instant he knew. "Get him. He'll have to take it out."

Tom looked at Margaret, and she waved her hand and he left.

Matthew asked, "Are you comfortable? Can we move you?"

"On my side, maybe."

Matthew turned him onto his right side while Margaret moved pillows to prop him up, and she replaced the cold packs while Matthew raised John's head and slipped a pillow beneath it.

John smiled. "This fever is making me light-headed."

"You've been fevered all night," Margaret said.

"Have you been up watching me?"

"We all have."

"That was a waste. One could have done it." He smiled and Margaret smiled at him.

John breathed deeply with the exertion, and suddenly he

coughed and winced and groaned at the pain of the big lead ball in his chest, and he swallowed and tasted warm salt blood. He reached for a wet cloth to wipe at his mouth, and he saw the flecks of bright red on the cloth. He folded it and held it in his hand away from the sight of the others. He looked out the window at the sunlight in the trees and blossoms, and the endless blue of the sky, and revelled in them.

"Beautiful day," he said quietly.

"Walter said you should drink something cold."

"Good. Is there any cider? You make good cider."

Matthew left and returned with a glass, and John sipped at it and smiled. "That's good." He sipped again, and coughed, and again swallowed and wiped and hid the red flecks in the folded cloth. He looked up at Margaret. "Was there any fighting in the streets yesterday?"

"No. We got news from time to time about the fighting in Concord, but there was no shooting here."

"What did you hear?"

"The British took a terrible beating."

John nodded. "They did."

"Joseph Warren came to see you in the night."

"What did he want?"

"To know if you were all right. And to tell us you did well yesterday. You and Tom."

"No more than the others."

"You led the Boston militia."

"We only tried to show them what we learned years ago."

The front door sounded, and Doctor Soderquist walked into the bedroom, dressed in fresh clothing. He walked to the bed and reached to touch John's head and face.

"On your stomach," he ordered, and John rolled onto his stomach. Walter lifted the cold pack and once more looked carefully at the large red splotch in the center. He laid his ear against John's back, then shifted and listened again. He pursed his mouth for a moment and then spoke to everyone else in the room. "I'll have to be alone now to do some things the rest of you should not see."

He waited until the room cleared, and then he closed the door and sat down beside John. His face was drawn, eyebrows peaked. "Can you feel that ball in your chest?"

"Yes, heavy. There's pain when I breathe, and when I cough it feels like something is tearing inside."

"It probably is. Can you taste blood?"

"All the time."

Walter exhaled and his shoulders slumped. "I hate it, John, but I have to tell you. I doubt you would survive an operation to get it out. And I doubt you'll survive if it is left in there. I don't know what to do."

"Let me take away your burden. I'm dying. I can feel it. I doubt I'll last the day."

"It's breaking my heart, John." Walter swallowed hard.

John smiled. "It wasn't your doing. You've served Boston well for forty years. I'm grateful to have you here."

Walter said nothing, and he slowly worked his hands together and stared at them as he sat in the shaft of sunlight, not knowing what to say next.

"Walter, how much time?"

Walter thought long before he answered. "Maybe an hour, maybe less. You're bleeding to death inside."

"I thought so. Would you do me a favor?"

"Anything."

"Can you bandage me and put me on my back so I can talk, and let me tell the family."

Ten minutes later Walter pulled the sheet and quilt up to John's shoulders as John lay on his back, propped up with pillows. "That bandage will hold. I'll bring them in."

Walter opened the door and said brusquely, "You can come back in," and they silently filed back in, wide-eyed, waiting for the doctor to speak.

"He'll be all right on his back. That bandage will hold for

today. I'll be back tonight to change it. His fever's dropped a little. He can talk when he wants. Let him drink when he wants it, and give him some bread and milk if he's hungry. If anything changes come get me."

He paused and reached to take John's hand, and he said quietly, "I'll see you soon, friend."

"Thank you."

When the front door closed behind the doctor, John smiled at the twins, Adam and Priscilla. "Aren't you supposed to be in school?"

"Mama said we should stay home today," Adam said. "Was there a battle yesterday?"

"Yes, there surely was."

"Were you in it?"

"Tom and I and Matthew were all in it, and Billy Weems too."

"Did you shoot at them?"

"We chased them from Concord clear back home."

"Did you win?"

"I think we did."

"Are you hurt?"

"Yes, I am. A British bullet hit me in the back."

Priscilla stared, wide-eyed. "Are you going to die?" she blurted.

"Not right away. I've got too much to do to die right now."

"Oh."

"If I tell you some things, will you both promise me to do them?"

"Uh-huh," they answered.

"Have your prayers every day and learn to read the Bible."

"Uh-huh."

"Take care of each other and Mother."

"Uh-huh."

Suddenly Priscilla and Adam understood that the others in the room were standing still, silent, and that John was talking to them alone, and they knew something was happening. They moved their feet and looked at the others with questions in their eyes, then looked back at their father.

"Will you try hard to learn to understand how to love others and God?"

"Yes."

"Will you learn to listen to that little voice inside of you that tells you what is right and what is wrong?"

"Uh-huh."

John smiled and nodded at them. For a moment he studied Priscilla's heart-shaped face and her blue eyes, and then Adam's blocky face and serious eyes, and he reached and they came to his bed. He gently touched each of their faces, and then he said, "You've promised. I'll expect you to do it."

John now turned to Caleb, who approached the bed, his face somber and his head bowed. "Caleb. Will you look after your younger brother and sister and see that they do the things they've promised?"

"Yes, sir," Caleb answered, his lower lip quivering.

"You will soon be a man. Your mother will need you to be strong. Will you be strong for her, son?"

"I will," Caleb said firmly.

John nodded. "Good." Then he spoke to Brigitte. "Same promises as your brothers and sister have made?"

Brigitte's chin trembled. "Yes."

She bent low and kissed him, and he smiled and looked at the lines of her face as though to memorize them as she backed away from the bed.

"Now, would you four go out into the parlor for a while. I have some serious things to talk over with your mother."

They waited until the door closed behind the children, and John turned to Tom.

"Thank you for everything."

Tom bit down hard against tears. "Don't thank me, John. Don't thank me."

John reached and Tom came to his bedside and sat beside him, and John grasped his thin, strong hand and held it.

"You've been a friend. My true friend."

Tom's chin trembled.

"Will you look in on Margaret and the family from time to time?"

Tom nodded but could not speak.

"One more thing. The battle yesterday—it was right. We stood on the right side. It was more than resisting the regulars. It was part of a bigger plan. It was a privilege to be by your side."

Tom's shoulders shook with silent sobs.

"Don't worry," John continued. "I'll be seeing you again soon. I promise."

Tom bowed his head, and the silent tears ran down his cheeks, and he clutched John's hand in both of his. He tried to speak and there were no words that would come, and he tried once more. "God bless you and keep you," he choked out.

John released his hand, and Tom rose and wiped his sleeve across his eyes and backed away from the bed.

John spoke to Matthew. "You did fine yesterday."

Matthew did not answer.

"You'll have to be master of the house. You can do it. Listen to your mother."

Matthew kneeled beside the bed and grasped John's hand in both of his, and John looked him full in the face.

"Matthew, try hard to understand what's going on all around you. There is a plan unfolding for this land. I see it in bits and pieces. Somehow the battle yesterday was a necessary part of it. You made the right choice when you joined in. Study the affairs of this country and watch. Something remarkable is going to happen. Will you do it?"

"Yes. I will."

"Stay close to God. Read his holy words. Pray. It will come to you." John paused and coughed, and could not hide the bright froth that showed at the corners of his mouth, and he wiped it away. "Have you talked with Kathleen since you got back?"

"She came here to see you."

"Did you two talk?"

"Yes. It's over. She chose it, not me."

The air went out of John, and for long moments he stared at the ceiling. "I am sorry to know that, but you must move on. You will do well."

Matthew leaned over John and kissed him on the cheek. "Father, I love you with my whole heart. You'll be with me as long as I live." His chin trembled and he swallowed. "God bless you." He rose and wiped silent tears.

John coughed once more and gritted his teeth against the violent stab of pain in his chest, and he quickly wiped at his mouth. His breath came in short gasps for a moment, then slowed. "Could I talk with your mother alone?"

Matthew and Tom walked from the room and closed the door.

"Margaret, come sit beside me."

She sat down and reached for his hand.

"I have little time, and there are some things I must tell you."

Her eyes were dry, her face soft, and her eyes shined as she listened.

"I love you with all that is in me. More than life, more than anything on this earth." His voice was weakening, but his eyes were bright, intense.

He paused, and her eyes widened in surprise. Never had he been so open with his feelings.

"I cannot imagine what my life would have been without you. You have been my greatest blessing, my friend, my wife. I cannot think of a virtue that you do not possess. I thank you for all you have been to me, and for the children you have borne and reared for me."

He paused to let his breathing settle, then continued. "Last Sunday after church we talked of heaven. Do you remember?"

"I remember." She raised his hand to her face and she kissed it and held it close.

"In my heart, I know some things that I dared not speak until now. I do not believe we are angels when we go to heaven. I do not believe we will spend eternity singing praises to God."

Margaret listened in startled silence.

"There will be no heaven for me without you. You and the children. I believe I will have you in heaven, and the children, and we will continue there as we are here, a husband and wife, and we will have our family. I cannot believe a just and kindly God would ever separate us. He would not do that."

Margaret's breath came short. "That is not the teaching."

"It is the teaching of every right thing inside of me! I know as I know I am here ready to leave this life that it is true, Margaret. I cannot bear the thought of being in eternity without you. That would be a torment I could not bear! I know it! I know it!"

He paused and wiped at his mouth, and the exertion left him panting for a moment before he could continue. "There is one more thing. The battle yesterday was necessary to the plan of God for this land. I know only a small part of the plan, but it is there. We had to fight that battle. Something is stirring in these colonies. A new spirit, a new feeling, a new direction for the world. Something will happen soon, something that will change this world forever. I don't know what it is, but it will happen."

His hand tightened on hers for a moment, then relaxed, and she felt his fingers begin to slip away. He licked his lips and forced his eyes to focus once more.

"I had to be part of it. Something inside. I had to do it. I would do it again. Can you forgive me?"

In the deepest chamber of her soul, where she lived alone with her conscience and her God, Margaret felt a stirring. It was as though a voice spoke to her quietly from within but the words could be heard in the room.

"Peace. My peace, not as the world."

A calmness came flowing, and a sense of peace she had never felt before spread from her heart and filled her and then reached beyond, into the room. Her breathing slowed and she looked about, and it seemed there was a brightness in the room beyond the sun streaming in the window. She looked into John's face and he was smiling and he was radiant.

"There is nothing to forgive," she said quietly. "You were doing His work."

She leaned over him and she took his face in her hands and she kissed him, and she put her cheek against his and said, "I love you." She felt his hand rise to touch her face and she drew back and he looked into her eyes.

"Thank you." His voice was faint and fading. "Thank you."

While she watched, his eyes shifted and he looked towards the far end of the room, and suddenly his eyes narrowed and he tried to speak. She leaned forward to listen, and she heard the whispered words, "You came!"

Slowly she turned and looked and she could see nothing, and she turned back to John. His eyes were fixed on someone, and she saw a joy in his face that defied all description. He sighed and the air left his body and his hand relaxed and she felt his life slip from him.

Margaret sat quietly at his side for a long time, aware only that inside the room was a peace and joy that transcended anything she had ever known. She had never seen happiness as she now saw it in John's face. Time passed, and it slowly began to withdraw, and she felt the deepest yearning of her life to seize it and never let it go, but it was beyond her power.

She gently reached to close John's eyes and then stood. For a moment she looked down at him, and she knew she would give all she had, all she was, to once again capture the peace and the joy she had felt.

She walked to the door and into the parlor.

"Children, come and see your father. Tom, you come with them."

CHAPTER XVII

★ ★ ★

*T*hick fog rolled in from the Atlantic during the night, and in the early morning a cold, thin drizzle of misty rain settled in. The heavens were a heavy, oppressive gray blanket, sealing out the sunrise, and Boston City wakened to dark, wet, somber streets. Only the necessary traffic moved, quick, anxious, while citizens stared from rain-streaked windows and disappeared when the silent, narrow-eyed British patrols came stamping in the rain-puddled streets. No birds sang; no squirrels chattered; no one called the usual carefree Saturday morning salutations in the strangely quiet city.

For three nights and two days both the British and the colonials had left the city with an unending stream of wagons or carriages or any vehicle they could find, to return later from the Concord Road with more of their dead and wounded. Every hospital room within ten miles was filled by midnight of April nineteenth. The enlisted men's barracks at the British military compound were jammed to the walls with wounded, and the dispossessed men slept in tents on the parade ground. Every church in Boston and Charlestown had been stripped of the pews and filled with cots. Every medical doctor, nurse, and orderly that could be found had been pressed into service. Wounded colonials were bedded in homes scattered for miles. By dawn of April twentieth every opiate and medicine in Boston and Charlestown had been used to dull the pain of amputations and stitching and probing for lead balls inside writhing bodies, and by order of General Gage the medicines and medical doctors on board every man-of-war in Boston Harbor and the Back Bay had been commandeered ashore. The colonials had taken every doctor and all medicines from every merchant ship they could find, no questions asked. Grave diggers had been busy in every available cemetery without ceasing, by light of day and by light of lantern at night. In an almost unending processional, clusters of silent people dressed in black moved through the streets to the graveyards, where they conducted brief graveside services, lowered the caskets, and quickly returned home to remain behind closed doors.

An unspoken, undefined truce had settled into place between the British and the colonials, born of desperate need on both sides.

The British command was utterly devastated, shattered by the unthinkable realization that a ragtag army of colonial farmers and merchants had met the flower of the proud British army head-on and had not just defeated them but chopped them to pieces in an eighteen-mile running ambush that by definition could be termed a massacre. General Gage knew that had the colonials been given three more hours of daylight on April nineteenth, not one British soldier returning from Concord would have reached Charlestown. Numbed, paralyzed, the British command was terrified that if they brought reprisals in the city, that same ragtag army, whom they now knew to be without fear, would swarm the Boston Peninsula and leave no soldier or sailor alive.

The colonials were overwhelmed by what they had done. Untested, untried, they had taken on the regulars with no advance hint of whether they or the army would take a beating, and they had nearly annihilated the army. With the battle now three days behind them, they were struggling with two questions. First, if the war continued, could they repeat their performance, or was it a colossal freak accident resulting from surprise? Second, with enough gunboats and cannon in the waters around Charlestown and Boston to level both towns in forty-eight hours, would the

British turn their firepower loose on the two towns? Tweaking the nose of a giant could bring disaster.

And both sides needed time to minister to their wounded and conduct the somber business of burying their dead. Thus it was that both sides silently walked the streets of Boston in the chill fog and drizzle of rain on that Saturday morning, to do what they must. Their faces were set, eyes flat as they met and silently passed each other, each fearful, tentative, neither side willing to provoke a confrontation.

In the quiet of her bedroom, Kathleen Thorpe finished buttoning her shoes, flounced her skirt to settle it, and peered into her mirror for a moment. She saw the faint shadows beneath her eyes from tormented days and sleepless nights. She took her hooded rain cape from her closet and slipped it around her shoulders as she walked out into the parlor and stopped beside the sofa where Phoebe lay against pillows with a quilt tucked about her.

"I'm going out for food. I'll be back in less than an hour. Will you be all right?"

Phoebe nodded weakly.

Kathleen turned to Charles, standing in the kitchen doorway, Faith behind him. "You and Faith be quiet and don't disturb Mother. Read a book to Faith if she needs it. Understand?"

Charles's face darkened and he asked, "Are you going? Why do you have to go?"

Kathleen saw the fear in his eyes. For Charles and Faith, the world had come crashing down when their father was arrested in the night. They could not understand why he was gone, or why their mother now seldom rose from the bed or sofa and could dissolve into tears at any time, or why their lifelong schoolmates called them strange names and shunned them. They only understood that Kathleen had become the center of their world—meals, washing, ironing, shopping, sleeping with Mother to quiet her when she woke wailing in the night, holding them when they cried, answering the knocks at the door to deal with hostile people and merchants who came to collect bills. Twice stones had smashed through the front window in the night, and the children had crept to see Kathleen sobbing while she swept broken glass by candlelight.

She walked to Charles, placed her hand on his shoulder, and looked into his eyes. "You're the man of the house now. You can do it. Be good to Faith, and get Mother a drink if she asks. I won't be long."

Charles swallowed and nodded his head, and his eyes dropped as Kathleen turned and picked the wicker shopping basket from the table and walked to the front door. She paused to look at the mantel clock, then looked once more at Charles and Faith watching her with forlorn eyes, and then she was gone. Outside, she glanced upward at the solid, dark overcast, and then up the street through the fog and drizzling mist, and pulled the hood over her head.

Ten minutes before eleven—funeral's at eleven—I can make it.

She moved north through the silent, light street traffic with long strides, past the vacant Dunson home and on north to the church. Slowing, she worked her way unnoticed through the people coming and going to tend to the wounded inside and moved to the far side of the churchyard. Cautiously she walked to the corner of the building and peered across the street, where the black wrought-iron picket fence enclosed the headstones and markers and monuments and the crypts of the church cemetery. Midway on the east side, through the dripping oak and maple trees and the fog, she made out the black shapes of many people gathered at the Dunson plot.

She could not hear the words. She stood where she was, alone in the cold rain, watching as Silas spoke briefly, then Joseph Warren. Afterward Silas led the group in a hymn that Kathleen could not hear clearly, and finally Silas dedicated the grave. She watched the men bend to lower the casket on the straps, and they committed the body of John Phelps Dunson back to mother earth. She felt the scalding tears running, dripping onto her cape, and she paid no heed. She watched the tall figure of Matthew cast the first shovel of earth into the grave, and she saw Margaret stiffen and

Brigitte grasp Adam and Priscilla close. Tom Sievers cast the second shovel of earth and stepped back and jammed the shovel upright into the large mound. Kathleen choked and sobbed with the deep pain of needing to be there, to hold Margaret, to comfort the children, to throw her arms around Matthew.

Too soon it was over. People slowly backed away from the grave site and walked the winding paths through the wet grass and the marble and granite stones to the street, and silently melted into the fog and were gone. Joseph Warren alone waited at the cemetery gate, head bowed, a lone, solitary figure. Kathleen stood where she was until only the Dunson family remained, and then she watched them turn and walk to the gate and onto the street. Joseph Warren stopped them and handed something to Matthew, and they talked for a moment before the family moved on towards home. Kathleen waited until they were all out of sight before she wiped her face with her handkerchief and crossed the street, passed through the gate, and walked to the Dunson plot where men were preparing to fill the grave with the sticky, wet gray-brown earth. On her approach they backed away while she walked to the head of the open grave and peered down.

Good-bye, John. I love you. I am so sorry. Forgive us. Forgive me. God bless you and keep you.

She waited until her tears stopped, and she wiped her face again and turned and walked rapidly from the cemetery, shopping basket clutched at her side.

At the Dunson home, Tom held the gate while Matthew led into the house, Margaret on his arm.

Tom stopped at the door. "I'll take my leave now, ma'am."

"Stay. Please stay," Margaret pleaded.

They wiped the rain from their shoes onto the braided rug inside the door and shook their wet raincoats out the door and hung them on coat trees to dry, and went to their bedrooms to change, Tom with Matthew.

At noon Matthew sat down at the dining table, a sealed envelope in his hand, his name written on it with a bold flourish.

"Is that from Joseph Warren?" Margaret asked.

Matthew nodded as he broke the seal, and Margaret and Tom sat down beside him while he silently read.

April 20th, 1775

My dear Mr. Matthew Dunson:

This will be delivered by Joseph Warren, our mutual friend.

I extend my deepest sympathies to your mother, Margaret, and yourself and family on the occasion of the loss of your father, John. The account I have received of his passing is an inspiration to all who love this land and have risen to secure our freedom. His name will forever be written with those of patriots and men of God.

However, I write for another purpose. I have received counsel from General George Washington of an immediate and critically urgent need for munitions, if he is to maintain the Continental army. He believes acquiring such munitions in quantities sufficient to his need depends almost entirely on immediately obtaining ships and crews capable of negotiating international waters to secure gunpowder and ordnance from British vessels and offshore allies. To meet his most urgent request we must have experienced maritime navigators who are also qualified to be naval officers. In this regard, discussions with knowledgeable men have led me to you.

It is with full knowledge of the extreme hardship this will place on your family that I must request of you that you set aside personal considerations and volunteer your services as a seasoned navigator in this effort. It is unknown how long your services will be needed, and there will be danger. Should you choose to comply with this request of General Washington, you can expect little more than his undying gratitude, and the eternal thanks of good men everywhere, and the blessings of a just God.

Regrettably, at this time of deep mourning for your family, I will need your response by Sunday, April 23, 1775, which must be in writing, delivered to Joseph Warren.

> With greatest respect,
> Your obdt. servant,
> Captain Soren Weyland

Matthew laid the letter before Margaret and settled against the back of his chair while she slowly read it aloud. When she was finished, she stared at it for long seconds, and then she set it on the table and looked at Tom. Tom looked into her eyes and then looked away as she spoke, quietly and without passion. "John is gone, and now they want Matthew."

No one spoke. Matthew returned the letter to its envelope and set it on the mantel and returned to his chair. The three of them sat in silence until a knock at the front door broke the somber quiet.

Matthew opened the door, and Dorothy Weems stood before him, shawl covering her head against the rain, slight vapors rising from her breath. She held a smoking, covered cooking pan, hot pads on both handles.

"Come in, please," Matthew said, and stepped aside. Dorothy followed Margaret into the kitchen and set the pan on the stove. She tried to speak to Margaret and could not and broke into tears, and the two women stood in an embrace for a time before Dorothy settled.

"It's a ham, Margaret. God bless you. If you need anything, if I can do anything, promise you'll send word."

"I will. Can't you stay for a time?"

"I've got dinner ready at home. I don't know what to say— how sorry I am. God bless you. God bless you all."

She turned and put her arms around Matthew for a moment, and then Tom. "You two saved my Billy. There is no way to thank you."

Three minutes after the door closed, Sarah Willums knocked and stood in the rain with a kettle of steamed vegetables, and tears. Five minutes later Mellie Potter left six smoking loaves of bread, and hugs, and as the afternoon wore on the food covered the dining table and spilled into the kitchen. Margaret set out stacks of plates and silverware and invited the steady stream of friends and loved ones to share with them.

In deep dusk the visiting slowed, and by dark it had ended. Once more Tom tried to leave, and once again Margaret pleaded with him to stay. They would make him a bed on the floor in Matthew's room. By nine o'clock the food had been stored and the dishes done. At nine-thirty they all knelt at the dining room table, and Matthew led them in prayer. At ten o'clock, with the children in bed, Margaret took the letter from the mantel and sat at the table, and the men, with Brigitte, sat with her and she read it aloud once more.

She turned to Matthew. "It's you they asked for. Do you have an answer?"

Matthew shook his head. "You and the family are the ones that will suffer if I go. What do you say?"

Brigitte leaned forward. "How would we manage—pay bills, eat? We have some money, but not enough for very long."

Margaret looked at Tom, and he hesitated for a moment before he spoke. "What would John do?"

At ten-thirty Margaret sighed and the conversation died, and she put the letter back in its envelope.

"I don't know how we would pay our bills and feed ourselves without Matthew," she said. "And I don't know how I would raise the children. They need a father, and theirs is gone. They can look to Matthew, but if he leaves . . ." She shook her head and didn't finish her thought, and they all saw the agony in her eyes. "I don't have an answer. We can talk about it in the morning before church."

Five minutes later Margaret sat on her bed in the yellow light of one lamp, shoulders slumped, her soul filled with impossible conflicts.

What should I do, John? I can't give them Matthew. If he were killed . . .

She clenched her eyes shut at the thought and forced it away. She heaved a great sigh and a heavy weariness settled, and suddenly she could hardly hold her head up. She slipped between the sheets and turned off the lamp and closed her eyes.

At midnight Matthew sat up and swung his feet onto the floor of his dark bedroom.

Tom's voice came whispering. "All right?"

"Yes. Can't sleep."

Matthew gathered his clothes and walked silently on bare feet to the parlor and dressed. He put on his damp raincoat and his hat and walked out the front door into a moonless night. The rain had stopped, and a cold Atlantic breeze turned his breath to vapor as he turned north in the silent, vacant street. Twice he turned corners to avoid British patrols, and then he was at the cemetery, standing at the head of the covered grave of his father. He took off his hat and stood with his head bowed.

What should I do? Where's my duty?

At one o'clock Margaret opened her eyes, suddenly wide awake, startled, wondering what had awakened her. She listened but could hear only the familiar sound of the night breeze and nothing more. She looked about the room—closed door, closed window, no other presence. Then the inner turmoil of the letter from Joseph Warren came flooding, and she turned on her back and closed her eyes and laid her arm over them, and tried to push it all away. Suddenly her thoughts settled, and a strong impulse drove her from her bed, onto her knees. She clasped her hands before her face and bowed her head and closed her eyes.

"Dear God, creator of us all, humbly I bow to thank thee . . ."

She got no further. It was as though a bright light burst in her soul. The peace she had felt with John on the day he died—the sweet peace that surpassed all other feelings she had ever known—began to rise in her heart. She was fixed to the spot and dared not move. The feeling grew and filled her very being, and once again she revelled in the spirit that seemed to fill the room. She opened her eyes but could see nothing.

Then from within came a quiet assurance that was more powerful, more certain than anything earthly she had ever known. Her breath came short, and she tried to speak but could not. She did not know how long she sat thus, unable to rise, unable to speak, possessed once again by a peace that transcended all earthly bounds. Then, as before, the spirit began to slowly withdraw, and finally she was left on her knees, yearning for a return of the sweetest peace she had ever known, but it had faded and was gone.

She remained on her knees for a time, and then again slipped into her bed and lay staring into the blackness. She did not remember when her eyes closed and she drifted into a deep, dreamless sleep.

In the cold wind of the dark cemetery, Matthew raised his hand to put his hat back onto his head, when he stopped, startled by an unexpected feeling that began in his breast and slowly spread. He looked upward into the black, moonless heavens and then into the trees and headstones about him, and saw nothing. The feeling filled him with a sense of light, and suddenly all inner turmoil settled and a peace seized him that was more powerful than anything in his life, and he understood in his heart what he must do.

He stood rooted, not moving for a time, and then the feeling subsided and was gone. He once again looked about, and there was nothing, no one. He settled his hat onto his head and slowly backed away from his father's grave, turned on his heel, and walked out of the cemetery.

Fifteen minutes later he stopped in the street in front of the Thorpe home, needing to awaken Kathleen and tell her what he had felt and what he must do. There was no light in the house; the windows were black, vacant, staring eyes. He stood in the cold wind for a time before he walked on to his home.

Inside the Thorpe home, Kathleen lay beside Phoebe, listening to mumbled snatches of sentences as Phoebe dreamed and tossed in her sleep. Clutched in Kathleen's hand was a small wooden figure of a white snow owl with round painted eyes, feathers, and two names carefully carved on the bottom of the square base: Kathleen and Matthew.

At six-ten A.M. Margaret was seated in the big rocking chair in the parlor when Matthew entered from his bedroom. She waited until he sat down on a chair facing her.

"You must go," she said quietly. "We will be all right."

"I know."

Part Two

★ ★ ★

CANADA

MASSACHUSETTS
(Maine)

NEW
HAMPSHIRE

Newburyport
Gloucester
Salem
Marblehead
BOSTON
ProvinceTown
Plymouth

NEW
ENGLAND
COLONIES

NEW YORK

MASS.

New
York

CONN.

R.I.

New
Bedford

Newport

PENNSYLVANIA

NEW JERSEY

Philadelphia

New
Haven

New
London

MIDDLE
COLONIES

Baltimore

MARYLAND

DEL.

VIRGINIA

Richmond

Norfolk

Yorktown

NORTH CAROLINA

SOUTH CAROLINA

Charleston

GEORGIA

SOUTHERN
COLONIES

Savannah

ATLANTIC OCEAN

Grand Bahama Is.

BAHAMAS

Nassau

N

WEST INDIES

CUBA

CHAPTER XVIII

★ ★ ★

*I*n muggy, late-afternoon mid-July heat, Matthew stood sweating on the worn deck of the old merchantman frigate *Buford* as she rose and settled with the gentle sea swells rolling into Boston Harbor from the Atlantic. The small door to the officers' quarters opened, and Matthew studied the leathery, lined face of Captain Nels Kirkegard as he looked at Matthew, then walked to face him and wait wordlessly while Matthew handed him a sealed envelope.

Matthew saw the faded blue eyes sharpen as the aging captain broke the seal and read the simple message:

> Request that you transport bearer, Matthew Dunson of Boston, north to the Massachusetts port of Beverly to Captain Soren Weyland of the schooner Esther, earliest. Most urgent business.
>
> Your obdt. servant,
> Gen. Geo. Washington.

Kirkegard raised eyes wise with forty-two years on the Atlantic to study Matthew, then his seaman's bag and the huge, flat forty-pound bundle bound in oilskins hung on a strap over his shoulder.

The captain gestured to the bundle. "Navigator?"

"Yes, sir. Charts."

"Weyland said you'd be coming. Do you know what this letter says?"

"I was told." Matthew could hear the slight Norwegian accent. "You know about the blockade?"

"Yes." British gunboats were strung in a line half a mile long at the mouth of Boston Harbor, with a second line farther out in Boston Bay, from Hull to Deer Island, cutting off all commerce, all trade, slowly strangling Boston Town.

Kirkegard refolded the letter as he spoke. "We run the blockade after dark, before moonrise. Stow your things in my cabin and make yourself acquainted with the ship. I'll need you tonight."

The *Buford* was 128 feet in length, bowsprit to stern, and thirty-two feet at the beam, with but two masts, mizzen and main, three yards per mast, all six sails furled and lashed, with rigging on the mainmast for a spanker sail. Food and water for the crew were stored in the hold but no cargo; empty, she rode high in the water, ready to move fast. She carried no cannon, no arms. Matthew finished his inspection and judged her to be old but sound.

With the sea dividing the sun in half, the officers took mess with the crew; then they all settled into their regular evening duties of lashing down all movable objects on the deck in the event of an unexpected night squall. In deep dusk Kirkegard gathered his officers and navigator at the mainmast with the crew behind. Matthew stood silently with the officers while the captain gave his terse orders.

"We're moving north to Port Beverly tonight, orders of General Washington. We run the blockade between full darkness and moonrise and we do it slow, on the mainsail only. No lights, no talking, no noise. Six men on the sail, first mate on the helm, the navigator on the bow with myself and Mr. Dunson, and bosun relaying the navigator's orders to the helm. Everyone else will be on the rail watching for anything that moves. What we don't need is to ram someone or something in the dark. Any questions?"

There were none.

"Once past the men-of-war we turn north. We should catch the Antilles current long before midnight and the westerlies soon after. When we do, we spread all six sheets and the spanker and run with the wind. We should sight the Marblehead lighthouse just before dawn, and we turn westward and should be in Beverly port by midmorning."

He paused for a moment, but there was no comment. "Does anyone know if Beverly is under blockade?"

No one knew.

"If she is, we go in anyway. We'll keep our canvas tight and should be able to outrun the gunboats. If we get past them, I doubt they'll follow us into port."

Matthew could hear fearless Viking blood ring in Kirkegard's voice.

Deep dusk gave way to full, moonless black, and on Kirkegard's signal, hard, experienced hands shoved capstan bars into their slots in the capstan to wind in the anchor while others unfurled the mainsail and set it to catch the light breeze. The first mate set the helm for a course due west, towards the line of lights at harbor's mouth. Slowly the old ship came about and crept forward. Her bow raised no curl, no sound, and she left no wake as she crawled steadily towards the lights of the British gunboats dead ahead.

Kirkegard stood at the bow rail. To his right stood his navigator, a nearly indiscernible shape in the blackness, Matthew to his left, gripping the rail. All three men had their heads thrust forward, breathing light, peering into the blackness, watching, listening for any sound. There was only the sigh of the breeze in the rigging and the quiet murmur of light waves lapping against the hull, and blackness.

They cleared the town, and the helmsman adjusted fifteen degrees south and the bow swung slightly, taking a heading that would divide in half the distance between the deck lights of the two nearest British gunboats at the mouth of Boston Harbor. The *Buford* inched forward and passed between the large lanterns on the stern of the gunboats, and Matthew heard quiet British voices from both men-of-war, strangely clear on the black water, as they slipped past one hundred fifty yards on either side. Then they were past the boats and Thompson Island, and the lights were three hundred yards astern. Kirkegard exhaled air, and they turned their faces east once more, towards the second line of lights out in Boston Bay.

Once again the helmsman selected two lights, this time in the gap between Deer Island and Long Island, and once again the *Buford* crept forward on the single sail. They had heard no sound from the crew, lined against the rails on either side of the ship, watching, listening in dead silence. Slowly the high deck lights of the British men-of-war approached and then passed, and then they were six hundred yards past Deer Island. The navigator turned and quietly called to the bosun, "Eighty degrees north," and the bosun softly relayed the order. The first mate made the adjustment on the helm, and the bowsprit of the old ship swung hard to port to miss Great Brewster Island and the Roaring Bulls, out in greater Massachusetts Bay and the open sea.

Five minutes later Kirkegard looked back half a mile at the British blockade and turned to the bosun. "Unfurl all canvas."

The bosun barked orders, and men leaped to the rope ladders and three minutes later were walking the ropes on the yards seventy feet above the deck in total blackness, jerking the lashings from the sails, letting them drop to catch the gentle breeze. On deck, other hard, experienced hands set the yard ropes to catch the breeze. Twenty minutes later Matthew felt the Antilles current catch and carry them into the Gulf Stream. Fifteen minutes later the westerlies curling northeast from the Horse latitudes came quartering in and turned north offshore, and for the first time the six sheets of sail on the two masts and the spanker all snapped and popped and filled, and the *Buford* leaped forward, running free with the current and the wind like something alive, her bow cutting a great white curl, her wake showing white water for a hundred yards. Half an hour later a quarter moon rose and the tides began to ebb, and the navigator gave the order—ten degrees north to compensate—and the helmsman adjusted.

For a moment Matthew felt a surge of pride and the incom-

parable thrill of running with the wind and current on the undu-
lating deck of a tall ship, with good men to handle her. He looked
into the face of Captain Kirkegard in the faint light of the quarter
moon, and he saw the deep satisfaction.

At one-fifty A.M. they passed East Point on the port side. At
four o'clock, with the moon already set, Kirkegard resumed his
position in the bow, peering into the black Atlantic night for the
first sighting of the Marblehead lighthouse. Matthew tipped his
head to study the heavens, located the Big Dipper, then the North
Star, and settled in to watch for the tiny fleck of light. At four
forty-five A.M. he pointed. "Marblehead." The helmsman brought
the bow on a line that kept the point of light fifteen degrees to
port. At five-thirty A.M., in the gray of dawn, Kirkegard used his
glass to search the waters north of Marblehead point for British
gunboats, then handed it to his navigator, then the first mate, then
Matthew.

There was no blockade on the stark, wild coast.

Half an hour later the frigate cleared the peninsula north of
Salem, furled all sails on the mizzen, worked west through the narrow channel, then moved north into the small port of Beverly, and
at eight-forty A.M. Kirkegard lowered a longboat without dropping anchor.

Matthew gathered his seaman's bag and charts and faced
Kirkegard at the rail. "Thank you, sir. I commend you and your
crew."

Kirkegard smiled and nodded.

"Do you plan to drop anchor for a while?"

Kirkegard shook his head. "We have to get out before they
decide to set a blockade. The *Esther*'s the last vessel to the north,
next to the dry dock."

The officers gathered to shake his hand while the bosun lowered Matthew's gear into the waiting longboat, and Matthew followed him and six sailors down the rope ladder and settled into
the longboat as it rocked, bumping against the hull of the *Buford*.
Ten minutes later he turned on the wharf to wave to the longboat

as the sailors put their backs into the oars on their return to the *Buford.* The bosun waved back.

The familiar sights and sounds and smells of a saltwater port washed over Matthew as he looped the strap of the heavy bundle of charts over his shoulder and picked up his seaman's bag and started north towards the empty dry dock at the end of the piers. Stolid eyes of bearded New England mariners watched him, silently questioning why a ship had entered the harbor only long enough to put him ashore. The sound of heavy crosscut saws and pounding sledges slowed Matthew for a moment, and he puzzled at ship's carpenters cutting sections at regular intervals out of the top deck railing of a merchantman. He paused, startled at the sight of cannon on deck, muzzles plugged while they waited to be fitted into the openings.

The *Esther* was moored to the last pier by four two-inch hawsers with double rat guards mounted. Matthew studied her while he walked down the pier to the gangplank. The *Esther* was a schooner, merchantman, yellow pine mainmast sixty feet, mizzen fifty feet, rigged with two jibs forward. About 160 feet, bow to stern, and about thirty-eight feet at the beam. She had been dry-docked while her hull was partly replaced where marine teredo wood bores had penetrated, the balance of the hull scraped clean of barnacles, then thick, tough tar paper sealed on, and light, hard copper sheathing attached to cover the hull to four inches above the high-water marking. The railing of her top deck had been cut nine times on both sides, and the ugly snouts of cannon protruded through the finished gun ports. Her canvas was all new. She had been repainted black except for the carved leaping gray porpoise that graced her bowsprit. Matthew calculated her burden at close to three hundred tons, but she was riding too high in the water to be loaded. She likely had munitions for the cannon, food and supplies for the crew, including the critical freshwater and lime juice and potatoes, and little else.

The aged gangplank sagged slightly with his weight as he walked to the ship's deck and faced the officer of the day. The clean-shaven, slender young man was dressed in the standard black coat, white shirt and black ribbon tie, and leather cap of a merchantman's first mate. His face was thin, chin long and pointed.

"You have business aboard the ship?"

"Matthew Dunson. Here to see Captain Weyland on orders of General Washington." Matthew handed him the envelope from Joseph Warren and glanced at the sailors who had paused from their duties to peer at him.

The young man quickly read the letter, then thrust out his hand. "I'm first mate Walter Riggins. Welcome aboard. We've been waiting for you. Follow me." He led Matthew to the stern of the ship, and rapped on a heavy oak door.

A gravelly voice called, "Enter," and Riggins opened the door and stepped into the captain's quarters, Matthew following, blinking while his eyes adjusted to the dim light of the small room.

"Sir," Riggins said, "Mr. Matthew Dunson is here."

Soren Weyland was average height, thick in the neck and shoulders, arms heavy, hands and fingers stubby, legs short, stocky, and his entire uniform seemed constrictive. He studied the letter for a moment, then peered intently at Matthew from beneath gray, bushy brows. Everything about the man and the cabin suggested hardheaded New England practicality and no-nonsense directness.

"Sit." He gestured to a chair facing his table, then sat down facing Matthew. Riggins closed the door as he left.

"There are some things we both need to know before we sail, and some of it can't leave this cabin. Kirkegard said I could trust you. Can I?"

"I think so, sir."

"Wonder why your letter was signed by George Washington, not a naval officer?"

"Yes."

"He's desperate. The army ran out of powder and shot at Bunker Hill, and right now there's not enough to fight another major engagement. Either he gets cannon and powder and shot, or his army will fail before winter. The colonies can't manufacture it fast enough, and there's only one way he knows to get it."

Matthew waited.

"From the men-of-war and merchant ships out of English ports." Weyland paused, his eyes points of light beneath his shock of gray hair. "Ever hear of letters of marque?"

"Yes, sir."

"What are they?"

"Letters issued by a government to citizens, authorizing them to do certain acts for the government."

"Correct." Weyland opened a drawer and tossed a heavy envelope to Matthew. "There isn't time to build ships, so Washington is going to use merchantmen for his navy. Those are my letters of marque from him. I'm to take British warships as prizes of war wherever I find them and deliver to the army their cannon and powder and shot and whatever else they have that's helpful."

Matthew did not move or speak.

"We fly the colonial flag. We're armed and there'll be fighting."

Matthew was incredulous. "This ship will be a colonial man-of-war?"

"It will."

"Who owns this ship?"

"Me."

"How are you compensated for all this?"

Weyland drew and released a great breath. "I'm not. Washington asked for my ship. I said yes."

Silence held for a moment while Matthew accepted the fact this bull of a man had given his life's work to the colonies.

Weyland waited until he saw Matthew's eyes settle. "Have you ever been under fire?"

"Once. Concord."

"Lost your father? Warren said you lost your father."

"I did."

Weyland's eyes lowered, and Matthew saw the pain, but Weyland said nothing.

"Is your crew trained for naval combat?"

"No. We have four army officers who know cannon, and they've had three days to train cannon crews on how to load and fire. But none of us have ever seen a naval engagement, let alone fought one."

"When did you get this ship out of dry dock?"

"Yesterday."

"Did you have her fitted for war?"

"No. She's a merchantman—India and China and back seven times. We're thin hulled. Cannonballs will come right on through anyplace they hit."

"You have copper sheathing on the hull to the waterline. She should be fast."

"She is. We can outmaneuver and outrun a British man-of-war, and that may be our best weapon."

"What happened to your navigator?"

"He didn't like the risks of combat."

"What's the pay?"

Weyland pursed his mouth for a moment before he answered. "We can sell anything the army doesn't want from the British ships and divide the money. Other than that, no pay. Government's broke."

Matthew slowly leaned back in his chair.

Weyland shrugged. "I don't like it, but that's the way it is." He leaned forward and interlaced his fingers. "You were graduated from Harvard and spent two summers at sea. Where?"

"Greenland to the West Indies."

"Who made your charts?" Matthew saw the intensity in the aging gray eyes. Nothing on board the ship was more important than the navigator's charts. Ocean currents and winds dictated seasons and directions of travel, and no one knew how many thousand ships lay on the bottom of the world's oceans covered with coral and sand because of a shoal or reef or a current or trade wind that did not appear on the navigator's charts. Endless sea stories spoke of ships whose navigators read currents and winds wrong and were never heard of again, or of the ship that sailed west from the Spanish coast in the wrong season, only to be blown back to port five months later without travelling ninety miles from home. And no ocean had currents or winds trickier than those of the Atlantic. Good navigators with good charts were prized, courted, sought after.

Matthew answered the question. "Laurie-Whittle in London, current through January of this year. Mercator projections, with circumnavigation charts by Byron, Wallis, Carteret, and Cook."

"The entire globe?"

"Yes. All oceans."

Weyland released relieved breath. Laurie-Whittle charts were the best available. "Ever see a naval engagement?"

"No, sir. I studied the history of naval warfare at Harvard."

A wry smile passed over Weyland's face. "That makes you our expert." The smile faded. "You've heard enough to know what you're getting into." He leaned back in his chair. "Will you take the position of navigator on this ship?"

Matthew straightened. "Yes, sir."

"Why?" Matthew saw the intensity rise in the old gray eyes.

"Personal reasons."

"Your father?"

"That, and more."

Captain Weyland bobbed his head once, and the conversation was closed. He spoke as he walked to the door. "We cast off tonight half an hour after full dark. If you were up last night on the *Buford*, you better get some rest." He opened the door and called Riggins. "Show Mr. Dunson to his quarters."

Men-of-war were designed to survive the devastating pounding of cannonballs. The hulls were double, the keel and rib timbers thick, the hold small and divided into compartments for the crew, with heavy bulkheads for storing the necessities of war and prolonged sea voyages. They were three-decked, with massive planking to support the cannon on every deck. They carried no cargo. The crew's quarters were adequate, the officers' quarters large and luxurious by sea standards.

Merchantmen were another matter altogether. They were designed for profit, not war, and profit depended on cargo tonnage. Consequently, they were single hulled, with lighter keels and ribs to accommodate a cargo hold as large as possible. The captain, first mate, and navigator each had small quarters in the stern of the main deck, while the balance of the crew had cramped quarters, separated by canvas walls, on the crowded, low-ceilinged second deck, between the stern and the mainmast. From the mainmast forward, the second deck was jammed with provisions, which often included a cow, sheep, pigs, and chickens for fresh meat as long as they lasted, and the air hung heavy, fouled by the stench of unbathed bodies and animals and their dung. Critical freshwater barrels were lashed to the hull on the second deck, with barrelled lime juice and fresh potatoes to prevent scurvy. The top deck could support cannon if ports were cut, but the second deck was too thin for cannon, and there was no third deck beneath.

Matthew unpacked his seaman's bag into a battered footlocker, removed the oilskin wrapping from his charts, and slipped the great two-feet-by-three-feet leather-bound volume into its drawer in the massive chart table that dominated one corner of the tiny room. He opened the polished mahogany box holding his octant, checked the eyepiece, replaced the instrument in its box and laid it beside the charts, then closed and locked the drawer and slipped the brass key into his pocket.

He walked back out into the bright sunlight on deck to the big eighteen-spoke rudder wheel at the stern in order to inspect the ship's compass nearby on its pedestal. It was an in-plane Pollock with a variable alidade for sighting. He walked the deck and studied the cannon set on their heavy oak carriages and thick wooden wheels. Centered amidships on both sides were two heavy thirty-two-pound Demi-Cannon, six-inch bore, each with a twelve-foot chase; all other cannon were smaller eighteen-pound Culverin with a five-and-one-half-inch bore and a ten-foot chase.

He took noon mess with the officers, who regarded him with typical stoic New England reserve, then went to his cabin. He lifted his logbook from the footlocker and sat at his chart table for a time while he made entries, then knelt beside the footlocker to replace it. He was rising when he saw the little flat waterproof paper, carefully folded and placed in one corner. He dropped back to one knee and tenderly picked it up and unwrapped it on the chart table.

The small royal blue watch fob shined in the shaft of sunlight from the window, and he touched the beautiful red white-edged letters, MD. A wave of nostalgia rose, and suddenly he could not remember why he was in strange quarters on a strange ship, away from his home, away from her. *What happened at Henry's trial? Guilty? Hanged? Deported? Was it a stroke Phoebe had, or just a fainting spell? How is Kathleen feeding them?* Her music students had dwindled to but a few. The washing and ironing were bringing in enough money for bread and milk until it slackened. *Have they lost their home?*

He folded the watch fob back inside its wrapping, and started to place it back in the footlocker. Then, on an impulse, he drew his leather wallet from his inside coat pocket and carefully inserted the folded paper with his valuable papers and slipped the wallet back into its place. He hung his coat on a peg set in the door and lay down on his bunk. He stretched tired muscles, felt the tensions begin to ebb and drain, and quietly drifted into sleep seeing Kathleen's eyes and dark hair.

He jerked awake with the sun low in the west and for a moment tried to understand where he was. He poured tepid water from the plain porcelain pitcher into the basin on the washstand and washed the light sweat from his face, then dried with a towel from the rack and combed his hair. He shrugged into his coat and looped the strap of his leather glass case over his shoulder, and walked out onto the deck. He took mess with the officers, then casually moved to the rail, watching the small port of Beverly end her day. Lights ashore flickered on in shadowy dusk, and the evening star emerged in the deep purple of the eastern sky, and by degrees the stars came alive, from east to west, until the heavens were a black vaulted dome filled with tiny diamonds. A shaft of yellow light flooded momentarily from the open door of Captain Weyland's quarters, then disappeared as he closed it and walked to the wheel.

"Cast off."

Hard, callused hands cast the four two-inch hawsers from the pier brackets, and seamen on board quickly reeled them in and coiled them on deck. The ten men in the longboat leaned into their oars, and the towrope between the longboat and the *Esther* rose dripping from the black water and tightened. Slowly the ship crept away from the pier, out into the harbor, due west past the lights of Salem Town in the distance on the starboard. On command the longboat dropped the towrope and came alongside the *Esther,* and five minutes later it was secured in its blocks on board and the oarsmen were standing to their duty stations on the deck of the dark ship.

"Unfurl all sails and hold her due west."

The Marblehead Peninsula slipped past on the starboard side, and ten minutes later the Gulf current and the westerlies caught the schooner and she leaped forward.

"Mr. Dunson, set a course for Gloucester."

"Yes, sir!" Matthew turned to the helmsman. "Hold her east by northeast for fifteen minutes, then northeast until we pick up the lights of Magnolia, shortly after midnight."

"Yes, sir." The helmsman turned the wheel a quarter turn and the bow corrected to starboard, then fifteen minutes later adjusted to port, and the *Esther* was flying on the open seas. The moon rose in the east, and Matthew waited for the first feeling of a shift in the tides and corrected one more time, ten degrees to port, and the ship continued, her bow throwing a curl on either side. Running empty and high, with copper sheathing to reduce friction, the *Esther* was the fastest ship Matthew had ever experienced. He stole a moment to relax, to revel in the feeling of running under the black-vaulted heavens, free, with the salt tang of the fresh westerlies blowing. He picked out the Dippers, then the North Star, and listened to the sound of the bow cutting a twenty-foot curl in the black waters, and he filled his lungs with the clean salt air and slowly released it.

At twenty minutes past midnight they sighted the lights of Magnolia.

"Three degrees east of due north," Matthew ordered, and once again the helmsman spun the wheel and the bow swung hard to port, allowing the three degrees for magnetic deviation, which meant the ship was driving due north.

"Sir," Matthew said to Weyland, "we'll be entering Gloucester Harbor within half an hour, and we'll make port by three A.M. Do you intend anchoring there tonight?"

"No. We stop half an hour before we reach Eastern Point, and wait for light."

"Are you expecting British ships?"

"I'm told they're up there harassing merchantmen."

Matthew drew his telescope from the scarred leather case, extended it, and glassed the blackness ahead. At ten minutes past two he leaned forward and studied the pinpoint of light dead ahead, then turned to Weyland. "Sir, we're about five miles from Eastern Point."

Ten minutes later all sails were furled and lashed to the yards, the ship died in the water, and the two bow anchors dropped splashing into the black waters. All deck lights were extinguished, and the *Esther* rocked with the swells and waves, nearly invisible in the night.

The first watch was ending before the stars in the eastern sky began to fade, and the officers gathered in the bow to glass the waters northward, Matthew with them. They all saw the tiny fleck on the horizon at the same instant, and it was Weyland who spoke. "Can you see her colors?"

Long minutes passed before Riggins spoke excitedly. "The Union Jack! She's an English man-of-war quartering southwest towards Gloucester Harbor."

"We'll wait here until she's at the bay entrance, then show our sails and colors," Weyland replied, and turned to the bosun. "Load the cannon and keep them out of sight, and keep the crews on standby. Then arm every man with a musket and ten rounds and tell them to load and prime."

Twenty minutes later Matthew said, "They'll be rounding Eastern Point and they'll be in the bay in ten minutes."

"Weigh anchors and unfurl all sails," Weyland barked.

The first arc of the rising sun cleared the eastern horizon as the last jib was tightened, and the early morning rays caught the rigging on both tall masts and turned the great sails to fire as the two anchors broke water and were secured under the bow. Three miles north, the British man-of-war slowed, then swung due south, tacking into the wind with the Union Jack glowing proudly in the sun.

"They've seen us," Weyland said. "Every man to his station. Mr. Riggins, run our colors up."

The oncoming three-masted gunboat rode deep and heavy in the water. She was high in the bow and stern, low and broad at the beam, double hulled, triple decked, thick keeled and ribbed, and Matthew judged her to have a burden well in excess of six hundred tons. She was slow and sluggish, her maneuvers ponderous.

At one mile Weyland asked, "Can you see any bow guns?"

"Two," Riggins said, his voice too high.

"How many decks show cannon?"

"Three," Matthew replied.

Weyland pursed his mouth and shook his head. They were closing with a ship more than twice their size, built for war, and they were outgunned three to one. A full broadside from three decks of cannon would shred the *Esther.*

Weyland licked dry lips. "With the wind from the southeast she'll have to turn nearly due west to bring her guns to bear. Mr. Riggins, tell the helmsman to keep a bearing head-on. She might think we're a merchantman until we turn and she sees our cannon ports."

At one-half mile neither ship had changed course. Aboard the *Esther* every officer, every seaman stood like a statue, frozen, white-knuckled, waiting for the oncoming man-of-war to make her move or for Weyland's orders to make his own.

At five hundred yards they saw the two puffs of white smoke on both sides of the bow, and a moment later waterspouts leaped fifty yards on either side of the bowsprit of the *Esther*, and then the sound of the two cannon shots rolled past. Seamen flinched and ducked and moved their feet, but stood to their posts. Weyland ignored the two cannonballs straddling his bow that were the universal demand to stop and strike colors and surrender.

"Steady as she goes," he shouted, and the *Esther* continued her headlong flight on a collision course with the oncoming British ship.

At two hundred yards they watched the British seamen finish reloading the two bow cannon and roll them back into their ports, and they saw the black-coated officer raise his hand and then throw it downward. The cannoneers touched their matches to the touchholes, and again the cannons blasted and belched white smoke. Again two geysers leaped, this time less than twenty feet on either side of the bow, and cold salt spray splattered the deck halfway to the mainmast. Men flinched and ducked, and for a moment murmured, then once more settled.

Weyland gripped the rail, knuckles white. "She won't ram us," he growled under his breath. "She'll turn. She has to turn." He pivoted his head to shout at the white-faced helmsman, "Steady as she goes."

Matthew did not realize he was crouched forward with a death grip on the rail, holding his breath, bracing himself for a head-on collision that would smash the *Esther* to kindling. At one hundred yards they were all looking upward at the high bow of the heavy ship, and they could see the beards and neckerchiefs of the excited British seamen. At ninety yards they could see the startled expressions on their faces. At eighty yards they saw the captain turn and heard his shout, but could not hear his order. Then, with a scant seventy yards separating the onrushing ships, the bow of the British vessel started to swing to the west, and the crew of the

Esther saw the line of cannon muzzles thrust from the gun ports on all three decks, twelve per deck, all thirty-six pounders.

Weyland's shouted order came instantly. "All cannon crews show your cannon and prepare to fire! Bosun, get crews onto the yard ropes and prepare to turn hard starboard, then hard port. Keep your muskets handy."

Men on either side of the cannon strained on the ropes and pulleys that rolled their gun forward into firing position, muzzles showing to the man-of-war, while other men looped the tether hawser around the butt of the cannon to take the recoil when they fired. Crews grabbed the ropes that controlled the yards and the sails, and stood with eyes locked onto Weyland, ready, anxious.

At fifty yards the bow of the man-of-war was into her slow, ponderous swing to the west to bring the snouts of her port-side cannon around to bear on the *Esther*, in a raking position, not broadside. Weyland's eyes were intent on the muzzle of the lead cannon, which would be the first to come into direct line. The instant before it reached firing position Weyland shouted, "Hard starboard!"

The helmsman spun the wheel, and the men on the yard ropes instantly adjusted sail to maintain capture of the southeasterlies to keep the canvas taut, full. The bow of the schooner swung violently towards the east, light, flying with the wind, and completed her turn, while the cumbersome man-of-war was less than half through her move to the west, and at forty yards the racing *Esther* flashed past the first four cannon ports, with the British gun crews watching in bewilderment, unable to collect their wits in time to line their cannon and fire. The schooner had passed the sixth column of cannon ports before the remaining British gun crews clacked their gaping mouths closed and came to life. They had no time to depress their gun muzzles to shoot downward at the hull of the *Esther*, a full ten feet lower than the bottom row of cannon. The cannoneers had time only to smack their matches down on the touchhole with a fervent prayer that the big thirty-six-pound ball would hit a mast or yard, and then the great guns bucked and roared.

The smoke from the muzzles reached halfway to the *Esther,* and the shock waves from the deafening blasts struck the white-faced crew on the schooner and they involuntarily hunched and took one step back to wait for the cannonballs to rip into them.

Matthew turned his face upward and watched the hits. Four whistling cannonballs punched holes through the mainsail, two more ripped through one jib, and one grazed the varnish on the starboard rail. The others whistled overhead through the rigging and touched nothing and raised geysers of water three hundred yards to starboard.

"Hard port!" Weyland shouted, and the helmsman wrenched the wheel back while the men on the yards strained to change sail direction, and once again the schooner dug into the dark waters in a violent left turn until she was directly behind the high stern of the British ship and closing fast.

"Does she have any stern cannon?" Weyland shouted, and Matthew shouted back, "No, sir. None."

The crew slowly understood they were no longer under the muzzles of British cannon. They had outwitted and outsailed the man-of-war and had taken half a broadside that only punched six holes in their canvas. The holes meant nothing; they could be repaired in fifteen minutes. Relief spilled out in talk and nervous laughter, and they all resumed their duty posts and waited for orders.

"Steady as she goes," Weyland called, and the bow steadied, with the stern of the huge warship dead ahead. At fifty yards Weyland shouted, "Hard starboard," and once again the little schooner darted right for one hundred yards before Weyland again shouted, "Hard port," and she turned back towards the heavier ship, coming in at an angle too far astern for any British guns to come to bear, and fully capable of outmaneuvering the big ship no matter what she did.

"Hold her steady," Weyland shouted, and the schooner bore down at an angle on the rear starboard quarter of the man-of-war.

The stern of the British ship was high, a full fifty feet above the water and twenty-five feet above the bow of the *Esther.* Delicate hand carvings of leaping porpoises and sea nymphs graced the hardwood backside, where two decks of nine windows each opened into the officers' quarters. Beneath the overhang of the bottom row of windows, the heavy, ironbound oak rudder, ten inches thick and two feet in breadth, ran from the superstructure down into the ship's wake. Above the window banks, between two carved sea nymphs, a craftsman had carved the name of the ship, *Stafford,* in beautiful English scroll.

The *Esther* was forty yards from the rear of the *Stafford* when the crew saw the first British seamen set a swivel gun in its socket in the stern rail and ram the powder charge home.

"Clear that rail," Weyland shouted, and every available man grabbed his musket. The British were seating three pounds of grapeshot against the powder in their swivel gun when the first musket volley blasted from the *Esther,* and every British seaman on the rail staggered back.

"Keep that rail clear," Weyland ordered, "and if they appear in those windows of the officers' quarters, shoot them!" The *Esther* crew reloaded their muskets and stood with the muzzles upward, ready. Twice more British seamen rushed the rail with swivel guns and muskets, and were driven back by the blasting volleys from the *Esther.*

"Sir," Riggins exclaimed, his voice high, excited, "we're going to ram!" He was white-faced, pointing.

Weyland raised his hand to quiet Riggins while he calculated distance, angle, and speed. "Starboard cannon, prepare to fire. We're going right under the stern and dump all wind from our sails. When your cannon come to bear, shoot the rudder."

Suddenly the reason for Weyland's confused maneuvers became crystal clear, and every man aboard the schooner jabbed a fist into the air, and from every throat rolled a resounding shout.

"Hard port!" Weyland cried, and the bow of the schooner veered left and started across the high stern of the *Stafford,* barely fifteen yards away. The rigging on the *Esther* mainmast was less than five yards from the *Stafford* when Weyland shouted, "Spill the sails!" The men released the yard ropes and the sails fluttered free, and the *Esther* instantly slowed, coasting slowly past the high stern of the man-of-war, whose rudder was exposed to the nine cannon on the starboard side of the schooner at point-blank range.

"Fire when you come to bear," Weyland ordered, and every eye on the little vessel watched as the first gun came on line with the rudder. The cannoneer touched his match to the touchhole, the cannon jumped and roared, and the ball raked a two-inch groove in the right side of the massive rudder. No one spoke or moved as the second cannon came on line and blasted. Wood splinters flew as the ball struck on the left side. Number three struck and wood shattered, but the rudder remained in commission. Numbers four and five were the heavy thirty-two-pound Demi-Cannon, and Matthew held his breath as number four came on line. The *Esther* was at a near standstill in the water, and the gunner stood directly behind the big gun, sighting down the barrel. He touched the match and the gun blasted and the huge ball smashed into the rudder dead center and ripped a groove eight inches deep. Three seconds later the second thirty-two-pounder jumped and roared, and the heavy ball split the rudder lengthwise and it sagged at an angle. The last four smaller guns fired in turn, and on the last shot, half the rudder fell into the sea, with the other half shot off its moorings, hanging at an angle, useless.

The *Stafford* was rudderless, adrift, at the mercy of wind and currents and of the *Esther.*

Matthew heard the triumphant shout well from his chest and then realized everyone on the *Esther* was shouting, unable to believe they had engaged the huge man-of-war and fatally crippled her, with only six harmless holes in their canvas. Matthew turned to Weyland, elated, grinning.

Weyland looked at Matthew and wiped sweat from his face and rounded his lips and blew air before he turned to the crew. "Hold your fire. She hasn't struck her colors yet."

He turned his face back to the warship. "Hello, *Stafford.*" He waited but there was no reply. "Hello, *Stafford*," he repeated. "Will you strike your colors?"

There was no reply from the silent *Stafford*.

He shook his head and turned back to his cannon crews. "Can you elevate your gun muzzles to the officers' quarters in the stern?"

"We can try, sir."

Weyland waited until the stern of the big ship had moved two hundred yards away, so that the *Esther* was out of effective range of any British muskets, before he ordered his cannoneers to fire. The first volley ripped into the lower deck of windows, and glass shards and wood splinters flew. The second volley caught the upper deck of windows and some of the carved images in the heavy wood and blasted them into splinters. Inside, the officers' quarters were a shambles.

"Hello, *Stafford!*" Weyland called. "Will you strike your colors?"

Again there was no reply, and Weyland shook his head, hating the necessity of chopping a helpless ship to pieces. He smacked his fist on the rail and turned to his cannon crews once more. "Reload."

"Sir," Matthew called, and pointed. Aboard the *Stafford*, the Union Jack was coming down, and a white flag was going up. While they watched, the first mate appeared on deck above the wreckage of the stern. He snapped to attention, his official English naval officer uniform gleaming in the sun, and they heard his shout. "Sir, we strike and we surrender."

A roar erupted from every voice on the *Esther*. Weyland removed his cap and wiped the sweat from his face and forehead. "Sir, are you disabled?" he called.

"We are disabled."

"I'm coming alongside to board you."

Twenty minutes later Captain Soren Weyland led Matthew and his bosun and thirty of his men, armed with muskets and pistols, onto the gently rolling decks of the *Stafford* and faced her captain while the British crew stood at attention, faces contorted and fists clenched as they struggled with their deep anger and resentment.

"Sir, I am Captain Soren Weyland of the *Esther*, authorized by letters of marque from General George Washington. In the name of the thirteen colonies I declare this vessel and all her stores to be a prize of war and the crew to be prisoners of war. What is your name, sir?"

"I am Captain Philip Edwards, His Majesty's Navy. I command the *Stafford*."

"I offer my ship's surgeon and medicines for your wounded, if you wish."

"It will not be necessary. We have sufficient."

"Very good. I will require your log, your navigation charts, your inventory of all stores, your octant, and your compass, sir. My bosun will accompany your first mate now to fetch those items." The bosun stepped forward and followed the ramrod-straight back of the first mate to the stern of the ship and disappeared.

Weyland gestured to the *Stafford*'s rigging. "My men will furl all sails at once and leave them furled while we tow you to Gloucester Port."

Captain Edwards's face reddened and he battled with control for a moment, then spoke through gritted teeth. "I am obliged to tell you, sir, that I cannot be responsible for the conduct of my crew. They consider the actions of your vessel to be high-seas piracy, and they may not be able to control their need to retaliate."

Weyland thrust his face forward. "And I am obliged to tell you, sir, that my crew considers your blockades of our ports to be cowardly, and they have an overpowering need to punish any ship flying the Union Jack that they find in colonial waters!" He made no attempt to hide his bitter contempt for the cruel hardships the British had inflicted on the small, struggling colonies.

The bosun and the British first mate returned carrying a loaded basket between them. "Sir," the bosun said, "I have the enumerated items."

Weyland nodded and again faced Captain Edwards. "You and all your officers will accompany me on the *Esther.* I will leave my bosun and twenty of my crew to furl the sails and handle this vessel. Your crew will go to their quarters and remain there until we reach Gloucester Port. They will destroy nothing, and they will not harm my men in any way. If they do otherwise, I will hang you and your entire staff of officers from the mainmast yard of the *Esther,* and then I will sink the *Stafford* with every one of your men aboard. This ship is rudderless and there's nothing your men could do to stop it. Am I clear, sir?"

Captain Edwards bit down on his temper. "Clear."

"Tell your men what I just said."

Captain Edwards turned and in terse, angry tones gave the orders to his men. For several moments there was murmuring, then open, hot, angry talk.

Weyland cocked his pistol and levelled it on Edwards's chest. "Your men have two minutes to be in their quarters, except for your officers. Tell them."

Edwards did not move as he barked out his orders. Slowly, reluctantly the talk dwindled, and then the crew turned and walked stiff-legged to the narrow gangways down to the lower decks and disappeared.

"Now you and your officers will take their places in the longboats while my crew takes charge of this vessel."

At three o'clock P.M., beneath a blazing sun, *Esther* sailed past Eastern Point and entered the wide mouth of Gloucester Harbor, and southwesterlies kept her sails tight as she moved the huge warship steadily on a straight line north towards the town. At four P.M. the schooner shortened the towrope from ninety feet to fifty feet for better control, and at four-forty P.M. furled all but two sails as she crept into the port.

Matthew was at the bow with Weyland and Riggins. Captain Edwards and his officers were clustered at the stern.

The ancient port of Gloucester had seen ships and seamen from every country and port in the world, and the stories told by old sailors on the docks and in the pubs spoke of wondrous and miraculous sights, but seldom had Gloucester seen anything to compare with the startling apparition that now crept into port. The activity on the docks, and on the ships riding at anchor or tied to the piers, slowed and stopped as sailors stood still and squinted in disbelief at the sight of a small merchantman schooner towing a man-of-war twice her size on a short tether, with the man-of-war flying the white flag of surrender, and her stern and rudder blasted to pieces.

Old sailors scratched scraggly gray beards until they read the unmistakable facts, and buzzing began and then rose to a crescendo as the *Esther* dropped anchor, and the two great anchors on the *Stafford* plunged into the water and the ships stopped. Eager hands caught the hawsers to tie Weyland's longboat to the pier, and men all over the docks shouted three great "hurrahs" for the crew of the small schooner as they wildly pounded Weyland and his officers on the back.

At nine P.M. Weyland called Riggins and Matthew into his quarters on the *Esther,* and they pored over the thick ledger of inventory of stores on the *Stafford.* At eleven-thirty P.M. Weyland pushed himself away from the small table and rose and stretched tired muscles. He closed the heavy ledger cover and glanced at the list he had dictated while Matthew wrote.

One hundred twelve kegs of powder, eighty pounds to the keg, seventy-two cannon, thirty-six-pounders, over two thousand rounds for the cannon, two hundred twenty muskets with ammunition, twelve swivel guns and shot, seven tons of salt beef, six tons of salt pork, sailcloth, uniforms, medicines, utensils, over one thousand pounds in English coin, and more, much more. He stared thoughtfully at the ledger on the table. "We'll unload the *Stafford* tomorrow and send word to General Washington. It should lighten the burden that man is carrying."

He turned to Riggins and Matthew. "There are a few items he won't need. We'll sell them ashore and divide the money equally, officers and seamen alike. Agreed?"

Both men nodded.

"Mr. Dunson, the navigational charts and equipment are yours."

"Thank you, sir."

Weyland loosened his black tie. "We were lucky today." He paused for a moment. "Either of you men superstitious?"

They shook their heads.

"Neither am I. But still, it flies in the face of what common sense I may have—the notion that we beat the *Stafford*."

Neither man spoke.

Weyland stood still in the yellow glow of the two lamps, eyes narrowed, brow drawn down, bulldog face lost in deep thought.

"I've got to tell you men something." He raised his eyes. "I didn't know how we were going to fight that ship today until she turned and showed us her cannon. From there, it came to me clear, like I had known it all along." His face was frank, open. "I don't think I was in command out there today."

His eyes bored into Matthew's, then Riggins's, and for long moments none of them spoke in the charged silence. Then Weyland heaved a weary sigh.

"Well, as I said, I'm not superstitious, but . . ." He stopped, and Matthew saw him consider his thoughts and change his mind. Weyland shifted his feet and looked for words, and tried to finish. "Nothing. Just a passing thought—nothing."

"I'd like to hear it, sir," Matthew said quietly.

Weyland stared at him intently. "If you think of it, you might mention it . . ." He stopped, and licked his lips, and did not finish.

Matthew said, "I will, sir. Tonight."

Weyland looked away, embarrassed at sharing his innermost thoughts, and his tough New England demeanor rose and the moment was past. He untied his black tie and pulled it from his neck.

"Men, we have a long day tomorrow. Get some rest."

"Sir," Matthew said, "when we've delivered the stores, what is your plan for the *Esther?*"

"Go looking for another British ship. We will do that until we get a change of orders from General Washington."

It was midnight when Matthew hung his coat on its peg in his quarters. He drew out his wallet and carefully removed and unfolded the small paper. The watch fob gleamed in the yellow lamplight, and he gently laid it in one palm and touched it with his fingertips.

Where is she tonight? Is she well? Is she well?

He refolded the paper and tucked it back inside the wallet and left it on the table. He turned to his bunk and dropped to his knees and clasped his hands and lowered his head.

"Dear God, for the blessings of this day I thank thee and praise thy name. And I beseech thee, dear God, to shed thy grace and mercies on Kathleen and her family, and on Mother and the children, and Tom. May Billy heal from his wounds. . . ."

Notes

General George Washington did grant letters of marque to privately owned American merchant ships for the purpose of sending them out under his authority to acquire munitions and other sorely needed supplies for his military needs. His orders to the captains of these small merchant ships included the directive to strenuously avoid engaging armed British vessels in favor of taking British merchant ships loaded with valuable cargoes, wherever possible. However, it appears that on occasion these American merchant ships, which had been armed with a few cannon on their main decks, may have found themselves having to engage armed British vessels. (See Knox, *A History of the United States Navy*, p. 10.) Hence the adventures of the *Esther* and her crew as depicted in the novel.

It must also be explained that the merchant ship *Esther* is a fictional ship and that her captain, Soren Weyland, is fictional. In the novel, the *Esther* participates in an amalgamation of events that are based largely on incidents experienced by other ships, captains, and crews of the time (and it should be noted that the *Esther*'s Revolutionary War career gets under way a couple of months before American merchant ships were actually engaged in such activities). This fictional ship was created to be representative of the great and often heroic service rendered by the ships and men who rose to the call of their country.

July 1775

Chapter XIX

★ ★ ★

*I*n soft yellow lamp glow, Margaret gently shook Brigitte's shoulder and waited. "Brigitte, it's time," she said quietly. Slowly the blue eyes opened, and for long moments Brigitte stared at her mother's face until she understood.

"Are you awake?" Margaret asked.

Brigitte nodded her head and threw back the bedcovers and swung her feet to the floor.

"Breakfast in fifteen minutes," Margaret said, and silently walked back to the kitchen, where oatmeal porridge simmered. Twenty minutes later Brigitte sat down at the table. Her hair was pulled back into one braid beneath a white scarf that covered her head. She wore a plain gray short-sleeved work dress and high-top lace-up work shoes. She glanced at the mantel clock as Margaret set a steaming bowl of porridge before her, with apple cider and sliced bread and honey. Brigitte sighed as she bowed her head, and Margaret stopped moving while Brigitte said grace. She ate in silence, and as she rose, Margaret glanced at the clock. Close to four A.M.

Brigitte walked to the front door and slipped her shawl about her shoulders.

"Go straight to the bakery, and move fast," Margaret said. "I'll watch as long as I can see you."

Brigitte nodded and walked out into the silvery light of a three-quarter moon. The air was hot, humid, still; the morning breeze from the Atlantic had not yet begun. She hurried through the gate, Margaret right behind, and Margaret watched until she disappeared in the shadows of the tree-lined sidewalk in the next block.

Margaret turned back through the gate and looked into the cloudless heavens at the countless points of light in the black dome and slowed for a moment, wondering. *Is he out there somewhere? Or is he still here, nearby?* She sighed as she closed the door and cleared Brigitte's breakfast dishes from the table. She returned to her bedroom and lay down, and wakened with a start at ten minutes past six, with bright late-July sun streaming through the east windows of the parlor. At seven o'clock she quietly stole into Caleb's room and shook his shoulder.

"Breakfast in twenty minutes."

Caleb rolled over and opened his eyes with a frown. "It's too early. I'll go later."

"Can't. Daniel's expecting you at eight. He has newspapers to deliver."

Caleb got his feet onto the rug and dug at his eyes with the heels of his hands. "Go on. I'll be out."

Margaret walked from the room, stopped, and turned back. Caleb had collapsed back onto the bed, one long, thin leg and oversized foot dangling over the edge.

"Stand up," she said, and there was iron in her voice.

He groaned as he once again dropped his feet to the floor and stood and tugged at his knee-length nightshirt. At seven-thirty he sat down at the table, dressed in work clothes, face washed, hair combed. At seven-forty he walked out the door into the dazzling sunlight, Margaret following, and twenty minutes later walked through the door into Daniel Knight's print shop.

At eight-twenty Margaret wakened Adam and Priscilla, and at nine o'clock she led them out the front door, around the corner, west two blocks, and rapped on the door of Enoch Parnum. The door opened a crack, and a faded eye beneath a bushy brow peered out suspiciously. "Who's there?" the scratchy voice demanded.

"Margaret Dunson. I've come for your laundry, Enoch."

"Is that you, Margaret?"

"It is."

"Oh. Well, if it's you, then you can come on in."

Slowly the door opened as Enoch shuffled backwards two steps. His long silver hair reached his shoulders, and his untrimmed brows nearly covered his sunken gray eyes. He had a two-week beard stubble, and wore a threadbare robe wrapped about his thin, aged, hunched frame.

He pointed across the parlor to a hall. "It's in there. Ruth'll help. I'll call her to help."

"I can get it, Enoch. No need to disturb Ruth." Margaret walked across the room and disappeared down the hall while Adam and Priscilla stood just inside the door, trying not to stare at Enoch. Their noses wrinkled at the musty, peculiar odor of a house that had been closed too long with an old man inside, alone. Margaret returned with a woven wicker basket filled with soiled clothing.

"Have you been eating, Enoch?" she demanded.

"Yes. Oh yes. Ruth makes me eat. Cooks all the time."

"When I come back with the laundry I'm going to bring some meat and bread and cheese. You see that you eat it. Do you hear?"

Enoch nodded. "I hear."

"Will you do it?"

"Yes. I will." He gestured at the basket. "Same price as before? I've got money. I can pay the money."

"Yes. Same price. I'll be back in two days. Now, you be sure to eat your meals."

He nodded vigorously. "I will, I will." He followed them to the door and watched until they turned on the sidewalk before he closed it.

"Mama, where's Ruth?" Priscilla looked up at Margaret.

"Ruth is Enoch's wife. She's in heaven. She died fourteen years ago."

"Then how can she cook?"

"She can't."

"But Enoch said—"

"For Enoch, Ruth is still there. Like your father. For me, he's still here."

"But you don't talk about him like that."

Margaret looked down into the innocent eyes. "Sometimes I do, when I'm alone, and sometimes I do when I'm with someone, but I do it silently."

A puzzled look crept over Priscilla's face.

"Enoch is nearly ninety-four years old. When you get that old, your mind gets tired and you forget some things. He knows Ruth is gone, but sometimes he just forgets, and he talks to her. It's all right."

Priscilla sighed and struggled to understand. Margaret shifted the basket from one hip to the other as they walked on. They turned the corner onto their block, and Margaret slowed for a moment as she studied the figure standing inside their fence.

"Someone's at our place," Adam said, pointing.

"It's Tom Sievers," Margaret replied, and hurried on. Tom met them at the gate.

"Good morning, ma'am. Can I carry the basket?"

"Thank you, Tom. It's heavy." She led them into the house and pointed. "Set it there, on the table."

Tom set it down, and his eyes dropped for a moment. "I just came for a minute, ma'am. There's news about Henry."

Margaret stopped in her tracks. "What is it?"

Tom glanced at the children. "Maybe I should wait."

"You two go change your clothes," Margaret directed, and Adam and Priscilla walked to their rooms.

"He was found guilty. This morning they sentenced him. He's banished."

Margaret's eyes closed and her shoulders slumped for a moment. "They aren't going to hang him?"

"No, ma'am."

"If he's banished, where does he intend going?"

"No one knows for sure. Maybe the West Indies."

"For how long?"

"Life."

"How do you know?"

"I was there."

"Was Phoebe there?"

"No, ma'am. Kathleen was."

Margaret groaned and slumped onto a chair. "That poor girl. Oh, that poor girl."

"She took it good, ma'am. Stood straight and walked to him before they took him out, and embraced him like always, and when he was gone she walked out with her head high."

Margaret wiped silent tears for a moment.

Tom moved his feet, not knowing what to do next. "I thought you should know."

"Tom, please let me prepare breakfast for you. Please."

"Thanks, ma'am, I've had breakfast."

"No you haven't. Give me five minutes."

Tom ate scrambled eggs and strips of ham, with bread and honey, and drank milk in ravenous silence while Margaret watched and smiled. He pushed himself away from the table and started to gather his dishes.

"I can do that," Margaret said. "Bring your wash in tomorrow."

Tom stood. "I thank you for the breakfast. I can take care of my wash."

"I know, but bring it in anyway."

Tom said nothing and started for the kitchen door into the backyard.

"Is there something out there?" Margaret asked.

"Caleb said the drum on the well was bumping."

"Oh. Yes. We can fix it."

Tom walked on into the yard, to the well house, and grasped the handle and slowly began to turn the drum. The rope tightened, and the bucket in the well began its upward climb, with Tom feeling the rotation of the axle drum through the handle. He felt the slight catch, then the sudden release, and heard the dull sound of wood dropping on wood. He looked at both ends of the axle, where it entered the rounded bearings, and walked back to Margaret standing in the door frame.

"Axle's worn crooked at one end. I can fix it tomorrow."

"Caleb and I can do it."

"I'll do it when I bring my wash."

"I'll pay you back for the wood."

"No need. I can make one." He walked back through the house, Margaret following to the front door.

"Come early in the morning and I'll have breakfast waiting," she called.

At the front gate Tom nodded and waved.

At ten minutes past two o'clock Brigitte thrust her arm into the warm, clouded water in the great, deep soapstone sink against the back wall of the bakery kitchen, and tugged the stopper from its hole and watched for a moment, hand and arm dripping, while the water level began to slowly settle. To her left, forty-eight battered copper bread pans were stacked on a slanted drain in orderly rows to dry, ready for use again tomorrow morning.

At four o'clock A.M. Calvin Fornier and his wife, Bess, and Brigitte would measure and mix the first batch of bread dough for the day. At five o'clock it would have risen, been punched, rolled out in three long rolls on the long wooden worktable, and cut into twenty-four measured one-pound sections. Each section would be powdered with flour and dropped plopping into the greased molds until it rose again, rounded above the pan tops.

Calvin would then carefully position each in the top compartment of the big three-tiered oven to bake while the next batch was rolled, cut, placed in the molds, and slipped into the next tier, and then the third batch would be prepared for the third tier. The second rotation would include tarts, cinnamon rolls, and sweet breads. At six o'clock Calvin's daughter and son would carefully line wicker baskets with cheesecloth and fill them with the first smoking loaves, and begin deliveries to taverns and inns and homes.

Outside, the still, hot, humid air lay over the Boston Peninsula like a great oppressive blanket. Inside the bakery kitchen, the huge oven piled heat on heat until the lard used in baking melted in the crocks, and those laboring tucked towels under their apron strings to wipe at sweat that ran dripping from their noses and chins. By ten o'clock, damp spots appeared on their clothing between their shoulder blades, and by noon, they were wet from the waist up.

Brigitte dipped fresh water to rinse the sink, then tugged at her apron strings. She wiped her face and arms in a clean towel, pulled the scarf from her head, tucked at her hair, and looked once more at the rows of pans. She was tired, clothes damp from perspiration, but a smile tugged at her mouth and her eyes as she looked at the clean molds and at the last rotation of perfect golden bread loaves cooling before they were placed in the glass cases in the front of the bakery for the afternoon trade. For a moment the sweat and weariness faded as a sense of pride and accomplishment rose. She loosened the tie-strings of her flour-covered apron and dropped it into the laundry basket by the back door, and faced Calvin.

He smiled. "Hot day. Why don't you take home a tart for the children."

She smiled back. "Thank you. See you in the morning." She said good-bye to Bess as she passed through the front of the bakery, then walked into the street and turned towards home with long strides.

At the Dunson home, Margaret glanced at the clock and frowned for a moment before she started for the front door to look up the street for Brigitte. She was reaching for the handle when the knock came, and she opened the door wide.

"Billy!"

Margaret stepped forward to wrap him in her arms for a moment, then stepped back. His face was thinner, ruddy skin sallow, and he stood slightly hunched, leaning on a cane. In his eyes she saw the hollow look of one who had spent thirty-two days in a bed feeling his life forces dwindle while his body fought to mend a bayonet wound and a bullet hole that had both penetrated deeply into his vitals. The wounds had drained for days and then stopped, and slowly the flesh knitted. Fifteen days later he could sit. Ten more days and he hobbled around the house, crouched over, leaning on a cane. A week later he took half an hour to walk the two blocks to the Dunson home. This was his third visit since, in the afternoon heat. Margaret had opened all the windows on the cool side of the house, hoping to capture any stir of air.

He smiled back at her. "Good afternoon, Mrs. Dunson. You're looking well, as always."

"Come in and sit down." She followed him to the table, and he settled onto one of the straight-backed chairs.

"Let me get you something cool to drink." She returned from the root cellar with a glass of buttermilk, and reached to cover his hand with hers for a moment. "It's so good to see you getting back your color and a little flesh. How are you feeling? Still have pain?"

He savored the buttermilk. "A little, but it's going away. Doctor says I can get rid of the cane soon."

"How's your mother? the children?"

"Good." He set the glass on the table and turned serious eyes to Margaret. "Have you heard about Henry?"

"Tom told me this morning. I can hardly bear the thoughts."

Billy shook his head. "Kathleen was there at court. She . . ." He shook his head again and didn't finish his thought, and then asked, "Is Brigitte here?"

"She should be here any time. Anything I can tell her?"

"She asked me to find what happened to the lieutenant she met from the regulars."

"I know. Did you find out anything?"

They both turned their heads at the sound of steps and the front door opening, and Brigitte walked in.

"Billy! You're looking better. How are you?"

"Still alive." He grinned.

Margaret eyed Brigitte. "You're late. I was starting to worry."

"What's planned for supper?" Brigitte asked as she walked into the kitchen and set the two wrapped tarts on the cupboard. She drank from the dipper and returned to sit with Margaret and Billy.

"Sliced meat and cabbage," Margaret answered. "Caleb likes cabbage. Did you work late?"

"A little. Calvin sent tarts for Adam and Prissy."

"Heard about Henry?" Billy asked.

Brigitte straightened. "No."

"Guilty. Banished."

"Banished! For how long? When?"

"Tomorrow. For life."

Brigitte's shoulders slumped and her eyes closed and her head dropped forward. "That poor family. What will they do?"

Billy shook his head sadly. There was no answer.

Brigitte turned to Margaret. "We better go down. Take food. Something."

"We tried," Billy said. "Kathleen won't take help from anyone."

"Yes she will!" Brigitte exclaimed. "This is ridiculous."

Margaret said, "Let a little time pass and we'll go. Time will help."

Brigitte settled, then turned to Billy. "Did you find anything about Lieutenant Buchanan?"

Billy leaned back in his chair. "He's at the hospital at the big military base."

Brigitte's face went white. "How bad?"

"Left arm was shattered above the elbow and he had a bad head wound."

She gasped and her hand covered her mouth for a moment. "Will he recover?"

"They saved the arm but it will be partly numb, and he won't have complete use. He was unconscious for nearly two weeks from a head wound, but it's healing. His memory's coming back. He'll be all right."

All the air went out of Brigitte, and her shoulders dropped for a moment before she again spoke. "Will he be released from the army?"

"No. Promoted to captain. The column of regulars stalled at Meno-tomy, and he got them moving before they were totally annihilated."

"How did you find out?"

For long moments Billy studied the buttermilk glass before he raised his eyes. "Kathleen."

"Kathleen?"

"She had to take work at the laundry at the British hospital. She asked a few questions three or four days ago."

Margaret slowly eased back against the chair. "Kathleen? Working for the British?"

Billy nodded. "Her music students quit coming, and no one brings laundry anymore. They need money. She's afraid they're going to have to sell the house." He waited a moment. "Phoebe's mind is beginning to wander."

For a moment they sat in silence, lost in their own somber thoughts, and then Adam and Priscilla came thumping from their bedrooms.

Brigitte looked inquiringly at Margaret, who nodded approval, and Brigitte spoke to the children. "Tarts on the kitchen cupboard."

They brightened and trotted into the kitchen.

"Be careful," Margaret called. "Take them into the backyard and don't spot your clothes."

Billy straightened. "Has Matthew written?"

"Yes." Margaret placed a letter on the table, and Billy eagerly opened it. For more than a minute his eyes glistened and a smile formed as he read, and then he refolded it.

"I wish I could be with him. I surely do."

"He wishes the same thing."

He pushed the envelope towards Margaret. "Caleb told me the drum on the well was starting to wobble. I'm going to look."

"Tom's coming to fix it."

"Good. We'll work on the yard this weekend." He did not look at Margaret directly as he continued. "Is everything all right here? Enough money?"

Brigitte answered. "I've got work, and Mama's doing ironing and sewing. Caleb's delivering papers and running errands for Daniel at the print shop. We'll manage."

"Promise you'll tell me if you need help? money?" Margaret interrupted. "Don't worry about us. We're fine."

He faced her directly. "Promise you'll tell me?"

She nodded. "Promise."

"When you write to Matthew, tell him I said hello, and to be careful."

"I will."

Billy rose and stood hunched over his cane for a moment, waiting for the injured muscles in his midsection to relax and allow him to move. He shuffled towards the door, and Margaret gently took his arm as he reached for the handle, and she spoke quietly. "Billy, thank you. For everything."

"No thanks necessary." He grinned, and for the first time in three months Margaret saw the gleam of the irrepressible, irresistible boy in him, and for a moment she felt a violent wave of nostalgia. She watched through the window as he patiently worked his way up the street, and then she turned back to Brigitte.

"Better get out of those clothes and wash yourself and lie down. You need your rest."

The heat of the day had passed and the sun was settling towards the western rim of the world when Brigitte came from her room, eyes still filled with sleep, hair damp against her forehead. Cabbage steamed on the stove, and Margaret had cut the cold leg of lamb and strips of cheese.

"Set the table," Margaret said, "and get the children washed for supper. Caleb should be home any time."

Caleb ate second helpings with abandon while Brigitte picked at her food. Margaret hovered over the twins until they cleaned their plates.

"It's too hot," Brigitte complained. "It was hot at the bakery and it's hot here."

"It's going to storm tonight," Margaret said. "I can feel it."

With supper finished, and shadows lengthening in the streets and yards, the two women cleared the table, and Margaret began washing the dishes in steaming suds while Brigitte rinsed and dried. Margaret finished and handed Brigitte the last pot. "Billy's looking better."

Brigitte nodded but said nothing as she dried the pot and set it in the cupboard.

Dusk settled and they lighted the lamps, and Margaret read to Adam and Priscilla. Caleb wandered aimlessly, restless, and finally settled at the table with one of Matthew's old college books.

Brigitte brushed her hair and spoke as she walked to the front door. "I'm going to see Billy."

Margaret raised her head. "It's getting dark and it's going to storm."

"I'll be all right."

"What do you need to see Billy about?"

"Captain Buchanan."

Margaret turned to Caleb. "Come read to the children for a minute." She walked out the front door with Brigitte and faced her in the deep shadows.

"Let go of it. Can't you see it will only bring heartache?"

Brigitte stared at her hands. "I can't help it, Mama. I can't."

"Sooner or later you'll have to. Do it now, before it's too late."

Brigitte shook her head.

Margaret sighed. "You're of age. I can't force you."

Impulsively Brigitte reached to grasp Margaret's arm. "I'll be all right, I promise. Don't worry about me."

"Huh!" Margaret grunted. "Just like that. Don't worry about me." Her voice rose. "I'll worry about you and the others as long as I'm alive!"

"I love you, Mama." Brigitte turned, and Margaret watched her move up the street with determined stride.

Brigitte entered at the white gate with the carved sign "WEEMS" on it and knocked on the door. Dorothy Weems cautiously opened it six inches.

"Who's there?"

"Me. Brigitte."

Dorothy opened the door wide. "Come in. Is anything wrong?"

"I'm fine. Could I speak with Billy?"

"Of course. Sit down. I'll get him." She called down the hallway, and Brigitte heard a door open and close, and Billy walked into the room, hunched over his cane.

"Brigitte!" He glanced at the clock on the fireplace mantel and sobered. "What a surprise. How are you?"

"I'm fine."

"Sit down."

Facing each other at the table, Billy waited.

"Billy," Brigitte began, "could you find out more about Captain Buchanan?"

Billy shrugged. "Depends."

"If I sent food, would he get it?"

Billy slowly straightened. "You want to send food?"

"A cake. Cookies."

Billy rounded his lips and blew air, and his forehead wrinkled. "You sure about this?"

"I'm sure."

A time passed while Billy weighed his words carefully. "I'm a little confused. John's gone, I was nearly gone, and Matthew's still fighting the regulars, and you're helping them." He raised his eyes to hers, testing.

Her head was high, her chin firm. She raised no defense, made no argument. "Will you do it?"

He studied her for a moment and then broke it off. "I'll find out."

Brigitte relaxed for a moment. "Is Kathleen still working in the laundry?"

"Yes."

"Can she find out?"

"I'll ask."

Notes

It will be remembered that Doctor Henry Thorpe, who appears in this volume as the informer who was delivering colonial secrets to General Thomas Gage, was actually Doctor Benjamin Church in history. Doctor Benjamin Church was discovered and went through a lengthy and bitter process of hearings, convictions, and appeals. A letter dated in 1782 states that he was finally "exiled to some Island in the West Indies, and threatened with death in case he [should] ever return" to the colonies. He boarded a small schooner under the command of a Captain Smithwick, sailed away, and was never heard of again. Historian Allen French writes that Doctor Church's father, "in a will dated November 18, 1780, bequeathed five pounds and his library to his son Benjamin, if alive, 'for alas; He is now absent—being cruelly banish'd his Country—and whither living or dead God only knows.' " (See *General Gage's Informers*, pp. 183–201.)

However, for purposes of accommodating the time sequences in this novel, the banishment of the fictional Doctor Henry Thorpe proceeds much more rapidly than that of the historical Doctor Benjamin Church.

CHAPTER XX

★ ★ ★

*T*he destruction of Colonel Francis Smith's elite column of regulars by the Massachusetts citizens' militia on the narrow country roads between Concord and Charlestown stunned the British empire, sent it reeling in disbelief. The dead and wounded filled the British military compound and spilled out into taverns and inns, which were commandeered at bayonet point. Desperate officers ordered squads of armed soldiers into the colonial homes of Boston and Charlestown to seize medicines and bandages and bedding wherever found. The terrible stain on the honor of the mightiest army on earth rode relentlessly on the shoulders of every British officer, every regular in the colonies like a great black suffocating cloud. General Thomas Gage was disoriented for days, unable to accept the obvious. When the horror of full realization set in, he wildly searched for any plan by which he could redeem himself, regain some shred of standing before the king.

Bunker Hill! The colonials have filled the streets of Boston and Charlestown, but they have not taken the high ground on the mainland that commands the entire peninsula. Seize the high ground! Take control! Redemption! Glorious redemption!

June 16, 1775, the British gunboats in the Back Bay moved towards Charlestown, and one anchored in the mouth of the Mystic River, another in the Charles River.

Thoughtful colonial eyes watched and reported. That night, one thousand militiamen silently moved to Breed's Hill and, just north of that, Bunker Hill. With picks and shovels, or their hands, or whatever they had, they dug rifle pits and trenches and built breastworks on Breed's Hill and threw up a fence at the base of Bunker Hill. Then they loaded their muskets and raised their flag.

In the bright morning sun of June 17, 1775, the roar of cannon from the British men-of-war shattered the silence on the Charles River, and for more than two hours, over eighty cannon blasted the colonial positions on the two hills while General Sir William Howe marshalled twenty-five hundred of the best officers and regulars on the continent. Charlestown was devastated, in flames. On his command, with fifes and drums pounding out the cadence, he started his army up the gentle slopes of Breed's Hill, his troops aligned row upon row, their white breeches and red coats and tall hats sparkling in the sun.

At the crest of the hill, General Israel Putnam and Colonel William Prescott, the latter having been designated as the one to command the colonials, stood on the colonial breastworks, watching the steady upward flow of the red-coated army, fully aware that the militia behind them had nearly no powder or shot. To their left, Colonel John Stark and his forces were lined up behind a rail fence extending down to the Mystic River. Among the colonials waiting in the breastworks was General Joseph Warren, who had volunteered to serve simply as another soldier under Prescott's command.

By the time the leading rank of redcoats reached the two-hundred-yard mark, General Putnam was riding up and down the lines of colonials, shouting, "Steady! Do not fire until you see the whites of their eyes! Make every shot count!"

The cannon from the British gunboats quieted, and Colonel Prescott stood on the breastworks, fully exposed, watching every step of the oncoming troops. At one hundred yards he turned his head and shouted, "Cock your muskets," and the clicks of drawn hammers rattled up and down the trenches and rifle pits, and narrow-eyed militiamen settled their muskets over the breastworks and began picking targets where the white straps crossed on the chests of the officers and surging regulars.

At fifty yards Prescott drew breath and shouted, "Fire!" and four hundred muskets blasted in unison and the front two ranks of regulars broke, staggering back against those behind. The return volley from the British ripped into the breastworks with little effect, and moments later the second colonial volley roared and two hundred regulars dropped in the third and fourth ranks. Wild confusion erupted. Half the officers were down. The dead and wounded in the first four ranks were piled like cordwood, and those behind were climbing over the bodies. Suddenly the ranks broke, and then they backed up and turned and ran down the hill like a great red tidal wave.

The colonial militia leaped up and raised triumphant fists and shouted their defiance.

General Howe rallied his army and once again started up the slope. There were no more drums or fifes. At one hundred yards General Howe ordered the first volley, and some militiamen jerked and went down. At fifty yards he ordered the second British volley, and once more some militiamen toppled. Then Colonel Prescott leaped to the top of the breastworks and in full sight of the oncoming British army shook his fist and shouted, "Fire!" and every colonial musket on Breed's Hill blasted. Thirty seconds later the second colonial volley roared, and to the British it seemed the entire front wall of their army collapsed. They turned and clambered over the bodies of their own dead in their second headlong retreat to the bottom of the hill.

"Warren!" someone shouted, and every eye turned.

Joseph Warren was down. Strong, gentle hands lifted him from atop the breastworks, opened his shirt, and felt for heartbeat, and then their eyes dropped.

Colonel William Prescott stood. "Report on ammunition!" he shouted.

There was none left.

"Withdraw! Down the back slope!"

Tom Sievers and ten picked men covered the escape.

The British lost over one-third of their 2,500 troops—one

thousand regulars and officers shot, with over two hundred of those being killed. The colonials lost some 450 men, with about 140 killed, and most of those casualties had been suffered after their ammunition was gone and they were forced to retreat from the two hills. General Gage declared the battle a resounding victory. King George declared it a resounding humiliation—just over one thousand colonials with nearly no ammunition had destroyed over one-third of the Boston fighting command in one day, and when their ammunition failed they had slipped away with less than half the casualties suffered by Gage's command.

General Thomas Gage was instantly relieved of command. General Sir William Howe, who had led the British into the battle, succeeded him.

When the report of the Bunker Hill battle was delivered to General George Washington, he realized he had to have powder and shot, and the only place he could see to get it was from the enemy. To do that, he had to have a navy. He began writing letters of marque, and thus it was that a general in the army created his own navy.

For the second time in two months, Boston and Charlestown were inundated with wounded and dying British regulars. General Howe gave orders to hire anyone the British could for the endless task of changing, washing, and drying the bedding and clothing and bandages necessary for care of the wounded. The colonials who accepted the work were shunned by many of their own as traitors.

For days Kathleen Thorpe had walked the streets of Boston to find honorable work, only to be turned away time and time again by shop owners with hard words and cold eyes when they learned her father was the infamous traitor under trial for treason. She sold much of the family silver to buy food for the children, until Phoebe discovered it and cursed her and slipped into a coma for two days. When Phoebe recovered, she began speaking in unfinished sentences, of things that had never happened.

Two days later Kathleen dressed well, spent time on her hair, and walked rapidly to the British compound, looking neither right nor left. The following day she reported for work at the laundry at midnight, to work until eight o'clock in the morning. Strong soap and scrubbing heavy, wet bedsheets on a scrub board had dried and cracked her hands. She slept when she could during the day, did the necessary housework, tried to console Phoebe, and cared for the children. Her cheeks were becoming hollow and her eyes sunken, and her clothing hung on her dwindling frame. She wept at her image in the mirror but could find no way to rise from the desolation that was destroying their home, their bodies, their lives. The pay from the laundry was poor, but it bought milk and bread for the children.

At seven fifty-five A.M. Major Avery Roy McMullen walked out of the officers' dining quarters and paused to look at the dark, overcast heavens. He wiped sweat from his hatband with a silk handkerchief, then wiped his forehead, and settled the hat back onto his head. The night had been sultry, and since five o'clock the thick gray clouds had been showing lightning flashes inland, but only in the past twenty minutes could the rumble of the distant thunder be heard in Boston.

Stocky, round faced, jowly, meticulous in every detail of his appearance, he glanced at his boots, shined each night by his orderly. He would have to instruct better attention to the sole dressing; it was sloppily done. The grumble of far thunder reached him as he walked with measured stride across the compound toward his quarters, and he muttered, "It's coming—hurricane season down south in the West Indies—storms." He wrinkled his nose, disliking the wind and rain that ruffled and spotted uniforms and sullied boots.

He glanced at movement to his right, past the flagpole, and as he walked he idly watched the eight o'clock laundry crew silently coming on duty and the midnight shift leaving. The laundry demands from the battles had resulted in quickly constructed wooden stands along the south and east walls. Twenty new large brass washtubs were set on the heavy timbered stands, and crews were hired for two shifts—midnight until eight A.M., eight A.M. until four P.M.—heating water, washing, hanging the wet, gathering the dry from the ten lines, thirty yards long, strung next to the stone wall of the compound.

McMullen's lip curled for a moment. *Colonials doing our dirty laundry—how appropriate.* He was turning towards his quarters, when something moving near the laundry building caught his eye and he slowed to look. It was a white scarf tied about the long dark hair of a tall girl who had finished her shift at the washtubs and was leaving the compound. Even at a distance he was struck by the grace of her movements and the clean, clear beauty of her face. He stopped, unaware he was staring at her. She stopped at the gate beside a corporal carrying a musket and showed her work card to a second corporal, who checked her off his work roster, and she quickly disappeared outside the compound walls.

Two minutes later McMullen slowed at the gate, and the corporal with the musket barked, "Attention!" and the corporal with the work roster jumped, surprised, and instantly snapped ramrod straight.

"Yes, sir," said the corporal with the musket. "What would the major want, sir?"

"The tall girl who left a minute ago—dark hair, white scarf— do you have her name?"

The corporal with the roster instantly ran his finger down the column. "Does the major mean the, uh, the . . . pretty one?"

The major sniffed. "That description would be accurate."

"Yes, sir, right here, sir. Thorpe. Kathleen Thorpe, sir."

"Address?"

The roster corporal glanced at the musket corporal for a moment, then back at the major. "Sir, is something wrong?"

"Not yet."

"We got only names, sir. Addresses are kept at the adjutant's office."

McMullen stopped at the adjutant's office before going to his office to resume his duties as officer in charge of base records, an assignment at which he could give full rein to his inherent need for perfection in all about him. Seldom were any of his records less than current or perfect. In matters related to his obsession for perfection in records, no one challenged or questioned his requests or orders. And seldom did anyone assigned to his office find more than revulsion and disgust for his petulant, unending demands and superior, condescending handling of his subordinates.

At ten minutes past ten o'clock a private rapped on his door. "Beggin' your pardon, sir, here's the address you requested."

McMullen waived off the private, opened the envelope, read the brief writing, tossed it on his desk, and called, "Orderly!"

Buck sergeant Aaron Brewster, tall, angular, rawboned, walrus mustache bristling, entered immediately and stood like a statue to stare at the crossed swords on the wall behind McMullen. "You called, sir?"

"In that envelope is a name and address of a colonial woman employed by the laundry detail. Find out what you can about her and make a written report."

"Anything else, sir?"

"Yes. The report is to be strictly confidential. No one is to know. Have it on my desk in two days. That is all."

"Very good, sir." Sergeant Brewster spun and marched from the office, heels clicking on the clean, polished hardwood floor.

By noon the deep purple clouds had sealed out all sunlight and settled, and the air was still, humid. The first wind stirred the trees shortly after one o'clock, and by two o'clock the higher branches were leaning to the north and citizens were clinging to their hats. At two-thirty the first great drops of rain came slanting, and by three o'clock the cobblestone streets of Boston were swamped and everyone not under cover was drenched.

Major McMullen stood in his office staring out the rain-streaked window, hands clasped behind his back, listening to the steady hum of wind and pelting of rain. He turned back to his desk, sat in his leather-covered chair for a moment, rose again, and paced, restless, agitated.

Thorpe. Thorpe. Where have I heard it? It's right there and it won't come back. The storm broke in the night, and by eight o'clock the morning sun was raising steam from the puddles and the mud. Major McMullen left the officers' mess and carefully picked his way to the laundry building, walking casually, appearing uninterested in the drudgery of scrubbing and hanging endless bedsheets and underwear, while his eyes darted, seeking the tall form of Kathleen. He slowed when he saw her, and for a moment his breathing constricted, and he licked his lips. Then he picked up the pace and arrived at the sentry post while she was yet fifty yards distant. The two corporals were intent on checking the midnight crew out and the morning crew in. The one with the musket snapped to attention when he saw McMullen.

"Sir, can I help the major?"

"Yes. May I see that roster? It appears two names may be incorrect."

Startled, the corporal with the roster handed it to McMullen, while the disgruntled civilians murmured and waited. McMullen stared at the page while he waited, covertly watching Kathleen approach. Her form, her movements, her dark eyes, dark hair—he felt his breathing constrict again.

She stopped in the growing crowd of workers, waiting, wondering, and McMullen suddenly raised his head and scanned the throng as though looking for someone. His eyes came to Kathleen's, and for a brief moment they locked, and then McMullen handed the roster back to the corporal.

"Thank you, Corporal. The names you have appear to be correct. Carry on."

Through the morning the image of the dark hair and the dark eyes and the way she moved rose to distract him, and again and again he felt the heady excitement, the grab in his chest. Kathleen Thorpe. Thorpe. At two-thirty he rose from his desk, agitated, searching, forcing his thoughts.

Where have I heard Thorpe? Where? Where? His compulsion for completeness, for control, for having all things resolved and in place, was driving him, would not let go. At four forty-five he suddenly looked up, dropped a file, and slapped the desktop with his open hand.

Of course! The colonials—Thorpe! Banished! Could it be . . . ? He ran to the door and threw it wide and nearly shouted, "Orderly!"

Sergeant Brewster jerked violently, and his pen and inkwell skittered across his desktop as he leaped to his feet. "Yes, sir."

"Didn't the colonials lately banish a man named Thorpe?"

Brewster pursed his mouth for a moment while he thought. "I believe that is so, sir."

"Could that man be related to the girl, the one I asked about?"

"Possible, sir."

"When will you have your report prepared?"

"I get the last information at six o'clock, sir, just before evening mess. I'll work on it tonight, and it will be on your desk tomorrow morning at seven o'clock as ordered, sir."

"See that it is! Tomorrow is Saturday, and this will not wait until Monday."

"Yes, sir. If I might ask, sir, wot's this girl done?"

"That's confidential."

"Yes, sir."

McMullen retreated into his office and closed the door, and Brewster waited until he heard him sit down at his desk.

"Confidential!" Brewster snorted under his breath. "In a pig's eye! Humph."

At two o'clock A.M. a steady breeze set in, and with it came more storm clouds, blotting out the stars from east to west as they moved inland from the Atlantic. Shortly after five A.M. the eastern cloud banks lightened from deep purple to gray; there was no sunrise. The air was suffocating.

At six-thirty A.M. McMullen walked the gravelled paths around the perimeter of the compound, stepping carefully to avoid spotting his impeccable boots with mud remaining from the previous storm, and slowed when he came to the laundry building, eyes darting as he searched, and then he saw her. He hesitated and felt the tightening in his chest as he stared at her. He passed slowly, watching her every move, every expression, his mouth twitching, eyes glowing, and then continued on to the officers' mess. At seven-fifteen he walked into the anteroom of his office, and Brewster rose to attention.

"Your report?"

"On your desk, sir." Brewster's back was ramrod straight, eyes locked on the cracking plaster of the wall behind McMullen.

McMullen marched through his door, slammed it, snatched the sealed envelope from his desktop, ripped it open, and read it twice. Then he tossed it back onto his desktop and barged back into the anteroom.

"When the night shift leaves the laundry in a few minutes, bring that girl here to my office. Do you understand?"

Brewster's eyes popped. "Here, sir? Under what authority? She's civilian."

"*Enemy* civilian, Sergeant. Suspicion of spying."

Brewster blinked. "Spying, sir? In the *laundry?*"

McMullen leaned forward, his mouth became ugly, and he jabbed a stubby finger at Brewster. "Bring her!"

Brewster recoiled. "Yes, sir!"

At ten minutes past eight o'clock Kathleen stopped at the gate and showed her name card to the corporal with the roster and he ran his finger down the page when the crisp command came from behind.

"Ma'am, you are to come with me."

The corporal's head jerked up, and he stared into the face of Sergeant Brewster, standing at full attention, chin up, eyes fierce, mustache bristling.

Kathleen turned and flinched in surprise. "Me? You want me to come with you?"

"Immediately."

"I . . . Who are you? What is this about?"

"Sergeant Aaron Brewster, orderly for Major Avery R. McMullen."

"I've never heard of him," Kathleen stammered. "For what reason?"

"He will explain that, ma'am. Come along, or I will order the corporal to assist." Brewster gestured to the corporal with the musket and bayonet.

Kathleen backed up one step. She was damp from perspiration. Her hands were wrinkled, drying, and small specks of blood were beginning to show at the cracks in her palms. Her legs ached, her back was alive with pain, and she felt light-headed. She was drained, empty, and she could endure no more, had nothing else to give. Her face flushed and her eyes flashed. "I don't know what this is about, and I'm not going with you until I do. I'm going home."

Brewster gestured to the corporal, who moved before Kathleen did and stopped three feet in front of her, musket held at the ready.

"Very well," Brewster said. "If you insist on knowing, Major McMullen wishes to question you about spying."

Both corporals were incredulous, and Kathleen's head thrust forward in utter surprise. "Spying? Me? How? When? Spying on whom?"

"Will you come peacefully or under armed guard?"

Kathleen stared at the corporal standing before her for long moments while her mind recovered from the numbness, and then she looked back at Brewster and her shoulders slumped. "Peacefully."

Five minutes later Brewster rapped on the office door marked "Major McMullen."

McMullen settled onto his great leather chair, tossed Brewster's report onto the center of his desk, assumed a casual expression, and said, "Enter."

The door opened and Brewster announced, "Miss Kathleen Thorpe, as you requested, sir."

McMullen leaned back. "Show her in."

Brewster stepped aside, and Kathleen cautiously walked three paces into the room to stand six feet from the front of McMullen's massive polished oak desk.

McMullen did not rise. He casually gestured to Brewster. "That will be all, Sergeant," and Brewster closed the door as he left.

Kathleen stood stock-still, studying McMullen, waiting for him to speak. She saw the immaculate hands, the snowy starched shirtfront, and the lace at his throat. His forehead was high, nose broad, mouth pinched. She looked into his eyes and they were inscrutable, and she felt a shudder.

"Please be seated," McMullen said softly, and Kathleen sat on a straight-backed upholstered chair facing his desk, and she noticed the sky-blue silk covering as she waited. He leaned forward to study the top sheet of the report.

Silence held for thirty seconds before McMullen raised his eyes. "Miss Kathleen Thorpe, I presume," he said. His smile was mechanical, a mask.

"Yes."

"I trust the sergeant did not mistreat you."

"Why am I here?" Her manner was direct, blunt.

He sighed and tapped the paperwork with his index finger, and his eyes narrowed. "It appears you have been engaged in some questionable activities on this base."

"Working at the laundry is questionable?"

McMullen smiled condescendingly and shook his head. "It isn't."

"Then what have I done?"

"It seems you have been secretly inquiring about the officers on the base." He leaned back, smiling slightly as he toyed with her.

"I have no idea what you're talking about."

"You don't?" Again he waited.

"No. I do not."

"Is it true you inquired about Captain Richard Buchanan?"

Kathleen's face clouded for a split second as she remembered. "That? Yes, I did. For a friend."

"A friend?" He attempted a smile. "Convenient. What did your friend want to know?"

"If he's alive or dead."

"For what reason?"

"I don't know."

"Who is your friend?"

"Just a friend."

"Male or female?"

Kathleen's eyes narrowed in anger and disgust. "Just a friend."

McMullen smiled broadly, and rose and walked to the window to stare outside at the confusion of people in the compound. He clasped his hands behind his back and slowly walked back to his chair. "It will be so much better if you would simply tell me. We'll find out anyway, you know."

Kathleen remained silent.

McMullen shrugged and his eyebrows peaked as if in pain. "I dislike the thoughts of arresting you. What would become of your family?"

Kathleen started. "What about my family?"

"Your father gone, your family dependent on you. Most unfortunate."

She tensed. "How do you know these things?"

He looked surprised. "It's my business to know."

"What do you want?" she demanded.

"Just a simple explanation of your interest in the officers on this base."

"I told you. A friend wanted to know if Captain Buchanan had died. That's all."

"Who was the friend, and why was that information wanted?"

"I don't know."

"You refuse to explain?"

"I know nothing more than what I've told you."

He settled back into his chair and sat in silence for long moments, reading from Brewster's report, letting Kathleen wait. Finally he raised his eyes to hers.

"I find myself in a hurtful position," he said quietly. "I have no desire to harm you, but I have my duty and I cannot ignore it. I need answers and I must get them, agreeably if possible, disagreeably if necessary. I regret that, but there's little I can do about it. Do you understand?"

Kathleen suddenly stood. "I'm going home. I've worked all night and I'm tired, and I have people to take care of."

He raised a hand. "Please sit down. I've been thinking. Perhaps there's a way to handle this."

Kathleen slowly settled back onto the front edge of the chair, waiting.

"I see no urgent need to conclude this investigation immediately," he said. "Perhaps I could be persuaded to take some time. Do it thoroughly."

Kathleen remained silent.

"May I make a suggestion? Go home and think it over until you report back for work Monday night. When you finish your shift Tuesday morning, Sergeant Brewster will escort you back here. Maybe that will give you enough time to think of a way you can persuade me to take more time with this investigation." He paused until she looked him in the eyes. "And, it is possible I could find much more appropriate work for you on this base than scrubbing soiled laundry, if you could persuade me. Much more appropriate."

For the first time his eyes were unveiled, frank, filled with lust.

For a split second Kathleen did not understand, and then the full implication exploded in her brain and she bolted to her feet. In two strides she was at his desk front and her clenched fist slammed down.

"You filthy animal!" Her words echoed off the walls and her eyes were like glowing coals. "You're insane!" She turned and strode to the door, threw it open, marched past a gaping Sergeant Brewster, jerked open the anteroom door, and crossed the compound without looking back.

McMullen waited until she was gone before he sauntered out

to Brewster in the anteroom, smiling. "She'll do a little thinking over the weekend, and Tuesday morning she'll be more agreeable. Bring her back then."

Kathleen worked her way through backstreets, marching ram-rod straight, mouth set, eyes blazing with outrage. She was three blocks from home before the first stir of hot breeze moved leaves in the trees, and she was rounding the corner of the last block before her chin began to tremble. She hurried through the gate and stopped at the front door, where she drew and released a great breath, closed her eyes for a moment to compose herself, and walked in.

"Kathleen, is that you?" came the muffled call from Phoebe's bedroom.

"Coming," Kathleen answered and walked to her room. Phoebe was still in bed in her nightgown, the children sitting on top of the great goose-down comforter.

Phoebe exhaled. "Where have you been? We've been worried sick!"

"The British were looking for spies at the base. It took a little time. I'll change and get breakfast."

At ten-thirty, Billy Weems opened the front door of his home and cast a squinted eye at the heavy purple overcast. The rising wind moaned in the trees, and he waited for a moment to see if raindrops had begun.

Dorothy called, "Where are you going?"

"To see Kathleen."

"About what?"

"For Brigitte."

"About that British officer?"

"Yes."

Dorothy shook her head. "Only trouble can come from that. Take your rain cape."

The wind was rising, and before Billy opened the gate to the Thorpe home, he was holding his hat jammed onto his head. Kathleen met him at the door.

"Billy, come in."

"Getting fierce out there," he said, smiling. He could hear the children quietly playing in the hallway. "How is Phoebe?"

"Asleep."

"How are you?" Only then did he notice the dead look in her eyes. "What's wrong? Something's wrong." He saw the slight tremor in her chin, and she swallowed.

"Sit down."

Facing him in a chair, Kathleen worked a handkerchief with her hands, folding and refolding it, eyes downcast, as she spoke. Neither of them was aware when the door into Phoebe's bedroom silently opened and she walked softly down the hall in her woolen slippers, toward the sound of the voices, and stopped two feet short of the archway, mesmerized by the story her daughter was quietly relating to Billy.

Kathleen's first silent tears came, and she wiped them with the handkerchief and continued. Billy listened without moving until he learned the reason McMullen had ordered Kathleen into his office, and he reared back in his chair, holding his anger until she finished.

"Tell this to the reverend!" he blurted. "He'll know what to do."

Kathleen shook her head. "No one will care. My name is Thorpe. It was my father who was banished."

"People *will* care!" Billy exclaimed. "You can't ignore it. We've got to do something!"

Kathleen drew a resolute breath and brought her eyes to Billy's. "I can do nothing. I must have that work at the laundry. Without the money, the children will not eat."

He saw the fear and the defeat and the desolation in her eyes, and it reached to touch him like something alive, and it struck pain into his heart.

Neither of them heard the silent movement as Phoebe retraced her steps to the library, where Henry's large desk and array of medical books had been untouched for three months. She sat in

Henry's large overstuffed chair and drew a piece of his professional stationery before her, reached for quill and inkwell, and began.

Saturday July 29th, A.D. 1775
The Monarch, the King of England

Your Royal Highness King George:

Begging your forgiveness for this unwarranted intrusion upon your Honorable Self, I humbly beseech you to consider my serious and most likely fatal plight.

My husband of twenty-four years, Doctor Henry Thorpe, lately of Boston in the colony of Massachusetts, in the face of much danger which I shall explain shortly, and with no thought for personal gain, repeatedly affirmed his absolute loyalty to King and Flag by risking his all in the cause of maintaining the right and the authority of the Crown over the colonies of New England. Finding himself in the Massachusetts legislature, and a leader on the Committee of Safety, he repeatedly delivered sensitive and vital information to General Thomas Gage, Governor of Massachusetts appointed by authority of Your Self, thus affording the good General opportunity to avoid many catastrophes.

Because of my husband's unswerving loyalty to the Crown, he was lately banished by Massachusetts courts, for life. As a consequence, I and my three children are now destitute, in want of the most fundamental of human needs. We are without funds for the necessities of sustaining life. The children weep daily for food. I am unable to write of the unbearable pain and daily conditions we now face.

I most humbly beseech Your Most Gracious Majesty to consider my condition, which can be confirmed by the slightest investigation of your loyal forces in Boston, and to find in your generous heart to allow myself and my children a small stipend sufficient to our basic needs, to relieve us of the unbearable conditions now existing in our lives. All through consideration by your Kind and Merciful Self for the unselfish service rendered to your cause by my husband, Doctor Henry Thorpe.

Signed,
Phoebe Thorpe

She blew on the letter until the ink had dried, folded it, sealed it inside an envelope, addressed it, then slipped it into the center desk drawer, locked it, and returned to her bedroom with the key.

In the parlor, Billy rose from his chair, leaning on his cane, eyes alive with anger. "What will you do Tuesday morning when that sergeant comes for you?"

Kathleen shook her head. "I don't know. Maybe demand someone come with me as a witness."

"Who? A British soldier?"

Kathleen shrugged her hopelessness. "That may be better than no one at all. All I know is, I must keep the work."

Billy's voice shook with rage. "If that officer touches you . . ."

Kathleen's shoulders trembled for a moment with silent sobbing before she regained control. The sounds of the children in the hallway stopped, and they appeared in the archway to stand wide-eyed, silently inquiring.

Kathleen quickly wiped red eyes and forced a smile. "I'll be there in a minute. Go on back." They disappeared.

Billy started for the door. "I should go, but I'll be back. I have to think on this."

"Why did you come?"

Billy looked at her for a moment, puzzled, before he understood the question. "Oh. Nothing. Brigitte had a question."

"What?"

"Nothing. Is there a way she could get food in to that officer, Buchanan?"

Kathleen shook her head. "I don't know. Is it important?"

"Forget it."

Billy reached for the door handle. "I'll be back. Kathleen,

please, please let us help. Money. Food. Take you to church. Anything."

She shook her head firmly. "You're not going to ruin everything for yourselves by helping the Thorpes. We are unclean. Traitors. Lepers. Banished."

He saw the bitter pain and the humiliation in her, and he could not stand it. "We don't care!" he exclaimed.

"I do!" she said.

He dropped his eyes for a moment and regained control. "I'll be back. Try not to worry."

At three o'clock P.M. Tom Sievers rapped on the back door of the Dunson home and Margaret opened it, holding it against the thrust of the howling wind. Tom entered, Caleb right behind, a rasp and screwdriver and hammer in his hand.

"Storm's coming," Tom said, "before nightfall."

"Rain with it?"

"A howler. Rain, lightning, likely. The axle on the well's fixed."

Caleb dipped water from the water bucket and drank. "'Bout blew us away." He walked back to his room.

"Laundry's on the table," Margaret said to Tom. "Thank you for letting Caleb help. He needs more of that."

They both heard the faint rapping and stopped to listen in the sound of the wind at the doors and windows and the whistling in the chimney, and Margaret walked briskly to the door.

"Come in, Billy, before you get blown away. What brings you?"

"Is Brigitte here?"

"Asleep. Got home from the bakery half an hour ago. Why?"

"She had a question." Billy stopped and his eyes dropped from Margaret's, and she saw the turmoil in him.

"What's wrong, Billy?"

Tom picked up the stack of folded laundry. "I ought to take my leave, ma'am." He started for the door as Billy spoke.

"It's Kathleen. Something happened at the British base this morning." His eyes dropped and he would not look directly at Margaret. "I hardly know how to talk about it."

Tom stopped with his hand on the door handle.

Margaret slowly sat down at the table. "You better tell."

Billy began, hesitantly at first and then rapidly as his anger rose. Margaret sat still, listening intently. She clapped her hand over her mouth in shock as Billy finished, unable to form a sentence.

Suddenly Tom was beside Billy. "What was the man's name?"

Billy looked up. "McMullen, I think."

"What rank?"

"She called him Major."

"What building was his office in?"

"She said the records building, whatever that is."

"Did she say what he looked like?"

"Only that he was a little shorter than she. His uniform was immaculate."

Tom dropped his laundry back on the table and spun and started for the door.

Margaret bolted from her chair. "Tom, what are you thinking? Tom, you come back here!"

Tom did not stop. He slammed the door as he darted out into the howling wind.

At four-thirty the torrential rain came rolling in from the Atlantic like a wall. Great bolts of lightning raced through the clouds, and thunder shook the ground. By five o'clock the streets of Boston were vacant and locked into an eerie darkness. Leaves and small branches were ripped from trees and whipped through the town, to be plastered against homes, buildings. By five-fifteen, half a dozen great branches had been shattered and were down in the streets, rolling crazily, knocking down fences until they smashed into a home or a building and stopped.

At the British base, the great copper laundry tubs had long since been blown from the wooden stands to roll clanging, tumbling across the compound, against the officers' quarters and west wall. The sentries had moved inside the gates and locked them, and stood with their backs against the wall, hunched over, heads down, holding their hats and muskets. The flag had been retired when the rain broke; the parade ground was utterly deserted. Lights showed in the windows of all barracks, and some of the officers' quarters; some officers were still in their duty offices, waiting for a break in the storm so they could go to their quarters.

At five forty-five, in the gathering gloom of the howling storm, no one saw the thin form of a man slip over the center of the east wall, nor did anyone see him sprint to the front of the office buildings and check them one at a time until he came to one with the sign "RECORDS" printed above the door. Inside the building one light remained burning. The man disappeared into the low bushes along the front wall of the building. At six-twenty the light extinguished, a moment later the door opened, and a rather short man stepped out into the maelstrom. His immaculate uniform was instantly drenched. He hunched his shoulders against the wind and slowly, carefully made his way to the building marked "OFFICERS' QUARTERS." Three minutes later a light flickered on in the corner window of the second floor.

At ten-thirty the last light in the officers' quarters extinguished. At eleven o'clock Tom Sievers forced the front door, unheard in the shrieking wind, and closed it quickly. Two minutes later he struck flint to steel and nursed the spark to a flame and read the name on the door of the corner room on the second floor: "MAJOR AVERY ROY MCMULLEN."

He waited until he saw lightning flash in the window at the end of the hall, and the instant the thunder boomed he kicked the door open. A moment later he was inside the room, the door closed behind him, and he stood still, waiting for the next lightning flash to take his bearings in the dark.

A high-pitched, terrified voice came from his right. "Who's there? Is someone there?"

Tom neither moved nor spoke. He heard the squeak of the lever lifting the chimney on a lamp and he drew his knife and crouched, ready, and at that moment lightning raced through the heavens over Boston and for three seconds the entire peninsula was lighter than midday.

In those three seconds, Tom saw McMullen, sitting bolt upright in his bed, hand working with a lamp on his bed stand.

McMullen saw a figure standing in the center of his room, dripping wet, clothes plastered to his thin frame, hair wild, beard scraggly, eyes dark hollows in his head. The knees were flexed, right arm extended, and in the right hand McMullen saw the unmistakable glint of light on the steel of a drawn knife blade.

An instant before the thunder clap shook the building, Tom heard the gasp, and the strangled attempt to cry for help was lost in the cracking thunder, and then Tom was at the man's bedside with his left hand locked onto the man's throat. He jammed the head back onto the pillow and dropped to one knee and brought his face down close.

"Do you remember Kathleen Thorpe?" Tom's voice was thick with rage.

There was no answer, and Tom smacked the cold flat of his knife blade against the man's cheek.

"Do you?"

"Yes, yes," came the choked, terrified answer.

"Never talk to her again. Never look at her again. Never say her name to anyone again. She is coming back to her work Monday and you will do nothing. Do you understand?"

Tom relaxed his stranglehold on the man's throat enough for the answer.

"Who are you?"

"I'm the man that'll cut your heart out if you don't leave her alone."

Lightning flashed and the room lighted and McMullen saw Tom's face crouched over his own, and for an instant he saw Tom's eyes.

"Yes!" he blurted. "Yes, I understand."

Thunder rolled as Tom backed away, and when the next lightning flashed, McMullen stared at an empty room. For a time he sat in his bed without moving, struggling to decide whether the awful minutes had been real or dreamed, and then with trembling fingers he lighted the lamp on his bed table. The center of the carpet was soaked wet in the middle of the room and at his bedside, and the doorjamb was splintered around the lock. McMullen loaded his pistol and wrapped himself in a blanket and sat in a chair in the corner throughout the night.

The storm moved inland and the lightning and thunder dwindled and died, and the Sabbath sunrise became a spectacular light and shadow display of golden shafts through purple clouds.

Phoebe insisted the family attend church at the North Chapel where they were less known, and Kathleen was busy with the children when Phoebe stopped at the door to offer her congratulations to the reverend for his sermon. She passed him an envelope and some currency, which he took, and nodded.

When Billy and Dorothy Weems returned from church, Tom was waiting at their gate.

"Tell Kathleen to not worry. McMullen won't bother her again."

Notes

The battle commonly known as the Battle of Bunker Hill actually included Bunker Hill and Breed's Hill. The battle was fought on June 17, 1775. British gunboats in the mouths of both the Charles River and the Mystic River bombarded the American entrenchments on the hills, and when American snipers were observed in Charlestown, the British cannonade continued until Charlestown was in flames and virtually destroyed. General Sir William Howe, under orders of General Gage, directed the British troops. General Israel Putnam and Colonels William Prescott and John Stark were prominent in the leadership of the colonial forces. Colonel Stark later played a critically important and heroic role in the battle of Trenton and subsequent battles, as will be shown in volumes yet to come in this series. General Joseph Warren, heroic patriot and renowned leader in Boston and Massachusetts, was killed while defending the breastworks with other colonials at the top of Bunker Hill. (See Leckie, *George Washington's War*, pp. 144–63.)

Reference is made in this chapter to the petition drawn by Phoebe Thorpe (actually the wife of Doctor Benjamin Church in history) and sent to King George of England, wherein she requested support for herself and her children as compensation for the services of her husband to the British Crown. The petition was granted, in the sum of one hundred and fifty pounds, a generous sum at that time. There is some evidence the pension was later reduced to one hundred pounds, presumably per year. While the substance of these events is true, the novel's necessarily limited scope prohibits a full accounting of the entire episode. For purposes of our story, the incidents are depicted within a much-reduced time frame. (See French, *General Gage's Informers*, p. 158.)

January 1776

CHAPTER XXI

★ ★ ★

*T*he four seamen on the four o'clock A.M. watch hunched their backs against the howling east wind that whistled through the ice-laden rigging of the *Esther* and plastered the backs of their heavy oilskins with stinging sleet and clogged their beards and brows with ice. The small schooner pitched and wallowed in the white-capped forty-foot waves, and her timbers groaned with the relentless wrenching of the wild January Atlantic storm, twelve miles off the northern coast of Massachusetts.

They had long since strung safety ropes inside the ship's railing, and the helmsman had tied himself to the ship's wheel, while the watchmen lashed one-inch ropes around their midsections and looped the other end around the nearest mast, with enough slack to allow them to reach the rail and no more. Standing at the rail, the watch hunched forward, eyes straining to pierce the black envelope of night that hid the peaks and valleys of the mountainous whitecaps.

On eleven prior missions the *Esther* had brought back British prizes taken on the high seas. On this, their twelfth search, they had sailed into the teeth of a killer Atlantic storm, with winds freezing salt spray and turning sails into frozen slabs. Captain Weyland cursed and ordered her about to run with the wind back to a safe harbor until the storm passed. He and first mate Riggins and Matthew clustered about the helmsman, as they had through the night, nerves tight as they held the ship on the east-northeast course Matthew had calculated when the storm broke and the heavens sealed. They were running for Newburyport, sailing cautiously and blindly, on Matthew's reckoning and instincts, with but one sail unfurled on the mainmast.

The entrance into the harbor was bordered on the south by the tip of Plum Island and on the north by two shoals, the first one two miles from the rocky coastline, the other less than one mile. The tip of Plum Island was above the water surface, but the shallow shoals were not. Belled buoys were anchored on both of them to warn away the unwary. No one knew how many tall ships had gone to watery graves with their hulls ripped open by the hidden granite rocks of the Newburyport shoals.

Twenty minutes before the gray of dawn the seaman on starboard bow watch tensed and his eyes narrowed in the gray-black gloom. He leaned forward, mittened hands clutching the ice-covered rail. Visibility was less than twenty yards, but he thought farther out he had caught a glimpse of a great, ghostly shape in the slanting sleet, closing with the *Esther.* A moment later he jerked straight and turned and worked his way back to the group of officers and thrust his head close to Weyland's ear to shout in the shrieking wind, while Riggins and Matthew crowded close.

"Sir, a ship close, starboard, likely a man-of-war." The man pointed.

Weyland recoiled. "Sure?" he bellowed.

"Sure."

"Her heading?"

"Same as us, sir—east-nor'east."

Weyland's eyes narrowed in hurried thought. "Back to your post and keep me informed." He turned to Riggins. "Get every hand on deck and unfurl the mainsail on the mizzenmast. Get the starboard cannon loaded."

Riggins gaped. "Sir, load and shoot in this weather?"

"Load! I can't come back to give the order to fire, so when we pass her, fire as our guns come to bear amidships and try to hull her below the waterline!"

Riggins started for the gangway as Weyland turned to Matthew. "Know where we are?"

"Close. About eleven miles east of Newburyport, if my guess on wind and currents is good."

"Locate those shoals and keep me informed."

"Yes, sir!"

Weyland worked his way to the starboard bow while the crew set the mizzenmast mainsail, and the *Esther* responded. The cannon crews threw sail canvas over the cannon and huddled under it to ram the powder measure home, then the cannonball, and prime the touchhole. They shoved loose cotton in the muzzles to stop the sleet, and rolled the guns forward and blocked them in firing position, with one man still under the canvas with the match.

Clinging to the rail with one hand and a safety rope with the other, Weyland and the seaman on watch rode the pitching bow as it rose high, then plunged until the bowsprit was awash and the freezing seas slammed into their knees, and the bow was again thrust upward, forty feet above the whipping waves. Minutes passed while the black of night softened to purple, then to deep gray, and visibility in the wind and sleet extended to fifty yards, then eighty, and suddenly Weyland's arm shot up, pointing.

"There!" He worked his way back to the helmsman, Riggins and Matthew following. "One of His Majesty's men-of-war, I think, one hundred yards, nearly dead ahead," he shouted in the wind. "I don't think she's seen us. We're going to fire as we pass her. If we can get her to chase us there's a chance we can get help and take her when the storm blows out."

He waited until he saw the helmsman understood. "When we come up on her I'll be up at the bow and won't have time to come back here and give orders. Pass along her port side, at twenty yards."

The helmsman started. "Twenty?"

"Twenty."

Weyland looked at Riggins. "Get ready to spread more canvas if we have to."

"Sir," Riggins stammered, "the masts might not take more canvas in this wind."

Weyland shrugged. "No choice. Get ready."

Matthew followed Weyland back to the starboard bow as the *Esther* bore down on the high stern of the big gunboat, both men gripping safety ropes to keep from being swept overboard. Suddenly Matthew pointed upward.

"She's a man-o'-war, three masts! The *Chelsea!*"

The flag atop the mainmast was the Union Jack, whipped to shreds in the wind, and on the port side were three rows of cannon, eleven per row. High on the stern was the carved name *Chelsea*. The *Esther* was a scant thirty yards behind and closing fast. The helmsman corrected and the bow of the *Esther* swung to port, then straightened, and was just over twenty yards from the *Chelsea* as she passed the stern.

"They've seen us," Matthew shouted, "but they're too late." Weyland bobbed his head as they both stared upward at the high deck of the big gunboat, where seamen scrambled desperately to put on more canvas and to load their cannon.

Ten seconds later Weyland and Matthew turned to watch Riggins, feet spread, braced, hunched over the nearest cannon. He was studying the peaks and valleys of the waves rolling in and the rise and fall of the two ships, side by side. A great swell rolled under the *Esther* and she rose, and she settled while the swell thrust the *Chelsea* upward. Riggins waited, watching, and as the next swell rolled under the *Esther*, he raised his arm, and a moment later he dropped it and shouted with all his strength, *"Fire!"*

All nine cannon bucked and roared as the *Esther* settled and the swell drove the *Chelsea* upward. The cotton muzzle plugs blew out into the sleet in flames, and all nine cannonballs punched gaping holes just below the waterline of the big gunboat. The cheer of every man on the decks of the *Esther* rose above the storm.

The small schooner cleared the bow of the man-of-war, Weyland signaled to Matthew, and they moved back to the helmsman. "Hold the course Mr. Dunson sets and hope she follows us."

The helmsman nodded, and Matthew moved quickly to his quarters, worked hastily with his divider and charts, then returned to the helmsman and pointed at the compass. "Correct to due nor'east."

The *Chelsea* was two hundred yards directly behind, and falling back. Weyland called to Riggins. "Spill the mizzen sail. Let her close a little."

The *Esther* slowed and the *Chelsea* crept forward. At one hundred yards the two bow guns on the gunboat fired, but no one knew where the shots struck in the churning waters. Three minutes later they fired again, and again the shots went wild into the stormy sea.

Standing at the stern rail, Weyland and Matthew recoiled in surprise as the *Chelsea* put on more sail. "She's too big, heavy," Weyland exclaimed. "They're risking their masts with more sail." Slowly the *Chelsea* gained speed, plowing ponderously through the heavy seas, and Weyland let her close slowly. He wiped ice from his brows and beard, and it was then that Matthew saw the rising concern in Weyland's face.

"Something's wrong," Weyland said. "They're risking a broken mainmast to catch us." He shook his head. "We're not worth it. I don't like it. Something's wrong." Matthew remained silent while Weyland studied the pursuing gunboat, and then Weyland turned to him. "How far from the shoals now?"

"I calculate six miles, a little over."

"Check your charts. Don't let us run aground."

"Yes, sir." Matthew worked his way to his quarters and for long minutes pored over his charts, wishing with all his soul the gray heavens would open long enough to get a sextant shot of the sun. At least that would fix the latitude, with some indication of how closely he had guessed current, tide, and drift.

On deck, Weyland allowed the high bow of the pursuing warship to come within thirty yards of the stern of the *Esther*, and held the interval, waiting, watching intently. At thirty yards the bow guns could hardly miss, yet the cannoneers stood in plain sight at the rail and the guns remained silent. Weyland ordered the mizzen sail tightened and spread the distance to one hundred yards, and stood shaking his head as the *Chelsea* continued to follow. "Something's wrong," he repeated to himself.

In his quarters, Matthew leaned over his charts, and suddenly paused. He jammed an index finger down on the entrance to Newburyport Harbor, then shifted it to the shoals. He thumped his fist on the chart table. Quickly he slipped cold hands back into his soaked mittens and emerged back on deck, gasping at the instant bite of the freezing wind. As he passed Weyland's quarters he glanced at the thermometer screwed to the door frame. Nine degrees above zero, Fahrenheit. Twenty-three degrees below freezing.

He grasped a safety rope and worked his way to Weyland. "Captain, can you come to my quarters for a minute?"

Inside his cramped cabin, Matthew shoved two more chunks of coal into the tiny stove and turned back to his charts. He wiped at his dripping nose as Weyland tugged off his soaked mittens.

Matthew tapped the large chart spread on his table. "Here's Newburyport." He moved his finger. "Here's the shoals."

Weyland waited.

"I think I know why the *Chelsea* is risking her mast to follow us."

Weyland raised his eyes in silent question.

"She's British, not familiar with these waters. She has charts that show the shoals, but can't find them in this storm. I think she wants us to lead her past them, into the harbor."

For long seconds Weyland studied the chart, then raised his eyes to Matthew and spoke quietly. "They intend dropping anchor in the harbor mouth and bottling it up and sinking everything afloat. Maybe even bombard the town."

Matthew bobbed his head emphatically. "That's what I think, sir."

Weyland slapped his hand flat on the table. "They can't find the shoals, so they'll follow us because we can!"

Matthew waited for a moment while Weyland settled.

"Sir, I think there's a way to handle this."

Weyland stopped, waiting.

Matthew once again placed his finger on the chart. "Don't come straight into the harbor. Come down from the north." He moved his finger slowly. "Distance the *Chelsea* about three hundred yards, and when we clear the shoals, make a hard turn to starboard, due west, and run for the harbor mouth." His finger retraced. "The *Chelsea* will be three hundred yards behind when we make our hard turn." He looked Weyland in the eyes. "What will she do when she sees us make that turn?"

Weyland pursed his mouth for a moment. "Take the shortest distance to us by cutting across."

"Exactly."

Weyland's brows rose. "And hit the shoals!"

"That's how I see it, sir."

"Will the shoals or the buoys be visible?"

"They'll be hard to see if this storm holds." Matthew pointed to a thick large book with "ATLANTIC TIDES AND CURRENTS" in block letters on the cover. "Right now the coastal tides are moving out. For the next two or three hours the shoals should be within three feet of the surface, but in this storm they'll be hard to see unless you know where they are or happen to see a buoy. The *Chelsea's* big and loaded heavy, with nine holes in her hull, and she's bound to have some water in her hold even with her pumps going. So right now I expect she must draw somewhere between twelve and fifteen feet."

Matthew waited and watched Weyland's mind work.

"Can you find those shoals?" Weyland asked.

"I think so, sir."

"How, with no sun, no landmarks, no coastline?"

Matthew blew air and pointed to the "TIDES AND CURRENTS" book. "Simple. We knew where we were when the storm hit thirty-six hours ago. We've got variable winds at our stern, gusting to seventy-two miles per hour, pushing us east, while the tides are pushing us west. We're in the Gulf Stream, which is moving us north at a variable rate up to two miles an hour. And we know our hold is empty, so we're high in the water and moving faster than usual. Put all that together and you can easily come out with an answer that puts us somewhere between two and twenty miles off the northern Massachusetts coast."

He paused, and Weyland snorted a laugh.

"From there you check with your viscera and your instincts, and you pray." He exhaled sharply and spoke decisively. "Sir, I've navigated these waters before. I think I can find those shoals."

For a moment their eyes locked and Matthew didn't flinch. A wry smile flickered on Weyland's face as he reached for the door handle. "Give the helmsman a heading, and get up on the bow."

For more than an hour they held a course while Matthew gripped the safety rope and the railing and rode the wildly plunging bow, swamped one moment, fifty feet high the next, staring intently eastward with his telescope, wiping ice from the lens, hoping in vain for a break in the storm that would show the bleak, rocky coastline in the distance. At the stern, the big gunboat doggedly followed while Weyland gave commands that kept her in sight.

"That's far enough," Matthew muttered to himself, and moved back to the helmsman. "Hard to port, due south."

The helmsman looked at him in question, and Matthew repeated it. The man spun the big wheel, and the bow of the *Esther* swung until the point on the compass needle split the large *S*. At the stern, Weyland turned to look and saw Matthew by the helmsman, and then turned back to watch the *Chelsea*, one hundred yards behind. Slowly the great gunship made her turn, once again following the *Esther*. Matthew returned to the bow, searching with his glass for yellow buoys that would be nearly invisible in the storm and for the telltale roiling of water that was the mark of rocks near the surface.

Minutes stretched to half an hour in which Matthew swept the pitching waters with his glass, searching, probing, and he finally muttered, "Too far—we've missed them. Where's the coast? If we could only see the—" He jerked erect and lunged against the safety rope while he searched again for a flash of yellow, and for a moment it was there, dancing in the ice and spray of the surging waves. His arm shot up, pointing as he shouted to himself. "There! Starboard! A buoy! There they are! Two hundred yards. The whole coast out there, and we found them." He spun, exuberant, and scrambled back to the helmsman. "Swing about ten degrees east of south and hold it steady. I'll tell you when to swing her starboard, due west. We found them," he exulted, "we found them."

The bow of the *Esther* swung hard to port and slammed into the incoming waves, and Weyland turned in question. Matthew waved his arms and pointed, and Weyland settled back against the stern rail to watch the course of the *Chelsea*. With less than one-fourth of her canvas unfurled she was slow, sluggish as she moved into her turn to follow the schooner, with the east wind battering her port side.

Weyland released held breath. *Keep coming—we'll show you where the port is—keep coming.* His eyes never left the bow of the big man-of-war as she plowed on, while the lighter schooner began to distance her. Five minutes later Weyland had to squint to see the great bow, three hundred yards behind, in the driving sleet and ice.

"Bring her to port, due west, and steady as she goes," Matthew shouted, and the helmsman spun the wheel, and the *Esther* swung due west and leaped before the wind. Matthew worked up the safety rope to the stern to stand beside Weyland, hardly breathing as he watched the man-of-war and both men stood like statues waiting for the *Chelsea* to make her move. Slowly she continued on her course due south for one hundred yards, then one hundred fifty yards, and Matthew said, "Turn—turn—you've got to turn—turn," and then the great, blunt bow dug into the seas and swung southwestward, and within seconds the sails on the mainmast and the foremast of the gunboat caught the wind slanting in from behind and she gained speed.

Matthew rounded his lips and blew relieved air, and Weyland wiped an icy mitten across his mouth as they watched the great ship increase speed in her sweeping turn.

Weyland said, "Will they see the buoys?"

"Probably, but in these seas maybe not until it's too late."

Far into the turn the bow of the gunboat straightened and then started to turn back to port, and Matthew shouted, "They saw the buoys but they're too late—she's going to hit!" Thirty seconds later Weyland gasped and Matthew flinched as the bow of the *Chelsea* jolted and raised out of the churning water and rammed forward another thirty feet, and the great ship lurched to a violent stop and settled, her keel broken, the front half angled slightly upward. Instantly both the mainmast and the foremast strained forward and then shattered, and the top fifty feet of each, with both sails and all the rigging, came smashing down on the deck. The mainmast toppled crazily into the sea, her sail and the ropes to her yards still tied to the ship.

For any man of the sea, the killing of a ship—no matter friend or enemy—is never a thing of joy. Everyone on the deck of the *Esther* spent a silent moment, feeling a sense of loss in their hearts as they stared at the *Chelsea*, mortally wounded with her spine broken and two of her three masts and her rigging in a splintered shambles on her decks and in the sea.

Weyland spun and barked orders to the helmsman. "Hard to port." He shouted at Riggins, "Spill all wind and furl all sails and drop anchor." With no sail, and the anchor at fourteen fathoms, the storm swung the *Esther* about until she was facing due east, bow into the wind, riding the storm but not moving. Every seaman was on her decks, grasping the safety ropes while they watched in awed silence, waiting to see if the *Chelsea* would try to launch her lifeboats, knowing there was little chance any of the longboats would survive the wild seas or the shoals. Minutes passed while the great waves battered the ship, settling her deeper onto the rocks, but no boats were launched. Half an hour passed with the *Esther* anchored, taking the storm head-on, watching, and the

Chelsea taking the battering broadside. The half hour became an hour before Captain Weyland finally turned to Riggins. "What's the time?"

Riggins pulled off a mitten and plucked his watch from inside his oilskins. "Eleven-twenty, sir."

"We ride out the storm anchored where we are. Get the assignments made to the crew."

All the seamen aboard the *Esther* took their orders and went to their duty posts or bunks with a quiet feeling of pride in the knowledge that their captain was waiting to see if the crew of the *Chelsea* would be forced to abandon their ship. If they did, they knew Weyland would risk his ship and they would risk their lives trying to save every one they could. They stood to their posts and they looked at the *Chelsea*, and they put the feeling away in a place in their hearts to be brought out later in a quiet moment and savored once more.

The winds slowed after one o'clock. By four o'clock, when the deck crew changed, the mountainous waves had dwindled to rough water that rocked the *Esther*, but the forty-foot swells were gone. When full darkness closed around them, they still had a headwind but were riding well at anchor. On Weyland's orders they built a fire on the deck, and ten minutes later an answering fire appeared in the blackness. The *Chelsea* had not yet broken up; her crew was surviving. At three o'clock in the morning Matthew pointed upwards at a break in the clouds and located the Big Dipper, then the North Star. Half an hour before sunrise Weyland raised signal flags, and the British answered. They were prisoners of war, their ship a prize of war.

With the first arc of the sun showing on the flat Atlantic skyline, the *Esther* closed to within two hundred yards of the *Chelsea* and again dropped anchor. Throughout the day the crews of both ships shuttled back and forth feverishly in every longboat they had, transferring the cannon and gunpowder and shot, ship's inventory, safe and log, navigational equipment, medicines, food stores, and clothing into the hold of the *Esther*. Weyland gave the

British captain a few moments alone with his crew on their ship before he took them all onto the *Esther*, and turned to Matthew. "Take us to Newburyport."

They tied up at the docks at ten minutes before eight o'clock and had the British crew delivered to the militia by eight-thirty. Weyland gave shore liberty to his men who wished it, while the others went to their bunks below decks. He took his supper in his quarters with Matthew and Riggins. At ten o'clock he set down his second cup of steaming tea, closed the inventory ledger of the *Chelsea*, and raised his eyes to Matthew and Riggins.

"Sixty-eight cannon, eighteen hundred pounds of gunpowder, thirteen hundred rounds of shot, six hundred pounds in gold, one hundred ninety uniforms, three hundred blankets, muskets, medicine . . ." He raised the steaming cup and squinted one eye as he sipped the searing-hot tea. "It didn't come easy, but it was worth it."

In the warmth of the cabin, a sense of weary satisfaction had mellowed and settled on all three men as they sat in dry clothing in the yellow lamplight, steaming tea cups on the table before them. Matthew and Riggins remained silent for a moment before Matthew spoke. "What about the *Chelsea*? Should we go back and blow her up? She might become a hazard if she breaks up and part of her remains afloat."

"We'll take a look when we leave. If she'll stay on those shoals we might leave her as a marker."

Riggins interrupted. "She was breaking up."

The words brought images in their minds, and for a moment each reflected on his own memory of a great ship driving onto hidden rocks—the shuddering jolt, the masts splintering, the rigging crashing, the wrenching sight of a proud thing broken and dying.

Weyland interrupted the reverie. "Mr. Riggins, where did you learn gunnery like that? Nine shots below the waterline in a storm."

Riggins shook his head and sipped at his tea. "I don't know. It just came."

Weyland raised his steaming cup. "Mr. Dunson, what were the odds of finding those shoals the way you did?"

Matthew considered for a moment. "Pretty poor."

Weyland pursed his mouth for a moment, and Riggins and Matthew brought their eyes to his, and for a moment they sat silently while something passed between them, and then Weyland said, "Do either of you think you . . ." He stalled for a moment. "Either of you think you did it alone?"

The instant he spoke all three men felt a subtle, indefinable impression fill the room, and they sat in silence for a time while their thoughts ran.

Riggins swallowed. "No, sir. Not alone."

Matthew spoke quietly. "I did not find those shoals alone, sir."

None of them knew or cared how long they sat thus, awed, humbled by their frank confessions and the profound implications of what had been said.

Weyland cleared his throat and tried to frame his thoughts. "I don't think I'm religious. I've never talked about such things much—a little embarrassing. It's just that since the colonies broke with the British, things have happened that don't make sense." He paused to look at his rough, square hands. "Like the *Chelsea*. It all seemed normal at the time, but looking back . . . Something's stirring. I can't explain it." He shook his head.

A sharp knock at the door jolted them all, and Weyland recovered and called, "Enter."

The deck watch opened the door, and his breath smoked in the freezing air as he spoke. "An officer from the militia to see you, sir."

"Send him in."

A man bundled in oilskins appeared in the doorway. "Captain Weyland?"

"Here."

"I'm Lieutenant Abel Haldeman of the Newburyport militia, sir. I have orders to deliver this to you personally." He handed a sealed envelope to the captain. "I will return in the morning for your reply."

Weyland nodded, and the door closed as Weyland tore open the envelope and flattened the two-page document on the table. Riggins and Matthew waited while he read it in silence, then tossed it on the table and again sipped from the smoking cup of tea. "Riggins, read it aloud."

Wednesday January 17th, A.D. 1776
Captain Soren Weyland:

In session on October 13, 1775, the Continental Congress voted to fit out ships for a Continental Navy. Time being critical, the following merchant ships were purchased to be fitted out as men-of-war: "Andrew Doria," "Alfred," "Columbus," "Cabot," "Providence," "Hornet," "Wasp," "Fly."

Receiving reliable intelligence that a large quantity of British munitions, including gunpowder, is stored on the Island of Providence in the West Indies, on November 29th, 1775, Congress ordered a special committee to secure it. On December 22, 1775, your humble servant Captain Esek Hopkins was appointed Commander in Chief of the fleet, with other officers for the remaining ships. After further advice from a secret committee assigned to execute the plan, a rendezvous has been scheduled at Abaco in the West Indies for March 1st or thereabouts, from which place the fleet shall proceed to the Island Providence to obtain the desired munitions, without which the Continental Army will face immediate and critical shortages.

Accordingly you are requested to add your schooner, the "Esther," to this expedition. The fleet will leave from the mouth of the Delaware River on or about February 17, 1776. All to remain in strictest confidence.

Would you kindly reply in writing into the hands of the bearer of this letter, earliest.

Your obdt servant,
Esek Hopkins, Commander.

Riggins turned to the second sheet.

To whom it may concern:

The Continental Congress of the Thirteen Colonies of America, in session met, did on December 22nd, A.D. 1775, regularly appoint and commission Esek Hopkins as Commander in Chief of the Continental Fleet.

Certified: Charles Thomson
Congressional Secretary

No one spoke for a time, and then Weyland set his cup down. "Less than three weeks. We'll have to unload the *Esther* and get provisioned." He glanced at Matthew. "Can you get us to the West Indies?"

"I think so, sir. I've been there."

"How do you know when to turn west?" Weyland was grinning.

"Easy. Go south until the butter melts, and turn west."

They laughed. Riggins stood. "I think I'll go to my quarters."

Weyland nodded, and Riggins put on his heavy coat. "Good night," they all said as he walked out into the freezing night.

Matthew reached for his heavy woolen coat. "Sir, when we get the *Esther* unloaded, could I have some time to go home? I left a family without a father."

Weyland turned in his chair and drew a small, heavy ironbound box from beneath his bunk, worked a key, and opened it. He counted silver coins into a leather purse and handed it to Matthew. "One hundred twenty pounds sterling. Take it. Be back before February seventeenth."

"I will. That's too much money."

Weyland shook his head. "With what you've saved and what's on the *Esther* right now, that's close to your share. I hope it helps your mother, family."

Matthew dropped the purse into his large coat pocket. "It will. Thank you, sir." He opened the door.

"Matthew," Weyland said, and Matthew closed the door and waited, startled. Weyland had never before called him by his first name. "Tell your mother I thank her for her sacrifices. For letting you come."

"I will, sir. I will."

In his small cabin, Matthew fed more coal into the stove and waited for the room to warm before he locked the purse in his instruments case and hung his heavy coat on the door peg. He drew out his leather wallet and carefully removed the small folded paper, laid it on his charts table, and unfolded it in the yellow lamplight. He gently laid the small watch fob on one palm and for long seconds studied the blue and red and white. He touched it gently with his fingers and then rewrapped and put it back, and then went to his knees beside his bunk, and clasped his hands before his bowed head.

CHAPTER XXII

★ ★ ★

ext."

Kathleen stood in the bright, frigid sun of late afternoon in early February and held out her mittened hand at the pay table of Helgestad Fish Company while Peter Helgestad dropped four silver coins clinking. Her feet were frozen numb inside her gum boots, and her breath was a vapor as she faced him on the east end of the Boston fish docks. She thrust the coins in the pocket of her heavy wool coat, untied the cord of the oilskin apron that covered her front from throat to ankles, and lifted the neck loop over the black knitted mariner's cap that was pulled low to her eyebrows and over her ears.

"Tomorrow?" she asked.

Helgestad studied her for a moment. He was bundled in a mariner's winter coat, his leather cap pulled low, and his breath rose in a cloud as he considered. Twenty-eight years building his fleet of twelve boats to ply the fisheries off the New England coast, and he could not remember hiring a woman to stand in the big, open shed on the docks eight hours at a time at sixteen degrees below freezing, doing the heavy, rough job of eviscerating cod at the big cleaning tables as his boats came in.

Three days ago, after the heavy storm passed through, the first of his boats returned from the Grand Banks to the north, their holds jammed to the hatches and a ton of cod held loose on the decks. Kathleen had come to the docks with the men, asking for work, and he had looked into her eyes and jabbed a thumb towards the long oak tables. He gave orders to the crew's Portuguese boss, who loaned her the big apron and the gum boots and elbow-length gum gloves, and gave her a short, thin knife. Patiently he showed her how to slit the fish from vent to gills, spill out all the entrails with one sweep of her thumb, shove the mess off the table splashing into a large metal tub, wash the inside of the fish clean in running water, and toss it down a chute to men waiting with wooden shipping crates and ice to pack them fresh for shipping to customers from Boston to the Gulf of Mexico. Helgestad had checked her twice that day, once the next day, and shook his head in wonder. She had worked steadily, watching, learning. She paid for the gum boots and apron and gloves with her third day's pay, and today she had held pace with the men without stopping, asking no quarter, saying nothing in her fierce concentration.

Helgestad's stubble beard moved as he spoke. "Tomorrow's the Sabbath."

"I know."

"Is it the money?"

She remained silent.

He glanced at the men standing behind her waiting for their day's pay, and they looked away while he quickly thrust four more coins into her hand and said gruffly, "Monday. Not tomorrow."

She looked at the coins. "I didn't earn this."

He looked away. "Monday. Go home," and he motioned for the next man.

She walked off the docks, leaving behind the stench of tons of fish entrails, into the wintry, narrow streets of Boston, steadily pacing off the blocks. Minutes later she looked left at the British base, four blocks away. After the Bunker Hill battle, the work at the military laundry dwindled as the wounded recovered, and by late August all civilian labor was stopped. Through the fall and early winter the British loosened their stranglehold on Boston. Their blockade of Boston Port dwindled, and fishermen went to sea, openly daring the British to interfere. Kathleen found work cleaning rooms at inns and taverns in Charlestown until the storms of January stopped most of the land travel, and then she went to the docks to take any work she could find from the incoming fishing boats.

She arrived at home with late-afternoon shadows lengthening, and spent half an hour washing herself, working to get the smell of fish from her hair and clothing. She made thick, hot soup for supper, fed the children, and carried a tray to Phoebe, who lay in bed. She finished the supper dishes and sat down at the dining table with a bottle of ointment given her by Doctor Soderquist and began working it into the stiff, dry skin and cracks in both hands, when a bold knock at the front door startled her and she jumped, then wiped her hands on a cloth and walked to the door.

She opened it eight inches and asked, "Who's there?"

"Colonel Arthur Wyans, Twenty-third Fusiliers, detailed to General Howe's command. I am accompanied by Captain Runyan."

Kathleen caught her breath. "On what errand?"

"I have a sealed message from General William Howe for Mrs. Phoebe Thorpe. Is that you, ma'am?"

"No. She is in bed. Could you return tomorrow?"

"I am sorry, I must deliver it tonight to her personally."

"Wait a moment."

Kathleen closed the door and dashed to Phoebe's bedroom. "A British colonel says he has a sealed message for you and must deliver it tonight! What is he talking about?"

Phoebe thought for a moment. "It could be from the king."

"*What?*" Kathleen shook her head emphatically. "No, Mama. You're imagining things again. Put on your robe and come to the door."

Phoebe thrust her chin forward. "Absolutely not. Show him in here—I will receive him here!"

In weary resignation, Kathleen returned to the door. "Mrs. Thorpe is not well. Do you wish to deliver the message in her bedroom?"

"Very well," Wyans said. Kathleen opened the door and the two officers followed her to the bedroom.

"Mrs. Phoebe Thorpe?"

"Yes."

"I herewith deliver a message to you from General William Howe, in the presence of Captain Runyan, my witness. I will return at one o'clock P.M. tomorrow for your answer in writing."

He bowed stiffly to Phoebe, turned on his heel, and marched back out the front door. Kathleen locked it behind him and ran back to Phoebe's bedroom as Phoebe finished reading the few lines on the parchment and turned triumphant eyes to Kathleen.

"General Howe has received instruction from King George to see me regarding my letter. He wishes an audience with me tomorrow at one o'clock P.M."

Kathleen clapped a hand over her mouth, dumbstruck. For a moment she could not gather her fragmented thoughts, and then she blurted, "*You* wrote to the king? When? How?"

"Weeks ago. He has authorized General Howe to make an investigation."

"An investigation of *what?*"

"My request that the king grant this family a stipend."

Kathleen stepped backwards in utter shock. "A *stipend?* You wrote the king of England for a *stipend?*"

"I did. England owes us that, at least until Henry gets back."

Kathleen's mouth dropped open. "A *stipend?* Help from the king of England? Mother! How could you do that?"

"We need it. Henry won't be back until fall, and we—"

"Mama!" Kathleen threw her hands in the air. "Father is not coming back—ever. He's gone, banished."

"The king wrote to General Howe—"

"How could you?" Kathleen's voice rang off the walls. "The British are our *enemies!* Our neighbors, our friends, have *died* fighting them. John dead, Joseph Warren, Billy wounded! It ruined us when Father was banished, but asking the British to give us *money*—we may as well declare ourselves loyal to the Crown and be banished!"

The door opened, and Faith and Charles stood with long faces, frightened at the raised voices. Kathleen spun. "Go back to the parlor and wait there." Charles quickly slammed the door, and Kathleen could hear Faith's soft whimpering as they walked away.

Phoebe's eyes flashed. "Nonsense! I did what had to be done! Look at yourself! A common fishmonger—look like a woman twice your age! And the children—can't even go to school, you have to teach them here—in the parlor now, crying! I did what I had to do!" She set her chin in defiance.

"Us live on British money while everyone else is suffering? Brigitte at the bakery. Billy can't even stand straight. Margaret taking in wash. Mama, can't you see what you've done? Can't you see?"

Phoebe turned her back to Kathleen in cold silence and pulled the comforter to her chin.

All the air went out of Kathleen and her shoulders sagged and her chin began to tremble and then the tears came. She dropped onto a chair in the corner and buried her face in her hands, and her sobbing moans frightened the children in the parlor.

They walked to the North Chapel for church services the following morning in stony silence, and ate their noon meal without allowing their eyes to meet. At twelve-thirty Phoebe confronted Kathleen in the kitchen.

"The appointment is in one-half hour. I'm leaving."

Kathleen remained silent.

"Are you coming?"

Kathleen shook her head and said nothing.

"Very well, I'll take the children and make whatever arrangements I can for us."

Kathleen placed her hands on her hips. "The children are not going."

Phoebe's eyes narrowed. "They are my children, not yours. They come."

"You are not in your right mind."

"Do you intend allowing Charles and Faith see us divided? Haven't they suffered enough? It is on your shoulders. Decide." She turned and called to the children. "Get your coats. We're leaving for a while."

The children stood in the archway, eyes wide in question as they stared at Kathleen, waiting for some indication from her. She saw the confusion and the hopelessness that had crept into their faces over the past months, and she could not bear thrusting more upon them.

"Get your coats."

The oak and maple trees that lined the streets were stark and bare, and their branches were like bony fingers reaching to claw at the frozen heavens. Vapor trailed from their faces as they walked to the British military compound, where a sentry at the main gate accompanied them to the office of the commanding general. They sat silently in the anteroom for a few moments before an officer opened the door with the sign "GENERAL SIR WILLIAM HOWE" written in scroll, and he ushered them inside, then closed the door as he left.

The general stood. "Mrs. Phoebe Thorpe, I presume," he said. He was taller than average, slender, restless eyes, regular features.

"I am Mrs. Thorpe," Phoebe said. "These are my children, Kathleen, Charles, and Faith."

The general nodded deeply. "Please be seated."

He sat back down in his large overstuffed chair behind a polished cherry wood desk and picked up a piece of paper. "I have been ordered by his Majesty King George to proceed with an investigation of a letter which he believes was written by yourself. Is that accurate, Mrs. Thorpe?"

"Yes. I wrote such a letter."

"Your husband is Henry Thorpe?"

"He is."

The general tapped a heavy brown envelope. "I have a transcript of the proceedings taken against him." He shook his head.

"Extremely disheartening." He waited a moment before raising his eyes again to Phoebe. "Your letter explains that because of the absence of your husband, you now find yourself in serious social and financial condition. Is that so?"

"Yes." Phoebe's chin was high, eyes bright, words clear. "When Henry returns this fall we shall recover."

The general's face clouded in question and he glanced at Kathleen. She held a steady gaze into his eyes and said nothing.

The general reflected for a moment before he looked back at Phoebe. "Do I understand correctly that your husband was banished for life by a Massachusetts court?"

"No. He is away on the king's business. He will return when it is finished."

The general leaned back in his chair and raised one hand to stroke his chin for a moment before he moved on. "You have no source of funds?"

"None. I must remain at home with the children. Kathleen has taken some positions to secure what funds she can, but they have been temporary. We have no more money and no way of getting any."

"Do you have relatives, perhaps?"

"None to whom we can go."

"What is it you wish the king to do for you?"

"Compensate us for the selfless service rendered the Crown by my husband. For years he has delivered invaluable information to the Crown at great risk to his life and welfare."

"Yes, so I understand. I ask again, what do you want the king to do?"

Phoebe drew a determined breath. "Give us a residence in England with a monthly stipend sufficient to our need."

Kathleen gasped and recoiled.

The general studied her for a moment, then turned back to Phoebe. "That is an extremely radical request. Do you know what you're asking?"

"I do."

"Leave your home, your friends, all with which you are familiar, to live in a new society where you are unknown—do you think you're prepared for such a thing?"

"I am."

He looked at Kathleen. "Do you think you and the children are prepared?"

Kathleen leaned forward on her chair. "May I have audience with the general alone?"

Phoebe cut her off. "Absolutely not."

"At least send the children from the room."

The general called his orderly, and he gently led the children into the anteroom.

Kathleen pointed at Phoebe. "She has not been in her right mind since Father was exiled. Somehow she has made herself believe he will return this fall. If you have read the court proceedings you know he was banished for the rest of his life. He will never return."

She paused for a moment. "I knew nothing of the letter she sent to the king. If I had, it would never have happened. We are having difficulties right now, but we will survive somehow. I can think of nothing—*nothing*—more insane than sending us all to England. I have no idea how the children would survive—"

Phoebe cut her off, her voice high, near hysteria. "The children will be fine. They're doing well in school. When Henry—"

Kathleen raised both hands, palms out, and exclaimed, "Stop! The children are not in school. Father is *gone!*" She turned back to General Howe. "Do you see how she is? Do you think she knows what she's asking the king to do?"

General Howe drew and released a great breath. "Do you have work, Miss Thorpe?"

"Yes."

"At Helgestad's fishery?"

Kathleen started. "How did you know?"

"The king asked me to investigate. You've also worked at inns and taverns in Charlestown—four of them—and at the laundry here at the base."

Phoebe gestured. "And look at her! She's becoming a shadow. If she continues she will become ill—permanently damage her health."

Kathleen turned. "I will be all right. I can—"

General Howe raised a hand and silenced them both. "I believe I have a grasp on this matter, at least sufficient to obey the orders sent to me by the king. Would you both wait in the foyer?"

They sat in the austere anteroom while Kathleen counted off thirty minutes on the mantel clock that ticked rhythmically in the silence. They heard the general walk to the door and it opened.

"Please come in and be seated."

They took their places, and General Howe leaned forward in his chair and clasped his hands on the desktop, and studied them for a moment before he raised his head.

"I was authorized by the king to take whatever action I deemed appropriate. He suggested the family may find comfort in England. I tend to agree with him, and that is what I am prepared to offer. You will have a small cottage near London and a monthly allowance sufficient to your needs. There is a British man-of-war, the *Britannia,* leaving for England with some of our wounded on February ninth, which is Friday next, five days from now. You will be allowed to take clothing and personal effects but none of your household furniture. You will have to dispose of your home any way you decide. This arrangement is extended to all of you. However, time is short. We will have to have all your luggage and personal effects no later than noon Thursday to be loaded, and I will have to know now if you wish to accept the king's hospitality."

He leaned back in his chair to give time for his offer to settle in.

"We accept!" Phoebe exclaimed.

Kathleen bolted to her feet. "We do *not* accept! This is insanity!"

General Howe again raised his hand for silence. "I refuse to be drawn into this conflict. However, I do believe you would be wise to consider one thing, Miss Thorpe."

Kathleen waited.

"If your mother goes alone, which she has the right to do, what would that do to you, and more important, the children, you living here and knowing nothing of your mother's condition or state of health?" He paused. "And if your mother takes the children, which she also has the right to do, how would you fare here, not knowing how the children were managing in a new and strange land? In short, if this family divides, what will that do to you, Miss Thorpe?"

Kathleen stared.

"Young lady," the general said quietly, "you have a difficult decision, and it may come down to the lesser of two evils. I am sorry I cannot give you time to ponder it, but I must know now if we need room for four passengers on the *Britannia,* or less."

Kathleen stood with hands clenched, eyes flat, dead. She settled back onto her chair and folded her hands in her lap and stared at them, and then looked at the children for a time, and finally spoke quietly. "Four."

At ten minutes past nine, the Reverend Mr. Silas Olmsted paused to listen, then hastened to open the outside door of his living quarters at the back of the church. His mouth fell open for a moment. "Kathleen! In heaven's name, come in, child. It's freezing out there."

He turned. "Millie, pour some hot tea." He guided Kathleen to a chair and sat opposite her in the small, sparse room in the light of two small lamps. "What brings you here this time of night?"

She leaned forward, eyes earnest. "I need your help. We will be leaving our home, and I need someone to sell it and the furniture. I don't know who to go to. Would you help?"

The reverend started. "Leaving? Going where?"

"That doesn't matter. I don't know when we'll be back. Perhaps never. Could you take care of the house until it's sold? We can compensate you from the sale money."

"Kathleen, I can't help if I don't know what's going on. Where are you going? Why?"

Kathleen bowed her head and tears came for a moment. She wiped at her nose and her downcast eyes. "England. Mother wrote the king without telling me. He's providing passage for us next Friday, and a home near London and a stipend, because Father was loyal to the Crown." She raised tortured eyes. "I am so sorry. Don't think ill of us. I don't know who else to turn to. Will you sell the house for us? I can write you with details as soon as I arrive there." She reached to clutch his arm. "And above all, Reverend, you must tell no one until we're gone. Promise me. No one."

Dawn broke clear and clean, and by midmorning the birds were singing their hearts out in temperatures nearing an unseasonable fifty degrees. Margaret hummed absentmindedly as she set one flatiron on the stove, picked up another, tested it with a wet finger, and continued ironing the yoke of a white shirt for Darren McGivey, a cantankerous old Scot who insisted his shirts be done just so. It was Tuesday, ironing day for all goodwives in Boston, and Margaret was alone in the house, kitchen window open to catch the fresh air and the first feeling of the awakening of earliest spring.

A rap at the front door stopped her, and she settled the iron back on the stove and hastened to open the door.

"Post, Mrs. Dunson." Arvin Fergus handed her two envelopes, and Margaret took them as she said, "Thank you," and eagerly looked at the addresses of the senders.

Her face clouded. "Captain Richard Arlen Buchanan," she said softly, "for Brigitte." She stared at it for long seconds. Brigitte had written two letters to him and sent three boxes of baked tarts and pumpkin cookies, none of which had been returned, but she had never received a letter or an acknowledgment from him. This was the first. Margaret felt a rise of concern.

She looked at the other envelope and her face blossomed. "Matthew! We have a letter from Matthew," she sang as she walked to the table and sat down. She opened the envelope and leaned forward on her arms while she read it slowly, savoring every word, every sentence. Halfway through she leaned back and exclaimed,

"He's coming home! Matthew's coming home! The eleventh or twelfth, for four or five days!" She revelled in the deep joy that surged through her being, then finished reading the letter. She read it all again, smiling, laughing, then looked at the mantel clock. Ten thirty-five, Tuesday, February 6, 1776. *Five more days. Sunday or Monday. Five more days. Matthew's coming home!*

She refolded the letter and tucked it back into the envelope, then laid both of them on the mantel.

The children arrived from school, and Caleb sat at the table to eat the bread and cheese strips Margaret placed before them. She beamed when she told them, "Matthew's coming home this weekend," and they broke into chatter as they drank their milk. Caleb finished and walked to the door while Margaret gave him his daily admonition, "Come straight home after work. And tell Daniel that Matthew's coming home." Caleb nodded and walked out and turned up the street, trotting towards the print shop, while the younger children changed their clothing and sat at the dining table, turning pages in a large picture book.

Half an hour later Brigitte walked in, smiling. "Isn't it nice outside?" she exclaimed as she hung her heavy sweater. The work at the bakery had been onerous at first, then endurable, then satisfying, and in the last month, to her profound surprise, she had found a sense of pride in working with the others, creating bread that came out of the ovens brown and steaming, and cakes and tarts that filled the air with rich aromas, and she sometimes paused and listened to the pleasant chatter from the front counter.

She started for her bedroom to change clothes, when Margaret gestured to the mantel. "You have a letter."

She stopped, startled. "Me?" The sudden realization struck her and she gasped. "From whom?"

"Your captain."

Brigitte flew to the mantel and snatched her letter, then trotted to her room and closed the door. She sat on the bed and opened it with trembling fingers and read it, scarcely breathing. Halfway through, her hand clamped over her mouth and she gasped in disbelief. She read it again, then once more, and leaped up and ran to the kitchen to Margaret, who was working on the last of Darren McGivey's shirts.

"He's well! He got my letters and my packages. He's being released from the hospital next Monday."

Brigitte's eyes were wide, wild with excitement. "Mama, please, please let me invite him here. Please."

Margaret continued stroking with the iron. "For what reason?"

"To meet you. And the family. Mama, you'll like him. I promise. Please." Brigitte's hands were clasped together under her chin as she pleaded.

Margaret laid the flatiron back on the stove and took the white shirt by the collar and lifted it to inspect the sleeves and front before she placed it on its wooden hanger. "You better read the letter from Matthew before you invite your captain. It's on the mantel."

"Matthew?"

"Yes. He's coming home next Sunday or Monday for a few days." She stopped and gave Brigitte a few seconds to understand. "You want a British captain here with your brother whose ship has taken twelve British gunboats and crews as prizes of war? I can hardly wait for *their* conversation."

Brigitte paused for long seconds as she struggled inside. "I still want him to come. Please, Mama."

Notes

Reference is again made to the petition, or request, made by the wife of Doctor Benjamin Church (Phoebe Thorpe in this volume) for a stipend, or pension, from King George of England in compensation for the doctor's services to the British Crown. It was her husband who had given colonial secrets to General Gage. His loyalty to the Crown had resulted in his arrest, trial, and eventual banishment from the colonies, leaving his wife and children in dire need. The details are more fully explained and supported by references in the notes for chapter 20.

CHAPTER XXIII

★ ★ ★

*M*atthew shouldered his seaman's bag, shook hands with the officer of the deck, and walked rapidly down the gangplank of the schooner *Penrod* onto the familiar east docks of Boston Town. His eyes were alive and shining as he strode thumping on the heavy planking in the five o'clock A.M. gray. Seagulls wheeled overhead and argued on the rocky beach over things the tides had left, and fishermen cast off the ropes that moored their boats to the docks, and prepared to work their way from Boston Harbor to the open sea. Each glanced at the eastern sky—red sky in the morning, sailor take warning—and, satisfied with the clear gray and the surprising warmth for February twelfth, began loosening the cords that lashed sails to lanyards. With the cod running up north, observance of the Sabbath would have to wait.

Matthew walked briskly through the narrow streets, a tight smile on his face, watching Boston Town begin to stir as the gray dawn turned to azure blue, and the sun, not yet risen, shot the low line of clouds through with reds and golds for a few brief moments. He turned onto the familiar street and looked two blocks ahead at the white fence, and his stride quickened at the thoughts of home. *Home. Family. Kathleen. Kathleen.*

He pushed through the front gate and set his bag down and tried the locked door, then rapped lightly. A moment later the curtain at the large front window stirred, and then Margaret flung the door open and threw herself into his arms and clung to him with all her strength. She kissed him on the cheek and said his name and remained within his arms, holding him, repeating his name softly.

She pushed herself away, still holding his arms, and looked at him from head to foot as though expecting somehow something should be wrong with him, but there was nothing, and words began to tumble. "You look wonderful. Come in. No one's up yet—I was just getting things ready for the Sabbath."

He walked in with her, arm tightly about her waist, and set his bag beside the dining table and followed her into the kitchen, where she fed wood to the stove.

"We got your letter," she said, "but I didn't expect you so early in the morning. Hungry?" She opened the cupboard for a bowl.

"Yes."

"Griddle cakes?" She took a large wooden spoon from a drawer.

"Good. I'll wait for the others. How are they?"

"Fine. Caleb's growing every day. Brigitte's working at the bakery. I think she's beginning to enjoy it."

Matthew took off his coat, drew his purse from the pocket, tossed the coat across a chair, and laid the purse thumping on the kitchen table. Margaret stopped to look.

"What's that?"

"One hundred twenty pounds sterling, for household use."

Margaret blinked in surprise. "That's a lot of money. Where did you get it?"

"My share of the prizes."

"That's a blessing. Thank you." She took the purse and disappeared for a moment in her bedroom, then returned. "How long can you stay?"

"Thursday the fifteenth. I sail on the *Penrod*. She brought me."

"Would you go get six eggs and some butter?"

Matthew took a bowl and disappeared into the root cellar, and returned and set the bowl and a butter crock on the table.

"I've been worried about you," he said. "How are you?"

She measured flour into a bowl and started cracking eggs on top, and looked at him in mild surprise. "Me?" She shrugged. "Fine. Just keep putting one foot ahead of the other." She stirred with the wooden spoon.

"I'll have time to help around the yard," he said.

"Tom's helped, and Billy's been here. Caleb's learning. We're getting along."

"Seen Kathleen?"

Margaret slowed. "No. She's working. We're all so busy we just don't see her."

"I'm going to see her." He waited. "This morning."

Margaret looked at him. "She's still pushing everybody away." She resumed stirring. "I feel so sorry for that family. You knew Henry was banished for life.".

"I heard." He stared vacantly at the mixing bowl for a moment. "Matthew!"

Brigitte rushed to throw her arms about him, and he held her close, then pushed her away. "You never looked better! The bakery did that for you?"

"Matthew!" she scolded, then brightened. "You look wonderful. We've read your letters a dozen times. How long can you stay?"

"Thursday."

She turned. "I'm going to get the children. They've been counting the days." Minutes later Adam and Prissy stood in the archway in their nightshirts digging fists into their eyes, squinting against the light until they saw him, and then they rushed to him and hugged him around the waist.

"I can't believe it," he said, an arm around each. "You've both grown up! Why, you're at least two inches taller."

"How long can you stay here?" Adam demanded.

"Thursday."

They both stood silent, staring up at him, waiting.

"What's this?" he demanded.

"Did you bring something?"

He chuckled. "Drag my bag in here and we'll see."

They both ran to his seaman's bag and tipped it over and began dragging it, when Caleb appeared in the archway.

Matthew straightened and looked at him. "Caleb! What happened to you?"

Caleb grinned, embarrassed. "Nothing."

"You're a foot taller!"

Margaret said, "He's delivering for Daniel Knight. Does a good job."

Matthew nodded his head in approval. "Well, come over here, little brother."

Caleb walked over and offered his hand, and Matthew avoided it and swept Caleb into his arms and held him tight. Caleb looked embarrassed and then didn't care and threw his long arms about his brother.

Matthew let him go, and Caleb walked to help the children with the bag, and Matthew lifted it to a chair. A moment later he had the laces open and rummaged around inside.

"For Adam." He handed him a small carved whale mounted on a pedestal.

Adam's eyes popped. "What's it made of?"

"Genuine whale's tooth."

"Genuine? Honest?"

"Honest."

Adam blew air. "Wait'll the others at church see *this!*"

"Prissy," Matthew said and handed her a comb of many colors.

"Mine? My own?"

"Your very own."

"What makes the colors?"

"That's made from abalone."

"Abalone! Oh! What's abalone? Mama, can I take it to church? Please? Please?"

Margaret smiled. "Abalone is seashell. You can take it to church."

"Caleb," Matthew said, and handed him a sextant.

Caleb beamed.

"That's a sextant we took from a British man-of-war. It's used for—"

Caleb interrupted. "I know what it is. I've been reading your books." Caleb ran his fingers over the fine precision instrument and his eyes shined. "Thanks."

"Brigitte." Matthew handed her a great white hand-knitted shawl with her name in royal blue in one corner.

"It's *beautiful*," she exclaimed. "Oh, thank you."

"Mother." He handed her a large vanity hand mirror, set in silver, with delicate roses and leaves engraved on the back and handle by a master silversmith, and a brush to match.

Margaret stopped in her tracks and her mouth dropped open for a second. "I've never seen anything so lovely!" she said softly. "Oh, son, they're just lovely." She caressed them for a time, feeling the polished silver and admiring the work.

Then she turned to the children. "Now, off with all of you. Put your gifts away for now and get ready for breakfast. Fifteen minutes."

With all of them standing at the table, Margaret nodded to Matthew. "Your turn."

They all knelt beside their chairs and Matthew clasped his hands. "Almighty God . . ."

The prayer was not long, and each said amen before they rose to sit, and it was then that each of them was suddenly aware of the vacant chair at the head of the table. Silent eyes turned to look, and an odd moment of unexpected quiet gripped them all as they worked with their own thoughts, their own memories of their father, and then Margaret cleared her throat.

"Matthew, John is here, but he can't sit at the head of the table anymore. Would you move to his chair? He expected you to do that."

It was done! In that peculiar moment, the healing that had gone on for nearly a year was completed, closed, behind them forever. Each drew a breath, and then they reached for the steaming platters.

Breakfast was a flood of questions and answers and exclamations and surprises and laughter that flowed around hot griddle cakes and melting butter and maple syrup and milk. Margaret and Brigitte did the dishes while Matthew took his bag to his room and unpacked, then walked back into the kitchen.

"I want to go see Kathleen for a few minutes before church," he said.

Margaret slowed. "She's still suffering—won't let anyone close. She's been attending church at the North Chapel. I think Phoebe's mind has been wandering. It might not be a good idea."

"I'll have to take a chance," Matthew said. "I have to see her."

Brigitte spoke. "Kathleen's been working wherever she could. The British laundry, at inns and taverns in Charlestown, and now she's working with the men at Helgestad's."

Matthew's head dropped forward. "Helgestad's? Cleaning cod?"

"Alongside the men."

"Why?"

Margaret stopped and faced him. "No one would give her work. No one. She worked at the British laundry because that was all she could find in Boston, and people called her a traitor just like her father. It's only gotten worse since. I don't know what's holding her together."

"Didn't anyone try to help?" Matthew's voice was high, excited.

"We all did. Me, Billy, Tom—but she refused. Simply refused."

"I'll be back in time for church," Matthew said as he walked to the door. Half a block from the Thorpe home Matthew saw the boards over the side windows, and his breath came short as he hurried on. He stopped at the front gate, appalled, stunned. There was no smoke from the chimney, the windows were all boarded, and a heavy wooden bar was bolted across the front door. A large padlock sealed the gate, and he vaulted it and trotted to the front door and banged hard with his clenched fist.

There was no greeting, no sound from within. He walked around the house, into the backyard, where the outbuildings were bolted shut and all windows were covered with boards. There was no cut kindling stacked against the back wall, no coal in the coal bin.

He vaulted the fence back into the street and trotted home and barged into the parlor, breathing hard.

Margaret came from the kitchen, hot pad in her hand, to stare at his face, frantic and wild. "What's wrong?" she demanded.

"The Thorpes are gone," he exclaimed, pointing.

"Gone?"

"The house is boarded up. Gone!"

Margaret was incredulous. Brigitte came trotting up the hall.

"Isn't there a sign on the door? Something?" Margaret asked.

"Nothing! Just a vacant house and yard."

Brigitte stood still, in shock. "Kathleen or the whole family?"

"All of them! Do you know anything about it?"

Brigitte shook her head violently. "No! I've been at the bakery."

"We've all been working," Margaret exclaimed. "I don't know a thing about it, but I can't believe they would do it—just leave without a word."

Matthew dropped into his chair, bewildered, unable to force his thoughts to a plan, a conclusion. "Somebody has to know! Billy? Would he know?"

Margaret answered. "Maybe. Let's go early and ask at church."

At nine twenty-five Matthew opened the tall doors to the church, and they entered to peer into the silent chapel. The sun streaming through the east bank of stained-glass windows cast a rainbow of color on the west wall.

"No one's arrived yet," Brigitte said.

"I'll go ask the reverend," Matthew replied. "You stay here and wait for Billy or someone and ask them." His heels clicked loud on the polished hardwood floor, and he stopped at the door behind the pulpit and rapped. A moment later it opened and the Reverend Silas Olmsted's bushy brows rose.

"Matthew! What a surprise! How good to see you! Won't you come in?"

"Thank you, Reverend, but I haven't come visiting. I need an answer to a question. I was down at the Thorpe home this morning and . . ."

Matthew saw the slight jerk of the reverend's head and the instant flex of the jaw muscles as his mouth tightened. He broke off his sentence and paused for one moment, then asked quietly, "Where are they?"

The reverend licked dry lips and stammered, "Won't you come in? We'll need to talk."

"Just tell me," Matthew said, and did not move.

The reverend straightened and looked him in the eye. "England. They sailed two days ago on the *Britannia.* The king granted them a home and stipend there."

For long seconds Matthew held the reverend's steady gaze, and then he repeated softly, "England?"

"Yes."

"I don't believe it."

"It's true. Kathleen left me with Phoebe's written authority to sell their house. She made me promise to tell no one—no one— until they were gone."

"Why did they go?"

"It was Phoebe, not Kathleen. Kathleen was bitter about it."

"But why?"

"Phoebe was becoming a recluse—not in her right mind."

"Couldn't someone stop her?"

"She wrote to the king. Directly to the king. He authorized General Howe to grant her passage and a home and money. There was no way to stop it without declaring her insane. Her mind wanders, but she's not insane."

"Why didn't Kathleen stay here, with the children?"

"Split the family? Separate the children from their mother? Worry about Phoebe forever?"

Matthew hesitated, then asked, "How long did she say they'd be gone?" He held his breath waiting for the answer.

"They won't be back. I'm to sell the house and forward the proceeds when Kathleen writes from England."

Matthew slowly exhaled and his shoulders dropped and he stood with face downcast, and he felt everything inside go dead. His heart turned to ashes. His mind quit functioning. He did not move or speak for more than one minute while Silas waited, giving him time.

Finally Silas touched his arm. "I'm so sorry. So sorry. Please come inside."

Still Matthew remained mute, unmoving.

"Matthew? Are you all right?"

Finally Matthew raised his head. "Thank you." He turned and walked slowly back up the aisle, out the door into the bright sunlight, where Margaret waited with the family.

Margaret sensed it. "Matthew! What's happened?"

He took her by the arm and walked her onto the grass, away from the entry, with Brigitte following. For three minutes he spoke quietly, haltingly, while both women covered their mouths with their hands and stood frozen like pillars.

Matthew finished and raised his eyes to Margaret, and she was speechless.

Brigitte broke the silence. "Gone? For always?" She shook her head, unable to grasp what was happening.

Margaret touched his arm. "Matthew, I am so sorry."

He looked at her and said nothing.

They turned at the sound of voices and watched a family in their Sunday best cross the street.

Margaret spoke. "Do you want to go home?" she asked.

Matthew shook his head. "No." He straightened and squared his shoulders. "Let's go inside."

By force of will Matthew and the family sealed off their inner devastation and abided the social requirements of greeting friends, and singing, and soberly listening to Silas Olmsted's sermon, and adding their "Amen" to his before rising to walk out into the February sunshine. Their façade succeeded with everyone save for one person. In the churchyard Billy Weems pulled Matthew aside.

"What's wrong?"

For three minutes Matthew talked low, and Billy felt the pain and his head dropped forward for a moment. "Last week, I talked to her, she didn't say a word."

"I've got to know some things. Why? How long, Billy? What am I going to do?"

"I don't know. I don't know. Let me think on it."

They worked their way back to their families, and with Margaret on his arm, Matthew led the children home. They changed clothes, and Margaret and Brigitte put on aprons. Brigitte tested the beef pie while Margaret slipped two apple pies into the oven. The children cornered Matthew in the parlor.

"Any sea battles?" Caleb asked.

Matthew nodded. "Quite a few."

Adam and Priscilla settled onto the sofa, wide-eyed, waiting.

"Did you capture any ships?"

"Several."

"What was the first one?" Caleb sat down facing Matthew on the sofa.

Half an hour later Margaret called, "Get washed for dinner."

Margaret said grace, and Adam declared, "Matthew caught some bad ships and brought 'em back with lots of gunpowder, and we're going to win the war because George Washington wanted the gunpowder." He looked fierce.

Matthew chuckled.

"Not Matthew," Prissy said, disgusted. "The captain of the ship."

"No sir," Adam declared, "it was Matthew." He turned large, pleading eyes upward. "Wasn't it?"

"Well," Matthew said, "it was Captain Weyland and me and the crew. We all did it."

Adam turned indignant eyes back to Prissy. "See! I told you."

"That's not the same as you said first," Prissy insisted.

"It is too," Adam declared.

"Hush, you two," Margaret said. "Matthew, when will you return from this next trip?"

"A month, six weeks."

"Where you going?" Caleb asked.

"West Indies."

"What for?"

"General Washington ordered it."

"Can't you tell us?"

"No."

Adam reared up in his seat. "A secret! Matthew's doing a secret for George Washington."

"He is not," Prissy retorted.

"He is so! He said!"

The talk flowed freely, uninhibited, in the bedrock security of the family.

Matthew turned to Brigitte. "Like working at the bakery?"

She answered without raising her eyes. "Yes. Fine."

"I'll get the custard," Margaret announced, and they all waited with spoons in hand while she disappeared out the back door, into the root cellar.

Again Matthew looked at Brigitte. "You haven't had much to say."

She wrinkled her nose and shrugged. "It's nice just listening. It's been so long since we've all been here."

With the dishes done and the shadows growing long in the streets, Matthew sat for a time at the dining table with a book, then rose to pace, running his hands through his hair.

"Kathleen?" Margaret asked.

Matthew nodded. "I can't leave it like this. I need to talk to her."

"Get her address from Silas when she writes to him, and send her a letter."

"That could be a year."

Margaret shrugged. "Sail one of your ships over there and find her." She turned to him. "Son, you may have to put this behind you without ever seeing her again. Don't get your heart too set."

Matthew sighed. "I'll see her again."

At eight-thirty Matthew called the family to the table and they knelt beside their chairs, and Margaret offered their evening prayer, then stood.

"To bed with you children," she said. "School tomorrow. Caleb, you too."

At nine-fifteen Margaret went into the kitchen to shake the grate in the stove, and Matthew followed her.

He spoke softly. "Is something wrong with Brigitte? Not ten words all day."

Margaret stared at the stove for a moment, deciding, then drew a determined breath. "Yes, there is." She walked back into the parlor to where Brigitte was sitting. "Come sit at the table. Matthew, you too." She waited. "Brigitte, you have something to tell Matthew."

Brigitte looked at her mother, and for a moment Matthew saw fear flicker in her eyes, and then she set her mouth and turned to him. "Yes, I do. Tuesday evening I have invited a guest for supper. Richard Arlen Buchanan, a captain in the regulars."

Slowly Matthew leaned back in his chair while he tried to make sense of it. "A British officer? What are you saying?"

"I invited him here. I want you and Mother to meet him."

Matthew shook his head slightly. "I don't understand what this is about." He looked at Margaret, face drawn in question.

Margaret looked at Brigitte. "Come to the point."

"I met him before Concord. He was wounded in the battle. I've written to him. I want him to come here."

Matthew's mouth fell open and he stared. "You're interested in this man?"

Brigitte's eyes were steady, firm. "Yes."

Matthew turned to Margaret, looking for help. "Is this true? An officer in the English army?"

Margaret nodded her head and remained silent.

"He was in the Concord battle?"

"Yes," Brigitte answered. "Nearly killed."

"Father *was* killed. Does he know that?"

"Not from me. I don't think he knows."

"Does he know I've spent the last eight months taking ships flying the Union Jack on the high seas?"

"No."

Matthew's voice was beginning to rise, hot. "What do you expect to come of it? Are you thinking of marriage?"

Brigitte's eyes fell and she remained silent, subdued.

"Brigitte! Think what you're saying!" Matthew leaned forward, concentrative, intent.

"A colonial girl and a British officer! It's insane! Could you forswear us, your home, this land, to become a British subject? the wife of a British officer? live in England?"

Brigitte would not raise her eyes.

"What do you know about him? How much time have you spent with him?"

"I know he's good and honorable."

"No, how much time? When have you talked with him?"

She shook her head. "Once."

"When? Where?"

"At the church."

"Church! He went to church with you?"

"No. That night they ransacked it."

"That was April of last year! You've never talked with him about all this?"

"I don't need to. I know what I know."

Matthew turned to Margaret, incredulous, angry. "She told you all this?"

"We've been through it half a dozen times."

"Can you see any good coming of it?"

Margaret shook her head emphatically. "I've told her. She's going to break her own heart."

Matthew turned back to Brigitte, loud. "What will it do to him when I tell him Father was killed in the Concord fight? that my ship's crew and I have killed British sailors, taken twelve British ships, given their guns and powder to George Washington to fight this man's king and country? What's he going to feel when he understands that Father or I or Billy or Tom would have killed him at Concord if we'd seen him?"

Margaret interrupted. "Not so loud. Don't wake the children."

Brigitte neither spoke nor moved.

Matthew lowered his voice. "That doesn't concern you?"

"Yes, it does. But it will not change things between him and me."

"Brigitte! Wake up! I might have to kill that man on the field of battle, or him me. Don't you see what you're doing?"

Brigitte swallowed but did not raise her eyes. "I've thought of all that."

"And you still invited him to break bread with us at our table?"

"Yes."

"I can't do that without telling him we're sworn enemies—about Father and me—that one day we may face each other in mortal combat. That would be utter hypocrisy!"

Matthew stood and paced for a moment. Then he turned and looked at Brigitte, and he felt the shock and anger dwindle. He sat down and gently took her hand in both of his. "Brigitte, look at me."

She raised tortured eyes and started at the deep compassion she saw in Matthew's face.

"If you think anything of this man, break this off now. It has only pain and heartbreak for both of you."

Brigitte's chin trembled for a moment, and her voice was strained. "I can't."

He tenderly touched the soft cheek and he stared into the pain in the blue eyes, and his voice was pleading. "I understand. Kathleen—gone—I understand the pain. But all the understanding doesn't change the truth. Don't do this to yourself."

"I can't help it."

For long moments they stared deep into each other's hearts. Then Matthew stood, and he raised her from her chair and pulled her to himself and held her. Her arms circled him tightly, and she sobbed. He gently stroked her hair and kissed her on the forehead and waited until the trembling stopped.

"Tuesday? What've you planned for supper? Mother's custard? We'll have to polish up a few things around here."

Brigitte stood on her tiptoes and threw her arms about his neck, and she kissed his cheek and a sob caught in her throat. "Thank you. Thank you."

"He's coming! He's coming!" Adam ran from the front window to the kitchen, shouting.

"Oh!" exclaimed Brigitte from the kitchen. "I look *awful!*" Her hands flew to tuck hair wisps, then to untie her apron, and she bolted from the room while Margaret chuckled and opened the oven door to thrust a fork into the baked ham, then watch the small trickle of steaming juices work their way down the side and disappear.

Matthew waited for the knock, then rose from his chair and opened the door, and for a moment the two men stood silent, Richard Buchanan surprised at the appearance of a tall young man at the door, and Matthew startled that Richard was dressed in a simple dark suit with starched white shirt and black tie at his throat, devoid of any indication of his military status or rank. He held a package loosely in his left hand.

"I'm Richard Buchanan. I'm looking for the residence of Miss Brigitte Dunson. Do I have the correct place?"

"You do. I'm Matthew Dunson, her brother." He thrust out his hand and felt the strong, sure grip. "Please come in. Brigitte will be out in a moment."

Richard stepped inside, into the rich aroma of roasting ham and the spicy taint of custard and hot maple sauce. His eyes swept the room, and he was aware of the quality of the furniture and the orderliness and the fine linens and place settings at the table. Matthew closed the door, and for an awkward moment they stood facing each other, unsure what should be said.

"Brigitte was helping in the kitchen," Matthew started. "She went to her room for a moment."

Richard nodded.

"Be seated," Matthew continued. "Dinner will be ready soon."

Richard began to sit in the nearest chair, when Margaret walked in from the kitchen, wiping her hands on her apron. Richard straightened and waited.

Matthew spoke. "Mr. Buchanan, I would like to present my mother, Margaret Dunson. Mother, this is Richard Buchanan."

Margaret finished wiping her hands as she walked, and shook hands with him. "Welcome. We're delighted you could come. Forgive me for appearing in my apron, and don't let the children overpower you."

He bowed. "I am honored, Mrs. Dunson." He raised the package. "Please accept this."

Margaret started. "For me?"

"Yes."

She looked at Matthew, then back at Richard. "Thank you. How nice. This is totally unexpected."

"Something for the house."

Margaret accepted the package. "I'll be a minute getting my apron off, and we will serve dinner shortly. Why don't you two sit down."

She started for the archway as Adam and Prissy came careening around the corner and stopped short, staring.

"Is this him?" Adam blurted.

Prissy gave her brother a dark look.

"Yes," Matthew answered, and smiled. "This is him. Mr. Buchanan, this is Priscilla and Adam, our twins. Children, this is Richard Buchanan."

Priscilla curtsied. "Pleased to meet you."

Adam took two steps forward, thrust out his hand, gave two perfunctory yanks on Richard's hand, and stepped back. "I am happy to meet you."

"I'm happy to meet both of you, too," Richard said.

Caleb appeared in the archway.

"And this is Caleb," Matthew concluded. "Caleb, this is Richard Buchanan."

Caleb stood eye to eye with Richard. "I am pleased to meet you, sir," he said, and thrust out his hand.

"I'm happy to meet you too," Richard answered as Caleb stepped back.

A door closed in the hallway, and Matthew listened to the rapid steps, and then Brigitte appeared in the archway. She wore a simple white ankle-length dress with a sash, and lace at her throat. Her hair was brushed and held back with a white ribbon, and her face was radiant. Richard felt his breath come short as she moved into the room, and Margaret saw the guarded admiration.

"How nice of you to come," Brigitte said, and offered her hand, and Richard grasped it and shook it.

"It's a privilege. I was unaware you have such a family."

Brigitte smiled. "I hope they haven't frightened you."

He looked at the children, and Matthew caught the slightest hint of a sadness, and a longing.

"Not at all. It has been my pleasure."

"Won't you sit down," Brigitte said, and gestured, and they all sat down just as Margaret walked back into the room. She carried two silver candlesticks, one in each hand, each handworked by a master silversmith. She set them gleaming on the mantel and turned to Richard.

"They are absolutely beautiful. Thank you."

Richard cast his eyes downward for a moment, and Margaret saw the flicker of pleasure in his face. "I'm happy if you like them," he murmured.

"Is your home and family in England?" Margaret asked.

"It was. Lichfield. A small coal mining town."

"Was?"

"Yes. My parents are gone. So is the home. I have no brothers or sisters."

"Oh." Margaret's eyes dropped for a moment. "I didn't know. I'm sorry about your parents—family."

"It's all right. It's been some time ago." He smiled his assurance.

An awkwardness touched them for a moment while their minds groped for something appropriate to say. The war, his wounds, his work, the loss of John, the politics between the colonies and England were all too divisive, too delicate.

Brigitte spoke. "I do hope you enjoy ham and potatoes. Mother does them so well."

"Brigitte did the ham," Margaret said bluntly.

"It's one of my favorites," Richard replied.

"We got custard for after," Adam blurted. "Mama makes it good."

Prissy gave him another dark look and they all laughed.

Richard turned to him. "With hot sauce?"

Adam nodded vigorously.

"That's the best there is," Richard said.

Margaret stood. "If any of you want to wash, Brigitte and I will get dinner on the table. Matthew, you show Richard where to wash."

With the roast ham and bowls of vegetables steaming on the table, they gathered and sat down, Matthew at the head, Margaret facing him, Richard and Brigitte seated opposite each other, with Adam and Priscilla on either side of Richard and Caleb beside Brigitte. Matthew spoke.

"Richard, we usually kneel to return thanks. Would you like to join us?"

Richard went to his knees beside his chair and bowed his head before clasped hands.

"Almighty God, we are thankful for the bounties of life before us and ask thy blessings upon them. Bless us with wisdom to use the good therefrom in righteousness. We are grateful for the guest in our home and ask thy blessings to be upon him. Amen."

Richard said his amen with the others, and for one instant he hesitated on his knees, and in that moment Margaret saw the longing, the need in him as he glanced at the others before rising.

Matthew cut smoking slices of ham while Brigitte started the bowls of potatoes and yams and squash around the table, then the sliced bread, and the mustard pickles to garnish the ham. Talk and laughter flowed uninhibited. Margaret covertly studied Richard. He took his portion as the platters and bowls passed and spoke when spoken to, but his eyes never stopped moving. He watched the children and Matthew and Margaret, and glanced at Brigitte, and he listened to the unending undercurrent of talk, and in his face Margaret saw the hunger that had built for years. He did not want to speak or interfere, only to quietly sit with them and feel his soul swell with the warmth of family and love.

He asked for second helpings and filled his plate, and he ate it slowly, savoring it all, while Margaret watched and smiled.

When his plate was clean, Adam grasped his spoon. "When do we get custard?"

"Adam, where are your manners?" Margaret scolded. "We'll have the custard later." She stood. "Give Brigitte and me a few minutes to clear the table," she said. "Why don't you men talk."

The shadows were long in the chill of a clear early evening. Matthew gestured. "Let me show you the yard." Richard followed him out the back door, to the circular bench that girdled the great oak, and they both sat.

For a long moment Matthew studied his hands on his knees, then spoke. "I sat at the head of the table because Father is gone. He was killed in the Concord battle."

He raised his eyes to Richard, who returned his steady gaze, and Matthew continued. "I was in the battle. So was Tom Sievers and Billy Weems. Friends. Billy was nearly killed—still partly crippled. We all killed British soldiers. Officers."

He paused.

"I've spent the last several months as navigator on a ship that has taken twelve British men-of-war, to get gunpowder and supplies for Washington's army. There were ten actions in which a lot of British sailors died, and some of ours."

He waited for Richard to respond, but he said nothing, and Matthew finished. "I'll continue the war against England until it's over. I thought you should know these things."

He stopped and waited.

For a long time Richard sat in the growing twilight and stared at the ground before he exhaled and his shoulders settled and he raised his eyes to Matthew's. "I didn't know about your father. I don't know what to say. I'm so sorry. So sorry." He shook his head and looked away for a moment. "I lost my parents years ago, and my home too. The army is my home, my family." He paused, trying to find a continuity to his thoughts. "I took serious wounds at Menotomy in the Concord fight, but I'm nearly recovered. When it was bad, Brigitte wrote and later sent food. She's the only person who did that, because I have no one else. She'll never know how much it meant."

He stopped for a moment to gather his thoughts. "I'll be a British soldier the rest of my life—I won't dishonor the oath I took as an officer."

He slowly rose. "My being here has been an awful burden on you. If I had known, I wouldn't have come, wouldn't have done this to you, or your mother and the children. I feel bad about it."

"Brigitte arranged this, not you."

"I know, but I should have asked, found out somehow. I've never sat at a table like today, and shared with a family like yours. And now I know it brought you all pain. I wish I had known before."

"Don't feel that way. We don't. You were welcome here, still are. In most ways it's been a blessing to us all."

For long moments Richard stared into Matthew's eyes. "Thank you," he said quietly.

In lengthening shadows Matthew led the way back to the house, and Brigitte and Margaret were waiting at the dining table in the light of half a dozen lamps.

"Take your seats for custard," Brigitte said.

Richard took his first taste and stopped and turned to Margaret. "That's the best I've ever tasted."

Margaret smiled, embarrassed, and shrugged. "Thank you. Eat your fill."

They cleared away the dishes and sat in the overstuffed chairs and on the sofa while Adam and Priscilla sat at the dining table with paper and pen, making crude drawings of animals. Adam held up his pad proudly. "Can you draw a dog?" he asked Richard.

"Not as good as that. But I can make one on the wall."

Adam's mouth dropped open. "On the wall?"

Richard gestured to a lamp and Matthew nodded, and Richard set it on the edge of the table, then knelt next to the wall. He positioned his hand, and the shadow cast on the wall was the head of a dog.

Adam and Priscilla were ecstatic. "A dog! He made a dog!"

Adam spoke, excited. "Can you make anything else?"

Again Richard shaped his hands, and the head of a rabbit appeared, with long ears that moved.

"A rabbit!" Priscilla exclaimed.

"I'll show you how," Richard said. He helped Adam shape his hands, and magically the head of the dog reappeared.

Adam nearly exploded. "I did it! A dog!" He did it again and again.

Richard helped Priscilla and the rabbit appeared, and Prissy squealed with delight.

Richard returned to his seat and watched for a moment while the children worked with their hands and began inventing their own shadow images. Then he turned and spoke to Matthew and Margaret. "With your permission I would like to talk with Brigitte for a few minutes, outside."

Seated on the oak bench in dark shadows of deep dusk, he spoke quietly. "Since I was hurt—your letters, the food—there are no words I know to tell you how they helped, lifted me. I will always be grateful."

"I'm so glad."

He took a deep breath. "Matthew told me about your father and himself and Billy Weems. I wish I had known earlier."

"You wouldn't have come, and I wanted you to come."

"I brought pain to this house."

"You brought healing."

"Seeing how you are—all of you—I don't belong here."

Impulsively she grasped his arm. "You *do!*"

He sat silently for a time, working with his thoughts, and Brigitte did not interfere. "The army is my life. I've sworn the oath of a British officer."

"I know. But the war will end sometime. It won't go on forever."

"The shooting will stop, but the differences will go on."

"They'll fade away."

He cleared his throat and moved his feet, and drew a small package from inside his coat. "Would you please accept this? It's nothing—just a little remembrance. I would like to know you have it."

Brigitte's hand flew to cover her mouth for a moment before she reached to accept it. "May I open it now?"

"If you wish."

Gently she worked the wrapping open, and in the fast-fading light she unfolded a handkerchief made of the finest linen trimmed with intricate lace. In one corner, in flawless royal blue needlepoint, were the initials "B. D." in beautiful scroll.

Brigitte held it in her hands for a moment, then laid it in her lap and tenderly touched it and smoothed it. "It's beautiful. So beautiful." Her eyes filled and she looked at him and once again she grasped his arm. "Thank you."

"It's little enough for what you've done. I'm pleased if you like it."

"It's a treasure."

He stood. "Let me take you inside."

She stood and faced him, and suddenly, impulsively, she stepped close to him and her arms circled his neck and she brushed a kiss on his cheek. He stiffened for a moment in surprise, and then he wrapped her inside his arms, and for a moment they stood in their embrace, and then he gently pulled back. "Shall we go inside?"

He took her hand and led her back to the house. Inside he looked at the mantel clock. "I was given leave until nine o'clock. I must be getting back to the base."

Matthew nodded, and Richard turned to Margaret.

"Mrs. Dunson, I don't know the words to tell you what all this has meant to me. It was the finest dinner I have ever had, and I will never forget the hours here with your family."

"It has been wonderful having you here. You must come again."

He turned to Matthew, and they shook hands warmly. "Thank you for everything."

"It was my privilege."

Finally he turned to Brigitte. "I am grateful you allowed me to come here to thank you and to meet your family. Thank you."

"Please, don't thank me. It was my pleasure."

He glanced once more at the clock. "I must be going." He opened the door and stopped to look at all of them. "It was wonderful being here. Good night."

No one spoke or moved for several seconds, and then Margaret sighed and turned towards the kitchen and Brigitte followed her.

"Mama, he gave me this." She handed her the handkerchief, and Margaret spread it in her hands.

"It's beautiful."

Before bed, they gathered and Margaret offered their evening prayer, then rose. "Off to bed, you three. School tomorrow."

Caleb grumbled, but Adam and Priscilla danced to their room and made shadow pictures on the wall until Margaret tucked them in and kissed them good night. Matthew was seated in the large overstuffed chair in deep thought when she returned to the parlor.

"Brigitte," Margaret called, and she came from her bedroom. "Sit down." She waited until Brigitte was seated, attentive, hardly breathing. "I think he's a fine boy," Margaret said. "Matthew?"

"I told him about Father, and me. He took it well. I like him."

Brigitte released her breath. "He's fine."

Matthew leaned forward. "He's fine, but that makes it worse, not better."

"How?" There was alarm in Brigitte's voice.

"He's a fine *Englishman* and he'll remain so. So would I, if I were him."

"The war will end! Things will get better," Brigitte exclaimed.

"The shooting may stop, but when will England and the colonies ever again embrace each other? In our lifetime? I doubt it."

Brigitte's eyes dropped, but she said nothing because she could think of nothing to say.

Matthew rose and touched her shoulder. "I wish with all my soul I could give this my blessing, but I can't. I love you, and I could accept Richard as my brother this minute, but that would not change the hard truth. His world and yours may never meet. You will have to follow your own heart, and know that I will support you in whatever you decide."

She reached to touch his hand on her shoulder, and she nodded her head but said nothing.

In his room, Matthew opened the closet door and drew his wallet from his inside coat pocket and removed the small folded paper. In the light of a single lamp, he unwrapped the small watch fob and laid it on his night table and stared at it for a long time, then touched it for a moment and rewrapped it.

Gone. Not coming back. Where is she tonight? How is she?

He sighed and replaced the folded paper in his wallet and pushed it back into his coat pocket, then drew out the written orders from Captain Soren Weyland and reread them carefully.

February seventeenth. The ESTHER—*down to the West Indies—nine of us. What's going to happen when we try to take munitions from a British fort? Who's going to live, and who's going to die?*

He replaced the written orders and dropped to his knees beside his bed and clasped his hands together before his bowed head.

"Almighty God, I thank thee for the bounties of my life. I humbly beseech thee to watch over and protect Mother and the children while I am gone, and to allow thy bounteous grace to guide and protect Kathleen and her family, and Richard . . ."

CHAPTER XXIV

★ ★ ★

*I*t's right there, sir, two days south of us."

Matthew leaned over a large chart on the big table in his small quarters and tapped the island of New Providence with the tips of his dividers and nearly shouted to be heard above the whistling gale that was battering the *Esther.* "And Nassau Town is right there." He carefully placed one of the points of the dividers on a small dot near the east tip of the island.

Captain Soren Weyland braced himself against the heavy pitch and roll of the small schooner and wiped with a towel at sea spray that dripped from his beard and oilskins.

"Can't see five hundred yards in this storm," he growled. "Haven't seen any of the others in our squadron since yesterday morning." He wiped at his face with the towel and scowled at the map. "I'm a China-India sailor, not familiar with these West Indies waters. We're supposed to rendezvous at Abaco Bay. Where is it?"

"There, sir—just about seventy miles due north of New Providence."

Weyland studied the large chart with the latitude markings and the depth soundings, and the West Indies islands, with the hundreds of tiny flecks scattered as if by a random and errant wind.

"Are these all islands?" He gestured with the sweep of his hand.

"Yes." Matthew worked with the points of his dividers. "Here's the North West Providence Channel—the one we take to thread our way through. It runs south through these straits between the mainland and the big island on the east, then due east towards Great Abaco Island, then angles off southeastward around this fishhook chain of islands and then curves back south to New Providence. Hardly any of these small islands have names—too many of them."

Weyland shook his head. "Are these depth markings accurate?"

"Pretty much. The whole West Indies system is just north of the equator. Just south of the equator, the south equatorial and the Canaries and the Guinea currents meet and cross the equator, and pretty much reverse themselves because of the earth's rotation on its axis, and that creates a big muddle of winds and currents that moves north into these islands and affects those depth soundings from time to time."

"Are these island locations correct?"

"The big ones, but those small islands are just mounds of sand above the surface. Beneath the surface are sandbars and coral reefs, and all of it shifts and moves when the winds and currents come up from the equator. Some small islands and reefs and sandbars on that chart are already gone, and new ones are there that are uncharted. The navigator who leads us through this had better know these waters."

Weyland wiped at his wet beard. "How do we get through them?"

"Whoever's in the crow's nest better know what to look for."

"Which is what?"

"White sand in blue water, in good weather. You can see the sandbars and reefs and islands from up there."

"What about in a storm like this?"

Matthew shook his head. "Sailing blind. The sea's the same color as the sky—gray—and you can't pick them out."

Weyland raised serious eyes to Matthew. "Can you get us into Abaco Bay?"

Matthew rounded his lips and blew air. "Yes, sir, I think I can. Two days."

Night gathers early in a sea storm and day breaks slowly. That day and the next, Matthew spent every daylight hour fifty-two feet up the violently pitching mainmast on the small circular deck of the crow's nest, dressed in his oilskins in the driving rain, lashed to the mast and the railing. His eyes seldom left his glass as he kept an unending vigil for landfall or sails. He gave hand signals to the helmsman on deck from time to time as they worked their way southward, then angled eastward, and finally due east toward Abaco Bay. At noon the second day the winds began to dwindle, and by four o'clock the first shafts of sunlight pierced the purple-gray overhead, and by five o'clock the *Esther* was riding in partial sunshine, steady on her course due east in little more than a stiff breeze.

At five-thirty Matthew's arm suddenly rose and he pointed and shouted, "Landfall! The Great Abaco Island, dead ahead. We'll be inside the bay in twenty minutes."

By dusk, visibility was three miles and they had sighted the masts and sails of two tall ships in the great bay, but they were too distant to recognize. Captain Weyland ordered anchor dropped, and the crew settled in for the night with double shifts on watch, straining to see the lights of ships, moving or at anchor. In the gray of dawn Matthew was again in the crow's nest, studying the anchored ships. While he watched, one hoisted anchor and spread canvas and swung around, taking a westward heading straight towards them in the bright early-morning sun. Matthew held his glass steady, breathing light, hoping, and suddenly he pointed and shouted down to Weyland.

"She's flying colonial colors, sir. She has to be one of ours." Fifteen minutes later he shouted, "She's the *Alfred*, sir. She's coming alongside. I think Commodore Hopkins is aboard."

Ten minutes later the *Alfred* slowed and furled her sails and stopped alongside the *Esther*, and Captain Dudley Saltonstall came to the rail with his horn.

"Hello, *Esther*. Are you sound?"

"We are sound," Weyland answered.

"The *Cabot* is anchored east of us. We have not seen the others since the storm set in. Have you seen them?"

"No. Only yourself and the *Cabot*."

Saltonstall handed the horn to Commodore Esek Hopkins. "Commodore Hopkins speaking. We three will take up positions across the mouth of the bay at regular intervals so we see everything entering or leaving, and can be seen. The *Esther* will take the west position, the *Alfred* the middle, the *Cabot* to the east. We will wait until tomorrow, four o'clock P.M., for the others and then make a plan accordingly. Confirm the order."

Weyland repeated the order, Hopkins approved it, the crews unfurled their canvas, and the ships moved to their positions at the mouth of Abaco Bay.

Shortly past noon the *Providence* hove into view and stopped alongside the *Alfred* for orders, then proceeded to take up a position halfway to the *Esther*. With the sun below the horizon, the *Columbus* came in from the west with her topsails shot golden by a sun already set and received her orders, to take up a position halfway to the *Cabot*. At dawn the *Andrew Doria* came in, the top twenty feet of her mizzenmast spliced and repaired. She stopped for her orders and dropped anchor one hundred yards from the *Alfred*. At noon the *Wasp* came in from the west riding deep in the calm waters of the bay, and Matthew and Weyland studied her sluggish movements.

"She's taking on water," Weyland said quietly. "She got hurt in the storm."

The slender schooner slowed and stopped beside the *Alfred*, while the others waited for the signals that were certain to follow, and twenty minutes later the many colored and shaped flags crept up the line fastened to the *Alfred*'s mainmast, while every eye in the squadron studied their message.

The *Wasp* needs repairs. The *Hornet* and the *Fly* have not been seen. Come to the *Alfred* immediately, and all captains, first mates, and navigators come on board. Urgent.

"Let's go," Weyland called to Riggins, and five minutes later four seamen had capstan bars in place and were winding in the anchor, while the mainsails on both the mainmast and the mizzenmast were unfurled. The bow of the *Esther* rose slightly as she knifed into the slow, glassy swells of the bay like something alive. Fifteen minutes later she spilled her sails and coasted to stop two hundred yards from the *Alfred*, while the other ships did the same. Twenty minutes later Weyland, Riggins, and Matthew were crowded into the quarters of Captain Saltonstall with eighteen other men and Commodore Esek Hopkins.

Hopkins stood and the room became silent.

"Thank you all for your presence. It is urgent I come directly to the point. The *Wasp* has a repairable crack in her hull but needs four pumps and one day to seal it. Do any of you have extra pumps?"

Six hands went up.

"Good. Captain Hallock will make arrangements to get them on board the *Wasp* immediately after I am finished."

He pursed his mouth for a moment. "The *Hornet* and the *Fly* have not been seen in nearly five days. I must presume they either sank in the storm or turned back. Either way, they are lost to us on this mission."

He paused while all the men in the room stared with flat eyes at the walls or their hands or the floor, and then raised their faces back to Hopkins.

"I had intended using the navigator on the *Fly* to lead us in, since he has been in these waters before and I thought him competent to get us to New Providence Island and then back home. So I must ask, have any of you navigators been in these waters before?"

Matthew and one other navigator raised their hands.

Hopkins looked at them both carefully. "Your name and your ship?"

The young blonde man came to attention and faced Hopkins. "Bernard Ambrose, of the *Andrew Doria*, sir."

"On how many occasions have you navigated these waters?"

"Once, sir. Three years ago. Assistant navigator."

He turned to Matthew, already at attention. "Your name?"

"Matthew Dunson, currently assigned to the *Esther.* I've navigated these waters twice before, sir. Chief navigator."

"Mr. Dunson, do you think you can lead this squadron through the West Indies to New Providence and back out?"

Matthew didn't flinch. "I think so, sir."

Hopkins faced Weyland. "Sir, may I borrow your navigator until this mission is completed?"

Weyland glanced at Matthew, then back at Hopkins. "Yes, sir, provided you return him in good repair."

Hopkins cracked a chuckle and every man in the room guffawed.

Hopkins spoke. "With the good graces of the Almighty, I intend doing that, sir." He sobered. "You who had the extra pumps, arrange with Captain Hallock now to get them onto his ship." He turned to Hallock. "Will your repairs be finished by three o'clock tomorrow afternoon?"

"I'll see to it, sir."

"Good. All of you return here tomorrow by four P.M. and we'll work out a plan and start at dawn the next morning. In the meantime, return to your positions across the bay."

As the day wore on, the seas became as glass, and long, slow swells came rolling. The sand and dirt and grit raised from the bottom by the storm settled, and the waters became clear and blue as the heavens. With the sun reaching for the clean line where ocean and sky meet, the air became heavy, steamy, oppressive. The seamen stood to their duties but with eyes that impatiently searched the western horizon for the first sign of a speck that might be the masts and sails of the missing ships, but none appeared. They volunteered for the crow's nest and sat on the platform straddling an iron post with their legs dangling while they worked the glass slowly across the horizon, then back again. Dusk settled and passed, and the black velvet dome of night closed over them, and they lighted their running lamps and continued peering to the west for lights that were not there.

Morning mess was somber, quiet, in the sweltering, oppressive air. Matthew stood at the bow with his glass, sweating, watching the crew of the *Wasp* in their tense battle with time to complete repairs. Twenty men were stripped to their drawers, taking turns diving into the clear waters, working twelve feet below the waterline to replace the cracked siding, reset the wooden pegs and eighteen-inch lag screws that bound it to the oaken ribs, and caulk every joint closed. With all her own pumps working, and six extras, the schooner began to rise in the water, and by two o'clock in the afternoon her waterline was visible. The crew cleared their makeshift diving platform from the side of the ship, pulled in all their safety lines, and scrambled barefoot and dripping onto the deck. Half an hour later Captain Hallock ran signal flags up the line.

Repairs completed. We're sound.

At four o'clock the captains, navigators, and first mates were again crowded in the quarters of Captain Saltonstall, quiet, intense, waiting. Commodore Hopkins stood with a wooden stick next to a large map he had nailed to one wall, and pointed with the stick as he spoke.

"Gentlemen, the munitions and powder we're after are located in two forts. Fort Nassau in the town and Fort Montague nearby outside town. The island of New Providence is inhabited largely by natives indigenous to the West Indies, and it is my guess they will have no stomach for a fight that concerns only British war supplies." He dropped his arm and looked at them. "I believe we can go ashore and get those supplies without firing a shot."

Dead silence gripped the room for a moment, and then buzzing broke out.

He raised his hands and the room quieted. "Here's the plan."

For more than an hour they listened, asked questions, gave, took, argued, and slowly hammered out the shape of their mission. At five-thirty P.M. Hopkins laid his stick on the table.

"Are we agreed? Do you all know your duty?"

They did.

"Good. At five o'clock A.M. this ship will leave. You all know your position in the column, and your interval." He turned to Matthew. "Will you get from the *Esther* whatever you consider necessary to your duties and return and remain on this ship until the mission is complete?" He turned to Weyland. "My navigator has agreed to replace Mr. Dunson on your ship, sir, if that is agreeable. Mr. David Pulliam."

Weyland nodded.

In deep dusk Matthew answered the knock on the door of his new quarters aboard the *Alfred.*

The man facing him was of average height, thin lipped, long, aquiline nose, penetrating, piercing eyes, dressed in navy uniform, epaulets of a lieutenant, older than Matthew. "Did you request to see Commodore Hopkins?"

"Yes."

"Come with me."

The man rapped on Hopkins's door and opened it on command, and Matthew followed him inside.

Commodore Hopkins rose. "You wanted to see me?"

Matthew squared his shoulders. "Yes, sir. With your permission I would like to volunteer to go ashore with the landing party tomorrow when we reach New Providence."

Hopkins's eyebrows arched and he studied Matthew for a moment. "What's your reason?"

"Personal, sir."

"There could be fighting."

"I know that, sir."

"Have you ever engaged in land combat?"

"I was at Concord."

Hopkins settled back onto his chair. "If I lost you, who would get us out of these islands?"

"Getting back won't be too difficult, sir. I can show someone what to watch for going in, and they can retrace our route."

"What happened at Concord?"

Matthew considered for a moment. "I lost my father."

Hopkins's eyes dropped. "I'm sorry."

"It isn't just that, sir."

"Then what?"

"Things are happening—I just have a feeling I should be going ashore to help get those munitions."

Hopkins eased back in his chair and interlaced his fingers on the table. His eyes locked with Matthew's and bored in. "Tell me about that feeling."

"I can't, sir. It's just something—there's something more happening than just breaking away from England. I sense it, but I don't care to try to explain it to someone else."

Hopkins leaned forward in the yellow light of the lamps. His eyes were like glowing embers, and he spoke softly. "Like the Almighty is moving to free this land? Like he has a plan far beyond ours?"

Matthew felt the hair on his neck stand up and the flesh on his arms crawl. He swallowed. "Yes, sir. That's what I mean."

"Permission granted." Hopkins stood and gestured to the lieutenant. "I'm not sure you've met Captain Saltonstall's first lieutenant."

"No, sir."

"Mr. Dunson, this is Lieutenant Jones. John Paul Jones. He's not familiar with these islands. Could you acquaint him with your charts and the route?"

Matthew grasped the strong, wiry hand. "I'm pleased to meet you, Lieutenant."

"It is my pleasure, sir," Jones replied. From his look and his crisp, assured manner, Matthew sensed in Jones decisiveness and self-confidence.

"If you have some time, I'll show you the charts—the North West Providence Channel."

"I'm at your command."

Matthew turned back to Hopkins. "Sir, thank you."

"No thanks necessary, Mr. Dunson. Be careful tomorrow."

Matthew led Jones back to his quarters and spread the West Indies chart out on the large table.

"We are here. We move south to the mouth of this channel, then bring her to port, nearly southwest through the narrows—here." He traced the route with his finger. "The Great Abaco Island is here, to the east, and on the south tip is the town of Cornwall, with a lighthouse. On the west is this fishhook formation of islands. We go between Abaco Island and these islands, due south, to New Providence. Nassau Town is right here, on the east end, with a small harbor. West of New Providence is Andros Island, with Nicolls Town on the north tip with a lighthouse. To the east is a string of scattered islands, some charted, some not, with Eleuthera Island and Governor's Harbor behind them, farther east."

In his fierce concentration, Jones had not moved. He raised his eyes to Matthew. "Where are the dangers?"

"Two things. First, missing a lighthouse. Remember, there's one at Nicolls Town to the west, one at Cornwall on the east. Keep them at the distances shown on this chart and you're in the channel. It gets narrow. Second, there will be small islands and sandbars scattered throughout, some charted, some not, some pushed up by this last storm. We can see them from the crow's nest if the weather's good."

"We ride the crow's nest?"

"We do."

Silently Jones placed his finger on the chart and worked it down through the channel, memorizing the lighthouse locations, the islands, the depth soundings. His lips moved soundlessly as he committed names, distances, directions to memory. He retraced the route once more, then raised his head.

"Very good. I have it."

"We'll go over it again in the morning."

Jones nodded. "I couldn't help overhearing your conversation with Commodore Hopkins. You feel this war has meaning beyond breaking from England?"

Matthew caught the slight Scottish accent. "Yes, I do."

"Deity has an interest in all this?"

"I believe the Almighty does."

A smile flashed on Jones's face. "I'll gain comfort from that when we try to take munitions from two British forts at the same time." He walked to the door. "Thank you for your help."

"Not at all."

For a moment Jones hesitated, groping. "I . . . I'm sorry about your father. Truly."

"Thank you. It's past."

"You . . . uh . . . losing him hasn't made you bitter about this war?"

"No. I think he expected he would not come back from the Concord fight."

"You have family?"

"Mother, two sisters, two brothers."

"Now without a father?"

"Yes. They're fine. You? A family, I mean."

"Three sisters. My brother and my parents are gone now. After age thirteen I saw little of my family. That's when I was apprenticed to a ship owner and went to sea—from Whitehaven, not far from my native Scotland." He stopped and drew and released a great breath. "I didn't intend digging into your personal affairs. I hope I didn't offend."

"Not at all."

"See you in the morning."

Matthew stared at the door for several seconds after it closed, then sat down at the chart table. For long minutes he stared unseeing at the spread of parchment while his thoughts reached back to the blasting sounds of the muskets at Concord, and the sick disbelief when he saw John in his bed and knew he was dying. He straightened and pushed the thoughts away, then drew his wallet from his coat and opened the tiny wrap of paper and for a moment studied the delicate lettering on the royal blue watch fob.

The sea was glassy smooth at four o'clock A.M. when they finished the morning mess, and twenty minutes later the northeasterly trade winds began to riffle the shining surface, hot and steamy.

"Hoist anchor," Captain Saltonstall ordered, and the anchor chain rattled as four seamen leaned into the capstan bars and began the rotation.

"Mainsails," he called, and barefooted seamen scaled the rope ladders like cats and jerked the knots holding the sails lashed to the yards, and they dropped. Able hands tied off the sails at the bottom, and they popped and billowed full, and the two masts creaked as the ship sliced through the crystal-clear blue waters.

Matthew led Jones up the rope ladder to the crow's nest near the top of the mainmast, and they lashed themselves to the swaying mast and the railing. They wore only their trousers and shirts in the muggy air. Fifty feet below, the seamen were miniature, and the ship left a long white wake as she cut through the sparkling waters. Both men breathed deep and for a moment felt the singular rise of joy at the feel of a tall ship with her mainsails filled, surging through good waters like a thing strong and separate and alive.

The ship entered the narrow channel, and both men raised their glass to peer north into her wake, and the *Esther* was there, one-half mile back, and one-half mile behind her, the *Providence*. The others were to follow at half-mile intervals to avoid raising fears among the islanders of an armada come to invade.

Matthew called down, "Furl the mizzen mainsail—dangerous water coming—we're moving too fast."

Seamen standing with bare feet curled around rope strung to the mizzenmast spilled the mainsail and lashed it to the yard, and stood waiting their next command.

The fishhook string of islands came into view to the west, and Matthew pointed and Jones nodded, and minutes later Matthew pointed to Great Abaco Island to the east. Suddenly he stiffened and raised his arm, and Jones followed his point. Half a mile ahead, port side, the waters were slightly lighter blue than those surrounding. Matthew called down to the helmsman, "Ten degrees starboard," and the ship instantly responded while Jones asked, "You saw something?"

"The water color is wrong—sandbar." Matthew waited thirty seconds, then called down again. "Now ten degrees port and hold her steady as she goes."

At two hundred yards the submerged sandbar defined itself and Jones licked his lips. "Was that one charted?"

"No. There'll be others. Keep a sharp eye."

Jones smiled with his newfound wisdom and leaned against the railing, eager for the life-and-death challenge of avoiding the hidden traps before they ripped the bottom out of the ship. Time passed, and suddenly Jones pointed eastward, and Matthew nodded. "Cornwall lighthouse?" Jones asked.

Matthew nodded and called down to the helmsman, "Take her due south by the compass," and the bow swung hard to starboard. Instantly Matthew tensed and again shouted, "Correct twenty degrees to port and steady as she goes."

Jones looked at him in surprise. "I missed something?"

"There," Matthew pointed. "Another sandbar or a reef. Must have moved from the fishhook islands during the storm."

Jones strained for several seconds. "I can't see the color change."

"The sun's wrong. But can you see how the water riffles over there? Calm around it, but small riffles?"

"That's not a school of fish?"

"Schools of fish move. That isn't moving."

A minute passed before Matthew called down once more, "Correct to due south by the compass and steady as she goes," and they studied the long, submerged sandbar as it slipped past, one hundred yards to starboard.

Jones looked at him but said nothing, and the small ship continued her course, working south to where the channel widened. Jones pointed west at Andros Island in the distance, with the lighthouse at Nicolls Town, and Matthew fixed his glass dead ahead at the horizon over the bowsprit. Five minutes later he pointed, and Jones glassed the distance.

"There it is," Matthew said quietly. "New Providence. We're

leaving the channel, and the waters become shallow fast, so watch sharp."

With the sun at its zenith they closed on the island, sweat dripping in the torrid, steamy heat, and twice more Matthew had to call course changes to the helmsman. Three miles from the island they veered southeast and swung in a slow arc to come in on the east tip of the landfall. At five hundred yards they furled all sails and dropped anchor. Less than one hour later all seven ships lay at anchor in a line offshore, and every officer stood at the bow of his ship, glassing the coast for anything that moved.

There was nothing.

Hopkins turned to Jones. "Hoist the signals. Get this operation under way."

"Aye, sir," Jones spat and turned on his heel. His orders were perfunctory, clear, and the seamen executed them instantly, without question. Matthew watched while the ships' crews put twenty longboats in the water, and two hundred marines under command of Captain Samuel Nicholas scrambled down nets into the boats and turned their faces upward to receive the muskets and ammunition and bayonets lowered in nets. They were followed by fifty seamen, Matthew among them, under the command of Lieutenant Thomas Weaver. The *Providence* and the *Wasp* swung their bows northward until they were broadside to the island, and on the signal of Commodore Hopkins aboard the *Alfred*, the men on the longboats put their backs into the oars and started for shore under the muzzles of the cannon.

They had one hundred yards yet to go when they heard the first far distant *whump* of cannon, and every head came up, probing the shoreline for a moment before they dug their oars back into the water.

Matthew stiffened. *Too far—not shooting at us.*

"Pull," shouted the officers in the boats. "We're not going to get caught in the water!"

The instant the bows of the boats hit the sand the crews were in the warm waters, dragging the boats above the high-tide line on the white, sandy beach, and then they grabbed their muskets and jerked out the ramrods and reached for their powder horns, while the officers watched the heavy foliage and the palm trees for any movement.

They waited behind their beached boats with their muskets at the ready, sweat running in the sweltering sun while their eyes probed, and minutes turned into a quarter of an hour, and still nothing moved. Captain Nicholas stood to give orders, but before he could speak, the sound of far-off cannon once again reached them. Nicholas crouched behind his boat, and again they waited while long minutes slowly ticked by.

Finally Nicholas stood. "Come on, men, follow me." He took two bold steps towards the green line of foliage and stopped in his tracks, staring.

A large native in full military dress of unknown nationality, but barefooted, had suddenly appeared as if by magic in the trees, and when Nicholas stopped, the man walked out onto the sandy beach and strode directly toward him, shoulders back, head up, indignant. Two smaller men in tattered canvas trousers and ragged cotton shirts followed him.

While the man was yet twenty yards distant, Nicholas shouted, "Do you speak English, sir?"

"I do." The British accent was unmistakable. "I have come to demand an explanation for this."

"What government do you represent, sir?"

"The people of this island."

"Your name?"

"My English name is Nathaniel. Your name, sir, and your country?"

"Captain Samuel Nicholas, the colonies of America."

The native frowned. "For what reason are you here?"

"For the British munitions at Fort Montague and Fort Nassau."

"What of the British munitions?"

"We will take possession of all the warlike stores on the island belonging to the Crown, but we have no desire to touch the property or the person of any of the inhabitants."

For a full minute the native studied the two hundred fifty armed men, and then the ships standing offshore, and then he spoke. "If you speak the truth, we will not resist you."

"You have fired cannon at us."

"No. We fired alarm shots to warn all on the island that you are here."

Matthew felt the tension rise.

Nicholas pursed his mouth for a moment in thought. "I thank you for your message. We will continue our march."

The native turned and within seconds had disappeared with his two companions in the dense green growth.

Nicholas signalled the other officers to come. "That man could be a decoy for an ambush." He paced nervously. "We haven't got time to find out. If there are British ships in these waters, our squadron may have to make a run for it, and if they do I aim to have you men on board. We're going ahead with the plan."

"Sir," Matthew said, and waited.

"What is it?"

"If there's an ambush it will be in the trees. What if we send ten or twenty men in there to spring the trap if there is one, and the rest of them travel on the beach? Nassau Town's right on the coast, about four miles west. I've been there."

Nicholas paused. "Might work."

"I volunteer," Matthew said, and countless other voices instantly joined him.

Nicholas quickly called out fifteen men and turned back to Matthew. "You've been to Nassau Town?"

"Yes, sir."

"Then you take command of this detail and move fast. We'll give you five minutes before we start up the beach. At the first sound of your fire, we come in after you."

"Yes, sir."

"Good luck."

Matthew turned to the volunteers. "Single file, and keep up the pace," he said. He led them trotting off the white sandy beach into the thick growth on the narrow footpath taken by the native and his two men, and he settled into the peculiar swinging gait he had learned from Tom and his father. He counted two hundred paces and stopped to listen; there was no sound other than the birds and the whisper of the trade winds in the trees. He counted two hundred more paces, stopped, continued, and repeated it again and again for three miles. Then he slowed and suddenly dropped to a crouch and stopped, and his men crowded around, breathing hard, sweating. He pointed through a break in the trees. "Fort Montague."

The square, ancient, crumbling structure with thick stone walls stood alone, cannon on the walls facing three directions. The Union Jack drooped in the heat from a flagpole on the west tower. Matthew studied the walls for half a minute; nothing moved.

He gave a hand signal and turned directly north and picked his way through the growth to the edge of the sandy beach, and his detail paused at the tree line to wait and watch and listen. The only sound was the birds and the wind and light surf. Matthew rose and walked boldly onto the beach, not stopping until he reached the water. There was no sign in the sand that two hundred thirty-five men had marched past, and Matthew looked east, searching, but there was nothing. He led his men back to the tree line and they hunkered down, eyes east, probing, wondering.

"There!" One of the seamen stood and pointed, excited.

Nicholas was leading, the marines and seamen following in rank and file. Nicholas waved lustily, and Matthew held his men in the trees until Nicholas arrived.

"Report," Nicholas said.

"No ambush, sir. Fort Montague is due west about five hundred yards. We saw nothing moving."

"Good work." Nicholas shaded his eyes to look at the westering sun, then pulled out his pocket watch. "We might get this finished before nightfall." He called the officers around him. "You know the plan. Break into your groups now and follow me. I'll position you, and then call to them and hope they parley."

They divided into fifteen groups of fifteen men, and the assigned officers took command. Nicholas led them into the heavy growth and moved west until they were within one hundred yards of Fort Montague, not visible in the trees and underbrush. He gave silent hand signals and the first group stopped. Nicholas turned due south and the remaining groups followed, and he paced off five long paces and signaled to the second group. They stopped, and the others followed as he continued west, dropping off a group every ten paces until the groups were in a straight line facing the east wall of the old fort.

Nicholas remained in the trees long enough to study the structure and the one hundred yards of fairly open ground that lay between the fort and his men, and then he took a great breath and exhaled it and stepped out into the open. "Hello, Fort Montague," he bellowed.

Three cannon on the top of the wall blasted, and the balls whistled harmlessly thirty feet over the heads of Nicholas's line and tore into the trees.

Nicholas instantly shouted, "Fire!" and two hundred and twenty-five muskets cracked. The .60-caliber lead balls knocked moss and stone chips from the top of the wall and left a dense cloud of white smoke hanging in a line one hundred yards long in the trees.

A head cautiously appeared above the wall, saw the long cloud of gun smoke, and then instantly disappeared.

"Reload!" Nicholas bawled.

A white flag tied to a musket bayonet was thrust above the wall and waved back and forth.

"Are you surrendering?" Nicholas called.

"Parley," a high-pitched voice answered.

"We will parley with you here," Nicholas shouted.

Five minutes later a heavy gate in the wall of the fort opened, and three natives in full uniform walked out under a white flag.

"Over here," Nicholas ordered, and they came. "You want to parley," he said sternly. "Make your statement."

"Sir, what is your purpose in being here?"

"We stated our purpose to the officer you sent to meet us. He said you would not resist, but you fired cannon at us."

"We did not fire at you. We fired over your heads to warn you to stop."

"We were stopped before you fired. I stood in the open and challenged you. You did not answer me. You fired."

The officer swallowed. "We did not mean to alarm you."

"You fired cannon and did not mean to alarm us? That is foolish."

The officer shook his head, unable to make a competent answer. "What is your purpose in coming to this place?"

"We are here to confiscate all British materials to do with war, and nothing more. We have no wish to engage you or anyone in the fort."

"You have not come to take the fort?"

"No. But we will have the British munitions."

Matthew was a scant twenty yards away, musket at the ready, eyes scanning the top of the wall as he listened intently. When Nicholas made his blunt demand, Matthew brought his eyes down, his thoughts racing. *We want your munitions—will you fight for them or not? How many soldiers do you have inside those walls? two hundred? five hundred? How many do you think we have? It all comes down to the next ten seconds.* He breathed light, waiting.

The native officer looked up and down the tree line where the smoke was vanishing. "How many soldiers have you brought?"

"Enough."

"We have five hundred in the fort."

Nicholas shrugged. "I thought seven hundred."

Matthew held his breath at the bold lie.

The native officer wiped at the perspiration on his face. "Give us half an hour."

"For what?"

"We will move the garrison to the fort in Nassau."

"We are going to take the munitions from that fort, too."

Matthew watched the eyes of the officer. They were flat, resigned, beaten.

"I will tell them."

He's afraid. He won't fight.

"You will leave your two men with us until we see you move the garrison. If you do not keep your word we will hang them here and take your fort by force."

"You do not trust my word?"

"You sent an officer to meet us. He said you would not resist. You fired cannon. I will keep your two officers until you move the garrison."

"How do I know you will release my men?"

"You don't. Make your choice."

For long, tense moments the officer stood expressionless before he turned to his two men. "You will remain here until they release you, and then come to the fort in Nassau."

One-half hour later the heavy front gates of the fort yawed open, and half a dozen officers led the garrison out in rank and file, turned them east, and marched them to the village of Nassau, with the fort and the governor's mansion near the center. Nicholas and his men counted them—two hundred—and they all grinned at the remembrance of the numbers bluff Nicholas had run at the parley.

Nicholas turned to Matthew. "Mr. Dunson, take your detail of men inside the fort and be certain of two things. First, that it is deserted. Second, that the munitions are secure and there is no timing device to explode them later."

"Yes, sir. May I make a request, sir?"

"What is it?"

"May I also take the two native officers with us? It would be interesting to see if they will open the door to the powder magazine."

A wry grin crossed Nicholas's face. "Granted. Move."

Matthew motioned the two native officers ahead of him and gave hand signals to his men, and they followed him running through the heavy gates into the compound, muskets and bayonets at the ready, eyes darting everywhere. A dog barked and slunk beneath an old toolshed, but there was no other sound or movement. Quickly Matthew scanned the buildings and pointed to one built of thick, aging stone and crumbling mortar, with a heavy lock in the hasp and a flaking, decaying sign, "MAGAZINE— KEEP OUT."

He stopped his detail and spoke to the two native officers. "You two will open the door to the powder magazine. Do it now."

Their eyes grew large, and they looked at each other in terror. One spoke. "The door is locked. I have no key."

"I'll take the lock off."

"I will not open the door."

"Is the powder magazine mined?"

"I do not know. I have been with you while the garrison prepared to leave. It is not possible to know the minds of the men as they prepared to abandon the fort."

"Do you trust your commanding officer?"

"In daily matters, yes. In such matters as mining the powder magazine, I have not had such experience to judge."

Matthew turned to the other officer. "You open the door."

The officer shook his head violently but said nothing.

Matthew looked at his men and paced for a moment in thought. "I'll open the door. Take these men and find cover. If the magazine blows, shoot them and report to Nicholas. Move."

A dozen voices rose in protest. "I'll open it, sir."

Matthew shook his head and pointed, and the men reluctantly seized the two native officers and moved rapidly behind the main blockhouse. Matthew waited until they were out of harm's way and then turned to the heavy door. He jammed his bayonet behind the hasp and threw his weight back, and the screws loosened in the heavy oaken doorjamb. He jerked once more and the hasp ripped out. Matthew lifted the latch and put his shoulder against the thick door and pushed, and it slowly swung open. He held his breath as he carefully walked into the gloom of the unlighted room, waiting for the explosion that would blow the building and half the compound to oblivion.

There was no sound, and he waited until his eyes adjusted. Then he stood straight and cautiously looked for anything that would detonate the powder, and there was nothing. He walked back to the door, into the sunlight, and motioned to his men, who cheered and came charging.

"Take a count and don't miss anything that might be left behind to set it off."

Ten minutes later he led them at a run back through the compound, out the front gate, to Nicholas. The captain exhaled air when he saw them burst through the gate, and the entire command broke into nervous, relieved exclamations.

"Report," Nicholas ordered.

"Sir, the compound is deserted. The powder magazine is intact and not mined. There is less powder than we expected, but more cannon and muskets and rounds of shot."

A spontaneous cheer erupted.

Nicholas turned to Lieutenant Weaver. "Take five men and go back to report to Commodore Hopkins, and promptly bring me his orders."

An hour later Weaver and his men returned to Captain Nicholas with Hopkins's written orders.

After quickly reading them, Nicholas faced one of his groups of men. "Group one, remain in the fort by the powder magazine. Load half a dozen of their cannon with grapeshot and arrange them near the powder magazine to cover each wall, with two on the gate. If anyone besides us tries to enter, fire. Use your muskets if necessary."

He turned to the others. "The rest of you, come with me. We're going on to Nassau before dark. By thunder, we'll have this business finished tonight!"

Within fifteen minutes the column was on the outskirts of Nassau, marching rapidly through streets nearly deserted. They approached the fort and Nicholas ignored it, and marched his men to the great red brick building near the center of the town, nestled on a five-acre estate surrounded by a white wrought-iron fence and graced with endless flower beds set in grass and sculpted trees. He stopped his men and ordered them into a square, facing all directions, with muskets at the ready. Then he proceeded up the red brick walkway towards the wide stairway that led to the twelve-foot white double doors covered by the portico and its six white columns.

Six natives in uniform gathered beneath the portico and advanced down the ten steps to meet him, faces stern, eyes narrowed, and their leader stepped forward. He was over six feet tall, thick in the chest, proud, defiant. "You approach the governor's mansion with arms. Do you intend forcing a battle?" His speech was flawless British.

"No," Nicholas answered loudly, "we do not. We intend taking all the warlike materials we find at the fort, and nothing more. We understand that is British property and not property of your people. We will harm no one or their property, if you do not resist."

"Under what guarantee?"

"A signed manifesto from my commander, if you demand such."

"Do you have it?"

"He is drafting one."

"It will be a piece of paper—meaningless if you do not intend to abide by it."

"You will have my word. I have kept my word to you thus far."

"Where are the two officers you refused to release?"

"They are here, safe. I will release them upon your written request."

The man's fierce expression did not change. "You will wait here." He turned on his heel and disappeared through the great white doors. Minutes stretched to a quarter of an hour, and Nicholas began to pace, nervous, impatient. He jerked around at the sound of the big doors opening, and the native officer strode to face him.

"You will deliver your commander's manifesto to me today for the consideration of the governor. He will have an answer for you by eight o'clock in the morning. You and your men will be here to receive it." He paused to thrust a scroll of paper to Nicholas. "This is the written demand of the governor to release our two officers immediately."

Nicholas unrolled the scroll and read the bold writing and the scrawled, illegible signature at the bottom. He considered for a moment, then turned to Weaver. "Release the two officers."

The two native officers marched stiff-legged up the stairs and turned to watch.

Nicholas spoke. "I will return to this place at eight o'clock this evening to deliver the manifesto you have requested. You will be here."

He watched the native officer bristle at the direct order, but Nicholas did not flinch or recant. "And while we are engaged in these negotiations you will be responsible for the safety of myself and my men."

The big uniformed native started to step forward, eyes flashing, and his hand locked onto his sword handle. Fifty muskets clicked onto full cock. The officer caught himself and settled and breathed heavily for a moment as he retained control. "I will be waiting."

Nicholas turned and gave orders and did not look back as he marched his men back to the edge of town into a grassy meadow.

"Lieutenant Weaver, did Commodore Hopkins say exactly when he would send a messenger with his manifesto?"

"Only that it would be soon, sir."

Nicholas nodded. "Have the men position themselves in a defensive circle while we wait."

Fifty minutes later three men arrived with the commodore's manifesto. Nicholas read over the document, then nodded his head. "That should do the job."

At eight o'clock Nicholas stopped his men before the governor's mansion and the big officer appeared on the steps. Nicholas marched forward and the officer raised his arm to stop him.

"You will give the document to my aide," he said.

A man rapidly descended the stairs, Nicholas handed him the tied scroll, and the man hastened to deliver it. The officer gave Nicholas the look of a superior to a subordinate, turned, and disappeared inside the doors. It took Nicholas ten minutes to realize he had been dismissed without a word. He stepped back to his men and gave orders.

"We will spend the night at Fort Montague."

They found food and bunks waiting, and kept a double guard on the walls throughout the night. In the early morning a cool easterly wind arose, and the temperature dropped to seventy degrees. They took morning mess at six-thirty, and at seven-fifteen Nicholas marched his men back to the governor's mansion. At eight o'clock the big native officer once again opened the doors, followed by his aide. The officer gave a hand gesture, and the aide descended the stairs and handed Nicholas a large envelope, then rapidly returned to the safety of the portico.

Nicholas broke the seal of the envelope, drew out a signed document, and read it carefully. He again opened the envelope and drew out a great brass key.

His shoulders dropped as the unbearable tension began to drain, and he rounded his lips and blew air before he raised his face to the big officer. "My compliments, sir. Tell your governor that we are deeply grateful for his hospitality and we will do nothing to breach his trust. We will be about our business immediately and leave the moment we are finished. If your governor has any complaints I will be happy to receive them, and I will offer redress for any wrongs. Tell him."

The big officer bowed stiffly, turned, and disappeared again.

Nicholas walked back to his men and held up the key. "He has turned the fort over to us."

Mouths dropped open and a rush of talk burst.

"Attention," Nicholas ordered. "Fall into our marching order. We're leaving for the fort now."

Ten minutes later Nicholas inserted the key in the great brass lock and turned it, and two men threw their shoulders into the heavy gates and they creaked open. The compound was deserted, as promised. Nicholas marched directly to the stone powder magazine and swung the doors open and stopped in his tracks. The large square room was jammed to the walls with munitions and supplies.

"Mr. Dunson," he bellowed, "take your detail of fifteen men back to the ships and tell them to come here as fast as they can and drop anchor in the bay, as close to shore as the tides will allow. Tell Captain Biddle of the *Andrew Doria* he's to circle this island once a day watching for British ships, and we will load him last before we leave."

"Yes, sir. May I ask a question, sir?

"What is it?"

"What did Commodore Hopkins say in that manifesto that persuaded the governor to turn the town over to us without a shot?"

Nicholas shrugged. "Nothing I can think of. I do remember his mentioning our fifteen men-of-war that we have coming one day behind us with seven hundred fifty cannon and three thousand marines. He suggested we would signal them to go back if the governor cooperated."

For fourteen days the longboats and men of the tiny American force sweated from gray dawn until dark, transferring cannon, mortas, shells, and other supplies from Fort Montague and Fort Nassau until the holds of the seven small ships were jammed to the hatches, and the last twenty cannons were lashed to the railings on deck. Unfortunately most of the gunpowder had recently been removed from the island so that the colonials could not get hold of it. Only twenty-four barrels remained. Nevertheless, the load of munitions and supplies was abundant, so much so that some of the seamen yielded their bunks and volunteered to cast their small straw-filled mattresses over some of the supplies and sleep on them during the voyage home.

By five-thirty in the morning of the fifteenth day the seven small vessels were hoisting anchors and unfurling sails. They rode deep in the water under a clear sky, in temperatures barely past seventy with a southeasterly breeze filling their sails, and talk was light and easy as every man went about his duties with the solid knowledge in their hearts of what they had done together.

Matthew and John Paul Jones sat in the crow's nest of the *Alfred* and led the column of ships back through the tricky island passage, past Abaco Bay, northwest. With the topsails shot through with a sun nearly set, Jones pointed. "Landfall."

Matthew smiled. "The mainland." He called down to the helmsman, "Starboard, two degrees east of due north, and hold her steady as she goes. Unfurl all sails. We're clear all the way home."

Eager hands added canvas, including the spankers, and the ships leaped, their bows cutting an eight-foot curl, with a white wake two hundred yards long behind their sterns. Matthew and Jones descended from the crow's nest for mess, and afterwards Matthew walked back to the mainmast and started back up to the crow's nest.

"Something wrong?" Jones asked.

"No. Just quiet up there. Peaceful. I won't be long."

He sat in the crow's nest with his back to the mainmast, legs dangling, the cool evening wind moving his long hair and the loose sleeves of his shirt. Dusk turned to black, and he studied the clear heavens, with her endless expanse of eternal stars, and the three-quarter moon rising in the east. He looked downward at the running lights and at the white, nearly phosphorescent wake of the *Alfred* fading two hundred yards behind. He squinted south and could see the fleck of light that would be the running lights of the *Esther,* and could make out her sails, half a mile behind, and knew the *Providence* would be behind her, and the other four.

Seven tiny ships—outbluffed the governor of New Providence—took two forts—never fired a shot in anger—jammed to the hatches with British munitions—impossible—impossible.

His thoughts came rolling, and he let them come on their own terms.

I wonder where Father is tonight. Was he right about all this? Is there a deeper plan than we know? Did we take those forts alone? Seven tiny ships? Two forts? The whole island of New Providence? Seven small ships didn't do that— couldn't do that.

Is Mother all right? She's all right—she knows. Brigitte? Who knows? Kathleen? England? Is that part of the plan? No, it can't be—she doesn't belong there—it's wrong—He doesn't do things wrong—how will He work it out? What is my part? What do I do? I don't know—it comes in bits and pieces— never know when—it just comes—I have to believe—wait and believe—do what I can when the moment arrives—trust—maybe that's my part—trust Him—is that faith? Is that what He expects?

Shortly past ten o'clock, with the moon casting a million diamonds on the clear Atlantic waters, Matthew descended the mainmast and made his way towards his quarters, and was startled by a voice from the shadows.

"Could I talk with you a minute?" He recognized the sure voice of John Paul Jones.

Matthew waited, and Jones spoke quietly. "The men told me about you volunteering to walk into any ambush, and about opening the powder magazine at Fort Montague."

Matthew said nothing, and there was an awkward time while Jones ordered his thoughts and came to the point. "Do you feel the Almighty was with us?"

Matthew drew a breath and released it. "Seven small vessels taking the island of New Providence and two forts without firing a shot in anger? Do you think he wasn't?"

Jones's voice was nearly inaudible. "I didn't hear a voice—saw no angel—felt nothing I haven't felt before."

Matthew realized the self-assured, confident Jones was laying bare some of his most personal, innermost thoughts, or fears, grasping, groping for an answer he had to have.

Matthew reached into his own soul. "Neither did I."

He saw Jones stiffen in the moonlight. "Then how can you say . . ." He did not finish his sentence, because he didn't have to.

Thirty seconds passed with only the quiet hiss of the bow cutting the water and the wind in the canvas.

"If you had been in command," Matthew said, "would you have tried to take two British forts on that island with seven converted merchant ships and two hundred fifty men?"

Jones lowered his face in deep thought but remained silent.

"Concord. We beat the mightiest army on earth."

Jones raised his face, eyes wide in the gloom.

"Bunker Hill."

Matthew waited, but Jones remained silent.

"Tell me from your heart we did all that alone."

A full minute passed as the two men stared at each other in the silvery moonlight, lost in something that held them, and then Jones spoke barely above a whisper. "Is that how He works?"

Slowly Matthew nodded. "I believe that's how He works, most of the time."

Silence held for a time, and finally Jones moved and the mood left as he once again assumed his sure, certain stance. He smiled and spoke. "General Washington will be pleased with the munitions."

The matter was closed between them, and Matthew could not gauge what impression it had made on Jones.

"He should be. With a little help, these men did a remarkable thing."

"See you in the morning."

Notes

The novel's depiction of the New Providence expedition is based on real events that took place in early 1776. A tiny fleet of ships, under the command of Commodore Esek Hopkins, did sail to the island of New Providence in the Bahamas and successfully acquire British munitions stored there in Fort Montague and Fort Nassau. Though the novel preserves the general tenor of these events, for the purposes of the story certain details have been altered or left out and some fictional elements have been added. The names of the vessels—the *Alfred*, the *Andrew Doria*, the *Wasp*, etc.—and the names of the commanders and other officers, such as Lieutenant John Paul Jones, are historically accurate. (See Knox, *A History of the United States Navy*, pp. 10–12; Miller, *Sea of Glory*, pp. 92–99, 107–12.)

In order to include Matthew Dunson as a participant in this dramatic incident of the Revolutionary War, the author has added to the small fleet of historical ships the fictional ship *Esther*, commanded by the fictional Captain Soren Weyland.

March 1776

CHAPTER XXV

★ ★ ★

*T*he front door slammed open, and Caleb burst into the parlor sweating, breathing hard from his run. "They're leaving! Leaving!"

Margaret turned from the stove in the kitchen and ran to him. "Who? What are you—"

"The British! All of them! Leaving town!"

"What on earth are—"

"Listen! You can hear the horses and the cannon in the streets! They're marching north! Daniel Knight's out getting the story for his newspaper right now!"

Margaret glanced at the mantel clock—nearly nine A.M., Saturday, March 17, 1776—and rushed past him. Caleb followed her out the front door and into the street, where people had dropped everything to walk unbelieving into the blustery March winds and to stand in the street and stare towards the unmistakable rumble of many men and horses and heavy cannon moving. Women wiped their hands in their aprons, and men abandoned their Saturday work to trot to the nearest corner to see the troop movement blocks away.

"Who said they're leaving?"

"Daniel Knight! He asked."

"Leaving Boston? Abandoning their military base?"

"Yes! Just leaving it behind."

"They're not coming back?"

"No. They're going north to stay."

Margaret cast her eyes to the sky. "Praise the Almighty!" She sobered with her thoughts and turned back to Caleb. "You better run up to the bakery and tell Brigitte. She'll want to know about Richard. And then get back to the print shop. Daniel will need you."

Caleb vaulted the fence and was gone. Adam and Priscilla walked out of the house.

"What's happening?" Adam asked, forehead drawn into a frown.

"Caleb said the British are leaving Boston. Can you hear?"

Adam cocked an ear. "Richard too?"

"Probably."

"Does that mean Matthew can come home?"

"Not right away. The war's not over. They're just moving north."

"When will Matthew and Richard come back?"

"Matthew soon. Richard, maybe a long time."

Prissy sighed and said nothing.

Caleb slowed as he came to the bakery, where Calvin and Bess stood in the street, hands and aprons white with flour, and Brigitte beside them, wiping her hands on a towel, eyes narrowed in question.

"Caleb! What are you doing here? What's happening? Why is everybody—"

"The British are leaving town. Daniel Knight said."

Brigitte stopped working her hands. "What?"

"Going north. Leaving."

"Richard! All of them?"

"Men, horses, cannon—everybody. Hear them?"

"Did you go look? Did you see Richard?"

"No, I ran home to tell Mama and she sent me here."

Without a word, Brigitte sprinted across the street, slowed at the corner, and ran the four blocks to the cobblestone street where the British column moved, soldiers in full uniform, muskets slung, marching to the cadence of fife and drum. The column filled the street and extended both directions as far as Brigitte could see. She moved as close to the cobblestones as she dared and peered into the faces of the oncoming troops, frantically searching. Minutes passed into half an hour, but she recognized no one in the passing parade of unknown faces, and she waited for the next officers, those in charge of cannon, to approach.

"Captain Richard Buchanan," she called, "have you seen him?"

The officer gave her the slightest shake of his head as he passed, and continued. She waited, and again called out, and again the officer shook his head and moved on without a word. An hour slipped by before the infantry and cavalry and cannon were past, and the endless wagons bearing supplies came on, and Brigitte's shoulders slumped. Slowly she turned and walked back to the bakery, desolate, staring unseeing at the ground.

Calvin met her at the bakery door. "We saw you run. You've been gone for two hours. Are you all right?"

"I'm sorry, Mr. Fornier. I guess I forgot everything when Caleb told me about the British," she said, without meeting his eyes.

"Something wrong at home?"

"No."

He looked at her dubiously, then asked, "Did you see them leaving?"

"Yes. I watched too long. I'm so sorry. I'll make up the time."

"No harm. Bess and I will probably close the bakery early. There's bound to be celebrating."

By one o'clock the rear of the British column had cleared the west edge of town, while the head of the column was well past the barricades at the Neck and had made the turn northward. In Boston people spilled into the streets from everywhere. Business was forgotten in the hurrahs and the tumult of a spontaneous outpouring of unbelievable relief from frustration and anger too long endured. Youth breached the gates and ran into the abandoned British compound and took souvenirs wherever they could be found. Fishermen and laborers left the docks to stream into the crowds, shouting, laughing. Ship bells clanged as captains and crews from merchantmen left their vessels half-loaded, or unloaded, and joined the outpouring of triumph and relief. They had outlasted the British! Beaten them! Once again the Bostonians owned their beloved Boston!

Calvin sent Brigitte home, and threw open the doors of his bakery and set trays of his goods on the counter and tables and let people take them, no questions asked. Taverns and pubs opened their doors and set out bottles and mugs for any takers.

Brigitte worked her way through the crowds and walked down the cobblestone street, past the trees with the green buds of spring swelling, through the gate, and into the parlor.

"Who's there?" came Margaret's call from the bedroom wing.

Brigitte dropped onto a dining table chair without answer, and Margaret appeared in the archway.

"What's wrong?"

Brigitte turned to her, face pleading. "He wouldn't leave like this, without telling me—a letter, something."

"Maybe he couldn't. He's an officer. Maybe he had orders."

"He would have found some way. Not just leave with nothing."

Margaret saw the pain, and she sighed and sat down facing her. "Good soldiers—officers—obey orders first, last, always. He was ordered to leave, and he left. If he didn't send you word, there has to be good reason. Trust him."

Brigitte's eyes dropped, and she began working her hands together in her lap. "How can I write to him?"

Margaret shook her head. "I have no idea."

Brigitte stood and walked into the kitchen. "I have to get cleaned up. Maybe there's someone left at the military base who can tell me."

Margaret sat at the table, listening to the children in the back-yard, wondering what she should do for Brigitte. She started at the unexpected rapping at the front door, rose, swung the door open, and faced a man she had never seen before.

"Are you Mrs. John Dunson?"

"I am."

"I was paid to deliver this to you personally, today after noon."

"What is it?"

"I was not told."

The man handed her a sealed brown envelope and turned and walked rapidly out the front gate. Margaret closed the door and quickly turned the envelope to read the name in the upper left corner, and she froze.

Captain Richard A. Buchanan.

She looked at the name of the person to whom it was sent.

Mrs. Margaret Dunson.

She slowly walked to the table and again examined the envelope, and then laid it on the table to stare at it as though it were something foreign, peculiar. Minutes later Brigitte walked through the archway, dress changed, hair brushed, and she slowed when she saw Margaret, then the letter.

"What's that?" she asked, then gasped. "Is it Matthew? Is Matthew all right?"

"It's not Matthew," Margaret said.

Brigitte rushed to the table and snatched up the letter. She read the name of the sender and began tearing it open, then read Margaret's name and stopped. A look of wonderment crossed her face. "For you? Not me?"

Margaret nodded but said nothing.

"Open it. Read it!"

Margaret drew a deep breath of foreboding and worked the envelope open. She unfolded the stiff paper and slowly, silently read the letter.

"Well?" Brigitte demanded.

Margaret began again, reading the brief writing aloud.

Thursday, March 15th, 1776.

Dear Mrs. Dunson:

A private courier will deliver this to you after the British military has evacuated the city of Boston. I could not leave without making my thoughts known to you, and your family, and to Brigitte.

It was my great blessing and privilege to share an evening with your family. I have never felt nor seen bonds of love to compare with those that were in your home that night. I will remember it always. I cannot imagine the joy if I were allowed to associate with such a family for the rest of my life, through your daughter Brigitte. I have never associated with young women before; however, in my heart I know I will have the strongest of feelings for Brigitte as long as I live.

Notwithstanding, the reality is, I am a British officer, and she is an American. I am unable to consider asking her to leave you, and your home, to live in England. While she may accept that offer now, I can see plainly that with the passage of time, she would yearn for you, and her family, and native land, which is only as it should be. My regard for her will not allow me to do that to her.

I know you can make her understand, and for that reason I address this letter to you. Please help her.

I hope I do not exceed my proper bounds when I express my love for you and your family, and for your daughter Brigitte.

Sincerely,
Captain Richard A. Buchanan

Margaret finished and laid the letter on the table, and Brigitte turned and folded her arms on the table and buried her face in them, and her unbridled sobs filled the room. Time was forgotten as Margaret sat still, hand on Brigitte's back, not knowing what to say or do to console her.

When Brigitte finally raised her head, her face and arms were wet from her tears. "I'll find him," she said, more to herself than Margaret. "I'll find him and I'll go to him."

Margaret said nothing as Brigitte took the letter and rose and walked to her bedroom and closed the door.

Half an hour later Billy came to be sure Margaret had heard of the British evacuation.

"Does Brigitte know?" he asked.

"Yes."

Billy sobered. "Did her captain tell her?"

"Yes."

"Is she all right?"

"Not right now. She needs time."

"Would you tell her I'm sorry? Truly sorry?" Margaret saw the hurt in Billy's eyes.

"Of course. Would you stay for supper?"

"Mother has our supper nearly ready. I just had to share the news with someone."

An hour later Tom knocked on the door. "The British are gone. There'll be celebrating in the streets. Will you be all right?"

"We'll be fine."

"I hope this means Matthew can soon be home."

"Wouldn't it be wonderful? Tom, please stay for supper."

She served beef stew, with nut cakes following, and took Brigitte's to her in the bedroom.

"Mama, can I go watch the celebration?" Caleb coaxed. "Everybody's out in the streets."

"There could be trouble," she replied.

"I'll watch him," Tom volunteered. "It will be something to remember."

Margaret stopped to look directly at Tom. "Always here when we need you." She looked at Caleb. "You mind Tom and get home early. Tomorrow's the Sabbath."

At ten o'clock, with the children in their beds and the coals banked in the fireplace and the early preparations for the Sabbath dinner completed, Margaret sat at the dining room table in the quiet solitude of yellow lamplight, with paper and quill before her.

At ten-thirty she took the quill in hand, squared a piece of paper, and carefully began to write.

Saturday, March 17th, 1776
Boston, Colony of Massachusetts
My dear Kathleen: . . .

The following morning, with church services ended, she made her way to Silas Olmsted as he stood by the tall front doors of the church, shaking hands with his congregation.
"Silas, has Kathleen written to you yet?"
"No."
"Will you send this to her with your first letter?"
Silas studied the envelope. "Yes. I will."
"Here's money for the postage." Margaret held out her hand.
"That's not necessary."

A raw April wind swept in from the Atlantic up the Thames River, driving a thin, drizzling rain slanting beneath a dull gray overcast. For two days the south half of the island of England, from Grimsby on the east coast to Liverpool on the west, had shivered in the chill wind and the fog. In the sprawling deep-sea port town of London, divided by the river, shop owners and factory workers made their way to work with shoulders hunched and coats tightly wrapped, walking cautiously on smooth-worn cobblestones slick with icy rain.

On the six great roads built by Romans seventeen centuries earlier, all leading to London from farms and villages for thirty miles in every direction, carts and wagons drawn by dripping, shaggy draft horses moved slowly, hauling their loads of cabbages and turnips and milk and mutton to the shops and inns and docks. The Westminster Bridge, beneath the great square tower, was jammed with the steaming, plodding horses and wagons. Dock laborers turned up the collars on their heavy coats and worked their way to load and unload the tall ships that were endlessly arriving with cargo from China, India, Europe, and the West Indies, and leaving, loaded with English wool, china, mutton, cutlery, steel, soft coal.

Seven miles west of London, and two miles south of the Thames River, Kathleen Thorpe stood at the front window of a small cottage on the outskirts of the old village of Bexley, a shawl pulled tight about her shoulders as she watched through the rain-streaked glass for Charles and Faith to appear, heads down and coats wrapped as they walked head-on into the wind and rain.

"Are they here?" came Phoebe's voice from the bedroom.

"Not yet. Be patient."

"Henry will be upset."

Kathleen did not answer. She shivered and drew the shawl tighter, and moved her feet impatiently, and then they were there, in the distance, slogging in the mud of the dirt road in their gum boots. She waited until they were walking up the gravelled path before she opened the door and they walked in.

She hung their oilskin coats and caps near the fire in the small fireplace to dry, sat the children at the small square dinner table, and brought hot milk and bread and honey.

"How was school?"

Charles sipped at his milk, then turned accusing eyes. "Do we talk funny?"

"Who said we talk funny?"

"Everybody. Just like last week. They point."

"We don't talk funny. Don't listen to them."

Faith wrapped her hands around her milk glass to warm them. "Charles can't go back to school Monday."

Charles scowled at her.

Kathleen straightened. "Why?"

"Let him tell."

Charles frowned and sipped at his milk.

"Well?" Kathleen demanded.

"Jacob said we talk funny and we don't belong here."

"Who's Jacob?"

"A boy."

"You can't go back to school because Jacob said that?"

Charles shook his head.

"Then why?"

Charles turned defiant eyes up to Kathleen and blurted, "Because he . . . because I pushed him down. That's why."

"Charles," Kathleen exclaimed, "you can't keep pushing people. This is the second time in three weeks. You'll just have to ignore what they say. I'll talk to your teacher."

"Won't do any good."

"Why?" There was alarm in Kathleen's voice.

"Mr. Humphrey said we're from the colonies and we're going back soon because the colonies are losing."

Kathleen stiffened. "Your teacher said that? In class?"

"Yes. The others said it after school."

"Well! We'll see about *that!* Now, drink your milk and eat your bread."

Phoebe called, "Is that Henry? Or the children?"

"The children are home. They're fine. I'll bring you some warm milk."

With supper finished, Kathleen read to the children before she took them into Phoebe's bedroom for prayer, then into their own bedroom and tucked them in. The wind and rain held, tapping and whispering at the east windows and moaning in the chimney. She banked the coals and sat in a rocking chair, head back while she waited for her thoughts to clear and her soul to gather strength for another day. Her eyes idly moved about the small room and into the adjoining darkness of the kitchen.

The little cottage was square, built of stone, with a parlor, kitchen, two bedrooms, and a pantry. The dirt street that passed in front was the last street on the east edge of the tiny village, and their nearest neighbor was one hundred yards south. There was little grass and no flowers left in the yard; rather, weeds and undergrowth had long since made their claim, and the back of the house opened into a field. There was no root cellar, but in one corner of the kitchen was a door in the floor, covering a hole that held a small amount of potatoes and cabbages and milk. The small fireplace in the parlor was the sole source of heat, save for the stove in the kitchen, with the oven. The outhouse was twenty yards south of the back door, the well ten yards north. Soft coal from the mines one hundred miles north provided the heat, and the soot that left a film.

She sighed and gave free reign to her thoughts.

Mother—addled—getting worse—what can I do? The children—hating school—no friends—nobody—hate the food—Faith won't eat half of it—the weather—we're all going to be sick—the church—cold—no one speaks to us—marked—the traitors—living off their taxes—talk funny—dress funny—no one cares—no one cares.

She closed her eyes and by force of will closed out the thoughts and sat for a time doing nothing, thinking nothing, asking only that her mind be empty. Later she started and sat bolt upright and looked at the clock. Ten minutes past two A.M. She checked on the children, then went to Phoebe's bedroom, where the double bed nearly filled the room, and silently slipped between the sheets next to her mother and listened to the slow breathing until her own eyes closed.

Saturday morning passed slowly while she kept the children busy with small chores and doing schoolwork. In the early afternoon she walked the half mile to the small shop where she bought bread and potatoes and cheese, then stopped at the next shop for milk and returned home, muddy to the tops of her shoes. The moment she opened the door a sense of foreboding stopped her.

She dropped the packages on the table and called, "Charles? Faith?"

Charles's voice answered from Phoebe's bedroom. "What's wrong with Mama? She looks at us but she won't talk."

In six strides Kathleen was in the bedroom and brushed the children aside and dropped to her knees beside the bed. Phoebe's head was on the pillow, face turned towards Kathleen, and her eyes moved to watch Kathleen; otherwise, nothing moved, nor did she speak.

"Mama!" Kathleen put the palm of her hand against Phoebe's cheek, then seized her hand. It remained limp while Phoebe stared at her, unblinking.

"Mama! Can you talk? Can you move?"

Phoebe neither spoke nor moved, and Kathleen saw the stark terror in her eyes. Kathleen jerked the bedcovers back and seized her arm and rubbed it roughly, then her leg.

"Mama, can you feel this?"

There was no sound, no movement. Kathleen could see the spreading dark place where Phoebe had fouled the bed. She threw the covers back up and ran to the kitchen to return with water and cloth, and paused only to brusquely order the children, "Go into the kitchen and wait!" They began to whimper and she shook a stern finger in their faces and they stopped and she pushed them on their way.

Twenty minutes later she emerged from the bedroom with the soiled sheets and Phoebe's nightgown and the pan of water, and set them on the kitchen floor and sat down at the kitchen table while she forced her shattered mind to focus. Two minutes later she stood the children before her and took Charles by the shoulders and peered directly into his face.

"I must go get the doctor. You both stay here, beside Mama's bed. If she says anything, do what she says. Do not let her fall out of bed, and do not cry! I will be back as soon as I can."

She banged out the front door and started towards town, running, trotting, slogging through the mud, heedless of the wind and rain at her back. People in the streets stopped to stare and point and she didn't care. She passed the church and the mayor's office, and stopped panting at the door of the small building with the sign next to the door, "Doctor Ulysses Potter." It was locked and she banged on it with her fist, but there was only silence.

She turned and ran back to the church, to the rear door where the Reverend Anders Kirby lived alone, and banged on the door. It opened and the tall, thin reverend looked down at her sternly.

"Yes?"

"I must find the doctor. Can you tell me where he lives?"

"He's not at his office?"

"No."

"His home is the fourth one past his office."

Kathleen spun on her heel and ran to the home and knocked loudly on the front door. A small, portly, aging woman opened it and said nothing, waiting.

"Is this the home of Doctor Potter?" Kathleen blurted. "I need him badly."

"He's not here."

From inside, Kathleen heard a man's voice call, "Who is it?"

The woman did not answer, but looked at Kathleen for a moment, then asked, "Aren't you the new ones in town? from the colonies?"

"Yes. Is that the doctor calling?"

"Wait here." The woman disappeared, and returned in two minutes. "The doctor is busy."

Kathleen's eyes narrowed and her mouth became a straight line. "Tell the doctor I will see him now or I will go to the mayor. My mother is critically ill and may be dying."

The woman recoiled, then composed herself, and once again retreated into the house. A minute later the door swung wide open and a stout, balding man stood before her, jowls hanging. "What is it?" he asked gruffly.

"My mother is critically ill. She needs help."

"Bring her to my office Monday."

"No! She needs your help now!"

"My office is closed today."

"Are you coming or do I go to the mayor?"

The man shrugged. "The mayor is my cousin. Go see him."

"My family is here under the protection of the king! If I have to I'll walk the eight miles into London this minute, and I'll sit in Buckingham Palace until I gain audience with the king, and your name will be the first one he hears. Now, are you coming or not?"

The man looked into her eyes and saw the wild anger and the

rock-solid determination, and he believed she would do exactly what she had threatened.

He bit down on his own anger and mumbled, "Wait here." Five minutes later he returned with his heavy coat and bowler hat and black bag, and led her to the back of his house, where he hitched a bay mare to a buggy.

He reined the mare in at the front of the small cottage, dropped the ten-pound weight tied to her bridle, and followed Kathleen up the gravelled path. Once they were inside, she took his coat, then led him to the bedroom, where she instructed the children to go to their bedroom and wait.

The doctor placed his black bag on the night table, while Kathleen reached for Phoebe's hand. The fingers moved, and then Phoebe's mouth moved, but no sound came.

"She tried to move," Kathleen exclaimed.

"What are her symptoms?" the doctor asked.

"Last night she was normal, but this morning she could not move. She could see us but could not move or speak."

The doctor took Phoebe's right hand in his. "If you can hear me, squeeze my hand," he said.

He felt a slight pressure. He took her left hand and repeated the command, but there was nothing. He released her hand, threw back the bedcovers, and exposed her feet. He ran his thumb up the bottom of her right foot, and it flinched. He repeated it with her left, and there was nothing. He put the bedcovers back into place, leaned closely over her face, opened her eyelid with his finger, and stared into her eye. Then he carefully worked the flesh of the right side of her face with his fingers, and then the left. He pressed his fingers into her wrist while he counted seconds on his pocket watch, then pushed her hand beneath the covers.

He raised his finger in front of her face and said, "Watch my finger," and he moved it slowly back and forth two times, while he watched her eyes. Both eyes tracked, but her left eye wandered slightly.

He leaned over and spoke to her directly. "What is your name?"

The right side of her mouth moved as she tried to frame the word *Phoebe*, but the left side did not.

The doctor drew a great breath and exhaled it, and picked up his black bag. He gave Kathleen a hand signal to follow him and walked to the dining table.

"I believe she has suffered a partial stroke that has affected the left side of her body. I think she will probably partially recover on the right side, but not the left. We do not know what causes these things, but we suspect it has to do with a blood clot in the brain, or something else interfering, and it is absolutely inoperable."

He opened the black bag and drew out a small bottle. "This will help her rest. Give her half a teaspoon when you put her to bed. Exercise all her limbs for fifteen minutes every eight hours— that is critical. Try to get her to speak and to squeeze your hand. Talk to her as usual. Make her comfortable. There is little else I know to tell you."

"Is she sane?"

"Yes, probably. She can hear, and she responds as well as she can."

"Should I tell her what you've said?"

"As soon as you think she can accept it."

He closed his black bag, and Kathleen asked, "How much do I owe you?"

The doctor shook his head and she saw the embarrassment in his face. "No charge." He raised his eyes to hers. "If you need me again, come find me, or send word. I'll come."

"Thank you."

She walked him to the front door and watched him wrap his coat close in the blustering rain. He picked up the weight from beneath the horse's head and dropped it thumping onto the floor of the buggy, then climbed to the driver's seat. He waved as he drove away, and she waved back.

She sat the children at the dining table and spoke calmly. "Mama has had a stroke. That means she can't move or talk very well. We're going to have to help her. You will have to be careful not to disturb her, and sometimes you'll have to help me with housework and to tend her. Mama will get better, but not all. Do you understand?"

Later Kathleen threw back the bedcovers, pulled up Phoebe's long nightshirt, and placed folded sheeting on her like a huge diaper, and smiled. "There. That should feel good." She saw the pleading in the frightened eyes, and she sat down beside her.

"Mama, the doctor said you've had a partial stroke. You'll get better. You should be able to talk soon, and move, but your left side might not recover too well. You're not to worry. I have some medicine, and we'll do fine. You must rest. I'll never be far."

The mouth opened and the lips moved, and Kathleen leaned over close to listen and heard the faint, lisped whisper. "Does Henry know?"

"Of course."

The eyes closed.

The wind died at suppertime, and the rain stopped when she put the children to bed. She sat rocking slowly in the rocking chair while the fire dwindled to glowing coals, and she banked the coals for morning, then settled back into the chair. At eleven o'clock she rose and blew out the lamp, and walked to the bedroom with a candle to change into her nightshirt. She checked the medicine on her nightstand, then opened the drawer and drew out the small carving of a snow owl. She sat quietly on the side of the bed for a time, touching the tiny owl tenderly. Then she clutched it tightly and knelt beside the bed and placed her hands together before her closed eyes.

"Dear God in Heaven, I thank thee for the goodness in my life. Please bless Mama to recover, and bless the children. I beg of thee, grant me the strength to do what must be done. And bless Matthew . . ." The warm tears came.

Notes

The British did evacuate Boston on March 17, 1776, which day became an annual holiday known as Patriot's Day. It has since been joined with St. Patrick's Day as a Boston holiday. General Howe ordered the evacuation in accordance with the general strategy created by the British commanders to move his troops north in an effort to trap George Washington's small army between two large British forces and annihilate the struggling colonial army. (See Leckie, *George Washington's War,* pp 239–41.)

June 1776

CHAPTER XXVI

★ ★ ★

*C*aptain Weyland needs you in his quarters. Urgent."

Matthew rose from the chart table in his small quarters on the *Esther,* slipped on his coat, and followed Riggins, who rapped on the door where the square brass plate with the engraved words "CAPTAIN SOREN WEYLAND" was fastened.

"Enter."

Inside, Matthew waited while his eyes adjusted from the brilliant late-June midmorning sunlight, and Weyland motioned him to a chair.

"Know where Lake Champlain is?"

"Yes, sir. North, between New York and Vermont."

"Ever navigated on it?"

"No, sir. I don't think you can reach it from the open sea."

"Do you have any charts for it? Depths, currents, islands?"

"Yes, sir."

"Could you navigate it if you had to?"

"I think so, but there's no need for an open-seas navigator. You can see both shores from the middle, most of the way."

"That may be, but let me tell you what's happening." Weyland leaned forward on his arms. "Some months ago, General Arnold tried to take Quebec with too few men, too little ammunition, and had to retreat. He then went to Lake Champlain, where Washington and Schuyler had ordered him to leave a few small vessels if he needed them. He's there, and as of now, Arnold controls the lake with those ships."

Matthew nodded and waited.

"While that was going on, General Howe evacuated Boston and went north. Now we know why. Look at this map." He pointed to a large map on his table and began tracing with his finger. "Washington's army is right there, and Howe and his Boston command are south of him, moving north up the Hudson River valley."

Matthew watched intently as Weyland's finger continued to move.

"We just found out the British have thirteen thousand troops right up here, at the top of Lake Champlain"—he tapped the map—"ready to move south under the command of a naval officer named Pringle. There are no roads, so Pringle's called in every shipbuilder in Quebec to build ships to move his thirteen thousand troops south."

He stopped and waited for Matthew.

Matthew's eyes narrowed as he studied the map, and suddenly he raised his face to Weyland. "Howe and Pringle mean to trap Washington between them." He straightened and Weyland saw the shock, and Matthew continued, his voice rising, alarmed. "The only thing stopping Pringle is Arnold's boats on Lake Champlain! How many boats?"

Weyland muttered, "Humph. Maybe six."

"You mean Arnold's holding the lake with six small boats? Washington better get out of the way."

"Where? There's no place he can go they can't follow, Howe from below, Pringle from above, and combined they outnumber and outgun Washington fifteen to one."

Matthew stood. "Then we better get men up there and build a few ships of our own!"

"Exactly," Weyland said. "Now, read this letter." He reached inside a drawer.

Wednesday, June 26, 1776

Captain Soren Weyland:

Through the misfortune of too few men and cannon, General Arnold did not succeed at Quebec and has brought his command to Lake Champlain, where he remains waiting my orders. I apprehend the British intend trapping my command between a large force under the command of Commodore Pringle, who has followed General Arnold, and the forces of General Howe, who is moving up the Hudson River valley. Lacking roads on which to move his command, Pringle is building ships to move south on Lake Champlain. I estimate that activity will conclude in the fall, perhaps early October. Should they succeed, I am convinced the Continental army will not survive.

Consequently, it is clear in my mind that we must build ships of our own in sufficient numbers to supply this obvious want of naval force. I do not believe we can match the number of shipbuilders employed by the British, and therefore expect that in October their naval forces on the lake will far exceed ours, and that we would not succeed in an open battle on the lake.

However, I do believe it is possible, through shrewd planning and device, and the kind mercies of the Almighty, to delay the British until the onset of winter, after which time they will not be able to proceed south until spring, by which time my army will be able to withstand theirs.

To perfect this delicate plan will require the services of a navigator who is trustworthy under severe battle conditions, and who can navigate Lake Champlain. Commodore Esek Hopkins has highly recommended Mr. Matthew Dunson, who was his chief navigator in a successful effort to seize British munitions in the West Indies. Commodore Hopkins advises this man is presently under your command.

I therefore earnestly make request of you that you send Mr. Dunson earliest to our forces at the south end of Lake Champlain, to assist in construction of ships and to serve as chief navigator under General Arnold when they are completed. I note, somewhat whimsically, the oddity of having a general of the army taking command of ships of the navy. However, in such times, we must meet the need with what we have and trust in God.

Further, should you know of any man who is acquainted with the forests and the Indians in and about northern New York and Vermont, and southern Quebec, and who has been in battle, his services would also be most welcome, since we are advised the British are bringing several hundred, perhaps thousands, of armed Indians to assist in their efforts.

Your earliest reply is urgently requested.

Your humble servant,
General George Washington.

Matthew stood still, silent, stunned.

"You better get your things packed," Weyland said gruffly.

"I never expected anything like this," Matthew breathed. "I've never seen Lake Champlain."

"You'll see a lot of new things before this war is finished. Know anybody who knows the north woods and the Indians?"

"Yes. Tom Sievers."

"Where is he?"

"Boston."

"Boston? How does he know the north woods? Indians?"

"It's a long story, but I can tell you he's the best fighting man in Massachusetts, and no one knows those north woods or the Indians like him. If I had to take one man into this fight, it would be Tom."

"Can you get him?"

"Yes."

"How will you get to Lake Champlain?"

"Any way I can."

At noon Matthew left his quarters, with charts, sextant, compass, clothing, and toiletries rolled inside a blanket, tied, with a loop slung over his shoulder. He paused for a moment to look at the familiar sights and sounds of the port of Gloucester in the late-June heat, then walked to the captain's cabin.

"I'm leaving, sir. Would you see to it this letter reaches my mother in Boston soon? She'll get it to Tom Sievers."

"How will he get to Lake Champlain?"

Matthew grinned. "Trot."

Weyland smiled, then sobered. "Washington's army lives or dies with you and Arnold on Lake Champlain. You have too much on your young shoulders. God bless you, Matthew." He thrust out his hand and Matthew grasped it warmly, then turned and strode to the gangplank and down onto the dock, and turned northwest.

For six days he walked on dirt roads or no roads, through tiny, unmapped hamlets and villages, rode on wagons and carts when he could, ate from fields or the bounteous tables of farmers when invited, bathed in streams, slept in straw stacks or barns, or beds when they were offered, and steadily made his way north and west, through the lush, overpowering beauty of the Green Mountains of New Hampshire and Vermont. On the seventh day he crested one of the endless ridges and to the north saw the waters of Lake Champlain glittering in the heat of the afternoon sun. At dawn he worked his way through a jumble of windfall timber to the rocky shores of the narrow south end of the lake and stopped to listen.

Jays argued in the trees, and nearby a woodpecker hammered out his incessant tattoo on a yellow pine. The morning breeze whispered in the pine boughs, and squirrels darted and chipmunks peered from branches, then disappeared in the blink of an eye. Eagles and hawks circled on great wings, patiently waiting, heads cocked and yellow-rimmed eyes focused on fish three feet below the lake surface. Matthew closed his eyes to concentrate, and sorted out the sound he sought, echoing across the smooth water—the sound of many axe blades being driven into the trunks of standing pines, and the incessant clanging of blacksmiths at their forges, along the east lakeshore.

He moved steadily on, following the sound, peering through the trees until he saw movement. He was a quarter mile from the camp when he stopped in his tracks, startled by the figure that silently appeared fifteen feet to his right, musket in hand.

"Tom! You got the letter—how are you?"

"Tolerable." He walked to Matthew and shook his hand warmly. He was dressed in worn buckskin hunting shirt and pants, and moccasins. "How are you?"

"Good. How's Mother, the family?"

"Sound. Good." He gave Matthew a head sign and they walked on towards camp while they talked.

"Heard anything about Kathleen?"

Tom shook his head.

"How long've you been here?"

"Yesterday morning."

"Met General Arnold yet?"

"Yes. Got a hundred fifty men or so up ahead building ships. Sent me to wait for you. Wants to see you as soon as you get here."

"Why?"

"He's army. Doesn't know about building ships."

"Doesn't he have some shipbuilders here?"

"One. Another one coming. A few carpenters. Mostly soldiers."

Tom walked him through the forest into a great clearing where the trees and stumps had been cut back one hundred yards up and down the lakefront for nearly half a mile, and a double string of tents was pegged down along the tree line. The area between the tents and the water's edge was organized with men driving oxen and mules to skid fresh-cut logs to three crews who worked with long, heavy crosscut saws to cut them into planking four inches thick, while other men stacked. At the north end, a thin line of smoke rose into the blue sky from three blacksmith forges, where sweating smithies pounded white-hot iron into brackets and bolts four feet long. Within twenty feet of the waterline, the keels of four small ships had been laid, ribs framed into place, and the planking on the sides begun.

A crew Matthew could not see was deeper in the forest, and he could hear their axes working. Wood chips and sawdust and tree bark were scattered everywhere, and the air was rich with the smell of fresh-cut pine logs and of pine gum. There was little conversation among the sounds of the ripsaws and of the heavy hammers driving the ribs into place and of the forges, while the carpenters continued the tedious work of measuring and boring the two-inch holes through which oak plugs would be driven to tie the ribs to the keel and to the deck. No man was more than thirty feet from his musket.

Tom picked his way through the men and timbers to the place where the first keel was laid and approached a well-built man in a shirt damp with sweat, poring over a crude drawing on a big, rough-cut pine table. Tom stopped and the man turned to him.

"General," Tom said, "this is Mr. Matthew Dunson."

General Benedict Arnold straightened and studied Matthew shrewdly for a moment with piercing blue eyes that missed nothing and in which Matthew could see traces of victories and defeats, joy and heartache. The man's chin and nose were prominent, attractive, and he moved with a sense of grace and authority. He thrust out his hand. "Welcome. We've been waiting for·you."

Matthew gripped the strong hand. "Thank you, sir."

"I take it you know why we're here—you've read General Washington's letter?"

"I have a copy."

Arnold's voice firmed. "We have about ninety days to prepare to stop the British on this lake, and I mean to do it. When Mr. Sievers has settled you in, come back and I'll acquaint you with what we're doing."

Tom walked Matthew to the east side of the clearing to a six-man tent. When they were inside, he pointed to a place in the corner. "Put your blanket there."

"Have you been helping with the ships?"

"No. Arnold told me to get fresh meat. There are two buck deer hung in the trees back there, and two more on spits roasting for supper."

They started back to Arnold's table.

"How'd you find deer with all this noise?"

"Found their salt lick two miles east. Borrowed a mule to pack them here."

Arnold straightened at their approach. "Find a place for your blankets?"

"Yes, sir."

"Good. Let me show you what we're doing." He turned a rough handmade drawing of a ship towards Matthew. "That was drawn by the only shipbuilder in camp. We're using it for a guide on these ships."

"Who's your shipbuilder?"

"Abraham Udell. He's built merchantmen before, but never a gunboat. I'd like your response to the drawing."

Matthew studied it for a minute. "Could I take some time to think about it?"

"Yes, but not much. I'd also like your thoughts on how best to meet the British on this lake, when the time comes. We know they'll have a superior force. The question is, what can we do to offset their advantage?"

"Could I study my chart of the lake for a while?"

"When can you have a report?"

Matthew shrugged. "Maybe tomorrow morning. Could I have that drawing for a couple of hours?"

For two hours Matthew studied his navigator's map of Lake Champlain, spread out on his blanket. Longitude, latitude, mean depth, deepest, shallowest, islands, sandbars, bays, coves, winds, currents, temperatures, seasonal shifts—he went over them again and again. Then he studied the drawing by which Arnold's tiny command was building their ships—length, width at the beam, height, mast height, deck structure, compartments in the hold, thickness of the hull, size of the sails.

He took one o'clock mess with Tom, then returned to his tent. At two o'clock he walked out and down to the shore, and watched the slow, tedious work of cutting the planking to fit the ribs of the ships. Then he hurried back to his tent and once again went over the dimensions on the ship drawing, and in the late afternoon sat cross-legged on his blanket writing pages of notes and a sketch of his own. At evening mess he returned the ship drawing to General Arnold.

"Sir, could I talk with you and Tom Sievers privately in the morning?"

Arnold looked at him, surprised. "Privately? Something wrong?"

"Not necessarily."

"Come find me after morning mess."

The cooks banged on brass kettles while the morning star was fading, and when the sun's rays caught the tops of the pines in the crisp, cool, clear air, the sounds of axes and saws and hammers were echoing through the trees and across the mirror surface of the lake.

"Come to my tent," Arnold invited, and Matthew and Tom followed and let the flap fall closed. They sat at a small table in the center of the large tent, Arnold's cot on one side, his aide's on the other.

Arnold leaned forward, arms on the table. "What is it?"

"I'll make this as short as I can," Matthew said.

Tom leaned back in his chair, missing nothing.

"How many ships do you already have?"

"Five serviceable," Arnold answered. "One is beyond repair."

"How many do you expect from the British?"

"Between twenty-five and thirty."

"How many will you have ready by then?"

"Half that number."

"Will you want to use your ships for anything when this is all over?"

"You mean maintain them on the lake? No."

"They're expendable?"

"Their sole purpose is to delay the British until winter."

"Do you know on which side of Grand Isle the British are working?"

"West side."

Matthew nodded his head and spread his chart of the lake on the table. "All right. This is how I see it."

For half an hour he led Arnold through the facts. Grand Isle divides the top of the lake—Valcour Island on the east side, the leeward side, of the isle at the southern tip—cove there—can hide several small vessels—the ships designed by Udell good but heavy—can't maneuver well—British bound to build heavy ones—we build lighter ones—outmaneuver them—hide ours in the Valcour Island cove—let British come past—come in behind them—ambush—leeward side—wind to our backs—they will have trouble turning into the wind—we can force them to come to us—move right in among them—use all cannon on both sides—best chance we have—tie them up as long as we can—do all the damage we can—then run for it to save our men if we survive—lighter ships can outrun heavier ones.

He finished and drew and released a great breath and fell silent, waiting.

Arnold slowly straightened. "Lighter and smaller?"

"Yes, sir. We can build six more then you've planned in the next ninety days, if we do. We can eliminate nearly everything below the main deck and save time and work."

"Can you make a sketch?"

"I have, sir." Matthew handed him the drawing.

"Fast, small ships, stripped down to only the necessaries for one severe battle. Is that it?"

"Yes, sir."

"What happens if they find out we're waiting in ambush in Valcour Island Cove?"

"If they do, we'll know it the moment they clear the south end of Grand Isle, because they'll have to make a hard turn to port—

east—to come get us, if that's what they intend to do. If they do that, we run north, and because we're lighter and smaller we'll out-run them. If they follow, we lead them up to Saint Albans, circle the island, and come right back to engage them, once again with the wind at our backs and able to outmaneuver them. If they split their force, half to follow us, half to go on south, we lead the half following us up to Saint Albans, circle the island, and make an all-out run through them, and catch the main group headed south, again with the wind at our backs and able to dictate the terms of the engagement."

Arnold studied the chart, and slowly a hint of a smile formed. "Let me study this for a while."

"There is something else."

Arnold raised his eyes. "What?"

"Send someone up there to see what they're doing, and count everything—officers, men, gunpowder, ships a-building, Indi-ans—everything."

"Who?"

"Tom."

Arnold turned to him. "Can you do that?"

"Shouldn't be much trouble."

"Both of you be back here in the morning before mess."

"Take up the slack. Easy, easy. You there, take up the slack. All right, she's true. Tie it off."

Matthew gave hand signals, and the men tied off the six guide ropes that held the forty-two-foot mizzenmast in place and exactly perpendicular in the big notch in the newly laid keel of the tenth ship, while craftsmen went to work with levels and drills and heavy iron brackets to bolt it in place. Then he backed away, sight-ing the mizzenmast against a straight, perpendicular stick to be sure the mast was not leaning. Satisfied, he wiped sweat with his sleeve and turned to get a dipper of water from the water barrel, and stopped, puzzled at the sounds of a running horse coming through the timber at the south end of camp. The work stopped as hands reached for muskets and waited to see what brought a horse and rider in at a run. The man reined the horse in near the big table and was on the ground before it came to a skidding stop.

"Where is General Arnold?" he demanded.

Fingers pointed, and he ran to the general. Matthew came trotting.

"Sir," the man panted, "I was sent to deliver this." He thrust an envelope to Arnold.

"From whom?"

"General Washington."

A sense of foreboding touched Benedict Arnold as he took the large brown envelope, looked briefly at the seal pressed on the flap, and nodded to the messenger. "Wait in camp. I might need to send an answer."

He settled onto a rough-cut pine stool in his tent and leaned forward, elbows on the large oak table covered with drawings of ship hulls and riggings. For a brief moment he stared at the bold, stiff cursive writing on the envelope, and his forehead wrinkled in concern. *From Washington? What's wrong? Has he surrendered? Are we beaten?*

He broke the seal and withdrew a sheaf of papers. With disciplined deliberation he laid them on the tabletop, smoothed them, and steadily read the first document, written in the hand of General Washington.

General Benedict Arnold:

On Tuesday, July 4th, 1776, the Congress of the United States adopted a Declaration of Independence, severing forever the thirteen colonies from England. The work of drafting Articles of Confederation for the new nation continues under the leadership of our Congress, and the beneficent eye of the Almighty. In my humble opinion, the document is unique. I send a copy for your consideration and whatever beneficial use you might find for it. You may wish to share it with your command.

I send this intelligence to you that you may know you are now free men, and the campaign in which you are engaged is for the purpose of maintaining the freedom we have so boldly declared and so dearly bought. Your success is critical to the survival of this new nation.

God bless you all.

Your obdt. servant,
General George Washington

Arnold felt a rise begin in the depths of his being. *Independence! They did it! Defied the British empire!*

Slowly he laid the letter aside and felt his breathing constrict as he read the bold printing centered at the top of the next page.

IN CONGRESS, JULY 4, 1776.
The unanimous Declaration of the thirteen united
States of America

States! Not colonies! Sovereign states! United! It surged through his brain, and he paused for a moment before he continued. Time and place were forgotten as he read. He finished and was oblivious to the sounds of axes and saws and men outside the tent as he again read the document, slowly, pausing, letting his thoughts run with the words and the concepts. Then he carefully read the signatures of the fifty-six men who had placed their lives and all that mortality holds dear on the block for the world to see and the British empire to crush and destroy if they could.

He gently picked up the letter and the document and walked out into the heat and the loud, ringing sounds of ships being built. He waved to Matthew. "Gather the men."

Five minutes later one hundred men had gathered, sweating, some stripped to the waist, axes and saws and hammers in hand while they waited in silence for their commander to speak.

"Men, the messenger brought a communication from General Washington." He paused and his eyes dropped to the documents.

"You need to know what these say. I'll read them for you. First, the letter written in the hand of General Washington."

His voice rang in the forest as he read. When he finished, there was not a sound from the men, and he continued.

"This is the declaration of independence he sent to us."

The only sounds were the jays in the trees and the squirrels scurrying.

" 'In Congress, July 4, 1776. The unanimous Declaration of the thirteen united States of America.' "

For a moment there was a hint of murmur among the men, and Arnold continued.

" 'When in the Course of human events, it becomes necessary for one people to dissolve the political bands which have connected them with another, and to assume among the powers of the earth, the separate and equal station to which the Laws of Nature and of Nature's God entitle them, a decent respect to the opinions of mankind requires that they should declare the causes which impel them to the separation.' "

Arnold paused for a moment to be certain of control before he continued.

" 'We hold these truths to be self-evident, that all men are created equal, that they are endowed by their Creator with certain unalienable Rights, that among these are Life, Liberty, and the pursuit of Happiness.' "

His chin quivered and he clamped his jaw shut and struggled for a moment.

" 'That to secure these rights, Governments are instituted among Men, deriving their just powers from the consent of the governed.' "

Again he stopped, and he raised his eyes to his command. Blacks and whites, professional men and craftsmen from cities standing beside farmers and illiterate backwoodsmen, shoulder to shoulder, sweating, hair plastered to their foreheads and shoulders, stunned by the words, feeling stirrings in their souls that none had ever experienced before.

He continued. " 'That whenever any Form of Government becomes destructive of these ends, it is the Right of the People to alter or to abolish it, and to institute new Government, laying its foundation on such principles and organizing its powers in such form, as to them shall seem most likely to effect their Safety and Happiness.' "

His voice held steady and strong as he continued, skipping over some of the words in order to focus on those statements that seemed to get at the heart of the matter. " 'Prudence, indeed, will dictate that Governments long established should not be changed for light and transient causes. . . . But when a long train of abuses and usurpations . . . evinces a design to reduce them under absolute Despotism, it is their right, it is their duty, to throw off such Government. . . . The history of the present King of Great Britain is a history of repeated injuries and usurpations. . . . To prove this, let Facts be submitted to a candid world.' "

He cleared his throat and continued. Institution of bad laws in defiance of good ones; denial of representation in government affairs; dissolving of Houses of Representatives at will and refusal to allow successor representatives to be elected; obstruction of laws allowing naturalization of citizens; refusal to allow the institution of judiciary powers; appointment of judges of the king's own choosing; creation of oppressive offices; placement of the military in control of the civil authorities; keeping a standing army in the homes of citizens; cutting off trade; institution of illegal and oppressive taxes and tariffs—Arnold continued until he had finished the enumerated offenses of King George against the colonies, then paused for a moment as he approached the conclusion.

" 'We, therefore, the Representatives of the united States of America, in General Congress, Assembled, appealing to the Supreme Judge of the world for the rectitude of our intentions, do, in the Name, and by Authority of the good People of these Colonies, solemnly publish and declare, That these United Colonies are, and of Right ought to be Free and Independent States. . . .' "

Again he paused, and raised his eyes once more to those of his men. He worked against the lump in his throat. Matthew was five feet to his left, mesmerized.

Arnold finished. " 'And for the support of this Declaration, with a firm reliance on the protection of divine Providence, we mutually pledge to each other our Lives, our Fortunes and our sacred Honor.' "

He took a breath. "This was signed by fifty-six men whom most of you know, who put everything, including their lives, at risk to do it."

He lowered the paper and looked at his men. His arms tingled with a feeling he had never before known or supposed existed, and he saw it rise in his men as the beginnings of understanding came into their eyes, and their hearts and minds leaped to grasp thoughts and feelings that were strange and yet somehow seemed to have always been locked away in some secret inner chamber, waiting, waiting.

No one knew how long they remained thus, seized by a spirit that bound them together in a newness of light. Strong men wiped at their eyes and looked about, unashamed.

Arnold wiped his sleeve across his mouth. "We will take one-half hour before evening mess to clean and prepare ourselves, and then we'll assemble here for a short meeting and a prayer to the Almighty, to be conducted by the camp chaplain." He lowered his head for a moment as though searching for words. "God bless you all. Let's get back to work."

He turned to the messenger. "You did well. Rest and care for your horse as long as you like; then draw provisions for your return trip and see me before you go. I'll have a message for General Washington."

Matthew followed Arnold into his tent, struggling to regain his voice. "General," he blurted, "did you feel it out there? Hear it? *All* men! Endowed by our Creator. Life, liberty, the pursuit of happiness. The consent of the people. The *common people.* That's where right government should derive its powers! Us! Not a king!"

He stopped, and Arnold remained silent, eyes locked with Matthew's as Matthew continued. "Fifty-six men! Our lives, our fortunes, our sacred honor, they said! Everything they are, everything they own, their sacred honor! Risked everything. *Everything.*"

Arnold dropped his eyes for a moment. "I felt it out there. I never read anything like it in my life. You know it's right when you hear it, and when we meet with the men, I'll put it to their vote as to whether we will make the same pledge as those fifty-six men did."

He slowly rose. "Right now the whole of it rests on our shoulders. We can do no less than those fifty-six men. Let's be about our business outside. You come back to my tent tonight and we'll talk."

The men hunched forward to pass from the tent into the noon heat and the sounds of men building ships.

The morning star was still bright when Matthew slipped out of his tent and walked silently to the lake's edge. The surface was a mirror of the starry heavens. Sounds came strangely unreal from far distances over the water. He heard the faint splashing of something big and four-legged walking through shallow water on the far shore, and then it stopped. Nighthawks did their incomparable acrobatics taking the numberless insects that flitted.

Matthew ran nervous fingers through his hair and paced on the sandy, rocky shore. *Too long—over two weeks. Have they caught him? Impossible—British can't catch him. Then where is he? Where?*

The stars faded, and the camp cooks pounded on the big brass kettles to awaken the camp and soon served steaming oat porridge with honey and brown bread. Shortly after six o'clock the sounds of the saws and axes and hammers resumed, and the squirrels and chipmunks became bolder as they darted to the rough-cut mess tables to snatch up bread crumbs.

Matthew settled in to the critical task of laying the deck of the number six ship, thick enough and braced well enough to bear cannon and men but no more. His eyes were incessantly moving, nervous, probing, watching, waiting for movement in the trees or on the lake that would be Tom returning.

At ten minutes past nine o'clock the carpenter next to him raised his head and shaded his eyes and pointed. "Is that something on the lake?"

Matthew stood and located the speck on the horizon, then leaped to the ground to sprint to his tent for his glass. One minute later he was at the lake's edge, hunched forward, studying the distant fleck, watching it grow with each passing second.

"Tom," he shouted. "It's Tom."

Arnold walked to his side. "He's back?"

"Yes, sir. In a canoe."

"A canoe? Sure it's not a Huron?"

Matthew shook his head, grinning his relief. "No, that's Tom."

Tom beached the canoe, and Matthew helped him drag it twenty feet ashore, and then, with half the camp watching, General Arnold led Tom and Matthew into his tent and gestured to chairs.

"Glad to have you back. Did you reach the British?"

"Yes."

"Report."

Tom laid four sticks on the table, each with notches. "They're up there, and they're building ships."

He picked up the longest stick and carefully ran his knife blade along the notches, counting. There were thirteen clicks.

"About thirteen thousand men in a big encampment, four miles north of the head of the lake."

He picked up the next stick and ran his knife blade over the notches. It clicked six times, then three more times.

"Six hundred more men at lakeshore, building thirty ships."

He picked up the next stick and counted twelve clicks. "Twelve hundred Huron up there in a camp. The British use them for scouts. They're not building anything—just waiting to come south and get into a fight with anyone the British say."

He ran his knife blade over the last stick. Two clicks, then eight clicks. "Two hundred cannon, and about eight hundred kegs of gunpowder, so far. More trickling in all the time."

Arnold leaned back in his chair, working with the facts.

"How big are their ships?" Matthew asked.

"One big, the rest smaller."

"How small? Any as small as ours?"

"No. Bigger. Mostly a lot bigger."

"Do they look like men-of-war or schooners?"

"Heavy timbered, heavy lines, like men-of-war."

Arnold asked, "How close are they to finishing work on their ships?"

"Half the hulls are done. Maybe five got decks in."

Arnold turned to Matthew. "When will they be ready to launch?"

Matthew shrugged. "If Tom's right, October, earliest. About like us."

Tom interrupted. "Those Huron got about two hundred war canoes up there, beached. I don't think they're too anxious to get onto those ships because they don't know how to sail one, and they hate not being in control."

Matthew leaned forward. "Do they know you were there?"

"No."

The questions and answers and discussion went on for half an hour before Arnold exhaled and leaned forward with his arms on the table. "Anything else?"

"Nothing more on what I saw."

"Mr. Dunson, has this changed your thoughts at all?"

"No, sir. Pretty much what we thought."

Arnold started to rise and Tom stopped him. "Might be one more thing we could talk about."

Arnold settled back onto his chair.

"Late September someone ought to go back up there. I think some things can be done to slow them down—maybe save us a lot of misery."

"Like what?" Arnold waited.

"Blow up some gunpowder. Maybe wreck a ship or two. Knock some holes in the bottom of two hundred war canoes. Fall storms start up there in late September—shouldn't be hard to do on a stormy night. Late September or early October wouldn't leave them time to do anything about it before spring. Might cut down their forces some."

A wry smile crossed Arnold's face. "Know anybody who could do that?"

Tom hunched his shoulders against the raw wind driving the freezing rain slanting in from the northwest and studied the dark camp.

For five days and five nights he had moved like a shadow among the trees, memorizing every detail of the British installation: the location of the regulars and the officers and the sentries in the big camp; the location of the Huron camp; the location of the construction camp and each of the thirty ships, now nearly completed; the cannon; the four powder magazines, buried and covered at two-hundred-yard intervals near the ships so one accident would not destroy it all; the latrines; the cook tents; the commissary and water barrels.

He had memorized the routine of each camp around the clock—where the sentries were located, how many, who, when they changed shifts, and which were British regulars and which were Huron. And he had waited for a storm.

The afternoon of the fifth day the temperature began to drop, and Tom watched monstrous purple clouds, bellies bulging with rain, move over the incredible beauty of the Adirondack Mountains on rising northwesterly winds. The British started their evening mess in early twilight and finished it in mud, with the wind tearing at their tents and the rain turning their camp into a morass of mud and puddles. Patiently Tom waited until the bugle sounded and the lights went out, and then in freezing rain so heavy he could not see five yards, he crept forward.

The first buried powder magazine—British sentry—one swing of a heavy pine stick—pry up the lock with the tomahawk—down eight steps into the magazine—four feet of fuse from the oilskin inside his shirt—flint and steel—the fuse hissing—back up the stairs—close the door—one hundred eighty paces in the dark—second magazine—sentry—pry up the lock—eight steps—second fuse—hissing—back up the steps—door closed—two hundred ten paces—third powder magazine—sentry down—lock broken open—down into the magazine—third fuse sputtering—up and out and close the door—fourth powder magazine—located between the cook tents, the latrines, and the tents of the sleeping construction gang—too many sentries—too much risk—still work to do.

Ninety paces to the construction site—pick a broadaxe from the rack—two hundred paces south into the trees—drop behind a great rock—wait—count breaths—watch.

He counted eighty breaths before the first powder magazine blew. Flame leaped two hundred yards into the air as nine tons of gunpowder packed in fifty-pound kegs erupted, six in quick succession, then all the remainder at once. The concussion wave knocked tents flat for two hundred yards, and two of the ships were knocked rolling, masts smashed, hulls cracked wide open. In the fires Tom saw men scattering in total, terrified disorganization, shocked, disoriented.

Twenty more breaths and the second powder magazine blew. Twelve more tons of gunpowder lifted flames into the rain-swept heavens, and the concussion wave knocked scrambling men thirty feet, sliding in the mud. Two more ships were lifted from their ramps and thrown like eggshells, smashed, gone.

Twenty-five more breaths and the third powder magazine exploded. Total panic seized the entire installation as eight more tons of gunpowder levelled half the tents at the construction site and blew running men in all directions. Two more ships were thrown down, hulls cracked, masts shattered.

For more than a minute Tom studied the pandemonium in the fires of the British camp and counted the ships destroyed. Then he crouched low and started south through the trees, the heavy broadaxe clutched in his left hand, right hand swinging free. He counted three hundred paces on the path through the woods and then angled left towards the lakeshore, where the two hundred Huron canoes were racked, bottoms up, along the shoreline. The fires at the camp cast a dull, eerie glow into the wet pines and the rain, and he slowed and crouched low and closed his eyes to listen.

He heard it. The sound of moccasins on soaked pine needles, moving fast, and he dodged off the path and dropped amid a tangle of windfall tree branches. In the dull glow he counted five Huron sentries trot past him going north to the fires.

The sixth one—they have six—where's the sixth one! He waited in the rain, breathing light, watching, and then suddenly the last one was there, crouched forward, moving cautiously, head swinging from side to side as he peered into the darkness.

Tom braced himself, ready, and drew his tomahawk. *He senses something—wait—wait—wait—let him pass—he'll pass—wait.*

The Huron stopped less than ten feet from Tom and suddenly turned his face towards the scramble of branches and Tom leaped. The Huron half turned before Tom's hurtling body knocked him backwards. The Huron grabbed frantically for his belt knife as they hit the ground, and it cleared the sheath at the moment Tom swung his tomahawk. Too late the Huron caught the flicker of firelight off the iron, and then the blade struck and he jerked and grunted and his body relaxed.

Instantly Tom jammed his tomahawk back into his belt and in two strides was back among the windfall trees. He seized the broadaxe and trotted to the lakeshore where the war canoes were lined, bottoms showing dully in the fires from the north.

For an hour Tom swung the broadaxe, chopping two gaping holes in the thin birch-bark bottoms of each canoe, then stopped to look and listen.

The Huron will miss the sixth sentry—come looking—seventy canoes left.

Forty minutes later he turned and for three seconds looked north up the quarter mile of canoes with their bottoms destroyed, except for the last one, beneath which he had cached his musket, bullet pouch, and powder horn. He heard the pounding feet one hundred yards north and spun and turned the last canoe over, dropped his musket and bullet pouch and powder horn and the broadaxe inside, grasped a cross-brace and threw all his weight against it, head down, legs driving, and rammed the canoe scraping into the water. When it floated free he leaped inside, settled onto his knees, and dug the paddle blade into the black, rain-whipped water with all his strength.

Ten seconds later the first musket cracked from the shore behind, and then he heard the high-pitched, warbling Huron war cries. Four more muskets cracked, and he heard one musket ball whistle past harmlessly. Five minutes later he eased up on the paddle and listened. There was no pursuit. He settled back on his haunches and let his shoulders slump for a time, then once again eased forward onto his knees and began a steady, rhythmic stroke with the paddle. The raw wind at his back would help him cover the one hundred twelve miles back to Matthew and Arnold by late afternoon the following day.

At seven-thirty A.M. General Arnold sat at his small table at the stern of his flagship, *Congress*, took quill in hand, and began his brief daily entry in the log.

Friday, October 11th, 1776.

His thoughts would not clarify, and he paused to look about. The tiny ship was anchored in the cove on the leeward side of Valcour Island, sails furled, with the fourteen ships in his small command behind him, all hidden, poised, waiting. They had finished a cold morning mess of hardtack and venison—no fires nor telltale smoke—and the crews of the fifteen vessels were waiting in tense, nervous silence for the appearance of the British fleet at the south point of the island. Of the fifteen ships, thirteen captains were civilian or army—no experience in handling ship, rudder, or sail. For two days Matthew had worked with them from dawn to dark, going over the fundamentals of maneuvering again and again, concerned that when the cannon were blasting and the cannonballs flying, they could not remain cool enough to think and remember.

Matthew stood at the bow of the *Congress*, watching through the mouth of the cove for the first sign of the British, waiting to see if their deck watch would discover the dwarf fleet hidden in the cove and turn east to try to trap them or continue south. Behind him men waited for his command to hoist the signal flags that would begin the engagement which would determine if Washington's Continental army lived or died.

The morning was clear, crisp, the lake calm, with a mist rising from the warm sun on the cold water. Arnold looked ashore at the glorious, incomparable beauty of the forests, ablaze with the rich reds and yellows and browns of leaves nipped by October frost, and he tasted the clean, clear air and then forced his mind back to the never-ending duty of keeping a daily log of his command.

> Expect to engage the British this date. We are as well pre-pared and trained as time and conditions allowed. Fifteen vessels, seven hundred fifty men. Held meeting last evening. Said our farewells, as we believe our small fleet will be so scattered by tomorrow's engagement that we will each have to find our own way to our homes at the conclusion, if any of us survive. Invoked the blessings of the Almighty. Fine spirit. Good men.

He shrugged, could think of nothing more to be added, closed the log, wrapped it in its oilskin and locked it back in his captain's chest, and walked forward to stand beside Matthew. "Anything?"

"Not yet."

Arnold walked back to his table and sat down. The beautiful morning wore on, and the men became nervous, then impatient as the sun climbed into the clear blue sky. Then at ten-twenty A.M. Matthew's arm shot up and he muttered, "There they are."

The bow of the big British flagship *Inflexible*, with her two decks of cannon, had cleared the point of the island, sails on the mainmast and the mizzenmast filled with the northwesterly breeze, on a heading due south.

Matthew turned and gave Arnold a violent hand signal and pointed and Arnold came trotting. They stood side by side, scarcely breathing, while they watched the British flagship *Inflexible*, three times the size of anything in their own fleet, plow through the calm waters.

Matthew's eyes never left the sails. If they were going to turn, the sails would have to be trimmed to the southeast to get full capture of the wind from the northwest.

The ship moved on, steady in her course, and Matthew counted—one hundred yards, two hundred, five hundred—and then he turned to Arnold, relief flooding. "She's not going to turn!" he whispered. "She didn't see us."

Arnold nodded and remained silent.

For twenty minutes they stood rooted, studying the line of ships as they came into view, counting cannon, masts, men they could see, and then they were all past.

"Twenty-five," Matthew said. "Nearly twice the ships and twice the cannon. I estimate about one thousand Huron and nearly that many regulars—ten times what we have. They intend to board us if they can."

"We'll see. When do we go after them?"

Three minutes later Matthew gave the command, and the signal flags were hoisted to the top of the mainmast, and men on the ships behind unfurled all mainsails. Arnold shouted orders, and the *Royal Savage* moved out of the mouth of the cove and took her heading south, following the British squadron. One minute later the four ships at the rear of the British fleet all turned hard to port and came about, beginning to tack into the wind, slowly moving north, and Arnold gave further orders and the column of ships moved out of the Valcour Island cove in a line.

At eleven o'clock the first British cannon boomed across the

water, and the mainmast of the *Royal Savage* shook and nine cannonballs ripped through her canvas. The remaining twenty-one
ships in the British fleet turned and began to beat upwind, tacking
back and forth, and as soon as they came into range they opened
up with all their cannon.

Matthew watched, scarcely breathing, to see if the commanders of the fifteen diminutive American ships would follow
the plan. He didn't realize he had shouted when he saw them
swing into a line, one hundred yards apart, and move south with
the wind and, when they came within range, begin their turns, first
port, then starboard, firing their cannon on either side as they
came to bear on any vessel flying the Union Jack.

For forty minutes the wild, confused battle raged, the British
trying to hold their formation while the smaller, faster American
craft flitted back and forth before their cannon, firing as they
turned, and then Matthew gaped as four British ships broke off.
Three headed for shore, the other a small island south of Valcour,
where they stopped long enough to set the entire contingent of
Huron on shore with their muskets.

"The Huron are afraid—won't stay on their ships!" Tom
shouted. The Indians quickly spread out on the shoreline and
began firing their muskets, and the balls raised small geysers in the
water two hundred yards short of the nearest American ships.

Then the four British ships returned to the British formation,
and the *Inflexible* ran signals up the mainmast, and the entire
squadron started the tedious maneuver of tacking into the wind,
back and forth, firing when an American target came under their
cannon.

Arnold looked at Mathew and Matthew nodded, and Arnold
ran a single red flag to the top of his mainmast and shouted to his
helmsman, "Go after the big one—their flagship."

All of the American commanders saw the red flag and
instantly trimmed their sails and took a heading directly into the
British ships nearest to them, helter-skelter, hit and run, fire at one
and pick another, precisely the way the militia and minutemen had

ripped into the British column at Concord. The British commanders shook their heads in bafflement as they tried to square with any American ship, only to have it blast them with ball and grapeshot and dance away to engage the next British ship. Time and time again the British ordered their troops to the rails while they tried to close with any American ship sufficiently to reach her with grappling hooks, and the Americans loaded their cannon with grapeshot and raked the British railings, stem to stern, knocking the troops backwards, and then changed course and were gone.

Matthew stood beside the helmsman on the *Congress*, shouting to him above the deafening din of the cannon. "Straight in! Don't turn! She doesn't have bow guns! Steady as she goes!" When the *Inflexible* was sixty yards away Matthew shouted, "Now, turn her to starboard—right!" He waited twenty seconds, then ordered, "Now, left, and bring us right down past her so close you think you're going to ram."

The white-faced helmsman followed the orders, and his eyes grew big as the small, low *Congress*, running with the wind, swept by the *Inflexible*, which was facing into the wind and nearly stalled, and every cannon on the port side of the *Congress* blasted holes in the hull of the larger ship, while the *Inflexible* emptied her cannon twenty feet above the decks of the *Congress*. One cannonball knocked splinters from the mainmast but did not cut it, and eight balls ripped through the rigging. Chunks and pieces came tumbling onto the deck, but the *Congress* did not falter and her mainmast held. A second ball shattered four feet out of the railing, and wood flew. Matthew felt the quick bite and sting on his left cheek, and his hand darted and he felt the jagged piece buried. He pulled it out and felt and smelled the blood running but could not stop to bandage it.

"Now," Matthew shouted at the helmsman. "Hard port—left, left—and hold her until she stalls in the wind." He turned to the cannoneers. "Reload! We're coming around for another broadside."

The *Congress* answered the rudder and cut violently to the left, around the stern of the *Inflexible*, and the cannoneers worked frantically while she continued the turn, and then she slowed and stalled in the wind. At the moment she came to a dead stop, she was off the rear quarter of the *Inflexible*, at an angle that brought her cannon to bear, while the *Inflexible* could not bring her guns to bear without turning to starboard. In that moment, Matthew shouted, "Fire," and once again the port cannon on the *Congress* blasted, and the balls smashed through the exposed hull of the big ship.

"Now, hard to port," Matthew called to the helmsman, who looked at him in question for a split second before he spun the wheel. The little vessel, bow in the wind, responded slowly. Then, as the wind began to catch the sails, she picked up speed. "Starboard cannon, get ready," Matthew shouted, and watched as the *Inflexible* began her right turn to bring her cannon to bear. Once again the cannon on the *Congress* came to bear before those of the *Inflexible*, and once again, in the five seconds during which he had the advantage, Matthew shouted, "Fire," and for the third time the guns on the *Congress* bucked and roared, and the *Inflexible* rocked slightly as the balls ripped into her.

"Now, hard port—left," Matthew called to the helmsman, "and pick a target."

He put his hand on his cheek and it was slick, and he glanced down his shirtfront and it was bloody from his shoulder to his waist. He looked and could find nothing, and he ripped his left sleeve from his shirt and pressed it hard against his cheek.

Minutes stretched to hours while the deafening sound of the cannon never ceased. American commanders stopped giving needless orders, allowing their helmsmen to pick the targets as they would, while the commanders took charge of the loading, aiming, and firing of the cannon. By two o'clock, seven of the British ships were burning, nine had their mainmasts shattered, four were listing, and twenty had been hulled and were taking on water.

Among the Americans, the decks and railings of four ships were a mass of shattered timbers. Six mainmasts were cut in half.

Most of the ships had holes blasted in their hulls and were taking on water. Grapeshot and cannonballs had shredded their sails. All of them had wounded on board; some officers were down, one commander dead.

And still, the tiny American command fought on, dumping the splintered masts and yards overboard, moving their dead out of the way, the wounded helping load and fire the cannon as fast as they could, manning the pumps below decks to keep from sinking. By four o'clock all of the Americans were stripped to the waist, sweating, faces grim, filthy from cannon smoke, beginning to count their shot and powder, dodging to avoid grappling hooks, clearing British troops away from the rails with grapeshot.

Matthew ran a grimy hand over his mouth and quickly counted the powder and shot remaining on the deck of the *Congress*, then turned serious eyes to gauge how many British ships were still in commission. And while he watched, his heart leaped.

The British were falling back! Regrouping!

He turned to Arnold, still commanding the starboard cannon. "They're falling back!"

It was exactly five o'clock P.M.

For more than a minute the two men stood rooted to the spot, unable to believe the British were withdrawing. They watched as the British ships fell back, downwind seven hundred yards, then formed into an east-west line with their starboard cannon coming to bear on the American ships.

Arnold gave orders and the red flag was quickly lowered and a royal blue one run up in its place, the signal for "Follow me." Those in command on all the American ships read it instantly and waited until the *Congress* made her turn to the northeast, and they all followed as Arnold led them away. Behind them the British cannon boomed and geysers erupted in the waters, but more than one hundred yards short. In the fading light, Matthew used his glass to carefully study the line of British ships, and then dusk settled into darkness and the cannon flashes stopped.

Arnold turned to Matthew. "How bad?"

"I don't know. It stopped bleeding. I washed it with lake water."

"Let me see." By lantern light Benedict Arnold carefully inspected the jagged tear, nearly an inch long. "I'll have the surgeon close it and bandage it. You'll have a scar." He waited for a moment. "You did well."

Arnold put out a call, and by ten o'clock those in command of the fifteen ships were on his deck, with Matthew and Tom.

"Report on damage," Arnold ordered.

The *Royal Savage* had beached on the southern tip of Valcour Island to save her crew. Her hull was cracked, mainmast shot away, and her rigging down. The *Washington* had lost her first lieutenant, with her captain and master wounded, mainmast shot through, and hull and decks battered by shot. The *Congress* had her mainmast hit and cracked, yard shot through, seven holes above the waterline, twelve at the waterline. The *New York* lost every officer except the captain and was riddled with grapeshot. The *Philadelphia*, shattered by grapeshot and wrecked by cannonballs, sank while Arnold was holding his conference. Her crew was picked up by the *Boston*. Every surviving ship was taking on water. They had sixty-one dead, ninety-three wounded, sixty-six of them disabled.

"Report on ammunition."

They had expended eighty percent of their powder and shot.

In the light of a three-quarter moon, Arnold turned to Matthew, with the white bandage bright in the moonlight. "Report on known damage to the British."

"Sixteen without serviceable masts, seventeen with rigging that must be repaired. Every ship among them has taken holes below the waterline. Thirteen are listing with water in their holds, and some of them will sink. Fourteen have fires on deck or below. I estimate four hundred of their troops are dead from grapeshot and cannon, and another three hundred wounded. Their flagship was hulled thirteen times below the waterline, and her pumps are keeping her afloat. I have no estimate of their remaining powder and shot."

"Will they be able to transport thirteen thousand troops the length of this lake before winter, in those ships?"

"No, sir. There is no way the British can bring in enough men and equipment to repair that fleet before spring. They will not move thirteen thousand troops south with those ships for at least nine months."

Murmuring broke out among the group, then dwindled.

"Gentlemen," Arnold said quietly, "we succeeded. I don't know who else will tell you, but I tell you now. It's probable you saved the Continental army today. History will not forget."

He paused and cleared his throat.

"We're out of ammunition and we're battered. We've done what we came to do. I propose the following plan." He turned to Matthew. "Can you navigate us around those British ships tonight, undetected?"

Matthew took a moment to collect his thoughts. "Yes, sir. I think so, after the moon sets. About two o'clock. "

Arnold turned back to his men. "After we've passed the British, each of you will take command of your own ship and go home any way you judge best. Beach your ships and walk, if you think it best. I'm going to Schuyler Island to try to make repairs. If I can't, I'll beach the *Congress* and walk home. Any of you who wish can follow me there, but you will be in command of your own crew and vessel."

He went around the circle, and in the crisp darkness of night, he shook hands with every man there, before each silently returned to his own command.

Notes

The survival of the Continental army under the comand of General George Washington, and therefore the survival of the newly declared independent colonies, hung in the balance at the first battle of Lake Champlain, fought in October 1776. The British intended bringing thirteen thousand troops south from Canada down Lake Champlain in order to trap General George Washington's meager army against the British forces under command of General Howe, which were moving north from Boston. To do so, the British had to move the thirteen thousand troops in boats down the 125-mile length of Lake Champlain. They had quickly built twenty-five boats, led by a sizeable man-of-war named *Inflexible*. To oppose this force, General Washington ordered General Benedict Arnold, assisted by General Philip Schuyler, to build as many craft as he could during the summer of 1776, with orders that whatever the cost, they had to stop or slow the British until winter set in, which would delay the movement of the troops in Canada to the following spring, 1777, giving George Washington sufficient time to prepare. General Washington did not care if they lost every ship; they had to stop the southward movement of the British troops.

October 11, 1776, Benedict Arnold led his fifteen hastily constructed craft against twenty-five British vessels. It was a desperate, do-or-die battle in which the British ships enjoyed an advantage of 70 percent more firepower than the small American fleet. Every American ship was sunk or destroyed, but the Americans succeeded in their mission. They stopped the British, and winter set in to delay the British movement south until the spring of 1777. (See Knox, *A History of the United States Navy*, pp. 17–19.)

It may surprise some readers to find Benedict Arnold, the infamous traitor, depicted here as having such devotion to the American cause. Before he turned traitor, Arnold was indeed one of the great heroes of the colonial army, a fact which made his eventual act of betrayal in 1780 all the more staggering to General Washington and the rest of the Americans.

December 1778

CHAPTER XXVII

★ ★ ★

*M*argaret picked up her saucer and balanced the cup of steaming rosebud tea from the kitchen to the dining table and set it down clinking on the tabletop, and wearily settled onto a chair. She pulled the scarf holding her hair and tossed it in a heap and slowly wrapped her hands around the warmth of the cup. She settled forward, arms resting on the tabletop, and she looked out the front windows at the stark, bare branches of the oak and maple trees tossing in the cold winds of early December, then glanced at the clock on the mantel.

Nearly two P.M., Wednesday, December 2, 1778.

The tea was sweet and pungent and hot, and she sipped gingerly and then held the cup between her palms while she sighed, and then settled back into her chair.

So tired, so weary. Three years and eight months without him—seems like forever. Wonder where he is today. Sometimes it feels like he's here—so close . . .

She wiped at the silent tears that came and then stopped, and a little smile formed.

Matthew's coming for Christmas. Home for Christmas. I wonder if that scar will look any better. That cannonball could have killed him.

She shuddered and pushed the memory away.

Where is Matthew today? What ship, what battles? Is he safe? God already has John. He wouldn't take Matthew too.

Her thoughts wandered and she let them go where they would.

Captain Richard Buchanan. Brigitte has written twenty letters, maybe more, with no answer. I wonder why, and where he is. When will Brigitte finally let go of it? She'll be coming home from school in two hours with the children. She's a good teacher—the best one they ever had at school. Nearly twenty-two years old, and half the young men in Boston would marry her in an instant if she would only let go of this thing with Captain Buchanan. Margaret shook her head. *So headstrong. Drove that wagon of blankets and medicine to Valley Forge in the dead of winter—Caleb with her. Nearly got herself hung. What does a mother do?*

She sipped at her tea and let her reveries run unchecked.

Her forehead wrinkled with deep concern. *What will become of Caleb? Begging every day to go with the army. Almost eighteen, the only man left in the house. One of these days he won't beg anymore. He'll just go. There's too much hurt, too much anger in him. Lost his father and just as well have lost his older brother to this war. God will help. He has to.*

She paused for a moment to listen to the wind moan in the chimney, and to glance at the fire.

Kathleen has written to Silas only once, and Silas can't sell their home. Will Matthew ever get her out of his heart? He must. That's a tragedy—a heartbreaking tragedy. I wonder how Phoebe is now, and Kathleen, and Charles and Faith.

Billy's back from his trip north to join Arnold and Stark and Schuyler and Gates to fight Burgoyne—when was it? a year ago? Can't be that long, but it was. Met them and beat them at Bennington and Freeman's Farm up in New York—New York or Vermont? New York. And then Burgoyne surrendered to Gates at Saratoga last year. Seems like last week. The British army included some of the soldiers from Boston—maybe Richard Buchanan was one of them. Billy was a while getting back, but he made it, unhurt. His old wounds from Concord have healed, thank the Almighty. Billy's become a good man.

She paused to shake her head in wonderment and sip again at her tea.

It wasn't long after that battle that France came into the war on our side. That was right after Saratoga. Ben Franklin talked them into it—Ben and his talk. He can talk anyone into anything. The war seemed to turn for us when France came in. Maybe we should send Ben to talk to King George. I'll bet if you gave Ben two months over there, England would be our fourteenth state.

She smiled at her own wry humor and drank at her tea as it cooled.

Silas was right in his vision. At least partly right. We've certainly had the war he saw coming, and we did declare our own independence. We have yet to see if we can give birth to the whole new bright land he saw. And we are paying a terrible price, just as he said. Nothing's the same—nothing. I hope Silas was right about the new land. John thought he was. That kind of thing can demand a terrible price in blood. John was willing to pay the price. I hope Silas was right.

She added kindling to the fire and sat back down to finish her warm tea.

Well, supper won't prepare itself, and this work never lets up, and I'm getting old and wrinkled and my bones are starting to hurt in the cold. Seems like twenty years since John left, and I look just that much older. I've got to roll out the dough for mutton pies, and I should make dessert, but I won't have time. Just too much to do. Too much ironing.

Movement on the street caught her eye and she started.

The postman. I can't let him see me looking like this.

She trotted to the bedroom and quickly brushed her hair and straightened her dress and peered at herself in the mirror. *Wrinkles and dark bags under my eyes. Where did they come from? I've got to do something about them.*

She reached the front door as the postman knocked.

"Package for Brigitte, letter for Matthew," he said, and handed her a package wrapped in stiff brown paper, and an envelope.

"Thank you." Margaret closed the door while she studied the name in the upper left corner of the letter. Captain John Paul Jones, United States Navy.

"Wonder where they want Matthew to go this time," she murmured.

She read the name in the left corner of the package for Brigitte and she stopped. Brigadier General William Howe, His Majesty's Royal Army.

British! Richard!

She placed the letter and the package on the mantel, beside the clock, and went to the kitchen and punched the dough. It settled and she rolled it out for mutton pie while a dark foreboding settled on her.

At ten minutes until four o'clock the door opened and Caleb walked in, followed by the twins.

"What are we having for supper?"

"Mutton pie."

Caleb and the children walked on through to their rooms to change clothes.

Brigitte closed the door and turned and saw Margaret and slowed. Margaret stood in the kitchen arch, feet spread slightly, arms hanging at her sides, face a blank.

Brigitte gasped, then recovered. "Mama, what's wrong?"

Without a word, Margaret took the package from the mantel and walked to Brigitte and handed it to her, then stepped back. Brigitte read the name of General Howe and suddenly her breathing constricted. She walked to the kitchen for a knife, cut the string, then returned to the table to tear open the paper and lift the lid from the box. Inside was a stiff document, a folded letter, and a smaller package tied with more brown paper. Scarcely breathing, she read the stiff parchment document first.

The beautiful cursive scroll writing at the top read, "Commission in the Military Forces of His Majesty the King of England." Quickly she scanned the lines. Richard Arlen Buchanan—duly qualified—granted commission—Captain—His Majesty's Army—Tuesday, January 30th, 1776.

She fumbled with the folds in the letter, then laid it flat on the table. Margaret sat waiting.

Thursday, October 8th, 1778.

Dear Miss Dunson:

I deeply regret to inform you that Captain Richard Arlen Buchanan, officer in the Royal Army, lost his life while serving with distinction at the battle of Freeman's Farm, State of New York, Tuesday, October 7, 1777.

He had declared no family in his military records, hence we were unable to find next of kin to whom we could forward his personal effects. However, four days ago, by chance we discovered a brief statement signed by Captain Buchanan, mixed into a bundle of letters he had received from yourself, in which he directed that in the event of his demise, his commission as a Captain in His Majesty's Army should be forwarded to you, together with his written statement, and your letters, which he treasured.

I tender my personal apologies that this arrives so long after his untimely death, and have undertaken this matter personally, immediately upon discovery of his statement above mentioned. I can only beg you to understand the difficulty of handling such matters in a time of war.

Your obdt. servant,
General William Howe.

Brigitte silently laid the letter on the table, untied the string around the small bundle, and removed the wrapping and counted. Twenty-one letters. He had received them all. Nine of them were dated after October 7, 1777.

The last document was the statement, and she unfolded it and read it.

Dated Thursday, September 18th, 1777.

Should I not survive the campaign under the command of General Burgoyne, now in progress, I hereby direct that my commission as a Captain in the armed forces of His Majesty, King George of England, should be delivered to Miss Brigitte Dunson, daughter of John P. Dunson and Margaret Dunson, of Boston City, Province of Massachusetts, together with this document, and her letters which will be found herewith. I have no other property, save my personal effects and military accoutrements, which I direct be disposed of as will best accommodate the army.

I will rest satisfied if I know that she will have these things that are my most cherished possessions. Would God have granted me one wish in this life, it would have been that I had been born in the colonies, or that she had been born in my beloved England.

Signed,

Captain Richard Arlen Buchanan.

Brigitte raised her eyes to Margaret's. "Richard is gone. He's been dead since October seventh of last year."

Dry-eyed, without another word, she carefully slipped the commission and the bundle of letters and the statement back into the box and walked steadily to her room and quietly closed the door.

Margaret sat at the table and listened to the sound of the chill December wind whisper in the chimney, and stared out the window at the bare branches of the trees as they moved.

The children came from their rooms and stopped and stared, waiting.

"Come sit down," Margaret said calmly. "There are some things I have to tell you."

Kathleen slowly, silently moved the bedcovers away and dropped her feet to the small braided rag-rug and leaned over to slip her feet into her slippers. She shivered in the damp cold as she took her robe from the closet and studied the still form of Phoebe, curled in bed, in the dim light of their bedroom. Quietly she opened the door and closed it behind her, walked to the fireplace, added wood chips to the banked coals, and waited for them to flicker and catch. Minutes passed while she waited, adding larger sticks, then kindling to the blaze.

Have to get the roast from the root cellar—not cellar, root pit—plum pudding and a roast of beef for Christmas dinner—children probably haven't slept all night—so excited—so excited—gifts wrapped . . .

She took blazing kindling to the stove and stuffed it in the firebox, added more, and returned to the fireplace to add the larger rungs of logs to the fire. Then she walked to the corner of the room and knelt to lift the door into the pit, where she kept their small supply of vegetables and milk and a roast of beef. She took the four-pound roast to the kitchen, where she washed it and placed it in a pan, then returned to the pit for carrots and potatoes to be washed and roasted with the beef.

While she waited for the fire to drive the damp chill from the room, she peered out the curtained window at the fog from the Thames River, at the bare trees and dead, ragged weeds and grasses, and at the dirt road.

When the warmth reached down the hall, Kathleen opened the door to the children's bedroom several inches, then silently entered her own bedroom to change into her dress and brush her hair, careful not to wake her mother. She heard the soft tread of feet and quickly walked back to the parlor, where the children stood, digging sleep from their eyes.

"Can we open the presents?"

"Get your robes on first, and we'll go into Mother's bedroom to open them with her."

One minute later the children were helping her carry the gifts—eight wrapped packages, two each—into the bedroom, where Phoebe lay unmoving. Kathleen pointed and they set their gifts on the foot of the bed and stepped back, eyes sparkling, faces alive with anticipation while Kathleen raised the blind to let the gray light of morning fill the small room, the children behind her. She leaned over the bed and gently laid her hand on the still shoulder of her mother, whose back was to her.

"Mother, it's Christmas morning. The children have surprises for you."

There was no movement.

Smiling, Kathleen shook the shoulder. "Mother! Time to wake up!"

The realization and the shock struck her at the same instant, and her hand darted to Phoebe's throat. It was cold and still. She turned the head to peer into the face, and the eyes were half-open, flat, lifeless, dead. Kathleen's head jerked back and her face turned white and her mouth clamped shut as she gasped air and held it.

For long seconds she did not move or speak while she waited for the numbing shock to fade, and then her thoughts came racing. *She's dead—the children—Christmas—their mother died on Christmas—how do I tell them on Christmas? Can't—can't . . .*

She leaned over the dead face and turned an ear downward and a moment later nodded her head. "All right, Mother, I understand. You rest. We'll go ahead."

She turned back to the children, smiling. "Mother's tired. She needs to rest. She says we should go ahead and open our gifts. She'll feel better in a while, and we can bring hers to her then."

They gathered at the fireplace, and Charles and Faith opened their simple gifts, beaming with the new mittens and scarves knitted by Kathleen. Faith unwrapped her smaller gift, and her eyes grew large as she held a beautiful silver bracelet with her name engraved on a heart. She threw her arms around Kathleen and exclaimed, "It's so beautiful!"

Charles unwrapped his smaller gift and stopped in disbelief at seeing the oak-handled pocketknife. He turned his grinning face to Kathleen and said nothing as he opened and closed the single blade.

"You've got to be careful," Kathleen warned.

"I will." He reached for a stick of kindling, and shaved splinters.

Kathleen opened her gift from the children, and exclaimed at the drawings they had made of each other in pencil and colors. She placed them upright on the mantel and smoothed the forgotten wrappings, and waited for a time while the children became accustomed to their newly arrived treasures.

"I better go check on Mama," she said, and disappeared into the bedroom, to emerge within half a minute. "Mama says she's feeling worse. I better go for the doctor."

She sat them both at the table. "I'll have to leave you here alone. Promise you'll not go into Mama's room, because she must sleep. I'll be back as soon as I can and put in the roast and we'll have a wonderful Christmas dinner this afternoon. Do you understand?"

She added logs to the fire and left, running, trotting to the door of Doctor Potter, and she banged with her fist. The door opened and warmth and the rich smells of baking tarts and ham came rolling, and she looked at Mrs. Potter.

"I believe my mother has just died. May I see the doctor?"

She rode beside the doctor in silence, with a man she did not know in the seat behind, through town, back to her cottage. The doctor dropped the weight tied to the mare's halter, and the man climbed from the backseat.

Kathleen spoke. "I didn't tell the children she was dead, only sick. I couldn't do that to them on Christmas."

"I understand. Don't worry."

They walked to the house, and Charles and Faith met them at the door.

Doctor Potter took off his hat and spoke. "I'm Doctor Potter. I understand your mother's not feeling well. I'm here to help. I might have to take her to my home where I can watch her for a while and give her medicine. Will that be all right?"

Charles nodded.

"Good. I thought you might like some Christmas candy—we have extra at my place and only me and my wife to eat it." He opened his black bag and placed a large brown sack on the table and spoke to Charles. "You look like the man of the house. You count that out, half for each of you. Can you do that?"

"Yes, sir."

"Good." He turned to Kathleen. "Shall we go see your mother?"

The three of them walked into the bedroom and closed the door.

Doctor Potter leaned over Phoebe for a few seconds. "She has passed on." He turned to Kathleen. "Do you have an extra blanket?"

Kathleen brought one from the closet, and Doctor Potter handed it to the man with him. "Wrap her in that and be certain her face is covered, and we'll take her out."

Three minutes later Kathleen held the door as they walked out of the bedroom. She opened the front door and the man walked out, while Doctor Potter stopped by the table where the candy was in two equal piles and Charles and Faith were eating their first pieces.

"I'll have to take your mother home for a while. You be good, and help your sister."

The children nodded but did not speak with their mouths full.

Kathleen followed the doctor out and closed the door. "I don't know how to thank you. What do I owe you?"

"We'll worry about that later. You did a remarkable thing, keeping this from those children. It would have ruined Christmas for them the rest of their lives."

Kathleen's chin trembled. "Thank you, Doctor." She threw her arms about him impulsively, and he patted her on the back, and turned and was gone.

Funeral services were held at graveside on Monday, December 28, 1778, in the far corner of the tiny Bexley cemetery. Seven people stood in the chill morning mist as the world said its final farewell to Phoebe Thorpe. Kathleen and the children, Doctor Potter and his wife, the Reverend Mr. Kirby, and the grave digger.

On Tuesday, Kathleen walked with the children to school, then continued the two miles to the docks on the Thames River where tall ships from every port of call in the world could be found. She walked to the first one flying the Union Jack and spoke to the officer of the deck, watching the gangplank.

"I'm inquiring about the fare for passage from here to the colonies in America."

A sneer crossed the man's face. "Sound like a colonial. You ought to know no English vessel uses American ports."

"Then where can I find a ship that does?"

"Take your pick." He pointed. "There're eleven miles of docks on up the Thames, clear past London Town."

At twelve-thirty P.M. Kathleen stopped before a large, squat, heavy ship and studied the flag—three bars, red, white, and blue—then walked up the gangplank to the officer waiting at the top.

"I'm inquiring about passage to the American colonies."

"Ja. Amerika. You vish to go?"

"Yes. Do you put in at American ports?"

"Sometime vi do. Talk vith Captain." He pointed, and Kathleen walked to a lean, grizzled veteran of forty years on the high seas in tall ships.

"I'm inquiring about passage to American ports."

"Ja."

"Do you put into American ports?"

"Ja."

"When will you be going there?"

The man's eyes narrowed and he shrugged. "Mitt good luck, seven, eight months. Vi go to India now, come back, leave for Amerika. You vait eight months. Vi take you."

"What country are you from?"

"Holland. Dutch."

"Do you know anyone leaving for America sooner than eight months?"

He shook his head. "Bad for ships in Amerika. British, French—fighting. Harbors closed, blockades. Bad."

"When do you sail for India?"

"Vun veek. Da six day of Januar."

"If I come back before then, can you mail a letter for me from the first port you visit that will carry it to America? I can bring you money for part payment of passage for myself and two children in eight months."

The man considered for a moment. "You bring da letter und ten pounds sterling und vi make arrangements. Ja?"

"What is the name of your ship?"

"*Van Otten.*"

"What is your name?"

"Jacob Schaumann."

"I will see you before Friday."

Kathleen trotted the four miles back to the small school with the white paint peeling, and was still breathing heavy when the bell clanged for dismissal, and the children came out, wrapping scarves and coats and putting on mittens.

After supper and prayers, she tucked the children into their beds and went back to the small dining table. With inkwell and paper before her and quill in hand, she thoughtfully began to write.

Tuesday, December 29th, 1778.

Dear Reverend Olmsted:

With heavy heart I write to inform you that my mother, Phoebe Thorpe, left us on Christmas Day, Friday, December 25th, 1778, and went to her final resting place in the cemetery at the village of Bexley, England.

Things are not well with the children, or myself, as long as we remain here. For that reason I write to tell you that I am making preparation to return to Boston in about eight months on a Dutch ship named the "Van Otten." The captain is Jacob Schaumann. If you have not sold the home which I inherited, would you please not do so pending my return. It is my intention to sell it myself for whatever price I can get, and use the money to begin a new life somewhere in America. I also beg of you, tell no one of this, since there is much time between now and my return, and too much can happen.

I am unable to find words to thank you for your kindnesses to myself and my family.

With kindest regards,
Kathleen Thorpe.

She went to the corner of the parlor and raised the door into the vegetable pit, and lifted a leather purse from beside a potato sack. She counted out ten pounds sterling, plus ten shillings, and laid them on the table with the letter.

Eight months—he didn't say how much passage would be—must get more money—can save it—from food and clothing money—I'll find a way—find a way.

She banked the coals in the fireplace, walked to her room, and slipped into her nightshirt. By the yellow light of a lantern, she opened the drawer to her nightstand and lifted out the small carved owl, and she stared at it for a long time, and touched it gently before she replaced it, and then slipped to her knees beside the bed.

CHAPTER XXVIII

★ ★ ★

*R*eport!"

Commodore John Paul Jones stood ramrod straight on the poop deck of the *Bonhomme Richard* facing Lieutenant Richard Dale in the late-afternoon September sun. To the west, the coastline of England rose barely visible twelve miles distant to interrupt the straight line where sea met sky. Seamen worked feverishly to clear the main deck of shattered rigging and to bring two fires under control.

"Sir," Lieutenant Dale said, "with the men taken prisoner at the engagements at the Shetlands and Orkneys, and the two prizes just taken, we have two hundred six British seamen locked in the third deck. The hold is nearly filled with gunpowder, cannon, medicine, salt beef, salt fish, lime juice, and fresh potatoes. We have some damage to the rigging, but the masts and yards are sound. We have one hole below the waterline that is repairable. The fires will be under control within the hour. We have four wounded, four dead."

"The British?"

"Both ships are sinking, sir. Twenty-eight dead, forty-one wounded and being tended by their ships' surgeons and ours. We have transferred everything we could to our own hold and to the *Alliance* and the *Pallas.* We cannot save either British ship."

"What damage to the *Alliance* and the *Pallas?*"

"All masts and hulls are sound. *Alliance* has two dead, six wounded; *Pallas* two dead, five wounded. Small fires that will be extinguished momentarily. We took the heaviest damage because we led the attack, sir."

"Very good, Mr. Dale, carry on." Jones turned to Matthew. "May I see you in my quarters?"

Inside the large, luxurious captain's quarters of the fourteen-year-old Indiaman, built by the French and given to the American navy to be converted to a man-of-war and renamed, Jones turned to Matthew. "Precisely where are we and how far are we from the nearest friendly port?"

Matthew stepped to the large Mercator map framed on the wall and traced with his finger. "We're right here, sir, about twelve miles from the east coast of England, and four miles north of Flamborough Head. The nearest friendly ports right now would be Trexel in Holland or Calais in France."

Jones paced as he considered. "How many days sailing time?"

"Loaded like we are, with good weather and the currents and winds holding, three days."

Jones stopped pacing and faced Matthew. "We've had good fortune on this voyage. Over one thousand miles within sight of the British Isles—Ireland, Scotland, the Orkneys, Shetlands, fifteen engagements, nineteen prizes so far, and no serious damage and only slight loss of men."

Matthew remained silent.

"We stung them at home and they're looking for us, so we'll have to keep moving. We'll hold here tonight and tomorrow for repairs, and then you can take us to Calais. The French will be impressed—ecstatic—with what we've done."

"A couple of more things, sir."

"Yes?"

"This vessel is fourteen years old, sir—waterlogged, leaking. Some of the ribs and part of the keel and hull are rotten. She needs to be dry-docked and have a lot of her wood replaced and a coat of tar and copper sheathing. She won't take much pounding in a heavy fight."

Jones's forehead wrinkled in deep concern. "I know. If we could stop the war for six months, we could fit her out like new." He shrugged. "But we can't, so she'll have to hold together for a while longer. There was something else?"

"Yes. The crews. By actual count, our crew now includes one hundred thirty-seven French marines, seventy-seven Irishmen, twenty-eight Portuguese, and a fair smattering of other nationalities, including some from India. The fifty-five Americans are mostly officers, and during this last fight some of the crew couldn't understand their orders. Things got a little confused a time or two. As you know, the *Alliance* has an American crew with the French captain Landais, and the *Pallas* crew is all French. They've both got the same problem with language."

Jones ballooned his cheeks and blew air. "I'm aware of it. When France came into the war this is what happened. I don't like it but I can't do anything about it except watch." He turned serious eyes to Matthew. "If you see things get snarled because of the language problems, take care of it on the spot. You have my full authority."

"Yes, sir."

Matthew turned to leave and Jones spoke once more. "Is Tom Sievers managing all right?"

"Tom's fine." Matthew grinned. "You should have seen the faces of five British seamen who tried to board us in the fight, when Tom met them at the rail with that Huron tomahawk."

Jones guffawed. "Good. Go back to your charts. We'll make sail sometime tomorrow after we've completed temporary repairs."

Sail makers and carpenters worked in shifts through the night, while the deck watch was doubled, peering into the night for the running lights of British men-of-war they knew would be combing the English coast looking for them. Morning found the three ships riding gentle swells at anchor, still making repairs in bright September sunlight while Jones and Dale and Matthew paced the deck nervously, eyes constantly on the horizon, waiting, watching. Noon mess was served, and the repairs continued. Matthew went to his quarters and once again checked latitudes, gulf current, winds, distances, channels, harbors. He opened the door and glanced back at the clock. Four-forty P.M., Thursday, September 23, 1779. The sun was dropping towards the low outline of the English mainland to the west when Matthew approached Jones.

"Sir, are repairs about completed?"

"We make sail in five minutes," Jones replied, "as soon as the crew over the side is back on deck."

Matthew watched the barefooted seamen, clad only in their drawers, water streaming, clamber onto the deck and pull up their rope ladder. The bosun's mate turned to Jones. "Sir, we're finished."

"Hoist anchor," Jones ordered, and eager hands shoved the capstan bars into their sockets, and the anchor chain rattled.

"Signal the *Alliance* and the *Pallas*."

Colored flags were run up the rope to the top of the mainmast.

"Unfurl all canvas."

Seamen already standing in the rigging with feet curled over the ropes jerked knots loose, and the great sails dropped from the yards flapping in the wind. Anxious hands tied them off at the bottom, and they popped and billowed, and the bow of the big ship rose slightly in the water as she came alive. Matthew looked, and the *Alliance* and the *Pallas* were moving, sails bulging, bows cutting a curl, sterns leaving a wake.

He exhaled and felt the tension begin to drain.

"Mr. Dunson, a heading, please."

"Due southeast until midnight."

"Southeast it is," the helmsman replied, and turned the wheel three-quarters of a turn and the bow swung to port.

The distant English coastline turned the sun red as it set, and then it was half gone, and the last arc was disappearing when the watchman in the crow's nest sang out, "Sails to the port side, stern," and raised an excited arm, pointing.

Matthew felt the knot in his stomach and raced to the stern

and grasped the rail with both hands, looking. The last rays of the setting sun caught sails on the horizon and set them glowing red, and Matthew's mouth became a straight line as he counted in disbelief. He darted to his quarters and snatched his glass and sprinted back to the rail and counted once more.

Forty-three sails!

He took control of his racing thoughts, and in the early dusk studied the incoming ships and their shape and their flags, and felt relief flood. He turned to Jones. "I think they're a fleet of merchantmen coming in from the Baltic, sir. I make out forty-one merchantmen with two men-of-war for escort. One big, one fair sized."

"Correct," Jones said crisply. He turned to Dale. "Signal the *Alliance* and the *Pallas* to form line for mutual support and follow us."

The signals went up immediately, and Matthew watched the ships behind maneuver, and suddenly his head thrust forward in disbelief. The *Alliance* was falling back, and the *Pallas* was turning to port.

Matthew turned to Jones. "They don't understand the signal, sir."

Jones watched for a moment, mouth clamped, then barked his next order. "Hold a course dead on the larger vessel," he called, and the helmsman corrected slightly to starboard.

Jones spoke to Dale and Matthew. "Count her guns as soon as you can."

Three minutes later Matthew called, "Fifty. Heavy."

"How many functional guns do we have?"

Dale answered, "Forty-two."

"Very good," Jones answered calmly. "Steady as she goes."

Matthew watched the distance between the ships dwindle, and glanced quickly to starboard, to see the *Pallas* setting a course to engage the other British man-of-war. The *Alliance* was behind at a safe distance.

Jones's eyes narrowed as he calculated distance, and at two

hundred yards he gave his next shouted command. "Hard to port and starboard guns prepare to fire."

The bow of the *Richard* swung left, and instantly the bow of the oncoming man-of-war swung the other direction. Within seconds the two ships were broadside to each other at just under two hundred yards.

"Fire!" shouted Jones, and in that instant all cannon on the starboard side of both ships blasted, and Matthew felt the shudder and saw the main deck near the bow erupt upwards for fifty feet, shattered, railing and decking splinters flying. Then through the swirling gun smoke he saw the gaping thirty-foot hole in the main deck and the fire beneath.

It took him three seconds to understand. Two of their three heaviest cannon on the second deck had exploded and blown a great hole in the side of the ship and a crater in the main deck. The crews were dead. Someone had misunderstood the powder measurement, or loaded two of the wrong-sized cannonballs. The *Richard* had but one more big gun. Matthew spun to hear Jones's order.

"Abandon that last big gun!" Jones shouted. "Do not fire it. It's unsafe!"

Matthew turned back to estimate the damage of the first broadside, while both ships frantically reloaded. Deck railings were shattered, sails punctured, rigging dangling, and he knew they had taken hits at the waterline.

The cannon roared again and the gun smoke billowed from both ships, but with the three big guns on the *Richard* out of action the exchange was pitifully lopsided. The heavy cannonballs from the British ship ripped into the second and third decks and silenced four more cannon and their crews, and Matthew felt the vibration as the *Richard* took nine more holes below her waterline. Fires began on the main and second decks, casting shadows on the tattered sails in the deep gloom of late dusk.

In fading light Jones gave his next command, "Hard starboard," and the helmsman spun the wheel. The *Richard* swung to her right, coming across the bow of the British man-of-war.

Matthew gauged speeds and distance and realized they were not going to get past the bow of the oncoming ship in time to make their turn to rake her with their cannon. He turned to watch Jones, who stood with feet planted apart, eyes narrowed as he gauged the distance, and Matthew made his own calculations and knew the oncoming man-of-war was going to ram them close to their stern. With the bowsprit of the oncoming man-of-war a scant fifty feet away, Matthew could read her name. The *Serapis.*

They lacked twenty feet of clearing the bowsprit when the *Serapis* plowed into the *Richard* with a shuddering, grinding *whump,* and the stern of the lighter *Richard* was knocked ten feet to starboard. Seamen on deck staggered to keep their footing.

Matthew could hardly believe the next command from Jones. "Tie us to their railing," he shouted, and stunned seamen obeyed without thought.

The British captain, Pearson, gaped when he saw the two-inch hawsers lashing the railings of the two ships together, and he recoiled, groping for the reason, understanding only that he needed distance for his cannon to take effect.

"Drop anchor," Pearson ordered. Startled British seamen jerked the locks from the chains, and they rattled as the anchor dropped into the black waters.

It flashed in Matthew's mind: *He thinks the tides will tear the ships apart—maybe they will—maybe.*

And then Jones's strategy clarified into Matthew's mind. His crippled ship could not outgun the big man-of-war, but with one hundred thirty-seven French marines on board, maybe they could storm the bigger ship and take her crew captive.

Riding the tide, the bow of the *Richard* slowly swung to port and she gathered speed, and while Captain Pearson of the *Serapis* gaped, the two ships slammed into each other, side by side, bows pointed in opposite directions. The cannon on both ships rammed into the hull of the other, the muzzles jammed tight. Overhead the yards and the rigging and the sails on both ships collided and meshed and tangled so badly they could not be separated.

It was five minutes past eight o'clock. The moon was not yet risen. The officers and crews of both ships suddenly understood that in the annals of naval warfare, never had two men-of-war found themselves sealed irrevocably to each other, hull to hull, locked in a deadly fight to the death, in total blackness.

Matthew looked desperately to starboard, probing for the *Pallas* in the darkness, and in the far distance saw gun flashes. He looked for the *Alliance,* and could not find her.

The heavy guns on the *Serapis* fired again, and the balls tore into the *Richard,* throwing the shattered, rotted timbers and planking in all directions. With one-fourth of her guns already silenced, the *Richard* returned fire, and wood from the hull and railing and decks of the *Serapis* flew.

Then Matthew heard the shouts from the *Serapis,* and half her crew came surging towards the railing. Matthew snatched up a sword and pistol from the wreckage and charged the railing, turning, shouting to the French marines, "Follow me," and then Tom was beside him. The marines came like a tidal wave, and they swarmed the oncoming British at the railings. For three brutal minutes the railings were lost in the tangle of bodies and flashing swords and cracking pistols as men fought to the death, close enough to feel the breath and see the terror in the eyes of the wounded and dying, and the British were thrown back onto their own decks.

The marines rallied and regrouped and charged the rails to storm the *Serapis,* and the British muskets blasted. Once again the two forces met at the railings, with swords flashing and pistols cracking, in a desperate hand-to-hand melee.

Matthew was at the rail and looked at the blood on his sleeves and saw that it was not his own. At that instant a cannonball whirred past his head and smashed into a British seaman on the *Serapis* railing, and Matthew froze in the realization the ball had come from behind him. He spun to look, and eight hundred yards off their port side he saw the winking of more cannon. Then the balls came smashing into the *Richard,* and Matthew screamed, "It's the *Alliance,*" and jammed, shoved his way through the mass of struggling men to the port rail. He grabbed a lantern and began to swing it wildly back and forth—the universal sign to cease fire.

There was a momentary pause, and then the next broadside came whistling from the *Alliance*. Matthew turned to look for Jones, and Jones was on the poop deck, swinging his own lantern violently. Then Tom was beside Matthew swinging a lantern, and they all shook their fists and shouted and kept the lanterns swinging until the next broadside came slamming into their rigging. They stopped the lanterns and ignored the *Alliance* because there was nothing more to do.

Fires were running out of control, and Matthew ran to shove a dislodged hatch cover back into place to prevent debris from falling below decks into the powder magazine or barrels. He turned back and saw Tom in front of the poop deck frantically shoving hand grenades inside his shirt, and then Tom stood and gave a sweep of his arm and shouted to the marines, "I'm going up," and started up the rigging like a cat. A dozen marines stuffed grenades in their shirts and followed, while twenty others rushed back to the rail with muskets to watch for any British seamen who raised their muskets to bear on Tom.

Fifty-five feet above the decks, caught in the flickering light of the fires on both ships, Tom stopped and wrapped his arms through the rope ladder and touched the smouldering cannoneer's match to the four-inch fuse of the grenade and threw it. The lighted fuse arced out and down, and one second after the grenade hit and bounced, it exploded and two British seamen staggered and went down.

As fast as he could light the fuses, Tom emptied his shirt of ten grenades, and the marines who followed him into the tangled rigging began throwing theirs. The British on deck took cover behind the mass of shattered wood and fallen yards and canvas. British marksmen stood on the decks of the *Serapis* and with their muskets took aim on the dim bodies in the rigging. The marines on the *Richard* fired, and some of the marksmen went down and others flinched and ducked for cover.

Suddenly the cannon from the *Alliance* stopped, and Matthew watched their running lights become clearer. *They're coming—they're coming—hold on—hold on* . . .

The blasting of the *Serapis's* cannon never ceased, and the planking of the old, rotten hull of the *Richard* began to separate under the endless battering. Water came pouring into the hold, and Matthew felt the deck settle with the weight below, where the crews were frantically pumping but unable to hold the water-line.

Again the British rushed the rails to board, and again the marines met them and pushed them back, while Tom and a dozen others lofted grenades downward from the rigging and musket balls whistled past them. Two groaned and grasped at the ropes, then released and tumbled downward.

In the wild confusion, Matthew suddenly realized Jones had left the poop deck and was on the main deck, commanding three cannon personally, and then Matthew understood they were the only guns on the main deck still working. A cannonball from the *Serapis* blew decking five feet from Jones, and Jones hunched his shoulders and gave the order to reload, when one of the cannoneers threw up his arms and shouted across the railings, "Quarter—we ask quarter—we surrender."

Jones jerked his pistol from his belt, closed with the cannoneer in one stride, and swung the pistol. Matthew heard the crack as it struck the seaman's head, and the man went down without a sound or movement.

Aboard the *Serapis*, Pearson heard the frightened, shouted request for quarter and seized his captain's horn and bellowed, "Verify the request—do you request quarter? Do you surrender?"

At that split second in time, Jones had but three guns working on his main deck (he did not know how many on the second deck); had four feet of water in the hold and rising; and had taken over twenty point-blank broadsides from the *Serapis*, as well as four from his own ship *Alliance*. He had fires burning out of control on two decks, men and shattered wood and rigging thick on his deck, mainmast and mizzenmast both splintered, sails shredded, and he did not know how many of his crew dead or disabled.

He pivoted to face Captain Pearson across the railings, and he thrust his clenched fist into the air and shouted with all his strength, "I have not yet begun to fight."

For a grain of time the defiant declaration hung in the air, and then it was lost in the sounds of battle, and Pearson gave the order, "Continue firing."

Again Matthew pointed over their port side at the incoming lights of the *Alliance*, convinced they had understood their mistake and were coming to join the fight against the *Serapis*. Then he saw the muzzle flashes, and once again four cannonballs ripped into the port side of the *Richard*, while a few whistled over her decks and slammed into the *Serapis*. Matthew ignored the incoming *Alliance* and raced to take the place of a fallen cannoneer, loading and firing one of the three remaining nine-pounders on the main deck.

Lieutenant Dale felt the *Richard* settling into the sea and realized it was only a matter of time, and in his mind flashed the faces of two hundred six British seamen locked below decks. He leaped to the nearest gangway and descended through the fires and the shattered timbers and took a bung starter and knocked the locks off the doors and released the prisoners—the unspoken law of the sea. They surged outward, and he retreated to the gangway upwards to freedom and stopped and faced them with a pistol in one hand and a sword in the other.

"You men will go down to the hold and man the pumps to save this ship, and if you do not, my next shot from this pistol will be into the powder stores beside you. Move." For two seconds that seemed an eternity he faced them before a dozen of them retreated to the gangway downward, and five minutes later the men were in the hold, manning every pump available.

It was ten minutes past nine o'clock.

At nine-twenty, Tom again loaded his shirt with grenades and scrambled back into the tangled rigging and crossed over to the rigging of the *Serapis*, where Lieutenant Stack had led marine marksmen to shoot down at the British below. With the sparking cannoneer's match Tom lighted the fuse of the first grenade and tossed it arcing downward. In the flash of the explosion on the deck, for the first time he noticed that a deck hatch cover had been blown partly out of place and there was a black opening, perhaps two feet wide and four feet long, down to the second deck.

Beneath him, marksmen raised their muskets and fired, and one ball left a black streak on the left hip of his trousers. The marine marksmen around him fired back. Tom wrapped his arms into the rigging to light the second grenade and tossed it carefully, and it hit the hatch cover six inches from the hole and rolled onto the deck before it exploded.

On the deck of the *Serapis* Matthew saw the arc of the burning fuse, and the explosion, and understood, and turned his face upward to peer into the rigging, and he saw Tom. He straightened, holding his breath, as Tom lighted the next fuse. One second later Tom tossed the grenade, and Matthew watched the sputtering fuse travel downward and disappear into the blackness of the open hatch.

On the second deck, the round grenade hit and rolled and stopped against a box of cartridges, and then it exploded. Instantly the box of cartridges erupted and the one next to it blew, and next to it were two kegs of gunpowder and they blew. In the next three seconds the explosions leaped from box to box of cartridges and barrel to barrel of gunpowder in one continuous, horrendous explosion.

Cannon were blown through their own ports into the sea. Fire blasted fifty feet out of every opening. On the main deck, every hatch cover was blasted out of sight into the black heavens. On the poop deck Captain Pearson grabbed for the rail to keep from being thrown down. It seemed every plank on the main deck rose half a foot, and through the cracks fire could be seen from below. Both the mainmast and the mizzenmast trembled. Not one cannon or one cannoneer on the second deck survived, and every cannon on the main deck was silenced.

Time seemed suspended while the seamen on both ships stopped, frozen, eyes wide in shock at the explosion that had shaken the great ship from stem to stern, and then the ragged firing resumed. Matthew looked upward to watch Tom, and he didn't realize he had raised one clenched hand and was holding his breath as Tom disengaged his arms from the ropes and began working his way back to the *Richard.*

From beneath, once again the British raised their muskets and fired, and Matthew saw Tom jerk, and then his shoulders slowly settled and his head fell forward and he clung to the tangled ropes. Matthew screamed, "Tom!" and leaped to the railing and started up the twisted ropes and rigging. He paid no heed to the musket balls whistling upward about him, and he was not aware the marines fired back and the British muskets stopped. Forty seconds later he was beside Tom, and he saw the great gout of black blood above the belt on his right side. He lifted the wiry body enough to slip the wrist and hand from the looped rope, and he put Tom over his shoulder and started back down.

He neither knew nor cared that the *Alliance* had finally arrived and by purest accident had taken a raking position on the *Serapis* that struck fear into Captain Pearson, or that at that moment the mainmast of the big man-of-war had shivered, or that Pearson was certain his ship was mortally wounded and sinking.

Matthew reached the deck of the *Richard,* and strong, gentle hands lifted Tom from his shoulder. They gathered sail canvas into a cushion and laid him on it, and Matthew leaned over the still form, hand spread on the chest, feeling for a heartbeat.

"Tom?" he said. "Tom—can you hear me?"

Matthew did not hear the shouted inquiry from Jones to Pearson, "Will you strike your colors?"

"Tom!" Matthew seized the limp hand.

He paid no attention when Captain Pearson answered Jones, "I will strike. I surrender my command."

Matthew gave hand signals, and men who had seen the grenade drop from the rigging into the open hatch tenderly picked up the cushion of canvas. Matthew led them to his quarters, and they laid Tom on Matthew's bunk. Matthew did not notice that the cannon had fallen silent. The battle was over.

"Get the ship's surgeon," he said, and two of them left.

Matthew leaned over the thin, leathery face and touched Tom's cheek gently with his fingers. Behind him, men wiped at their eyes and said nothing. The door opened and the balding doctor dropped to one knee beside the still form, and he tucked two fingers carefully under Tom's jaw and closed his eyes to concentrate. He frowned, and adjusted his fingers. He rolled Tom onto his side and ripped the bloody shirt wide open, and his face fell when he saw the purple welt surrounding the hole made by the .75-caliber ball. He closed his eyes and for a moment shook his head, then turned to Matthew. "Did you see it happen?"

"Most of it."

"Was the ball travelling upward?"

"Yes."

Slowly the surgeon rose and stood with his hands at his sides, and Matthew stood to face him.

"The ball is somewhere in his chest. I think by his heart." He paused, hating his next words. "I can't get it out."

"Is he dead?"

The surgeon shook his head. "There is a slight heartbeat but it's fading."

"Is there any chance?"

"None."

"Thank you." Matthew dropped to his knees beside the bunk and leaned over to peer intently at the weathered face, as though to memorize every line.

Behind him, the men quietly backed away and walked out the door, except for the last man, who paused. "Some of us saw what he did. We won't forget."

The door closed, and Matthew brought the lamp from the table to the nightstand, and drew a chair over by the bunk, and settled onto it and leaned forward, one hand on Tom's. Time meant nothing, and Matthew was vaguely aware when the door behind him opened and closed softly. Time passed and then Jones's voice came from behind. "Is he alive?"

"Yes."

"They told me what he did."

Matthew did not turn or speak.

"The British surrendered. That man saved us."

Matthew nodded his head.

"We're sinking. We'll have to move him to the *Serapis* by morning."

"I'll stay with him."

Jones quietly left and Matthew glanced at the clock. It was twenty minutes past eleven o'clock P.M., Thursday, September 23, 1779.

At two o'clock A.M. Jones returned to stand quietly in the yellow lamp glow. "We're moving everything to the *Serapis*. We have perhaps five or six more hours."

Matthew nodded.

"Is he still alive?"

"I think so."

"I'll come when it's time."

Jones turned to go, and then he heard a sigh and a whisper. "Matthew?" He turned and watched.

Matthew was instantly on his knees beside the bunk, one hand holding Tom's, the other against his cheek, ear close to Tom's face. "I'm here, Tom."

The eyes fluttered open for a moment. "Are you all right?"

"I'm fine."

A smile formed. "I promised Margaret."

"Don't talk, Tom. Listen. They surrendered. You saved us."

Matthew watched the look of deep weariness settle on the pale face.

"Not me. Him. He saved us."

The voice was fading. Matthew gently slipped his arm beneath the neck and raised the head to him as he would a child and listened intently as the mouth worked to form whispered words.

"Came back. Promised to tell you."

Matthew's ear was inches from Tom's mouth.

"Saw John. Splendid. Tell Margaret saw John."

A sob caught in Matthew's throat, and he felt the warm tears on his cheeks as he began to slowly rock back and forth, holding the frail body.

Tom's eyes opened wide and his face took on a radiance. "Elizabeth. There waiting. And Jacob! A man. Grown. My Jacob! Knew me—called me by name. All white and shining. Peaceful."

He settled back in Matthew's arms and he was smiling and his eyes were alive, filled with wonder. "John said tell you. Going back now. Elizabeth waiting. Jacob."

Matthew watched the glow fade from the face as Tom left his body and it slowly relaxed, smiling, eyes wide.

Matthew did not know how long he remained on his knees, holding Tom to his chest while the tears wet his face and fell into the tangled hair. Finally he laid the head back on his pillow and tucked the hair into place, and pulled the blanket up to the chin, but did not cover the face. He studied Tom for a time before he covered the face.

He turned at a sound from behind and Captain Jones was still there. Matthew stood and wiped his face with his sleeve and looked calmly into Jones's face.

"Matthew," Jones said softly, "may I inquire?"

Matthew waited.

"Did he mention John?"

"My father. Tom brought him back from the Concord battle. He died the next day."

"Elizabeth?"

"Tom's wife. Dead nearly thirty years. Huron Indians."

"Jacob?"

"His son. Died with his wife."

"Do you believe he saw them?"

Matthew looked directly into Jones's eyes. "He saw them."

Jones swallowed and remained silent and unmoving for a time, then spoke once again. "At the first, he said he didn't save us. Someone else did. Who?"

Matthew did not flinch. "The Almighty."

"But it was Tom who climbed the rigging—threw the grenade."

"Tom knows who saved us."

Jones did not move for a long time, staring into Matthew's eyes, and then he walked towards the door.

"Captain," Matthew said.

Jones turned.

"I would like to take Tom home for burial, near his wife. Could you instruct the surgeon to prepare the body?"

Jones swallowed but could not speak. He nodded his head and walked out the door into the night.

Notes

This chapter addresses what is historically one of the most famous sea engagements in modern times. The American ship *Bonhomme Richard*, forty-two guns, under the command of Commodore John Paul Jones, engaged the British man-of-war *Serapis*, fifty guns, off Flamborough Head on the east coast of England as dusk approached on the evening of September 23, 1779. The *Richard* was a French vessel that had previously been a merchantman for thirteen years under the name *Le Duc de Duras*, plying between Europe and China. Although refitted, the ship was slow and cumbersome, with many waterlogged and rotting timbers, and was substantially inferior in both size and quality to the *Serapis*. Nonetheless, Jones closed with the larger ship and cut across her bow, causing the *Serapis* to ram the *Richard*. Jones ordered his crew to lash the railings of the two ships together, and the tides swung them until they were side by side, bound together, bows pointing in opposite directions.

In total darkness, the cannon roared at point-blank range for more than two hours before a member of Jones's crew called for quarter and Captain Pearson, commander of the *Serapis*, asked Jones to repeat the request. It was at that point Jones shouted back that he had not asked for quarter, followed by the now immortal words, "I have not yet begun to fight."

Shortly after 9:30 P.M., while the *Richard* was slowly sinking with five feet of water in her hold, a crewman from the *Richard* threw a hand grenade from the rigging, which dropped through an open hatch into the second deck of the *Serapis*, igniting barrels of gunpowder in quick succession and blowing out the entire second deck. Captain Pearson feared that his ship was sinking, and on Jones's demand he struck his colors and surrendered. Jones's men worked to save the *Richard*, but after one day and a night, it was obvious she would not last. So Jones transferred the wounded and the desired munitions and supplies to the *Serapis*, jury-rigged the captured ship's battered mast, and made other emergency repairs. During the morning of September 25, 1779, to Jones's regret the *Richard* finally sank, and he sailed the *Serapis*, with prisoners, to a Dutch port and thence to the United States. (See Knox, *A History of the United States Navy*, pp. 32–36; Jobé, ed., *The Great Age of Sail*, p. 151.)

October 1779

CHAPTER XXIX

★ ★ ★

*M*atthew dropped the shovel into the wagon bed, wiped the sweat from his face, and took his coat from the wagon seat. He buttoned it while he walked back to the fresh mound of dark earth, and he stopped and stood quietly in the silence and looked about the valley, peaceful in the warm autumn sun.

October frosts had nipped the oak and maple trees, and the gently rolling hills were ablaze with red and orange. The grasses of summer had come to full head and were yellow and nodding heavy. To the east, Marsden Creek was lined with willows and brown summer-cured cattails where it worked its way through the low ground and disappeared at the south end of the valley. Shaggy squirrels darted to snatch up seeds and nuts and crowd them into their cheeks before they stopped for a second to inspect with beady eyes the intruder, then made their run to store their winter supply in a tree hollow. A mother raccoon led two little ones with rings on their tails to the creek and watched patiently while they washed their faces and paws and then settled down to wait patiently for a fish to venture too close. Four hundred yards to the north, a doe and yearling fawn raised their dripping muzzles from the creek, long ears pointed, twitching while they studied Matthew, and then they lowered their muzzles once more.

Matthew looked at the small marble headstone with the inscription. "THOMAS SIEVERS. DIED SEPTEMBER 24,

1779. BELOVED HUSBAND, FATHER, FRIEND, PATRIOT."

He went to one knee beside the fresh-turned mound and placed one hand on it.

"It's the best I could do, Tom. From what Father said, the church was over there, and your home should have been about here. I hope we're close to where Elizabeth and Jacob are sleeping."

He crumbled moist clods between his fingers.

"Mother and Billy wanted to come, but somehow I thought you and I should do this together, just the two of us. They said their good-byes yesterday before I left. I hope you don't mind."

He brushed dirt crumbs from his hands.

"I told Mother what you said about Father, and it did her good. She said sometimes he's so close she feels like she can reach out and touch him."

He looked about for a moment. "Your little valley is beautiful. You'll like it here."

He stood and rubbed the palms of his hands against his trouser legs. "Wish I could see you with Jacob. That must be something, after twenty-five years. Really something."

He felt the warm sun on his face and shoulders, and drew and released a great breath. "I have to go now. I'll be back soon, and I'll bring Mother and the family, and Billy."

A strange feeling rose in his breast, and for a moment he knew Tom was there, close, and he smiled down at the mound. "I know, Tom. I'd stay if I could. You wait, and we'll be back soon."

The moon was full overhead when Matthew unhitched the mare at the Boston livery and emptied a gallon of oats and two forks of hay into her feed manger, and pushed the wagon against the back wall of the shed. It was ten minutes before one o'clock A.M. when he opened the front door and walked softly into the twilight of the parlor.

Margaret started and rose from the rocking chair. "Are you all right?"

Matthew nodded. "Good."

"Hungry?"

Matthew shrugged, and Margaret opened the oven and set a plate of hot roast beef and potatoes and gravy before him.

"Tell me about it."

For twenty minutes Matthew ate and spoke slowly, quietly, and a deep sense of peace and rightness settled in the room.

When he finished, Margaret wiped her eyes. "I'm so glad," she said. She sighed and stood. "Well, tomorrow's the Sabbath. It's late. We better get to bed." They knelt together for their evening prayers, and then walked through the archway to their bedrooms.

In the glow of the single lamp on his nightstand, Matthew lifted his wallet from his coat and laid it on his pillow and opened it. A moment later the small watch fob lay on the white pillowcase, delicate and beautiful. He touched it gently, and his thoughts came: *Three years. Where is she? her family? Are they safe? warm?*

He carefully rewrapped it and pushed the wallet back into his coat and turned out the lamp as he slipped into his bed.

Dawn found Margaret humming while she stirred the banked coals in the fireplace and added wood shavings, then kindling, and transferred fire to the oven in the kitchen. Matthew got squash from the root cellar while Brigitte sliced fresh apples for dumplings, and Margaret worked cloves into the pork roast.

The family stood for Matthew's inspection before they walked out into the street, and none of them could remember a more beautiful, exhilarating October day, air still in the warm sunshine, leaves so many colors they nearly hurt their eyes. Greetings were called and chatter abounded. Silas led them in song and sermon, then prayer, and the congregation emerged again into the bright sunlight to gather in small groups, feeling the touch of magic in the crisp air, needing release, to talk and laugh, reluctant to leave.

Billy and Dorothy stood with Matthew and Margaret and Brigitte, while Adam and Prissy sought their own to tease and run on the thick grass.

It was Matthew who saw Silas approach with an envelope in hand, and he saw the concern in Silas's eyes and sobered.

"Matthew, could I see you for a moment?"

Matthew looked at Margaret, then Billy, then back at Silas. "Something wrong?"

"I don't wish to alarm you, but could I see you?"

"Of course."

He followed Silas back into the vacant chapel, where the sun streamed through the stained-glass windows to transform the sparse room into a kaleidoscope of color.

Silas led him to one corner and spoke quietly. "I'm deeply concerned about Kathleen."

Matthew started, instantly tense, focused. "Kathleen? What's happened?"

"I received a letter from her the last week in September. It was written ten months ago, in January. I have no idea why it was so long getting here."

Matthew took control of his racing thoughts, fears. "What was in the letter?"

Silas looked toward the door, then reached inside his robe. "Read it. Maybe you'll understand."

Matthew opened the frayed envelope and silently read the letter, and his shoulders slumped for a moment. "This is the last you heard from her?"

"Yes. Now do you see my concern?"

"She said she would be here in eight months. That was ten months ago. Is that it?"

"Yes. You know about ships and the ocean. What could be wrong?"

"Too many things. Storms, shipwreck, white slavers, high-seas pirates, a lying captain—too many things. Why didn't you tell me sooner?"

"You've been home only a few days, and she wanted no one to know. What can be done?"

Matthew skimmed the letter once more. "Captain Jacob Schaumann, of the *Van Otten*. I'll go to the docks and find out all I can about the ship and the captain, and everything available about the weather in the North Atlantic for the past two months. October is bad for storms."

"Will you do it?"

"I'll need this letter."

"Take it."

Matthew refolded the letter and jammed it into his inside coat pocket and started for the door, when Silas grasped his arm.

"Don't make this generally known."

"I'll have to tell Mother, and probably Billy. He can help."

"Do what you have to do. If that poor child is gone . . ." Silas's eyes were pleading.

Matthew said nothing as he walked out the door, directly to the waiting families. "We have a little emergency. Billy, can you come with me now? Maybe for the rest of the day?"

Billy's eyes widened at the rare request. "Of course."

"Mother, will you take the family home and finish the day without me? I don't know when I'll be home."

Margaret's face paled. "What's happened? Trouble?"

"Don't worry. I'll tell you as soon as I can."

He turned to Dorothy. "I'm sorry to take Billy. I'll explain later."

Dorothy shrugged. "Any danger?"

"No. We'll be at the docks."

The two left the churchyard, and Matthew handed the letter to Billy, who read it as they hurried northeast onto Franklin, then east to India Street and down to the east docks of the Boston Peninsula.

"She's two months late?" Billy asked.

"Yes. I've got to know why. Come with me and listen."

Matthew trotted south on the docks to the first ship tied up unloading, strode up the gangplank, and faced the officer of the deck, Billy at his shoulder.

"Sir, I am Matthew Dunson. I'm a navigator. I've just received news of an overdue ship from either Holland or London. Have you come in from the North Atlantic?"

"Yes."

"What was your port of origin?"

"Cherbourg."

"What was the weather?"

"Bad. Delayed four weeks."

"Hear of any ships lost?"

"Three."

"Any of Dutch registry?"

"One."

"What name?"

"The *Amsterdam*. Went down with all hands one hundred twenty miles northwest of La Coruña. Hurricane. We turned back, but she didn't. Have you lost someone?" The narrowed eyes softened.

"Maybe. Heard anything of a Dutch ship called the *Van Otten*?"

The man pondered for a moment. "Heard of her, but nothing this trip."

"Thank you, sir."

The man watched as Matthew led Billy back to the heavy oak planking of the docks and stopped.

"If we separate, we can cover twice as many ships. This is Sunday and not every ship is going to have the gangplank down and someone on deck, but some of them will. The Dutch flag is three bars, red on top, white, blue on the bottom. Watch for that flag especially. If the office of a shipping company is open, go on in. Can you handle it?"

"Yes."

"You work south, I'll go north. One more thing. Don't get caught on these docks after dark. Too many crews from foreign ports will cut your throat for the coins in your pockets and hide your body under the docks. Meet me back here at six o'clock."

The docks ran for four miles, from the Colony Depot on the east side of the peninsula to Fruit Street on the west, with ships moored on one side of the street, and on the other, weathered warehouses of brick or frame and office buildings with names of national and international shipping companies printed in square letters across the windows or on signs above. The two men patiently walked the gangplanks of the ships that were loading or unloading, and entered the doors of shipping companies when lights showed inside, patiently inquiring. The day wore on and the sun dipped to the west and set, and they each retraced their steps to meet back at India Street.

"Anything?" Matthew asked, and Billy shook his head.

"Can you help tomorrow?"

Billy thought for a moment. "Beginning at noon. I've got to finish balancing accounts and a profit or loss statement for Bingham Foundry—one of our biggest clients—and then I think Mr. Becksted will give me the rest of the day off. I'll go to the accounting office early."

"Your mother will need to know about all this, but try to not let it go further."

Billy nodded.

At full dark Matthew walked into the parlor and closed the door. Margaret and Brigitte were waiting. Margaret set a hot supper on the table, and they sat down, the women silent, waiting.

Matthew laid Kathleen's letter on the table in front of Margaret and began eating.

Margaret read silently, gasped, and put her hand over her mouth. "Phoebe's gone!" she exclaimed softly. Brigitte started, then settled, and Margaret finished and handed her the letter, and said quietly, "You and Billy went down to the docks to find out about that ship?"

"Yes."

"Did you learn anything?"

"There was bad weather in the North Atlantic—hurricane—three ships went down. We'll go back tomorrow. I've got to know what happened."

Dawn came clear and calm, and the Boston docks were alive with tall ships moving in and out and with dockworkers dressed in woolen sweaters going to and coming from the vessels being loaded or unloaded. Matthew worked his way through the crowds and patiently continued his search. At one o'clock Billy found him and they separated.

At three-forty P.M. Billy studied a ship newly arrived under a flag he did not recognize, tied to the Aspinwall Wharf, next to the landing of the Winnisimmet Ferry. He walked up the gangplank and stopped before the deck officer.

"Sir, I am Billy Weems. I have need to inquire about a ship that is long overdue. Do you come from Europe?"

"Lisbon. Portugal." Billy was aware of the strong Spanish-Portuguese accent.

"Do you know anything of the *Van Otten?* Dutch registry."

The small, bearded Portuguese officer thought for a moment. "Sailed from London three months ago?"

Billy came to an instant focus. "Yes."

"Hurricane in the North Sea—she was damaged—put in at Lisbon for repairs. I saw her."

"Is she still there?"

"No. She sailed the day we sailed."

"Has she arrived here yet?"

"No. We distanced her. One day or two days behind us."

"What ship is this?"

"*Ferdinand.*"

"Thank you!" Billy spun and ran thumping down the gang-plank onto the dock and started west, working his way through the stacks of crates and cargo and the milling throng. At four-thirty P.M. he caught up with Matthew, panting, breathless.

"There's a Portuguese ship—the *Ferdinand*—at Aspinwall Wharf. They saw the *Van Otten.*"

With the sun casting long shadows from the masts of the tall ships, Matthew trotted up the gangplank of the *Ferdinand*, which rose and fell gently with the incoming tide, and faced the deck officer.

"I'm Matthew Dunson, a navigator. Do you have knowledge of the *Van Otten?*"

The man glanced at Matthew, then studied Billy for a moment before recognition showed. "The *Van Otten* should be in tomorrow or the next day."

"Do you know which company her captain trades with?"

The man pursed his mouth for a moment. "DePriest, I think."

"Thank you." He spun and Billy followed him trotting, three hundred yards south, stopping before a square, weathered brick building with a peeling sign across the front, "DEPRIEST INT'L. TRADING, LTD." Inside, a man in black tie and shirt-sleeves had just locked the door, and Matthew banged.

Irritated, the man opened the door a foot. "Yes?"

"Are you expecting the *Van Otten?*"

The man sobered. "Yes. Have you heard something?"

"The deck officer of the *Ferdinand* says she'll probably be in within two days."

"He told us."

"Do you know Captain Jacob Schaumann?"

"We know him."

"Is he reliable?"

"Been fair with us. What's your interest in this?"

"Does Schaumann take on passengers?"

"Sometimes. Are you expecting someone?"

"Maybe. Thank you. Very much."

The man locked the door and disappeared in the office.

Matthew turned to face Billy, excitement rising. "She might be on it. Kathleen might be coming home!" He turned and looked east, out towards the mouth of the harbor to the open sea. "You go on home. I'm going to stay. She could arrive yet today. Tell Mother I'll be home after dark."

"Want me to wait with you?"

"I've taken you too much the past two days. You go on."

It was past ten o'clock when Matthew pushed through the door into the parlor, and minutes later Margaret set a bowl of steaming beef broth before him while they talked.

At five-thirty A.M. Matthew was back on the docks, his

telescope in his coat pocket, peering intently eastward into the gray dawn, watching the mist rise from the sea. The rising sun came in calm, clear skies, and the mists stopped, and Matthew stood with his telescope extended, moving constantly back and forth for any speck that might appear on the horizon. He paid no heed to the incessant sounds and sights and smells of merchant-men unloading tea and silk and spices from the East, or porcelain and wool from Europe.

Three times before noon he stiffened and tracked a fleck on the horizon until it became sails and then a ship and then a schooner or a frigate from New York or the West Indies. He was unaware when the sun reached its zenith and began to set towards the western horizon, nor did he care that he had not eaten. In his heart and mind was but one thought. *She might be coming—she might be coming . . .* It repeated like an unending chant, and he could hear nothing else.

At two-thirty P.M. Billy walked up beside him, and Matthew looked at him and then resumed scanning the horizon with his tele-scope. At three P.M. Matthew turned to Billy. "No need to stay."

"Sure?"

"Go on home. She might not come in until tomorrow, or the next day."

Billy turned to go, and at that instant Matthew started and then his breath constricted, and Billy stopped.

For two full minutes Matthew studied the incoming sails and the cut of the ship. Square sails, squat, square ship, unlike the slim lines of schooners or frigates.

"She might be Dutch," Matthew said quietly. He was scarcely breathing.

Billy stood staring, unmoving, waiting while minutes passed.

Suddenly Matthew hunched forward and for an instant dropped his telescope from his eye and looked, then raised the scope again. "Her colors are Dutch! Dutch!" he exclaimed. "Red, white, blue! It has to be her."

Billy turned on his heel and was gone, and Matthew realized it but did not move, standing like a statue waiting for the name on the bow of the ship to come into focus large enough to read.

Minutes became a quarter of an hour, and Matthew waited until he was certain and then exclaimed, "*Van Otten!* It's the *Van Otten!* She might be on it—has to be on it."

The ship came steadily on, square sails full, blunt bow cutting a wake, and Matthew studied the rail through his telescope, and there were only the seamen, making ready for the pilot boat to meet them and bring them into the harbor. Hawsers were cast, and the pilot boat caught them and turned and began the slow work of bringing the ship through the channel into her dock. Matthew's eyes did not leave the railing, searching for the figure of a woman, or children, but there were only seamen on the main deck and two officers by the helmsman. He licked dry lips, suddenly fearful.

The pilot boat made her turn and headed for the Lewis Dock, and Matthew ran to it and waited, watching the rail.

Behind him he heard his name and turned, and Billy was there with Margaret and Brigitte and Adam and Prissy, working through the crowd. Matthew turned back and watched as seamen cast their hawsers, and rough hands tied the ship. One man raised the hinged section of railing for the gangplank, and four men moved it forward and lowered it into position, thumping on the dock, and locked it.

Matthew stood rooted, eyes sweeping the rail, and there was no woman there. Then two seamen came with trunks and set them by the gangplank, and suddenly she was there behind them, and she moved forward with the children beside her.

Matthew leaped to the gangplank, and she saw him and her hand flew to her mouth as he raced upward. Then he was on the deck, and he swept her into his arms, and she threw her arms about him and buried her face in his shoulder. She clung to him and he held her with all his strength, and they stood in the warm early-November afternoon sun, eyes closed, lost in each other, aware only that the pain was gone, and they were whole, and they were home.

SELECTED BIBLIOGRAPHY

★ ★ ★

Birnbaum, Louis. *Red Dawn at Lexington: "If They Mean to Have a War, Let It Begin Here!"* Boston: Houghton Mifflin, 1986.

Bunting, W. H., comp. *Portrait of a Port: Boston, 1852-1914.* Cambridge, Mass.: Harvard University Press, 1971.

Colbert, David, ed. *Eyewitness to America: 500 Years of America in the Words of Those Who Saw It Happen.* New York: Pantheon Books, 1997.

Cutler, Carl C. *Queens of the Western Ocean.* Annapolis, Md.: United States Naval Institute, 1961.

Fischer, David Hackett. *Paul Revere's Ride.* New York: Oxford University Press, 1994.

French, Allen. *The Day of Concord and Lexington: The Nineteenth of April, 1775.* Boston: Little, Brown, and Co., 1925.

———. *General Gage's Informers.* Ann Arbor, Mich.: University of Michigan Press, 1932.

Furnas, J. C. *The Americans: A Social History of the United States, 1587-1914.* New York: G. P. Putnam's Sons, 1969.

Galvin, John R. *The Minute Men: A Compact History of the Defenders of the American Colonies, 1645–1775.* New York: Hawthorn Books, 1967.

Jobé, Joseph, ed. *The Great Age of Sail.* Translated by Michael Kelly. New York: Crescent Books, 1967.

Knox, Dudley W. *A History of the United States Navy.* Revised edition. New York: G. P. Putnam's Sons, 1948.

Leckie, Robert. *George Washington's War: The Saga of the American Revolution.* New York: HarperCollins, 1992.

Miller, Nathan. *Sea of Glory: A Naval History of the American Revolution.* Annapolis, Md.: Naval Institute Press, 1992.

Outhwaite, Leonard. *The Atlantic: A History of an Ocean.* New York: Coward-McCann, 1957.

Ulrich, Laurel Thatcher. *Good Wives: Image and Reality in the Lives of Women in Northern New England, 1650–1750.* New York: Vintage Press, 1991.

————. *A Midwife's Tale: The Life of Martha Ballard, Based on Her Diary, 1785–1812.* New York: Vintage Press, 1990.

Acknowledgments

Richard B. Bernstein, a constitutional historian specializing in the Revolutionary generation, made a tremendous contribution to the historical accuracy of this work, for which the writer is deeply grateful. The staff of the publisher, Bookcraft, most notably Garry Garff, editor, and Jana Erickson, art director, spent many hours immersed in the details of preparing the manuscript for publication. Harriette Abels, consultant and mentor, graced this volume with her wisdom and encouragement and, ultimately, her approval.

And finally, the spirit of those heroes of so long ago seemed to reach across time and touch the words as they formed on the pages.

Without all of these, this volume would have been lacking.